A Grammar of Contemporary Polish

A GRAMMAR OF
CONTEMPORARY POLISH

OSCAR E. SWAN

Bloomington, Indiana, 2002

SLAVICA

Technical Editors: Jennifer J. Day, Andrea Rossing McDowell

ISBN: 0-89357-296-9

Slavica Publishers
Indiana University
2611 E. 10th St.
Bloomington, IN 47408-2603
USA

[Tel.] 1-812-856-4186
[Toll-free] 1-877-SLAVICA
[Fax] 1-812-856-4187
[Email] slavica@indiana.edu
[www] http://www.slavica.com/

Contents

Preface

This present work grew out of the first two editions of the author's more modest and now out-of-print *Concise Grammar of Polish*. The overall length of this work in its new form ruled out the continuation of the original title. This reference grammar is primarily intended for English-speaking learners of Polish. It is a practical grammar, designed to facilitate the learning of forms and to explain their uses in a way that will be accessible to the non-specialist. At the same time, this book aims to be a fairly complete and reliable technical guide to the rules, regularities, and principles which underpin Polish grammar, taking into account important exceptions and irregularities. No attempt is made to simplify or gloss over matters which are in actuality complex, as many matters of Polish grammar are. The aim is to present complex things as simply as possible, and not to make simple things seem more complex than they are in actuality. A special attempt has been made to describe facts relating to the social implementation of grammatical forms, a point of view which is often inadequately represented in grammars of Polish written by Poles, for whom such matters may seem obvious.

Working on the present version of this book has given me a renewed appreciation for how nothing of this nature can ever aim at being a complete description. Something as simple as the description of use of a single preposition like **w** *in*, to do it justice, could be continued for pages and pages. I have tried to be sensible as to the point of cut-off of various discussions, using my best judgment both as to where a potential user's interest naturally wanes, and as to what can realistically be accomplished by a written description of living language phenomena.

In my work on this book, I am indebted to nearly every Polish speaker with whom I have ever come into contact. I know of no country more linguistically friendly to foreigners than Poland, and no body of speakers more linguistically astute and willing to help one learn their language than the Poles.

Oscar E. Swan
Pittsburgh, 2002

Acknowledgments

Special thanks, in chronological order, to Linda Ewbank, Wiesław Oleksy, Mark Lauersdorf, Grażyna Kabat, Robert Henshew, and an anonymous reader for reading major parts of the manuscript, for catching many errors, and for making many useful suggestions. Zygmunt Saloni of Warsaw was available by e-mail for resolving various knotty problems of grammatical correctness. The entire manuscript benefitted from the careful reading, insightful suggestions, and occasional creative solutions of Jolanta Łapot, Kościuszko Foundation Scholar at the University of Pittsburgh during the years 1999–2002. Remaining mistakes and imprecisions are the author's responsibility alone.

Many years after their initial publication, I continue to find W. Doroszewski and H. Kurkowska, *Słownik poprawnej polszczyzny* (Warszawa: PWN, 1973) and J. Stanisławski and W. Jassem, *Wielki słownik polsko-angielski* (Warszawa, Wiedza Powszechna, 1969) invaluable sources of information on contemporary Polish. Toward the end of my work I was able to consult some of the many new works now appearing on Polish, including especially A. Markowski, ed., *Nowy słownik poprawnej polszczyzny* (Warszawa: PWN, 1999) and B. Dunaj, *Słownik współczesnego języka polskiego* (Warszawa: Wilga, 1996).

Polish and Poland

The Polish language is spoken by around 35-40 million speakers in the country of Poland (offical name: RZECZPOSPOLITA POLSKA *Republic of Poland*). The capital city is Warsaw, with a population of over 1.7 million and growing. Poland is bounded on the north by the Baltic Sea; on the west by Germany (where the natural boundary is the Oder (ODRA) River); on the south by the Czech Republic and Slovakia (where the natural boundary is formed by the Sudeten and Carpathian Mountains); on the east by Ukraine, Belarus, Lithuania); and, in the northeast, by a fragment of Russia. In addition to Poland, Polish is spoken to one or another extent by several million people outside Poland in Western Europe; in South and especially North America; and in such countries as Australia, New Zealand, and South Africa. Polish ranks 17th among world languages as to number of speakers.

Polish belongs to the Slavic group of Indo-European languages. Among the major Slavic languages Polish is most closely allied with Slovak and Czech, and also has many features in common with Ukrainian, an East Slavic language with which it has been in close contact for centuries. Christianity was brought to Poland by Czech missionaries and was adopted under the Polish ruler Mieszko I in 966. The earliest Polish writing goes back to the 14th-15th centuries. The Polish language attained status as a means of accomplished literary expression by individual writers in the 16th century, and attained full maturity as a language of education, science, jurisprudence, public debate, and other broad social functions in the 17th–18th centuries. The boundaries of Poland have undergone many changes over its history, including a period in the 18th and 19th centuries when the country was entirely incorporated into the territories of its neighbors. Present-day Poland resembles in large part the shape of Polish lands in the Middle Ages.

Contemporary Standard Polish, based in the main on the Warsaw variant of the language, is spoken or at least understood over the entire country. Due to mass education and communication, together with sizable movements in population from one part of the country to another, especially following the Second World War, the standard language has largely replaced strikingly different regional varieties. The most significant regional dialect is that of the Kraków-Silesia-Poznań area, characterized by a subtly different way of voicing and devoicing consonants between words. The Silesia region itself has a noticeably different dialect, characterized among other things by its non-standard treatment of nasal and certain other vowels. The Góral dialect of the high south mountains is quite distinct both in vocabulary and, mainly, in its lack of differentiation between such consonants as **cz** and **c**, **ż** and **z**, **sz** and **s**.

Abbreviations

adj	adjective	oth(er)	non-masculine personal
det	determinate verb	part	participle
dim	diminutive	pass	passive
fem	feminine	pej	pejorative
imper	imperative	pers or p	personal or person
impf	imperfective aspect	pf	perfective aspect
indet	indeterminate verb	pl	plural
masc	masculine	refl	reflexive
mppl	masculine personal plural	sg	singular
neut	neuter	def	defined

N	Nominative case	I	Instrumental case
G	Genitive case	L	Locative case
D	Dative case	V	Vocative case
A	Accusative case		

Incorrect forms may be prefixed with an asterisk (*); substandard or stylistic unusual forms may be indicated with a preceding exclamation mark (!).

Chapter 1

**Sounds, Spelling, and
Pronunciation**

THE POLISH ALPHABET

a ą b c ć d e ę f g h i j k l ł m n ń o ó p r s ś t u w y z ź ż

Digraphs (letter-combinations representing single sounds) include **ch, cz, dz, dź, dż, rz, sz**. The combinations **bi, ci, fi, gi, ki, mi, ni, pi, si, wi, zi** plus a following vowel, representing **b'** (bj), **ć, f'** (fj), **g', k', m'** (mj), **ń, p'** (pj), **ś, w'** (wj), **ź**, respectively, may also be considered digraphs. The combination **dzi** plus a following vowel, representing **dź** (as in **dziadek** *grandfather*), is a tri-graph. Di- and trigraphs are alphabetized the same as any other letter-combinations. The Polish alphabet does not ordinarily make use of Q (= **k**), V (= **w**) or X (= **ks**), although these letters, especially **v**, may be found in renderings of foreign words, names, and phrases as in *Quo vadis whither goest thou?* (title of novel), **video** *video*, **Pan X** "iks" *Mr. X*.

OVERVIEW OF POLISH SOUNDS

Letter & Approx. sound in American English	Examples
a *father*	**tak** *yes*, **kara** *punishment*
ą *dome*	**są** *they are*, **wąż** *snake*

The nasal-vowel sound **ą** is pronounced rather like *om*, except that the lips or tongue are not completely closed to pronounce the *m*, leaving a final glide "w" with a nasal resonance instead: "oɯ̃". The nasal resonance actually begins slightly ahead of the glide. Before stop and affricate consonants, **ą** is decomposed into **o** plus a following nasal consonant; see further below.

b *big*	**bok** *side*, **doba** *24-hr. period*
bi- *beautiful*	**bieg** *gear, speed*, **nabiał** *dairy products*
c *fits*	**co** *what*, **noc** *night*, **taca** *tray*
ch *hat*	**chata** *cottage*, **dech** *breath*, **ucho** *ear*

The sound of *ch* is much raspier and noisier than English *h*, but it is not as harsh as German *ch* or Russian *x*.

ci- *cheek*	**ciasto** *cake*, **cicho** *quietly*, **Kasia** *Kate*
cz *chalk*	**czas** *time*, **beczka** *barrel*, **oczy** *eyes*
ć *cheek, teach*	**choć** *although*, **ćma** *moth*

The letters **ć** and **ci-** represent the same sound. The spelling **ci-** is used before a vowel, except that only **c** is written before **i**. Remember: the letter **c** before **i** is pronounced **ć**. The sound of **ć**/**ci-**, pronounced with the mouth and tongue in the position of English "y", is distinct from the sound of **cz**, pronounced with the mouth and tongue in the position of English "r". See further discussion.

d	*do*	**data** *date*, **lada** *counter*
dz	*odds*	**cudzy** *foreign*
dzi-	*jeans*	**dziadek** *grandfather*, **dziki** *wild*, **Tadzio** *Teddy*
dź	*jeans*	**wiedźma** *witch*
dż	*jaw*	**dżem** *jam*, **radża** *rajah*

The letters **dź** and **dzi-** represent the same sound. The spelling **dzi-** is used before a vowel, except that only **dz** is written before **i**. Remember: the letters **dz** before **i** are pronounced **dź**. The sound of **dź**/**dzi-**, pronounced with the mouth and tongue in the position of English "y", is distinct from the sound of **dż**, pronounced with the mouth and tongue in the position of English "r"; see further discussion. The sound **dż** is infrequent, and occurs mainly in words of foreign origin, like **dżez** *jazz*, **dżudo** *judo*. In Polish words, it is always preceded by **ż**, as in **jeżdżę** *I ride*.

e	*ever*	**echo** *echo*, **ten** *that*, **dobrze** *fine*

It is important not to reduce or change the quality of the sound **e** at the end of a word. It is pronounced clearly and distinctly in all positions; hence **dobrze** "dobże", not "dobżuh".

ę	*sense*	**gęś** *goose*, **tęsknić** *long for*

The sound **ę** is pronounced rather like *em*, except that the lips or tongue are not completely closed to pronounce the *m*, leaving a final glide "w" with a nasal resonance instead: "ew". The nasal resonance actually begins slightly ahead of the glide. At the end of a word, the letter **ę** is normally pronounced the same as **e**; or, at least, its nasality is strongly reduced. Before stop and affricate consonants, **ę** is decomposed into **e** plus a following nasal consonant; see further below.

f	*felt*	**farba** *paint*, **lufa** *rifle barrel*
fi-	*few*	**fiołek** *violet*, **kalafior** *cauliflower*
g	*get*	**guma** *erase*, **noga** *legr*
gi-	*tug you*	**magiel** *mangle*, **gips** *plaster*
h	*hat*	**hak** *hook*, **aha** *oh yes*

The letter **h**, pronounced the same as **ch**, appears mainly in words of foreign origin and in certain exclamations (as **aha** *oh yes!*).

i	*cheek*	**igła** *needle*, **list** *letter*, **czyli** *whether*
j	*you, boy*	**jak** *as*, **moja** *my-fem.*, **raj** *heaven*
k	*keg*	**kupa** *pile*, **foka** *seal*, **tak** *yes*
ki-	*like you*	**kiedy** *when*, **kit** *bushy tail*
l	*leaf*	**las** *forest*, **kula** *ball*, **dal** *distance*

The letter l is pronounced rather like French or German l, with the front of the tongue, not like English "dark" l, as in *ball*, not as "soft" as Russian /ļ/.

ł	*wag, bow*	łyk *swallow*, **bryła** *clod*, **był** *he was*
m	*moth*	**mama** *mama*, **tam** *there*
mi-	*mew*	**miara** *measure*, **miska** *bowl*
n	*not*	**noc** *nigh*, **szyna** *rail*, **syn** *son*
ni-	*canyon*	**nie** *no*, **nikły** *faint*, **kania** *kite (bird)*
ń	*canyon*	**koń** *horse*, **tańczyć** *to dance*

The letters ń and ni- represent the same sound. The combination ni- is used before a vowel. The letter n before i is pronounced like ń/ni-.

o	*pore*	**okno** *window*, **pot** *sweat*, **to** *that-neut.*

Polish o is pronounced more or less halfway between the *o* in English *poke* on the one hand and *pot* on the other hand, with the brevity of the latter.

ó	*toot*	**ósmy** *eigth*, **ból** *pain*

The letter ó is pronounced the same as u. This letter does not occur word-finally.

p	*pup*	**pas** *belt*, **łapa** *paw*, **słup** *pole*
pi-	*pew*	**piana** *foam*, **pić** *drink*, **konopie** *hemp*
r	*arriba* (Span.)	**rada** *advice*, **nora** *burrow*, **bór** *grove*

The sound r is pronounced by lightly trilling the tip of the tongue, but not as vigorously as in Spanish, Italian, or Russian.

rz	*pleasure*	**rzeka** *river*, **morze** *sea*, **wierzba** *willow*

The sound of rz is exactly the same as that of ż; see below. For example, **morze** *sea* and **może** *he can* are identical in pronunciation.

s	*sad*	**sam** *oneself*, **las** *forest*, **rasa** *race*
si-	*sheep*	**siano** *hay*, **sito** *sieve*, **Basia** *Barb*
sz	*shark*	**szal** *frenzy*, **kasza** *kasha*, **tusz** *mascara*
ś	*sheep*	**nośny** *portable*, **oś** *axle*

The letters ś and si- represent the same sound. The spelling si- is used before a vowel, except that only s is written before i. Remember: the letter s before i is pronounced ś. The sound of ś/si-, pronounced with the mouth and tongue in the position of English "y", is distinct from the sound of sz, pronounced with the mouth and tongue in the position of English "r". See further discussion.

t	*top*	**tak** *yes*, **pot** *sweat*, **data** *date*
u	*toot*	**but** *shoe*, **tu** *here*
w	*vote*	**wata** *wadding*, **kawa** *coffee*
wi-	*view*	**wiara** *belief*, **wiosna** *spring*

y	ill	**dym** *smoke,* **ty** *you*
z	zoo	**zupa** *soup,* **faza** *phase*
zi-	azure	**ziarno** *grain,* **zima** *winter*
ź	azure	**woźny** *porter*
ż	pleasure	**żaba** *frog,* **kałuża** *puddle,* **ciżba** *throng*

The letters **ź** and **zi-** represent the same sound. The spelling **zi-** is used before a vowel, except that only **z** is written before **i**. Remember: the letter **z** before **i** is pronounced **ź**. The sound of **ź/zi-**, pronounced with the mouth and tongue in the position of English "y", is distinct from the sound of **ż/rz**, pronounced with the mouth and tongue in the position of English "r"; see further discussion.

CONSONANT AND VOWEL PHONEMES

"Phoneme" is the technical name for a sound unit native speakers of a language recognize as belonging to their language. Phonemes are the sounds out of which words are composed, regardless of how consistently these sounds are represented by letters according to the orthographic conventions of the language. Each phoneme of a language is distinct from every other phoneme. Phonemes consist of consonants and vowels. Vowels by definition have a syllabic quality to them. Consonants form syllables only in combination with vowels. In Polish, consonants usually occur at the beginning of syllables, before a vowel.

CONSONANT PHONEMES

By +v is meant "voiced", pronounced with the participation of the larynx. By –v is meant "not voiced". On the sounds ŋ, ŋ', see further below.

	Labial	Palato-labial	Dental	Palatal	Back-pal.	Velar	Palato-velar
Stops							
–v	p	p'	t			k	k'
+v	b	b'	d			g	g'
Spirants							
–v	f	f'	s	ś	sz	ch/h	ch'/h'
+v	w	w'	z	ź	ż/rz		
Affricates							
–v			c	ć	cz		
+v			dz	dź	dż		
Sonants							
Nasal	m	m'	n	ń		(ŋ)	(ŋ')
Liquid			r	l			
Semivowels	ł			j			

Hard and Soft Sibilants and Affricates Contrasted

Closest American English sound	Hard (back-palatal) "r-position"	Soft (palatal) "y-position"
"ch" (*church*)	cz	ć (ci-)
"j" (*jury*)	dż	dź (dzi-)
"sh" (*sure*)	sz	ś (si-)
"zh" (*pleasure*)	ż/rz	ź (zi-)

The English sounds are approximately "in the middle" between the Polish hard and soft correspondents, possibly more like the hard than the soft.

Contrast:

"ch"	**czas** *time*	**ciasto** *cake*
"j"	**dżungla** *jungle*	**dziura** *hole*
"sh"	**proszę** *please*	**prosię** *piglet*
"zh"	**barze** *bar Lsg.*	**bazie** *base Lsg.*

English sounds are closest to the Polish soft sounds before the vowel *ee*, as in *cheek, jeans, sheep*. Nevertheless, using Polish spelling, Poles would still transcribe English *cheek* as "czik", i.e., with the consonant sound of **cz** and the vowel sound of **i** (which ordinarily does not occur after **cz**). It is the sounds of **ć, dź, ś, ź** which require the most attention for speakers of English.

Notes

a. The voiceless stop consonants **p, t, k** are pronounced with considerably less aspiration (plosive force) than their English counterparts, to the untrained ear making them sound somewhat similar to **b, d, g**. Plosive force may be tested by holding a piece of paper loosely in front of one's mouth. The consonants **p, b, k** should not move the paper to any greater extent than **b, d, g**.

b. The consonant sounds **p', b', f', w', m', ć, dź, ś, ź, ń, l, k', g', ch', j** are phonetically soft, meaning that they are pronounced with the tongue and mouth oriented toward the hard palate just behind the dental ridge (the English "y" position). Polish **l** is only moderately palatal. Consonants other than the above are phonetically hard. The acute mark used above **ć, dź, ś, ź, ń** is called in Polish a **kreska**. The names for the other diacritics are: **ogonek** 'tail' or **haczek** 'hook' for the mark under **ę** and **ą**; **kropka** 'dot' for the dot above **ż**; and **bar** 'bar' for the line through **ł**.

c. The soft (palato-, palatalized) labials **p', b', f', w', m'** and the palato-velars **k', g'** occur only before vowels, hence in practice they are always spelled **pi, bi, fi, wi, mi, ki, gi** (or without i before the vowel i) The palato-velar **ch'/h'** occurs infrequently, in foreign borrowings and in verb derivation: **Chiny** *China*, **wymachiwać** *wave about*, **higiena** *hygiene.*

d. In standard Polish, the soft labials **p′, b′, f′, w′, m′** are usually pronounced **pj, bj, fj, wj, mj**: **piana** "pjana" *foam*, **biały** "bjały" *white*, **miara** "mjara" *measure*. Palatalized **p′, b′, f′, w′, m′** not followed by **j** occur before the vowel **i**: **pić** "p′ić" *drink*, **film** "f′ilm" *film*.

e. The letters **ż** and **rz** represent the same sound; **może** *he can* and **morze** *sea* are pronounced exactly the same. The spelling **rz** is used when the sound is etymologically related to **r**, for example **morze** *sea*, compare **morski** *maritime*. The letter **ż** is used otherwise. It is etymologically related to **g** or **z**; see **mogę** *I can*, **możesz** *you can*; **wóz** *cart-noun*, **wożę** *I cart*.

f. The letter **h** is occasionally used for the sound **ch** in foreign borrowings and in some exclamations: **hybryda** *hybrid*, **aha** *aha*. The pronunciation of this letter as voiced **h** (g) in borrowings from Czech or Ukrainian is totally artificial.

g. Before spirants and affricates, the sound **ń** is preceded by a nasalized **j**-glide, while **ń** itself may become weakened: **cieńszy** "ćej^{n}szy" *thinner*, **koński** "koj^{n}ski" *equine*, **słońce** "słoj^{n}ce" *sun*. In **hańba** *disgrace*, the **ń** assimilates to **m** before the **b**: "hajmba".

h. The symbol **ŋ** represents the sound of English *ng* in *bang*. In Polish this sound is not independent but merely an optional variety of **n** before **k** and **g**: **bank** "bahk" or "bank" *bank*. Before soft **k′** and **g′**, **ŋ** may be pronounced **ŋ′**: **banki** "baŋ′k′i". Warsaw pronunciation tends to pronounce **n** before **k** or **g** in foreign words as **ŋ**, hence **bank** "baŋk", **tango** "taŋgo", but as **n** in native words or in well assimilated borrowings, especially if the **n** may be separated from the following velar by a mobile vowel: **łapanka** "łapanka" *roundup* (cf. Gpl. **łapanek**), **ratunku!** "ratunku" *help!* (cf. Nsg. **ratunek**). Kraków-Silesia-Poznań pronunciation tends to pronounce **ŋ** everywhere.

i. The letter **u** may be used to render the sound of **ł** in foreign borrowings: **autobus** *bus* "ałtobus", **Europa** *Europe* "ełropa". Contrast with **nauka** *learning* "na-u-ka".

j. The sound of **ł** in the east or "Kresy" regions (contemporary Belarus, Lithuania, and Ukraine) is similar to English "dark" l as in *cold*. This pronunciation is also referred to as "stage *l*", since it was, and to an extent still is, used in the theater, especially in productions of older works. The pronunciation of this sound as a bilabial glide (English "w") goes back as far as the 16th century.

k. *Geminate (double) consonants* are not common but, when they occur, they are pronounced as such; that is, they are held for about one-and-a-half times as long as a single consonant. In careful pronunciation, double consonants may be pronounced as literally double: **dzienny** *daily*, **netto** *net amount*, **pełłem** *I weeded-masc.* Borrowed words with spelled double consonants (whatever their actual pronunciation in the source language) tend to be pronounced with double consonants; see **hobby** *hobby* "hobbi". Eventually, foreign words may be assimilated to single-consonant pronunciation, with corresponding changes in spelling; see former **kollega**, contemporary **kolega** *colleague*.

VOWEL PHONEMES

	Front	Central	Back
High	i	~ y	u/ó
Mid	e		o
Nasal	ę		ą
Low		a	

Notes

a. The vowel phoneme represented by the letters **i** and **y** occupies a fairly wide area in the front-central region. The pronunciation and spelling depend on the quality of the preceding consonant, whether phonetically hard or soft; see further discussion under spelling rules. Polish endings will sometimes be represented as beginning in **-y/i**, meaning 'y or i , depending on spelling rules.'

b. The letters **u** and **ó** are pronounced exactly the same. The letter **ó** ("kreska o") is used when the sound is etymologically related to **o**, as in **ból** *pain*; compare **boleć** *hurt*. The letter **ó** never occurs in word-final position, and almost never in grammatical endings. Many words show an alternation between **ó** in some forms and **o** in others, as **stół** *table*, **stoły** *tables*.

c. Polish oral (non-nasal) vowels **a, e, i~y, o, u/ó** are all pronounced with the same short length, achieved by not moving the lips or tongue after the onset of the vowel, as happens, for example, in English long vowel-sounds *ee* (*knee*), *oe* (*toe*), *oo* (*boot*). Correct pronunciation of the vowels as "pure" is the single most important key to a good accent in Polish. Practice the difference by contrasting:

English	Polish	(do not move the tongue or lips after
clean	**klin** *wedge*	the onset of the vowel)
dome	**dom** *house*	
boom	**bum** *boom*	

The Polish words are much shorter than the English.

d. Polish vowels do not change or reduce in quality according to stress, as happens in English. Unstressed vowels are pronounced with approximately the same clarity as vowels under stress. This observation applies

equally well to unstressed vowels in word-final position, which are pronounced as clearly as other unstressed vowels.

e.   The nasal vowels **ą** and **ę**, alone among the vowels, are pronounced long,
the length usually being due to the rounding of the lips when forming the
nasal glide "w" at the end:

gęś "gewś" *goose*
wąż "wowsz" *snake*.

Bear in mind that the letter **ą** represents nasal **o**, not nasal **a**. See further
below on the pronunciation of the nasal vowels before certain consonants.

f.   The vowel **a** is pronounced in the mid-to-back region. It is not as far back
as *a* in English f*a*r, nor as far front as *a* in English f*a*t.

g.   **-aj** at the end of a word is pronounced regionally as "-ej"; see **wczoraj**
"fczorej" *yesterday*, **dzisiaj** "dźiśej" *today*, **tutaj** "tutej" *here*.

SPELLING RULES

1.   Most spelling-adjustment rules have to do in one way or another with the
letter **i**. The letter **i** has four main functions: (a) it can identify the vowel **i**;
(b) it can both identify the vowel **i** and be a marker of preceding consonant softness; (c) it can be a marker of preceding consonant softness before vowels other than **i**; (d) it can represent the sound **j**.

a.   About the only instances where the letter **i** represents the vowel sound **i**
by itself are in word-initial position and after vowels: **igła** *needle*; **moi** *my*
(mp. pl.).

b.   When consonant letters **p, b, f, w, m, k, g, ch/h** occur before the vowel **i**,
the **i** indicates pronunciation as **p', b', f', w', m', k', g', ch'/h'**, respectively:
pić "p'ić" *drink*, **kino** "k'ino" *cinema*. On **p, b, f, w, m** before **i**, see further
below, e.

c.   When the consonants **ń, ć, dź, ś, ź** occur before the vowel **i**, they lose in
spelling the special indication of softness (the kreska). The **i** then serves
both to represent the vowel **i** and to indicate preceding consonant soft-
ness: **ani** "ańi" *neither*, **cicho** "ćicho" *quiet*, **dziki** "dźik'i" *wild*, **sito** "śito"
sieve, **zima** "źima" *winter*.

d.   When the soft consonant sounds **p', b', f', w', m', ń, ć, dź, ś, ź, k', g', ch'/h'**
occur before vowels other than **i**, a following **i** will be written: **ciasto**
"ćasto" *dough*; **nie** "ńe" *no*, **kiedy** "k'edy" *when*, **giętki** "g'entki" *supple*.

e.   When the soft labials **p', b', f', w', m'** occur before vowels other than **i**, the
i both replaces the softness indicator and represents **j**: **pawie** "pawje" *pea-*
cocks; **miasto** "mjasto" *town*.

f. Regarding the spelling **ni** before vowels, most speakers make a distinction according to whether the word is borrowed or native, differentiating, for example, between **panią** "pa-ńą" *lady-Isg.* and **manią** "mań-ją" *mania-Isg.* In such instances the orthography is ambiguous.

g. The letter **i** also represents **j** after **r** and **l** before vowels other than i: **Maria** "marja", **bulion** "buljon" *bouillon.* After letters other than **n** which can carry a kreska (**s, z, c**), where a following **i** representing **j** would be confusing, **j** is spelled **j**: **akcja** *action*, **Rosja** *Russia*, **Azja** *Asia.*

> To sum up: the letter **i** after a consonant infrequently represents merely i. In practice, its most frequent function is to indicate that a preceding consonant is soft, whether before the vowel **i** or before another vowel.

h. In unassimilated foreign borrowings, the letter **i** can occur after hard dental consonants, where it will either be pronounced as **y** or, usually, as **i** preceded by a slightly palatalized hard dental; see **holding** "hold'iŋk" *holding company*, **rifle** "r'ifle" *Rifle jeans.* The ability of both **i** and **y** to occur after hard dentals suggests a tendency toward the independent phonemic status of **i** and **y**.

Rules Governing the Spelling of i/y

2. When choosing in spelling between **i** and **y**, the letter **i** is written after phonetically soft consonants (**p', b', f', w', m', ć, dź, ś, ź, ń, l, j**). The letter **y** is written elsewhere, except that **k** and **g** automatically soften before **y** to **k'** and **g'** which take **i**, so that in practice only the combinations **ki** and **gi** occur, never *ky or *gy. Either **i** or **y** may follow **ch/h**.

   Confusion may be occasioned by the ambiguity of the letter **c**. By itself **c** designates the sound "ts" and takes **y**, as in **cygaro** *cigar.* The letter **ć** before **i** loses its kreska, yielding **ci** (for example **cicho** "ćicho" *quiet*), making it appear that **c** can take either **i** or **y**. Actually, **c** takes only **y**, and **ć** takes only **i**, but is spelled **c** before **i**.

   The letter **l** is phonetically soft and can only be followed by **i**, never by **y**. By contrast, the letters **cz, sz, dz, rz, ż** are phonetically hard and are followed only by **y**, never by **i** (except rarely, in foreign-influenced spellings like **reżim** *regime*, **Hiroszima**).

> In sum, these consonants take **i** (and lose the softness marker, if any): **p', b', f', w', m', ć, dź, ś, ź, ń, l, k', g', ch'/h'.j.**

The converse of the i/y rule is just as important. The letter **i** after **p, b, f, w, m, c, dz, s, z, n, k, g, ch** indicates that the preceding sounds are **p', b', f', w', m'** (or **pj, bj, fj, wj, mj**), **ć, dź, ś, ź, ń, k', g', ch'**.

> A minor exception is that verbs beginning with **i** may take the Perfectivizing prefix **z-** without changing the pronunciation of **z** to **ź**: **irytować** *irritate*, prefixed Perfective **zirytować** "z'i-ry-to-wać".

3. Stem-final **j** after a vowel is dropped before **i** (in both spelling and pronunciation): **kolej-i: kolei** *railway-Gsg.*, **stoj-i: stoi** *he/she stands.*

4. *Unassimilated Spellings:* In growing numbers, Polish contains words which retain their foreign (usually, English) spelling and rely on the speaker to know the correct pronunciation (for example, that **pepsi** is pronounced "peps'i", not "pepśi"). See also **outsider, coca cola, musical, non-iron, peugeot, pizza, poncho**, and many, many more. Sometimes such words may have more or less assimilated versions; see **igloo** "iglo-o", "iglo", or "iglu".

AUTOMATIC CHANGES IN PRONUNCIATION

By automatic changes in pronunciation are meant phonemically significant sound-changes (i.e. the change of one phoneme to another) that are not connected to the grammatical shape of the word, and which are not normally reflected in the spelling. Unless otherwise noted, the following rules reflect the pronunciation of standard Warsaw Polish.

Voiced and Corresponding Voiceless Consonants

+v	b	w	d	dz	dź	dż	rz	z	ź	ż	g
–v	p	f	t	c	ć	cz	sz	s	ś	sz	k

a. In word-final position, voiced consonants **b, w, d, dz, dź, dż, rz, z, ź, ż, g** are devoiced to **p, f, t, c, ć, cz, sz, s, ś, sz, k**, respectively: **dziób** "dźup" *beak*, **paw** "paf" *peacock*, **twarz** "tfasz" *face*, **mąż** "mąsz" *husband*, **gwóźdź** "gwuść" *nail*. Before the imperative ending **-my**, consonants behave as at word end: **róbmy** "rupmy" *let's do it.*

b. Word-final **r** and **ł** do not necessarily protect a preceding consonant from devoicing: **bóbr** "bupr" *beaver*, **mógł** "mugł" or "muk" *he could*, **wiózł** "wjuzł" or "wjus" *he carted.*

c. Inside a word, voiced consonants are devoiced before voiceless consonants: **łóżko** "łuszko" *bed*, **podpiszę** "potpiszę" *I'll sign*, **gąbka** "gom(p)ka" *sponge*; and voiceless consonants are voiced before voiced consonants. The latter happens most often before the conditional particle **by**: **choćby** "chodźby" and the emphatic particle **że: jednakże** "jednagże" *however*. The sound **ch/h** can also become voiced (symbol: γ) before voiced consonants, this being the only place where this sound occurs: **klechda** "kleγda" *folk tale*, **Bohdan** "boγdan" (first name).

d. For purposes of voicing and devoicing, basic (mainly, one-syllable) prepositions are treated as part of the following word. Thus, **od niego** *from him* is pronounced "odńego"; **pod oknem** *beneath the window* is "podoknem"; **pod strzechą** *beneath the roof* is "potstszechą"; **przez Tadka** *by Tadek* is "pszestatka"; and so on. For further information on the pronunciation of prepositions, see below under stress.

e. In normal colloquial speech a voiceless consonant at the end of a word is often lightly voiced before a voiced consonant of a following word in the same sentence, providing there is no pause between them: **los Dariusza** "loz darjusza" *Dariusz's fate* ; and a voiced consonant is not totally devoiced: **wóz Dariusza** "wuz darjusza" *Dariusz's car.*

f. Under Kracjw-Silesia-Poznan pronounciation, voiceless consonants are lightly voiced not only before a voiced consonant of a following word, but also before a vowel or resonant consonant (**l, ł, m, n, ń, r, j**): **brat ojca** "brad ojca" *father's brother*, **brat matki** "brad matk'i" *mother's brother.* Voiced consonants retain their voice in this position: **już jutro** "już jutro" *already tomorrow*. Standard Warsaw Polish does not observe this rule, hence "brat ojca", "brat matki", "jusz jutro".

g. After a voiceless consonant in the same word, the sounds **rz** and **w** are devoiced to **sz, f**, respectively: **przy** "pszy" *near*, **trzy** "tszy" *three*, **krzesło** "kszesło" *chair*, **chwała** "chfała" *praise*, **twarz** "tfasz" *face*, **kwiat** "kfjat" *flower*, **ćwierć** "ćfjerć" *quarter*, **swój** "sfuj" *one's own.*

h. The consonants **p', b', w', m'** automatically harden at the end of a word. As a result, word-final **p, b, w, m** are structurally ambiguous: some instances represent **p, b, w, m**, while others represent potential **p', b', w', m'** (or **pj, bj, wj, mj**). The difference becomes apparent when adding endings to words. For example, the Genitive sg. of **staw** *pond* is **stawu**, whereas the Genitive sg. of **szczaw** *sorrel* is **szczawiu** "stawju".

i. The consonants **t** and **d** are normally assimilated to **cz** and **dż**, respectively, before **sz** and **rz**: **trzy** "tszy" or "czszy" *three*, **drzewo** "dżewo" or "dżżewo" *tree*. Contrast **trzy** "tszy" or "czszy" to **czy** "czy". Pronunciations such as "czeba" for **trzeba** occur, but are considered careless and substandard (pronounce instead "tszeba" or "czszeba"). Word-final **trz**, however, is pronounced **cz**: **popatrz** *look!* "popacz", **mistrz** "miscz" *master*. The consonants **s** and **z** before **cz, sz, rz/ż**, and **dż** may be pronounced **sz** and **ż**, respectively: **z czego** "szczego" *from what*, **z dżungli** "żdżungli" *out of the jungle.*

j. Before **ć, ś, ź** or **dź**, the consonant **z** (usually the final consonant of one of the verbal prefixes or prepositions **przez, roz, z**) may may undergo voicing/palatalization assimilation to **ś** or **ź**: **przez ciebie** "psześćebje" *through you*, **Zdzisław** "żdźisłaf" (first name), **rozdzielać** "roźdźelać" *distribute,*

rozcieńczać "rośćeńczać" *dilute,* and so on. The assimilation of **z** or **s** to **ś** is often reflected in the spelling: **ściąć** "śćońć" *cut down* (from **z-ciąć**), **Bośnia** *Bosnia.*

k. In rapid speech, **ł** is dropped between consonants and after consonants other than **r** at the end of words: **jabłko** "jabłko" or "japko" *apple,* **mógł** "mugł" or "muk" *he could,* but usually **umarł** "umarł" *he died.*

Nasal Vowels

l. Before stops and affricates, the nasal vowels **ę** and **ą** (which, recall, consist in their basic form of **e** and **o** plus a nasal glide **w̧**), decompose into **e** and **o** plus a nasal consonant, according to the following rules:

Before labial stops (including palatalized labial):	**ę: em**	**tępy** "tempy" *dull*
		głębia "głembja" *depth*
	ą: om	**dąb** "domp" *oak*
Before dental stops and hard affricates (whether dental or backpalatal):	**ę: en**	**kręty** "krenty" *twisted*
		ręce "rence" *hands*
	ą: on	**kąt** "kont" *corner*
		pączek "ponczek" *bud*
Before palatal dental affricates:	**ę: eń**	**chęć** "cheńć" *desire*
	ą: oń	**bądź** "bońć" *be (imper.)*
Before velar stops:	**ę: eŋ**	**ręka** "rehka" *hand*
	ą: oŋ	**bąk** "bohk" *gadfly*
Before palato-velar stops:	**ę: eŋ'**	**ręki** "reh'k'i" *hand-Gsg.*
	ą: oŋ'	**bąki** "boh'k'i" *gadflies*

It follows from the above that full nasal vowels occur only before **f, w, s, z, ś, ź, sz, rz/ż,** (c)h and, in the instance mainly of **ą**, in word-final position; see **kęs** *piece,* **wąsy** *mustaches,* **węszyć** *sniff,* **dążyć** *tend.* Between soft consonants, the sound of **j** will often follow the nasal vowel: **siąść** "śąⁱść" *sit down,* **więzienie** "w'eⁱźeńe" *prison,* **są** *they are.*

m. In informal colloquial speech **ę** and **ą** before **f, w, s, z, ś, ź, sz, rz/ż,** (c)h are often shortened to near the length of an oral vowel by eliminating the labial glide: **wąż** "wǫsz" or "wow̧sz" *snake,* **węża** "węża" or "wew̧ża" *snake-Gsg.;* **mężczyzna** "mew̧szczyzna", "męszczyzna", or even "meszczyzna" *man.*

n. Nasal vowels lose nasality before **l** and **ł**: **gięli** "gieli" *they bent,* **zdjął** "zdjoł" *he took off.* The nasal vowels, while not pronounced here, are still spelled as nasals.

o. The vowel **ę** is usually partially or completely denasalized in word-final position, particularly in rapid speech: **proszę** "prosze" or "proszę" *please,*

nogę "noge" or "nogę" *leg-Asg.*, **się** "śe" or, pedantically, "śę" *self.*
Consistent nasal pronunciation of word-final **ę** is pedantic and affected.
Whether or not the **ę** is pronounced, it is still spelled **ę**.

> The fact that the children of Polish-speakers living abroad as a rule
> totally lose the ability to distinguish between word-final **e** and **ę**
> suggests that the distinction in the country itself is maintained only
> under the pressure of formal education and, to an extent, mass media.

p. After **n**, word-final **ą** may be denasalized to "oł", as in **krzykną**
    "kszyknoł" *they'll shout*, i.e. the same as **krzyknął** *he shouted*. In very
    relaxed and rapid speech, final **ą** may be denasalized to "oł" after other
    consonants as well. Word-final **ą** should not be pronounced as "om", this
    being regional (Silesian and Western Małopolska), dialectal, and sub-
    standard.

q. Ad hoc nasal vowels often arise in speech when an oral vowel is followed
    by **n** plus a spirant: **awans** "awans" or "awąs" *raise in salary*, **czynsz**
    "czynsz" or "czywsz" *rent*, **dżinsy** "dżinsy" or "dżiwsy" *jeans*, **kunszt**
    "kunszt" or "kuwszt" *craftsmanship*. Vowel plus **m** before **w** or **f** may also
    produce a nasal vowel: **emfaza** "ęfaza" *emphasis*, **tramwaj** "trąwaj" *trolley*.
    Note that the sign *ą* in these examples stands for nasal *a*, not nasal *o*.

SYLLABLE DIVISION

By syllable division is meant the way speakers divide words into syllabic
pulses during speech, not how words are divided between lines of print
(although it is correct to split words between lines according to speech syllables). Polish words tend toward an open-syllable structure, meaning that syllables gravitate toward the structure C(C)V. That is, syllables tend to begin
with (C)onsonants and to end with (V)owels. A syllable will be closed (ended
with a consonant) under the following circumstances:

a. if a consonant or consonants end the word, e.g. **ogród** o-gród ("o-grut")
    garden.

b. if a word-internal consonant cluster potentially begins with a resonant (**l**,
    ł, m, n, ń, r, j), e.g. **pełny** peł-ny *full*, **lampa** lam-pa *lamp*, **twardy** tfar-dy
    hard, **trójka** trój-ka ("truj-ka") *triplet;*

c. if a nasal vowel precedes a consonant cluster: **tęsknię** tęs-knię *I long;*

d. if a double consonant occurs inside the word, e.g. **wonny** won-ny *aro-
    matic;*

e. if two different contiguous stop or affricate consonants share the same
    general place of articulation: **bodźca** bodź-ca *stimulus-Gsg.;*

f. if the first of the consonants ends a prefix, e.g. **podwieść** pod-wieść *lead up to*, **odjechać** od-jechać *drive away*. Compare **odzysk** od-zysk *salvage*, where the **od** represents a prefix, to **wodze** wo-dze *reins* (where **dz** is a unit phoneme).

Aside from these circumstances, syllables tend to end with vowels, and consonants are carried over to the beginning of the next syllable (up to the end of the word, where consonants, if present, close the final syllable). The principle of open syllable structure often carries over to the pronunciation of words in sequence in the same sentence. Word-final consonants will often be carried over to the beginning of the next word of the sentence, provided there is no pause:

dużo innych wyrazów określających *many other modifying expressions* "du-żo-in-ny-gwy-ra-zu-fo-kre-śla-jon-cych"

> The principle of open syllable structure has important consequences for the correct pronunciation of Polish words in sequence, and differs markedly from English where, for example, **crude ox** and **crew docks** are pronounced slightly differently, no matter how rapidly spoken.

STRESS

Polish words have one main place of stress; even very long words do not develop a strong secondary stress, as in English. Pronouncing Polish words with English-like secondary stress sounds sing-song. Stress in a Polish word is fixed and predictable; it falls on the next-to-last syllable: **sprawa** SPRA-wa *matter*, **Warszawa** War-SZA-wa *Warsaw*, **gospodarka** go-spo-DAR-ka *economy*, **zadowolony** za-do-wo-LO-ny *satisfied*. When a word is extended by multisyllablic suffixes or endings, the stress shifts accordingly to the right: **kobieta** ko-BIE-ta *woman*, **kobietami** ko-bie-TA-mi-*Ipl.*, **czytam** CZY-tam *I read*, **czytają** czy-TA-ją *they read*.

Only a few instances violate this general rule:

a. Enclitics such as the past-tense personal endings **-śmy** and **-ście** and the conditional particle **by** do not, in standard Polish, cause the stress to shift to the right: **znali** ZNA-li *they knew*, **znaliśmy** ZNA-li-śmy *we knew*, **znaliście** ZNA-li-ście *you knew*, **znalibyśmy** ZNA-li-by-śmy *we would have known*. Stress on the next-to-last syllable in such forms is considered substandard. The imperative endings **-cie** and **-my**, by contrast, *do* cause stress to shift to the right: **przeczytajmy** prze-czy-TAJ-my *let's read*.

b. Past-tense verb enclitics **-em -eś -eśmy -eście** do not affect the place of stress of a word to which they may be attached: **nieraześ mi to już mówił** NIE-ra-ześ mi to już MÓ-wił *you have already said that to me a number of times*.

c. The item **-set** *100* in compounds like **kilkaset** KIL-ka-set *several hundred*, **pięciuset** PIĘ-ciu-set *five hundred-m.p.pl.*, and so on, does not affect the place of stress.

d. Basic one-syllable prepositions, including their two-syllable alternates ending in **e**, combine with a following pronoun for purposes of pronunciation and stress. If the following word is of one syllable, the stress will fall on the preposition (which then occupies the next-to-last syllabic position): **dla niej** DLA niej *for her*, **beze mnie** be-ZE mnie *without me*. The two-syllable prepositions **ponad** *up above* and **poza** *besides* are also proclitic in this sense: **ponad nim** po-NA-dnim *up above him*, **poza mną** po-ZA-mną *besides me*. Contrast with **przeciwko mnie** prze-CI-wko mnie, **mimo woli** MI-mo WO-li *beyond one's control*.

e. Assimilation in softness does not occur between **z** and a following pronoun beginning in **ń**: **bez niej** "BEZ-niej", i.e., not *"BE-źniej".

f. The stress situation of one-syllable prepositions before nouns other than pronouns is somewhat fluid. The noun may carry independent stress, but in certain fixed expressions the stress can fall on the preposition: **do dna** DO dna *to the bottom*, **na dół** NA dół *downstairs*, **na wieś** NA wieś *to the country*; **za mąż** ZA mąż in the expression **wyjść za mąż** *get married (of a woman)*.

g. Short-form personal pronouns **go, mu, mi, ci, cię** and the reflexive particle **się** cannot be emphasized or stressed. They also do not affect the place of stress of words next to which they occur. Other personal pronouns may be either stressed or not, according to whether or not they are emphasized. An exception would be the expression **jak się masz?**, somewhat jocularly treated as a single word: jak SIĘ masz? *how are you?*

h. Similarly to basic prepositions, the negative particle **nie** is normally not stressed and combines with a following verb for purposes of stress. If **nie** precedes a one-syllable verb form, stress will fall on the **nie**: **nie wiem** NIE wiem *I don't know*, **nie chcę** NIE chcę *I don't want*, **nie bój się** NIE bój się *don't be afraid*. Such pronunciation is obligatory, and has nothing to do with emphasis. Note that the negative particle **nie** may never be separated by another word from a verb it modifies.

i. The enclitics **no** (exhortative) and **-że** (emphatic) do not influence the place of stress: **chodźcie no** CHODŹ-cie-no *well come on! (impatient)*, **powiedz że nam** PO-wiedz że nam *come on and tell us*.

j. Borrowed words containing suffixes **-yk-/-yka** or **-ik-/-ika** tend to stress the syllable preceding **-yk-**: **elektryka** e-LEK-try-ka *electrician-GAsg.*, **klinika** KLI-ni-ka *clinic*, **muzyka** MU-zy-ka *music*, **polityka** po-LI-ty-ka *politics*. In the Instrumental pl., stress will fall on the next-to-last syllable: **klinikami** kli-ni-KA-mi.

k. Isolated words and expressions: **opera** o-PE-ra or O-pe-ra *opera* (but only **operami** o-pe-RA-mi), **w ogóle** W O-gó-le *in general*, **dobra noc** do-BRA noc *good-night*, **prezydent** PRE-zy-dent *president* (but GAsg. **prezydenta** pre-zy-DEN-ta, etc.), **uniwersytet** u-ni-WER-sy-tet *university* (but Gsg. **uniwersytetu** u-ni-wer-sy-TE-tu, etc.). Some words regularly stressed on the third-from-last syllable have developed next-to-last syllable stress in idiomatic meanings; see **oPEra** *hoopla*, **muZYka** *band*, **gimnaSTYka** *dodging and darting*.

Chapter 2

Morphophonemics
(Sound Changes)

THE IDEA OF MORPHOPHONEMICS

Morphophonemics has to do with sound-changes or sound-replacements related to the changing grammatical forms of words. By a "morphophoneme" is meant a phoneme that either conditions or itself undergoes a change to (a replacement by) another phoneme in a given grammatical position. In addition to morphophonemes that have an existence as phonemes, there are in Polish a few morphophonemic "operators", most importantly the "plain zero" (-Ø), "softening zero" (-'), and "null; absolute end of word" (-#). Morphophonemic changes take place at or near junctures between morphemes, i.e. meaningful parts of words such as stems, suffixes, and endings. Morpheme-junctures are indicated in technical transcription with a hyphen (-). An important purpose of morphophonemic description is to be able to point to a particular shape of a given morpheme as being basic, simultaneously specifying how other forms of the morpheme are related to it.

For example, **k, c**, and **cz** all appear in the same root-final position in the related words **ręka** *hand-Nsg.*, **ręce** *hand-Lsg.*, and **ręczny** *manual-adj.* The root of the word could be described as consisting of **ręk- ~ ręc- ~ ręcz-**, where by ~ is meant "alternates with". In a more concise approach, it is preferable to state that the root of the word is **ręk-**, specifying at the same time the rules which describe where **k** in some grammatical positions goes to **c**, and in other grammatical positions to **cz**. Morphophonemics thus systematizes the sound-relationships one finds among related words, and related forms of the same word.

CONSONANT MORPHOPHONEMES

The most important division among Polish consonant morphophonemes is into "primary" and "derived". Primary consonants are **p, b, f, w, m, t, d, s, z, ł, r, n, k, g, ch/h, j**. Except for **j**, this is also the class of "functionally hard consonants". All other consonants, including **j**, are "functionally soft", and are derived, which means that in the native Polish word-stock they are derived from one of the primary consonants. For example, as seen above with the example of **ręka, ręce**, and **ręczny, c** and **cz** are derived from **k**, hence **k** is primary with respect to **c** and **cz**; and **c** and **cz** are derived with respect to **k**. The sound **j** alone is outside the system of primary-derived consonants.

Derived consonants are not always related to a primary consonant. For example, in **mecz** *match*, the **cz** is not derived from any primary consonant but has been borrowed together with the word from English *match*. Additionally, inside roots, certain consonants may have been historically derived from a primary consonant, but there is no need to recognize this fact, since the consonant never appears in its primary form in a related word. Inside roots, then, it is usually expedient to carry out primary-to-derived sound-changes in advance of the description of the root. Thus the root of **czesać** *to comb* is represented as **czes-**, not, say, as ***kes-**, changing everywhere to **czes-**.

CONSONANT REPLACEMENTS

Consonant replacements take place almost exclusively at morpheme junctures before vowels and morphophonemic operators. Most often, consonant replacements occur at the end of a word-stem before a grammatical ending, almost all of which begin with a vowel. Since different kinds of consonant replacements may take place before the same vowel phoneme in different grammatical positions, it becomes necessary to distinguish among vowel morphophonemes which emerge ultimately as the same phoneme. For the most dramatic such example, based on the behavior of the velar consonants **k**, **g**, and **ch** before the phoneme **e**, there are five different morphophonemes **e**, which may be represented as **e, ě₁, ě₂, è**, and **ė**:

> -**e** conditions the changes **k: cz** and **g: ż**, as in **piek-esz: pieczesz** *you bake*, **mog-esz: możesz** *you can*.

> -**ě₁**, which occurs in nominal morphology, conditions the changes **k c**, **g: dz**, and **ch:sz**, as in **ręk-ě: ręce** *hand DLsg.*, **nog-ě: nodze** *foot-DLsg.*, **cech-ě: cesze** *trait-DLsg.* The subscript here refers to consonant-replacement type R1, on which see further below.

> -**ě₂**, which occurs in verbal morphology and inside roots, conditions the changes **k: cz, g: ż**, and **ch:sz**. The subscript refers to consonant-replacement type R2, on which see further below. The main difference between **e** and **ě₂** (before both of which R2 replacement occurs) is that **ě₂** participates in the alternation **e~a**, whereas **e** does not. See **krzyk-ě₂-ć: krzyczeć** *shout*, 3.p.sg.masc. past **krzyk-ě₂-ł-Ø: krzyczał**.

> -**è** conditions the changes **k: k'** and **g: g'**, as in **rok-èm: rokiem** *year Isg.*, **dog-èm: dogiem** *great Dane-Isg.*

> -**ė** has no effect on a preceding **k** or **g**. Since **ė** occurs inside roots, there is usually no need to indicate this **e** with a special diacritic device; see **keks** *biscuits*, **generał** *general*. However, **ė** occurs at a morpheme juncture in masculine past-tense singular verb-endings **-em** and **-eś** which, when detached and added to a word ending in **k** or **g**, have no softening effect on the preceding **k** or **g**: **jakem myślał** *as I thought*; hence the endings may be represented as **-ėm, -ėś**.

Overall, four main types of consonant-replacement occur in Polish. The order in which they are listed, and designated as R1–R4, is based on frequency of occurrence, hence on the overall importance of the consonant-replacement in the grammar.

➢ **R1** replacements take place before the vowel morphophonemes -$\check{e}_1$ and -ĭ.

➢ **R2** replacements take place before the vowel morphophonemes **e** and **i** and before the softening operator -'-. In verb conjugation, R2 replacement occurs before $\check{e}_2$.

➢ **R3** replacements take place before **j** (remember: only across morpheme boundaries). After conditioning an R3 replacement, **j** is dropped.

➢ **R4** replacement refers to the palatalization of **k** and **g**, and rarely of **ch** (to **k'**, **g'**, **ch'**, respectively) before **y** or **è**. Non-velar consonants do not have R4 replacements.

For purposes of describing the various consonant-replacements, it is helpful to divide the consonants into groups: labials-and-sonants; dentals; velars; and clusters:

a. Labials and Sonants: Dental sonants:

Primary (R0):	p	b	f	w	m	n	ł	r
R1, R2, R3:	p'	b'	f'	w'	m'	ń	l	rz

Note that the item **ł** is "dental" only in a historical-functional sense.

b. Dental Stops and Fricatives

Primary (R0):	t	d	s	z
R1, R2:	ć	dź	ś	ź
R3:	c	dz	sz	ż

c. Velars: Marginal:

Primary (R0):	k	g	ch	h
R1:	c	dz	sz/ś	ż/ź
R2, R3:	cz	ż	sz	ż
R4:	k'	g'	ch'	h'

Notes on Velars:

i. Observe that **c, dz, sz, ż**, in addition to their occurrence in the chart of velars, also occur in the R3 row of dentals.

ii. The consonant **ch** goes to **sz** before the vowel morphophoneme $\check{e}_1$, but to **ś** before ĭ; cf. **much-**$\check{e}_1$: **musze** *fly-DLsg.*, **Czech-ĭ: Czesi** *Czech-Npl.*

iii. In some historical borrowings from Ukrainian or Czech, the consonant **h** has a separate morphophonemic status, independent from **ch**, and goes to **ż** before **ě**$_1$ and to **ź** before **ǐ**: **watah-ě**$_1$: **wataże** *band (of Cossacks)-DLsg.*, **blah-ǐ**: **blazi** *trivial-m.p.pl.* Mutation according to the rules for **ch** is optional with such words and, in such instances, **h** and **h'** may be viewed as spelling variants of **ch** and **ch'**.

d. Clusters:

Primary (R0):	st	zd	sn	zn	sm	sł	zł	sk	zg
R1`:	źć	źdź	śń	źń	śm'	śl	źl	sc	zdz
R2:	"	"	"	"	"	"	"	szcz	żdż
R3:	szcz	żdż	"	"	"	"	"	"	"

The cluster **zm** has an optional R1 **źm'**, which is not normally spelled, although it is almost always pronounced: **kataklizmie** "katakliźmie" *cataclism-Lsg.* from **kataklizm**. The combination **łł** does not soften past the right-most **ł** in **pełli** *they weeded-masc. pers. pl.*; however, the adjective from **Jagiełło** (name of king) is **jagielloński** *Jagiellonian*; the DLsg. of **mułła** *mullah* is **mulle**.

Detailed illustrations of sound-replacements rules are given at the end of this chapter.

Note on the Morphophoneme *c*

The morphophoneme **c** presents something of an anomaly. On the one hand **c** is the R1 counterpart of **k** and the R3 counterpart of **t**. On the other hand, in some words **c** acts as a primary consonant, having **cz** as an R2 counterpart (before **e, i,** and **-'**):

    ojciec *father*, Vocative **ojc-e**: **ojcze**
    tablica *blackboard*, diminutive **tablic-'k-a**: **tabliczka**
    koniec *end*, **kon'c-i-ć**: **kończyć** *to finish*
    walc *waltz*, diminutive **walc-ik**: **walczyk**

In sum, **c** functions mainly as a derived consonant under **k** and **t**, but it can also function as a quasi-primary consonant, having **cz** as an R2 counterpart. As a marginal phenomenon, **dz** functions as a primary consonant, changing to R2 **ż**, in, say, **ksiądz** *priest*, Vocative **księże**; **pieniądze** *money*, **pieniężny** *monetary*.

FUNCTIONALLY HARD AND FUNCTIONALLY SOFT CONSONANTS

From the point of view of morphophonemics, it is not the literal phonetic hardness or softness of consonants that is important but their historical hardness or softness, or what from the contemporary point of view may be called their "functional" hardness/softness. Many inflectional processes, especially in nominal declension, continue to be sensitive to the historical status of certain consonants as soft, even though today these consonants are phonetically hard. For example, feminine noun declension specifies one Locative sg. ending, $-\check{e}_1$, for (functionally) hard-stems, and another, $-y/i$, for (functionally) soft-stems. Briefly, all primary consonants other than **j** are functionally hard; all derived consonants, and additionally **j**, are functionally soft.

In sum:

Functionally Hard: **p, b, f, w, m, t, d, s, z, n, r, ł, k, g, ch**

Functionally Soft:

    Phonetically Soft: **p', b', f', w', m', ć, dź, ś, ź, ń, l, j**

    Phonetically Hard: **c, cz, dz, dż, rz, sz, ż**

VOWEL MORPHOPHONEMES

Rather than primary and derived, vowel morphophonemes may be divided into "primary" and "shifted", since vowel replacements do not result in new vowels but rather in the shift of one primary vowel to another. Not every vowel participates in the primary-shifted system. The vowel-shifts are not as consistent in their operation as are the consonant-replacements.

Primary:	**a**	**e**	**ě**	**è**	**i**	**ĭ**	**y**	**u**	**o**	**ę**	**ą**
Shifted:		**o**	**a**						**ó**	**ą**	

When **o** shifts to **u**, the result is spelled **ó** to indicate its derivation from **o**. A shifted vowel becomes a primary vowel in its new value and may take part in a subsequent shift, but in no more than one such additional shift. For example, if **e** shifts to **o**, this new **o** may may subsequently shift to **ó**. One may observe such a double-shift in a series like **nieść** *carry,* **niosę** *I carry,* **niósł** *he carried,* all of which have an original root **nies-** as a point of departure.

In active morphophonemics, $\check{e}_1$ occurs mainly in nominal morphology, while $\check{e}_2$ occurs in verbal morphology and inside roots. Both $\check{e}_1$ and $\check{e}_2$ may participate in the **e~a** alternation (see further discussion). Because of the distributional predictability of $\check{e}_1$ and $\check{e}_2$, it is possible to dispense with the subscripted notation in most discussions, as below; i.e., assume that **ě** as a Dative or Locative noun ending is $\check{e}_1$ and, unless otherwise mentioned, any other **ě** is $\check{e}_2$.

In addition to the vowel morphophonemes, one distinguishes the morphophonemic operators "plain zero" (Ø) and "softening zero" ('). These operators have vowel-like distributional properties, and they can condition or undergo shifts in ways similar to vowels. The null operator (#) participates in vowel-shifts only as an outcome; i.e., if Ø or ' do not shift to a vowel, they can be considered to go to #, i.e. to disappear; see further discussion.

VOWEL-SHIFTS

1. **e: o** and **ě: a.**

The vowel morphophonemes **e** and **ě** often shift to **o** and **a**, respectively, before primary dentals (**t, d, s, z, n, ł, r**). Note that for this rule, sonants **n, ł, r** count as dentals. This shift encompasses both $ě_1$ and $ě_2$.

Compare with:

bier-ę:	**biorę** *I take*	**bier-esz**:	**bierzesz** *you take*
jěd-ę:	**jadę** *I ride*	**jěd-esz**:	**jedziesz** *you ride*

In these examples, the 1.p.sg. ending **-ę** does not soften the dentals **r** and **d**, hence the shift-rule operates. By contrast, the 2.p.sg. ending **-esz** softens the dentals (to R2), hence the vowel does not shift.

In nominal and adjectival declension, where almost all forms of a word (including the dictionary form) display a primary dental at the end of the stem, and only one or two forms show a softened dental, this rule appears to operate in reverse:

Stem:	Dictionary form:	Unshifted vowel:	
spalen-:	**spalony** *burnt*	**spalen-ĭ**:	**spaleni** *Npl. mp.*
lěs-:	**las** *forest*	**lěs-$ě_1$**:	**lesie** *Lsg.*
miěr-:	**miara** *measure*	**miěr-$ě_1$**:	**mierze** *DLsg.*
miěst-	**miasto** *town*	**miěst-$ě_1$**:	**mieście** *Lsg.*

In such words, the morphophonemic stem which one needs to establish in order to describe this shift is, statistically speaking, isolated and exceptional in the declension of the word.

The **ě: a** alternation is prominently visible in the past tense of verbs with infinitives in **-eć** (**-$ě_2$-ć**), with **e** occurring in the masc. pers. pl. forms, before softened **ł: l**:

widzieć *see*	**widział** *he saw*	**widzieli** *they (masc. pers. pl.) saw*
mieć *have*	**miał** *he had*	**mieli** *they (masc. pers. pl.) had*

This alternation does *not* occur in the adjective or participle, where stem-final **'a** (**a** preceded by a functionally soft consonant) is generalized everywhere; see **mile widziani** *welcome (masc. pers. pl.)*.

Inside many words, the shifted vowel has been generalized to all forms of the word, including forms where one might expect to find the primary vowel. For example, in **wiosna** *spring*, the **e** has gone to **o** everywhere, including in the Dative-Locative sg., which is no longer *wieśnie but **wiośnie**. Similarly, in **jezioro** *lake*, the Locative sg. is **jeziorze** instead of expected (and archaic) *jezierze. In such words, the basic vowel of the stem is, then, no longer **e** but **'o** (**o** preceded by a functionally soft consonant). One may occasionally observe different realizations of original **e** or **ě** within the same root from one word-class to another. For example, one may observe the original unshifted **e** in the second syllable of **jezioro** in the related word **pojezierze** *lake district*. The word **piana** *foam, DLsg.* **pianie** has generalized shifted **a** (from **ě₂**) everywhere, while the related verb **pienić się** *to foam* has unshifted **e** before soft **ń** everywhere.

2. **o: ó and ę: ą**

The vowel **o** often shifts to **ó** (phonemic **u**), and **ę** to **ą**, before a consonant at the end of a word or before two consonants within a word. These vowel shifts are conditioned by a following **Ø** (plain zero) operator, whether the operator occurs between two consonants or at the end of a word, as illustrations to follow show. These changes occur especially frequently before originally voiced consonants which have become devoiced according to the rules of automatic phonemic adjustment, but they occasionally take place before unvoiced consonants as well. In addition, these shifts may occur before **r, ł, l,** and **j,** which are not subject to devoicing.

		Compare with:	
cnot-Ø:	**cnót** *virtue-Gpl.*	**cnot-a:**	**cnota** *Nsg.*
głow-Ø:	**głów** *head-Gpl.*	**głow-a:**	**głowa** *Nsg.*
kor-Ø:	**kór** *bark-Gpl.*	**kor-a:**	**kora** *Nsg.*
koz-Ø:	**kóz** *goat-Gpl.*	**koz-a:**	**koza** *Nsg.*
pol-Ø:	**pól** *field-Gpl.*	**pol-e:**	**pole** *Nsg.*
zorz-Ø:	**zórz** *dawn-Gpl.*	**zorz-a:**	**zorza** *Nsg.*
ręk-Ø:	**rąk** *hand-Gpl.*	**ręk-a:**	**ręka** *Nsg.*
wstęg-Ø:	**wstąg** *ribbon-Gpl.*	**wstęg-a:**	**wstęga** *Nsg.*

From the point of view of masculine noun declension, where the Nominative sg. form (i.e., the dictionary form) contains the shifted vowel, this rule appears to operate in reverse:

bor-Ø:	**bór** *woods-NAsg.*	**bor-u:**	**boru** *Gsg.*
stoł-Ø:	**stół** *table-NAsg.*	**stoł-u:**	**stołu** *Gsg.*
dęb-Ø:	**dąb** *oak-NAsg.*	**dęb-u:**	**dębu** *Gsg.*
wąż-Ø:	**wąż** *oak-Nsg.*	**węż-a:**	**węża** *GAsg.*

In such instances, only the Nominative-inan. Accusative sg. of the word will contain the shifted vowel; other forms will contain the primary vowel. These changes do not usually occur before originally unvoiced consonants, nor before devoiced consonants in words felt to be borrowings: **rok-Ø: rok** *year-NAsg.*, **tog-Ø: tog** *toga-Gpl. of* **toga**. The change **o: ó** usually does occur before word-final **j**: **boj-Ø: bój** *fight*, Gsg. **boju, stroj-Ø: strój** *costume*, Gsg. **stroju**. An incorrectly applied **o: ó** shift before voiceless consonants in the Gpl of feminine-declension nouns is the subject of frequent normative correction. For example, dictionaries recommend **rosa** *dew*, Gpl **ros** (not ***rós**), **rota** *oath*, Gpl **rot** (not ***rót**), but do accept either **kop** or **kóp** as the Gpl of **kopa** *stack*.

The vowel-shifts **o: ó** and **ę: ą** often occur before devoiced consonants, and before **j** and **ł**, before the suffix **-Øk-**. When these changes occur, they tend to be generalized to all forms of the word, including forms where Ø is realized as **e**, and where consequently one would not expect the shift:

Regular shift:

głow-Øk-a: **główka** *head-dim.*
boj-Øk-a: **bójka** *fight-dim.*
wstęż-Øk-a: **wstążka** *ribbon-dim.*

Analogical shift in Gpl.:

głow-Øk-Ø: **główek** *Gpl.*
boj-Øk-Ø: **bójek** *Gpl.*
wstęż-Øk-Ø: **wstążek** *Gpl.*

Compare with **dęt-Øk-a: dętka** *inner tube*, where the shift does not take place before the originally unvoiced **t**. With masculine-declension nouns, the vowel-shift occurs less regularly. If it does occur, the shift appears naturally in the majority of forms and is projected into the Nominative-Accusative sg., presumably originally by analogy:

Regular shift:

woz-Øk-a: **wózka** *pram-Gsg.*

Analogical shift in Nsg.:

woz-Øk-Ø: **wózek** *Nsg.*

Compare with **kłęb-Øk-a: kłębka**, not *kłąbka *puff of smoke-Gsg.*, or with **doł-Øk-a: dołka**, not *dółka *pit-Gsg.*, where the shift does not occur even though the requisite conditions are present. Among neuter-declension nouns, the **o: ó** shift occurs before the suffix **-Øk-**, for example, in:

Regular shift:

koł-Øk-o: **kółko** *circle-dim.-NAsg.*
słow-Øk-o: **słówko** *word-dim.-NAsg.*

Analogical shift in Gpl.:

koł-Øk-Ø: **kółek** *Gpl.*
słow-Øk-Ø: **słówek** *Gpl.*

The vowel-shift **ę: ą** may be lacking even when all conditions appear to be favorable. For example, the Genitive pl. of **potęga** *power* is **potęg**, not expected *potąg; similarly for **pręga** *stripe*, Gpl **pręg**, not *prąg. The Nominative sg. of 'swan' is **łabędź**, not *łabądź; **rząd** *Gsg.* **rzędu** *row* contrasts with **rząd** *Gsg.* **rządu** *government*; and so on. Before **rz** and **l**, the shift **o: ó** shift may or may not occur; if it does, it will usually occur in all forms of the word: **tchórz** *coward-Nsg.*, **tchórza**-*GAsg.*; compare **węgorz** *eel-Nsg.* **węgorza**-*GAsg.*, **ból** *pain-NAsg.*, **bólu**-*Gsg.*; compare to **boleć** *to hurt*. In the instance of the word **król** *king-Nsg.*, **króla**-*GAsg.*, where all forms of the root have generalized **ó**, including in all related words, the vowel can be considered to be basic **u**, merely spelled **ó** according to tradition.

Apart from nominal inflection, the shifts **o: ó** and, less often **ę: ą** may be observed in the imperative of some verbs before softening zero ('):

Before -'

rob-': **rób** *do-imper.*
stoj-': **stój** *stand-imper.*
będ-': **bądź** *be-imper.*

Compare with:

rob-i-sz: **robisz** *you do*
stoj-i-sz: **stoisz** *you stand*
będ-e-sz: **będziesz** *you are*

but:

chod-':   chodź *come-imper.*   chod-i-sz: chodzisz *you come*
pęd-':   pędź *rush-imper.*   pęd-i-sz: pędzisz *you rush*

An example of the **e: o** shift feeding into the **o: ó** shift may be seen in the word **kościół**:

e: o shift, leading to: **o: ó** shift
kościeł-Ø: kościoł-Ø: kościoł-Ø: kościół *church NAsg.*

Compare with other forms:

e: o shift: No shift:
kościeł-a: kościoła *Gsg.*   kościeł-ĕ: kościele *Lsg.*

The Locative sg. **kościele**, then, is the only form of this word to contain the unshifted vowel (the root with **e** may also be seen in the adjective **kościeł-'n-y: kościelny**).

MOBILE VOWELS

By "mobile vowel" is meant a vowel (usually, phonemic **e**) which alternates with # (null, nothing) in different forms of the same morpheme. Most often, the mobile vowel appears between two consonants at the end of a word before the grammatical ending **-Ø**; see **sen** *dream-NAsg.*, **snu**-*Gsg.*; **mydło** *soap-NAsg.*, **mydeł**-*Gpl.*; **książka** *book-Nsg.*, **książek**-*Gpl.* As these examples show, from the point of view of masculine noun declension, it appears that the mobile vowel, which appears in the dictionary form, is being lost in the oblique case forms. From the point of view of neuter and feminine nouns with a mobile vowel in the Genitive pl., the mobile vowel appears to split the final two consonants of the stem in this one form. In either instance, one has to do with the grammatical ending **-Ø**, and a single form in the word's inflection that contains the mobile vowel.

The mobile vowel **e** may represent either morphophonemic **e** or **è**. The difference between **e** and **è** can be determined by looking at the effect on a preceding consonant. R2 replacement appears before mobile **e**, while only R4 replacement (the change of **k, g** to **k', g'**) occurs before mobile **è**:

R2 replacement before mobile **e**:   Compare with:
pies *dog-Nsg.*   **psa** *GAsg.*
orzeł *eagle-Nsg.*   **orła** *GAsg.*
dzień *day-NAsg.*   **dnia** *Gsg.*
kwiecień *April-Nsg.*   **kwietnia** *Gsg.*

R4 (velars only) replacement before mobile **è**:   Compare with:
łeb *noggin-NAsg.*   **łba** *Gsg.*
den *bottom-Gpl.*   **dno** *NAsg.*
okien *window-Gpl.*   **okno** *NAsg.*
ogień *fire-NAsg.*   **ognia** *Gsg.*

It is apparent that the mobile vowel rules are a kind of shift-rule, analogous to the vowel-shift rules described above:

Primary: Ø   '
            | |
Shifted: è   e

Conditioning factor: before a consonant followed by an unshifted Ø or '. Otherwise, the operators Ø and ' are dropped. Here are some examples; for further illustrations, see the end of this chapter:

Form with **e** from ' before ending -Ø:	Form without **e** before vowel ending:
p'ń-Ø: pień-*stump-NAsg.*	**p'ń-a:** **pnia** *Gsg.*
chłop'c-Ø: **chłopiec**-*boy-Nsg.*	**chłop'c-a:** **chłopca**-*GAsg.*
Form with **è** from Ø before ending -Ø:	Form without **è** before vowel ending:
mØch-Ø: mech-*moss-NAsg.*	**mØch-u:** mchu-*Gsg.*
krØw'-Ø: krew *blood-NAsg.*	**krØw'-y/i:** krwi-*Gsg.*

As is the case with the other vowel-shifts, the product of a mobile-vowel shift may feed into another (at most, one other) shift-rule. For example, the product of the ': e shift may feed into the e: o shift, resulting in what amounts on the surface to a mobile **o**:

': e shift, leading to:	e: o shift:
kot'ł-Ø: **kocieł-Ø:**	**kocieł-Ø:** **kocioł** *pot-NAsg.*

Observe that the form **kocioł** Gsg. **kotła** *pot* does not go further to *kociół (as one might expect by looking at **kościół**). Since two shifts have already occurred, ': e and e: o, the further shift of o to ó is thwarted.

Hard/Soft Consonant Alternations in Stems with Mobile Vowels

In stems containing the mobile-vowel operator ' ("softening zero"), the rules for whether or not the ' will result in an R2 replacement in forms where the shift to **e** does not occur are fairly complex:

a. labials **p'**, **b'**, **w'**, **m'** (not including **ł**) always harden: **p's-a: psa** *dog-GAsg.*, compare with **p's-Ø: pies** *Nsg.*; **ow's-a: owsa** *oats-Gsg.*, compare with **ow's-Ø: owies**-*NAsg.*

b. **ł** always softens: **pał-'c-a: palca** *finger-Gsg.*, compare with **pał-'c-Ø: palec** *NAsg.* See the root **pał-** in related **pałka** *stick.*

c. dental stops and the dental sonant **r** harden before other dentals, but otherwise soften: **d'ń-a: dnia** *day-Gsg.*, compare with **d'ń-Ø: dzień** *NAsg;* **t'm-a: ćma** *moth-Nsg.*, compare with **t'm-Ø: ciem** *Gpl.*; **kor'c-a: korca** *bushel-Gsg.*, compare with **kor'c-Ø: korzec**-*NAsg.*

d. **n** hardens before **n**: **pan'n-a: panna** *miss-Nsg.*, compare with **pan'n-Ø: panien**-*Gpl.*

e.   velars always soften to R2: **tek-'k-a**: **teczka** *briefcase-Nsg.*, compare with
     tek-'k-Ø: **teczek** *Gpl.* See the root **tek-** in related **kartoteka** *cardfile.*

It follows that stems with dental consonants before other dental consonants (here, including **r**, **n**, and the historical-functional dental **ł**) require the
greatest attention. Here are some examples:

With mobile **e** (o) and softened dental:	Rorm with zero and hard dental:
dworzec *station-NAsg.*	**dworca** *Gsg.*
grudzień *December-NAsg.*	**grudnia** *Gsg.*
kocioł *pot-NAsg.*	**kotła** *Gsg.*
korzec *bushel-NAsg.*	**korca** *Gsg.*
kozioł *goat-Nsg.*	**kozła** *GAsg.*
krosien *loom-Gpl.*	**krosno** *NAsg.*
kwiecień *April-NAsg.*	**kwietnia** *Gsg.*
marzec *March-NAsg.*	**marca** *Gsg.*
orzeł *eagle-Nsg.*	**orła** *GAsg.*
wzorzec *model-NAsg.*	**wzorca** *Gsg.*

> As a rule, mobile vowels occur in only one place in a noun's declension:
> before the ending -**Ø**. Where they do occur, they compensate, as it were,
> for the lack of an overt ending, becoming, in effect, a surrogate gram-
> matical marker. Mobile-vowel mistakes will often be incomprehensible
> from the point of view of a speaker of Polish. As a consequence, among
> possible sources of grammatical errors, mobile vowels are deserving of
> the especially careful attention of the foreign-speaking learner.

Mobile Vowels after Prepositions

The prepositions **bez**, **(z)nad**, **od**, **(s)pod**, **(s)przed**, **przez**, **w**, and **z** end in
an underlying -**Ø**, which will be realized as mobile **e** under limited circumstances, not necessarily involving the presence of ' or **Ø** in a following syllable.

a.   The preposition **w** becomes **we** before **w** or **f** followed by another conso-
     nant:

we Francji *in France*   **we wrześniu** *in September*
we Wrocławiu *in Wroclaw*   **we wsi** *in the village*
we wszystkim *in everything*   **we Włoszech** *in Italy*
Compare:
w Szwecji *in Sweden*
w Warszawie *in Warsaw*

b.   The preposition **z** (in whichever meaning) becomes **ze** before **s**, **z**, **ś**, **ź**, **ż**,
     sz, **wz**, **ws** followed by another consonant:

ze względu na *with regard to*   **ze szczęścia** *from happiness*
ze wstrząsem *with a shock*   **ze wstydem** *with shame*

ze zdrowiem *with health*   **ze złością** *with anger*
ze swojego pokoju *from his room*

Compare:

z(e) wszystkim *with everything*   **z wszą** *with a louse*
z psem *with a dog*

Also contrast **we Francji** *in France* with **z Francją; w Szwecji** *in Sweden*
with **ze Szwecji** *from Sweden.*

c. All of the above prepositions may take a following **e** before asyllabic sur-
    face stems of nouns and pronouns, in particular including oblique forms
    of **ja** *I* beginning with **mn-: ze mną** *with me,* **przede mną** *in front of me,*
    nade mną *over me,* and so on. See also:

    we śnie *in a dream*   **ze łzami** *with tears*
    we łby *in the heads*   **we mchu** *in the moss*
    spode łba *from beneath one's brow*   **we mnie** *in me,* and so on

d. Occasionally mobile vowels will occur in set expressions but not in regu-
    lar collocations, as in **z krwi** *from one's blood* but possible **ze krwi i kości**
    in one's very bones, as in **Polak ze krwi i kości** *a Pole through and through;* **w
    dniu** *on the day,* but **we dnie i w nocy** *by day and night.*

e. *Mobile vowels after verb prefixes.* Consonantal verbal prefixes will take a fol-
    lowing mobile **e** before asyllabic verb-stems, as in **nade[jd]ę** *I'll approach,*
    ode[rw]ać *tear off,* **ode[tch]nąć** *take a breather,* **pode[jm]ę** *I'll undertake,*
    roze[pn]ę *I'll unpin,* **ze[tn]ę** *I'll cut off,* and so on.

f. *Words with two mobile vowel positions.* Occasionally, a word will contain
    some combination of two mobile-vowel operators, whether Ø or ', in
    which case there will be two alternative positions for mobile-vowel inser-
    tion, depending on whether the ending is zero or vocalic:

    przedØd'ń-Ø: przeddzień *eve of event*   **przedØd'ń-a: przededna** *Gsg.*

Mobile ę and ą

When either of the two operators ' or Ø precede **n** or **m** followed by a consonant, a nasal vowel will result, either **ę** or **ą**. Additionally, the combination
en will go to **ę** before a consonant (in practice, **t**) or **#** (end of word). An **ę** from
either '/Ø+n/m or **en** may feed into the **ę: ą** shift rule; hence this change is
similar to vowel-shifts already examined, in that two may be chained
together.

Primary:	'+n/m, Ø+n/m	en	ę
	|	|	|
Shifted:	ę/ą	ę	ą

Whether the vowel from '+n/m or Ø+n/m will be ę or ą is either unpredictable, or is governed by grammatical factors rather than by phonological environment. In practice, mobile ę occurs most often. Mobile ę/ą is usually found in verb conjugation. Here are some examples in some verb roots, where it makes most sense to assume that the vowel is first ę, changing to ą before consonant+Ø:

Stem:	Form before -ł-a, showing ę:	Form before -ł-Ø, showing ą:	Form before -ę, showing n/m:
dØm- *puff*	dęła	dął	dmę
gØn- *bend*	gięła	giął	gnę
p'n- *pin*	pięła	piął	pnę
t'n- *cut*	cięła	ciął	tnę
wØz'm- *take*	wzięła	wziął	wezmę
zacz'n- *begin*	zaczęła	zaczął	zacznę
ż'm- *press*	żęła	żął	żmę
ż'n- *reap*	żęła	żął	żnę

In gØn-ł-a: gięła, one assumes the same R4 replacement (g: g') before ę that one finds before è. Assuming ę: ą before -ł-Ø, then, explains the occurrence of g' before ą in giął. In wØz'm- *take*, one sees a combination of two internal mobile-vowel slots, with correspondingly two alternate positions for mobile vowel appearance; compare

wØz'm-ć: wziąć *to take*   **wØz'm-ę: wezmę** *I will take*

The lack of the expected softening z: ź in **wezmę** (not *weźmę) is anomalous.

The change en(t)-#: ę is restricted to neuter-gender nouns of the **imię** *name* and **zwierzę** *animal* types. These types are of interest for showing the different development of en(t) before # on the one hand, and before Ø on the other:

Nsg. **im-en-#: im'-en-#: imię**
Gpl. **im-en-Ø: im'en-Ø: im'on** (e: o before n), spelled **imion**.

Nsg. **zwier-ent-#: zwierzęt-#: zwierzę**
Gpl. **zwier-ent-Ø: zwierzęt-Ø: zwierząt**

For fuller discussion of these noun types, see Chapter 5.

Distribution of Ø and ' in Grammatical Affixes

Here are the grammatical positions where the operators ' and Ø most frequently occur:

a. Ø occurs as a grammatical ending in nominal inflection:

zeszyt-Ø: **zeszyt** *notebook-NAsg.*
lamp-Ø: **lamp** *lamp-Gpl.*
koł-Ø: **kół** *wheel-Gpl.*

b.   Ø occurs as the first component of the derivational suffix **-Øk-**:

     książ-Øk-Ø: **książek** *book-Gpl.*
     ołów-Øk-Ø: **ołówek** *pencil-NAsg.*
     koł-Øk-Ø: **kółek** *wheel-dim.-Gpl.*

c.   ' occurs as a stem-extension in the fem. declension in -Ø:

     kost-'-Ø: **kość** *bone-NAsg.*

d.   ' can be imputed as a stem-extension in the soft masc. declension in -Ø:

     rys-'-Ø: **ryś** *lynx-Nsg.*

e.   ' occurs as a singular stem-extension in the neut. declension in -#:

     im-en-'-a: **imienia** *name-NAsg.*

f.   among noun suffixes, ' occurs most prominenently as the first part of the suffix **-'c-**:

     łow-'c-Ø: **łowiec** *hunter-Nsg.*

g.   among adjective suffixes, ' occurs most prominenently as the first part of the adjective suffix **-'n-**:

     mąk-'n-y: **mączny** *flour-adj.*

h.   ' occurs as an imperative verb ending:

     nos-':   **noś** *carry-imper.*

i.   ' occurs as a stem-extension in verbal-noun formation:

     ży-t-'-e: **życie** *life*
     mieszka-n-'-e: **mieszkanie** *apartment*

THE MERGER OF VOWEL MORPHOPHONEMES INTO PHONEMES

Following the sound-changes which the vowel morphophonemes either condition or undergo, they lose their separate status and merge into a smaller number of vowel phonemes. The signs ě, è, ĭ, ', Ø, and # are not written other than in technical analyses. Specifically,

a.   e, ě, and è merge into e; thus, the phoneme e in the words **nieść** *carry*, **jeść** *eat*, and **teść** *father-in-law* derives from morphophonemic e, ě, and è, respectively.

b.   i, ĭ, and y merge into the same phoneme i~y. The letters i and y become subject to a phonetically conditioned spelling rule (see Chapter 1), and no longer reflect original i, ĭ, or y. Thus, the letter y in the words **dobry** *good-Nsg.-masc.* and **wielcy** *great-Npl.mp.* reflects original y and ĭ, respectively. The letters i and y in **wielki** *great-Nsg.masc.* and **dobry** *good-Nsg.masc.* reflect original y. In the words **nosić** *carry* and **uczyć** *teach*, the i and y derive from original i; and so on.

c. The morphophonemic operators ' and Ø either become mobile **e** and **è**, respectively (which then merge into phonemic **e**), or disappear completely (according to rules discussed above under Mobile Vowels).

DIFFERENT LEVELS OF MORPHOPHONEMIC ABSTRACTION

It is possible to carry out the analysis of words to different degrees of completeness or abstraction. For example, **książka** *book* may be analyzed on one level as **książk-a**; on another as **książØk-a**; on another as **księg-'k-a**; on another as **ks'ng-'k-a**; and this does not exhaust the possibilities for the increasingly abstract description of this word. In general, one carries out a structural analysis to the point necessary for the elucidation of a particular problem. For example, the form **książØk-a** suffices for elucidating the mobile vowel in **książek** *Gpl*. The form **księg-'k-a** helps to demonstrate the relationship of the word to **księga** *tome*. Any further levels of abstraction than this would be helpful mainly in demonstrating the history of the word; its connection to related words in other Slavic languages; or its historical origin: it goes back to an old (Scandinavian? Central Asian?) borrowing into Slavic.

In practical works such as the present one, one often makes use of two pragmatic levels of morphophonemic description, "shallow" and "deep(er)". The shallow description is appropriate for describing the inflection of the word by itself, while the deep(er) description is used for showing the etymological or derivational relationship of the word to other related word-forms in the given language. For example, for purposes of describing the declension of the word **kość** *bone,* it is not necessary to analyze the word any further than to say that its stem is **kość-** and its ending is -**Ø**. However, for relating this word to, say, **skostniały** *ossified,* it is necessary to analyze the stem further, into **kost-** plus the softening formant -'- (plus the ending -**Ø**: **kost-'-Ø**).

Conventions adopted in the present work are designed to cast light on particular problems while preserving the recognizability of forms. It is for this reason that sound-changes have been carried out inside roots. For our purposes there would be little value in claiming that the root of, say, **czytać** *read* is ***kit-**; in particular, there is no evidence that speakers of Polish might feel that this is the deep root of this word. The noun **kit** means 'putty', so the suggestion might even strike one as amusing.

INDO-EUROPEAN MORPHOPHONEMIC VESTIGES

The Slavic languages among which Polish belongs derive historically from the Indo-European family of languages. Indo-European morphophonemics were characterized by a series of vowel replacements and lengthenings which are reflected only vestigially in contemporary Polish. The most important reflections in Polish of the earlier system are the alternations **o~a**, **'~i**, and **Ø~y**, which were originally based on vowel lengthening, and which are still visible and to an extent active in Imperfective verb derivation:

	Perfective verb:		Imperfective verb:
o~a	za-pros-i-ć		**zapraszać** *invite*
'~i	wy-t′n-ć:	wyciąć	**wycinać** *cut out*
∅~y	wy-sØch-n-ąć:	wyschnąć	**wysychać** *dry out*

Totally lacking in vitality are alternations based on Indo-European vowel gradation, which consisted in the interchange of ∅, e, and o in the same root. An alternation e ~ (o~ó) can be observed in:

wybierze *he'll choose*	**wybór** *choice*
cieknie *flows*	**potok** *stream*
niesie *carries-det.*	**nosi** *carries-indet.*

The alternation ∅ ~ e can be seen in

brać *take*	**bierze** *takes*
prać *wash*	**pierze** *washes*
pleć *weed*	**piele** *weeds*

An alternation between i and o~ó can be traced to an Indo-European alternation between *ei and *oi:

piję *I drink*	**napój** *drink*
wiję *I wind*	**zwój** *roll*
gniję *I rot*	**gnoić się** *to fester*

While the elucidation of such facts belongs to the description of Polish broadly considered, their detailed discussion is beyond the scope of the present work.

PHONOLOGICAL IRREGULARITIES

Sound correspondences among related Polish words are remarkably regular and predictable. However, occasionally sound-relationships, or the internal sound-structure of a Polish word, do not follow regular patterns and must be described on a case-by-case basis.

The irregular distribution of o versus ó and ę versus ą has already been mentioned. The distribution of ę and ą in particular often seems little better than haphazard. For example, ę will always be replaced by ą before final -ć in the infinitive of a verb, as in ciąg-n-ę-ć: ciągnąć *tug*, even though ć is not a devoiced consonant. By contrast, ę has not gone to ą before final ć in pięć *five*, while ę in the same root is replaced by ą in an open syllable in piąty *fifth*. One sees a similar situation in the verb zamącić *stir up* vs. the related noun zamęt *muddle*. Several doublets arbitrarily show ą or ę, for example gęsior/gąsior *gander*, kręg *vertebra* vs. krąg *circle*, kęsek/kąsek *morsel*. Many facts relating to the irregular distribution of o~ó and ę~ą can be traced to prehistoric occurrences connected with the loss of certain vowels, and with changes in original vowel length and pitch. Such facts cannot be described completely systematically from the point of view of the modern language, or at least so it would appear.

As we have seen, some phonological irregularities derive from inconsistencies in derivational strategies followed from one word to another. For example, on the basis of **róg** *horn*, diminutive **rożek**; **wór** *sack*, diminutive **worek**, **kłąb** *puff*, diminutive **kłębek**, one might expect **wóz** *cart*, diminutive ***wozek**. However, the diminutive of this word is **wózek**. The pressure of existing forms often impedes the regular operation of sound-changes. For example, the pejorative augmentative of **wódka** *vodka* is **wóda**, a word which preserves **ó** under the pressure of the base word and also to distinguish it from **woda** *water*. Sometimes rules may be formulated to describe how sound-changes will be affected in word-derivation; sometimes the linguistic facts are truly irregular and must be described on a case-by-case basis. For example, there is no apparent reason why **ě** does not shift to **a** in the 1.p.sg. of **wleźć wlezę wleziesz** *creep in*, stem **wlěz-**; see 3.p.sg. masc. past **wlazł**, with expected **a**. Often enough, even if systematic rules may be formulated, they are so complex as to make it preferable to treat the material as irregular anyway.

SUMMARY OF POLISH "ACTIVE" VOWEL AND ZERO/NULL MORPHOPHONEMES

Morphophoneme and Most Important Characteristics:

➢ -# conditions preceding **en** or **ent**: **ę**

➢ -Ø conditions a mobile-vowel shift (to **e**) and preceding R4 consonant replacement

➢ -' conditions a mobile-vowel shift (to **e**) and preceding R2 consonant replacement

➢ -e conditions preceding R2 consonant replacement, and may shift to **o** before hard dentals

➢ -ě$_1$ conditions preceding R1 consonant replacement, and may shift to **a** before hard dentals

➢ -ě$_2$ conditions preceding R2 consonant replacement, and may shift to **a** before hard dentals

➢ -è conditions preceding R4 consonant replacement

➢ -ė does not condition any changes

➢ -ę may shift to **ą** under various conditions, and prompts a preceding R4 consonant replacement

➢ -i conditions a preceding R2 consonant replacement

➢ -ï conditions a preceding R1 consonant replacement

➢ -y (-y/i) conditions a preceding R4 consonant replacement

➢ -o may shift to **ó** (= **u**) under various conditions

ILLUSTRATIONS OF SOUND-REPLACEMENT AND SPELLING RULES

The following examples, in addition to illustrating sound-replacement rules, also illustrate techniques used to establish underlying stems of words.

1. Consonant-replacement type R1

    a. Examples using the fem. DL sg. ending -ě$_1$:

    łąka *glade*

    Step 1. Subtract the ending **-a** from **łąka** to obtain the stem; add the ending **-ě** to the stem: **łąk-ě**.

    Step 2. Replace the stem consonant **k** with its R1 counterpart **c**, simultaneously merging **ě** with **e: łąc-e: łące**.

    lada *counter*

    Step 1. Subtract the ending **-a** from **lada** to obtain the stem; add the ending **-ě** to the stem: **lad-ě**.

    Step 2. Replace the stem consonant **d** with its R1 counterpart **dź**, simultaneously merging **ě** with **e: ladź-e**.

    Step 3. Spell **dź** as **dzi** before the vowel **e: ladzi-e: ladzie**.

    b. Examples using the Npl. masc. pers. ending -ĭ:

    biolog *biologist*

    Step 1. Subtract the ending (here, zero) from **biolog** to obtain the stem and add the ending **-ĭ** to the stem: **biolog-ĭ**.

    Step 2. Replace the stem consonant **g** with its R1 counterpart **dz**, simultaneously merging **ĭ** with **y/i: biolodz-y/i**.

    Step 3. Spell **y** after **dz: biolodz-y: biolodzy**.

    Czech *Czech*

    Step 1. Subtract the ending (here, zero) from **Czech** to obtain the stem and add the ending **-ĭ** to the stem: **Czech-ĭ**.

    Step 2. Replace the stem consonant **ch** with its R1 counterpart (in this instance, **ś**), simultaneously merging **ĭ** with **y/i: Cześ-y/i**.

    Step 3. Spell **i** after **ś**, and spell **ś** as **s** before **i: Czes-i: Czesi**.

2. Consonant replacement type R2. Illustrations using the 2.p.sg. verb ending

    -esz (1st conjugation) and **-isz** (2nd conjugation):

    piec piekę pieczesz *bake (1st conjugation)*

    Step 1. Obtain the stem from the 1.p.sg. pres. by subtracting **ę** from **piekę** and add the ending **-esz** to it: **piek-esz**

    Step 2. Replace **k** with its R2 counterpart **cz: piecz-esz: pieczesz**

iść idę idziesz *go-det. (1st conjugation)*

Step 1. Obtain the stem from the 1.p.sg. pres. by subtracting **-ę** from **idę** and add the ending **-esz** to it: **id-esz**

Step 2. Replace **d** with its R2 counterpart **dź**: **idź-esz**.

Step 3. Spell **dź** as **dzi** before the vowel **e**: **idzi-esz**: **idziesz**.

lubić lubię lubisz *like*

Step 1. Obtain the stem from the infinitive **lubić** by subtracting **-ić** from it and by taking the resulting stem-consonant **b'** back to its primary state **b**. Add the ending **-isz** to the stem: **lub-isz**

Step 2. Replace **b** with its R2 counterpart **b'**: **lub'-isz**.

Step 3. Spell **b'** as **b** before the vowel **i**: **lub-isz**: **lubisz**.

3. Consonant replacement type R3.

   a. Illustration using the 1.p.sg. link+ending **-j-ę**:

chodzić chodzę chodzisz *walk*

Step 1. Obtain the stem from the infinitive by subtracting **-ić** from **chodzić**; take the stem-consonant **dź** back to its primary state **d**. Add the link+ending **-j-ę** to the stem: **chod-j-ę**

Step 2. Replace **d** with its R3 counterpart **dz**, simultaneously erasing **j**: **chodz-ę**: **chodzę**.

   b. Illustration using the present-stem formant **-j-**:

pisać piszę piszesz *write*

Step 1. Obtain the stem from the infinitive by subtracting **-ać** from **pisać**: **pis-**. Add the formant **-j-** + any ending to the stem: **pis-j-ą**

Step 2. Replace **s** with its R3 counterpart **sz**, simultaneously erasing **j**: **pisz-ą**: **piszą**.

4. Consonant replacement type R4. Illustration using the masc. Isg. ending **-èm**.

rok *year*

Step 1. Obtain the stem by subtracting the ending (here, zero) from **rok**, and add **èm** to the stem: **rok-èm**.

Step 2. Replace **k** with its R4 counterpart **k'**, simultaneously merging **è** with **e**: **rok'-em**.

Step 3. Spell **k'** as **ki** before the vowel **e**: **roki-em**: **rokiem**.

5. Mobile **e** before consonant plus **Ø**. Illustrations from masculine and feminine noun declension.

pies psa *dog*, illustration of Nsg.

Step 1. Obtain the stem by comparing the N and G forms **pies psa** and add **-Ø** to the resultant stem **p's-**: **p's-Ø**.

Step 2. Replace ' with **e**, simultaneously dropping Ø: **p[e]s**.

Step 3. Replace **p** before **e** with its R2 counterpart **p'**: **p'[e]s**.

Step 4. Spell **p'** as **pi** before the vowel **e**: **pies**.

książka Gpl. **książek** *book*, illustration of Gpl.

Step 1. Obtain the deep stem by comparing the two forms of the word to each other, and to related **księga**; the implied stem is **księg-'k-**. Add Ø: **księg-'k-Ø**.

Step 2. Replace ' with **e**, simultaneously dropping Ø: **księg-ek**.

Step 3. Replace **g** before **e** with its R2 counterpart **ż**: **księżek**.

Step 4. Replace **ę** with **ą** by analogy with the other forms in this noun's declension, which show shifted **ę: ą: książek**.

6. The **e: o** and **ě: a** vowel shifts before hard dentals.

a.   Example from the 1.p.sg. of the 1st conjugation, ending **-ę**.

nieść niosę niesiesz *carry*.

Step 1. Obtain the stem by comparing all forms of the word; **niosę niesiesz**, masc. 3.p.sg. past **niósł** imply the stem **nies-** Add **-ę**: **nies-ę**.

Step 2. Replace **e** with **o** before the hard dental: **nios-ę: niosę**.

b. Example from the DLsg. of feminine noun declension.

miara *measure*

Step 1. Obtain the stem by comparing all forms of the word, including DLsg. **mierze**. The implied stem is **miěr-**. Add any non-softening ending, for example Nsg. **-a: miěr-a**

Step 2. Replace **ě** with **a** before the hard dental: **miar-a**.

7. The **o: ó** and **ę : ą** vowel shifts before devoiced consonants plus Ø. Illustrations from masculine and feminine noun declension.

głowa *head*.

Step 1. Obtain the stem by subtracting the ending **-a** from **głowa: głow-**. Add the Gpl. ending **-Ø** to the stem: **głow-Ø**.

Step 2. Replace **o** with **ó** before devoiced **w**, simultaneously erasing Ø: **głów**.

dąb dębu *oak*.

Step 1. Obtain the stem by comparing the N and G forms; **dąb dębu** imply **dęb-**. Add Ø to the stem: **dęb-Ø**.

Step 2. Replace **ę** with **ą** before devoiced **b**, simultaneously erasing Ø: **dąb**.

Chapter 3

Feminine-Gender Noun Declension

GRAMMATICAL GENDER IN POLISH

In Polish, gender is a feature of a noun largely defined by whether one may replace the noun with **on** (masculine), **ona** (feminine), **ono** (neuter), **oni** (masculine-personal plural), or **one** (other plural). Noun gender is of importance primarily for: adjective-noun agreement (see **dobra krowa** *good cow-fem.*, **dobry koń** *good horse-masc.*, **dobre dziecko** *good child-neut.*); and for past-tense verb agreement (see **krowa była** *the cow was*, **koń był** *the horse was*, **dziecko było** *the child was*). With rare exceptions, the gender of a noun is inhererent to that noun, and is not affected by what the noun refers to. For example, **osoba** *person* is of feminine gender, whether it refers to a man or a woman.

Words referring to specifically male persons are masculine in gender, and words for female persons are of feminine gender. Occasionally, a word of masculine gender can be used as a nickname, slang term, or an ad hoc means of referring to a female. In such instances, one usually follows grammatical gender, although reference by natural gender may also be encountered. Thus, **Żuczek** *Bug* used as a girl's slang nickname will most often take masculine agreement. The same goes for **babsztyl** *hag*, **kopciuch** *slattern*, **kotek** *chick*, and words like **mańkut** *lefty* or **mazgaj** *dawdler* when used of women. Words for barnyard animals usually have masculine and feminine names corresponding to a difference in sex; see **kura** *hen*, **kogut** *rooster*; **krowa** *cow*, **byk** *bull*. Other than for these general principles, gender is assigned to nouns on an arbitrary basis as far as their reference to objects is concerned. For example, **gwiazda** *star* is feminine, **księżyc** *moon* is masculine, and **słońce** *sun* is neuter.

To a large extent, the gender of a noun can be determined by the superficial form of the Nominative singular. Most words ending in **-a** are feminine (but see **mężczyzna** *man-masc.*, and many other such male personal nouns); most words ending in **-o, -e, -ę, -um** are neuter (but see **Józio** *Joey-masc.*); and words ending in a functionally hard consonant are masculine. The gender of nouns ending in a functionally soft consonant must be determined individually. For example, **mysz** *mouse* is feminine, while **kosz** *basket* is masculine. Such nouns may occasionally cause indecision for Poles themselves. For example, **magiel** *ironing mangle* is traditionally masculine, but in the south of Poland it may be found treated as feminine, especially in reference to a shop with a mangle in it. Similarly, **patrol** *patrol-masc.* is often mistakenly treated as feminine; one may encounter substandard **ten** or **ta pomarańcz** *this orange* for standard **ta pomarańcza**; and so on. There are very few true gender-doublets in standard Polish. Some examples would be **frędzla** or **frędzel** *fringe*, **kapsel** or **kapsla** *bottlecap*, **kluska** or **klusek** *noodle*, **krawat** or, regionally, **krawatka** *necktie*, **morga** or **mórg** *morga (measure of land)*, **nagietek** or **nagietka** *marigold*, **przerębel** or **przerębla** *ice-hole*, **rodzynek** or **rodzynka** *raisin*, **zawias** or **zawiasa** *hinge*. Entirely idiosyncratic is the doublet **łupież** Gsg. **łupieży** *plunder-fem (archaic)* vs. **łupież** Gsg. **łupieżu** *dandruff-masc.*

To a predominant extent, the declensional type of a noun (the set of case-number endings used by the noun) is determined by the gender to which the noun belongs, so that, as a convenient organizational principle, one is entitled to speak of feminine-gender, masculine-gender, and neuter-gender declensions (even though, for example, certain masculine nouns may in fact have a mostly feminine-like declension, as **kolega** *colleague*).

FEMININE GENDER AND DECLENSION

A test for a "noun of feminine gender" is to determine whether one may substitute for the noun with the 3rd person singular pronoun **ona** *she*. Feminine-gender nouns belong to one of three declensional subtypes:

a. hard stems with Nsg. in **-a**, as **kobieta** *woman*, **noga** *leg*.

b. functionally soft stems with Nsg. in **-a** or **-(yn)i** as **ulica** *street*, **ziemia** *earth*, **gospodyni** *landlady*.

c. functionally soft stems with Nsg. in **-∅**, as **kość** *bone*, **twarz** *face*. Functionally soft stems include stems in potentially soft labials like **krew krwi** *blood*.

Feminine soft-stems derive for the most part from the underlying presence in the stem of a suffix **-j-** or **-'-**, as in **ziemia**, deep stem **ziem-j-a**, **kość**, deep stem **kost-'-**. See further below under Common Feminine Softening Word Formatives.

THE SURFACE STEM OF FEMININE-GENDER NOUNS

The surface stem of nouns with Nsg. in **-a** is obtained by subtracting the ending **-a** and by comparing all forms of the noun to one another, with a view to establishing a single form from which all forms can be be predicted by means of regular sound-change rules. In most instances this amounts merely to subtracting **-a**: **kobieta** *woman*, stem **kobiet-**. If the stem ends in two consonants, one may expect a mobile vowel in the stem in the Gpl. before the ending **-∅**, as in **matka** *mother*, Gpl. **matek**, hence stem **mat∅k-**; **panna** *maiden*, Gpl. **panien**, hence stem **pan'n-**. Whether or not a mobile vowel appears in the Gpl. must, of course, be checked. If the **ě: a** shift is visible in the DLsg. (as indicated by **e** here and **a** in other forms), then the stem-vowel may be established as **ě**: **miara** *measure*, Lsg. **mierze**, hence stem **miěr-**.

The surface stem of nouns with Nsg. in **-∅** is usually the same as the Nsg.: **twarz** *face*, stem **twarz-**, **noc** *night*, stem **noc-**. Since the NAsg. ending is **-∅**, the NAsg. may contain a mobile vowel; a hardened labial consonant; the result of an **o: ó** or **ę: ą** shift; or some combination of these: **krew** *blood*, Gsg. **krwi**, stem **krØw'-; sól** *salt*, Gsg. **soli**, stem **sol-; głąb** *depth*, Gsg. **głębi**, stem **głęb'-; wesz** *louse*, Gsg. **wszy**, stem **wØsz-**. The surface stem of nouns in -(yn)i ends in **-yń-**: **gospodyni**, stem **gospodyń-**.

All feminine nouns without exception have identical DLsg. and NAVpl. forms. Given this, the most differentiated feminine declensional type as to endings are hard-stems in **-a**, the least differentiated feminine nouns in **-Ø**. Feminine nouns of all three types take the same ending in the Gsg. (**-y/i**), the Isg. (**-ą**) and the same endings in the DILpl. (**-om, -ami, -ach**):

FEMININE DECLENSIONAL ENDINGS

		Hard stems in -a	Soft stems in -a, -i	Soft stems in -Ø
Sg.	N	-a	-a	-Ø
	G	-y/i	←	←
	DL	-ě	-y/i	-y/i
	A	-ę	←	= N
	I	-ą	←	←
	V	-o	← (-u, -i)	-y/i
Pl.	NAV	-y/i	-è	-e (-y/i)
	G	-Ø	←	-y/i
	D	-om	←	←
	I	-ami	←	←
	L	-ach	←	←

By ← is meant "same as the ending to the left". In the sg., a useful rule of thumb for ending-prediction is the zig-zag method. Lay out the endings of hard-stems in **-a** and soft stems in **-Ø** next to one another, placing endings shared between the two in the middle. Next, draw a line zig-zagging back and forth between the left and the right. These will be the endings of soft-stems in **-a**. Except for the Nsg., soft stems in **-i** take the same endings as soft-stems in **-a**.

Sg.		Hard-a	Soft-a	Soft-Ø
	N	-a		-Ø
	G		-y/i	
	D	-ě		-y/i
	A	-ę		-Ø
	I		-ą	
	L	-ě		-y/i
	V	-o (-u, -i)		-y/i

DISTRIBUTION OF ENDINGS

1. The Vsg. of soft-stem personal affectionate names is **-u: Basia**, Vsg. **Basiu; babcia** *grandma*, Vsg. **babciu; mamusia** *mommy*, Vsg. **mamusiu**. Personal nouns with Nsg. in **-i** take Vsg. **-i: gospodyni** *landlady*, Vsg. **gospodyni**. The Vocative occurs mainly with names for persons, political entities (**Polska Polsko, Warszawa Warszawo**, etc.), and certain abstractions such as **wolność wolności** *freedom*, **młodość młodości** *youth*, and so on. However, the Vocative exists as a potential form for any noun, and there is no justification for leaving it out of any noun's declension.

2. The NAVpl. for many common feminine soft-stems in **-Ø** is **-y/i** instead of expected **-e: brew** *brow* NAVpl. **brwi; mysz** *mouse*, NAVpl. **myszy; gęś** *goose*, NAVpl. **gęsi; myśl** *thought*, NAVpl. **myśli; odpowiedź** *answer*, NAVpl. **odpowiedzi; rzecz** *thing*, NAVpl. **rzeczy; wesz** *louse*, NAVpl. **wszy;** and others. All feminine nouns in **-(o)ść** take **-y/i: kość** *bone*, NAVpl. **kości; przykrość** *unpleasantness*, NAVpl. **przykrości; część** *part*, NAVpl. **części; powieść** *novel*, NAVpl. **powieści;** and others. A number of feminine soft stems may take either **-y/i** or **-e**, for example, **postać** NAVpl. **postaci** or **postacie** *shape, character*.

3. Stems in **j** with Nsg. in **-a** regularly take Gpl. in **-y/i: nadzieja** *hope*, Gpl. **nadziei; ostoja** *bulwark*, Gpl. **ostoi; konferencja** *conference*, Gpl. **konferencji**. This rule extends to nouns where **j** is spelled **i: hierarchia** "hi-er-ar-chja" *hierarchy*, Gpl. **hierarchii** "hje-ar-chji". An older tradition used **-y/ij** here: **lekcyj, hierarchij**. Exceptions: **knieja** *forest* Gpl. **kniej, żmija** *adder (snake)*, Gpl. **żmij; zgraja** *gang* Gpl. **zgraj**.

    Some soft-stems in **-a** take Gpl. in **-y/i**, including in particular many words in **-la: czapla** *heron*, **dola** *fate, lot*, Gpl. **doli; grobla** *dam*, Gpl. **grobli** or **grobel; kontrola** *control*, Gpl. **kontroli; kropla** *drop*, Gpl. **kropli** or **kropel; muszla** *mussel*, Gpl. **muszli** or **muszel; skrzela** *gill*, Gpl. **skrzeli; szabla** *saber*, Gpl. **szabli** or **szabel**. Also: **babcia** *grandma*, Gpl. **babci** (or **babć**).

    Nouns in **-lnia** and **-rnia** take either **-y/i** or **-Ø**. Most often, both endings are possible: **cukiernia** *candy-shop*, Gpl. **cukierni** or **cukierń; księgarnia** *book-store*, Gpl. **księgarni** or **księgarń; piekarnia** *bakery*, Gpl. **piekarni** or **piekarń; uczelnia** *school*, Gpl. **uczelni; szatnia** *cloakroom*, Gpl. **szatni, pracownia** *workshop*, Gpl. **pracowni; latarnia** *lantern*, Gpl. **latarni** or **latarń**.

4. The Ipl. of a few nouns in **-Ø** is **-mi**, almost always occurring alongside optional and expansive **-ami: gałąź** *branch*, Ipl. **gałęźmi** or **gałęziami; dłoń** *palm of hand*, Ipl. **dłońmi; kość** *bone*, Ipl. **kośćmi; nić** *thread*, Ipl. **nićmi; gęś** *goose*, Ipl. **gęśmi** or **gęsiami; sieć** *net(work)*, Ipl. **sieciami** or archaic **siećmi**.

SOUND-CHANGES OCCURRING IN FEMININE DECLENSION

When declining feminine-declension nouns, the following sound-changes should be kept in mind:

1. **k** and **g** will be replaced by **k'** and **g'**, respectively, before **y/i**: **ręka** *hand*, Gsg. **ręk-y/i**: **ręk'-y/i**. Spelling rules select **i**: **ręki**. Similarly: **noga** *leg*, Gsg. **nog-y/i**: **nog'-y/i**: **nogi**.

2. Hard stem consonants exhibit an R1 replacement before **ě**: **ręka** *hand*, DLsg. **ręk-ě**: **ręce**, **kawa** *coffee*, DLsg. **kaw-ě**: **kawie**, **kobieta** *woman*, DLsg. **kobiet-ě**: **kobiecie**, and so on.

3. The vowel-shift **ě**: **a** before hard dentals is exhibited in a few hard-stems, in which case **ě** will be preserved (in the form of **e**) in the DLsg., while all other forms will contain **a**: **wiara** *belief*, DLsg. **wierze**, stem **wiěr-**.

4. Mobile vowels and the **o**: **ó** and **ę**: **ą** shifts can occur before the ending **-Ø** in the Gpl. of nouns in **-a** or in the NAsg. of nouns in **-Ø**:

   a. Mobile vowels: **matka** *mother*, Gpl. **matek**, stem **matØk-**; **miotła** *broom*, Gpl. **mioteł**, stem **miotØł-**; **wesz** *louse*, Gsg. **wszy**, stem **wØsz-**; **poszwa** *pillow-case*, Gpl. **poszew**, stem **poszØw-**. Consonants that soften (to R2) before the mobile vowel **e** (from **'**) usually appear as hard when the mobile vowel is absent: **panna** *maiden*, Gpl. **panien**, stem **pan'n-**; **trumna** *coffin*, Gpl. **trumien**, stem **trum'n-**; for details, see Chapter 2.

   b. **o**: **ó** and **ę**: **ą**: **głowa** *head*, Gpl. **głów**, stem **głow-**; **sól** *salt*, Gsg. **soli**, stem **sol-**; **szkoła** *school*, Gpl. **szkół**, stem **szkoł-**; **wstęga** *ribbon*, Gpl. **wstąg**, stem **wstęg-**; **głąb** *depth*, Gsg. **głębi**, stem **głęb'-**.

5. Soft labial consonants harden in final position: **ziemia** *earth*, stem **ziem'-**, Gpl. **ziem**.

6. Stem-final **j** is dropped after a vowel before **-y/i**: **kolej** *railway*, Gsg. **kolei**; **ostoja** *bulwark*, Gsg. **ostoi**; **szyja** *neck*, Gsg. **szyi**.

EXAMPLES OF REGULAR FEMININE NOUNS

Hard-Stems in -*a*

lampa *light, lamp* (**p**-stem)

	Sg.	Pl.
N	lampa	lampy
G	lampy	lamp
D	lampie	lampom
A	lampę	lampy
I	lampą	lampami
L	lampie	lampach
V	lampo	lampy

osoba *person* (**b**-stem, **o**: **ó**)

	Sg.	Pl.
N	osoba	osoby
G	osoby	osób
D	osobie	osobom
A	osobę	osoby
I	osobą	osobami
L	osobie	osobach
V	osobo	osoby

szafa *cupboard* (**w**-stem)

	Sg.	Pl.
N	szafa	szafy
G	szafy	szaf
D	szafie	szafom
A	szafę	szafy
I	szafą	szafami
L	szafie	szafach
V	szafo	szafy

zima *winter* (**m**-stem)

	Sg.	Pl.
N	zima	zimy
G	zimy	zim
D	zimie	zimom
A	zimę	zimy
I	zimą	zimami
L	zimie	zimach
V	zimo	zimy

glista *worm* (**st**-stem)

	Sg.	Pl.
N	glista	glisty
G	glisty	glist
D	gliście	glistom
A	glistę	glisty
I	glistą	glistami
L	gliście	glistach
V	glisto	glisty

gwiazda *star* (**zd**-stem, **ě: a**)

	Sg.	Pl.
N	gwiazda	gwiazdy
G	gwiazdy	gwiazd
D	gwieździe	gwiazdom
A	gwiazdę	gwiazdy
I	gwiazdą	gwiazdami
L	gwieździe	gwiazdach
V	gwiazdo	gwiazdy

głowa *head* (**w**-stem, **o: ó**)

	Sg.	Pl.
N	głowa	głowy
G	głowy	głów
D	głowie	głowom
A	głowę	głowy
I	głową	głowami
L	głowie	głowach
V	głowo	głowy

gazeta *newspaper* (**t**-stem)

	Sg.	Pl.
N	gazeta	gazety
G	gazety	gazet
D	gazecie	gazetom
A	gazetę	gazety
I	gazetą	gazetami
L	gazecie	gazetach
V	gazeto	gazety

broda *beard* (**d**-stem, **o: ó**)

	Sg.	Pl.
N	broda	brody
G	brody	bród
D	brodzie	brodom
A	brodę	brody
I	brodą	brodami
L	brodzie	brodach
V	brodo	brody

kiełbasa *sausage* (**s**-stem)

	Sg.	Pl.
N	kiełbasa	kiełbasy
G	kiełbasy	kiełbas
D	kiełbasie	kiełbasom
A	kiełbasę	kiełbasy
I	kiełbasą	kiełbasami
L	kiełbasie	kiełbasach
V	kiełbaso	kiełbasy

koza *goat* (z-stem, o: ó)

	Sg.	Pl.
N	koza	kozy
G	kozy	kóz
D	kozie	kozom
A	kozę	kozy
I	kozą	kozami
L	kozie	kozach
V	kozo	kozy

szkoła *school* (ł-stem, o: ó)

	Sg.	Pl.
N	szkoła	szkoły
G	szkoły	szkół
D	szkole	szkołom
A	szkołę	szkoły
I	szkołą	szkołami
L	szkole	szkołach
V	szkoło	szkoły

siostra *sister* (r-stem, o: ó)

	Sg.	Pl.
N	siostra	siostry
G	siostry	sióstr
D	siostrze	siostrom
A	siostrę	siostry
I	siostrą	siostrami
L	siostrze	siostrach
V	siostro	siostry

łąka *meadow* (k-stem)

	Sg.	Pl.
N	łaka	łąki
G	łąki	łąk
D	łące	łąkom
A	łąkę	łąki
I	łąką	łąkami
L	łące	łąkach
V	łąko	łąki

żona *wife* (n-stem)

	Sg.	Pl.
N	żona	żony
G	żony	żon
D	żonie	żonom
A	żonę	żony
I	żoną	żonami
L	żonie	żonach
V	żono	żony

góra *mountain* (r-stem)

	Sg.	Pl.
N	góra	góry
G	góry	gór
D	górze	górom
A	górę	góry
I	górą	górami
L	górze	górach
V	góro	góry

apteka *pharmacy* (k-stem)

	Sg.	Pl.
N	apteka	apteki
G	apteki	aptek
D	aptece	aptekom
A	aptekę	apteki
I	apteką	aptekami
L	aptece	aptekach
V	apteko	apteki

córka *daughter* (k-stem, m. vowel)

	Sg.	Pl.
N	córka	córki
G	córki	córek
D	córce	córkom
A	córkę	córki
I	córką	córkami
L	córce	córkach
V	córko	córki

noga *leg, foot* (**g**-stem, **o: ó**)

	Sg.	Pl.
N	noga	nogi
G	nogi	nóg
D	nodze	nogom
A	nogę	nogi
I	nogą	nogami
L	nodze	nogach
V	nogo	nogi

cecha *trait* (**ch**-stem)

	Sg.	Pl.
N	cecha	cechy
G	cechy	cech
D	cesze	cechom
A	cechę	cechy
I	cechą	cechami
L	cesze	cechach
V	cecho	cechy

Soft-Stems in -*a*

ziemia *earth* (**m′**-stem)

	Sg.	Pl.
N	ziemia	ziemie
G	ziemi	ziem
D	ziemi	ziemiom
A	ziemię	ziemie
I	ziemią	ziemiami
L	ziemi	ziemiach
V	ziemio	ziemie

parafia *parish* (**j**-spelled-**i**-stem)

	Sg.	Pl.
N	parafia	parafie
G	parafii	parafii
D	parafii	parafiom
A	parafię	parafie
I	parafią	parafiami
L	parafii	parafiach
V	parafio	parafie

ciocia *aunt* (**ć**-stem, Vsg. **-u**)

	Sg.	Pl.
N	ciocia	ciocie
G	cioci	cioć
D	cioci	ciociom
A	ciocię	ciocie
I	ciocią	ciociami
L	cioci	ciociach
V	ciociu	ciocie

gosposia *maid* (**ś**-stem, Vsg. **-u**)

	Sg.	Pl.
N	gosposia	gosposie
G	gosposi	gospoś (or gosposi)
D	gosposi	gosposiom
A	gosposię	gosposie
I	gosposią	gosposiami
L	gosposi	gosposiach
V	gosposiu	gosposie

koszula *shirt* (**l**-stem)

	Sg.	Pl.
N	koszula	koszule
G	koszuli	koszul
D	koszuli	koszulom
A	koszulę	koszule
I	koszulą	koszulami
L	koszuli	koszulach
V	koszulo	koszule

kuchnia *kitchen* (**ń**-stem, Gpl. **-y/i**)

	Sg.	Pl.
N	kuchnia	kuchnie
G	kuchni	kuchni (or kuchen)
D	kuchni	kuchniom
A	kuchnię	kuchnie
I	kuchnią	kuchniami
L	kuchni	kuchniach
V	kuchnio	kuchnie

świnia *pig* (ń-stem)

	Sg.	Pl.
N	świnia	świnie
G	świni	świń
D	świni	świniom
A	świnię	świnie
I	świnią	świniami
L	świni	świniach
V	świnio	świnie

tablica *blackboard* (c-stem)

	Sg.	Pl.
N	tablica	tablice
G	tablicy	tablic
D	tablicy	tablicom
A	tablicę	tablice
I	tablicą	tablicami
L	tablicy	tablicach
V	tablico	tablice

zorza *dawn* (rz-stem, o: ó)

	Sg.	Pl.
N	zorza	zorze
G	zorzy	zórz
D	zorzy	zorzom
A	zorzę	zorze
I	zorzą	zorzami
L	zorzy	zorzach
V	zorzo	zorze

plaża *beach* (ż-stem)

	Sg.	Pl.
N	plaża	plaże
G	plaży	plaż
D	plaży	plażom
A	plażę	plaże
I	plażą	plażami
L	plaży	plażach
V	plażo	plaże

owca *sheep* (c-stem, mobile vowel)

	Sg.	Pl.
N	owca	owce
G	owcy	owiec
D	owcy	owcom
A	owcę	owce
I	owcą	owcami
L	owcy	owcach
V	owco	owce

tęcza *rainbow* (cz-stem)

	Sg.	Pl.
N	tęcza	tęcze
G	tęczy	tęcz
D	tęczy	tęczom
A	tęczę	tęcze
I	tęczą	tęczami
L	tęczy	tęczach
V	tęczo	tęcze

susza *drought* (sz-stem)

	Sg.	Pl.
N	susza	susze
G	suszy	susz
D	suszy	suszom
A	suszę	susze
I	suszą	suszami
L	suszy	suszach
V	suszo	susze

ostoja *bulwark* (j-stem)

	Sg.	Pl.
N	ostoja	ostoje
G	ostoi	ostoi
D	ostoi	ostojom
A	ostoję	ostoje
I	ostoją	ostojami
L	ostoi	ostojach
V	ostojo	ostoje

kolacja *supper* (j-stem)

	Sg.	Pl.
N	kolacja	kolacje
G	kolacji	kolacji*
D	kolacji	kolacjom
A	kolację	kolacje
I	kolacją	kolacjami
L	kolacji	kolacjach
V	kolacjo	kolacje

* In older orthography, **kolacyj**.

tragedia *tragedy* (j-spelled-i stem)

	Sg.	Pl.
N	tragedia	tragedie
G	tragedii	tragedii
D	tragedii	tragediom
A	tragedię	tragedie
I	tragedią	tragediami
L	tragedii	tragediach
V	tragedio	tragedie

Maria *Mary* (j-spelled-i-stem)

	Sg.	Pl.
N	Maria	Marie
G	Marii	Marii
D	Marii	Mariom
A	Marię	Marie
I	Marią	Mariami
L	Marii	Mariach
V	Mario	Marie

Zosia *Zofia-dim.* (ś-stem)

	Sg.	Pl.
N	Zosia	Zosie
G	Zosi	Zoś
D	Zosi	Zosiom
A	Zosię	Zosie
I	Zosią	Zosiami
L	Zosi	Zosiach
V	Zosiu	Zosie

Functionally Soft-Stems with Nsg. in -Ø

głąb *depth* (b'-stem, ę: ą)

	Sg.	Pl.
N	głąb	głębie
G	głębi	głębi
D	głębi	głębiom
A	głąb	głębie
I	głębią	głębiami
L	głębi	głębiach
V	głębi	głębie

brew *brow* (w'-stem, mob. vowel)

	Sg.	Pl.
N	brew	brwi
G	brwi	brwi
D	brwi	brwiom
A	brew	brwi
I	brwią	brwiami
L	brwi	brwiach
V	brwi	brwi

nić *thread* (ć-stem)

	Sg.	Pl.
N	nić	nici
G	nici	nici
D	nici	niciom
A	nić	nici
A	nicią	nićmi (!)
L	nici	niciach
V	nici	nicie

kość *bone* (ś-stem, Npl. -y/i)

	Sg.	Pl.
N	kość	kości
G	kości	kości
D	kości	kościom
A	kość	kości
I	kością	kośćmi (!)
L	kości	kościach
V	kości	kości

łódź *boat* (**dź**-stem)

	Sg.	Pl.
N	łódź	łodzie
G	łodzi	łodzi
D	łodzi	łodziom
A	łódź	łodzie
I	łodzią	łodziami
L	łodzi	łodziach
V	łodzi	łodzie

wieś *village* (**ś**-stem, mob. vowel)

	Sg.	Pl.
N	wieś	wsie
G	wsi	wsi
D	wsi	wsiom
A	wieś	wsie
I	wsią	wsiami
L	wsi	wsiach
V	wsi	wsie

sól *salt* (l-stem, **o: ó**)

	Sg.	Pl.
N	sól	sole
G	soli	soli
D	soli	solom
A	sól	sole
I	solą	solami
L	soli	solach
V	soli	sole

jesień *fall, autumn* (**ń**-stem)

	Sg.	Pl.
N	jesień	jesienie
G	jesieni	jesieni
D	jesieni	jesieniom
A	jesień	jesienie
I	jesienią	jesieniami
L	jesieni	jesieniach
V	jesieni	jesienie

gęś *goose* (**ś**-stem, Npl. **-y/i**)

	Sg.	Pl.
N	gęś	gęsi
G	gęsi	gęsi
D	gęsi	gęsiom
A	gęś	gęsi
I	gęsią	gęsiami (or gęśmi)
L	gęsi	gęsiach
V	gęsi	gęsi

więź *bond* (**ź**-stem, Npl. **-y/i**)

	Sg.	Pl.
N	więź	więzi
G	więzi	więzi
D	więzi	więziom
A	więź	więzi
I	więzią	więziami
L	więzi	więziach
V	więzi	więzi

myśl *thought* (l-stem, Npl. **-y/i**)

	Sg.	Pl.
N	myśl	myśli
G	myśli	myśli
D	myśli	myślom
A	myśl	myśli
I	myślą	myślami
L	myśli	myślach
V	myśli	myśli

kolej *railway* (**j**-stem)

	Sg.	Pl.
N	kolej	koleje
G	kolei	kolei
D	kolei	kolejom
A	kolej	koleje
I	koleją	kolejami
L	kolei	kolejach
V	kolei	koleje

noc *night* (c-stem)

	Sg.	Pl.
N	noc	noce
G	nocy	nocy
D	nocy	nocom
A	noc	noce
I	nocą	nocami
L	nocy	nocach
V	nocy	noce

twarz *face* (rz-stem)

	Sg.	Pl.
N	twarz	twarze
G	twarzy	twarzy
D	twarzy	twarzom
A	twarz	twarze
I	twarzą	twarzami
L	twarzy	twarzach
V	twarzy	twarze

wesz *louse* (sz-st., m.v. Npl. -y/i)

	Sg.	Pl.
N	wesz	wszy
G	wszy	wszy
D	wszy	wszom
A	wesz	wszy
I	wszą	wszami
L	wszy	wszach
V	wszy	wszy

rzecz *thing* (c-stem, Npl. -y/i)

	Sg.	Pl.
N	rzecz	rzeczy
G	rzeczy	rzeczy
D	rzeczy	rzeczom
A	rzecz	rzeczy
I	rzeczą	rzeczami
L	rzeczy	rzeczach
V	rzeczy	rzeczy

mysz *mouse* (sz-stem, Npl. -y/i)

	Sg.	Pl.
N	mysz	myszy
G	myszy	myszy
D	myszy	myszom
A	mysz	myszy
I	myszą	myszami
L	myszy	myszach
V	myszy	myszy

Note: substandard **mysza**, Asg. **myszę** may occasionally be found.

podróż *journey* (ż-stem)

	Sg.	Pl.
N	podróż	podróże
G	podróży	podróży
D	podróży	podróżom
A	podróż	podróże
I	podróżą	podróżami
L	podróży	podróżach
V	podróży	podróże

SPECIAL DECLENSIONAL TYPES AND EXCEPTIONS

1. Nouns of the **brew brwi** *brow* type comprise a fairly sizable category of functional soft stems in **-Ø**, even if few have great frequency. Many or most have been replaced by formations in **-a**. Included in this type are **brzoskiew** *variety of cabbage,* **cerkiew** *Orthodox Church,* **chorągiew** *banner* (usually **chorągiewka**), **konew** *jug* (usually **konewka**), **kotew** *anchor* (usually **kotwica**), **krew** *blood,* **krokiew** *rafter,* **marchew** *carrot* (usually **marchewka**), **Narew** *Narew River,* **panew** *bushing, pan* (usually **panewka**), **rzodkiew** *radish* (usually **rzodkiewka**), **żagiew** *torch,* and perhaps a dozen more. NAVpl. is usually **-e** (e.g., **cerkwie, chorągwie**), although **brew**, for example, shows **brwi**.

2. Feminine personal nouns with Nsg. in -i.

gospodyni *hostess, landlady*

	Sg.	Pl.
N	gospodyni	gospodynie
G	gospodyni	gospodyń
D	gospodyni	gospodyniom
A	gospodynię	gospodynie
I	gospodynią	gospodyniami
L	gospodyni	gospodyniach
V	gospodyni	gospodynie

pani *lady, Mrs. Ms.*

	Sg.	Pl.
N	pani	panie
G	pani	pań
D	pani	paniom
A	panią (!)	panie
I	panią	paniami
L	pani	paniach
V	pani	panie

Similarly: **bogini** *goddess,* **mistrzyni** *mistress,* **monarchini** *monarch,* and others. Words ending in **-yni** often correspond to words for males in **-wca**; see **wykonawca** *executor,* **wykonawczyni** *executrix;* **zbawca** *saviour (m.),* **zbawczyni** *(f.);* **zdrajca** *traitor,* **zdrajczyni** *traitoress,* etc. However, the formant **-yni** is felt to be archaic and is not always used where it might be expected. For example, **kłamca** *lier,* **wykładowca** *instructor* and **ludożerca** *cannibal* are used for both males and females. The formant **-yni** has a certain amount of productivity in forming female variants of male words in **-ek**; see **członek członkini** *member,* **skoczek skoczyni** (or **skoczka**) *ski-jumper.*

3. Vowel stems with Nsg. in **-a** take the same endings as stems in **j**, except that **statua** takes GDLsg. in **-i** or **-y** and Npl. in **-y**:

idea *idea* (vowel-stem)

	Sg.	Pl.
N	idea	idee
G	idei	idei
D	idei	ideom
A	ideę	idee
I	ideą	ideami
L	idei	ideach
V	ideo	idee

statua *statue* (vowel-stem)

	Sg.	Pl.
N	statua	statuy
G	statuy (or -i)	statui
D	statui	statuom
A	statuę	statuy
I	statuą	statuami
L	statui	statuach
V	statuo	statuy

The word **posąg** is more often used for 'statue', thereby avoiding the awkwardness of the declension of **statua**.

4. Feminine personal nouns with mixed nominal and adjectival declensions.

księżna *duchess*   **królowa** *queen*

	Sg.	Pl.
N	księżna	księżny (-e)
G	księżny (-ej)	księżnych
D	księżnie (-ej)	księżnym
A	księżnę (-ą)	księżny (-e)
I	księżną	księżnymi
L	księżnie (-ej)	księżnych
V	księżno	księżny (-e)

	Sg.	Pl.
N	królowa	królowe
G	królowej	królowych
D	królowej	królowym
A	królową	królowe
I	królową	królowymi
L	królowej	królowych
V	królowo	królowe

With **księżna**, the nominal endings are traditional; the adjectival endings are expansive and probably more often used today. The declension of **królowa** *queen* is regular adjectival except for Vsg. **-o**. Similarly to **królowa** are declined **bratowa** *sister-in-law*, **cesarzowa** *empress*, **krawcowa** *seamstress*, **generałowa** *general's wife*, **teściowa** *mother-in-law*, **wójtowa** *Vojt's wife*. By contrast, the declension of **królewna** *princess* is wholly nominal, except for a possible, as yet unsanctioned, adjectival ending in the Ipl. and Lpl:

królewna *princess*

	Sg.	Pl.
N	królewna	królewny
G	królewny	królewien
D	królewnie	królewnom
A	królewnę	królewny
I	królewną	królewnami (?królewnymi)
L	królewnie	królewnach (?królewnych)
V	królewno	królewny

See also further below under last names in **-owa** and **-ówna**.

5. *Feminine-gender adjectival nouns.* Some feminine-form adjectives are used as nouns. These include names for lines and numbers (presumably in original agreement with **linia** *line* and **liczba** *number*), and various personal nouns:

sieczna *secant*   **znajoma** *acquaintance*

	Sg.	Pl.
N	sieczna	sieczne
G	siecznej	siecznych
D	siecznej	siecznym
A	sieczną	sieczne
I	sieczną	siecznymi
L	siecznej	siecznych
V	sieczna	sieczne

	Sg.	Pl.
N	znajoma	znajome
G	znajomej	znajomych
D	znajomej	znajomym
A	znajomą	znajome
I	znajomą	znajomymi
L	znajomej	znajomych
V	znajoma	znajome

Similarly: **krzywa** curve, **krewna** relative, **narzeczona** fiancée, **prosta** straight line, **salowa** ward nurse, **średnia** average, **wytyczna** guideline, **wygrana** winnings, **wytyczna** guideline, **zmienna** variable, and others.

6. *Names of streets.* Names of streets are of two general types, Genitive or, more often, adjectival. If adjectival, the adjective is usually feminine, in agreement with **ulica** *street* (abbreviated **ul.**), which may be reinstated; see **ul. Ogrodowa** *Ogrodowa (Garden) Street.* In practice, the adjectival form by itself may function as an ad hoc adjectival noun of feminine gender: **Mieszkam na Ogrodowej** *I live on Ogrodowa Street.* **Niech pan jedzie Ogrodową.** *Go along Ogrodowa Street.* and so on. Streets named after people are usually Genitival; see **Ulica Szopena** *Chopin Street,* **Ulica Bohaterów Westerplatte** *Heroes of Westerplatte Street.* The Genitive form often functions as an ad hoc indeclinable noun of presumably feminine gender: **Mieszkam na Sienkiewicza** *I live on Sienkiewicz Street.* **Jedzie się Sienkiewicza.** *One goes along Sienkiewicz Street.*

7. The word **ręka** *hand* has various irregularities. The NAVpl. form **ręce** comes from an old dual form, as does the optional Ipl. **rękoma**. The optional Lpl. form **ręku** also derives from a former dual form. It is used in the sense of 'both hands' and in set expressions such as **dziecko na ręku** *child in arms*. Note the ę: ą shift in the Gpl., exceptional before unvoiced **k**:

ręka *hand, arm* (k-stem, ę: ą)

	Sg.	Pl.
N	ręka	ręce (!)
G	ręki	rąk (!)
D	ręce	rękom
A	rękę	ręce (!)
I	ręką	rękami (or rękoma)
L	ręce (ręku)	rękach (ręku)
V	ręko	ręce (!)

The historically dual form **rękoma** is still usually used in logically dual uses: **własnymi rękoma** *with one's own (two) hands.* The historically dual form **ręku** is today widely interpreted as singular. It can be found in the expression **dziecko na ręku** *child-in-arms.* Traditionally and pedantically, **ręku** takes Lpl. adjective agreement (**w moich ręku** *in my hands*), but Lsg. masc.-neut. agreement (**w moim ręku**) also has tradition behind it and is more often used today.

8. The noun **rzeczpospolita** *republic,* with stress usually on the syllable "rzecz-po-SPO-li-ta", alternatively on the next-to-last syllable, has the following declension, in which the endings of the nominal component occur optionally (preferred usage keeps the endings).

rzeczpospolita *republic*

	Sg.	Pl.*
N	rzeczpospolita	rzecz(y)pospolite
G	rzecz(y)pospolitej	rzecz(y)pospolitych
D	rzecz(y)pospolitej	rzecz(y)pospolitym
A	rzeczpospolitą	rzeczypospolite
I	rzecz(ą)pospolitą	rzecz(y)pospolitymi
L	rzecz(y)pospolitej	rzecz(y)pospolitych
V	rzeczypospolita	rzecz(y)pospolite

* Since this noun is usually used in reference to the country of Poland (**Rzeczpospolita Polska**), except for the NAVpl., the plural forms of this noun verge on the hypothetical.

9. Other feminine nouns with various irregularities include:

   a. **kuchnia** *kitchen,* Gpl. **kuchni** or **kuchen; suknia** *gown,* Gpl. **sukien** or **sukni. wiśnia** *cherry,* Gpl. **wisien** (or **wiśni**). Note in all instances the hard final **n.**

   b. **cześć** *honor,* GDLVsg. **czci,** *sg.* **czcią;** no plural.

   c. **szansa** *chance,* NAVpl. **szanse.**

   d. **nuda** *boredom,* Gpl. **nudów.**

   e. **Wielkanoc** *Easter* (NA), GDL **Wielkanocy** or **Wielkiejnocy,** I **Wielkanocą** or **Wielkąnocą.**

   f. **brandy** *brandy,* **pepsi** *Pepsi,* **whisky** *whisky:* indeclinable feminine nouns; cf. **francuska brandy** *French brandy,* **szkocka whisky** *Scotch whisky,* **zimna pepsi** *a cold Pepsi.*

   g. the borrowed indeclinable title **miss** *Miss,* referring to the winner of a beauty or talent pageant, takes the Gsg. of the locality: **Miss Bydgoszczy** *Miss Bydgoszcz.* Exception: **Miss Polonia** *Miss Polonia (Polonia referring to Poles abroad).*

FEMALE LAST NAMES AND TITLES

10. Probably no socio-linguistic subject provokes as much discussion and occasions as much difficulty, whether in practice or in self-help articles, as does the proper form and declension of female surnames and titles.

    a. About the only type of female last name not subject to some form of difficulty are those in **-ska, -cka, -dzka,** whose declension is straightforwardly adjectival (the use of **-o** in the Vocative of such last names counts as a grammatical error):

Jarocka *Jarocka*

	Sg.	Fem. Pl.
N	Jarocka	Jarockie
G	Jarockiej	Jarockich
D	Jarockiej	Jarockim
A	Jarocką	Jarockie
I	Jarocką	Jarockimi
L	Jarockiej	Jarockich
V	Jarocka	Jarockie

Dąbrowska *Dabrowska*

	Sg.	Fem. Pl.
N	Dąbrowska	Dąbrowskie
G	Dąbrowskiej	Dąbrowskich
D	Dąbrowskiej	Dąbrowskim
A	Dąbrowską	Dąbrowskie
I	Dąbrowską	Dąbrowskimi
L	Dąbrowskiej	Dąbrowskich
V	Dąbrowska	Dąbrowskie.

b. Other adjectival female surnames traditionally were declined; however, there is an increasing tendency not to decline female last names based on common adjectives, combined with the device of allowing the title **pani** *Ms.* to serve as the case-marker; hence either

Mała *Small* or **Mały** *Small*

	Sg.	Pl.
N	Mała	Małe
G	Małej	Małych
D	Małej	Małym
A	Małą	Małe
I	Małą	Małymi
L	Małej	Małych
V	Mała	Małe

	Sg.	Pl.
N	Pani Mały	Panie Mały
G	Pani Mały	Pań Mały
D	Pani Mały	Paniom Mały
A	Panią Mały	Panie Mały
I	Panią Mały	Paniami Mały
L	Pani Mały	Paniach Mały
V	Pani Mały	Panie Mały

c. Last names based on male names ending in a consonant, and last names based on regular nouns, even when of feminine gender, are ordinarily not declined:

Pani Nowak *Ms. Nowak*

	Sg.	Pl.
N	Pani Nowak	Panie Nowak
G	Pani Nowak	Pań Nowak
D	Pani Nowak	Paniom Nowak
A	Panią Nowak	Panie Nowak
I	Panią Nowak	Paniami Nowak
L	Pani Nowak	Paniach Nowak
V	Pani Nowak	Panie Nowak

Pani Zima *Ms. Zima*

	Sg.	Pl.
N	Pani Zima	Panie Zima
G	Pani Zima	Pań Zima
D	Pani Zima	Paniom Zima
A	Panią Zima	Panie Zima
I	Panią Zima	Paniami Zima
L	Pani Zima	Paniach Zima
V	Pani Zima	Panie Zima

Undeclined **Pani Zima** contrasts with a potential figurative use Miss "Winter" (a person dressed in costume as the season), which would be declined. Similarly for last names such as **Buszko**: NGDLVsg. **pani Buszko**, AIsg. **panią Buszko**, etc. See **Dałem Nowak piątkę.** *I gave Nowak a 5 (an A):* since the name is not declined, one infers that Nowak is a woman.

d. Both elements of a hyphentated female surname are succeptible to declination, as NV **Pawlikowska-Jasnorzewska**, GDL **Pawlikowskiej-Jasnorzewskiej**, AI **Pawlikowską-Jasnorzewską**; compare to NA **Dębowska-Król**, GDL **Dębowskiej-Król**, AI **Dębowską-Król**.

e. The suffixes **-owa** 'wife of' (with an adjectival declension) and **-ówna** 'Miss, daughter of' (nominal declension) are not much used today. When encountered, they have the status of a virtually independent last name; for example **Nowakowa, Nowakówna**:

adjectival declension:
Nowakowa *Mrs. Nowak*

nominal declension:
Nowakówna *Miss Nowak*

	Sg.	Pl.		Sg.	Pl.
N	Nowakowa	(adjectival)	N	Nowakówna	Nowakówny
G	Nowakowej		G	Nowakówny	Nowakówien
D	Nowakowej		D	Nowakównie	Nowakównom
A	Nowakową		A	Nowakównę	Nowakówne
I	Nowakową		I	Nowakówną	Nowakównami*
L	Nowakowej		L	Nowakównie	Nowakównach*
V	Nowakowa		V	Nowakówno	Nowakówny

* Many today would used adjectival endings Ipl. **-ymi** and Lpl. **-ych**.

Nowak would be the standard surname today for both men and women, with **Nowak** being undeclined when used of women (see the example above). Apparently some divorced women adopt names in **-owa**, and give their daughters names in **-ówna**, to set themselves apart from the husband or father. The endings **-owa** and **-ówna** have a certain, although limited, current use in referring to the wives or daughters of famous men; see **Wałęsowa** *Wałęsa's wife*; **Wałęsówna** *Wałęsa's daughter* (traditionally the endings here would have been **-ina** and **-'anka**; see just below). Professional couples working in the same field may use the female suffix to distinguish the woman's work from the man's, for example, in linguistics the couples **Puzyn** and **Puzynina**, or **Żgołka** and **Żgołkowa**.

The traditional suffixes **-ina** ('wife of') and **-'anka** ('daughter of'), used in forming female surnames from male names in **-a**, have almost entirely gone out of use. See older **Zaręba Zarębina Zarębianka**, **Zasada Zasadzina Zasadzianka**; also **sędzina** 'judge's wife' or, jocularly, 'woman judge' (from **sędzia** *judge*), **starościna** *starost's wife*, **starościanka** *starost's daughter* (from **starosta** *village head*), **wojewodzina** *voivode's wife*, **wojewodzianka** *voivode's daughter* (from **wojewoda** *voivode*), all declined as nouns.

f. Originally male titles such as **doktor** *doctor*, **profesor** *professor*, and so on, are not declined in reference to women but are usually preceded by a declined form of **pani**, similar to the use with last names described just above: NGDLVsg. **pani doktor Szulc**, AIsg. **panią doktor Szulc**, etc. Nouns like **doktorowa** or **profesorowa** would imply 'doctor's or professor's wife'. One finds words in **-owa** primarily in older literature, as also **generałowa** *general's wife*, **młynarzówna** *miller's daughter*, **wójtowa** *vojt's (community head's) wife*, and so on. The suffix **-owa** has a certain limited productivity in the formation of female occupation-names such as **krawcowa** *dress-maker*, **szefowa** *boss*.

g. Even when standard female versions of occupation-names exist, one may expect women to prefer the male title instead of the female form, particularly in the white-collar or creative professions, and in formal situations and contexts of honorific mention (professional meetings, business stationery, funeral speeches, grave-markers, awards ceremonies, etc.). Hence one might expect **Zofia Kowalska**, *polski lekarz* (**dziennikarz, rzeźbiarz, malarz**) **światowej renomy** *Zofia Kowalska, a Polish physician (journalist, sculptor, painter, etc.) of world renown*, even though the female-specific nouns **lekarka, dziennikarka, rzeźbiarka, malarka**, and so on are in common use. Other than on formal occasions, adjective agreement with feminine-reference masculine-form occupation-names occasions awkwardness and indecision. The grammatically and normatively correct **ładny elektryk** *pretty electrician* sounds incongruous; **ładna elektryk** is considered substandard or slang; while **ładna pani elektryk** is pretentious. The women's magazine *Twój styl* makes a femininst statement by displaying on the masthead **redaktor naczelna** *editor-in-chief*, instead of **redaktor naczelny**.

FEMALE FIRST NAMES AND DIMINUTIVES

There are around 500 female first names in use in Poland. Most have standard nickname forms, used more or less automatically among friends and family. Most first names have child's or intimate family forms; some are regionally or socially colored; some are more in use for small children; some are used as chiding or deprecatory forms. From **Maria**, one finds **Marysia** (standard), **Maryla** (old-fashioned), **Marysia** (child's) **Marysieńka** (child's or old-fashioned), **Mania** (countrified or child's), **Mańka** (chiding, slightly disrespectful). Some female first names are subject to possible mocking augmentation with **-isko**, as **Beacisko** from **Beata**, resulting in a noun of neuter gender. Here is a list of common female first names, listed in the order: formal; standard nickname; child's or intimate form; chiding form.

Agata, Agatka
Agnieszka, Agunia, Agusia, Aga
Aleksandra, *Ola* Ala, Oleńka, Olka
Alicja, *Ala* Alusia, Alka
Alina, *Ala*, Alusia, Alka
Aneta, Anetka
Aniela, Anielka

Anna, *Ania*, Hanka, Anka
Barbara, *Basia*, Baśka
Beata, Beatka
Bogdana, Bogdanka
Bogumiła, *Bogusia*
Bogusława, *Bogusia*
Bożena, Bożenka, Bożusia

Brygida, Brygidka
Cecylia, Cyla, Cylka
Danuta, *Danusia*, Danka
Dominika, Domiczka
Dorota, Dora, Dorotka
Edyta, Edytka
Elżbieta, *Ela*, Elunia
Emilia, Emilka
Ewa, Ewunia, Ewcia, Ewusia, Ewka
Felicja, *Fela*, Felka
Franciszka, *Frania*, Franka
Gabriela, *Gabrysia*, Gabryśka
Genowefa, *Gienia*, Gieńka
Grażyna, Grażynka
Halina, Hala, Halka, Halusia, Halinka
Hanna, *Hania*, Hanusia, Hanka
Helena, *Hela*, Helenka, Helcia
Henryka, *Henia*, Heńka
Irena, Irenka,Ircia, Irusia, Irka
Iwona, Iwonka
Izabela, *Iza*, Izunia, Izka
Jadwiga, *Jadzia*, Jaga, Jadźka, Jadwisia
Janina, *Janka*, Janinka
Joanna, Joaśka, Aśka
Jolanta, *Jola*, Jolusia, Jolcia, Jolka
Józefa, *Józia*, Józka
Judyta, Judytka
Julia, Jula, Julcia, Julka
Justyna, Justynka
Karolina, Karolcia, Karolinka
Katarzyna, *Kasia*, Kasieńka, Kaśka
Kazimiera, *Kazia*
Kinga, Kinia
Klara, Klarusia, Klarcia

Kornelia, Kornelka
Krystyna, *Krysia*, Kryśka
Leokadia, *Lodzia*, Loda, Leosia
Lidia, *Lidka*
Liliana, *Lila*, Lilcia, Lilka
Lucyna, Luca, Lucusia, Lusia, Lucynka
Ludwika, Lusia, Ludka
Magdalena, *Magda*, Madzia, Magdusia
Małgorzata, *Małgosia*, Gosia, (Mał)gośka
Maria, *Marysia*,
Marta, Marcia, Martunia
Maryl(ka), Mariol(ka) vars. of **Maria**
Marzena, Marzenka
Mirosława, *Mirka* , Mirusia
Monika, Moniczka, Monisia, Nika
Natalia, Tala, Natalka
Olga, *Ola*, Oleńka, Olka
Regina, Reginka
Renata, Renia, Renatka
Róża, Rózia, Różyczka
Sabina, Saba, Sabinka
Stanisława, *Stasia*, Staśka
Stefania, *Stefa*, Stefcia, Stefka
Sylwia, Sylwiunia
Teresa, Teresia, Renia, Terenia, Tereska
Urszula, *Ula*, Urszulka
Wanda, Wandzia
Weronika, Weroniczka, Weronka
Wiesława, *Wiesia*, Wieśka
Wiktoria, Wika, Wiktorka
Zofia, *Zosia*, Zosieńka, Zośka
Zuzanna, *Zuzia*, Zuzka

For female relation-names, see under Names of Relations in Chapter 4.

DIMINUTIVIZATION

The commonest word-formative device among nouns is the creation of a diminutive from a base noun, as **książeczka** *booklet* from **książka** *book* (itself a formal diminutive from **księga** *tome*). The word **ława** refers to a judicial bench, **ławka** to a bench in the park or to a school desk, and **ławeczka** to a footstool. In the instance of both **książka** and **ławka**, these historically diminutive forms have acquired the status of independent words, no longer felt to be diminutives. The formation of spontaneous diminutives in the sense of 'cute', 'sweet', or 'nice', often used when talking to small children, is characteristic of colloquial, melodramatic, and somewhat affected speech, and cannot usually be imitated successfully by a foreigner. Although nouns of any gender are subject to diminutivization, feminine-gender diminutives usually strike the foreigner first; see **kawka** *coffee-dim.*, **herbatka** *tea-dim.*, **bułeczka** *roll-dim.*, **rączki** *tiny hands,* **nóżki** *tiny feet,* **wódeczka** *vodka-dim.*, **kawiareńka** *café-dim.*, and so on.

SECOND-DEGREE DERIVATIONS

In Polish, second-degree derivations (derivations based on other derivations) are often based not on the deep stem or root but on the derived form of the first degree. Sound-changes already in place in the derivation of the first degree are often preserved in the derivation of the the second degree, whether or not they are motivated in the new environment. For example, **wstążeczka** *little ribbon* is based on **wstążka** *ribbon* (itself based on **wstęga** *large ribbon*), by adding a second suffix -'k-: (wstąż-'k-)'k-a. It would appear that once the vowel **ę** in **wstęga** has shifted to **ą** in **wstążka**, it loses the ability to shift back to original **ę** when the motivation for the shift to **ą** (the devoiced **ż** before **k**) is removed. However, the same is not true of the mobile-vowel operator ' in **wstąż'k-a**, which remains operant and shifts to **e** when it occurs before consonant plus ' in the derivation of the second degree: **wstąż'k-'k-a**: **wstążeczka**. Observe, however, that this **e** is now frozen: it does not revert to ' and then to # in the Gpl., where conditions for the change ': **e** are lacking: **wstąż'k-'k-Ø**: **wstążeczek**, not *wstążczek. Thus, second-degree derivations can sometimes "look at" the inner structure of the words on which they are based, and sometimes not.

COMMON FEMININE SOFTENING WORD FORMATIVES

Below are listed the most frequently encountered feminine-noun word-formatives which can condition the replacement ("substitutive softening") of a preceding consonant.

a. **-j-**
    władza (analyzed stem **wład-j-**) *authority,* cf. **władać** *possess*
    świeca (analyzed stem **świet-j-**) *candle,* cf. **świecić** *shine,* **światło** *light*
b. **-'-**
    kość (analyzed stem **kost-'-**) *bone,* cf. **kostka** *little bone, dye*
    głębia (analyzed stem **głęb-'-**) *depth,* cf. **głęboki** *deep*
    poręcz (analyzed stem **po-ręk-'-**) *railing,* cf. **ręka** *hand*

c. -'k-

wstążka (analyzed stem wstęg-'k-) *ribbon*, cf. wstęga *band*.
teczka (analyzed stem tek-'k-) *briefcase*, cf. teka *portfolio*
muszka (analyzed stem much-'k-) *gnat*, cf. mucha *fly*

d. -ic-

stolica (analyzed stem stoł-ic-) *capital*, cf. stół *table*
macica (analyzed stem mat-ic-) *womb*, cf. matka *mother*

e. -'arń- (occurs alongside non-softening -arń-)

mleczarnia (analyzed stem mlek-'arń-) *dairy*, cf. mleko *milk*
druciarnia (analyzed stem drut-'arń-) *wire factory*, cf. drut *wire*

CONTINENTS, COUNTRIES, AND INHABITANTS

Names for the continents and almost all countries are feminine in gender.
For the declension of the male-inhabitant names, see the following chapter.

	Continent	Adjective	Inhabitant (m./f.)
America	Ameryka	amerykański	Amerykanin, Amerykanka
Africa	Afryka	afrykański	Afrykanin, Afrykanka
Antarctica	Antarktyda	antarktyczny	
Asia	Azja	azjatycki	Azjata, Azjatka
Australia	Australia	australijski	Australijczyk, Australijka
Europe	Europa	europejski	Europejczyk, Europejka
	Country		
Afganistan	Afganistan	afgański	Afgan, Afganka
Albania	Albania	albański	Albańczyk, Albanka
Angola	Angola	angolski	Angolijczyk, Angolijka
Argentina	Argentyna	argentyński	Argentyńczyk, Argentynka
Australia	Australia	australijski	Australijczyk, Australijka
Austria	Austria	austriacki	Austriak, Austriaczka
Belgium	Belgia	belgijski	Belg, Belgijka
Bosnia	Bośnia	bośniacki	Bośniak, Bośniaczka
Brazil	Brazylia	brazylijski	Brazylijczyk, Brazylijka
Bulgaria	Bułgaria	bułgarski	Bułgar, Bułgarka
Belarus	Białoruś	białoruski	Białorusin, Białorusinka
Canada	Kanada	kanadyjski	Kanadyjczyk, Kanadyjka
Chile	Chile	chilijski	Chilijczyk, Chilijka
China	Chiny	chiński	Chińczyk, Chinka
Columbia	Kolumbia	kolumbijski	Kolumbijczyk, Kolumbijka
Croatia	Chorwacja	chorwacki	Chorwat, Chorwatka
Cuba	Kuba	kubański	Kubańczyk, Kubanka
Czech Rep.	Czechy	czeski	Czech, Czeszka
Denmark	Dania	duński	Duńczyk, Dunka
Egypt	Egipt	egipski	Egipcjanin, Egipcjanka

	Country	Adjective	Inhabitant (m./f.)
England	Anglia	angielski	Anglik, Angielka
Estonia	Estonia	estoński	Estończyk, Estonka
Finland	Finlandia	fiński	Fin, Finka
France	Francja	francuski	Francuz, Francuzka
Germany	Niemcy	niemiecki	Niemiec -mca, Niemka
Great Brit.	Wielka Brytania,	brytyjski	Brytyjczyk, Brytyjka
Greece	Grecja	grecki	Grek, Greczynka
Holland	Holandia	holenderski	Holender, Holenderka
Hungary	Węgry	węgierski	Węgier, Węgierka
India	India	hinduski	Hindus, Hinduska
Iraq	Irak	iracki	Irakijczyk, Irakijka
Iran	Iran	irański	Irańczyk, Iranka
Ireland	Irlandia	irlandzki	Irlandczyk, Irlandka
Israel	Izrael	izraelski	Izraelczyk, Izraelka
Italy	Włochy	włoski	Włoch, Włoszka
Japan	Japonia	japoński	Japończyk, Japonka
Korea	Korea	koreański	Koreańczyk, Koreanka
Latvia	Łotwy	łotewski	Lotysz, Łotyszka
Lithuania	Litwa	litewski	Litwin, Litwinka
Macedonia	Makedonia	makedoński	Makedończyk, Makedonka
Marocco	Maroko	marokański	Marokańczyk, Marokanka
Mexico	Meksyk	meksykański	Meksykańczyk, Meksykanka
Mongolia	Mongolia	mongolski	Mongoł, Mongołka
N. Zealand	Nowa Zelandia	nowozelandzki	Nowozelandczyk, -landka
Norway	Norwegia	norweski	Norweg, Norweżka
Peru	Peru	peruwiański	Peruwiańczyk, Peruwianka
Poland	Polska	polski	Polak, Polka
Portugal	Portugalia	portugalski	Portugalczyk, Portugalka
Romania	Rumunia	rumuński	Rumun, Rumunka
Russia	Rosja	rosyjski	Rosjanin, Rosjanka
Scotland	Szkocja	szkocki	Szkot, Szkotka
Serbia	Serbia	serbski	Serb, Serbka
Slovakia	Słowacja	słowacki	Słowak, Słowaczka
Spain	Hiszpania	hiszpański	Hiszpan, Hiszpanka
Sweden	Szwecja	szwedzki	Szwed, Szwedka
Switzerland	Szwajcaria	szwajcarski	Szwajcar, Szwajcarka
Turkey	Turcja	turecki	Turek, Turczynka
Ukraine	Ukraina	ukraiński	Ukrainiec, Ukrainka
Uruguay	Urugwaj	urugwajski	Urugwajczyk, Urugwajka
USA	Stany Zjednoczone	amerykański	Amerykanin, Amerykanka*

* or: **mieszkaniec (mieszkanka)** or **obywatel (obywatelka) Stanów Zjednoczonych**
inhabitant (citizen) of the United States.

By a "noun of masculine gender" is meant a noun for which one may substitute the 3rd person singular pronoun **on** *he*. Most masculine-gender nouns share a distinct set of endings which, for convenience, may be referred to as the masculine declension. The Nsg. is typically **-Ø**. The following main subtypes are distinguished:

a. Functionally hard stems, as **zeszyt** *notebook*, **stół** *table*, **dąb** *oak*
b. Velar stems, as **sok** *juice*, **róg** *horn*, **strych** *garret*
c. Functionally soft stems, as **płaszcz** *coat*, **nóż** *knife*, **hotel** *hotel*

Velar stems have no unique endings, but borrow the LVsg. ending in **-u** from the (functionally) soft stems. In all formal types one also distinguishes among inanimate, animate, and personal nouns, distinguished mainly according to the treatment of the noun in the Accusative case; see further discussion.

Some masculine-gender nouns referring to males have Nsg. in **-a**, and have a feminine-like declension, at least in the sg., for example **mężczyzna** *man*, **kolega** *colleague*, **poeta** *poet*. Some male first names may take Nsg. in **-o**, otherwise following a masculine declension, for example, **Józio**, **Stasio**. All such nouns, of either type, take masculine personal pronominal, adjectival, and verb agreement. In other words, as far as grammatical agreement is concerned, male reference takes preference over declensional type .

MORPHOSYNTACTIC CATEGORIES OF MASCULINE NOUNS

Among masculine-gender nouns, one needs to distinguish the following morphosyntactic types, defined according to case syncretisms: "inanimate" (A = N), "animate" (Asg = Gsg, Apl = Npl), and "personal" (A = G). See further discussion and chart on page 125.

THE SURFACE STEM

The surface stem of masculine-declension nouns usually has the same form as the Nsg.: **zeszyt** *notebook*, stem **zeszyt-**; **koń** *horse*, stem **koń-**. Since the Nsg. ending is **-Ø**, the Nsg. form may show a mobile vowel, the result of the **o:** **ó** or **ę:** **ą** shift, or a potentially soft labial consonant: **sen** *dream*, Gsg. **snu**, stem **sØn-**; **pies** *dog*, Gsg. **psa**, stem **p's-**; **stół** *table*, Gsg. **stołu**, stem **stoł-**; **wąż** *snake*, Gsg. **węża**, stem **węż-**; **paw** *peacock*, Gsg. **pawia**, stem **paw'-**.

REGULAR MASCULINE DECLENSIONAL ENDINGS

		Hard stems	Velar stems	Soft stems
Sg.	N	-ø	←	←
	G	-u or -a	←	←
	D	-owi	←	←
	A	= N/G	←	←
	I	-èm	←	←
	LV	-ě	-u	-u
Pl.	NV	-y/i or -ĭ	←	-è
	G	-ów	←	-y/i (-ów)
	D	-om	←	←
	A	= N/G	←	←
	I	-ami	←	←
	L	-ach	←	←

DISTRIBUTION OF REGULAR ENDINGS

Where a choice in ending is indicated in the above chart:

1. The Gsg. for animate nouns (masculine-gender nouns referring to animate beings, including persons) is -a, with the exceptions of **wół** *ox*, GAsg. **wołu** and **bawół** *buffalo*, GAsg. **bawołu**; see **szczur** *rat*, GAsg. **szczura**; **słoń** *elephant*, GAsg. **słonia, klient** *customer*, GAsg. **klienta**. Inanimate nouns tend to take Gsg. in -u, e.g. **zeszyt** *notebook*, Gsg. **zeszytu; hotel** *hotel*, Gsg. **hotelu.** However, many inanimate nouns take -a, for example, **ołówek** *pencil*, Gsg. **ołówka; chleb** *bread*, Gsg. **chleba; kościół** *church*, Gsg. **kościoła**, and others. For further details see below under The Choice Between -a and -u in the Gsg.

2. Inanimate nouns take the Asg. like the Nsg. (no matter what the Gsg.): **stół** *table*, NAsg. **stół; ręcznik** *towel*, NAsg. **ręcznik.**

3. Animate nouns take the Asg. like the Gsg. (which will be -a): **koń** *horse*, GAsg. **konia; student** *student*, GAsg. **studenta.**

4. Most hard-stem personal nouns take NVpl. in -ĭ (before which an R1 consonant replacement will occur) **biolog** *biologist*, NVpl. **biolodzy** (alongside **biologowie**); **student** *student*, NVpl. **studenci; Szwed** *Swede*, NVpl. **Szwedzi.** Soft-stem nouns take NVpl. in -è, regardless of whether personal or non-personal: **hotel** *hotel*, NVpl. **hotele; lekarz** *doctor*, NVpl. **lekarze.** There are numerous exceptional endings for masculine personal nouns; for details see further below under Personal Nouns with Special Endings or Inflections.

5. Hard-stem nouns take Gpl. (with personal nouns, GApl.) in -ów: **samochód** Gpl. **samochodów** *car*, **stół** Gpl. **stołów** *table*, **student**, GApl. **studentów** *student*. Additionally, nouns with stems in **c, dz,** and **j** usually take -ów, as **walec** Gpl. **walców** *steam-roller*, **widelec** Gpl. **widelców** *fork*, **wieniec** Gpl. **wieńców** *wreath*, **wódz wodzów** *leader*, **kraj krajów** *country*,

zdrój Gpl. **zdrojów** *spring.* Soft-stem nouns tend to take **-y/i**, although there is much variation: **czerw** Gpl. **czerwi** *maggot,* **tokarz** GApl. **tokarzy** *turner,* **żyrandol** Gpl. **żyrandoli** *chandelier,* **judasz** Gpl. **judaszy** or **judaszów** *peep-hole.* For further details, see below under the Choice between **-y/i** and **-ów** in the Gpl.

6. Personal nouns (not nouns which are merely animate) take the Apl. like the Gpl.: **student** *student,* GApl. **studentów; nauczyciel** *teacher,* GApl. **nauczycieli.** Animate non-personal nouns take the Apl. like the Npl., just like inanimate nouns: **kot** *cat,* NApl. **koty; stół** *table,* NApl. **stoły; hotel** *hotel,* NApl. **hotele.**

SOUND-CHANGES OCCURRING IN MASCULINE DECLENSION

When declining masculine nouns the following sound-changes should be kept in mind:

1. Hard stem consonants exhibit an R1 replacement before LVsg. **-ĕ: zeszyt** *notebook,* LVsg. **zeszyt-ĕ: zeszycie; mur** *wall,* LVsg. **mur-ĕ: murze; pył** *dust,* LVsg. **pył-ĕ: pyle,** and so on. This rule does not apply to velar stems, which take the ending **-u,** as **rok** *year,* LVsg **roku.**

2. Hard, including velar, consonants will be replaced by their R1 counterparts before the masc. pers. NVpl. ending **-ĭ.** The item **ĭ** merges with **y/i** and is subject to the **y/i** spelling rule: **student-ĭ: studenć-y/i: studenci; lektor-ĭ: lektorz-y/i: lektorzy; lotnik-ĭ: lotnic-y/i: lotnicy.**

3. **k** and **g** will be replaced by **k'** and **g',** respectively, before Isg. **-èm** and NApl. **-y/i: buk** *beech,* Isg. **buk-èm: buk'-em: bukiem;** NApl. **buk-y/i: buk'-y/i: buki; katalog** *catalog,* Isg. **katalog-èm: katalog'-em: katalogiem;** NApl. **katalog-y/i: katalog'-y/i: katalogi;**

4. The **ĕ: a** vowel-shift before hard dentals is exhibited in a few hard dental-stems, in which case **ĕ** will be preserved (in the form of **e**) in the LVsg., while the other forms will contain **a: kwiat** *flower,* LVsg. **kwiecie,** stem **kwĕt; las** *forest,* LVsg. **lesie,** stem **lĕs-; obiad** *dinner,* LVsg. **obiedzie,** stem **obiĕd-; powiat** *local district,* LVsg. **powiecie,** stem **powiĕt-; świat** *world,* LVsg. **świecie,** stem **świĕt-; zjazd** *congress,* LVsg. **zjeździe,** stem **zjĕzd-.** This change does not occur everywhere it might be expected, cf. **dział** *division,* LVsg. **dziale.** In case the hard dental-stem is a personal noun, the **ĕ: a** shift will be found in the NVpl. as well: **sąsiad** *neighbor,* LVsg. **sąsiedzie,** NVpl. **sąsiedzi,** stem **sąsiĕd-.**

5. The **e: o** vowel-shift is not normally exhibited in the form of **e** in the LVsg. of masculine nouns, cf. **dzięcioł** *woodpecker,* LVsg. **dzięciole; gruczoł** *gland,* LVsg. **gruczole; przedmiot** *object,* LVsg. **przedmiocie, wieczór** *evening,* LVsg. **wieczorze.** However, **e** does occur in the word 'church': **kościół,** LVsg. **kościele,** stem **kościeł-** (this word also exhibits the **o: ó** shift in the NAsg.). The **e** of the **e: o** vowel-shift is found in the LVsg. and NVpl. of **anioł** *angel,* LVsg. **aniele,** NVpl. **anieli** (or **aniołowie**), stem

aniel-, and in the NVpl. of adjectival nouns from participles in **-ony**: **uczony** NVpl. **uczeni** *scholar(s)*.

6. The **o**: **ó** and **ę**: **ą** vowel-shifts often occur in the NAsg. before the ending **-Ø**: **stół** *table*, Gsg. **stołu**, stem **stoł-**; **wół** *ox*, Gsg. **wołu**, stem **woł-**; **strój** *costume*, Gsg. **stroju**, stem **stroj-**; **dąb** *oak*, Gsg. **dębu**, stem **dęb-**; **urząd** *office*, Gsg. **urzędu**, stem **urzęd-**. The **ę**: **ą** shift often does not occur where expected, cf. **rząd** *row*, Gsg. **rzędu** vs. **rząd** *government*, Gsg. **rządu**; **łabędź** (not *łabądź) *swan*, GAsg. **łabędzia**.

7. The mobile-vowel shifts **Ø**: **è** and **'**: **e** can occur before the NAsg. ending **-Ø**: **ołówek** *pencil*, Gsg. **ołówka**, stem **ołówØk-**; **błazen** *clown*, GAsg. **błazna**, stem **błazØn-**; **łokieć** *elbow*, Gsg. **łokcia**, stem **łokØć-**; **palec** *finger, toe*, Gsg. **palca**, stem **pal'c-**; **owies** *oats*, Gsg. **owsa**, stem **ow's-**. Here are some common monsyllables exhibiting the **Ø**: **e** shift (the second form is the Gsg.): **bez bzu** *lilac*, **dech tchu** *breath*, **dzień dnia** *day*, **kieł kła** *fang*, **łeb łba** *animal head*, **lew lwa** *lion*, **mech mchu** *moss*, **pień pnia** *stump*, **sen snu** *dream*.

8. As was the case with feminine-declension nouns, when a noun is suffix-ally derived from another noun, the **o**: **ó** and **ę**: **ą** shifts and the mobile-vowel are not always predictable. For example, **wózek** *baby carriage* retains **ó** in the NAsg. against the rule, presumably based on the **ó** of the other forms (**wózka**, etc.) and of the NAsg. of the base-word **wóz** *carriage*. By contrast, **rożek** G **rożka** *croissant* does not preserve the **ó** of **róg** *horn* but rather the **o** of the stem **rog-**; **kłębek** *tuft* G **kłębka** does not preserve the **ą** of **kłąb** *skein* but of the stem **kłęb-**. The word **piesek** *doggy* retains the vowel **e** which is mobile in **pies** *dog*; one might expect *psek. By con-trast, **psisko** *big dog* treats the vowel as mobile and drops it. See also **bąbel bąbla** *blister*, diminutive **bąbelek** (not *bąblek).

9. Consonants that soften (to R2) before the mobile vowel **e** may appear as hard when the mobile vowel does not occur: **marzec** *march*, Gsg. **marca**, stem **mar'c-**; **mędrzec** *wise man* Gsg. **mędrca**, stem **mędr'c-**; **orzeł** *eagle*, GAsg. **orła**, stem **or'ł-**; **pies** *dog*, GAsg. **psa**, stem **p's-**. As a rule, conso-nants other than **l** appear as hard, hence **smalec** *lard*, Gsg. **smalcu**, but **dworzec** *station*, Gsg. **dworca**, **grudzień** *December*, Gsg. **grudnia**. See fuller discussion in Chapter 2.

10. Soft labial consonants harden in final position: **paw** *peacock*, GAsg. **pawia**, stem **paw'-**; **Wrocław** *Wroclaw*, Gsg. **Wrocławia**, stem **Wrocław'-**; **gołąb** *pigeon*, GAsg. **gołębia**, stem **gołęb'-** (this word also shows the **ę**: **ą** shift).

11. Stem-final **j** is dropped (in pronunciation and spelling) after a vowel be-fore **-y/i**: **pokój** *room*, Gpl. **pokoi** (**pokoj-y/i**: **poko-i**: **pokoi**).

EXCEPTIONAL ENDINGS

See also below under Personal Nouns with Special Endings or Inflections.

1. Dsg. **-u**. The following nouns take Dsg. in **-u**: **Bóg** *God*, Dsg. **Bogu**, **brat** *brother*, Dsg. **bratu**; **chłop** *peasant*, Dsg. **chłopu**; **chłopiec** *boy*, Dsg. **chłopcu**; **czart czartu** *devil*, **diabeł** *devil*, Dsg. **diabłu**; **kat** *hangman*, Dsg. **katu**; **kot** *cat*, Dsg. **kotu**; **ksiądz** *priest*, Dsg. **księdzu**; **lew** *lion*, Dsg. **lwu**; **ojciec** *father*, Dsg. **ojcu**; **osioł** *donkey*, Dsg. **osłu**; **pan** *sir*, *Mr.*, Dsg. **panu**; **pies** *dog*, Dsg. **psu**; **świat** *world*, Dsg. **światu**. The Dsg. ending **-u** occurs alongside **kwiatowi** with **kwiat** *flower*. The Dsg. for other masculine-declension nouns is **-owi**.

2. Lsg. **-u** with hard-stems. The following three hard-stem nouns take this ending: **dom** *house*, Lsg. **domu** (Vsg. **domie**); **syn** *son*, LVsg. **synu**; **pan** *sir*, *Mr.*, Lsg. **panu** (Vsg. **panie**). Archaic **bór** Lsg. **boru** *woods*, today **borze**. However, the Lsg. of the television serial title **"Dom"** is **w "Domie"**.

3. Vsg. **-u** with hard stems. In addition to **syn**, this ending may occasionally be found with **dziad** *old man*, Vsg. **dziadzie** or colloquial **dziadu**, **lud** *people, folk*, Vsg. **ludu**.

4. Vsg. **-e** with certain stems in **c** and **dz**. Before this exceptional ending, **c** will be replaced by **cz** and **dz** by **ż** (**g**, **k** will be replaced by **ż**, **cz**, respectively, as expected). This ending occurs with the four common nouns **ojciec** *father*, Vsg. **ojcze**, **chłopiec** *boy*, Vsg. **chłopcze**, **ksiądz** *priest*, Vsg. **księże**, **Bóg** *God*, Vsg. **Boże**. The Vsg. form **krawcu** (from **krawiec** *tailor*) is expanding at the expense of **krawcze**, as is **naukowcu** (from **naukowiec** *scientist*) instead of **naukowcze**; **Niemcu** (from **Niemiec** *German*) instead of **Niemcze**; and so forth for other such nouns. In older writing, the ending **-e** may occasionally be found on stems in **k** or **c**, with **k** or **c** going to **cz**: **Kozak** *Cossack*, Vsg. **Kozaku** or archaic **Kozacze**, **człowiek** *man*, Vsg. **człowieku** or archaic **człowiecze**, **jeździec** Vsg. **jeźdźcu**, older **jeźdźcze**.

5. Vsg.= Nsg. The Nominative can almost always be used in place of the Vocative. Importantly, last names do not form a Vocative, including those with a nominal inflection. Thus, the Vocative of **Duraj** (**Duraja Durajowi**, etc.) is **Duraj**.

6. NVpl. **-è** after hard-stems. This is the NVpl. ending of a few (not all) nouns ending in **-ans** or **-ons**: **anons anonse** *announcement(s)*, **awans awanse** *promotion(s)*, **fajans fajanse** *porcelain(s)*, **kwadrans kwadranse** *quarter-hour(s)*, **niuans niuanse** *nuance*, **seans seanse** *showing(s) (of movie)*. Some such nouns take either **-e** or **y**, as **ambulans** *ambulance*, **dyliżans** *stagecoach*, **dystans**, us. **dystansy** *distance*.

7. NVpl. **-a**. This uncommon ending occurs with **akt akta** *deed(s)*, **grunt grunta** *ground(s)*, **cud cuda** (or **cudy**) *miracle(s)*, **koszt koszta** or **koszty** *cost(s)*, **organ** *organ* 1. 'body part', 2. 'partisan newspaper', *pl.* **organy**, 3. 'administrative unit' *pl.* **organa** or **organy**, as in **organa** (**organy**) **ścigania** *investigative units*; 4. plural-only **organy** Gpl. **organów** *organ*. For **brat** *brother*, NVpl. **bracia**, see below under the declensional illustrations.

8. Ipl. **-mi**. **brat** *brother*, Ipl. **braćmi; gość** *guest*, Ipl. **gośćmi; koń** *horse*, Ipl. **końmi; ksiądz** *priest*, Ipl. **księżmi; liść** *leaf*, Ipl. **liśćmi; pieniądz** *coin, money*, Ipl. **pieniędzmi; przyjaciel** *friend*, Ipl. **przyciaciółmi; ludzie** *people*, Ipl. **ludźmi**. Optionally: **gwóźdź** *nail*, Ipl. **g w o ź d ź m i** (usually gwoździami).

9. Ipl. **-y**. An archaic ending surviving in a few songs and phrases, as **z wszystkimi znaki** *with all signs* (from a Christmas carol), **dawnymi czasy** *in olden times*, **dziw nad dziwy** *wonder above wonders*.

THE CHOICE BETWEEN -U AND -A IN THE GSG.

The occurrence of **-u** or **-a** in the Gsg. of inanimate nouns is determined by historical, semantic, and morphological factors which are impossible to unravel completely. For some nouns usage is not definitely established; see, for example, **abażur abaszuru** or **abażura** *lampshade*, **bunker bunkru** or **bunkra** *bunker*, **chlew chlewu** or **chlewa** *pigsty*, **daszek daszku** or **daszka** *peak of cap*, **dywan dywanu** or **dywana** *carpet*, **konar konara** or **konaru** *corona of tree*, **łachman łachmana** or **łachmanu** *rag*, **portfel portfela** or **portfelu** *billfold*, **wieczór wieczora** or **wieczoru** *evening*, **balon balonu** or **balona** *baloon*, **bambus bambusa** or **bambusu** *bamboo*, **bilard bilardu** or, increasingly, **bilarda** *billiards*; **zamek zamka** occurs in the meaning 'lock', while **zamek zamku** is used in the sense 'castle'. The following guidelines will resolve most instances of indecision.

The Gsg. ending **-u** is the expected ending for inanimate nouns: **dom domu** *house*, **hotel hotelu** *hotel*, **zeszyt zeszytu** *notebook*, etc. The Gsg. ending **-u** almost always occurs with names for large and especially amorphous objects (**gmach gmachu** *large building*, **kraj kraju** *country*, **ocean oceanu** *ocean*; substances (**miód miodu** *honey*, **piasek piasku** *sand*, **płyn płynu** *liquid*); forces, intangibles, and abstractions (**fach fachu** *trade, profession*, **pokój pokoju** *peace*, **temat tematu** *subject*, **wiatr wiatru** *wind*); and nouns formed on verbal roots (**postój postoju** *stop, stand*; **przelot przelotu** *flight*, **utwór utworu** *creation*).

The Gsg. ending **-a** occurs with all animate nouns (other than **wół wołu** *ox* and **bawół bawołu** *bison*). For the GA of **wół**, see **Jednego wołu i dwa cielce zakropił**. *A single ox and two calves he sprinkled [slauthered]*. A. Mickiewicz, *Pan Tadeusz*. Without the support of normative grammar and older works of literature, the GA of **wół** and **bawół** would long ago have been replaced by **woła, bawoła**, which do occur as colloquial forms.

The following rules concern inanimate nouns taking **-a**.

1. All facultative animate nouns (referentially inanimate nouns treated as grammatically animate) take GAsg. **-a**: **papieros papierosa** *cigarette*, **kac kaca** *hangover*, **pech pecha** *bad luck*, **rydz rydza** *agaric mushroom*, **walc walca** *waltz*. See further below under Facultative Animate Nouns.

2. Many (but by no means all) names for trees, nuts, fruits (especially exotic), vegetables, and berries take Gsg. **-a**: **ananas** *pineapple*, **arbuz** *water-*

melon, **banan** *banana*, **burak** *beet*, **daktyl** *date*, **kartofel kartofla** *potato*, **pomidor** *tomato*, **migdał** (or **migdału**) *almond*, **ogórek ogórka** *cucumber*, **orzech** *nut*, **rodzynek rodzynka** *raisin*. Some trees: **buk** *beech*, **jawor jawora** (or **jaworu**) *sycamore*, **kasztan kasztana** (or **kasztanu**) *chestnut*, **modrzew modrzewia** *larch*, **świerka** *spruce* (but: **cedr cedru** *cedar*, **dąb dębu** *oak*, **dęba** occurring in some phrases). Most masculine-gender flowers take **-a**, for example: **aster astra** *aster*, **fiołek fiołka** *violet*, **irys irysa** *iris*, **narcyz narcyza** *narcissus*, **tulipan tulipana** *tulip*, but **bławat bławatu** *cornflower*, **żonkil żonkilu** (alongside **żonkila**) *daffodil*.

3. Serially produced food items, especially delicacies, tend to take Gsg. **-a**: **cukierek cukierka** *candy*, **gofer gofra** *waffle*, **hamburger** *hamburger*, **herbatnik** *tea-cookie*, **hotdog** *hotdog*, **klops** *meatball*, **kołacz** *Easter bread*, **pączek pączka** *doughnut*, **wafel wafla** *wafer*. Cuts of meat can sometimes take either **-a** or **-u**; thus **befsztyk** *beafsteak*, **filet** *filet*, **zraz** *chop*, etc., but only **kotlet kotleta** *cutlet*, **sznycel sznycla** *cutlet*.

4. Most masculine names for tools, pegs, implements, appliances, mechanical parts, poles, pots, pans, containers, rope, wire, twine, furniture, articles of household use take **-a**: **cybuch** *pipe stem*, **cyngiel cyngla** *trigger*, **cyrkiel cyrkla** *compass*, **czekan** *ice-ax*, **czop** *spigot*, **ćwiek** *hobnail*, **drut** *wire*, **dyszel dyszla** *wagon tongue*, **dzban** *jug*, **filar** *pillar*, **fotel** *armchair*, **garnek garnka** *pot*, **gwóźdź gwoździa** *nail*, **kabel kabla** *cable*, **kapsel kapsla** *bottlecap*, **kielich** *chalice*, **kij** *stick*, **klawisz** *key (of piano, etc.)*, **klin** *wedge*, **klocek klocka** *block*, **klucz** *key*, **komin** *chimney*, **kosz** *basket*, **kół koła** *pike*, **kubek kubka** *mug*, **kufel kufla** *stein*, **młot** *hammer*, **nóż noża** *knife*, **ołówek ołówka** *pencil*, **otwieracz** *opener*, **parasol** *umbrella*, **piec** *oven*, **pług** *plow*, **rondel rondla** *saucepan*, **sierp** *sickle*, **słój słoja** *jar*, **słup** *pole*, **szczebel szczebla** *rung*, **sznur** *cord*, **świder świdra** *drill*, **tapczan** *day-couch*, **wentyl** *valve*, **wór wora** (or **woru**) *sack*, **żyrandol** *chandelier*; and so on (but: **oszczep oszczepu** *javelin*, **stół stołu** *table*).

5. Masculine-gender names for parts of the body, whether human or animal, including protuberances and eruptions, take Gsg. **-a**: **bak** *sideburn*, **bąbel bąbla** *blister*, **brzuch** *paunch*, **dziób dzioba** *beak*, **guz** *bruise*, **język** *tongue*, **kciuk** *thumb*, **kędzior** *curl*, **kieł kła** *fang*, **łokieć łokcia** *elbow*, **nos** *nose*, **ogon** *tail*, **ozór ozora** *animal tongue*, **palec palca** *finger*, **paznokieć paznokcia** *fingernail*, **pazur** *talon*, **pieg** *freckle*, **pryszcz** *pimple*, **wąs** *mustache*, **włos** *a hair*, **ząb zęba** *tooth*. However: **kark karku** *nape or back of neck*, **róg rogu** *horn*.

6. Masculine-gender articles of, or parts of, apparel or haberdashery take Gsg. in **-a**: **cylinder cylindra** *top hat*, **fartuch** *apron*, **guzik** *button*, **kaftan caftan**, **klips** *clip-on earring*, **kapelusz** *hat*, **kaptur** *hood*, **kołnierz** *collar*, **kożuch** *sheepskin coat*, **krawat** *necktie*, **melonik** *bowler hat*, **monokl** *monacle*, **szalik** *scarf*, **guzik** *button*, **pasek paska** *belt*, **płaszcz** *coat*, **szal** *shawl*. However: **beret beretu** *beret*, **gorset gorsetu** *corset*, **mankiet mankietu**

cuff; **portfel portfela** or **portfelu** *billfold.* Footwear in **-a: but** *shoe,* **drewniak** *clog,* **kalosz** *galosh,* **pantofel pantofla** *house-slipper,* **sandał** *sandal,* **trzewik** *slip-on shoe.*

7. Names of the months take Gsg. in **-a: grudzień grudnia** *December,* **czerwiec czerwca** *June,* **listopad listopada** *November,* etc. Masculine-gender days of the week take **-u: poniedziałek poniedziałku** *Monday,* etc.

8. Weights, measures, and monetary units take Gsg. in **-a: amper ampera** *amper,* **funt** *pound,* **kilogram** *kilogram,* **kilometr** *kilometer,* **korzec korca** *bushel,* **lir lira** *lira,* **litr** *liter,* **mórg morga** *morg (of land),* **rubel rubla** *ruble,* **tuzin** *dozen,* **wat** *watt,* etc. Monetary units are facultatively animate; see below.

9. Games, dances, and many sports terms, many or most of which are facultatively animate (see further below), take Gsg. in **-a: as** *ace,* **gol** *goal,* **kier kiera** *heart (in cards),* **oberek oberka** *oberek dance,* **palant** *batball,* **pik** *spades (in cards),* **wist** *whist.*

10. Most Polish towns, especially those ending in soft consonants and in the suffixes **-in-** and **-ow-**, take Gsg. in **-a: Gdańsk Gdańska, Kraków Krakowa, Lublin Lublina, Olsztyn Olsztyna, Poznań Poznania, Radom Radomia, Rzeszów Rzeszowa, Szczecin Szczecina, Toruń Torunia, Wałbrzych Wałbrzycha, Wrocław Wrocławia.** Contrast with **Hel Helu, Sopot Sopotu, Białystok Białegostoku, Szczyrk Szczyrku.** Among foreign town-names, these take **-a: Berlin Berlina, Paryż Paryża** *Paris,* **Wiedeń Wiednia** *Vienna.* (but, for example, **Londyn Londynu, Rzym Rzymu, Nowy Jork Nowego Jorku.**

11. Nouns ending in **ć, ń, dź, c, dz, rz, ż,** unless they name abstractions or substances, tend to take Gsg. in **-a: cmentarz** *cemetery,* **czyściec czyśćca** *purgatory,* **dworzec dworca** *station,* **dzień dnia** *day,* **grobowiec grobowca** *tomb, sepulcher,* **grzebień grzebienia** *comb,* **hamulec hamulca** *brake,* **tydzień tygodnia** *week,* **egzemplarz** *copy,* **jęczmień jęczmienia** *oats (even though a substance),* **kaganiec kagańca** *muzzle,* **kalendarz** *calendar,* **kamień kamienia** *rock,* **kolec kolca** *thorn,* **komentarz** *commentary,* **krzyż** *cross,* **księżyc** *moon,* **liść liścia** *leaf,* **miesiąc** *month,* **miesień mięśnia** *muscle,* **pieniądz** *coin.* Contrast with substance-nouns in **-u: kurz kurzu** *dust,* **miedź miedziu** *copper,* **mosiądz mosiądzu** *bronze,* **smalec smalcu** *lard,* **tytoń tytoniu** *tobacco;* **kopeć** *lampblack* allows either **kopcia** or **kopciu.**

12. Many nouns in **-ak, -yk, -ik, -ek,** unless they name substances, take Gsg. in **-a.** Many of these nouns also fall under some other class taking **-a: cukierek cukierka** *hard candy,* **durszlak** *strainer,* **haczyk** *hook,* **język** *tongue,* **ogryzek ogryzka** *apple core,* **patyk** *stick,* **pojemnik** *container,* **pomnik** *monument,* **kłębek kłębka** *tuft of yarn* (contrast with **kłąb kłębu** *skein*), **krzak** *bush,* **stolik** *end table* (contrast with **stół stołu**), **wiatrak**

windmill, **wózek wózka** *baby carriage* (contrast with **wóz wozu** *cart*). The substance-noun **piasek piasku** *sand* takes Gsg. **-u.**

13. Many nouns in **-ar, -er** or **-or,** especially those naming equipment, take Gsg. in **-a: bojler** *boiler,* **helikopter** *helicopter,* **kaloryfer** *radiator,* **kanister kanistra** *fuel can,* **komputer** *computer,* **lewar** *jack,* **skuter skutera** *scooter,* **telewizor** *television set,* **tornister tornistra** *schoolbag,* **traktor** *tractor,* **tranzystor** *transistor,* etc.

14. Some common inanimate nouns taking Gsg. in **-a** not clearly following one of the above rules include **afisz** *playbill,* **bandaż** *bandage,* **chleb** *bread,* **chlew** *pigsty,* **owies owsa** *oats,* **kawał** *piece,* **kęs** *chunk,* **kleks** *inkspot,* **komin** *chimney,* **kościół kościoła** *church,* **knot** *wick,* **krzak** *bush,* **młyn** *mill,* **owies owsa** *oats,* **piorun** *thunderbolt,* **ser** *cheese,* **szpital** *hospital,* **świat** *world,* **węgiel węgla** *coal,* **węzeł węzła** *knot,* **wiersz** *line of poetry,* and many more.

THE CHOICE BETWEEN -Y/I AND -ÓW IN THE GPL.

1. Gpl. **-ów.**

   a. Hard-stem nouns take **-ów: zeszyt** *notebook,* Gpl. **zeszytów; student** *student,* Gpl. **studentów; stół** *table,* Gpl. **stołów; dąb** *oak,* Gpl. **dębów;** and so on. This rule extends to masculine personal nouns with Nsg. in **-a,** with the single exception of **mężczyzna** *man,* GApl. **mężczyzn;** see **kolega** *colleague,* GApl. **kolegów; dentysta** *dentist,* GApl. **dentystów; wojewoda** *voivode,* GApl. **wojewodów, zwycięzca** GApl. **zwycięzców** *victor.*

   b. Personal nouns with NVpl. in **-owie** (see further below), even if soft-stems, take GApl. in **-ów: ojciec ojcowie ojców** *father,* **król królowie królów** *king,* **paź paziowie paziów** *page,* **widz widzowie widzów** *viewer,* **więzień więźniowie więźniów** *prisoner;* **wódz wodzowie wodzów** *leader.* Personal adjectival nouns taking **-owie** (like **budowniczy budowniczowie** *builder*) do not follow this rule but take adjectival **-ych:** GApl. **budowniczych.**

   c. Nouns ending in **-c** and **-dz** take GApl. **-ów: koc** Gpl. **koców** *blanket;* **kupiec** *merchant* GApl. **kupców; materac** Gpl. **materaców** *mattress;* **pałac** Gpl. **pałaców** *palace;* **palec** Gpl. **palców** *finger;* **piec** Gpl. **pieców** *stove;* **rydz** Gpl. **rydzów** *agaric mushroom;* **szewc** *cobbler,* GApl. **szewców; sztuciec** Gpl. **sztućców** *utensil (us. pl.);* **taniec** Gpl. **tańców** *dance;* **widelec widelców** *fork,* **wieniec wieńców** *wreath,* **wódz wodzów** *leader,* **znawca** *connoisseur* GApl. **znawców.** The following nouns in **-ąc** or **-ądz** take the Gpl. in **-ęcy, -ędzy,** respectively: **miesiąc** *month,* Gpl. **miesięcy; pieniądz** *coin, money,* Gpl. **pieniędzy; tysiąc** *thousand,* Gpl. **tysięcy; zając** *hare,* Gpl. **zajęcy.**

2. Gpl. **-y/i**. The Gpl. ending among masculine soft-stem nouns is in a con-
tinuous state of flux. For a while it appeared as though **-ów**, being unam-
biguously Gpl., was the expansive ending, destined eventually to drive
out **-y/i**. More recently, however, **-y/i** has been making a comeback at
the expense of **-ów**, driving out even well-established **-ów** among certain
nouns. There is a substantial discrepancy between contemporary usage
and that, say of nineteenth century literature (which continues to be read,
possibly influencing current usage). Many doublets can be encountered,
for example **materac** *mattress*, Gpl. **materacy** instead of standard
materaców; mecz *sports match*, Gpl. **!meczy** instead of **meczów, strój** *costume*, Gpl. **!stroi** instead of **strojów**; and so on. In practice, much depends
on the individual consonant and word. Contemporary normativists allow
considerable leeway.

a. Stems in **-l** tend to take **-i**: **hotel** Gpl. **hoteli** (alongside **hotelów**) *hotel;*
kowal GApl. **kowali** *smith;* **motyl** Gpl. **motyli** *butterfly;* **szczebel** Gpl.
szczebli *rung,* **trzmiel trzmieli** *bumblebee,* **żonkil żonkili** *daffodil,*
żyrandol żyrandoli *chandelier.* With some nouns in **-l**, **-ów** is a less
common alternative: **badyl** *stalk,* **bakcyl** *bacillus,* **kufel** *stein,* **kumpel**
buddy, **pudel** *poodle,* **portfel** *billfold,* **skalpel** *scalpel,* **ul** *beehive.* The Gpl.
of **cel** *goal* is only **celów**.

b. Stems in **-j** tend to take **-ów**, but there are many exceptions and alternative possibilities; see **gronostaj** Gpl. **gronostai** or **gronostajów** *er-
mine;* **bobslej** *bobsled,* Gpl. **boblejów** or **bobslei** *bobsled;* **kraj** Gpl.
krajów *country;* **skraj** Gpl. **skrajów** *edge;* **urodzaj** Gpl. **urodzajów** *harvest,* **kij** Gpl. **kijów** *stick;* **burżuj** GApl. **burżujów** *bourgeois.* Words in
-ój occasion the most difficulty; see **bój** Gpl. **bojów** *fight,* but **pięciobój**
Gpl. **pięcioboi** or **pięciobojów** *pentathlon.* These take only **ów**: **nastrój**
Gpl. *mood;* **przebój** *hit song;* **rój** *swarm;* **strój** *costume.* These can take
either **-ów** or **-i**: **napój** *drink,* **nabój** *cartridge,* **pokój** *room,* **zwój** *roll.*

c. Stems in phonetically soft dentals **ć, dź, ń, ź** and soft labials **b', p', m',
w'** usually take **-i**: **paznokieć** Gpl. **paznokci** *fingernail;* **papuć** Gpl.
papuci *slipper;* **śledź** Gpl. **śledzi** *herring;* **żołądź** Gpl. **żołędzi** *acorn,*
miesień Gpl. **mięśni** *muscle;* **pień** Gpl. **pni** *stump;* **karp** Gpl. **karpi** *carp;*
modrzew Gpl. **modrzewi** *larch;* **paw** Gpl. **pawi** *peacock,* **żółw** Gpl.
żółwi *tortoise.* A number of stems in **-ń** take **-ów** as an alternative, including **cień** Gpl. **cieni** or **cieniów** *shadow;* **dureń** GApl. **durniów** or
durni *fool,* **cierń** Gpl. **cierni** or **cierniów** *thorn.* Some nouns in **ś** take
-ów as a preferred choice: **rabuś** GApl. us. **rabusiów** *robber,* **struś** Gpl.
us. **strusiów** *ostrich,* **żartowniś**, GApl. us. **żartownisiów** *joker,* **harnaś**
GApl. us. **harnasiów** *Tatra mountain brigand leader.*

d. Stems in **cz, rz, sz, ż** show the greatest variety. Nouns in **cz**, while they
usually take **-y**, often take **-ów** as a less common alternative, and
sometimes **-ów** is preferred; see **bogacz** *rich man,* **deszcz** us. **deszczów**

rain, **dreszcz** *shiver*, **gąszcz** *thicket*, **kurcz** *spasm*, **mecz** only **meczów** *sports match*, **miecz** *sword*, **nietoperz** *bat*, **płacz** Gpl. only **płaczów** *wailing*, **płaszcz** *coat*, **skecz** *sketch*, **świerszcz** *cricket*, **trębacz** *trumpeter*, **tłuszcz** only **tłuszczów** *fat*. Nouns in **rz** often take -**y** with -**ó w** occurring as a substandard form. This includes **dziennikarz** *journalist*, **harcerz** *scout*, **lekarz** *doctor*, **plotkarz** *gossiper*, **ślusarz** *locksmith*, **talerz** *plate*, **tancerz** *dancer*, **weterynarz** *veterinary*. Nouns in **sz** and **ż** often have -**ów** as a less-common alternative, as **fałsz** *falsehood*, **jubileusz** *anniversary*, **kosz** *basket*, **smakosz** *gourmand*, **wiersz** only **wierszy** *verse*, **bandaż** *bandage*, **papież** *pope*, **pasaż** *mall*, **pejsaż** *landscape*, **sondaż** *poll*, **tatuaż** *tattoo*. Gpl. in -**ów** is usual with **afisz** *playbill*, **tchórz** *coward*, **tusz** *mascara*, **wieprz** *hog*, **zamsz** *chamois*.

FACULTATIVE ANIMATE NOUNS

A fairly large number of masculine nouns referring to inanimate objects take GAsg. in -**a**, similar to animate nouns. So-called facultative animate nouns may be divided into those for which the animate ending is virtually obligatory (hence the nouns are grammatically animate, even if referentially inanimate), and those where the Asg. ending -**a** is merely optional. With the latter group, the use of the animate ending is characteristic of an informal colloquial style.

Among facultative animates the following categories may be distinguished:

1. Metonymically animate nouns, including
   a. Inanimate nouns when figuratively applied to people: **bas** *base*, **geniusz** *genius*, **ideał** *ideal*, **oryginał** *original*, **parawan** *cover*, **typ** *type*, **szkielet** *skeleton*, **sopran** *soprano*, **skarb** *treasure*, **grzyb** *old so-and-so*; etc. Except for **grzyb** *mushroom*, which is in any case facultatively animate with GAsg. in -**a**, the foregoing nouns have -**u** in the non-figurative Gsg.
   b. Idols and objects of human shape: **bałwan** *snowman*, **chochoł** *straw man*, **manekin** *mannequin*, **robot** *robot*, **strach** *scarecrow*.
   c. Ghosts, mythical beings: **demon** *demon*, **potwór potwora** *monster*, **amor** *cupid*, **smok** *dragon*, **upiór upiora** *phantom*, **krasnoludek krasnoludka** *fairy*. Note that most such items are animate, but not necessarily masculine personal. The Apl. of **demon**, for example, is usually **demony**, not *demonów.
   d. Planets, stars, constellations, geographical features named after people or mythological beings: **Mars** *Mars*, **Saturn** *Saturn*, **Syriusz** *Sirius*, **Wodnik** *Aquarius*, **Mnich** *Monk (mountain peak)*.

e. Works of artistic creativity named after the author: **Mozart** *work by Mozart,* **Polański (A Polańskiego)** *film by Polanski,* **Rubens** *painting by Rubens.*

f. Animate nouns figuratively applied to things, as **motyl** *butterfly/bow tie,* **pająk** *spider/brachiated light fixture,* **wąż węża** *snake/water hose.*

2. Virtually obligatory (not strongly colloquial) facultative animates:

a. Reified mental states: **bzik** *mania,* **fioł** *craze,* **kac** *hangover,* **pech** *bad luck,* **strach** *fear.*

b. Smacks, pinches, kisses: **całus** *kiss,* **klaps** *smack,* **kopniak** *kick,* **prztyczek prztyczka** *fillip,* **szczutek szczutka** *pinch.*

c. Automobile brands and models: **fiat** *fiat,* **ford** *ford,* **gokart** *go-cart,* **jeep** *jeep,* **mercedes** *Mercedes.* Not: **samochód** *automobile.*

d. Cigarettes and cigarette brands: **papieros** *cigarette,* **pet** *butt,* **skręt** *roll-your-own,* **camel** *Camel,* **giewont** *Giewont,* **wawel** *Wawel.* Not usually **niedopałek** *butt.*

e. Brand names of appliances and equipment: **grundig** *Grundig radio,* **parker** *Parker pen,* **koral** *Coral TV,* **panasonic** *"panasonik" Panasonic stereo,* **sharp** *Sharp electronic appliance,* **telefunken** *Telefunken radio,* **zenit** *Zenith camera.*

f. Space ships and artificial satellites: **Discoverer, Łunnik, Sputnik,** also **satelita** Asg. **tego satelitę** *satellite.*

g. Dances: **fokstrot** *foxtrot,* **menuet** *minuet,* **oberek oberka** *oberek,* **polonez** *polonaise,* **walc** *waltz.*

h. Monetary units: **dolar** *dollar,* **dukat** *ducat,* **forint** *forint,* **funt** *pound,* **reński reńskiego** *florin, tip,* **rubel rubla** *ruble,* **złoty złotego** *zloty.*

i. Sports, games, and gaming terms: **as** *ace,* **brydż** *bridge,* **gol** *goal,* **golf** *golf,* **hokej** *hockey,* **pik** *spade,* **ping-pong** *ping-pong,* **poker** *poker,* **rober robra** *rubber,* **set** *set,* **tenis** *tennis,* **totalizator** *lottery.*

j. Certain dramatic movements and gestures: **drapak** *slip,* **kozioł** *somersault,* **nur** *dive,* **sus** *leap.* Not usually: **piruet** *pirouette,* **zygzak** *zig-zag.*

k. Mushrooms: **borowik** *boletus,* **grzyb** *mushroom,* **prawdziwek prawdziwka** *type of boletus,* **rydz** *agaric.*

l. Pastries: **gofer** *waffle,* **naleśnik** *pancake,* **pączek pączka** *donut,* **pieróg pieroga** *meat pie,* **rogalik** *croissant.*

m. Pegs: **ćwiek** *hobnail,* **czop** *plug,* **klin** *wedge.* Not usually **gwóźdź** *nail.*

n. Bruises, bodily afflictions: **guz** *bruise,* **platfus** *flatfoot,* **siniak** *bruise,* **siniec** *black eye,* **strupek** *scab,* **zez** *cross-eye.*

o. Pieces of junk: **grat** *junk furniture,* **gruchot** *rattle-trap,* **klekot** *rickety object.*

p. Wine and certain drinking terms: **bełt** *rot-gut wine*, **burgund** *burgundy*, **drink** *alcoholic drink*, **szampan** *champagne*. Increasingly: **vermut** *vermouth*; masculine-gender beer names, e.g. **pilzner** *pilsener*, **żywiec** **żywca** *Żywiec beer*.

q. Exotic fruits and vegetables: **ananas** *pineapple*, **banan** *banana*, **daktyl** *date*, **grejpfrut** *grapefruit*, **melon** *melon*. Less often: **kokos** *coconut*, **migdał** *almond*, **rodzynek** *raisin*.

r. Candies: **batonik** *candy bar*, **cukierek cukierka** *candy*, **lizak** *sucker*, **miętowy** (GAsg. **miętowego**) *mint*, **miodynek miodynka** *honey drop*.

s. Miscellaneous: **bąk** *goof*, **figiel** *trick*, **judasz** *peep-hole*, **karniak** *penalty*, **latawiec** *kite*.

3. Among occasional (rather more colloquial) facultative animates are:

a. Measures of alcohol: **kielich** *jigger*, **klin** *shot*, **litr** *liter (of vodka)*, **łyk** *swallow*, **strzemienny** GA **strzemiennego** *one for the road*.

b. Non-leafy individual vegetable items: **burak** *beet*, **kalafior** *cauliflower*, **ogórek ogórka** *cucumber*, **pomidor** *tomato*, **ziemniak** *potato*.

c. Marks on paper: **kleks** *inkspot*, **kulfon** *misshapen letter*, **zawijas** *flourish*.

d. Dread diseases (many slang): **syf** *syphilis*, **tężec tężca** *lockjaw*, **tryper trypra** *clap*, **hiv** *HIV*.

e. Serially produced food items of various sorts: **chips** *chip*, **hamburger** *hamburger*, **hotdog** *hotdog*, **klops** *meatball*, **krokiet** *croquet*, **sandwicz** *sandwich*, **serdelek serdelka** *link sausage*, **zraz** *chop*.

f. Skin afflictions: **pieg** *freckle*, **pieprzyk** *mole*, **pryszcz** *pimple*, **wągier wągra** *blackhead*.

e. Flowers: **goździk** *carnation*, **irys** *iris*, **tulipan** *tulip*.

d. Footwear: **but** *shoe*, **bucior** *clodhopper*, **drewniak** *clog*, **kalosz** *galosh*, **pantofel pantofla** *slipper*, **sandał** *sandal*.

e. Individualized names for teeth, hair, nose: **mleczak** *milk tooth*, **nochal** *shnoz*, **pejs** *side curl*, **ryj** *snout*, **trzonowy trzonowego** *molar*, **włosek włoska** *a hair*.

f. Various nouns in **-ak**, **-ec**: **brukowiec brukowca** *trashy novel*, **gościniec gościńca** *coming-home present*, **korkowiec korkowca** *pop gun*, **siwak** *gray earthenware pot*, **składak** *folding bicycle*, **straszak** *cap pistol*.

g. Miscellaneous: **cybuch** *pipe stem*, **jasiek jaśka** *throw pillow*, **samograj** *sure-fire hit*, **smoczek smoczka** *baby's pacifier*, **sopel sopla** *icicle*, **śmierdziuch** *smelly cheese*.

Some idioms appear to contain facultative animate constructions, as **dać drapaka** *give a scratcher, i.e. decamp*, **dostać kosza** *get the basket, i.e., turned down by a woman*, **iść gęsiego** *walk goose-like, i.e. single file*, **włosy stanęły dęba** *hair* *stood an oak, i.e. on end,* and others. Many other semantic classes of nouns can on occasion be used as facultative animates, including names for ships, airplanes, buildings, plant parts, trees, shrubs, knives, tools, jewelry, sticks, and various isolated nouns. The status of a noun as potentially facultatively animate can rarely be ascertained from an ordinary dictionary. It may often only be learned through experience or the careful interviewing of speakers.

PERSONAL NOUNS WITH SPECIAL ENDINGS OR INFLECTIONS

1. NVpl. **-owie**. This is the usual ending for **dziad dziadowie** *forefather(s)*.

   a. male relations: **mąż mężowie** *husband(s)*, **ojciec ojcowie** *father(s)*, **syn synowie** *son(s)*, **wujek wujkowie** *uncle(s)*, **teść teściowie** *father(s)-in-law*, etc.; also: **kum kumowie** *god-father(s)*, **swat swat** *matchmaker(s)*.

   b. deities and august rulers: **anioł aniołowie** (or, less often, **anioły** or **anieli**) *angel(s)*, **bóg bogowie** *god(s)*, **car carowie** *tsar(s)*, **król królowie** *king(s)*, **monarcha monarchowie** *monarch(s)*, **szach szachowie** *shah(s)*.

   c. officer ranks and some civilian titles: **generał generałowie** *general(s)*, **kapitan kapitanowie** *captain(s)*, **major majorowie** *major(s)*, **oficer oficerowie** (less often, **oficerzy**) *officer(s)*, **porucznik porucznikowie** *lieutenant(s)*, **poseł posłowie** *envoy(s)*, **szef szefowie** *boss(es)*, **wójt wójtowie** *village head(s)*. Compare the non-officer ranks **kapral kaprale** *corporal(s)*, **sierżant sierżanci** *sergeant(s)*.

   d. titles and names of professions used as titles or honorifically: **ambasador ambasadorowie** or, as non-title, **ambasadorzy** *ambassador(s)*; similarly **biolog biologowie** or **biolodzy** *biologist(s)*, **doktor doktorowie** or **doktorzy** *doctor(s)*, **pan panowie** *sir(s)*, **prezes prezesowie** *chairman (-men)* (but: **prezydent prezydenci** *president(s)*), **profesor profesorowie** or **profesorzy** *professor(s)*, **szejk szejkowie** *sheik(s)*, etc.;

   e. non-adjectival last names: **Nowak Nowakowie, Buszko Buszkowie**, etc.; also see discussion of **Mały** under i. below.

   f. names for certain nationalities and tribes: **Arab Arabowie** *Arab(s)*, **Awar Awarowie** *Avar(s)*, **Belg Belgowie** *Belgian(s)*, **Hun Hunowie** *Hun(s)*, **Wiking Wikingowie** *Viking(s)*, etc.;

   g. some personal nouns with Nsg. in **-a**, as **baca bacowie** *flock-master(s)*, **doża dożowie** *doge*, **gazda gazdowie** *Carpathian farmer(s)*, **joga jogowie** *yogi(s)*, **monarcha monarchowie** *monarch(s)* (but **despota despoci** *despot*), **patriarcha patriarchowie** *patriarch(s)*, **wojewoda wojewodowie** *voivode*, etc.;

   h. a random assortment of other personal nouns, e.g. **członek członkowie** *member(s)*, **eunuch eunuchowie** *eunuch(s)*, **pasażer pasażerowie** *passenger(s)*, **patron patronowie** *patron(s)*, **potomek potomkowie** *descendant(s)*, **sobek sobkowie** *egoist*, **świadek** świadkowie *witness(es)*, **uczeń uczniowie** *pupil(s)*, **widz widzowie** *spectators(s)*, **więzień więźniowie** *prisoner(s)*, **wódz wodzowie** *leader(s)*, **wróg wrogowie** *enemy (enemies)*.

i. The ending **-owie** is used with adjectival professional names ending in **-niczy: budowniczy budowniczowie** *builder*; and it is often used with basic adjectives used as last names, e.g. **Mały Małowie** *Small(s)*.

j. With male first names, the ending **-owie** may indicate the man and his wife: **Jan** *Jan*, **Janowie** *Jan and wife*.

2. Nouns in **-anin**, NV pl. **-anie**. Many names for tribes, nationalities, sects, and inhabitants of regions and towns belong to this type. The singulative suffix **-in-** is dropped in the plural, and the NVpl. ending is **-e**, as in **Słowianin** *Slav*, NVpl. **Słowianie**. The Gpl. is usually **-Ø**, although several take **-ów**, for example **Amerykanin Amerykanów** *American*. See the inflection of **Rosjanin** *Russian* in the declensional illustrations.

3. NVpl. in **-e**. Besides nouns in **-anin** (see above, 2), a few other personal nouns take NVpl. in **-e**, for example **Cygan Cyganie** *Gypsy (Gypsies)*, **Hiszpan Hiszpanie** *Spaniard(s)*, **krajan krajanie** *countryman (-men)*, **młodzian młodzianie** *young man/men (archaic)*.

4. NVpl. in **-y** with stems in c-. Masculine personal nouns with stems in **-c**, if they do not take NVpl. **-owie**, take NVpl. in **-y: chłopiec chłopcy** *boy(s)*, **kłamca kłamcy** *liar(s)*, **kupiec kupcy** *merchant(s)*, **ludożerca ludożercy** *cannibal(s)*, **naukowiec naukowcy** *scholar(s)*, **przedsiębiorca przedsiębiorcy** *entrepreneur(s)*, **sprzymierzeniec sprzymierzeńcy** *ally (allies)*, **znawca znawcy** *connoisseur(s)*, etc.

5. A few random masculine personal nouns, containing other irregularities, take NVpl. in **-a: brat** *brother*, NVpl. **bracia; ksiądz** *priest*, GA **księdza**, NVpl. **księża; książę** *prince*, GA **księcia**, NVpl. **książęta**.

6. Masculine personal nouns with Nsg. in **-a**. The class of masculine personal nouns with Nsg. in **-a**, and with a singular declension like that of feminine nouns, is quite numerous due to the productivity of the suffixes **-yst-a** and **-w'c-a**, as in **dentysta** *dentist* and **znawca** *connoissseur*. Other nouns in **-a** include **despota** *despots* Npl. **despoci, poeta** *poet* Npl. **poeci**. The NVpl. ending is usually **-ï** (sometimes **-owie**; see above) and the GApl. ending is **-ów**, cf. **dentysta dentyści dentystów, znawca znawcy znawców**. The only noun of this type to take GApl. in **-Ø** is **mężczyzna** *man*, Npl. **mężczyźni** GApl. **mężczyzn**. The VSg. is **-o: dentysto, znawco, mężczyzno**. Nouns requiring special treatment are **sędzia** *judge*, **hrabia** *count*, **margrabia** *margrave*, **cieśla** *carpenter*, GApl. **-i** or **-ów**, Npl. **cieśle**; see inflectional illustrations further below.

7. Couples in **-ostwo**. Certain titles and relation-names form masculine personal plural nouns in **-ostwo** referring to man and wife: **generałostwo**

general-and-wife, **doktorostwo** *doctor and wife*, **księstwo** *prince and princess*, **profesorostwo** *professor-and-wife*, **wujostwo** *uncle and wife*, and others. The declension and agreement properties are the same as for **państwo** (Chapter 7).

8. Personal nouns in **-niczy**. This suffix forms a few names of professions. The declension is adjectival, except that the NVpl. is **-owie: budowniczy** *builder*, NVpl. **budowniczowie**, GApl. **budowniczych**. Some others are **leśniczy** *forester*, **łowczy** *hunter*, **motorniczy** *tram-driver*. To this declensional type also belongs **chorąży** *standard-bearer, ensign*, and such antique titles as **koniuszy** *equerry*, **podczaszy** *cup-bearer*, **podkanclerzy** *deputy exchequer*, **podkomorzy** *chamberlain*, **podstoli** *lord high steward*.

9. A number of masculine personal nouns follow a purely adjectival declension, for example **bagażowy** *porter*, GAsg. **bagażowego**, NVpl. **bagażowi**, GApl. **bagażowych**. Similarly: **biegły** *expert*, **borowy** *forester*, **gajowy** *gamekeeper*, **krewny** *relative*, **myśliwy** *hunter*, **narzeczony** *fiancée*, **pieszy** *pedestrian*, **plutonowy** *platoon leader*, **podróżny** *traveller*, **posterunkowy** *constable*, **poszkodowany** *disaster victim*, **przyjezdny** *visitor*, **przysięgły** *jury-member*, **radny** *councillor*, **służący** *servant*, **szeregowy** *rank-and-file soldier*, **wojskowy** *military man*, **znajomy** *acquaintance*; and others. To these may be added various adjectives naming debilities which have acquired a common nominal use, as **chory** *patient*, **głuchy** *deaf person*, **kulawy** *lame person*, **niemy** *deaf person*, **niewidomy** *sightless person*, **ranny** *wounded person*, **stary** *old person*, **ślepy** *blind person*, and so on; such words most often occur in the plural. For further examples of adjectives as nouns, see Chapter 6; on the use of participles as nouns, see Chapter 12.

FIRST NAMES

1. First names ending in consonants take a regular nominal inflection: N **Zenon** GA **Zenona** D **Zenonowi** I **Zenonem** LV **Zenonie**; N **Tomasz** GA **Tomasza** D **Tomaszowi** I **Tomaszem** LV **Tomaszu**.

2. Affectionate first names and relation-names in **-'o-** like **dziadzio** *gramps*, **wujcio** *uncle*, **Józio** *Joey*, and so on, follow a masculine declension in the sg. In the pl., they follow the declension of masculine personal names with NVpl. in **-owie: dziadzio** GAsg. **dziadzia**, Dsg. **dziadziowi**, Isg. **dziadziem**, LVsg. **dziadziu**, NVpl. **dziadziowie** GApl. **dziadziów**, etc.

3. First names with endings interpretable as adjectival take an adjectival declension with NVpl. in **-owie: Ignacy** *Ignatius*, GAsg. **Ignacego**, **Jerzy** *George*, GAsg. **Jerzego**; **Konstanty** *Constantine*, GAsg. **Konstantego**; **Antoni** *Anthony*, GAsg. **Antoniego**; **Eddie** *Eddie*, GAsg. **Eddiego**. Foreign first names in **-e, -y, -i** take a similar declension, except that names in **-e** take ILsg. in **-em: Dante**, GAsg. **Dantego**, ILsg. **Dantem**. Persons unsure of themselves, and conscious of the foreign provenience of a name, will sometimes not decline it even when a recognized pattern exists.

4. Latin first names in **-o**. The first names **Bruno** GA **Brunona, Gwido** GA
    Gwidona, Hugo GA **Hugona, Iwo** GA **Iwona, Nero** GA **Nerona, Otto**
    GA **Ottona**, following Latin tradition, form stems in **n**. However, the cur-
    rent younger generation tends not to be familiar with this formation, and
    often even people bearing these names follow different customs. For ex-
    ample, a person named **Hugo** may prefer the Vocative forms **Hugo** or
    Hugu instead of (best) **Hugonie**. The name for the Latin orator **Cyrero(n)**
    is stressed on the first syllable.

LAST NAMES

1. Last names in **-ski, -cki, -dzki** take a regular adjectival declension, hence
    Zawadzki, GAsg. **Zawadzkiego**, NVpl. **Zawadzcy**, GApl. **Zawadzkich**.
    Adjectival last names based on regular adjectives tend to take NVpl. in
    -owie (but GApl. in **-ych**), e.g. **Mały**, NVpl. **Małowie** (less often **Mali**)
    GApl. **Małych**.

2. Last names in consonants take a regular nominal inflection: NV **Tokarz**
    GA **Tokarza** D **Tokarzowi** I **Tokarzem** L**Tokarzu**. Consonantal last
    names do not form a special Vocative even when preceded by a title that
    is in the Vocative; hence **doktor Klimczak**, V **doktorze Klimczak**. Foreign
    last names ending in consonants will normally be adapted to a nominal
    declension. If the foreign last name ends in a "silent vowel", an apostro-
    phe will separate the ending, except sometimes in the Locative before **-e**:
    NV **Verne** "Vern", GA **Verne'a** D **Verne'owi** I **Verne'em**, but L **Vernie**;
    NV **Montaigne** GA **Montaigne'a** D **Motaigne'owi** I **Montaigne'em** L
    Montaigne'u.

3. Last names in **-a** and **-o** take a feminine-like declension in the sg., with
    NVpl. in **-owie** and GApl. in **-ów**: NVsg. **Wojtyła** NVpl. **Wojtyłowie**
    GApl. **Wojtyłów**; NVsg. **Fredro** GAsg. **Fredrę**, DLsg. **Fredrze**, Isg. **Fredrą**,
    NVpl. **Fredrowie** GApl. **Fredrów**, etc.

4. Compound last names decline only the second part: **Szut-Mechrzyński**,
    Gsg. **Szut-Mechrzyńskiego**, Dsg. **Szut-Mechrzyńskiemu**, etc.

5. Foreign last names ending in **-e** or **-i** are adapted to the adjectival inflec-
    tion: NV **Kolbe** GA **Kolbego** D **Kolbemu** IL **Kolbem**.

6. Last names based on recognizable common nouns, especially names for
    animals, often do not participate in sound changes characteristic of the
    common noun. Compare **kozioł** *goat*, GAsg. **kozła** to **Kozioł** *(surname)*,
    GAsg. **Kozioła**, NVpl. **Koziołowie**; however, **Kozła, Kozłowie** can also
    be found. The surname **Gołąb** NVpl. **Gołąbowie** contrasts with the noun
    gołąb GAsg. **gołębia** *pigeon;* see also **Dąb** GAsg. **Dąba** (not **Dęba*), NVpl.
    Dąbowie, Mech GAsg. **Mecha** (not **Mcha*). However, the last name
    Grudzień *December* will usually have the mobile vowel, similar to the
    noun: GAsg. **Grudnia** (less often, **Grudzienia**), NApl. **Grudniowie** (less

often, **Grudzieniowie**). Such determinations must be made on a name-by-name and person-to-person basis. The popular singer **Czesław Niemen**, named after the river **Niemen Niemna**, prefers GAsg. **Niemena**.

COMMON-GENDER NOUNS (EPICENES) IN -*A*

A number of personal nouns with Nsg. in -**a** can refer to either males or females, and take correspondingly masculine or feminine agreement, according to reference. So-called epicenes are essentially all inherently pejorative; they include, for example, **ciapa** *sluggard*, **fajtłapa** *galoot*, **gaduła** *chatterbox*, **gapa** *lout*, **hulaka** *rabble-rouser*, **kanalia** *blackguard*, **mądrala** *wiseguy*, **niedojda** *bungler*, **niedołęga** *klutz*, **oferma** *milksop*, **pierdoła** *old fart*, **przybłęda** *vagabond*, **szelma** *rascal*, **znajda** *foundling*, and others.

In the singular, epicenes optionally take feminine agreement, even in reference to males, in order to bring out the deprecatory coloration of the word; hence either **ten ciapa** *that m. sluggard* Asg. **tego ciapę** or, usually, **ta ciapa** *that f. sluggard* or *that m. sluggard-pejorative*, A **tę ciapę**. The Gpl. of epicenes in -**a** with male reference is usually -**ów**; -**Ø** is used with females and, deprecatorily, with males: **tych ciapów** *sluggard-masc.pers. Gpl.* or **tych ciap** *sluggard-fem. or masc. pers. pej.* Apl. is **tych ciapów** (male) or **te ciapy** (female or especially pejorative male). None of these nouns take a softened NVpl.

Perhaps the most useful way to approach these nouns is to divide them into referentially male declensions on the one hand, and referentially female (or especially pejorative male) declensions on the other.

	Male:		Female, especially pejorative male:	
	Sg.	Pl.	Sg.	Pl.
N	ten ciapa	te ciapy	ta ciapa	te ciapy
G	tego ciapy	tych ciapów	tej ciapy	tych ciap
D	temu ciapie	tym ciapom	tej ciapie	tym ciapom
A	tego ciapę	tych ciapów	tę ciapę	te ciapy
I	tym ciapą	tymi ciapami	tą ciapą	tymi ciapami
L	tym ciapie	tych ciapach	tej ciapie	tych ciapach
V	ciapo	ciapy	ciapo	ciapy

The main difference between one declension and the other is found in the Gpl. (male in -**ów**, fem. in -**Ø**), and in the feature Apl.= Gpl. (male) vs. Apl.= Npl. (female). The word **kanalia** *blackguard* has G(A)pl. only in -**ii**: **kanalii**. Increasingly, the tendency is to use the female forms only (the right-hand, more pejorative, declension above), whether with male or female reference.

The following words must be described individually:

➢ **idiota** *idiot*. This noun has approximately the same alternative declensional possibilities as **ciapa** above, but without the possibility of literal female reference, since a separate female form **idiotka** exists. Gpl. is only **idiotów**. NVpl. **idioci** is usual, alongside non-softened especially pejorative **idioty**. Apl. is either **idiotów** or, especially pejoratively, **idioty**. See the declension at the end of this chapter.

➢ **kaleka** *cripple*. This noun has the same alternative declensions and gender-agreement as **ciapa** above, except that an optional softened NVpl. male form is available: **kalecy** (usually, however, **kaleki**). The standard Gpl. is **kalek**, although **kaleków** occurs as a substandard form. However, **kaleków** is standard in the Apl. in reference to men, making this possibly the only masculine noun with Apl. in **-ów** not corresponding to **-ów** in the Gpl. With reference to females (and to especially pejoratively treated males), the Apl. is **kaleki**. See the declension at the end of this chapter. As a neutral substitute one may use **osoba niepełnosprawna** *handicapped individual*, or simply the adjectival noun **niepełnosprawny** *a handicapped person*.

➢ **sierota** *orphan*. This word is usually feminine, even in reference to males, similarly to **osoba** *person*. Masculine agreement in the singular is theoretically possible, but uncommon. In the plural, only a feminine-like declension is available: NAVpl. **sieroty**, G **sierot** (regionally, **sierót**). See the declension at the end of this chapter.

➢ **sługa** *servant*. This (obsolete) noun may show either masculine or feminine agreement in the singular. In the plural, an optional softened male form is available: **słudzy**. Gpl. is only **sług**, and Apl. is only **sługi**, whatever the reference. See the declension at the end of this chapter.

PEJORATIVE MASCULINE PERSONAL NOUNS WITHOUT SOFTENING IN THE NV.PL.

Certain inherently or potentially pejorative hard-stem masculine personal nouns take nonsoftening **-y** in the NVpl. instead of the expected softening **-ĭ**, as if to underscore the pejorative coloration. The Accusative plural will usually be identical to the Genitive plural, although, with reference to women and for especially pejorative effect with males, the Apl. may take the form of the unsoftened Npl. Because of the slightly different treatment of such nouns in the plural with female reference, such nouns may be referred to as SEMI-EPICENES. Whether or not such a noun allows a softened NVpl., even in reference to males, must be examined on an individual basis. Some such nouns have specifically female variants. Examples: **bękart bękarty** *bastard(s)*, **brudas brudasy** (or, less frequently, in reference to males only, **brudasi**) *slob*, **błazen błazny** (less often, **błaźni**) *clown*, **bufon bufony** (less often, **bufoni**) *buffoon*, **cham chamy** *cad, cur*, **chuligan chuligani** (less often, **chuligany**) *hooligan, hoodlum*, **ciemniak ciemniaki** (less often, males only, **ciemniacy**) *ignoramus*, **dryblas dryblasy** (less often, males only, **dryblasi**) *beanpole*, **gbur gbury** *churl*, **karzeł karły** *dwarf*, **leniuch leniuchy** *lazy-bones*, **liliput lipiputy** (or **lilipuci**) *dwarf* (female is **liliputka**), **łajdak łajdaki** (or, less often, **łajdacy**) *rogue* (female is **łajdaczka**), **łobuz łobuzy** (less often, males only, **łobuzi**) *rascal(s)*, mańkut mańkuty (less often, males only, mańkuci) *left-hander,* młokos młokosy (less often, males only, młokosi) *milksop,* mieszczuch *city-dweller,* nieborak nieboraki (less often, males only, nieboracy) *wretch,* nierób Npl. nieroby *idler,* oszust *swindler* Npl. oszusty (less often, males only, oszuści); snob snoby (less often, males only, snobi) *snob,* śpioch śpiochy *sleepy-head,* zabijak zabijaki *rabble-rouser,* and many others.

Here is the declension of **snob** *snob:*

Sg. Pl.		Pl.	
Male or female ref.:		**Male reference:**	**Female or especially pej. male ref.:**
N	**ten snob**	**ci snobi**	**te snoby**
G	**tego snoba**	**tych snobów**	←
D	**temu snobowi**	**tym snobom**	←
A	**tego snoba**	**tych snobów**	**te snoby**
I	**tym snobem**	**tymi snobami**	←
L	**tym snobie**	**tych snobach**	←
V	**snobie**	**snoby**	←

Here is the declension of **karzeł** *dwarf:*

Sg. Pl.		Pl.	
Male or female ref.:		**Male reference:**	**Female or especially pej. male ref.:**
N	**ten karzeł**	**te karły**	←
G	**tego karła**	**tych karłów**	←
D	**temu karłowi**	**tym karłom**	←
A	**tego karła**	**tych karłów**	**te karły**
I	**tym karłem**	**tymi karłami**	←
L	**tym karle**	**tych karłach**	←
V	**karle**	**karły**	←

One should note that, whatever the actual reference, unsoftened pejorative forms take non-masculine-personal modifers and past-tense verb agreement: **te okropne snoby** *those horrible snobs,* **łobuzy jedne** *those rascals;* and non-non-masculine personal past-tense verb agreement: **Te łobuzy porozbijały wszystkie żarówki.** *Those hooligans broke out each and every one of the lightbulbs.* Compare to softened, hence masculine-personal: **Ci łobuzi porozbijali wszystkie żarówki.** *(idem).* If the noun is a soft-stem, pejorative coloration can only be signaled by the modifier or (past-tense) verb-form: **mazgaj** *dawdler,* **te mazgaje były** *those dawdlers were* (alongside **ci mazgaje byli** *idem*), **niechluj** *slovenly person,* **te niechluje były** *those slovenly persons were* (alongside **ci niechluje byli** *idem*).

SEMI-MASCULINE-PERSONAL NOUNS

Nouns with either a pejorative or a neutral connotation can take either the non-softening or the softening NVpl. ending according to intent and, occasionally, connotation: **Szwab Szwabi** (or **Szwabowie**) *Swabian* or **szwab szwaby** *Kraut;* **garbus garbusi** or **garbusy** *hunchback;* **chłop chłopi** *peasant* or **chłopy** *guy, man;* **kat kaci** or, expressively, **katy** *hangman,* **krewniak krewniacy** or **krewniaki** *kinsman,* and so on. The noun **pasierb** *step-son* takes NVpl. **pasierbowie** or, when referring to step-sons and step-daughters together, **pasierby.** Apl. is **pasierbów** or, with with reference to both sexes, **pasierby.** The independent word for 'step-daughter' is **pasierbica.**

The nouns **chłopak** *lad, guy, boyfriend,* **chłopczyk** *boy,* **dzieciak** *child, kid,* **jedynak** *only child,* **kuchcik** *cook's assistant,* **nastolatek nastolatka** *teenager,* **noworodek noworodka** *new-born,* and **przedszkolak** *preschooler* have usual NVpl. **chłopaki** (less often, **chłopacy**), **chłopczyki, dzieciaki, jedynaki, kuchciki, nastolatki, noworodki, przedszkolaki,** but without special pejorative coloration. The usual Apl. forms are **chłopaków, chłopczyków, kuchcików, nastolatków,** but **dzieciaki, jedynaki, noworodki, przedszkolaki,** respectively. See the declensions of **chłopak** and **dzieciak** in the declensional illustrations below (p. 101).

NAMES FOR DEAD PEOPLE

The nouns **denat** *corpus delicti,* **duch** *ghost,* **nieboszczyk** *dead person, the late,* **topielec** *drowned man,* **trup** *corpse,* **umrzyk** *corpse,* and **wisielec** *hanged man* are treated roughly similarly to nouns like **brudas** NVpl. **brudasy** *slob,* except that plural forms must be described individually: GAsg. **denata, ducha, nieboszczyka, topielca, trupa, umrzyka, wisielca;** NVpl. **denaci** (or **denaty**), **duchy, nieboszczycy** (pejoratively, **nieboszczyki**), **trupy, topielcy** (not *topielce), **umrzyki, wisielcy** (not *wisielce); Gpl. **denatów, duchów, nieboszczyków, topielców, trupów, umrzyków, wisielców;** Apl. **denatów** (pejoratively, **denaty**), **duchy, nieboszczyków** (pejoratively, **nieboszczyki**), **topielców, trupy** (rarely, **trupów**), **umrzyki** (rarely, **umrzyków**), **wisielców.**

EXAMPLES OF MASCULINE-DECLENSION NOUNS

Hard Stems

sklep *store* (p-stem)

	Sg.	Pl.
N	sklep	sklepy
G	sklepu	sklepów
D	sklepowi	sklepom
A	sklep	sklepy
I	sklepem	sklepami
L	sklepie	sklepach
V	sklepie	sklepy

chłop *peasant* (p-stem, pers.)

	Sg.	Pl.
N	chłop	chłopi*
G	chłopa	chłopów
D	chłopu	chłopom
A	chłopa	chłopów
I	chłopem	chłopami
L	chłopie	chłopach
V	chłopie	chłopi

* In the sense 'guy, lad': **chłopy**

chleb *bread* (**b**-stem, Gsg. **-a**)

	Sg.	Pl.
N	chleb	chleby
G	chleba	chlebów
D	chlebowi	chlebom
A	chleb	chleby
I	chlebem	chlebami
L	chlebie	chlebach
V	chlebie	chleby

sposób *way, manner* (**b**-stem, **o: ó**)

	Sg.	Pl.
N	sposób	sposoby
G	sposobu	sposobów
D	sposobowi	sposobom
A	sposób	sposoby
I	sposobem	sposobami
L	sposobie	sposobach
V	sposobie	sposoby

krzew *shrub* (**w**-stem)

	Sg.	Pl.
N	krzew	krzewy
G	krzewu	krzewów
D	krzewowi	krzewom
A	krzew	krzewy
I	krzewem	krzewami
L	krzewie	krzewach
V	krzewie	krzewy

film *film, movie* (**m**-stem)

	Sg.	Pl.
N	film	filmy
G	filmu	filmów
D	filmowi	filmom
A	film	filmy
I	filmem	filmami
L	filmie	filmach
V	filmie	filmy

łeb *anim. head* (**b**-stem, m.v., Gsg. **-a**)

	Sg.	Pl.
N	łeb	łby
G	łba	łbów
D	łbowi	łbom
A	łeb	łby
I	łbem	łbami
L	łbie	łbach
V	łbie	łby

dąb *oak* (**b**-stem, **ę: ą**)

	Sg.	Pl.
N	dąb	dęby
G	dębu	dębów
D	dębowi	dębom
A	dąb	dęby
I	dębem	dębami
L	dębie	dębach
V	dębie	dęby

lew *lion* (**w**-stem, m. vow., anim.)

	Sg.	Pl.
N	lew	lwy
G	lwa	lwów
D	lwu	lwom
A	lwa	lwy
I	lwem	lwami
L	lwie	lwach
V	lwie	lwy

sufit *ceiling* (**t**-stem)

	Sg.	Pl.
N	sufit	sufity
G	sufitu	sufitów
D	sufitowi	sufitom
A	sufit	sufity
I	sufitem	sufitami
L	suficie	sufitach
V	suficie	sufity

kwiat *flower* (t-stem, ě: a)

	Sg.	Pl.
N	kwiat	kwiaty
G	kwiatu	kwiatów
D	kwiatowi	kwiatom
A	kwiat	kwiaty
I	kwiatem	kwiatami
L	kwiecie	kwiatach
V	kwiecie	kwiaty

kot *cat* (t-stem, anim.)

	Sg.	Pl.
N	kot	koty
G	kota	kotów
D	kotu	kotom
A	kota	koty
I	kotem	kotami
L	kocie	kotach
V	kocie	koty

listopad *November* (d-stem, Gsg. -a)

	Sg.	Pl.
N	listopad	listopady
G	listopada	listopadów
D	listopadowi	listopadom
A	listopaD	listopady
I	listopadem	listopadami
L	listopadzie	listopadach
V	listopadzie	listopady

rząd *row* (d-stem, ę: ą)

	Sg.	Pl.
N	rząd	rzędy
G	rzędu	rzędów
D	rzędowi	rzędom
A	rząd	rzędy
I	rzędem	rzędami
L	rzędzie	rzędach
V	rzędzie	rzędy

but *shoe* (t-stem, Gsg. -a)

	Sg.	Pl.
N	but	buty
G	buta	butów
D	butowi	butom
A	but	buty
I	butem	butami
L	bucie	butach
V	bucie	buty

student *student* (t-stem, pers.)

	Sg.	Pl.
N	student	studenci
G	studenta	studentów
D	studentowi	studentom
A	studenta	studentów
I	studentem	studentami
L	studencie	studentach
V	studencie	studenci

ogród *garden* (d-stem, o: ó)

	Sg.	Pl.
N	ogród	ogrody
G	ogrodu	ogrodów
D	ogrodowi	ogrodom
A	ogród	ogrody
I	ogrodem	ogrodami
L	ogrodzie	ogrodach
V	ogrodzie	ogrody

obiad *dinner* (d-stem, ě: a)

	Sg.	Pl.
N	obiad	obiady
G	obiadu	obiadów
D	obiadowi	obiadom
A	obiad	obiady
I	obiadem	obiadami
L	obiedzie	obiadach
V	obiedzie	obiady

zjazd *congress* (**zd**-stem, **ě: a**)

	Sg.	Pl.
N	zjazd	zjazdy
G	zjazdu	zjazdów
D	zjazdowi	zjazdom
A	zjazD	zjazdy
I	zjazdem	zjazdami
L	zjeździe	zjazdach
V	zjeździe	zjazdy

czas *time* (**s**-stem)

	Sg.	Pl.
N	czas	czasy
G	czasu	czasów
D	czasowi	czasom
A	czas	czasy
I	czasem	czasami (czasy)
L	czasie	czasach
V	czasie	czasy

las *forest* (**s**-stem, **ě: a**)

	Sg.	Pl.
N	las	lasy
G	lasu	lasów
D	lasowi	lasom
A	las	lasy
I	lasem	lasami
L	lesie	lasach
V	lesie	lasy

obraz *picture* (**z**-stem)

	Sg.	Pl.
N	obraz	obrazy
G	obrazu	obrazów
D	obrazowi	obrazom
A	obraz	obrazy
I	obrazem	obrazami
L	obrazie	obrazach
V	obrazie	obrazy

sąsiad *neighbor* (**d**-stem, pers.)

	Sg.	Pl.
N	sąsiad	sąsiedzi
G	sąsiada	sąsiadów
D	sąsiadowi	sąsiadom
A	sąsiada	sąsiadów
I	sąsiadem	sąsiadami
L	sąsiedzie	sąsiadach
V	sąsiedzie	sąsiedzi

nos *nose* (**s**-stem, Gsg. **-a**)

	Sg.	Pl.
N	nos	nosy
G	nosa	nosów
D	nosowi	nosom
A	nos	nosy
I	nosem	nosami
L	nosie	nosach
V	nosie	nosy

pies *dog* (**s**-stem, mob. v., Dsg. **-u**)

	Sg.	Pl.
N	pies	psy
G	psa	psów
D	psu	psom
A	psa	psy
I	psem	psami
L	psie	psach
V	psie	psy

wóz *car* (**z**-stem, **o: ó**)

	Sg.	Pl.
N	wóz	wozy
G	wozu	wozów
D	wozowi	wozom
A	wóz	wozy
I	wozem	wozami
L	wozie	wozach
V	wozie	wozy

artykuł *article* (ł-stem)

	Sg.	Pl.
N	artykuł	artykuły
G	artykułu	artykułów
D	artykułowi	artykułom
A	artykuł	artykuły
I	artykułem	artykułami
L	artykule	artykułach
V	artykule	artykuły

orzeł *eagle* (ł-stem, mob. vow.)

	Sg.	Pl.
N	orzeł	orły
G	orła	orłów
D	orłowi	orłom
A	orła	orły
I	orłem	orłami
L	orle	orłach
V	orle	orły

kocioł *pot* (ł-stem, mob. vow., e: o)

	Sg.	Pl.
N	kocioł	kotły
G	kotła	kotłów
D	kotłowi	kotłom
A	kocioł	kotły
I	kotłem	kotłami
L	kotle	kotłach
V	kotle	kotły

pomysł *thought* (sł-stem)

	Sg.	Pl.
N	pomysł	pomysły
G	pomysłu	pomysłów
D	pomysłowi	pomysłom
A	pomysł	pomysły
I	pomysłem	pomysłami
L	pomyśle	pomysłach
V	pomyśle	pomysły

stół *table* (ł-stem, o: ó)

	Sg.	Pl.
N	stół	stoły
G	stołu	stołów
D	stołowi	stołom
A	stół	stoły
I	stołem	stołami
L	stole	stołach
V	stole	stoły

kościół *church* (ł-stem, e: o, o:ó)

	Sg.	Pl.
N	kościół	kościoły
G	kościoła	kościołów
D	kościołowi	kościołom
A	kościół	kościoły
I	kościołem	kościołami
L	kościele	kościołach
V	kościele	kościoły

kozioł *goat* (ł-stem, mob. vow., e: o)

	Sg.	Pl.
N	kozioł	kozły
G	kozła	kozłów
D	kozłowi	kozłom
A	kozła	kozły
I	kozłem	kozłami
L	koźle	kozłach
V	koźle	kozły

ocean *ocean* (n-stem)

	Sg.	Pl.
N	ocean	oceany
G	oceanu	oceanów
D	oceanowi	oceanom
A	ocean	oceany
I	oceanem	oceanami
L	oceanie	oceanach
V	oceanie	oceany

sen *sleep, dream* (**n**-stem, mob. vow.)

	Sg.	Pl.
N	sen	sny
G	snu	snów
D	snowi	snom
A	sen	sny
I	snem	snami
L	śnie	snach
V	śnie	sny

mur *wall* (**r**-stem)

	Sg.	Pl.
N	mur	mury
G	muru	murów
D	murowi	murom
A	mur	mury
I	murem	murami
L	murze	murach
V	murze	mury

ser *cheese* (**r**-stem, Gsg. **-a**)

	Sg.	Pl.
N	ser	sery
G	sera	serów
D	serowi	serom
A	ser	sery
I	serem	serami
L	serze	serach
V	serze	sery

sweter *sweater* (**r**-st., m.v., Gsg. **-a**)

	Sg.	Pl.
N	sweter	swetry
G	swetra	swetrów
D	swetrowi	swetrom
A	sweter	swetry
I	swetrem	swetrami
L	swetrze	swetrach
V	swetrze	swetry

cukier *sugar* (**r**-stem, mob. vow.)

	Sg.	Pl.
N	cukier	cukry
G	cukru	cukrów
D	cukrowi	cukrom
A	cukier	cukry
I	cukrem	cukrami
L	cukrze	cukrach
V	cukrze	cukry

bór *woods* (**r**-stem, o: ó)

	Sg.	Pl.
N	bór	bory
G	boru	borów
D	borowi	borom
A	bór	bory
I	borem	borami
L	borze	borach
V	borze	bory

wiatr *wind* (**r**-stem, ě: a)

	Sg.	Pl.
N	wiatr	wiatry
G	wiatru	wiatrów
D	wiatrowi	wiatrom
A	wiatr	wiatry
I	wiatrem	wiatrami
L	wietrze	wiatrach
V	wietrze	wiatry

kelner *waiter* (**r**-stem, pers.)

	Sg.	Pl.
N	kelner	kelnerzy
G	kelnera	kelnerów
D	kelnerowi	kelnerom
A	kelnera	kelnerów
I	kelnerem	kelnerami
L	kelnerze	kelnerach
V	kelnerze	kelnerzy

Velar Stems

bank *bank* (**k**-stem) **rynek** *market* (**k**-stem, mob. vow.)

	Sg.	Pl.
N	bank	banki
G	banku	banków
D	bankowi	bankom
A	bank	banki
I	bankiem	bankami
L	banku	bankach
V	banku	banki

	Sg.	Pl.
N	rynek	rynki
G	rynku	rynków
D	rynkowi	rynkom
A	rynek	rynki
I	rynkiem	rynkami
L	rynku	rynkach
V	rynku	rynki

ptak *bird* (**k**-stem, anim.)

	Sg.	Pl.
N	ptak	ptaki
G	ptaka	ptaków
D	ptakowi	ptakom
A	ptaka	ptaki
I	ptakiem	ptakami
L	ptaku	ptakach
V	ptaku	ptaki

czytelnik *reader* (**k**-stem, pers.)

	Sg.	Pl.
N	czytelnik	czytelnicy
G	czytelnika	czytelników
D	czytelnikowi	czytelnikom
A	czytelnika	czytelników
I	czytelnikiem	czytelnikami
L	czytelniku	czytelnikach
V	czytelniku	czytelnicy

pociąg *train* (**g**-stem)

	Sg.	Pl.
N	pociąg	pociągi
G	pociągu	pociągów
D	pociągowi	pociągom
A	pociąG	pociągi
I	pociągiem	pociągami
L	pociągu	pociągach
V	pociągu	pociągi

róg *horn, corner* (**g**-stem, **o: ó**)

	Sg.	Pl.
N	róg	rogi
G	rogu	rogów
D	rogowi	rogom
A	róg	rogi
I	rogiem	rogami
L	rogu	rogach
V	rogu	rogi

biolog *biologist* (**g**-stem, pers.)

	Sg.	Pl.
N	biolog	biolodzy (biologowie)
G	biologa	biologów
D	biologowi	biologom
A	biologa	biologów
I	biologiem	biologami
L	biologu	biologach
V	biologu	biolodzy

dach *roof* (**ch**-stem)

	Sg.	Pl.
N	dach	dachy
G	dachu	dachów
D	dachowi	dachom
A	dach	dachy
I	dachem	dachami
L	dachu	dachach
V	dachu	dachy

mech *moss* (**ch**-stem, mob.vow.)

	Sg.	Pl.
N	mech	mchy
G	mchu	mchów
D	mchowi	mchom
A	mech	mchy
I	mchem	mchami
L	mchu	mchach
V	mchu	mchy

Czech *Czech* (**ch**-stem, pers.)

	Sg.	Pl.
N	Czech	Czesi
G	Czecha	Czechów
D	Czechowi	Czechom
A	Czecha	Czechów
I	Czechem	Czechami
L	Czechu	Czechach
V	Czechu	Czesi

Soft-Stems

karp *peacock* (**p'**-stem, anim.)

	Sg.	Pl.
N	karp	karpie
G	karpia	karpi
D	karpiowi	karpiom
A	karpia	karpie
I	karpiem	karpiami
L	karpiu	karpiach
V	karpiu	karpie

gołąb *pigeon* (**b'**-stem, ę: ą, anim.)

	Sg.	Pl.
N	gołąb	gołębie
G	gołębia	gołębi
D	gołębiowi	gołębiom
A	gołębia	gołębie
I	gołębiem	gołębiami
L	gołębiu	gołębiach
V	gołębiu	gołębie

paw *peacock* (**w'**-stem, anim.)

	Sg.	Pl.
N	paw	pawie
G	pawia	pawi
D	pawiowi	pawiom
A	pawia	pawie
I	pawiem	pawiami
L	pawiu	pawiach
V	pawiu	pawie

łokieć *elbow* (**ć**-stem, Gsg. -a, m.v.)

	Sg.	Pl.
N	łokieć	łokcie
G	łokcia	łokci
D	łokciowi	łokciom
A	łokieć	łokcie
I	łokciem	łokciami
L	łokciu	łokciach
V	łokciu	łokcie

łabędź *swan* (**dź**-stem, anim.)

	Sg.	Pl.
N	łabędź	łabędzie
G	łabędzia	łabędzi
D	łabędziowi	łabędziom
A	łabędzia	łabędzie
I	łabędziem	łabędziami
L	łabędziu	łabędziach
V	łabędziu	łabędzie

ryś *lynx* (**ś**-stem, anim., Gpl. **-ów**)

	Sg.	Pl.
N	ryś	rysie
G	rysia	rysiów
D	rysiowi	rysiom
A	rysia	rysie
I	rysiem	rysiami
L	rysiu	rysiach
V	rysiu	rysie

gość *guest* (**ść**-stem, pers.)

	Sg.	Pl.
N	gość	goście
G	gościa	gości
D	gościowi	gościom
A	gościa	gości
I	gościem	gośćmi (!)
L	gościu	gościach
V	gościu	goście

hotel *hotel* (**l**-stem)

	Sg.	Pl.
N	hotel	hotele
G	hotelu	hoteli
D	hotelowi	hotelom
A	hotel	hotele
I	hotelem	hotelami
L	hotelu	hotelach
V	hotelu	hotele

kufel *beer mug* (**l**-st., Gsg. **-a**, m.v.)

	Sg.	Pl.
N	kufel	kufle
G	kufla	kufli (-ów)
D	kuflowi	kuflom
A	kufel	kufle
I	kuflem	kuflami
L	kuflu	kuflach
V	kuflu	kufle

dzień *day* (**ń**-stem, m.v., Gsg. **-a**)

	Sg.	Pl.
N	dzień	dni (or dnie)
G	dnia	dni
D	dniowi	dniom
A	dzień	dni (dnie)
I	dniem	dniami
L	dniu	dniach
V	dniu	dni (dnie)

gwóźdź *nail* (**źdź**-stem, o: ó)

	Sg.	Pl.
N	gwóźdź	gwoździe
G	gwoździa	gwoździ
D	gwoździowi	gwoździom
A	gwóźdź	gwoździe
I	gwoździem	gwoździami
L	gwoździu	gwoździach
V	gwoździu	gwoździe

Optional I pl.: **gwoździmi**

cel *goal* (**l**-stem, Gpl. **-ów**)

	Sg.	Pl.
N	cel	cele
G	celu	celów
D	celowi	celom
A	cel	cele
I	celem	celami
L	celu	celach
V	celu	cele

marzyciel *dreamer* (**l**-stem, pers.)

	Sg.	Pl.
N	marzyciel	marzyciele
G	marzyciela	marzycieli
D	marzycielowi	marzycielom
A	nauczyciela	marzycieli
I	marzycielem	marzycielami
L	marzycielu	marzycielach
V	marzycielu	marzyciele

koń *horse* (**ń**-stem, anim.)

	Sg.	Pl.
N	koń	konie
G	konia	koni
D	koniowi	koniom
A	konia	konie
I	koniem	końmi
L	koniu	koniach
V	koniu	konie

kraj *country* (j-stem, Gpl. pl. -ów)

	Sg.	Pl.
N	kraj	kraje
G	kraju	krajów
D	krajowi	krajom
A	kraj	kraje
I	krajem	krajami
L	kraju	krajach
V	kraju	kraje

plac *town square* (c-stem)

	Sg.	Pl.
N	plac	place
G	placu	placów
D	placowi	placom
A	plac	place
I	placem	placami
L	placu	placach
V	placu	place

koniec *end* (c-stem, mob. vow.)

	Sg.	Pl.
N	koniec	końce
G	końca	końców
D	końcowi	końcom
A	koniec	końce
I	końcem	końcami
L	końcu	końcach
V	końcu	końce

płaszcz *overcoat* (cz-stem, Gsg. -a)

	Sg.	Pl.
N	płaszcz	płaszcze
G	płaszcza	płaszczy (-ów)
D	płaszczowi	płaszczom
A	płaszcz	płaszcze
I	płaszczem	płaszczami
L	płaszczu	płaszczach
V	płaszczu	płaszcze

pokój *room* (j-stem, o: ó)

	Sg.	Pl.
N	pokój	pokoje
G	pokoju	pokoi (-ojów)
D	pokojowi	pokojom
A	pokój	pokoje
I	pokojem	pokojami
L	pokoju	pokojach
V	pokoju	pokoje

koc *blanket* (c-stem, Gsg. -a)

	Sg.	Pl.
N	koc	koce
G	koca	kocy (koców)
D	kocowi	kocom
A	koc	koce
I	kocem	kocami
L	kocu	kocach
V	kocu	koce

rydz *agaric mushroom* (dz-stem, fac. an.)

	Sg.	Pl.
N	rydz	rydze
G	rydza	rydzów
D	rydzowi	rydzom
A	rydza	rydze
I	rydzem	rydzami
L	rydzu	rydzach
V	rydzu	rydze

deszcz *rain* (cz-stem, Gpl. -ów)

	Sg.	Pl.
N	deszcz	deszcze
G	deszczu	deszczów
D	deszczowi	deszczom
A	deszcz	deszcze
I	deszczem	deszczami
L	deszczu	deszczach
V	deszczu	deszcze

lekarz *doctor* (**rz**-stem, pers.)

	Sg.	Pl.
N	lekarz	lekarze
G	lekarza	lekarzy
D	lekarzowi	lekarzom
A	lekarza	lekarzy
I	lekarzem	lekarzami
L	lekarzu	lekarzach
V	lekarzu	lekarze

grosz *grosh* (**sz**-stem, Gsg. **-a**)

	Sg.	Pl.
N	grosz	grosze
G	grosza	groszy
D	groszowi	groszom
A	grosz	grosze
I	groszem	groszami
L	groszu	groszach
V	groszu	grosze

Fac. anim. Asg.: **grosza**.

nóż *knife* (**ż**-stem, Gsg. **-a**)

	Sg.	Pl.
N	nóż	noże
G	noża	noży
D	nożowi	nożom
A	nóż	noże
I	nożem	nożami
L	nożu	nożach
V	nożu	noże

talerz *plate* (**rz**-stem, Gsg. **-a**)

	Sg.	Pl.
N	talerz	talerze
G	talerza	talerzy
D	talerzowi	talerzom
A	talerz	talerze
I	talerzem	talerzami
L	talerzu	talerzach
V	talerzu	talerze

listonosz *mailman* (**sz**-stem, pers.)

	Sg.	Pl.
N	listonosz	listonosze
G	listonosza	listonoszy
D	listonoszowi	listonoszom
A	listonosza	listonoszy
I	listonoszem	listonoszami
L	listonoszu	listonoszach
V	listonoszu	listonosze

wąż *snake* (**ż**-stem, anim., **ę: ą**)

	Sg.	Pl.
N	wąż	węże
G	węża	węży (-ów)
D	wężowi	wężom
A	węża	węże
I	wężem	wężami
L	wężu	wężach
V	wężu	węże

Illustrations of Masculine Personal Nouns with Special Endings

Npl. -owie

ojciec *father*

	Sg.	Pl.
N	ojciec	ojcowie
G	ojca	ojców
D	ojcu	ojcom
A	ojca	ojców
I	ojcem	ojcami
L	ojcu	ojcach
V	ojcze	ojcowie

syn *son*

	Sg.	Pl.
N	syn	synowie
G	syna	synów
D	synowi	synom
A	syna	synów
I	synem	synami
L	synu	synach
V	synu	synowie

mąż *husband*

	Sg.	Pl.
N	mąż	mężowie
G	męża	mężów
D	mężowi	mężom
A	męża	mężów
I	mężem	mężami
L	mężu	mężach
V	mężu	mężowie

kawaler *bachelor*

	Sg.	Pl.
N	kawaler	kawalerowie
G	kawalera	kawalerów
D	kawalerowi	kawalerom
A	kawalera	kawalerów
I	kawalerem	kawalerami
L	kawalerze	kawalerach
V	kawalerze	kawalerowie

dziadek *grandfather*

	Sg.	Pl.
N	dziadek	dziadkowie
G	dziadka	dziadków
D	dziadkowi	dziadkom
A	dziadka	dziadków
I	dziadkiem	dziadkami
L	dziadku	dziadkach
V	dziadku	dziadkowie

pan *gentleman*

	Sg.	Pl.
N	pan	panowie
G	pana	panów
D	panu	panom
A	pana	panów
I	panem	panami
L	panu	panach
V	panie	panowie

teść *father-in-law*

	Sg.	Pl.
N	teść	teściowie
G	teścia	teściów
D	teściowi	teściom
A	teścia	teściów
I	teściem	teściami
L	teściu	teściach
V	teściu	teściowie

Jan *Jan*

	Sg.	Pl.
N	Jan	Janowie
G	Jana	Janów
D	Janowi	Janom
A	Jana	Janów
I	Janem	Janami
L	Janie	Janach
V	Janie	Janowie

Stasio *Stan (first name)*

	Sg.	Pl.
N	Stasio	Stasiowie
G	Stasia	Stasiów
D	Stasiowi	Stasiom
A	Stasia	Stasiów
I	Stasiem	Stasiami
L	Stasiu	Stasiach
V	Stasiu	Stasiowie

Nowak *(surname)*

	Sg.	Pl.
N	Nowak	Nowakowie
G	Nowaka	Nowaków
D	Nowakowi	Nowakom
A	Nowaka	Nowaków
I	Nowakiem	Nowakami
L	Nowaku	Nowakach
V	Nowak	Nowakowie

NVpl. forms like **Janowie, Stasiowie** etc. are used in the sense 'Stasio and wife'.

Moniuszko *(surname)*

	Sg.	Pl.
N	Moniuszko	Moniuszkowie
G	Moniuszki	Moniuszków
D	Moniuszce	Moniuszkom
A	Moniuszkę	Moniuszków
I	Moniuszką	Moniuszkami
L	Moniuszce	Moniuszkach
V	Moniuszko	Moniuszkowie

Fredro *(surname)*

	Sg.	Pl.
N	Fredro	Fredrowie
G	Fredry	Fredrów
D	Fredrze	Fredrom
A	Fredrę	Fredrów
I	Fredrą	Fredrami
L	Fredrze	Fredrach
V	Fredro	Fredrowie

Wojtyła *(surname)*

	Sg.	Pl.
N	Wojtyła	Wojtyłowie
G	Wojtyły	Wojtyłów
D	Wojtyle	Wojtyłom
A	Wojtyłę	Wojtyłów
I	Wojtyłą	Wojtyłami
L	Wojtyle	Wojtyłach
V	Wojtyło	Wojtyłowie

Sapieha *(surname)* h-stem

	Sg.	Pl.
N	Sapieha	Sapiehowie
G	Sapiehy	Sapiehów
D	Sapieże	Sapiehom
A	Sapiehę	Sapiehów
I	Sapiehą	Sapiehami
L	Sapieże	Sapiehach
V	Sapieho	Sapiehowie

Note the exceptional change in **Sapieha** of h to ż in the traditional DLsg.: **Sapieże**. More common today: DLsg. **Sapiesze**.

Npl. -*an* and -*anin* types; NVpl. in -*e*

Cygan *(Gypsy)*

	Sg.	Pl.
N	Cygan	Cyganie
G	Cygana	Cyganów
D	Cyganowi	Cyganom
A	Cygana	Cyganów
I	Cyganem	Cyganami
L	Cyganie	Cyganach
V	Cyganie	Cyganie

Rosjanin *(Russian)*

	Sg.	Pl.
N	Rosjanin	Rosjanie
G	Rosjanina	Rosjan
D	Rosjaninowi	Rosjanom
A	Rosjanina	Rosjan
I	Rosjaninem	Rosjanami
L	Rosjaninie	Rosjanach
V	Rosjaninie	Rosjanie

Similarly to **Rosjanin**: **chrześcianin** *Christian*, **Indianin** *(American) Indian*, **krakowianin** *Cracovian*, **mieszczanin** *burgher*, **poganin** *pagan*, **powodzianin** *flood victim*, **Słowianin** *Slav*. Assume Gpl. in -∅; however, these, among others, have -ów: **Amerykanin** *American*, **anglikanin** *Anglican*, **luteranin** *Lutheran*, **Meksykanin** *Mexican*, **Afrykanin** *African*, **purytanin** *puritan*, **wegetarianin** *vegetarian*.

chłopiec *boy*

	Sg.	Pl.
N	chłopiec	chłopcy
G	chłopca	chłopców
D	chłopcu	chłopcom
A	chłopca	chłopców
I	chłopcem	chłopcami
L	chłopcu	chłopcach
V	chłopcze	chłopcy

człowiek *man*

	Sg.	Pl.
N	człowiek	ludzie
G	człowieka	ludzi
D	człowiekowi	ludziom
A	człowieka	ludzi
I	człowiekiem	ludźmi
L	człowieku	ludziach
V	człowieku	ludzie

brat *brother*

	Sg.	Pl.
N	brat	bracia
G	brata	braci
D	bratu	braciom
A	brata	braci
I	bratem	braćmi
L	bracie	braciach
V	bracie	bracia

rodzice *parents*

	Sg.*	Pl.
N	rodzic	rodzice
G	rodzica	rodziców
D	rodzicówi	rodzicom
A	rodzica	rodziców
I	rodzicem	rodzicami
L	rodzicu	rodzicach
V	rodzicu	rodzice

Archaic Vsg. **człowiecze**. The sg. form ***rodzic** *parent, forebear* is possible but not common.

przyjaciel *friend.*

	Sg.	Pl.
N	przyjaciel	przyjaciele
G	przyjaciela	przyjaciół
D	przyjacielowi	przyjaciołom or, substandard, **przyjacielom**
A	przyjaciela	przyjaciół
I	przyjacielem	przyjaciółmi or, substandard, **przyjacielami**
L	przyjacielu	przyjaciołach or, substandard, **przyjacielach**
V	przyjacielu	przyjaciele

ksiądz *priest*

	Sg.	Pl.
N	ksiądz	księża
G	księdza	księży
D	księdzu	księżom
A	księdza	księży
I	księdzem	księżmi
L	księdzu	księżach
V	księże	księża

książę *prince*

	Sg.	Pl.
N	książę	książęta
G	księcia	książąt
D	księciu	książętom
A	księcia	książąt
I	księciem	książętami
L	księciu	książętach
V	księże	książęta

Archaic sg. uncontracted forms for **książę**: GA **książęcia** DL **książęciu** I **książęciem**, V still **książę**.

Nsg. -*a*

mężczyzna *man* (GApl. -Ø)

	Sg.	Pl.
N	mężczyzna	mężczyźni
G	mężczyzny	mężczyzn
D	mężczyźnie	mężczyznom
A	mężczyznę	mężczyzn
I	mężczyzną	mężczyznami
L	mężczyźnie	mężczyznach
V	mężczyzno	mężczyźni

artysta *artist*

	Sg.	Pl.
N	artysta	artyści
G	artysty	artystów
D	artyście	artystom
A	artystę	artystów
I	artystą	artystami
L	artyście	artystach
V	artysto	artyści

monarcha *monarch*

	Sg.	Pl.
N	monarcha	monarchowie
G	monarchy	monarchów
D	monarsze	monarchom
A	monarchę	monarchów
I	monarchą	monarchami
L	monarsze	monarchach
V	monarcho	monarchowie

sędzia *judge*

	Sg.	Pl.
N	sędzia	sędziowie
G	sędziego	sędziów
D	sędziemu	sędziom
A	sędziego	sędziów
I	sędzią	sędziami
L	sędzi(m)	sędziach
V	sędzio	sędziowie

kolega *colleague*

	Sg.	Pl.
N	kolega	koledzy
G	kolegi	kolegów
D	koledze	kolegom
A	kolegę	kolegów
I	kolegą	kolegami
L	koledze	kolegach
V	kolego	koledzy

znawca *coinnoisseur*

	Sg.	Pl.
N	znawca	znawcy
G	znawcy	znawców
D	znawcy	znawcom
A	znawcę	znawców
I	znawcą	znawcami
L	znawcy	znawcach
V	znawco	znawcy

gazda *(Carpathian) farmer*

	Sg.	Pl.
N	gazda	gazdowie
G	gazdy	gazdów
D	gaździe	gazdom
A	gazdę	gazdów
I	gazdą	gazdami
L	gaździe	gazdach
V	gazdo	gazdowie

cieśla *carpenter*

	Sg.	Pl.
N	cieśla	cieśle
G	cieśli	cieśli (-ów)
D	cieśli	cieślom
A	cieślę	cieśli
I	cieślą	cieślami
L	cieśll	cieślach
V	cieślo	cieśle

Similarly: **hrabia** *count*, **margrabia** *margrave*. Archaic or sometimes with women judges: GDLsg.: **sędzi**; optional feminine NAVpl.: **sędzie**.

NOUNS WITH EMOTIVE COLORATION

See detailed discussion of these nouns above, in the body of this chapter.

chłopak *boy, lad,* usual declension:*

	Sg.	Pl.
N	chłopak	chłopaki
G	chłopaka	chłopaków
D	chłopakowi	chłopakom
A	chłopaka	chłopaków
I	chłopakiem	chłopakami
L	chłopaku	chłopakach
V	chłopaku	chłopaki

* NVpl. rare **chłopacy**, Apl. especially pej. **chłopaki**.

dzieciak *child, kid,* usual declension:

	Sg.	Pl.
N	dzieciak	dzieciaki
G	dzieciaka	dzieciaków
D	dzieciakowi	dzieciakom
A	dzieciaka	dzieciaki
I	dzieciakiem	dzieciakami
L	dzieciaku	dzieciakach
V	dzieciaku	dzieciak

znajda *foundling,* usual declension:*

	Sg.	Pl.
N	znajda	znajdy
G	znajdy	znajdów
D	znajdzie	znajdom
A	znajdę	znajdów
I	znajdą	znajdami
L	znajdzie	znajdach
V	znajdo	znajdy

* Sg.: m. **ten znajda** or f. **ta znajda**, etc. fem. or pej. male Gpl. **znajd**, Apl. **znajdy**

sługa *servant,* usual declension:*

	Sg.	Pl.
N	sługa	słudzy
G	sługi	sług
D	słudze	sługom
A	sługę	sługi
I	sługą	sługami
L	słudze	sługach
V	sługo	słudzy

* Sg.: m. **ten sługa** or f. **ta sługa**, etc. NVpl. fem. or pej. male **sługi**

sierota *orphan,* usual declension:*

	Sg.	Pl.
N	sierota	sieroty
G	sieroty	sierot
D	sierocie	sierotom
A	sierotę	sieroty
I	sierotą	sierotami
L	sierocie	sierotach
V	sieroto	sieroty

* Sg.: rarely: m. **ten sierota**, etc. Pl.: either male or fem. ref.

idiota *idiot,* usual declension:*

	Sg.	Pl.
N	idiota	idioci
G	idioty	idiotów
D	idiocie	idiotom
A	idiotę	idiotów
I	idiotą	idiotami
L	idiocie	idiotach
V	idioto	idioty

* Sg.: only **ten idiota** (fem. **ta idiotka**) NAVpl. pej. **idioty**

kaleka *cripple*, usual declension:*

	Sg.	Pl.
N	kaleka	kaleki
G	kaleki	kalek(ów)
D	kalece	kalekom
A	kalekę	kaleków
I	kaleką	kalekami
L	kalece	kalekch
V	kaleko	kaleki

* Sg.: m. **ten kaleka** or f. **ta kaleka**, etc. NVpl.:
optional male ref.: **kalecy**. Gpl. for males
kaleków is substandard. Apl. for males
kaleków is standard. Apl.: fem. or pej. male ref.:
kaleki.

mańkut *lefty*, usual declension:*

	Sg.	Pl.
N	mańkut	mańkuty
G	mańkuta	mańkutów
D	mańkutowi	mańkutom
A	mańkuta	mańkutów
I	mańkutem	mańkutami
L	mańkutcie	mańkutach
V	mańkucie	mańkuty

* Sg.: only **ten mańkut**, etc. (m. or f. ref.).
NVpl. optional male ref.: **mańkuci**.
Apl.: fem. or pej. male ref. **mańkuty**.

ADJECTIVAL

księgowy *book-keeper*

	Sg.	Pl.
N	księgowy	księgowi
G	księgowego	księgowych
D	księgowemu	księgowym
A	księgowego	księgowych
I	księgowym	księgowymi
L	księgowym	księgowych
V	księgowy	księgowi

bliźni *fellow-man*

	Sg.	Pl.
N	bliźni	bliźni
G	bliźniego	bliźnich
D	bliźniemu	bliźnim
A	bliźniego	bliźnich
I	bliźnim	bliźnimi
L	bliźnim	bliźnich
V	bliźnI	bliźni

chorąży *ensigN*

	Sg.	Pl.
N	chorąży	chorążowie
G	chorążego	chorążych
D	chorążemu	chorążym
A	chorążego	chorążych
I	chorążym	chorążymi
L	chorążym	chorążych
V	chorąży	chorążowie

uczony *scholar*

	Sg.	Pl.
N	uczony	uczeni
G	uczonego	uczonych
D	uczonemu	uczonym
A	uczonego	uczonych
I	uczonym	uczonymi
L	uczonym	uczonych
V	uczony	uczeni

woźny *janitor*

	Sg.	Pl.
N	woźny	woźni
G	woźnego	woźnych
D	woźnemu	woźnym
A	woźnego	woźnych
I	woźnym	woźnymi
L	woźnym	woźnych
V	woźny	woźni

rabbi *rabbi*

	Sg.	Pl.
N	rabbi	rabbiowie
G	rabbiego	rabbich
D	rabbiemu	rabbim
A	rabbiego	rabbich
I	rabbim	rabbimi
L	rabbim	rabbich
V	rabbi	rabbiowie

SURNAMES

Jarocki *(surname)*

	Sg.	Pl.
N	Jarocki	Jaroccy
G	Jarockiego	Jarockich
D	Jarockiemu	Jarockim
A	Jarockiego	Jarockich
I	Jarockim	Jarockimi
L	Jarockim	Jarockich
V	Jarocki	Jaroccy

Mały *(surname)*

	Sg.	Pl.
N	Mały	Małowie
G	Małego	Małych
D	Małemu	Małym
A	Małego	Małych
I	Małym	Małymi
L	Małym	Małych
V	Mały	Małowie

Nowak *(as male surname)*

	Sg.	Pl.
N	Nowak	Nowakowie
G	Nowaka	Nowaków
D	Nowakowi	Nowakom
A	Nowaka	Nowaków
I	Nowakiem	Nowakami
L	Nowaku	Nowakach
V	Nowak	Nowakowie

Król *(as male surname)*

	Sg.	Pl.
N	Król	Królowie
G	Króla	Królów
D	Królowi	Królom
A	Króla	Królów
I	Królem	Królami
L	Królu	Królach
V	Król	Królowie

FIRST NAMES

Adam *(first name)*

	Sg.	Pl.
N	Adam	Adamowie
G	Adama	Adamów
D	Adamowi	Adamom
A	Adama	Adamów
I	Adamem	Adamami
L	Adamie	Adamach
V	Adamie	Adamowie

Karol *(first name)*

	Sg.	Pl.
N	Karol	Karolowie
G	Karol	Karolów
D	Karolowi	Karolom
A	Karola	Karolów
I	Karolem	Karolami
L	Karolu	Karolach
V	Karolu	Karolowie

Jerzy *(first name)*

	Sg.	Pl.
N	Jerzy	Jerzowie
G	Jerzego	Jerzych
D	Jerzemu	Jerzym
A	Jerzego	Jerzych
I	Jerzym	Jerzymi
L	Jerzym	Jerzych
V	Jerzy	Jerzowie

Antoni *(first name)*

	Sg.	Pl.
N	Antoni	Antoniowie
G	Antoniego	Antonich
D	Antoniemu	Antonim
A	Antoniego	Antonich
I	Antonim	Antonimi
L	Antonim	Antonich
V	Antoni	Antoniowie

The oblique pl. forms for male first names are mostly hypothetical. The NVpl. forms would usually mean 'Jerzy (Antoni) and wife'.

MASCULINE-GENDER NOUNS WITH VARIOUS IRREGULARITIES

➤ **Białystok** *Białystok* (town name). Both parts of the name decline: G **Białegostoku,** D **Białemustokowi,** L **Białymstoku.** The D form **Białystokowi** can be heard in informal speech.

➤ **czas** *time,* optional Ipl. **czasy,** especially in phrases, alongside regular **czasami.** See **dawnym czasy** *in olden days,* vs. **Interesuję się czasami najnowszymi.** *I'm interested in the most recent times.*

➤ **dech** *breath,* G **tchu** D **tchowi** I **tchem** LV **tchu** (plural lacking). The devoicing of the **d** is exceptionally reflected in the spelling.

➤ **deszcz** *rain,* archaic Gsg. **dżdżu** (usually **deszczu**).

➤ **dzień** *day,* NApl. **dnie** or **dni,** but only **dwa, trzy, cztery dni.** Archaic Lsg. in the phrase **we dnie i w nocy** *by day and night.*

➤ **Kraków,** Dsg. **Krakowu** in the expression **ku Krakowu** (alongside **ku Krakowowi**) *toward Krakow.*

miesiąc *month,* Gpl. **miesięcy:**

	Sg.	Pl.
N	miesiąc	miesiące
G	miesiąca	miesięcy
D	miesiącowi	miesiącom
A	miesiąc	miesiące
I	miesiącem	miesiącami
L	miesiącu	miesiącach
V	miesiącu	miesiące

Similarly: **zając** *hare* (GAsg. **zająca**).

tysiąc *thousand,* Gpl. **tysięcy:**

	Sg.	Pl.
N	tysiąc	tysiące
G	tysiąca	tysięcy
D	tysiącowi	tysiącom
A	tysiąc	tysiące
I	tysiącem	tysiącami
L	tysiącu	tysiącach
V	tysiącu	tysiące

Occasional substandard Dsg.: **tysiącu.**

➤ **pieniądz** *coin, (in pl., money),* Gpl. **pieniędzy,** Ipl. **pieniędzmi**

	Sg.	Pl.
N	pieniądz	pieniądze
G	pieniądza	pieniędzy
D	pieniądzowi	pieniądzom
A	pieniądz	pieniądze
I	pieniądzem	pieniędzmi
L	pieniądzu	pieniądzach
V	pieniądzu	pieniądze

➤ **raz** *once, one time,* Gpl. **razy,** as in **wiele razy** *many times*

> **rok** *year*, pl. **lata**

	Sg.	Pl.
N	rok	lata
G	roku	lat
D	rokowi	latom
A	rok	lata
I	rokiem	latami or laty
L	roku	latach
V	roku	lata

The Ipl. form **laty** is used in expressions like **przed laty** *years ago*, **dawnymi laty** *in olden days*. Compare with **Interesuję się latami pięćdziesiątymi** *I'm interested in the 1950s*.

> **satelita** *satellite*. Except for Gpl. **satelitów**, this masculine-gender noun has a purely feminine-like declension, but takes masculine animate agreement, e.g. GAsg. **tego satelitę**. Note that **planeta** *planet* is regular feminine.

> **tydzień** *week*, stem **tygodń-**:

	Sg.	Pl.
N	tydzień	tygodnie
G	tygodnia	tygodni
D	tygodniowi	tygodniom
A	tydzień	tygodnie
I	tygodniem	tygodniami
L	tygodniu	tygodniach
V	tygodniu	tygodnie

> **wół** *ox* and **bawół** *buffalo*: GAsg. in **-u**: **wołu, bawołu** (colloquially also **woła, bawoła**).

RELATION-NAMES

Both male and female names of both blood relations and relations by marriage are given here.

Male
krewny *relative, relation*
ojciec *father*
tata *dad*
tatuś *daddy*
brat *brother*
braciszek *diminutive)*
dziadek *grandfather*
dziadziuś *granddaddy*
pradziadek *great-grandfather*

Female
krewna
matka *mother*
mama *mom*
mamusia *mommy*
siostra *sister*
siostrzyczka *(diminutive)*
babcia, babka *grandmother*
babunia, babusia *granny*
prababcia *great-grandmother*

Male	Female
mąż *husband*	**żona** *wife*
mężuś, mężulek *(diminutives)*	**żonka, żoneczka** *(diminutives)*
syn *son*	**córka** *daugher*
synek, syneczek *(diminutives)*	**córeczka, córeńka, córunia** *(dim.)*
wnuk *grand-son, grand-child*	**wnuczka** *grand-daughter*
wnuczek *(diminutive)*	**wnusia** *(diminutive)*
wuj or **wujek** *(maternal) uncle*	**wujenka** *(maternal) aunt*
stryj(ek) *(paternal) uncle*	**stryjenka** *(paternal) aunt*
wujek *(generalized) uncle*	**ciocia, ciotka** *(generalized) aunt*
bratanek *nephew on brother's side*	**bratanica** *niece on brother's side*
siostrzeniec *nephew on sister's side*	**siostrzenica** *niece on sister's side*
brat stryjeczny *paternal cousin*	**siostra stryjeczna** *paternal cousin*
brat cioteczny *maternal cousin*	**siostra cioteczna** *maternal cousin*
kuzyn *(generalized) cousin*	**kuzynka** *(generalized) cousin*
szwagier *brother-in-law*	**bratowa** *sister-in-law*
zięć *son-in-law*	**synowa** *daughter-in-law*
teść *father-in-law*	**teściowa** *mother-in-law*

The formal diminutives **wujek** and **ciocia** are in common use for 'uncle' and 'aunt' in general (also in the sense: friend of the family), as is **kuzyn(ka)** for 'cousin'. Collective relational names include the masculine-personal nouns **rodzeństwo** *brothers-and-sister*, **stryjostwo** and **wujostwo** *(uncle and wife)*, **małżeństwo** *husband and wife*. Step-relations include

ojczym *step-father*	**macocha** *step-mother*
pasierb *step-son*	**pasierbica** *step-daughter*
przyrodni brat *half-brother*	**przyrodnia siostra** *half-sister*

God-relations are expressed with the adjective **chrzestny**: **matka chrzestna** *god-mother*, **ojciec chrzestny** *god-father*, **córka chrzestna** *god-daughter*, **syn chrzestny** *god-son*.

POLISH FIRST AND LAST NAMES

Ancient Polish first names (**imiona**) often had a composite character. Of those still used, most end in **-dan** 'gift', **-sław** 'glory' or **-mir, -mierz** 'peace', as **Bogdan** 'god-gift', **Bogusław** 'God-glory', **Bronisław** 'weapon-glory', **Czesław** 'honor-glory', **Sławomir** 'glory-peace', **Włodzimierz** 'authority-peace', and so on. Female variants of such names are formed by adding **-a**: **Bogdana, Bogusława, Bronisława, Sławomira**, and so forth. Following the acceptance of Christianity in 966, names tended to be taken from the Bible or medieval saints, as **Adam, Daniel, Grzegorz, Jan, Józef, Piotr, Stefan, Tomasz**, etc. (or, for women, **Anna, Ewa, Maria**, Elżbieta, Barbara, Małgorzata, Zofia, etc.). The names of the early Polish saints **Wojciech** and **Stanisław** (fem. **Stanisława**) have always been popular. Beginning in the 18th century, names often became drawn from classical or contemporary literature and culture, as **Emil, Ernest, Horacy, Oskar, Ryszard; Emilia, Flora, Julia, Malwina, Laura**, etc. Although both tradition and the office of vital statistics discourages the giving of non-traditional first names, according to a recent census there are eleven Polish men named **Elwis**, two named **Ringo**, and 54 named **Dastin** (presumably after Dustin Hoffman).

The universal use of surnames (**nazwiska**) became established in Polish only in the 18th century. The landed gentry and richer merchants with a need for broader recognizability were the first to use stable last names. Surnames in **-ski** were often based on the name of an estate or village belonging to the estate; **Orłowski** could mean 'from the village of **Orłowo** or **Orłów**'. Patronymic surnames in **-owicz** or **-ewicz** are also common, **Janowicz** being more or less the equivalent of Johnson. Many last names originated as sobriquets, as **Biały** 'white', **Mazgaj** 'dawdler' **Mądrala** 'wiseguy', **Niemiec** 'German', **Smakosz** 'gourmand', **Węgrzyn** 'Hungarian', and so on. Surnames in **-ak, -an, -czyk** often refer to places of origin, as **Krakowian, Poznańczyk, Radomiak, Warszawiak**. Many animal names occur: **Baran** 'ram', **Czyżyk** 'finch', **Kania** 'kite', **Kozioł** 'goat', **Kruk** 'raven', **Łoś** 'elk', **Wróbel** 'sparrow'. Names of crafts are another major source: **Bednarz** 'cooper', **Budarz** 'builder', **Kowal** 'smith', **Rymarz** 'harness-maker', **Szewc** 'cobbler', **Tokarz** 'turner', etc. Diminutive suffixes in **-ek, -ik, -czyk** were often used patronymically; in individual cases **Kowalik** could have meant 'smith's son'; **Rymarek** 'harness-maker's son'; and so on. Many surnames underwent a process of gentrification through the addition of **-ski**, as **Kowalski. Baranowski** could mean 'from **Baranów** or **Baranowo**', or it could have originated from the addition of **-owski** to **Baran. Bednarski** was gentrified from **Bednarz; Tokarski** from **Tokarz**, and so on. Due to German settlement stretching back to the Middle Ages, German surnames have a long tradition of use in Poland: **Braun, Szulc, Werner**, etc.

MALE FIRST-NAMES AND DIMINUTIVES

There are around 700 male first names in use in contemporary Poland. Male first names may form conventional, child's, and chiding or mocking diminutives, according to patterns that have to be described for each noun. For example, **Ryszard** *Richard* forms **Rysiek** (conventional), **Ryś** or **Rysio** (child's), **Rycho** (augmentative, slightly mocking). Not all names form a complete set, even of the first two possibilities. Diminutives and augmentatives in **-o** often use the Vocative form in **-u** (**Rysiu, Rychu**) as a de facto Nominative. Here is a list of commonly used Polish male first names, *standard nicknames* (when different from the formal name), and affectionate forms.

Adam, Adaś, Adasiek
Aleksander, *Olek*, **Oluś, Alek**
Andrzej, Andrzejek, Jędrek
Antoni, *Antek*, **Antoś**

Artur, Arturek
Bartłomiej, *Bartek*, **Bartosz, Bartuś**
Bogdan, Bogdanek, Boguś
Bogusław, Boguś

Bolesław, *Bolek*, Boluś
Bronisław, *Bronek*
Cezary, *Czarek*, Czaruś
Czesław, *Czesiek*, Czesio
Daniel, Danielek
Dariusz, *Darek*, Daruś
Dominik, Domek
Edward, *Edek*, Edzio
Emil, Emilek, Milek, Miluś
Eugeniusz, *Gienek*, Geniuś, Gienio
Feliks, *Felek*, Feluś
Filip, Filek, Filipek, Filuś
Florian, *Florek*, Floruś
Franciszek, *Franek*, Franuś, Franio
Fryderyk, Frydek, Fryc
Grzegorz, *Grzesiek*, Grzesio
Gustaw, *Gutek*, Gucio
Henryk, *Heniek*, Henio, Heniuś
Ignacy, Ignacek, Ignaś
Jarosław, *Jarek*, Jaruś
Ireniusz, *Irek*, Iruś
Jacek, Jacuś
Jakub, *Kuba*, Jakubek
Jan, *Janek*, Jasiek, Jasio
Janusz, Januszek
Jarosław, *Jarek*
Jerzy, *Jurek*, Jureczek
Józef, *Józek*, Józeczek, Józio, Juzuś
Julian, Julianek
Juliusz, *Julek*
Karol, Karolek
Kazimierz, *Kazik*, Kazio
Konrad
Konstanty, *Kostek*, Kostuś
Krzysztof, *Krzysiek,*, Krzyś
Leon
Lech, *Leszek*, Lesio
Lucjan, *Lucek*
Ludwik, *Ludek*
Łukasz, Łukaszek
Maciej, *Maciek*
Marcin, Marcinek

Marek, Mareczek, Maruś
Marian, Marianek, Maryś
Mariusz, Mariuszek
Mateusz, Mateuszek
Michał, Michałek
Mieczysław, *Mietek*
Mikołaj, Mikołajek
Miron, *Mirek*
Mirosław, *Mirek*
Paweł, Pawełek
Piotr, *Piotrek*, Piotruś
Rafał, Rafałek
Robert, Robuś
Roman, *Romek*, Romeczek, Romuś
Ryszard, *Rysiek*, Rysio, Ryś
Sławomir, *Sławek*
Stanisław, *Stasiek*, Stasio, Staś,
    Stacho
Stefan, Stefek
Szczepan, Stefek
Szymon, *Szymek*, Szymuś
Sylwester, *Sylwek*, Sylwuś
Tadeusz, *Tadek*, Tadzio
Teodor, *Dorek*, Teodorek
Tobiasz, Tobiaszek
Tomasz, *Tomek*
Wacław, *Wacek*
Waldemar, *Waldek*
Walery, Walerek
Wawrzyniec, *Wawrzek*, Wawrzuś
Wiesław, *Wiesiek*, Wiesio
Wiktor, Wiktorek
Wincenty, *Wicek*, Wicuś
Witold, *Witek*, Wituś
Władysław, *Władek* , Władzio
Włodzimierz, *Włodek*
Wojciech, *Wojtek*, Wojtuś
Zbigniew, *Zbyszek*, Zbynio, Zbysio,
    Zbych
Zdzisław, *Zdzisiek*, Zdziś
Zenon, *Zenek*
Zygmunt, Zygmuś

STEM AND ROOT TRUNCATION IN DERIVATIONS

The term truncation refers to the violation of the integrity of the root or stem of a base word in the adding-on of suffixes. For example, the formation of **Jasio** *Johnny* from **Jan** involves cutting the root off before stem-final **n** and inserting, as it were, **ś** as a new stem consonant: **Jaś-**. Truncation is a frequent formative device in the derivation of affectionate names, pejoratives (belittling words), and augmentatives (meaning 'big' or 'crude'). Often truncation involves the replacement of one consonant by another, not etymologically related to it. The phonetically soft consonants **ć, ś, dź, ń, l** and the velar fricative **ch** are those most frequently involved in such consonant substitutions. Following are some examples of truncative formations in masculine noun derivation:

nochal *shnoz,* from **no|s** *nose*
wujcio *uncle (affectionate,* from **wuj|ek** *uncle)*
Stasio or **Staś** *Stan* from **Sta|nisław**
paluch *stubby finger* from **pa|lec** *finger*
pet *cig,* from **p|apieros** *cigarette*
ptaszek *birdie* from **pta|k** *bird*
piach *sand* from **pia|sek** *sand*

Derivation through truncation is best illustrated by masculine-declension nouns, but it also may be found among feminine and neuter nouns, for example,

Joasia from **Joa|nna** *Joanna*
ciacho *cake (pejorative or augmentative)* from **cia|sto** *cake.*

THE MOST IMPORTANT MASCULINE-NOUN SOFTENING FORMANTS

1. **-j-**

   wódz (analyzed stem **wod-j-**) *leader,* cf. **wodzić** (**wod-i-ć**) *lead*
   gąszcz (analyzed stem **gęst-j-**) *thicket,* cf. **gęsty**. This word shows an unpredictable shift of **ę** to **ą**.

2. **-'-**

   łabędź (analyzed stem **łabęd-'**) *swan*
   łoś (analyzed stem **łos-'**) *elk*

3. **-'k-** (alongside non-softening **-Øk-**)
   The variant **-'k-** occurs primarily with velar roots:

   boczek (analyzed stem **bok-'k-**) *ham,* cf. **bok** *side*
   móżdżek (analyzed stem **mózg-'k-**) *bird-brain,* cf. **mózg** *brain*
   twarożek (analyzed stem **twarog-'k-**) *cottage cheese-dim.,* cf. **twaróg** *cottage cheese*

4. -ik-

bilecik (analyzed stem bilet-ik-) *ticket-dim.*, cf. bilet *ticket*
walczyk (analyzed stem walc-ik-) *waltz-dim.*, cf. walc *waltz.*

5. -'c-

starzec (analyzed stem star-'c-) *old man*, cf. stary *old*
nosorożec (analyzed stem nos-o-rog-'c-) *rhinoceros*, cf. róg *horn.*

NAMES FOR INHABITANTS OF TOWNS

Various suffixes are in use for forming names of persons from towns. The most productive and stylistically neutral suffix is -'anin (fem. -'anka) but more colloquial nouns in -'ak (fem. -'anka) and -'czyk (fem. -ka or -'anka) may also be found, especially with foreign town names. Such nouns are not capitalized:

Town	Male resident	Female resident
Berlin	berlińczyk	berlinianka
Białystok	białostocczanin	białostoczanka
Kraków	krakowianin or krakowiak	krakowianka
Londyn	londyńczyk	londynka
Łódź	łodzianin	łodzianka
Nowy Jork	nowojorczyk	nowojorczanka
Oświęcim	oświęcimianin	oświęcimianka
Paryż *Paris*	paryżanin	paryżanka
Poznań	poznanianin or poznaniak, poznańczyk	poznanianka
Rzym *Rome*	rzymianin	rzymianka
Toruń	torunianin	torunianka
Warszawa	warszawianin or warszawiak	warszawianka
Wrocław	wrocławianin or wrocławiak	wrocławianka

DAYS OF THE WEEK

The days of the week (tydzień tygodnia *week*, adj. tygodniowy) are mostly masculine in gender with Gsg. in -u. Names of the days of the week are not capitalized. The names of the days of the week have associated adjectives which are used where English tends to use the noun (as niedzielny koncert *Sunday concert*, sobotni wieczór *Saturday evening*, etc.):

	Noun	Adjective
Monday	poniedziałek -działku	poniedziałkowy
Tuesday	wtorek wtorku	wtorkowy
Wednesday	środa środy (fem.)	środowy
Thursday	czwartek czwartku	czwartkowy
Friday	piątek piątku	piątkowy
Saturday	sobota soboty (fem.)	sobotni
Sunday	niedziela niedzieli (fem.)	niedzielny

MONTHS

The names for the months (**miesiąc miesiąca** *month*, adj. **miesięczny**) are masculine in gender and, except for the adjectival form **luty**, have Gsg. in **-a**. Names of the months are not capitalized. The related adjectives are used in attributive position where English tends to use the noun, as illustrated by **styczniowa pogoda** *January weather*, **powstanie listopadowe** *November Uprising*, etc.).

	Noun	Adjective
January	styczeń stycznia	styczniowy
February	luty lutego	lutowy
March	marzec marca	marcowy
April	kwiecień kwietnia	kwietniowy
May	maj maja	majowy
June	czerwiec czerwca	czerwcowy
July	lipiec lipca	lipcowy
August	sierpień sierpnia	sierpniowy
September	wrzesień września	wrześniowy
October	październik -a	październikowy
November	listopad listopada	listopadowy
December	grudzień grudnia	grudniowy

COMPASS DIRECTIONS

	Noun	Adjective
North	północ północy (fem.)	północny
South	południe południa (neut.)	południowy
East	wschód wschodu	wschodni
West	zachód zachodu	zachodni
South-West	południowy-zachód	południowozachodni
South-East	południowy-wschód	południowowschodni
North-West	północny-zaschód	północnozachodni.
North-East	północny-wschód	północnowschodni

Neuter-Gender and Plural-Only Noun Declension

By a "noun of neuter gender" is meant a noun for which the 3rd. personal singular pronoun **ono** *it* may be substituted. By a "noun of neuter declension" is meant any inflected noun of neuter gender.

STEM TYPES

For the most part, neuter-declension stem types are the same as for masculine nouns: hard, velar, and (functionally) soft. In addition, neuter declension exhibits two special extended-stem (**en-** and **ent-**) types which are soft in the sg. and hard in the pl. (as **imię** Gsg. **imienia** NAVpl. **imiona** *name* and **zwierzę** Gsg. **zwierzęcia** NAVpl. **zwierzęta** *animal*). For hard, velar, and soft stems, the surface stem is obtained by subtracting the NAVsg. ending **-o** or (with soft-stems) **-e**: **słowo** *word*, stem **słow-**; **wieko** *lid*, stem **wiek-**; **pole** *field*, stem **pol-**; **zdanie** *opinion*, stem **zdań-**. For stems ending in two consonants, the Gpl. should be checked for a possible mobile vowel before **-Ø**, as in **okno** *window*, Gpl. **okien**, stem **okØn-**; **płótno** *cloth*, Gpl. **płócien**, stem **płót'n-**. No simple surface stem can be derived for nouns of the extended-stem types; the deep stems of such nouns are discussed further below. Endings of the neuter declension are either identical to those of, or at least occur as exceptional endings in, masculine noun declension.

NEUTER DECLENSIONAL ENDINGS

		Hard stems	Velar stems	Soft stems	Extended stem
Sg.	NAV	-o	←	←	-#
	G	-a	←	←	←
	D	-u	←	←	←
	I	-èm	←	←	←
	L	-ě	-u	-u	←
Pl.	NAV	-a	←	←	←
	G	-Ø	←	← (-y/i)	-Ø
	D	-om	←	←	←
	I	-ami	←	←	←
	L	-ach	←	←	←

Neuter-declension nouns without exception have the same form in the NAVsg. and NAVpl. The rule for the distribution of the Lsg. ending, **-ě** or **-u**, is the same as for masculine-declension nouns: soft and velar stems take **-u**, non-velar hard-stems take **-ě**. By **-#** in the NAVsg. of extended-stem neuters is meant the "null ending". This ending is different in its effect from the zero ending **-Ø** in the Gpl.; compare NAVsg. **im-en-#: imię** to Gpl. **im-en-Ø: imion.**

EXCEPTIONAL NEUTER-DECLENSION ENDINGS

1. NAVpl. **-y/i: dziecko dzieci** *child(ren)*, **oko oczy** *eye(s)*, **ucho uszy** *ear(s)*. Optionally for **oczko** *eye-dim.*, pl. **oczka** or **oczki; uszko** *ear-dim.*, pl. **uszka** or **uszki.**

2. Gpl. **-y/i.** This is the expected ending for neuter nouns with an underlying stem-suffix **-'-.** Most of these nouns are either originally collective in meaning or are names for areas or places, for example **osiedle** *settlement*, deep stem **osiedł-'-,** Gpl. **osiedli; ostrze** *blade*, deep stem **ostr-'-,** Gpl. **ostrzy; podwórze** *courtyard*, deep stem **podwor-'-,** Gpl. **podwórzy;** and so on. Some common nouns taking Gpl. in **-y/i** are **naręcze** *armful*, Gpl. **naręczy; narzędzie** *tool*, Gpl. **narzędzi; nozdrze** *nostril*, Gpl. **nozdrzy; oblicze** *face-fig.*, Gpl. **obliczy; pojezierze** *lake district*, Gpl. **pojezierzy; popołudnie** *afternoon*, Gpl. **popołudni; przedszkole** *pre-school*, Gpl. **przedszkoli; wybrzeże** *seacoast*, Gpl. **wybrzeży; stulecie** *centenary*, Gpl. **stuleci; zaplecze** *supply base*, Gpl. **zapleczy; zbocze** *slope*, Gpl. **zboczy.**

3. Gpl. **-ów.** This ending is regular with neuters in **-um** and **-io**, as **muzeum** *museum*, Gpl. **muzeów, studio** *studio*, Gpl. **studiów** (see below under special declensional types); and with animate augmentatives in **-isko.** Nouns in **-isko** referring to male persons may take either masculine or neuter agreement and syntax, hence either NAsg. **to chłopisko** *that boy* or, less often **ten chłopisko,** Asg. **to chłopisko** or, less often, **tego chłopiska,** Npl. **te chłopiska,** Gpl. **tych chłopisków,** Apl. **te chłopiska** or, less often, **tych chłopisków.** Augmentative names in **-isko** referring to female persons (e.g., formed from first names, like **Beacisko** from **Beata**) take a regular neuter declension.

4. Ipl. in **-y.** This archaic ending is found with the word **słowo** *word* in the set expression **innymi słowy** *in other words.* See also **przed laty** *years ago*, **dawnymi laty** *in former times*, and other expressions where the plural of **lato** *summer* functions as the suppletive plural of **rok** *year.*

SOUND-CHANGES TAKING PLACE IN NEUTER DECLENSION

1. Primary consonants are replaced by their R1 counterpart before the Lsg. ending **-ě: słow-ě: słowie** *word*, **biur-ě: biurze** *office.* Velar consonants do not occur before this ending but instead take Lsg. **-u: pudełko** *box*, Lsg. **pudełku.**

2. **k** and **g** soften to R4 **k'** and **g'** before the Isg. ending **-èm: ok-èm: okiem.**

3. In the declension of **oko** *eye* and **ucho** *ear*, the changes **k: cz** and **ch: sz** occur throughout the plural: **oko oczy** *eye(s)*, **ucho uszy** *ear(s).*

4. The mobile vowel, reflecting either stem-internal Ø or ', can be expected to occur between two consonants at the end of the stem before the Gpl. ending **-Ø**. In neuter declension, the mobile vowel is usually **è** (from Ø), not **e** (from '). It typically occurs before a stem-final resonant consonant (**ł, r, m, n**) following another consonant: **jarzmo** *yoke*, Gpl. **jarzem** (or **jarzm**); **mydło** *soap*, Gpl. **mydeł; krzesło** *chair*, Gpl. **krzeseł; okno** *window*, Gpl. **okien; pismo** *document*, Gpl. **pisem** (or **pism**), **wiadro** *bucket*, Gpl. **wiader.** Mobile **e** (') may be seen in **krosno** Gpl. **krosien** *loom*, **płótno** *cloth*, Gpl. **płócien.** The mobile vowel occurs most frequently in the diminutive suffix **-Øk-** as in **kółko** *circle*, Gpl. **kółek; pudełko** *box*, Gpl. **pudełek**, and others.

5. The **o: ó** shift can occur in the Gpl. before the ending **-Ø: czoło** *brow*, Gpl. **czół; morze** *sea*, Gpl. **mórz, pole** *field*, Gpl. **pól, koło** *wheel*, Gpl. **kół, słowo** *word*, Gpl. **słów.** Note: **jezioro** *lake*, Gpl. **jezior.**

6. The **ę: ą** shift occurs before the Gpl. ending **-Ø** in **święto** *holiday*, Gpl. **świąt** (but not in **mięso** *meat*, Gpl. **mięs**); and in nouns of the **ent-** type: **zwierzę** *animal*, NAVpl. **zwierzęta**, Gpl. **zwierząt.**

7. The **e: o** shift can be found in certain nouns with soft stems in the sg. and hard stems in the pl.: **nasienie** *seed*, NAVpl. **nasiona, ziele** *herb*, NAVpl. **zioła, imię** *name*, Gsg. **imienia**, Npl. **imiona.** The shift is often missing where it might be expected in the Lsg., as in **jezioro** *lake*, Lsg. **jeziorze** (not occasionally heard *jezierze). Compare the Lsg. of **czoło** *brow*, Lsg. **czole** to archaic **czele** in the phrase **na czele** *at the head of.*

8. The **ě: a** shift can be found in the Lsg. of a few nouns, for example **ciało** *body*, Lsg. **ciele; ciasto** *dough*, Lsg. **cieście; gniazdo** *nest*, Lsg. **gnieździe, lato** *summer*, Lsg. **lecie; miasto** *town*, Lsg. **mieście.** The shift is often absent, as in **działo** *cannon*, Lsg. **dziale, kolano** *knee*, Lsg. **kolanie; siano** *hay*, Lsg. **sianie, wiadro** *bucket*, Lsg. **wiadrze.**

EXAMPLES OF REGULAR NEUTER NOUNS

Hard Stems

piwo *beer* (w-stem)

	Sg.	Pl.
N	piwo	piwa
G	piwa	piw
D	piwu	piwom
A	piwo	piwa
I	piwem	piwami
L	piwie	piwach
V	piwo	piwa

czasopismo *periodical* (m-stem)

	Sg.	Pl.
N	czasopismo	czasopisma
G	czasopisma	czasopism
D	czasopismu	czasopismom
A	czasopismo	czasopisma
I	czasopismem	czasopismami
L	czasopiśmie	czasopismach
V	czasopismo	czasopisma

błoto *mud* (t-stem)

	Sg.	Pl.
N	błoto	błota
G	błota	błot
D	błotu	błotom
A	błoto	błota
I	błotem	błotami
L	błocie	błotach
V	błoto	błota

miasto *town* (st-stem, ě: a)

	Sg.	Pl.
N	miasto	miasta
G	miasta	miast
D	miastu	miastom
A	miasto	miasta
I	miastem	miastami
L	mieście	miastach
V	miasto	miasta

mięso *meat* (s-stem)

	Sg.	Pl.
N	mięso	mięsa
G	mięsa	mięs
D	mięsu	mięsom
A	mięso	mięsa
I	mięsem	mięsami
L	mięsie	mięsach
V	mięso	mięsa

koło *wheel* (ł-stem, o: ó)

	Sg.	Pl.
N	koło	koła
G	koła	kół
D	kołu	kołom
A	koło	koła
I	kołem	kołami
L	kole	kołach
V	koło	koła

stado *herd* (d-stem)

	Sg.	Pl.
N	stado	stada
G	stada	stad
D	stadu	stadom
A	stado	stada
I	stadem	stadami
L	stadzie	stadach
V	stado	stada

gniazdo *nest* (zd-stem, ě: a)

	Sg.	Pl.
N	gniazdo	gniazda
G	gniazda	gniazd
D	gniazdu	gniazdom
A	gniazdo	gniazda
I	gniazdem	gniazdami
L	gnieździe	gniazdach
V	gniazdo	gniazda

wiadro *bucket* (r-stem, mob. vow.)

	Sg.	Pl.
N	wiadro	wiadra
G	wiadra	wiader
D	wiadru	wiadrom
A	wiadro	wiadra
I	wiadrem	wiadrami
L	wiadrze	wiadrach
V	wiadro	wiadra

biuro *office* (r-stem)

	Sg.	Pl.
N	biuro	biura
G	biura	biur
D	biuru	biurom
A	biuro	biura
I	biurem	biurami
L	biurze	biurach
V	biuro	biura

wino *wine* (n-stem)

	Sg.	Pl.
N	wino	wina
G	wina	win
D	winu	winom
A	wino	wina
I	winem	winami
L	winie	winach
V	wino	wina

okno *window* (n-stem, mob. vow.)

	Sg.	Pl.
N	okno	okna
G	okna	okien
D	oknu	oknom
A	okno	okna
I	oknem	oknami
L	oknie	oknach
V	okno	okna

krzesło *chair* (ł-stem, mob. vow.)

	Sg.	Pl.
N	krzesło	krzesła
G	krzesła	krzeseł
D	krzesłu	krzesłom
A	krzesło	krzesła
I	krzesłem	krzesłami
L	krześle	krzesłach
V	krzesło	krzesła

jezioro *lake* (r-stem)

	Sg.	Pl.
N	jezioro	jeziora
G	jeziora	jezior
D	jezioru	jeziorom
A	jezioro	jeziora
I	jeziorem	jeziorami
L	jeziorze	jeziorach
V	jezioro	jeziora

Gpl. **jeziór** is considered to be substandard.

Velar Stems

biurko *desk* (k-stem, mob. vow.)

	Sg.	Pl.
N	biurko	biurka
G	biurka	biurek
D	biurku	biurkom
A	biurko	biurka
I	biurkiem	biurkami
L	biurku	biurkach
V	biurko	biurka

lotnisko *airport* (k-stem)

	Sg.	Pl.
N	lotnisko	lotniska
G	lotniska	lotnisk
D	lotnisku	lotniskom
A	lotnisko	lotniska
I	lotniskiem	lotniskami
L	lotnisku	lotniskach
V	lotnisko	lotniska

echo *echo* (ch-stem)

	Sg.	Pl.
N	echo	echa
G	echa	ech
D	echu	echom
A	echo	echa
I	echem	echami
L	echu	echach
V	echo	echa

tango *tango* (g-stem)

	Sg.	Pl.
N	tango	tanga
G	tanga	tang
D	tangu	tangom
A	tango	tanga
I	tangiem	tangami
L	tangu	tangach
V	tango	tanga

Soft Stems

przyjęcie *reception* (ć-stem)

	Sg.	Pl.
N	przyjęcie	przyjęcia
G	przyjęcia	przyjęć
D	przyjęciu	przyjęciom
A	przyjęcie	przyjęcia
I	przyjęciem	przyjęciami
L	przyjęciu	przyjęciach
V	przyjęcie	przyjęcia

pole *field* (l-stem, o: ó)

	Sg.	Pl.
N	pole	pola
G	pola	pól
D	polu	polom
A	pole	pola
I	polem	polami
L	polu	polach
V	pole	pola

miejsce *place* (c-stem)

	Sg.	Pl.
N	miejsce	miejsca
G	miejsca	miejsc
D	miejscu	miejscom
A	miejsce	miejsca
I	miejscem	miejscami
L	miejscu	miejscach
V	miejsce	miejsca

południe *afternoon* (ń-stem, Gpl. -y)

	Sg.	Pl.
N	południe	południa
G	południa	południ
D	południu	południom
A	południe	południa
I	południem	południami
L	południu	południach
V	południe	południa

mieszkanie *apartment* (ń-stem)

	Sg.	Pl.
N	mieszkanie	mieszkania
G	mieszkania	mieszkań
D	mieszkaniu	mieszkaniom
A	mieszkanie	mieszkania
I	mieszkaniem	mieszkaniami
L	mieszkaniu	mieszkaniach
V	mieszkanie	mieszkania

morze *sea* (rz-stem, o: ó)

	Sg.	Pl.
N	morze	morza
G	morza	mórz
D	morzu	morzom
A	morze	morza
I	morzem	morzami
L	morzu	morzach
V	morze	morza

słońce *sun* (c-stem)

	Sg.	Pl.
N	słońce	słońca
G	słońca	słońc
D	słońcu	słońcom
A	słońce	słońca
I	słońcem	słońcami
L	słońcu	słońcach
V	słońce	słońca

wybrzeże *seacoast* (rz-stem, Gpl. -y)

	Sg.	Pl.
N	wybrzeże	wybrzeża
G	wybrzeża	wybrzeży
D	wybrzeżu	wybrzeżom
A	wybrzeże	wybrzeża
I	wybrzeżem	wybrzeżami
L	wybrzeżu	wybrzeżach
V	wybrzeże	wybrzeża

SPECIAL DECLENSIONAL TYPES AND EXCEPTIONS

1. NAsg. in **-um, -io.** Neuter nouns in **-um** and **-io** are not declined in the sg. In the pl., they are declined like regular neuter nouns, except that the Gpl. ending is **-ów**. Some nouns in **-um** are vowel-stems, for example **muzeum** *museum*, stem **muze-**, NVpl. **muzea**, Gpl. **muzeów**, etc.

<table>
<tr><td colspan="3">centrum town center (-um-type)</td><td colspan="3">studio studio (-io-type)</td></tr>
<tr><td></td><td>Sg.</td><td>Pl.</td><td></td><td>Sg.</td><td>Pl.</td></tr>
<tr><td>N</td><td>centrum</td><td>centra</td><td>N</td><td>studio</td><td>studia</td></tr>
<tr><td>G</td><td>centrum</td><td>centrów</td><td>G</td><td>studio</td><td>studiów</td></tr>
<tr><td>D</td><td>centrum</td><td>centrom</td><td>D</td><td>studio</td><td>studiom</td></tr>
<tr><td>A</td><td>centrum</td><td>centra</td><td>A</td><td>studio</td><td>studia</td></tr>
<tr><td>I</td><td>centrum</td><td>centrami</td><td>I</td><td>studio</td><td>studiami</td></tr>
<tr><td>L</td><td>centrum</td><td>centrach</td><td>L</td><td>studio</td><td>studiach</td></tr>
<tr><td>V</td><td>centrum</td><td>centra</td><td>V</td><td>studio</td><td>studia</td></tr>
</table>

Similarly to **centrum: archiwum** *archive*, **audytorium** *audience*, **liceum** *lyceum*, **medium** *medium*, **muzeum** *museum*, **plenum** *plenary session* (no pl.), and others. Some words in **-um** are masculine and are declined as such, for example, **album** *album*, Gsg. **albumu; kostium** *suit*, Gsg. **kostiumu.** Similarly to **studio: folio** *folio*, **patio** *patio*, **radio** *radio*. These nouns sometimes show endings such as Lsg. in **-u**, as **w radiu, w studiu.** The word **auto** *car*, formerly indeclinable in the singular, today regularly takes endings: Gsg. **auta**, Isg. **autem**, Lsg. **aucie.**

2. Extended stem **(-en-** and **-ęt-)** types. A small number of nouns are declined according to the models of **imię** *name* and **zwierzę** *animal*. Most nouns of the latter type refer to animal young.

<table>
<tr><td colspan="3">imię first name (-en-type, e: o)</td><td colspan="3">zwierzę animal (ęt-type, ę: ą)</td></tr>
<tr><td></td><td>Sg.</td><td>Pl.</td><td></td><td>Sg.</td><td>Pl.</td></tr>
<tr><td>N</td><td>imię</td><td>imiona</td><td>N</td><td>zwierzę</td><td>zwierzęta</td></tr>
<tr><td>G</td><td>imienia</td><td>imion</td><td>G</td><td>zwierzęcia</td><td>zwierząt</td></tr>
<tr><td>D</td><td>imieniu</td><td>imionom</td><td>D</td><td>zwierzęciu</td><td>zwierzętom</td></tr>
<tr><td>A</td><td>imię</td><td>imiona</td><td>A</td><td>zwierzę</td><td>zwierzęta</td></tr>
<tr><td>I</td><td>imieniem</td><td>imionami</td><td>I</td><td>zwierzęciem</td><td>zwierzętami</td></tr>
<tr><td>L</td><td>imieniu</td><td>imionach</td><td>L</td><td>zwierzęciu</td><td>zwierzętach</td></tr>
<tr><td>V</td><td>imię</td><td>imiona</td><td>V</td><td>zwierzę</td><td>zwierzęta</td></tr>
</table>

Similarly to **imię: znamię** *banner*, **ramię** *shoulder*, **ciemię** *crown of head*, **plemię** *tribe*, **brzemię** *burden*, **siemię** *seed*, **strzemię** *stirrup*, **wymię** *udder*.

Similarly to **zwierzę: cielę** *calf*, **dziecię** *child*, **jagnię** *lamb*, **kocię** *kitty*, **pisklę** *chick*, **szczenię** *puppy*, **prosię** *piglet*, **źrebię** *foal*, and so on. Over much of Poland, names for animal young in **-ę** are supplanted by masculine nouns in the suffix **-ak: cielak** *calf*, **dzieciak** *child*, **kurczak** *chick*, szczeniak *puppy*, źrebak *foal*, and so on. Nouns of the **ęt-** type form diminutives in **-'t-Øk-o**, with the shift of **ę** to **ą**: **zwierzątko** *beastie*, Gpl. **zwierzątek**. Observe that the nouns **chłopię** *boy* and **dziewczę** *girl*, despite reference to persons, are of neuter gender: **to chłopię, to dziewczę**. For further analysis of these types, see further below.

3. The following two nouns have irregular plural stems based on defunct dual forms:

<table>
<tr><td colspan="3">**oko** *eye* (irreg. pl.)</td><td colspan="3">**ucho** *ear* (irreg. pl.)</td></tr>
<tr><td></td><td>Sg.</td><td>Pl.</td><td></td><td>Sg.</td><td>Pl.</td></tr>
<tr><td>N</td><td>oko</td><td>oczy</td><td>N</td><td>ucho</td><td>uszy</td></tr>
<tr><td>G</td><td>oka</td><td>oczu</td><td>G</td><td>ucha</td><td>uszu</td></tr>
<tr><td>D</td><td>oku</td><td>oczom</td><td>D</td><td>uchu</td><td>uszom</td></tr>
<tr><td>A</td><td>oko</td><td>oczy</td><td>A</td><td>ucho</td><td>uszy</td></tr>
<tr><td>I</td><td>okiem</td><td>oczami</td><td>I</td><td>uchem</td><td>uszami</td></tr>
<tr><td>L</td><td>oku</td><td>oczach</td><td>L</td><td>uchu</td><td>uszach</td></tr>
<tr><td>V</td><td>oko</td><td>oczy</td><td>V</td><td>ucho</td><td>uszy</td></tr>
</table>

Optional Ipl. **oczyma**. Archaic Gpls. **ócz, oczów**.

Archaic Gpl. **uszów**. Archaic Ipl. **uszyma**

4. The following two nouns contain a softening formant in the sg. only:

<table>
<tr><td colspan="3">**nasienie** *seed* (irreg., **e: o**)</td><td colspan="3">**ziele** *herb* (irreg., **e: o: ó**)</td></tr>
<tr><td></td><td>Sg.</td><td>Pl.</td><td></td><td>Sg.</td><td>Pl.</td></tr>
<tr><td>N</td><td>nasienie</td><td>nasiona</td><td>N</td><td>ziele</td><td>zioła</td></tr>
<tr><td>G</td><td>nasienia</td><td>nasion</td><td>G</td><td>ziela</td><td>ziół</td></tr>
<tr><td>D</td><td>nasieniu</td><td>nasionom</td><td>D</td><td>zielu</td><td>ziołom</td></tr>
<tr><td>A</td><td>nasienie</td><td>nasiona</td><td>A</td><td>ziele</td><td>zioła</td></tr>
<tr><td>I</td><td>nasieniem</td><td>nasionami</td><td>I</td><td>zielem</td><td>ziołami</td></tr>
<tr><td>L</td><td>nasieniu</td><td>nasionach</td><td>L</td><td>zielu</td><td>ziołach</td></tr>
<tr><td>V</td><td>nasienie</td><td>nasiona</td><td>V</td><td>ziele</td><td>zioła</td></tr>
</table>

5. The word 'child' is of neuter gender. The stems in the sg. and pl. are different:

<table>
<tr><td colspan="3">**dziecko** *child* (irregular pl.)</td></tr>
<tr><td></td><td>Sg.</td><td>Pl.</td></tr>
<tr><td>N</td><td>dziecko</td><td>dzieci</td></tr>
<tr><td>G</td><td>dziecka</td><td>dzieci</td></tr>
<tr><td>D</td><td>dziecku</td><td>dzieciom</td></tr>
<tr><td>A</td><td>dziecko</td><td>dzieci</td></tr>
<tr><td>I</td><td>dzieckiem</td><td>dziećmi (!)</td></tr>
<tr><td>L</td><td>dziecku</td><td>dzieciach</td></tr>
<tr><td>V</td><td>dziecko</td><td>dzieci</td></tr>
</table>

6. The word 'sky' has an irregular plural stem extension -'os-, and certain optional archaic plural forms:

niebo *sky, heaven* (irregular pl. stem)

	Sg.	Pl.
N	niebo	niebiosa or archaic niebiosy
G	nieba	niebios or archaic niebiosów
D	niebu	niebiosom
A	niebo	niebiosa
I	niebem	niebiosami
L	niebie	niebiosach or archaic niebiesiech
V	niebo	niebiosa or archaic niebiosy

Npl. **nieba** occurs in exclamations of the type **O wielkie nieba!** *O great (=merciful) heavens!*.

7. The noun **zło** *evil* has the anomalous Lsg. form **złu**.

8. Neuter indeclinables. A large number of words ending in **-o, -i, -y, -e**, and vowel plus **-a** are neuter in gender and do not take endings in either singular or plural. Among neuter indeclinables are such words as **bikini** *bikini*, **boa** *boa*, **canoe** *canoe*, **etui** *glasses case*, **grafitti** *grafitti*, **hobby** *hobby*, **jury** *jury*, **kombi** *station wagon*, **salami** *salami*, and many others. It is striking that foreign borrowings in consonant plus **o** often do not assimilate to regular neuter noun declension. For example, the following words are indeclinable: **awokado** *avocado*, **dżudo** *judo*, **gestapo** *Gestapo*, **igloo** *igloo*, **karo** *diamond card-suit*, **mango** *mango-fruit*, **molo** *breakwater*, **porto** *portwine*. By contrast, **auto** *car*, **kino** *cinema*, **palto** *overcoat*, **rondo** *round-a-about*, *hat-brim*, **tango** *tango*, and some others are declined; **kapo** *prison-camp foreman* and **poncho** *"ponczo" poncho* are usually not declined, but can be.

   The animals **gnu** *gnu*, **kudu** *kudu* are either feminine or neuter; **okapi** *okapi* is either masculine or feminine. The animal **kiwi** *kiwi* is masculine, while the fruit is neuter.

9. Acronyms (letter-abbreviations) ending in vowel sounds will either be treated as neuter indeclinables or as indeclinables of the gender of the head-noun of the abbreviation. For example, **CDT** (**Centralny Dom Towarowy**), pronounced and often written "**Cedete**", may take either neuter or masculine (because of **dom**) verb and modifier agreement. In speech, it will usually be declined, hence Lsg. **w cedecie**. Similarly, **PKO** (**Polska Kasa Oszczędności** *Polish Savings Association*) "**Pekao**", will not be declined and may take either neuter or feminine (because of **kasa**) verb and modifier agreement. In general, day-to-day life as a reader in Poland depends more on a knowledge of acronyms than in many other countries.

hobby *hobby* (indeclinable)

	Sg.	Pl.
N	hobby	hobby
G	hobby	hobby
D	hobby	hobby
A	hobby	hobby
I	hobby	hobby
L	hobby	hobby
V	hobby	hobby

Pekao *Pekao* (neuter or feminine indeclinable)

	Sg.	Pl.
N	Pekao	Pekao
G	Pekao	Pekao
D	Pekao	Pekao
A	Pekao	Pekao
I	Pekao	Pekao
L	Pekao	Pekao
V	Pekao	Pekao

10. Neuter adjectival nouns. A few place names are neuter adjectival in form, for example **święcone** *Easter delicacies*, **Zakopane** *(town name)*. Names for voivodeships are neuter adjectival: **Warszawskie** *Warsaw Voivodeship*, **Poznańskie** *Poznan Voivodeship*, **Krakowskie** *Crakow Voivodeship*, etc. The ILsg. of such words ends in the old (pre-1936) neuter sg. adjective ending **-em**:

Zakopane *(town name)*

	Sg.	Pl.
N	Zakopane	—
G	Zakopanego	—
D	Zakopanemu	—
A	Zakopane	—
I	Zakopanem	—
L	Zakopanem	—
V	Zakopane	—

Krakowskie *(voivodeship name)*

	Sg.	Pl.
N	Krakowskie	—
G	Krakowskiego	—
D	Krakowskiemu	—
A	Krakowskie	—
I	Krakowskiem	—
L	Krakowskiem	—
V	Krakowskie	—

Some other neuter-gender adjectival nouns would be **komorne** *rent*, **wpisowe** *membership fee*, **odjezdne** or **odchodne** *point of leaving*, as in **na odjezdnym/odchodnym** *in parting*, **odczepne** as in **na odczepne** *in getting rid of someone*.

THE MAIN NEUTER-FORMING SOFTENING FORMANTS

1. **-j-** Compare:

   morze *sea* (analyzed stem **mor-j-**)   **morski** *maritime*
   pole *field* (analyzed stem **poł-j-**)   **połać** *tract*

2. **-ʹ-**

   życie *life* (analyzed stem **żyt-ʹ-**)   **żyto** *rye*
   narzędzie *tool* (analyzed stem **narzęd-ʹ-**)   **narząd** *organ*

3. **-isk-**

   psisko *big dog* (analyzed stem **pʹs-isk-**)   **pies** *dog*
   łożysko *river-bed* (analyzed stem **łog-isk-**)   **nałóg** *addiction*

4. **-'-ąt-Øk-**

    wilczątko *wolf cub* (stem **wilk-'-ąt-Øk-**)   **wilk** *wolf*
    jagniątko *lamb* (analyzed stem **jagn-'-ąt-Øk-**)   **jagnię** *lamb*

5. **-idØł-**

    świecidło *spangle* (analyzed stem **świět-idØł-**)   **światło** *light*
    straszydło *fright* (analyzed stem **strach-idØł-**)   **strach** *fright*

The Deep Stem of Nouns of the *imię* and *zwierzę* Types

Nouns of the **imię** and **zwierzę** types exhibit a stem-forming suffix **-en-** or **-ent-** (becoming **-ęt-**), respectively. In word-final position (in the NAsg., before #), both suffixes are replaced by **-ę**. In the sg., **en** softens to **eń**, and **ęt** to **ęć**, before the formant **-'-**. In the pl., in the **-en-** type the **e: o** shift occurs before the hard dental **n**. In the **-ęt-** type, the **ę: ą** shift occurs before Gpl. **-Ø**:

		Spelled
NAVsg.	im-en-#: im'-en-#: im'-ę:	imię
Gsg.	im-en-'-a: im'-eń-a:	imienia
NAVpl.	im-en-a: im'-en-a: im'-on-a:	imiona
Gpl.	im-en-Ø: im'-en-Ø: im'-on-Ø:	imion
NAVsg.	zwier-ent-#: zwierz-ęt-#: zwierz-ę:	zwierzę
Gsg.	zwier-ent-'-a: zwierzęt-'-a: zwierz-ęć-a:	zwierzęcia
NAVpl.	zwier-ent-a: zwierz-ęt-a:	zwierzęta
Gpl.	zwier-ent-Ø: zwierz-ęt-Ø: zwierz-ąt-Ø:	zwierząt

PLURALIA TANTUM (PLURAL-ONLY NOUNS)

Some nouns occur only in the plural and therefore do not exhibit gender in the same way as other nouns (since gender is primarily of significance for the singular). Nevertheless, for convenience in listing, plural-only nouns may be grouped according to whether they follow a feminine-like, masculine-like, or neuter-like declension. Some soft-stems, like **binokle** G **binokli** *binocles*, **lędźwie** G **lędźwi** *loins*, could be equally well assigned to the feminine-like or the masculine-like group; here they are placed in the masculine-like group. Some plural-only nouns, like **okowy** G **oków** or **okowów** *fetters, chains*, have alternate Genitive endings, placing them in one group or the other.

1. Plural-only nouns with feminine-like endings include **andrzejki** G **andrzejek** *melted wax divination ceremony*, **chrzciny** G **chrzcin** *baptism*, **ciarki** G **ciarek** *creeps*, **dożynki** G **dożynek** *harvest festival*, **drzwi** G **drzwi** *door*, **ferie** G **ferii** *inter-term holidays*, **gratulacje** G **gratulacji** *compliments, congratulations*, **idy** G **id** *Ides*, **imieniny** G **imienin** *name-day*, **kajdany** G **kajdan** *shackles*, **kolonie** **kolonii** *summer camp*, **kombinerki** G **kombinerek** *pliers*, **konopie** **konopi** *hemp*, **koszary** G **koszar** *barracks*, **łaskotki** G **łaskotek** *the tickles*, **majtki** G **majtek** *panties*, **nożyczki** G **nożyczek** *scissors*, **odwiedziny** G **odwiedzin** *visit*, **oględziny** G **oględzin**,

postrzyżyny G **postrzyżyn** *hair-clipping ritual*, **przeprosiny** G **przeprosin** *apology*, **rajstopy** G **rajstop** *tights, panty-hose*, **regaty** regat *regatta*, **skrzypce** G **skrzypiec** *violin*, **sanie** G **sań** I **sańmi** (or *saniami*) *sleigh*, **spaliny** spalin *exhaust* **spodnie** G **spodni** *trousers*, **suchoty** suchot *consumption*, **szczypce** **szczypiec** *pincers*, **urodziny** G **urodzin** *birthday*, **wakacje** G **wakacji** *vacation(s)*, **widły** G **wideł** *pitchfork*, **gacie** G **gaci** *drawers*.

Town names in **-ce** belong to this type: **Chojnice** G **Chojnic**, **Dębice** G **Dębic**, **Kielce** G **Kielc**, **Katowice** G **Katowic**, **Siedlce** G **Siedlec**, and so on. Some other geographical names with a feminine-like declension would be **Ateny** G **Aten** *Athens*, **Alpy** G **Alp** *The Alps*, **Bieszczady** G **Bieszczad** *Bieszczady Mountains*, **Filipiny** G **Filipin** *The Phillipines*, **Karpaty** G **Karpat** *The Carpathian Mtns.*, **Kujawy** G **Kujaw** *Kujawy Region*, **Mazury** G **Mazur** *Mazury Region*, **Morawy** G **Moraw** *Moravia*, **Prusy** G **Prus** *Prussia*, **Tatry** G **Tatr** *Tatra Mountains*, **Teby** G **Teb** *Thebes*.

Some of the foregoing may have been historically masculine with an old Gpl. ending **-∅**; such is the case with these country-names: **Chiny** G **Chin** *China*, **Czechy** G **Czech** *Bohemia*, **Niemcy** G **Niemiec** L **Niemczech** *Germany*, **Prusy** G **Prus** *Prussia*, **Węgry** G **Węgier** L **Węgrzech** *Hungary*, **Włochy** G **Włoch** L **Włoszech** *Italy*. Note with two of these words the archaic Lpl. ending **-ech**.

2. Plural-only nouns with masculine-like endings include **bary** G **barów** *shoulders*, **bokobrody** G **bokobrodów** *side-whiskers*, **chaszcze** G **chaszczów** or **chaszczy** *thicket*, **cięgi** G **cięgów** *drubbing*, **ciuchy** G **ciuchów** *duds*, **cugle** G **cugli** *reins*, **dzieje** G **dziejów** *history*, **dżinsy** **dżinsów** *jeans*, **finanse** G **finansów** *finances*, **flaki** G **flaków** *tripe*, **fochy** G **fochów** *whims, airs*, **fumy** G **fumów** *whims*, **fusy** G **fusów** *coffee or tea grounds*, **grabie** G **grabi** *rake*, **hantle** G **hantli** *dumbells*, **ineksprymable** G **ineksprymabli** **(ineksprymablów)** *inexpressables (underwear)*, **kalesony** **kalesonów** *underwear*, **kleszcze** G **kleszczy** *tongs*, **kudły** G **kudłów** (rarely **kudeł**) *curls*, **kuluary** G **kuluarów** *corridors-fig.*, **lejce** G **lejców** *reins*, **manowce** G **manowców** *tractless land*, **modły** G **modłów** *prayers*, **nieszpory** G **nieszporów** *vespers*, **obcęgi** G **obcęgów** *pliers*, **okulary** G **okularów** *eyeglasses*, **organy** G **organów** *organ*, **otręby** G **otrębów** or **otrąb** *bran*, **penaty** G **penatów** *Penates*, **pikle** G **piklów** or **pikli** *pickle*, **plecy** G **pleców** *shoulders*, **powijaki** **powijaków** *swaddling*, **rajtuzy** G **rajtuzów** (or **rajtuz**) *riding breeches*, **slipy** **slipów** *bathing shorts*, **szarpie** G **szarpi** *lint*, **szorty** G **szortów** *shorts*, **wczasy** **wczasów** *holiday vacation*. Among geographical names are **Andy** G **Andów** *The Andes*, **Bałkany** G **Bałkanów** *The Balkans*, **Karkonosze** G **Karkonoszy** *The Karkonosze Mountains*, **Sudety** G **Sudetów** *The Sudeten Mtns.*

3. There are only a few plural-only nouns with neuter-like endings, including **gusła** G **guseł** *sorcery*, **usta** G **ust** *mouth*, **warzywa warzyw** *vegetables*, **wrota** G **wrót** *gate*. To these may be added various Latin borrow-

ings in **-ia**: **genitalia** *genitalia* G **genitaliów**; similarly: **juwenalia** *(annual university-student costume pageant)*, **juwenilia** *juvenile works*, **realia** *realia*, **regalia** *regalia*, etc.

4. A few plural-only nouns have an adjectival declension, for example, **dane** G **danych** *data*, **drobne** G **drobnych** *small change*, **kieszonkowe** G **kieszonkowych** *pocket change*.

SYNTHETIC CHART OF REGULAR NOUN ENDINGS

		Feminine			Masculine			Neuter		
Sg.	N	*-a* (*-i*)	or	**-Ø**		**-Ø**		**-o**	or	**-e**
	G		**-y/i**		-u	or	-a		-a	
	D	**-ě**	or	*-y/i*		**-owi (-u)**			-u	
	A	**-ę**	or	**-Ø**		= N/G			= N	
	I		**-ą**			**-èm**			←	
	L		= D		-ě	or	-u		←	
	V	*-o* (*-u*)	or	**-y/i**		= L			= N	
Pl.	NV	**-y/i**	or	*-è*	(**-y/i** or **-ĭ**)	or	**-è**		**-a**	
	G	**-Ø**	or	**-y/i**	**-ów**	or	**-y/i**	**-Ø** (**-y/i**)		
	D		→			**-om**			←	
	A		= N			= N/G			= N	
	I		→			**-ami**			←	
	L		→			**-ach**			←	

Distribution of Endings

1. *Feminine.* Hard-stems in **-a** take left-hand endings; soft-stems in **-Ø** take right-hand endings; soft-stems in **-a** or **-i** take italicized alternates. Soft-stem diminutive and affectionate first names take Vsg. in **-u**.

2. *Masculine.*

   a. Animate nouns take Gsg. in **-a**. Most inanimates take Gsg. in **-u**. There are many exceptions.

   b. Animate nouns take Asg. like the Gsg. in **-a**. Inanimates take Asg.= Nsg. in **-Ø**.

   c. A small handful of nouns take Dsg. in **-u**

   d. Velar and soft stems take LVsg. in **-u**; others take LVsg. in **-ě**.

   e. Hard-stem nouns take NVpl. in (**-y/i** or **-ĭ**), with personal nouns taking **-ĭ**. Soft-stems take **-è**. Names for titles and relations tend to take NVpl. in **-owie**.

   f. Hard stems take Gpl. in **-ów**. Soft-stems take Gpl. in **-y/i**, although some, especially stems in **c**, **dz**, and **j**, take **-ów**.

   g. Personal nouns take Apl.= Gpl. All others take Apl.= Npl.

3. *Neuter*. Soft-stems take NAVsg. in **-e**; hard stems take NAVsg. in **-o**. Some soft-stem neuters with a collective meaning, or naming areas or spaces, take Gpl. in **-y/i**. A very few neuters, most importantly those in **-um**, do not decline in the sg. and take Gpl. in **-ów**. A few neuters have NAsg. in **-#** and have soft stems in the sg., hard stems in the pl. (the **imię, zwierzę** types).

SUPPLEMENT: MORPHOSYNTACTIC TYPES OF MASCULINE NOUNS, arranged from lower to higher "status".

Nsg	Gsg.	Asg	Npl	Gpl	Apl

1. Inanimate: A = N

a. Gsg. **-u** : **zeszyt** *notebook*

zeszyt	zeszytu	zeszyt	zeszyty	zeszytów	zeszyty

b. Gsg. **-a**: **młot** *hammer*

młot	młota	młot	młoty	młotów	młoty

2. Animate: Gsg. **-a** , Asg=Gsg, Apl=Npl.

a. Facultatively animate: **papieros** *cigarette*

papieros	papierosa	papierosa	papierosy	papierosów	papierosy

b. Referentially animate: **opos** *opossum*

opos	oposa	oposa	oposy	oposów	oposy

c. Especially pejorative personal: **młokos** *milksop*

młokos	młokosa	młokosa	młokosy	młokosów	młokosy

3. Personal: A=G

a. Pejorative personal: non-softening Npl: **brudas** *slob*

brudas	brudasa	brudasa	brudasy	brudasów	brudasów

b. Personal: softening Npl: **student** *student*

student	studenta	studenta	studenci	studentów	studentów

c. Honorific personal: Npl **-owie**: **Arab** *Arab*

Arab	Araba	Araba	Arabowie	Arabów	Arabów

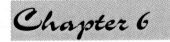

ADJECTIVES

For purposes of describing declension, adjectives may be divided into hard, velar, and soft stems. Since all adjectives share the same endings, this division is only of use for distinguishing spelling-types. The adjective declensional endings are as follows:

		Masculine	Neuter	Feminine
Sg.	NV	**-y/i**	**-è**	**-a**
	G	**-ègo**	←	**-èj**
	D	**-èmu**	←	**-èj**
	A	= N/G	= N	**-ą**
	I	**-y/im**	←	**-ą**
	L	**-y/im**	←	**-èj**

		Masculine personal		All others
Pl.	NV	**-ĭ**		**-è**
	GL		**-y/ich**	
	D		**-y/im**	
	A	= G		= N
	I		**-y/imi**	

Neuter endings ILsg. **-èm** and Ipl. **-èmi** (also sometimes feminine) were eliminated by spelling reform in 1936. The ILsg. ending **-èm** may still be found on certain adjectival place names, e.g. **Zakopane**, ILsg. **Zakopanem**. Feminine endings in **-èj** are regionally pronounced close to **-yj** or even **-y**.

THE FEATURE "MASCULINE PERSONAL" FOR ADJECTIVES

The noun category "masculine personal" refers to (a) all-male groups of people; (b) groups of people with perceived mixed male and female constituency; (c) sometimes, groups of people and other things. As far as adjectives are concerned, this category is of relevance in the Npl., where a special ending applies, and in the Apl., which agrees with the masculine-personal noun in taking the form of the Gpl. Compare:

To są [dobrzy, mili, zajęci, zadowoleni] studenci.
Those are good, nice, busy, satisfied students-N-m.p.pl.

To są [dobre, miłe, zajęte, zadowolone] studentki.
Those are good, nice, busy, satisfied students-Npl.fem.

Pamiętam wszystkich moich dobrych studentów.
I remember all my good students-m.p.pl.

Pamiętam wszystkie moje dobre studentki.
I remember all my good students-fem.

ADJECTIVE-NOUN AGREEMENT

Adjectives agree with the noun modified as to gender, number and (almost always) case, whether or not the adjective is in close proximity with the modified noun. Thus, an adjective occurring by itself in the predicate will still refer in gender to the noun with which the adjective is connected:

Oboje moi rodzice są młodzi. *Both my parents are young.*

Ojciec jest młody, ale matka jest jeszcze młodsza. *Father is young- masc., but mother is even younger-fem.*

Miałem go za człowieka bardziej inteligentnego. *I took him for a more intelligent person.*

As a partial exception to the case-agreement principle, in old-fashioned usage the Instrumental case can be found in the predicate after certain verbs and in certain constructions instead of or alongside the possibly expected Nominative, as in

On okazał się *zdolnym. He-N turned out to be talented-I.*

This usage is more common after the infinitive **być**, although here, too, in contemporary Polish, the Nominative occurs in such contructions.

Ona chce być *szczęśliwą. She-N wants to be happy-I.*

In some constructions, the principle of grammatical agreement of a predicate adjective with the noun of reference is quite strong. See such expressions as the following, discussed in Chapter 8:

Moich pięć sióstr jest zadowolonych. *My five sisters-Gpl. are satisfied-Gpl.*

The metalinguistic use of an item may prompt neuter agreement:

Autorskie ja **pojawia się dopiero w końcu opowieści.** *The authorial "I" turns up only at the end of the story.*

Spośród wszystkich dźwięków polskich, *cz* **jest szczególnie** *trudne. Out of all the Polish sounds, "cz" is especially difficult.*

ADJECTIVE-NOUN ORDER

Qualitative adjectives (adjectives directly modifying a noun as to some quality) are normally placed in front of the noun: **słodka herbata** *sweet tea,* **duże przesiębiorstwo** *large enterprise,* **wymagający dyrektor** *a demanding manager,* **wolny kraj** *free country,* **białe ściany** *white walls.* Adjectives referring to the type of a thing rather than some quality of it usually occur after the noun: compare **zwykły kleszcz** *an ordinary tick* to **kleszcz zwykły** *The Common Tick*; **teatralny gest** *a theatrical gesture* to **gest teatralny** *a gesture used in the theater*; **piękna literatura** *beautiful literature* to **literatura piękna** *belles lettres*. Usually type-adjectives are derived from a noun, as **choroba dziecięca** *childhood disease*, **gitara elektryczna** *electric guitar*, **fryzjer męski** *men's hairdresser*, **hymn narodowy** *national anthem*, **drzewo iglaste** *coniferous tree*. If more than one type-adjective occurs with a noun, the outer modifying adjective(s) will be moved in front of the noun: **Państwowe Monopol Spirytusowy** *State Liquor Monopoly*, **Polskie Towarzystwo Językoznawcze** *Polish Linguistic Society*.

Qualitative adjectives often become placed after the noun in set expressions, as in **dzień dobry** *hello*, (but **dobra noc** *"do-BRA-noc" good night*), **Pismo Święte** *Holy Scripture*. Language adjectives usually follow **język** *language, tongue:* **język polski** *the Polish language*. Post-nominal position may also be used for emphasis, as though expressing a relative clause: **dyrektor wymagający** *a manager who is demanding*, **polszczyzna piękna i poprawna** *Polish which is beautiful and correct*.

SOUND-CHANGES IN ADJECTIVAL DECLENSION

1. **k** and **g** go to **k'** and **g'** before endings beginning with **y** or **è**: **wielk-y**: **wielk'-y/i**, spelled **wielki**; **wielk-è**: **wielk'-e**, spelled **wielkie**.

2. Hard (primary) consonants are replaced by their R1 counterparts before the NV masc. pers. pl. ending **-ĭ**: **dobr-ĭ**: **dobrz-y/i**, spelled **dobrzy**; **chud-ĭ**: **chudź-y/i**, spelled **chudzi**; **wielk-ĭ**: **wielc-y/i**, spelled **wielcy**; **cich-ĭ**: **ciś-y/i**, spelled **cisi** *quiet*.

3. Also before **-ĭ**, **ż** is replaced by **ź** in the instance of **duży**: **duż-ĭ**: **duź-y/i**, spelled **duzi** *large*; **sz** is replaced by **ś** in **pieszy**: **piesz-ĭ**: **pieś-y/i**, spelled **piesi** *pedestrian*. Otherwise, soft consonants remain unchanged before **-ĭ**: **gorąc-ĭ**: **gorąc-y/i**, spelled **gorący** *hot*; **zajęcz-ĭ**: **zajęcz-y/i**, spelled **zajęczy** *hare's*; **cudz-ĭ**: **cudz-y/i**, spelled **cudzy** *foreign*; **chyż-ĭ**: **chyż-y/i**, spelled **chyży** *fleet*; **hoż-ĭ**: **hoż-y/i**, spelled **hoży** *comely*

4. The **e: o** shift is visible in the NV masc. pers. pl. of passive participles ending in **-ony** and in the word **wesoły**, in which instances only the NV masc. pers. pl. form retains the original vowel **e: zmęczony** *tired*, NVm.p.pl. **zmęczeni; wesoły** *merry*, NV m.p.pl. **weseli**. The NVm.p.pl. of the non-participle **czerwony** *red* is **czerwoni**; however, the NVm.p.pl. of **zielony** *green* is **zieleni** (or sometimes **zieloni**). The **ě: a** alternation does not occur in the adjective; see **biały** *white*, NVm.p.pl. **biali; śmiały** *bold*, NVm.p.pl. **śmiali; mile widziany** *welcome*, NVm.p.pl. **mile widziani**.

EXAMPLES OF DECLINED ADJECTIVES

Representatives of most stem-types are given. The potentially most distinct form from type to type is that of the NVm.p.pl.

skąpy *stingy* (p-stem)

	Sg.			Pl.	
	Masc.	Neut.	Fem.	Masc. pers.	Other
NV	skąpy	skąpe	skąpa	skąpi	skąpe
G	skąpego	←	skąpej	skąpych	←
D	skąpemu	←	skąpej	skąpym	←
A	= N/G	skąpe	skąpą	skąpych	skąpe
I	skąpym	←	skąpą	skąpymi	←
L	skąpym	←	skąpej	skąpych	←

słaby *weak* (b-stem)

	Sg.			Pl.	
	Masc.	Neut.	Fem.	Masc. pers.	Other
NV	słaby	słabe	słaba	słabi	słabe
G	słabego	←	słabej	słabych	←
D	słabemu	←	słabej	słabym	←
A	= N/G	słabe	słabą	słabych	słabe
I	słabym	←	słabą	słabymi	←
L	słabym	←	słabej	słabych	←

chciwy *greedy* (w-stem)

	Sg.			Pl.	
	Masc.	Neut.	Fem.	Masc. pers.	Other
NV	chciwy	chciwe	chciwa	chciwi	chciwe
G	chciwego	←	chciwej	chciwych	←
D	chciwemu	←	chciwej	chciwym	←
A	= N/G	chciwe	chciwą	chciwych	chciwe
I	chciwym	←	chciwą	chciwymi	←
L	chciwym	←	chciwej	chciwych	←

łakomy *thirsty* (m-stem)

	Sg.			Pl.	
	Masc.	Neut.	Fem.	Masc. pers.	Other
NV	łakomy	łakome	łakoma	łakomi	łakome
G	łakomego	←	łakomej	łakomych	←
D	łakomemu	←	łakomej	łakomym	←
A	= N/G	łakome	łakomą	łakomych	łakome
I	łakomym	←	łakomą	łakomymi	←
L	łakomym	←	łakomej	łakomych	←

bogaty *rich* (**t**-stem)

	Sg.			Pl.	
	Masc.	Neut.	Fem.	Masc. pers.	Other
NV	bogaty	bogate	bogata	bogaci	bogate
G	bogatego	←	bogatej	bogatych	←
D	bogatemu	←	bogatej	bogatym	←
A	= N/G	bogate	bogatą	bogatych	bogate
I	bogatym	←	bogatą	bogatymi	←
L	bogatym	←	bogatej	bogatych	←

chudy *thin, scrawny* (**d**-stem)

	Sg.			Pl.	
	Masc.	Neut.	Fem.	Masc. pers.	Other
NV	chudy	chude	chuda	chudzi	chude
G	chudego	←	chudej	chudych	←
D	chudemu	←	chudej	chudym	←
A	= N/G	chude	chudą	chudych	chude
I	chudym	←	chudą	chudymi	←
L	chudym	←	chudej	chudych	←

łasy *avid, greedy* (**s**-stem)

	Sg.			Pl.	
	Masc.	Neut.	Fem.	Masc. pers.	Other
NV	łasy	łase	łasa	łasi	łase
G	łasego	←	łasej	łasych	←
D	łasemu	←	łasej	łasym	←
A	= N/G	łase	łasą	łasych	łase
I	łasym	←	łasą	łasymi	←
L	łasym	←	łasej	łasych	←

czysty *clean* (**st**-stem)

	Sg.			Pl.	
	Masc.	Neut.	Fem.	Masc. pers.	Other
NV	czysty	czyste	czysta	czyści	czyste
G	czystego	←	czystej	czystych	←
D	czystemu	←	czystej	czystym	←
A	= N/G	czyste	czystą	czystych	czyste
I	czystym	←	czystą	czystymi	←
L	czystym	←	czystej	czystych	←

ścisły *precise* (sł-stem)

Sg.

	Masc.	Neut.	Fem.
NV	ścisły	ściśle	ścisła
G	ścisłego	←	ścisłej
D	ścisłemu	←	ścisłej
A	= N/G	ściśle	ścisłą
I	ścisłym	←	ścisłą
L	ścisłym	←	ścisłej

Pl.

	Masc. pers.	Other
NV	ściśli	ściśle
G	ścisłych	←
D	ścisłym	←
A	ścisłych	ściśle
I	ścisłymi	←
L	ścisłych	←

wesoły *merry* (oł-stem)

Sg.

	Masc.	Neut.	Fem.
NV	wesoły	wesołe	wesoła
G	wesołego	←	wesołej
D	wesołemu	←	wesołej
A	= N/G	wesołe	wesołą
I	wesołym	←	wesołą
L	wesołym	←	wesołej

Pl.

	Masc. pers.	Other
NV	weseli	wesołe
G	wesołych	←
D	wesołym	←
A	wesołych	wesołe
I	wesołymi	←
L	wesołych	←

zły *bad, angry* (zł-stem)

Sg.

	Masc.	Neut.	Fem.
NV	zły	złe	zła
G	złego	←	złej
D	złemu	←	złej
A	= N/G	złe	złą
I	złym	←	złą
L	złym	←	złej

Pl.

	Masc. pers.	Other
NV	źli	złe
G	złych	←
D	złym	←
A	złych	złe
I	złymi	←
L	złych	←

biały *white* (ł-stem)

Sg.

	Masc.	Neut.	Fem.
NV	biały	białe	biała
G	białego	←	białej
D	białemu	←	białej
A	= N/G	białe	białą
I	białym	←	białą
L	białym	←	białej

Pl.

	Masc. pers.	Other
NV	biali	białe
G	białych	←
D	białym	←
A	białych	białe
I	białymi	←
L	białych	←

biedny *poor* (n-stem)

	Sg.			Pl.	
	Masc.	Neut.	Fem.	Masc. pers.	Other
NV	biedny	biedne	biedna	biedni	biedne
G	biednego	←	biednej	biednych	←
D	biednemu	←	biednej	biednym	←
A	= N/G	biedne	biedną	biednych	biedne
I	biednym	←	biedną	biednymi	←
L	biednym	←	biednej	biednych	←

zmęczony *tired* (participle on-stem)

	Sg.			Pl.	
	Masc.	Neut.	Fem.	Masc. pers.	Other
NV	zmęczony	zmęczone	zmęczona	zmęczeni	zmęczone
G	zmęczonego	←	zmęczonej	zmęczonych	←
D	zmęczonemu	←	zmęczonej	zmęczonym	←
A	= N/G	zmęczone	zmęczoną	zmęczonych	zmęczone
I	zmęczonym	←	zmęczoną	zmęczonymi	←
L	zmęczonym	←	zmęczonej	zmęczonych	←

czerwony *red* (non-participle on-stem)

	Sg.			Pl.	
	Masc.	Neut.	Fem.	Masc. pers.	Other
NV	czerwony	czerwone	czerwona	czerwoni	czerwone
G	czerwonego	←	czerwonej	czerwonych	←
D	czerwonemu	←	czerwonej	czerwonym	←
A	= N/G	czerwone	czerwoną	czerwonych	czerwone
I	czerwonym	←	czerwoną	czerwonymi	←
L	czerwonym	←	czerwonej	czerwonych	←

wczesny *early* (sn-stem)

	Sg.			Pl.	
	Masc.	Neut.	Fem.	Masc. pers.	Other
NV	wczesny	wczesne	wczesna	wcześni	wczesne
G	wczesnego	←	wczesnej	wczesnych	←
D	wczesnemu	←	wczesnej	wczesnym	←
A	= N/G	wczesne	wczesną	wczesnych	wczesne
I	wczesnym	←	wczesną	wczesnymi	←
L	wczesnym	←	wczesnej	wczesnych	←

chory *sick* (**r**-stem)

Sg.

Pl.

	Masc.	Neut.	Fem.	Masc. pers.	Other
NV	chory	chore	chora	chorzy	chore
G	chorego	←	chorej	chorych	←
D	choremu	←	chorej	chorym	←
A	= N/G	chore	chorą	chorych	chore
I	chorym	←	chorą	chorymi	←
L	chorym	←	chorej	chorych	←

brzydki *ugly* (**k**-stem)

Sg.

Pl.

	Masc.	Neut.	Fem.	Masc. pers.	Other
NV	brzydki	brzydkie	brzydka	brzydcy	brzydkie
G	brzydkiego	←	brzydkiej	brzydkich	←
D	brzydkiemu	←	brzydkiej	brzydkim	←
A	= N/G	brzydkie	brzydką	brzydkich	brzydkie
I	brzydkim	←	brzydką	brzydkimi	←
L	brzydkim	←	brzydkiej	brzydkich	←

długi *long* (**g**-stem)

Sg.

Pl.

	Masc.	Neut.	Fem.	Masc. pers.	Other
NV	długi	długie	długa	dłudzy	długie
G	długiego	←	długiej	długich	←
D	długiemu	←	długiej	długim	←
A	= N/G	długie	długą	długich	długie
I	długim	←	długą	długimi	←
L	długim	←	długiej	długich	←

cichy *quiet* (**ch**-stem)

Sg.

Pl.

	Masc.	Neut.	Fem.	Masc. pers.	Other
NV	cichy	ciche	cicha	cisi	ciche
G	cichego	←	cichej	cichych	←
D	cichemu	←	cichej	cichym	←
A	= N/G	ciche	cichą	cichych	ciche
I	cichym	←	cichą	cichymi	←
L	cichym	←	cichej	cichych	←

błahy *trite, trivial* (**h**-stem)

	Sg.			Pl.	
	Masc.	Neut.	Fem.	Masc. pers.	Other
NV	błahy	błahe	błaha	błazi or błasi	błahe
G	błahego	←	błahej	błahych	←
D	błahemu	←	błahej	błahym	←
A	= N/G	błahe	błahą	błahych	błahe
I	błahym	←	błahą	błahymi	←
L	błahym	←	błahej	błahych	←

głupi *stupid* (**p'**-stem)

	Sg.			Pl.	
	Masc.	Neut.	Fem.	Masc. pers.	Other
NV	głupi	głupie	głupia	głupi	głupie
G	głupiego	←	głupiej	głupich	←
D	głupiemu	←	głupiej	głupim	←
A	= N/G	głupie	głupią	głupich	głupie
I	głupim	←	głupią	głupimi	←
L	głupim	←	głupiej	głupich	←

The masc.pers. forms of many of the following adjectives can be formed, but do not normally occur for logical-semantic reasons.

pawi *peacock's* (**w'**-stem)

	Sg.			Pl.	
	Masc.	Neut.	Fem.	Masc. pers.	Other
NV	pawi	pawie	pawia	pawi	pawie
G	pawiego	←	pawiej	pawich	←
D	pawiemu	←	pawiej	pawim	←
A	= N/G	pawie	pawią	pawich	pawie
I	pawim	←	pawią	pawimi	←
L	pawim	←	pawiej	pawich	←

olbrzymi *giant* (**m'**-stem)

	Sg.			Pl.	
	Masc.	Neut.	Fem.	Masc. pers.	Other
NV	olbrzymi	olbrzymie	olbrzymia	olbrzymi	olbrzymie
G	olbrzymiego	←	olbrzymiej	olbrzymich	←
D	olbrzymiemu	←	olbrzymiej	olbrzymim	←
A	= N/G	olbrzymie	olbrzymią	olbrzymich	olbrzymie
I	olbrzymim	←	olbrzymią	olbrzymimi	←
L	olbrzymim	←	olbrzymiej	olbrzymich	←

łabędzi *swan's* (**dź**-stem)

Sg.

	Masc.	Neut.	Fem.
NV	łabędzi	łabędzie	łabędzia
G	łabędziego	←	łabędziej
D	łabędziemu	←	łabędziej
A	= N/G	łabędzie	łabędzią
I	łabędzim	←	łabędzią
L	łabędzim	←	łabędziej

Pl.

	Masc. pers.	Other
NV	łabędzi	łabędzie
G	łabędzich	←
D	łabędzim	←
A	łabędzich	łabędzie
I	łabędzimi	←
L	łabędzich	←

pszczeli *bee's* (**l**-stem)

Sg.

	Masc.	Neut.	Fem.
NV	pszczeli	pszczele	pszczela
G	pszczelego	←	pszczelej
D	pszczelemu	←	pszczelej
A	= N/G	pszczele	pszczelą
I	pszczelim	←	pszczelą
L	pszczelim	←	pszczelej

Pl.

	Masc. pers.	Other
NV	pszczeli	pszczele
G	pszczelich	←
D	pszczelim	←
A	pszczelich	pszczele
I	pszczelimi	←
L	pszczelich	←

przedni *anterior, front* (**ń**-stem)

Sg.

	Masc.	Neut.	Fem.
NV	przedni	przednie	przednia
G	przedniego	←	przedniej
D	przedniemu	←	przedniej
A	= N/G	przednie	przednią
I	przednim	←	przednią
L	przednim	←	przedniej

Pl.

	Masc. pers.	Other
NV	przedni	przednie
G	przednich	←
D	przednim	←
A	przednich	przednie
I	przednimi	←
L	przednich	←

gorący *hot* (**c**-stem)

Sg.

	Masc.	Neut.	Fem.
NV	gorący	gorące	gorąca
G	gorącego	←	gorącej
D	gorącemu	←	gorącej
A	= N/G	gorące	gorącą
I	gorącym	←	gorącą
L	gorącym	←	gorącej

Pl.

	Masc. pers.	Other
NV	gorący	gorące
G	gorących	←
D	gorącym	←
A	gorących	gorące
I	gorącymi	←
L	gorących	←

cudzy *alien, another's* (**dz**-stem)

	Sg.			Pl.	
	Masc.	Neut.	Fem.	Masc. pers.	Other
NV	cudzy	cudze	cudza	cudzy	cudze
G	cudzego	←	cudzej	cudzych	←
D	cudzemu	←	cudzej	cudzym	←
A	= N/G	cudze	cudzą	cudzych	cudze
I	cudzym	←	cudzą	cudzymi	←
L	cudzym	←	cudzej	cudzych	←

czczy *empty, vain* (**cz**-stem)

	Sg.			Pl.	
	Masc.	Neut.	Fem.	Masc. pers.	Other
NV	czczy	czcze	czcza	czczy	czcze
G	czczego	←	czczej	czczych	←
D	czczemu	←	czczej	czczym	←
A	= N/G	czcze	czczą	czczych	czcze
I	czczym	←	czczą	czczymi	←
L	czczym	←	czczej	czczych	←

szczurzy *rat's* (**rz**-stem)

	Sg.			Pl.	
	Masc.	Neut.	Fem.	Masc. pers.	Other
NV	szczurzy	szczurze	szczurza	szczurzy	szczurze
G	szczurzego	←	szczurzej	szczurzych	←
D	szczurzemu	←	szczurzej	szczurzym	←
A	= N/G	szczurze	szczurzą	szczurzych	szczurze
I	szczurzym	←	szczurzą	szczurzymi	←
L	szczurzym	←	szczurzej	szczurzych	←

hoży *comely* (**ż**-stem)

	Sg.			Pl.	
	Masc.	Neut.	Fem.	Masc. pers.	Other
NV	hoży	hoże	hoża	hoży	hoże
G	hożego	←	hożej	hożych	←
D	hożemu	←	hożej	hożym	←
A	= N/G	hoże	hożą	hożych	hoże
I	hożym	←	hożą	hożymi	←
L	hożym	←	hożej	hożych	←

duży *large* (ż-stem, Npl. masc.pers.pl. **-zi**)

	Sg. Masc.	Neut.	Fem.	Pl. Masc. pers.	Other
NV	duży	duże	duża	duzi	duże
G	dużego	←	dużej	dużych	←
D	dużemu	←	dużej	dużym	←
A	= N/G	duże	dużą	dużych	duże
I	dużym	←	dużą	dużymi	←
L	dużym	←	dużej	dużych	←

SHORT-FORM MASCULINES

A number of adjectives optionally take Nsg. masc. in **-Ø** in predicate or immediate post-nominal position. Other than **pewien** *certain* instead of **pewny**, short forms are nowadays going out of use; some are already obsolete. Such adjectives include **ciekawy** or **ciekaw** *curious*, **godny** or **godzien** *worthy*, **gotowy** or **gotów** *ready*, **łaskawy** or **łaskaw** *gracious, kind*, **pełny** or **pełen** *full*, **pewny** or **pewien** *certain*, **próżny** *empty, vain* or obsolete **próżen**, **syty** or obsolete **syt** *satiated*, **świadomy** or **świadom** *conscious, aware*, **wart** *worth*, **wesoły** or **wesół** *merry, gay*, **winny** or **winien** *to blame, owing*, **zdrowy** or **zdrów** *healthy, well*, **żywy** or **żyw** *alive*. The short form, if it occurs, will usually be in predicate or post-nominal position:

Bądź wesół i zdrów. *Be happy and well.*

Jesteś pewien? *Are your sure?*

Czy już jesteś gotów? *Are you ready yet?*

Pan będzie łaskaw ciszej mówić. *Be so kind as to talk more quietly.*

To jest człowiek godzien uwagi. *That's a man worthy of attention.*

To był dzień pełen przygód. *It was a day full of adventure.*

Pewien instead of **pewny** occurs in pre-nominal position in the sense 'a certain':

Zjawił się pewien człowiek z teczką. *A certain man with a briefcase showed up.*

The adjectives **rad** *happy* and **wart** *worth* occur only in predicate position, and, in the masculine, have only short forms:

Rad jestem, że mogę to zrobić dla ciebie. *I'm glad that I can do that for you.*

Dzisiaj nie jestem nic wart. *I'm not worth anything today.*

A nearly defunct possessive adjective with a short Nsg. masc. form can be derived from male nouns and first names, as in **Michałów dom** *Michael's home*, **Michałowa siostra** *Michael's sister*, **Michałowe łóżko** *Michael's bed* (from **Michał**).

DIMINUTIVE ADJECTIVES

Many common Polish adjectives form a diminutive, typically with an affectionately intensifying force, as **cichuteńki** *nice and quiet*, **młodziutki** *real young*, **mokrzuteńki** *good and wet*, and so on. The usual suffixes involved are **-eńki**, **-'utki**, and **-'uśki**, the first possibly extended by **-'uś-**. A preceding stem consonant is usually, but not always, softened. Diminutive forms of adjectives may arise spontaneously. They are characteristic of colloquial speech, and are used more often by women than by men. Their overuse sounds affected. Here are some examples:

cichutki, cichuteńki cicheńki, cichuśki *quiet*
czyściutki, czyściuteńki *clean*
głupiutki, glupiuteńki *stupid*
króciutki, króciuteńki *short*
malutki, maluteńki, maluśki, malusieńki *small, teeny, tiny*
mięciutki, mięciuteńki, mięciuseńki *soft*
milutki, miluśki, milusieńki *nice*
nowiuteńki, nowiuśki, nowiutki *new*

pijaniutki, pijaniuteńki *drunk*
równiutki, równiuteńki *level*
prościutki, prościuteńki *simple*
słabiutki, słabiusieńki, słabeńki *weak*
słodziutki, słodziuteńki, słodziusieńki *sweet*
spokojniutki, spokojniuteńki *calm*
świeżutki, świeżuteńki *fresh*
szybciutki, szybciuteńki *quick*
tłuściutki, tłuścieńki *fat*
wolniutki, wolniuśki *slow*

and others

TEMPERED ADJECTIVE OPPOSITES; NEGATIVES WITHOUT POSITIVES

One may relatively freely negate an adjective by prefixing **nie-** to it, creating a 'mild or tempered opposite': **niedobry** *not exactly bad, but not good either*. Similarly, **niezły** *not bad*, **nieładny** *not pretty*, **nieświeży** *not fresh*, **niebogaty** *not rich*, **niegłodny** *not hungry*, **niedaleki** *not far*, **niedelikatny** *indelicate*, and so on. A few negative adjectives do not have positive variants, for example, **niebywały** *unheard-of*, **niechlujny** *slovenly*, **niepomierny** *immeasurable*.

INDECLINABLE ADJECTIVES

A small number of adjectives are indeclinable (do not take endings). These include **kontent** *content*, **fair** "fer" *fair* (as in **To nie jest fair** *That's not fair*), **blond** *blond*, **beż** *beige* (alongside **beżowy**), **bordo** *bordeaux* (alongside **bordowy**, a color) and certain other names of exotic colors; **maksi** "maks-i" *maxi (to-the-ankle, in women's clothing)*, **mini** *mini*. Such adjectives follow the noun they modify: **włosy blond** *blond hair*, **sukienka mini** *minidress*.

ADJECTIVES USED AS AD HOC NOUNS

In addition to the question of adjectives which are in essence nouns (so-called substantivized adjectives like **gajowy** *gamekeeper*; see Chapter 4), personal adjectives are often used by themselves in the function of nouns, for example **biały** *white man, Causasian,* **biedni** *the poor-pl.,* **bogaci** *the rich-pl.,* **chory** *sick person, patient,* **chudy** *the thin man,* **czarny** *black man,* and so on. Ad hoc substantivization occurs especially often with personal participles; see Chapter 12.

RELATIONAL ADJECTIVES

By 'relational' adjective is meant an adjective derived from a noun in the meaning "relating, pertaining, or belonging to" the noun. Relational adjectives are usually absolute in meaning, in the sense that they are not compared other than in exceptional circumstances (for example jocularly, as in **bardziej polski niż Polak** *more Polish than a Pole*).

1. *Place-name adjectives.* Polish uses place-name adjectives, especially adjectives based on town names, in situations where English simply uses the name of the town. The usual deriving suffix is **-ski**, before which velar consonants, **s**, and **z** are dropped, and various other stem-consonant simplifications take place. Town-name adjectives are not capitalized:

Białystok	białostocki	**Racibórz**	raciborski
Bydgoszcz	bydgoski	**Rzeszów**	rzeszowski
Elbląg	elbląski	**Sieradz**	sieradzki
Gdańsk	gdański	**Szczecin**	szczeciński
Kalisz	kaliski	**Toruń**	toruński
Katowice	katowicki	**Wałbrzych**	wałbrzyski
Łódź	łódzki	**Warszawa**	warszawski
Olsztyn	olsztyński	**Wrocław**	wrocławski
Opole	opolski	**Zielona Góra**	zielonogórski
Poznań	poznański		

Mobile vowels and irregular stem-changes may occasionally be observed in the adjective; see

Bielsko-Biała	bielski	**Kielce**	kielecki
Leszno	leszczyński	**Lublin**	lubelski
Moskwa	moskiewski	**Nowy Sącz**	nowosądecki
Siedlce	siedlecki		

2. *Type-adjectives.* Type-adjectives are a heterogeneous group consisting of adjectives used to qualify a noun as to type. They are usually derived from nouns; however, ordinary adjectives may acquire a typing function as well. Type-adjectives generally go together with an accompanying noun in a fixed expression, the adjective usually following the noun. The suffix is usually **-ow-** or **-'n-**:

Fixed expression	Related noun
burak cukrowy *sugar beet*	**cukier**
kleszcz zwykły *Common Tick*	—

pałka gumowa *rubber truncheon*	guma
roślina wodna *water plant*	woda
sezon zimowy *winter season*	zima
wino białe *white wine*	—
życie rodzinne *family life*	rodzina

Type adjectives do not normally occur by themselves in the predicate; hence one would not normally say *Życie jest rodzinne.

3. *Substance adjectives.* Common formants for deriving adjectives from names for substances include -'an- and -ow-:

Substance adjective:	Related noun:
gliniany *of clay*	glina
metalowy *of metal*	metal
miedziany *of copper*	miedź
stalowy *of steel*	stal
szklany *of glass*	szkło
wełniany *of wool*	wełna
Also:	
srebrny *of silver*	srebro
złoty *of gold, golden*	złoto

4. *Quality adjectives.* Suffixes used to form adjectives referring to a noun's characteristic quality include -'asty, -at-y, -ist-y, -owat-y:

Quality adjective:	Related noun:
iglasty *needle-bearing (= coniferous)*	igła
językowaty *tongue-shaped*	język
kudłaty *shaggy*	kudło
kulisty *ball-shaped*	kula
liściasty *leaf-like*	liść
pienisty *foamy*	piana
piegowaty *freckled*	pieg
srebrzysty *silvery*	srebro
szklisty *glassy*	szkło

5. *Animal-possessive adjectives.* When describing traits of animals, Polish generally uses a possessive adjective where English would normally use the noun. The suffix is usually -'-:

Animal-possessive adjective:	Related noun:
łabędzia szyja *swan-like neck*	łabędź
łabędzi śpiew *swan song*	łabędź
kocie łby *cat-heads (cobble-stones)*	kot
lisi ogon *fox's tail*	lis
lwia część *lion's share*	lew

ośle uszy *donkey's ears*	osioł
owczy ser *sheep's cheese*	owca
psia natura *dog's nature*	pies psa
wilczy apetyt *wolf-like appetite*	wilk
żabie oko *frog-eye*	żaba

Anomalous stem:

ptasie mleko *bird's milk*	ptak, dim. ptaszek

6. *Personal adjectives.* Well-known last names form possessive adjectives more often in Polish than in English, which tends to make more use of the noun by itself. The usual Polish suffix for forming personal possessives is **-owsk-**, used with non-adjectival last names:

czasy stanisławowskie *Stanislavian times* (after King Stanslaw August Poniatowski)
poemat Mickiewiczowski *a Mickiewicz narrative poem*
powieść Reymontowska *a Reymont novel*
styl szopenowski *the Chopin style*
dramat szekspirowski *Shakespearian drama*
fresk Rafaelowski *a Rafael fresco*, and so on

Capitalization depends on whether the adjective is perceived as pertaining to the individual or has an established existence as an independent adjective with a more general reference, for example, to a style.

COMPOUND ADJECTIVES

Adjectives are compounded to one another with the help of the linking suffix **-o-**:

społecznopolityczny *sociopolitical*
szczerozłoty *pure gold*
wysokogórski *high-mountain*, and so forth

COMMON ADJECTIVAL SOFTENING FORMANTS

1. **-j-**. This suffix may be distinguished from **-'-** only after dental consonants, which distinguish R2 from R3:
related noun:

chłopięcy (chłopięt-j-)	chłopię chłopięcia *boy*
cudzy (cud-j-) *foreign, strange*	cud *miracle*
sierocy (sierot-j-) *orphan's*	sierota *orphan*

2. **-'-**. One may assume the suffix **-'-** when it is not demonstrably **-j-**:

boży (bog-'-) *god's*	bóg boga *god*
koci (kot-'-) *cat's*	kot *cat*
lwi (lØw-'-) *lion's*	lew *lion*

psi (p's-'-) *dog's*   pies psa *dog*
ślimaczy (ślimak-'-) *snail's*   ślimak *snail*

One may also interpolate -'- in possessive adjectives derived from soft-stem animal names:

niedźwiedzi (niedźwiedź-'-) *bear's*   niedźwiedź *bear*
pawi (paw-'-) *peacock's*   paw pawia *peacock*

Non-softening -#-. A few derivations show adjective endings, strikingly, added directly to a velar noun-stem: **wielooki** (alongside **wielooczny** *multocular*) **kaleki** *dwarf,* **dwunogi** (alternatively **dwunożny**) *bipedal,* **czwororęki** (alongside **czwororęczny**) *four-handed.*

3. -'n-. Before this suffix, velar consonants, s, and z change to R2:

bezbrzeżny (bezbrzeg-'n-) *boundless*   brzeg *shore*
brudny (brud-'n-) *dirty*   brud *dirt*
chłodny (chłod-'n-) *chilly*   chłód chłodu *cold*
głośny (głos-'n-) *loud*   głos *voice*
mroźny (mroz-'n-) *frosty*   mróz mrozu *frost*
muzyczny (muzyk-'n-) *musical*   muzyka *music*
senny (sen-'n-) *sleepy*   sen *sleep*

4. -'sk- . Before this suffix, various consonant substitutions take place: ł goes to l; n goes to ń; s, z, k, g drop; t, d combine with -sk- to form -ck-, -dz-; rz reverts to r:

boski (bog-'sk-) *divine*   bóg boga *god*
diabelski (diabØł-'sk-) *devilish*   diabeł diabła *devil*
ludzki (lud-'sk-) *human*   lud *folk, people*
malborski (malbork-'sk-)   Malbork
pański (pan-'sk-) *lord's, sir's*   pan *lord, sir*
raciborski (racibor-'sk-)   Racibórz (racibor-j-)
studencki (student-'sk-) *student's*   student *student*

5. -ist-. R2 replacements occur, as expected:

kościsty (kost-ist-) *bony*   kostka *die*
mglisty (mgØł-ist-) *foggy*   mgła *fog*
mszysty (mØch-ist-) *mossy*   mech mchu *moss*
soczysty (sok-ist-) *juicy*   sok *juice*
spadzisty (spad-ist-) *precipitous*   spad *slope*

6.-'an-, -'ast-. Before these suffixes, R2 replacements occur:

druciany (drut-'an-) *of wire*   drut *wire*
gąbczasty (gąbØk-'ast-) *spongelike*   gąbka *sponge*
kraciasty (krat-'ast-) *checkered*   kratka *check*
wełniasty (wełØn-'ast-) *woolly*   wełna *wool*
wełniany (wełØn-'an-) *woolen*   wełna *wool*

COMPARISON OF ADJECTIVES

Attributive adjectives form an adjective of the comparative degree either by adding a comparative suffix to the adjective stem (-'sz- or -ejsz-) or by using separate words for 'more' (**bardziej**), 'most' (**najbardziej**).

COMPARATIVE DEGREE

1. *Suffixal comparative.* The comparative suffix -ejsz- may be added only to stems ending in two consonants, and it is added to most such stems. R2 consonant replacements occur before it. The suffix -'sz- occurs after stems ending in single consonants, and after a few stems ending in two consonants. Before -'sz-, stem consonants **ł**, **n**, and **g** soften to R2 **l**, **ń**, **ż**; other consonants are unchanged.

-ejsz-:	-'sz-
bystry bystrzejszy *fast -er*	**długi dłuższy** *long -er.*
ciepły cieplejszy *warm -er*	**gruby grubszy** *fat fatter*
dorosły doroślejszy *adult more ad.*	**miły milszy** *nice nicer*
gęsty gęściejszy *thick -er*	**drogi droższy** *dear, dearer*
łatwy łatwiejszy *easy easier*	**nowy nowszy** *new -er*
mądry mądrzejszy *wise wiser*	**stary starszy** *old -er*
ostry ostrzejszy *sharp -er*	**twardy twardszy** *hard -er*
uprzejmy uprzejmiejszy *polite*	**zdrowy zdrowszy** *healthy -ier*

The stem consonants **ch** and **h** remain unchanged before -'sz-: **błahy błahszy** *trivial, more trivial,* **cichy cichszy** *quiet quieter,* as does **k** in the few instances where it occurs before -'sz-: **wielki większy** *large larger.*

Of adjectives taking -**ejsz**-, those ending in consonant plus the suffix -'n- are extremely numerous:

ciemny ciemniejszy *dark -er*	**sprytny sprytniejszy** *clever -er*
grzeczny -niejszy *polite, more p.*	**trudny trudniejszy** *difficult, more d.*
jasny jaśniejszy *bright -er*	**wolny wolniejszy** *free, freer,*
ładny ładniejszy *pretty prettier*	and many, many more

Adjectives with stems in -**st**- often form the comparative either way: **czysty** *clean* **czystszy** or **czyściejszy** *cleaner;* **gęsty** *thick* **gęstszy** or **gęściejszy** *thicker;* **prosty** *simple* **prostszy** or, substandard, **prościejszy** *simpler ;* **tłusty** *fat* **tłustszy** or **tłuściejszy** *fatter.*

Notes on the Suffixal Comparative

a. The adjectival suffixes -**k**-, -**ek**-, -**ok**- are dropped before -'sz-:

brzydki brzydszy *ugly, uglier*	**płytki płytszy** *shallow, shallower*
cienki cieńszy *thin, thiner*	**prędki prędszy** *rapid*
ciężki cięższy *heavy, heavier*	**rzadki rzadszy** *rare, rarer*
daleki dalszy *far, farther*	**szeroki szerszy** *wide, wider*

głęboki głębszy *deep, deeper*
miękki miększy *soft, softer*
słodki słodszy *sweet, sweeter*

szybki szybszy *quick, quicker*
wysoki wyższy *high, higher*

Irregular consonant and/or vowel substitutions occur in

bliski bliższy *near, -er*
lekki lżejszy *light, -er*

niski niższy *low, -er*
wąski węższy *narrow, narrower*

b. The **e: o** and **ě: a** shifts may be visible before the suffix **-'sz-**, with the comparative form displaying the unshifted vowel:

biały bielszy *white, whiter*
śmiały śmielszy *bold ,-er*
blady bledszy *pale, paler*

wesoły weselszy *merry, merrier*
zielony zieleńszy *green, greener*
czerwony czerwieńszy *red, redder*

c. The following adjectives, in addition to some already listed, form either suppletive or irregular comparatives:

dobry lepszy *good, better*
zły gorszy *bad, worse*
gorący gorętszy *hot hotter*

mały mniejszy *small smaller*
wielki or **duży większy**
great/large, greater/larger

2. *Analytic comparative.* The analytic comparative using **bardziej** *more* is used with most adjectives formed from nouns or verbs, and with many longer adjectives. Most adjectives with the suffixes **-ow-, -sk-, -at-, -'ast-, -ist-** form the comparative analytically:

celowy, bardziej celowy *purposeful, more purposeful*
garbaty, bardziej garbaty *hunched, more hunched*
gliniasty, bardziej gliniasty *clayish, more clayish*
pijany, bardziej pijany *drunk, drunker*
przemakalny, bardziej przemakalny *permeable, more permeable*
słoneczny, bardziej słoneczny *sunny, sunnier*
wodnisty, bardziej wodnisty *watery, more watery*

NOTES ON THE ANALYTIC COMPARATIVE

a. The analytic comparative is used with participles and with adjectives based on participles:

zajęty, bardziej zajęty *busy, busier*
interesujący, bardziej interesujący *interesting, more interesting*
zaniedbany, bardziej zaniedbany *neglected, more neglected*

An exception: **kochany najukochańszy** *most beloved, dearest*

b. A number of adjectives, including several in **-ki,** form the comparative in **bardziej** as well, including

bosy *barefoot*	**mokry** *wet*	**suchy** *dry* (or: **suchszy**)
chory *sick*	**nagi** *naked*	**szary** *gray*
gorzki *bitter*	**płaski** *flat*	**słony** *salty*
łysy *bald*	**rześki** *brisk*	**żywy** *alive*
mokry *wet*	**śliski** *slippery*	

c. Color-adjectives usually form the comparative analytically: **bardziej czerwony** (alongside **czerwieńszy**) *redder*, **bardziej zielony** (alongside rare **zieleńszy**) *greener*, **bardziej żółty** *yellower*, **bardziej niebieski** *bluer*, etc.

d. Generally speaking, most adjectives allow the analytic comparative as an option instead of the synthetic comparative with little or no difference in nuance or correctness, Polish being more liberal in this respect than English. Often the analytic comparative will be preferred in figurative uses; see **w bardziej wysokim stylu** *in a higher style* vs. **na wyższym piętrze** *on an upper floor*; however, see **bardziej żywy** *more alive* vs. **żywszy** *livelier*.

THE SUPERLATIVE

3. The superlative form of the adjective is formed by adding the prefix **naj-** either to the suffixal comparative or to the analytic comparative word **bardziej**:

łatwy *easy*	**łatwiejszy** *easier*	**najłatwiejszy** *easiest*
zepsuty *spoiled*	**bardziej zepsuty** *more spoiled*	**najbardziej zepsuty** *most spoiled*

4. *The comparative and superlative of lesser amount* are formed analytically with **mniej** *less* and **najmniej** *least*:

drogi *dear*	**mniej drogi** *less dear*	**najmniej drogi** *least dear*
ciekawy *curious*	**mniej ciekawy** *less curious*	**najmniej ciekawy** *least curious*

5. *Among adjectival upgraders and downgraders*, most important are **bardzo** *very*, **trochę** *a little, slightly*, **dość** *rather*, **nieco** *somewhat*, **całkiem** *quite*, **zbyt** *too*, **niezbyt** *not particularly*. Upgraders frequently occurring with comparatives include **o wiele** *by a lot*, **znacznie** *considerably*, **jeszcze** *even more*, **dużo** *a lot*:

znacznie bardziej inteligentny *much more intelligent*
o wiele bardziej pracowity *much more industrious*
dużo intensywniejszy *a lot more intensive*
jeszcze bardziej twórczy *even more creative*

The upgrader **dość** *rather, fairly* exists in a kind of reciprocal relationship with the downgrader **nie zbyt** *not too*:

On jest dość inteligentny. *He is rather intelligent.*

On nie jest zbyt inteligentny. *He is not too intelligent.*

ADJECTIVAL ADVERBS

Adjectival adverbs are, in effect, adjectives unmarked for gender- number, and case, since they are used to modify items without these inherent features: verbs, adverbs, and other adjectives. See

szybko reagować *respond quickly* (adverb modifying a verb)
wyjątkowo mądrze powiedziane *exceptionally well said* (adverb modifying an adverb)
świeżo malowany *freshly painted* (adverb modifying an adjective)

1. *The formation of adverbs from adjectives.*

   a. Velar and soft-stem adjectives form the adverb with the ending **-o**:

suchy sucho *dry*	**głupi głupio** *stupid*
tęgi tęgo *stout*	**tani tanio** *cheap*
wysoki wysoko *high*	**świeży świeżo** *fresh*

   The form **wysoce** *highly* is used in figurative expressions like **wysoce zabawny** *highly amusing.*

   b. Non-suffixed adjectives with stems in **p, b, s, t, d** also take the adverbial ending **-o**:

bogaty bogato *rich*	**czysty czysto** *clean*
bosy boso *barefoot*	**słaby słabo** *weak*
chudy chudo *thin*	**tępy tępo** *dull*

   c. Most adjectives with stems ending in a consonant plus **n** take **-'e**, although some take **-o**:

delikatny delikatnie *delicate*	**okrutny okrutnie** *cruel*
grzeczny grzecznie *polite*	**silny silnie** *strong*
ładny ładnie *pretty*	**sztywny sztywnie** *stiff*

   Compare with

ciemny ciemno *dark*	**pilny pilno** *urgent*
dawny dawno *former*	**trudny trudno** *difficult*

   d. Other adjectives form the adverb either in **-o** or in **-'e**, and it is difficult or impossible to give rules:

   With **-o**:

łatwy łatwo *easy*	**późny późno** *late*
mokry mokro *wet*	**szary szaro** *gray*
nowy nowo *new*	**zielony zielono** *green*

   With **-'e**:

dobry dobrze *good*	**szczęśliwy szczęśliwie** *happy*
mądry mądrze *wise*	**szczery szczerze** *sincere*
miły mile *nice*	**zły źle** *bad*

Occasionally, both endings, -'e and -o, will be found with the same adjective, differentiated in style or use:

mglisty *foggy,* adv. usually **mglisto,** but **wyrazić się mgliście** *express oneself unclearly*

wysoki *high,* adv. usually **wysoko,** but **wysoce pożądany** *highly desirable*

miły *nice, kind.* **miło** or **mile,** the former in impersonal expressions, the latter in strictly adverbial uses: **Miło było panią poznać** *It was nice to meet you.* **Byłem mile zaskoczony.** *I was pleasantly surprised.*

nudny *boring,* **nudno** or **nudnie,** the latter in strictly adverbial uses, the former always in impersonal constructions: **nudno mi** *I'm bored,* **nudnie pisać** *write boringly.*

smutny *sad* **smutno** or **smutnie,** the latter more often in strictly adverbial uses, the former in impersonal constructions: **smutno mi** *I'm sad,* vs. **smutnie wyglądać** *look sad.*

srogi *stern, severe* **srogo** or **srodze**

pilny *urgent* **pilno pilnie,** with analogous distribution to **miło, nudno, smutno: pilno** (impersonal) **pilnie** (optionally, adverbial): **pilno mi** *it's urgent for me,* **pilnie się uczyć** *study diligently*

OTHER ADVERBIAL FORMATIONS

1. Adjectives in **-ski** create a manner adverbial with **po** plus the ending **-u**:

polski *Polish*	**po polsku** *in Polish*
chłopski *peasant's*	**po chłopsku** *peasant-style*
myśliwski *hunter's*	**po myśliwsku** *hunter-style,* and others

2. A similar expression using **po** plus the neuter Dative adjective ending can be formed from some adjectives:

domowy *home-adj.*	**po domowemu** *home-style*
swój *one's own*	**po swojemu** *in one's own way*
pijany *drunk*	**po pijanemu** *while drunk,* and others

3. A relatively small number of adjectives can form adverbial expressions with **z** plus an archaic Genitive ending **-a**:

daleki *far*	**z daleka** *from afar*
lekki *light*	**z lekka** *lightly, slightly*
ostrożny *cautious*	**z ostrożna** *cautiously*
wolny *slow*	**z wolna** *slowly, gradually*
nagły *sudden*	**z nagła** *of a sudden*
lewy *left*	**z lewa** *on the left,* and some others

One may also mention here idiosyncratic expressions composed of **za** or **po** plus **-u,** as in **za młodu** *while young,* **po cichu** *on the sly,* and others.

4. Passive participles in -ty and -ny do not often form adverbs. The participle form in -o has a use as an impersonal verb. Thus **zaniedbano** means 'someone neglected (something)'; **przyjęto** means 'someone accepted (something)'; and so on (see Chapter 12). After the verbs **wyglądać** *look, appear* and **czuć się** *feel*, which ordinarily take adverbial complements, participles take **na** plus the Accusative: **wyglądasz na zmęczonego** (f. **zmęczoną**) *you look tired.* The lack of an adverb for a participle can be remedied with phrases such as **w sposób zaniedbany** *in a neglected way.* In case the participle has become a de facto independent adjective, adverbial forms in -'e may be found, especially with negated items:

nieoczekiwany *unexpected*	**nieoczekiwanie** *unexpectedly*
niespodziewany *unexpected*	**niespodziewanie** *unexpectedly*
niezbity *irrefutable*	**niezbicie** *irrefutably*
szalony *insane*	**szalenie** *insanely*

5. Various idiomatic expressions, most commonly cooking terminology, utilize **na** plus adverbs in -o:

podać na gorąco (na zimno) *serve hot (cold)*
jajka na miękko (na twardo) *soft (hard) boiled eggs*
malować na zielono *paint green*
Wszystko wykalkulował na zimno. *He worked everything out in cold blood.*

Cf.: **na nowo** anew, **na prawo** to the right, **na lewo** to the left, on the sly

DIFFERENCES BETWEEN POLISH AND ENGLISH IN THE USE OF ADVERBS

The Polish adverb in -'e or -o corresponds only roughly to the English adverb in *-ly*, for various reasons. Most importantly, it is primarily English manner and time adverbs that take *-ly*. English adverbs of place tend to be identical in form to the adjective: *highly qualified* vs. *fly high.* Both corresponding forms in Polish will take the adverbial form: **wysoko wykwalifikowany**, **lecieć wysoko.** In general, Polish requires the speaker to be more sensitive to the difference between adjective and adverb than English, in which the distinction is often blurred. Here are some specific ways in which Polish and English differ as to the use of adverbs:

1. English often drops *-ly* with certain adverbs in informal speech, a process without any analogue in Polish: *speak softly* or, colloquially, *speak soft*, but only **cicho mówić.**

2. Certain verbs which, in English, take adjectival complements, take adverbial complements in Polish, most important being **wyglądać** *look, appear* and **czuć się** *feel:*

You look funny.	**Śmiesznie wyglądasz.**
I feel bad.	**Źle się czuję.**

3. The English impersonal adjective has an adverbial correspondent in Polish:

    It's late (quiet, hot).   **Jest późno (cicho, gorąco).**

    In Polish, only factual impersonals are expressed with an adjective (in the neut. sg.):

    It's surprising that he doesn't   **Jest dziwne, że on nie zna lepiej**
    know French any better.   **francuskiego.**

4. Polish impersonal adverbs with personal Dative complements, expressing feelings and sensations, are generally expressed in English with personal predicate adjectives:

    I'm cold (sad, hot).   **Jest mi zimno (smutno, gorąco).**

5. Manner adverbs are typically placed before the verb instead of after, as in English:

    I know him well.   **Dobrze go znam.**
    You look nice.   **Ładnie wyglądasz.**
    I see poorly.   **Źle widzę.**

THE COMPARISON OF ADVERBS

Another way in which Polish is more sensitive than English to the adverbial vs. adjectival status of a word is in the use of comparative forms. English tends to blur the distinction between adjective and adverb under comparison, and often has no separate way of expressing a comparative adverb as opposed to a comparative adjective:

sing more prettily or (colloquially) *sing prettier*   **ładniej śpiewać**
be better vs. *do better* (not *weller*)   **być lepszy, robić lepiej**

A fairly reliable rule for forming the comparative of the adverb in Polish is to drop **-szy** from the comparative adjective and add **-ej** to those forms that do not already end in **-ej**.

Positive adjective	Comparative adjective	Comparative adverb
dobry *good*	**lepszy** *better*	**lepiej**
gruby *fat*	**grubszy** *fatter*	**grubiej**
jasny *bright*	**jaśniejszy** *brighter*	**jaśniej**
twardy *hard*	**twardszy** *harder*	**twardziej**
wysoki *high*	**wyższy** *higher*	**wyżej**

In case the comparative adjective is formed analytically with **bardziej**, the adjective is merely put in the adverbial form:

| **łysy** *bald* | **bardziej łysy** *balder* | **bardziej łyso** |

If added to a primary consonant stem, the suffix **-ej** is preceded by R2:

młody *young*	**młodszy** *younger*	**młodziej**
zły *bad*	**gorszy** *worse*	**gorzej**

Irregular:

duży *large*	**większy** *larger*	**więcej**
gorący *hot*	**gorętszy** *hotter*	**goręcej**

Adjectives containing a suffix with **-k-** drop the suffix and, often, have unpredictable stems in the comparative adverb:

bliski *near*	**bliższy** *nearer*	**bliżej**
brzydki *ugly*	**brzydszy** *uglier*	**brzydziej**
cienki *thin*	**cieńszy** *thinner*	**cieniej**
daleki *far*	**dalszy** *farther*	**dalej**
głęboki *deep*	**głębszy** *deeper*	**głębiej**
krótko *short*	**krótszy** *shorter*	**krócej**
lekko *light*	**lżejszy** *lighter*	**lżej**
miękki *soft*	**miększy** *softer*	**mię(k)cej**
płytki *shallow*	**płytszy** *shallower*	**płycej**
prędki *swift*	**prędszy** *swifter*	**prędzej**
rzadki *rare*	**rzadszy** *rarer*	**rzadziej**
szeroki *wide*	**szerszy** *wider*	**szerzej**
szybki *quick*	**szybszy** *quicker*	**szybciej**
wysoki *high*	**wyższy** *higher*	**wyżej**

The superlative adverb is formed by adding **naj-** either to the comparative adverb or to **bardziej**:

Positive adjective	Comparative adjective	Comparative adverb
jasny *clear*	**jaśniej**	**najjaśniej**
żywy *alive, lively*	**bardziej żywo**	**najbardziej żywo**

COMMON EXPRESSIONS USING COMPARATIVES AND SUPERLATIVES

1. *than* is translated either by **od** plus the Genitive or with the conjunction **niż**; od+G tends to be used unless clauses are being compared instead of nouns.

   On jest starszy ode mnie. *He is older than I.*

   On jest starszy niż ja. (possible but clumsy in the same meaning)

   Ona śpiewa lepiej ode mnie. *She sings better than I.*

   Ona śpiewa lepiej niż ja. (more acceptable, because the comparison is more clearly implicitly clausal).

   On jest starszy niż przypuszczałem. *He is older than I supposed.*

   Ona śpiewa ładniej niż myślałem. *She sings more prettily than I thought.* (the only possibilities, since the comparison is clausal)

2. *even (more)* is translated by **jeszcze** in combination with the comparative form of the adjective or adverb:

   Ta walizka jest ciężka, ale tamta jest jeszcze cięższa. *That suitcase is heavy, but that other one is even heavier.*

   On czyta szybko, ale ona czyta jeszcze szybciej. *He reads quickly, but she reads even more quickly.*

3. *more and more* is translated by **coraz** plus the comparative form of the adjective or adverb:

   Życie robi się coraz trudniejsze. *Life is getter more and more difficult.*

   Czytasz coraz szybciej. *You're reading faster and faster.*

4. *the... the...* is translated by **im... tym...**:

   Im starsza książka, tym cenniejsza. *The older the book, the more valuable (it is).*

   Im bardziej przepis niezrozumiały, tym lepszy. *The more incomprehensible a regulation is, the better.*

   Im szybciej, tym lepiej. *The quicker the better.*

   Im głębiej, tym chłodniej. *The deeper (you go), the colder (it gets).*

5. *as... as possible* is translated by **możliwie, jak,** or **jak można** plus the superlative form of the adjective or adverb:

   Proszę o jak (or możliwie) najtańszą wódkę. *I'd like the cheapest possible vodka.*

   Pilot wybierze możliwie najodpowiedniejsze miejsce. *The pilot will choose the most appropriate place.*

   Napisz mu jak najszybciej. *Write him as soon as possible.*

   Wszystko ułożyło się jak najlepiej. *Everything worked out as well as possible.*

   Napiszę ci to jak można najkrócej. *I'll write it for you as briefly as possible.*

6. *-est of all* in the sense 'more than anyone' is expressed with the comparative of the adjective or adverb, accompanied by **ze wszystkich**:

   Ze wszystkich pływaczy on jest najlepszy. *Of all the swimmers, he is the best.*

   In the sense 'better than anything' *most or best of all* is usually expressed simply with **najbardziej**:

   Najbardziej lubię muzykę klasyczną. *I like classical music best of all.*

7. *all the more* is expressed with **tym bardziej**:

Ten zwrot jest tym bardziej niezrozumiały, że jest wyjęty ze swojego normalnego kontekstu. *This expression is all the more incomprehensible in that it is taken out of its usual context.*

8. *by how much* is expressed with **o**+A:

Marek jest wyższy ode mnie o całą głowę. *Marek is a whole head taller than I am.*

Matka jest o rok młodsza od ojca. *Mother is a year younger than Father.*

9. The question-adverb **jak** *how, as* and the adverbial modifier **tak** *as* are used with adjectives to ask for or to help specify the degree of an adjective or adverb. In the second sentence below, note the use of the particle **aż** in combination with **tak**:

Jak długo będziesz w Paryżu? *How long will you be in Paris?*

Nie będę tam aż tak długo. *I won't be there all that long.*

The adverb **jak** is not used as often with adjectives as it is with adverbs, some other expression often being substituted for the adjective, as in

Ile lat ma twój pies? *How many years does your dog have (= how old is your dog)?* instead of

!Jak stary jest twój pies? *How old is your dog.*

Jak długo się jedzie do Łodzi? *How long does it take to get to Lodz?* instead of

!Jak długa jest podróż do Łodzi? *How long is the trip to Lodz?*

and so on.

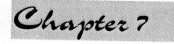

Pronouns, Pronominal Adjectives, and Pro-Adverbs

PERSONAL PRONOUNS

The class of personal pronouns consists of the following items:

1. 1st and 2nd person pronouns

	ja *I (1st pers. sg.)*		**my** *we (1st pers. pl.)*
N	**ja**	N	**my**
G	**mnie (mię)**	G	**nas**
D	**mnie, mi**	D	**nam**
A	**mnie (mię)**	A	**nas**
I	**mną**	I	**nami**
L	**mnie**	L	**nas**

The GA short form **mię** is often spoken but is not written (as a written form, **mię** is archaic). The oblique-case forms of **ja** beginning with **mn-** (**mnie, mną**) condition the appearance of a mobile vowel after prepositions ending with a consonant: **beze mnie** *without me*, **nade mną** *over me*, **ode mnie** *from me*. Stress falls on the mobile vowel: "be-ZE mnie". For the choice between long and short forms, see following discussion.

	ty *you (2nd pers. sg.)*		**wy** *you (2nd pers. pl.)*
NV	**ty**	NV	**wy**
G	**ciebie, cię**	G	**was**
D	**tobie, ci**	D	**wam**
A	**ciebie, cię**	A	**was**
I	**tobą**	I	**wami**
L	**tobie**	L	**was**

FORMAL AND INFORMAL ADDRESS

a. The 2nd-person sg. pronoun **ty** *you* is used in informal address among family members, close friends, school-mates and, often but not always, among co-workers. Using **ty** with a person amounts to being on a familiar first-name basis with that person. Otherwise, one prefaces the person's first name with **pan** *Mr., sir,* **pani** *Ms., lady, madam,* or some other title. Since 1st and 2nd-person pronouns are usually omitted in speech (see further below), "being on a **ty** basis" with someone (**być z kimś na "ty"**) usually amounts to using 2nd-person sg. verb endings with that person, and calling that person by his or her first name without a title.

b. Children and most university students address one another automatically informally (with **ty** or with informal verb-forms), and children are addressed informally by adults. However, among adults conventions of formal address (using **pan, pani**) apply unless a mutual agreement has been made to use informal address. Generally speaking, among adults (age aside), it is up to a woman to initiate such a proposal to a man. Otherwise, age or status determines the initiative. It is safest to use formal address with a person until specifically invited to use informal address.

c. One "goes over" to using **ty** with a person (**przejść z kimś na "ty"**) by repeating first names, often drinking a shot of liquor with right arms entwined (**wypić bruderszaft**), and exchanging kisses on both cheeks (including men to men). Once one has "gone over" to **ty** with a person, it is rare to return to formal address, short of an unpleasant break-off of relations, or in case one person rises very high over another person in rank or title.

d. Needless to say, indecision often arises concerning the proper form of address, whether formal or informal. After all, situations may fall somewhere in between complete informality on the one hand and radical formality on the other; and some situations may be difficult to evaluate. In such instances, when a relationship of formality or informality has not been established among people, one may avoid using verb forms which express either one situation or the other, often by employing impersonal or indirect modes of speech. Observe how the following statements omit "you":

Czy nalać herbatę? *May I pour some tea?*

Trzeba tam jeszcze raz zadzwonić. *One should call there again.*

Można zawsze spróbować. *One may always try.*

Gdzie tu się kupuje mydło? *Where does one buy soap around here?*

e. The 2nd-person pl. pronoun **wy** is the plural of **ty**, but it may be more easily used to address a group, the members of which would not be addressed individually with **ty**. In certain isolated rural regions, especially in the south, **wy** functions with singular reference as a form of polite address. The use of **wy** for singular address was formerly used toward servants and staff. Additionally, it is (mainly, was) used among Communist and Socialist Party members for singular, "comradely" address. This mannerism never caught on in Poland outside these narrow circles. For these reasons in almost all settings **wy** sounds jarring when used for singular address, whether formal or informal. For formal address with singular reference, one uses the 3rd-person pronouns of polite address **pan, pani** (see further below).

LONG VS. SHORT 1ST AND 2ND-PERSON PRONOUNS

f.   In instances where there is a choice between a long and a short form of the pronoun, the short form, inherently unstressed, is used unless emphasis or contrast is intended:

Szukam cię. *I'm looking for you.*

—Kogo szukasz? —Ciebie szukam. *Who are you looking for? I'm looking for you.*

g.   Long forms are required regardless of other considerations at the beginning of a clause:

Mnie jest łatwo. *It's easy for me-D.*

Tobie już to powiedziałem. *You-D I already told that to.*

Short forms of pronouns avoid occurrence in clause-final position if possible (as long as they are not placed in clause-initial position). Occurrence after the verb is necessary in a two-word sentence.

Pamiętam cię. *I remember you.*

Pomóż mi. *Help me.*

h.   Long forms are required after prepositions:

Tu jest coś dla ciebie *Here is something for you-G.*

Co masz przeciwko mnie? *What do you have against me-D?*

OMISSION OF 1ST AND 2ND-PERSON PRONOUNS

i.   In ordinary colloquial speech, 1st and 2nd-person pronouns are usually omitted when they are the subject of a verb unless contrasted with another pronoun, or unless emphasis is intended:

Trochę się niepokoję. *I'm a little worried.*

Gdzie idziesz? *Where are you-sg. going?*

Chcemy odpocząć. *We want to relax.*

Macie czuć się jak u siebie w domu. *You-pl. are to feel as if in your own home.*

Under emphasis or contrast:

Jeśli ty będziesz oglądał ten mecz, to ja sobie pójdę. *If you're going to watch that game, then I'll be on my way.*

While 1st and 2nd-person pronouns occur frequently in live speech in contexts that are not clearly emphatic or contrastive, their over-use sounds strange and should be avoided.

2. 3rd-person pronouns

    on *he (3rd-pers. masc.)*   **ono** *it (3rd-pers.neut.)*   **ona** *she (3rd-pers. fem.)*

N	**on**	**ono**	**ona**
G	**jego, niego, go**	←	**jej, niej**
D	**jemu, niemu, mu**	←	**jej, niej**
A	**jego, niego, go**	**je, nie**	**ją, nią**
I	**nim**	←	**nią**
L	**nim**	←	**niej**

    oni *they (3rd-pers.m.p.pl.)*   **one** *they-non-m.p.pl.*

N	**oni**	**one**
G	**ich, nich**	←
D	**im, nim**	←
A	**ich, nich**	**je, nie**
I	**nimi**	←
L	**nich**	←

3RD-PERSON PRONOMINAL REFERENCE

a. Third-person pronouns agree in grammatical gender (not in sex) with the antecedent. For example, one refers to a lamp as **ona** *she*, since the word **lampa** *lamp* is feminine in gender. Similarly, one refers to a notebook as **on**, since **zeszyt** is masculine; or to a tree as **ono**, since **drzewo** is neuter.

b. The noun category 'masculine personal', or 'virile' as it is sometimes called, refers to (a) all-male groups of people; (b) groups of people with mixed male and female constituency; (c) sometimes, groups of people and other things. Thus, the masc. pers. form **studenci** *students* could refer to male-only students or to a mixed group of students of whom at least one is male. A group of men and horses is still treated as masculine personal. By contrast, a group of women and horses, or women and infants, is treated as non-masculine personal. Some will use masculine personal agreement with such mixed-sex/gender groups, but such use is considered substandard. The 3rd-person pronoun used to refer to masculine-personal groups is **oni**, Accusative **ich** (after prepositions, **nich**). All other plural groups are referred to with **one**, Accusative **je** (after prepositions, **nie**).

    Czy widzisz tych chłopców? *Do you see those boys?*
    Tak, widzę *ich.* **Martwię się o** *nich.* *Yes, I see them. I'm worried for them.*

    Czy znasz te dziewczyny? *Do you know those girls?*
    Tak, znam *je.* **Martwię się o** *nie.* *Yes, I know them. I'm worried for them.*

NOTES ON THE USE OF 3RD PERSON PRONOUNS

a. The same rules apply to the choice between long and short forms (**jego** vs. **go, jemu** vs. **mu**) as apply to analogous choices with the 1st and 2nd person pronouns. That is, short forms are used unless emphasis or contrast is intended; long-forms are required after prepositions, emphasis aside, and in clause-initial position. If there is a choice, forms in **n-** are used after prepositions:

Widzę go. *I see him.*

Jego jednego nie widzę. *Him, alone I don't see.*

Czekam na ciebie (na niego). *I'm waiting for you (for him).*

b. As noted, third-person pronominal forms beginning with **n-** are used after prepositions:

Musimy pójść bez niego. *We have to go without him.*

Kupiłem coś dla niej. *I've bought something for her.*

Czekam na nią. *I'm waiting for her.*

Boję się o nie. *I'm afraid for them-non-masc.pers.pl.*

Wszystko, co umiem to dzięki niemu. *Everything I know how to do is thanks to him.*

c. In writing, especially in older, more formal writing and in poetry, the masc. Accusative form **niego** after prepositions ending in vowels may be reduced to **ń: doń** = **do niego** *to it;* **dlań** = **dla niego** *for it,* **nań** = **na niego** *on it,* **odeń** = **od niego** *from it;* cf. **Pada nań deszcz.** *Rain falls on it (e.g.,* **na kapelusz** *on a hat).*

d. When the pronoun has only one syllable, stress will fall on a preceding syllabic preposition: **bez niej** "BEZ-niej", **o nich** "O-nich", **na nią** "NA-nią".

e. The use of **go** for the Accusative of **ono** instead of **je** is encountered more and more frequently, and may be on the verge of acceptability, but it is still decidely better to avoid **go** and use **je**.

f. The item **on-** was once a demonstrative pronoun in Old Polish, taking pronominal adjective endings (**onego, onemu, onej**, etc.; see further below).

OMISSION OF 3RD-PERSON PRONOUNS

g. When the subject of a sentence, 3rd-person pronouns are usually used the first time in a paragraph. In subsequent use in the paragraph they are omitted as long as reference remains clear:

Tam jest pan Sosnowski. On jest adwokatem. Jest bardzo zapracowany. *That is Mr. Sosnowski over there. He is a lawyer. (He) is very overworked.*

THIRD-PERSON POSSESSIVE PRONOUNS

h. The Genitive forms of the 3rd-person pronouns: **jego** *his, its,* **jej** *her(s),* **ich** *their(s)* function as indeclinable possessive pronouns (and do not take a preceding **n-**): **w jego obecności** *in his presence,* **bez jej wiedzy** *without her knowledge,* **w ich domu** *in their home.*

3. Reflexive pronoun (all persons)

siebie *oneself*

N	——(się?)
G	**siebie, się**
D	**sobie (!se)**
A	**siebie, się**
I	**sobą**
L	**sobie**

The item **się** occupies a quasi-nominal position in impersonal constructions like **Jak to się pisze?** *How is this written?* The Dative short form **se** is highly marked stylistically, being considered "hick". However, educated speakers often color their speech by using it. It does not follow the same rules as the other pronominal short forms **go, mu, cię, ci,** which are used automatically unless emphasized, or unless after a preposition.

MEANING AND USE OF *SIEBIE*

a. The reflexive pronoun **siebie** *oneself* has either a reflexive or a reciprocal meaning:

Reflexive ('oneself'):

If a pronoun in the complement position is referentially identical to the subject of the sentence, the reflexive pronoun must be used:

On jest bardzo zadowolony z siebie. *He's very satisfied with himself.*

Nie mam pieniędzy przy sobie. *I don't have any money on me.*

Nie mogę przyjść do siebie. *I can't come to myself, i.e. to my senses.*

Ona myśli tylko o sobie. *She thinks only about herself.*

Probably most frequent is the instance when the indirect object position is identical to the subject, calling for the Dative-case form **sobie** (more or less the equivalent of **dla siebie** *for oneself*)

Zapiszę sobie pana adres. *I'll take down your address for myself.*

Myślę, że kupię sobie nowy płaszcz. *I think I'll buy myself a new coat.*

Zamów sobie coś do picia. *Order yourself something to drink.*

Wynajmiemy sobie pokój w Zakopanem. *Let's take out a room for ourselves in Zakopane.*

Reciprocal ('each other'):

Kupili sobie prezenty. *They bought each other presents.*

Ciągle się ze sobą kłócą. *They are always quarreling with one another.*

Opowiadamy sobie plotki. *We tell each other gossip.*

Nie podajemy sobie rąk. *We don't shake hands with each other.*

My tylko przeszkadzamy sobie. *We're just getting in each other's way.*

SIEBIE VS. SIĘ

b. In the Accusative, the long form **siebie** is used more often than the short form **się**, in order to distinguish the Accusative of the reflexive pronoun from the reflexive particle **się** (which historically derives from the Accusative of **siebie**, but which synchronically is a different item). Hence one will usually say:

Lubię *siebie* **w tym swetrze.** *I like myself in this sweater.*

But: **Nie widzę** *cię* **w tym swetrze.** *I don't see you in this sweater.*

For uses of the reflexive particle **się**, see Chapters 12 and 14.

SOBIE AS A SPECIFYING DATIVE

c. The Dative reflexive **sobie** is often used colloquially to lend a nuance of casualness, subjectivity, aimlessness, perverseness, or disregard to an action:

Jak sobie chcesz. *If you really want to.*

Pójdę sobie. *I'll be going on my way.*

On sobie siedzi i pracuje. *He's sitting there and (sort of) working.*

Usiądź sobie, ja zaraz wrócę. *Just have a seat. I'll be right back.*

Spędzimy sobie dwa tygodnie na wsi. *We'll spend a couple of weeks in the country.*

See also the fairy-tale phrase:

Był sobie król. *Once upon a time there was a king.*

SOBIE ATTACHED TO CERTAIN VERBS

d. The item **sobie** forms fixed phrases with a number of verbs, for example **folgować sobie** *luxuriate,* **kpić sobie** *mock,* **przypomnieć sobie** *recall,* **rościć sobie** *have pretensions,* **uświadomić sobie** *realize,* **używać sobie** *have the time of one's life,* **wyobrażać sobie** *imagine,* **wypraszać sobie** *not put up with,* **zdawać sobie sprawę** *realize,* **życzyć sobie** *desire,* and others.

INTERROGATIVE PRONOUNS

4. The 3rd-person interrogative pronouns consist of words for 'who' and 'what', and their negative answers 'no one' and 'nothing':

Negative:

	kto *who*		**nikt** *no one*
N	**kto**	N	**nikt**
G	**kogo**	G	**nikogo**
D	**komu**	D	**nikomu**
A	**kogo**	A	**nikogo**
I	**kim**	I	**nikim**
L	**kim**	L	**nikim**

Negative:

	co *what*		**nic** *nothing*
N	**co**	N	**nic**
G	**czego**	G	**niczego, nic**
D	**czemu**	D	**niczemu**
A	**co**	A	**nic**
I	**czym**	I	**niczym**
L	**czym**	L	**niczym**

REFERENCE AND AGREEMENT OF *KTO* AND *CO*

a. The pronoun **kto** *who* is always of masculine gender, regardless of reference. In order to avoid awkwardness, **która z was** *which of you* may be used for specifically feminine reference:

Dziewczyny: *która* **z was miała** (instead of *kto* **z was miał**) **wczoraj dyżur?** *Girls: which one of you was on duty yesterday?*

However, sentences like the following, in which **kimś** and **jej** refer to the same female person, are possible:

Czy rozmawiałaś z *kimś* **o** *jej* **pracy?** *Have you spoken to anyone about her (i.e. the same person's) work?*

b. In oblique cases, **kto** and **co** are followed by adjectives of the same case, often separated from them by an adverbial phrase of manner:

Nad *czym* **tak szalenie** *interesującym* **pracujesz?** *What are you working on that's so terribly interesting?*

Kogo **poznałaś tak bardzo** *interesującego?* *Who(m) did you meet (that was) so very interesting?*

c. In direct (Nominative or Accusative) cases, **co** (but not **kto**) is followed by the Genitive of a following adjective:

Co jeszcze tam usłyszałeś tak *interesującego?* *What else did you hear there of such interest?*

It is not usually correct to use **kogo** as a possessive pronoun in the sense 'whose'. Use forms of **czyj czyja czyje** *whose* instead.

KTO AND *CO* AS RELATIVE PRONOUNS

d. **Kto** is normally used as a relative pronoun when in coordination with **ten** or with some other pronoun or pronominal adjective, as in

Tylko ten, *kto* (not !który) ma własne dzieci, może je zrozumieć. *Only he who has his own children is able to understand them.*

Otherwise, **który** substitutes for **kto** in the sense 'who(m)' as a relative pronoun:

Nie znam studenta, o *którego* (not *o kogo) pytasz. *I don't know the student you are asking about .*

Similarly, **co** is used in relative clauses when coordinated with **to** or another pronominal adjective:

Z tego, *co* wiem, on jest w Paryżu. *From what I know he is in Paris.*

Co is often used as a relative pronoun with sentential content:

Lubię teatr, *co* jednak nie znaczy, że chcę dzisiaj pójść do teatru. *I like the theater, which doesn't mean, however, that I want to go to the theater today.*

On powiedział, że widział mnie, *co* było nieprawdą. *He said that he saw me, which was an untruth.*

In normal conversational speech, **co** is often used as a universal Nominative-case relative pronoun (instead of forms of **który**):

Ci, *co* (instead of **którzy) kradli drzewo zabili go.** *The ones who stole the wood killed him.*

To wina tego pana, *co* (instead of **który) za mną stoi.** *It's the fault of the man standing behind me.*

In substandard (although commonly heard) speech, in oblique-case uses, **co** as a relative pronoun is followed by a 3rd-person pronoun serving as the case marker:

Zgubiłem pieniądze, *co* mi *je* (instead of **które) dałaś.** *I lost the money you gave me.*

Pamiętasz dziewczynę, *co* ją (instead of **którą) u Ryśka poznałem?** *Remember the girl I met at Rysiek's?*

SPECIAL USES OF *CO*

e. **Co** can function as an accusatory expression for 'why?':

Co ty dzisiaj tak wcześnie wstajesz? *What are you getting up so early for?*

f. **Co** plus nouns naming periods of time is used to express 'every day', 'every month', etc. The noun may occur in the Nominative, Accusative or, with **rok** *year*, in the Genitive: **co dzień** *every day*, **co tydzień** *every week*, **co miesiąc** *every month*, **co godzina** or **co godzinę** *every hour*, **co chwila** or **co**

chwilę *every moment,* **co rok** or **co roku** *every year.* See also **co pewien czas** *every so often,* **co któryś wyraz** *every expression or so,* **co jakieś zdanie** *every sentence or so.*

g. **Co** often translates the English conjunction *as* in sentences like the following:

To nie był ten sam człowiek, *co* **wczoraj.** *It was not the same man as yesterday.*

h. The construction **co za**+N may be used as a substitute for **jaki**:

Co to za pies? *What sort of dog is that?*

Co to za ludzie? *What sort of people are they?*

Co za zaszczyt! *What an honor!*

i. Various idioms with **co** include **co do** +G *as far as X is concerned,* **dopiero co** *only just,* **co do jednego** *down to the last one,* **co lepsze** *only the better,* **co najmniej** *at the least,* **no to co?** *well so what?* and others.

NIKT AND NIC

j. The occurrence of **nikt** and **nic** in a sentence requires that the verb be negated, whether these items appear in subject or object position:

Nikt nic nie wie. *No one knows anything.*

Nikogo nie widzę. *I see no one (I don't see anyone).*

Nic nie rozumiem. *I understand nothing (I don't understand anything).*

Nic właściwie mi nie dziwi. *Nothing actually surprises me.*

k. The Accusative forms **nikogo** and **nic** cannot easily be distinguished from the Genitive, since these items occur mainly in contexts requiring the Genitive case (especially, after negated verbs):

Nic nie mam. *I don't have anything-G.*

Nie widzę tu nikogo. *I don't see anyone-G here.*

Forms after Accusative-requiring prepositions are clearly Accusative:

Nie zrobię tego za nic na świecie. *I wouldn't do that for anything in the world.*

Nie czekam na nikogo. *I'm not waiting for anybody.*

l. After Genitive-requiring prepositions, the specifically Genitive long form **niczego** will usually be used: **bez niczego** *without anything,* **do niczego** *good for nothing.* **Niczego** is also often encountered after Genitive-requiring verbs, as in **niczego** (or **nic**) **się nie boję** *I'm not afraid of anything.,* **niczego** (or **nic**) **nie używam** *I don't take anything.* Otherwise, **niczego** is used for emphasis; hence either **Nic tu nie widzę** or, less frequently, **Nie widzę tu niczego** *I don't see anything here.*

m. In Nominative-Accusative uses **nic** takes the Genitive of a following qual-
ifying adjective:

Nic tak *strasznego* **się nie stało.** *Nothing-N so terrible-G happened.*

Otherwise, a following adjective will agree in case with **nikt** or **nic**:

O nikim (niczym) *innym* **nie myślę.** *I'm not thinking about anyone
(anything) else-L.*

3RD-PERSON PRONOUNS OF POLITE OR TITLED ADDRESS

As forms of polite address, Polish uses the titles **pan** 'Mr.' or **pani** 'Ms.' (=
Mrs. or Miss) plus the first name. Both **pan** and **pani** have plural forms, and a
special plural pronoun **państwo** refers to mixed gender groups, i.e. conjunctions of **pan** and **pani**. The titles concerned are the following:

	pan *Mr., sir*		pani *Mrs., Miss, Ms.*		państwo *Mr. and Mrs., ladies and gentlemen*
	Sg.	Pl.	Sg.	Pl.	M.p.pl. only
N	pan	panowie	pani	panie	państwo
G	pana	panów	pani	pań	państwa
D	panu	panom	pani	paniom	państwu
A	pana	panów	panią	panie	państwa
I	panem	panami	panią	paniami	państwem
L	panu (!)	panach	pani	paniach	państwu (!)
V	panie	panowie	pani	panie	państwo

THE USE OF *PAN, PANI, PANNA, PAŃSTWO*

a. The title **panna** *Miss*, Gpl. **panien** is not much used today other than in
set expressions such as **panna młoda** *bride*, **stara panna** *old maid*. Note
also the phrases **pan młody** *bridegroom*, **państwo młodzi** *the young couple*.
A girl on the threshold of womanhood may be affectedly referred to as
panna, especially by those who are much older. Unmarried women of all
ages and status are regularly referred to and addressed as **pani**.

b. The titles **pan** and **pani** may be combined with either the first or last
name; however, especially in the presence of the person concerned, they
are usually combined with the first name: **pan Jan, pani Maria.** Use with
the last name occurs more often in lists (like class rolls) than in direct address. Direct address with the last name is used only in situations of extreme formality, for example in client or petitioner situations:

Pan Zieliński? Proszę, niech pan wejdzie. *Mr. Zieliński? Come right in.*

c. Even though **pan** and **pani** plus the first name belong to formal address,
one still needs to know fairly well the person one addresses in this manner, and to be on a level of social equality (or superiority). For example, a
cleaning lady will not easily address her employer as **pani Zosia**, but

rather simply as **pani**. On the other hand, the employer might well address the cleaning lady as, say, **pani Jagusia**.

d. The form **państwo** means either 'ladies and gentlemen' (equivalent to the plural of **pan + pani**) or, more narrowly, especially with last names, 'Mr. and Mrs.':

Witam państwa! *Greetings, ladies and gentlemen!*

Tu mieszkają państwo Bobrowscy. *This is where Mr. and Mrs. Bobrowski live.*

In the sense 'ladies and gentlemen', **panie i panowie** may also be used. **Państwo** has a singular-like declension but takes masculine personal plural agreement:

To są państwo Zielińscy. *That is Mr. and Mrs. Zieliński.*

Państwo Durkaczowie byli spóźnieni. *The Durkaczes were running late.*

e. When used in direct address, **pan** and **pani** occur in the Vocative case. The use of the Vocative with both the title and first name is obligatory:

Dzień dobry, panie Janie! (pani Mario!) *Hello, Jan (Maria)!*

By themselves, **pan** and **pani** may often be translated as 'sir', 'madam' (southern U.S. *ma'am*). With the greeting **dzień dobry** *hello*, these items occur in the Dative case:

Dzień dobry panu (pani, państwu)! *Hello, sir (madam, ladies and gentlemen).*

f. The titles **pan, pani, państwo** take the 3rd-person form of the verb; **państwo** takes masculine-personal verb and adjective agreement:

Wie pan(i) co? *Do you know-3.p.sg. what?*

Czy państwo rozumieją? *Do you (people) understand?*

Państwo są zmęczeni, prawda? *You (people) are tired, right?*

g. The use of **pan** with the 2nd-person sg. form of the verb is a form celebrated as representing the speech of Warsaw cab-drivers (and other such workers); it should not be emulated by persons outside this narrow social and dialect group:

Wsiadaj pan! *Have a seat, sir!*

h. In relaxed social settings, **państwo** may be used with 2nd-person plural verb agreement; indeed, 3.p.pl. agreement may sound in some instances distant:

Gdzie państwo mieszkają? or, more relaxed, **Gdzie państwo mieszkacie?** *Where do you (people-formal) live?*

In even more relaxed and informal settings, **wy** may be used as the plural of persons one would address in the singular with **pan** and **pani**, as in:

Gdzie (wy) mieszkacie? *Where do you live?*

i. Unlike the 3rd-person pronouns **on, ona, oni, one**, the forms **pan, pani, państwo** are rarely left out. However, they may be omitted in the second part of a complex sentence when they occur as the subject of both clauses, as in

Pan widocznie nie rozumie, co (pan) mówi. *You evidently don't understand what you are saying.*

In certain social settings, **pan, pani, państwo** of the first clause may be represented by 3rd-person pronouns **on, ona, oni** in the second clause, although this sounds extremely formal and distant, as in

Pan rozumie, że w ten sposób przepada *mu* (better: **pana**) **stypendium.** *You realize that this way you lose your fellowship.*

Pytam panią o *jej* (better: **pani**) **zdanie w tej sprawie.** *I'm asking you (f.) about your opinion in this matter.*

j. The Genitive forms **pana, pani, państwa** are used as de facto indeclinable possessive pronouns; **pana** and **pani** are placed before the noun, while **państwa** is placed after the noun: **pana kapelusz** *your (masc.) hat,* **pani mąż** *your (fem.) husband,* **dom państwa** *your (masc. pers. pl.) house.* The possessive adjective **pański** may be used as a more formal, rather old-fashioned, possessive of **pan:**

Tu są pańskie (less high-handedly, **pana**) **dokumenty.** *Here are your documents, sir.*

k. When used in combination with the demonstrative pronoun **ten ta to**, **pan, pani,** and **państwo** take on the meaning of nouns in the sense of 'gentleman', 'lady', 'people', respectively:

Co mówi ten pan? *What is that man saying?*

Kim była ta pani? *Who was that lady?*

Ci państwo nic nie rozumieją. *Those people don't understand anything.*

OTHER TITLES USED IN DIRECT ADDRESS

Polish makes considerably more use of titles, whether academic or professional, than does English, at least the American variant of English. While a full discussion of titles and titling in Polish exceeds the scope of this work, here are some guidelines:

a. Frequent use is made of official titles, often accompanied by **pan, pani, państwo**, as de facto 2nd-person pronouns of respect, similar to the use of **pan, pani, państwo** by themselves. Americans are apt to think such usage exaggerative and affected, but it sounds quite normal in Polish.

Czego pan minister sobie życzy? *What do you desire, your excellency?*

(alternatively: **Czego pan sobie życzy, panie ministrze?**)

Co mogę panu profesorowi podać? *What may I serve you, professor?*

(alternatively: **Co mogę panu podać, panie profesorze?** *What may I offer you, professor-V?*).

b. The words **kolega** (f. **koleżanka**) *colleague,* **obywatel** (f. **obywatelka**) *citizen,* and (among Communist Party members) **towarzysz** (f. **towarzyszka**) *comrade* when used as forms of address combine with 2.p.pl. verb-forms, masc.pers.pl. only, no matter what the reference:

Kolego! Macie zapałkę? *Hey buddy! Do you have a match?*

Towarzyszko! Nie byliście na zebraniu! *Comrade-f.: you weren't-m.p.pl. at the meeting!*

Such usage today is strictly out of fashion.

c. With women, most academic and professional titles use the unaltered male title preceded by **pani: pani magister Ewa Nowak, pani doktor Maria Dębowska**.

d. In most families, children refer to older relations by their (usually affectionate) relation-name and use it as a de facto pronoun:

Czy mama gdzieś się wybiera? *Are you going out somewhere, mom?*

Czy mogę tacie pomóc? *May I help you, dad?*

With adult friends of the family, the words **wujek** *uncle* and **ciocia** *aunt* are used by children as titles of respectful address:

Czy wujek przeczyta mi bajkę? *Would you read me a story, "uncle"?*

Przywitaj się z ciocią Heleną, Agatko. *Say hello to "aunt" Helen, Agatka.*

e. In a few isolated rural areas, it is possible to encounter the honorific use of masc. pers. pl. forms in agreement with singular family titles, as **ojciec** (or **matka**) **poszli** *father (mother) has left.* Such usage is alien to the standard language.

f. Among other common titles are **ojciec** *father* and **siostra** *sister,* used with priests and nuns; **siostra** is also used in hospitals as the title 'nurse'.

g. When addressing letters, or people in an official speech, Poles make greater use than Americans of such preceding adjectives as 'worthy', 'honored', 'venerable', and so on. The standard introduction in a letter is **Szanowny Panie (Szanowna Pani, Szanowni Państwo)** 'Respected Sir (Madam, Gentlemen)'. To a friend or relative one uses **Drogi** *Dear* or **Kochany** *Dear, Beloved.* Other adjectives of respect used to address persons and groups include **czcigodny** *venerable, revered,* **łaskawy** *gracious,* **dostojny** *worthy.* A sentence such as

Czego szanowny pan sobie życzy? *What does the gracious gentleman desire?* (as spoken by a salesperson to an older customer) is old-fashioned, but not as archly so as the English translation implies.

SUMMARY: ELEVEN WAYS OF SAYING "WHERE ARE YOU GOING?"

The following sentences in Polish would all be translated by *Where are you going?* in English (here using **dokąd** *where to* instead of possible **gdzie** *where*):

Dokąd (ty) idziesz?	2.p.sg. informal
Dokąd (wy) idziecie?	2.p.pl. informal
Dokąd pan idzie?	3.p.sg. of polite address (male)
Dokąd panowie idą?	3.p.pl. of polite address (male)
Dokąd panowie idziecie?	3.p.pl. of polite relaxed address (male)
Dokąd pani idzie?	3.p.sg. of polite address (female)
Dokąd panie idą?	3.p.pl. of polite address (female)
Dokąd panie idziecie?	3.p.pl. of polite relaxed address (female)
Dokąd państwo idą?	3.p.pl. of polite address (m.p.pl.)
Dokąd państwo idziecie?	3.p.pl. of polite relaxed address (m.p.pl.)
Dokąd mama(etc.) idzie?	3.p.sg. of titled address.

PRONOMINAL ADJECTIVES

Pronominal adjectives belong to the class of grammatical determiners, i.e. noun-modifiers with a mainly discourse or identifying function rather than attributive meaning. They are often used literally pronominally, to take the place of the noun referred to (analogously to English *mine, his, hers, its, theirs.* Inflectionally, pronominal adjectives have declensions similar to regular adjectives, except that the Nsg. masculine ending is often **-Ø**.

1. **Possessive pronouns**

czyj czyja czyje *whose* (poss. of **kto**)

	Sg.			Pl.	
	Masc.	Neut.	Fem.	Masc. pers.	Other
N	czyj	czyje	czyja	czyi	czyje
G	czyjego	←	czyjej	czyich	←
D	czyjemu	←	czyjej	czyim	←
A	= N/G	czyje	czyją	czyich	czyje
I	czyim	←	czyją	czyimi	←
L	czyim	←	czyjej	czyich	←

mój moja moje *my, mine* (poss. of **ja**)

	Sg.			Pl.	
	Masc.	Neut.	Fem.	Masc. pers.	Other
NV	mój	moje	moja	moi	moje
G	mojego	←	mojej	moich	←
D	mojemu	←	mojej	moim	←
A	= N/G	moje	moją	moich	moje
I	moim	←	moją	moimi	←
L	moim	←	mojej	moich	←

twój twoja twoje *your, yours* (poss. of **ty**)

		Sg.			Pl.	
		Masc.	Neut.	Fem.	Masc. pers.	Other
NV		twój	twoje	twoja	twoi	twoje
G		twojego	←	twojej	twoich	←
D		twojemu	←	twojej	twoim	←
A		= N/G	twoje	twoją	twoich	twoje
I		twoim	←	twoją	twoimi	←
L		twoim	←	twojej	twoich	←

Old-fashioned or bookish contracted forms based on the stems **m-** and **tw-** may occasionally be encountered, as:

		Sg.			Pl.	
		Masc.	Neut.	Fem.	Masc. pers.	Other
NV		(twój)	twe	twa	(twoi)	twe
G		twego	←	twej	twych	←
D		twemu	←	twej	twym	←
A		= N/G	twe	twą	twych	twe
I		twym	←	twą	twymi	←
L		twym	←	twej	twych	←

Similarly: (**mój**) **me ma** *my*. In contemporary Polish, these shortened forms are encountered most often in songs, where they are used for the sake of meter.

nasz nasza nasze *our, ours* (poss. of **my**)

		Sg.			Pl.	
		Masc.	Neut.	Fem.	Masc. pers.	Other
NV		nasz	nasze	nasza	nasi	nasze
G		naszego	←	naszej	naszych	←
D		naszemu	←	naszej	naszym	←
A		= N/G	nasze	naszą	naszych	nasze
I		naszym	←	naszą	naszymi	←
L		naszym	←	naszej	naszych	←

wasz wasza wasze *your, yours* (poss. of **wy**)

		Sg.			Pl.	
		Masc.	Neut.	Fem.	Masc. pers.	Other
NV		wasz	wasze	wasza	wasi	wasze
G		waszego	←	waszej	waszych	←
D		waszemu	←	waszej	waszym	←
A		= N/G	wasze	waszą	waszych	wasze
I		waszym	←	waszą	waszymi	←
L		waszym	←	waszej	waszych	←

NOTES ON *CZYJ, MÓJ, TWÓJ, NASZ, WASZ*

a. As observed earlier, the use of **kogo** in place of all forms of **czyj** should be avoided as decidedly less elegant, hence:

Czyj to jest płaszcz? *Whose coat is that?*

not: !**Kogo to jest płaszcz?**

A possible exception would be in a phrase like **u kogo w mieszkaniu** *at whose apartment*, although **w czyim mieszkaniu** is probably better.

b. The same rules of use as to formality/informality apply to **twój, wasz** as to the pronouns **ty, wy**; see above under Formal and Informal Address.

c. The use of possessive pronouns is much less frequent in Polish than in English. With persons, pets, and accoutrements, the possessive relation is not normally mentioned unless there is a need for clarity:

Idzie brat ze znajomym. *Here comes (my) brother with (his) friend.*

Uciekł mi kot. *My cat ran away.*

Gdzie zostawiłam parasol? *Where did I leave my umbrella?*

d. Depending on whether they modify a noun or are used predicatively, possessive pronouns are translated as 'my/mine', 'your/yours', 'our/ours', 'their/theirs':

To jest mój zeszyt. *That is my notebook.*

On jest mój. *It (the notebook) is mine.*

e. Recall that the 3rd-person forms **jego, jej, ich, pana**, and **pani** function as possessives of **on/ono, ona, oni/one, pan**, and **pani**. These forms do not usually occur in predicate position. Thus, one will more often use

Ten zeszyt należy do niego. *That notebook belongs to him.*

or: **To jest jego zeszyt.** *That is his notebook.*

than: **Ten zeszyt jest jego.** *That notebook is his.*

swój swoja swoje *one's own* (possessive of **siebie**)

	Sg.			Pl.	
	Masc.	Neut.	Fem.	Masc. pers.	Other
NV	swój	swoje	swoja	swoi	swoje
G	swojego	←	swojej	swoich	←
D	swojemu	←	swojej	swoim	←
A	= N/G	swoje	swoją	swoich	swoje
I	swoim	←	swoją	swoimi	←
L	swoim	←	swojej	swoich	←

NOTES ON *SWÓJ SWOJA SWOJE*

a. **Swój swoje swoja** *one's own* is used when a 3rd-person possessive in the predicate refers to the subject of the sentence:

On ma swoje zalety. *He has his good points.*

The use of **jego** *his* here is not impossible, but it would imply that the person has someone else's good points. With personal subjects, this rule is virtually ironclad, and may be broken only in case of doubt as to the true subject, cf.

Czy on sam bierze udział w obchodach swoich (or **jego**) **urodzin?** *Is he himself taking part in the celebration of his birthday?*

Here, since other people are celebrating the birthday along with the celebrant, one might make a case for being able to use **jego**.

With impersonal subjects, this rule may be broken more easily, although it is always safer to abide by it; see

Dyplom ten upoważnia swojego (or **jego**) **posiadacza do podejmowania pracy we wszystkich szkołach podstawowych.** *This diploma entitles its bearer to undertake work in all elementary schools.*

The problem of ambiguous predicative reference is not a logical problem in the 1st and 2nd persons, where one may use either the 1st or 2nd-person possessive forms or, usually better, **swój**:

Ja mam swoje powody. *I have my own reasons.*

Dziękuję za książkę, ale już mam swoją. *Thanks for the book, but I already have my own.*

The respective use of **moje, moją** here would not be totally wrong, but it would not be the best choice unless emphasis on the possessor is intended.

b. For emphasis, **swój** may occur with **własny**:

Ja mam swój własny rower. *I have my own bicyle.*

c. **Swój** can have the meaning 'of one's own kind or sort':

Adam to swój chłopak. *Adam is our kind of guy.*

d. The neut. sg. form **swoje** has various idiomatic uses in the sense of 'one's own way or thing', for example

On wszystko robi po swojemu. *He does everything in his own way.*

On zawsze robi swoje. *He always does his own thing, in his own way, has his own way.*

pański *your* (old-fashioned poss. of **pan**)

	Sg.			Pl.	
	Masc.	Neut.	Fem.	Masc. pers.	Other
NV	pański	pańskie	pańska	pańscy	pańskie
G	pańskiego	←	pańskiej	pańskich	←
D	pańskiemu	←	pańskiej	pańskim	←
A	= N/G	pańskie	pańską	pańskich	pańskie
I	pańskim	←	pańską	pańskimi	←
L	pańskim	←	pańskiej	pańskich	←

Pański is considerably more stiff and formal than the 3rd-pers.sg. **pana** in the same function:

To jest pański pomysł, prawda? *That's your idea, right? (accusatory)*

To jest pana pomysł, prawda? *That's your idea, right? (same meaning, but more sympathetic).*

2. **Pronominal adjectives with neuter sg. in -o.**

ten ta to *this, that* (demonstrative pronoun)

	Sg.			Pl.	
	Masc.	Neut.	Fem.	Masc. pers.	Other
NV	ten	to	ta	ci	te
G	tego	←	tej	tych	←
D	temu	←	tej	tym	←
A	= N/G	to	tę	tych	te
I	tym	←	tą	tymi	←
L	tym	←	tej	tych	←

NOTES ON *TEN TA TO*

a. **Ten ta to** *this, that* is used in the sense of both 'this' and 'that', although **tamten tamto tamta**, with a declension similar to that of **ten ta to**, is available to express specifically 'that other, that over there'.

b. The Asg. fem. is increasingly often pronounced "tą", even by speakers on radio and TV, bringing it into conformity with the other pronominal adjectives, but it is nevertheless spelled **tę**. By contrast, the Asg. fem. of **tamten tamta tamto** is always **tamtą**, not *tamtę.

c. In 3rd-person narratives, **ten** and **ta** occasionally take the place of **on** and **ona** in order to indicate specifically the second of two persons:

Jarek zapytał profesora, ale ten nie odpowiedział. *Jarek asked the professor, but he (the professor) didn't answer.*

d. When a phrase with **ten ta to** is the topic of discussion, head-modifier position is usually reversed:

Wczoraj przeczytałem ciekawy artykuł. *Artykuł ten* **napisał niejaki profesor Korbe.** *Yesterday I read an interesting article. The article was written by some professor Korbe.*

e. **Ten ta to** often occurs as a specifier with other adjectives and with certain other pronominal adjectives:

Proszę o *ten* **biały** (e.g. **ser**). *I'd like that white one (e.g. cheese).*

To nie jest *ten* **sam człowiek** *That's not the same person.*

Zaskakuje mnie *ta* **jego nieuczciwość.** *That lack of integrity of his surprises me.*

f. **Ten ta to** is often placed before proper nouns and identifier-phrases to suggest slight irony or affection:

Ten **twój brat to zdolny facet.** *That brother of yours is a talented guy.*

Jak żyjecie w *tej* **Warszawie?** *How are you getting on in that Warsaw of yours?*

g. The neuter form **to** often occurs as a sentential pronoun:

—**On zdobył najwyższą nagrodę.** *He won the highest award.*

—*To* **wcale mi nie dziwi.** *That doesn't surprise me at all.*

h. **to..., to...** is used to express "now this, now that":

Zawsze ktoś ciekawy przyjeżdża: to ksiądz, to dyrektor, to jakaś aktorka. *There's always someone interesting coming: sometimes a priest, sometimes a director, sometimes some actress.*

i. In sloppy speech, **ten** in its various forms is often used to substitute for a noun the speaker cannot recall at the moment:

Wiesz, wczoraj u tego, cośmy go w zeszłym roku poznały na tych... *You know, yesterday, at that (guy's) that we met last year at that (name-day party?) ...*

In a similar informal use, the form **tego** serves as an all-purpose substitute for virtually any unstated item in the Nominative-Accusative, or a sentential item:

Jego żona się obraziła i powiedziała, że tego, rozumiesz, bo ona jest zazdrosna. *His wife got offended and said, like, you understand, because she is jealous.*

sam sama samo *-self, same, very, alone* (intensifying pronoun)

	Sg.			Pl.	
	Masc.	Neut.	Fem.	Masc. pers.	Other
NV	sam	samo	sama	sami	same
G	samego	←	samej	samych	←
D	samemu	←	samej	samym	←
A	= N/G	samo	samą	samych	same
I	samym	←	samą	samymi	←
L	samym	←	samej	samych	←

NOTES ON *SAM SAMA SAMO*

a.   This word functions as an intensifying pronoun often translatable as '(by) oneself, itself':

Zrób to sam *Do it yourself.*

Nie uda im się samym. *They won't be able to manage by themselves.*

Dom sam się rozwalił. *The house fell down of its own accord.*

b.   In the sense of 'the same', this word usually occurs with **ten ta to**:

To była ta sama dziewczyna. *That was the (very) same girl.*

Czy to nie jest ten sam film pod innym tytułem? *Isn't that the same film under a different title?*

c.   The neuter form **samo** can function adverbially in construction with **tak** and **tyle**:

Zrób tak samo, jak ja. *Do the same as I do.*

Podróż do Nowego Jorku kosztuje tyle samo, ile do Frankfurtu. *A trip to New York costs as much as one to Frankfurt.*

These constructions can often be reduced to shorter versions by trimming items down to **jak** or **ile**:

Zrób tak samo, jak ja. > Zrób tak, jak ja. Zrób, jak ja.

Podróż kosztuje tyle samo, ile do Frankfurtu. > Podróż kosztuje tyle, ile do Frankfurtu. > Podróż kosztuje, ile do Frankfurtu.

d.   **Sam sama samo** is also used in the sense of 'alone', 'by oneself':

Czy pani mieszka sama? *Do you live by yourself-fem.?*

Został sam na świecie. *He was left alone in the world.*

Nie wystarczą same dobre zamiary. *Good intentions alone aren't enough.*

A special use in this sense employs the Dative-case forms **samemu** or **samej**, as though the subject of an infinitive:

Przyjemnie jest tu siedzieć samemu (samej). *It's pleasant to sit here by oneself.*

Jestem na tyle dorosły (dorosła), żeby to samemu (samej) zrobić. *I am sufficiently grown-up to do it on my own.*

Compare **Chcę to zrobić sam(a)** *I want to do it myself* to **Nie chce mi się tego robić samemu (samej)** *I don't feel like doing that myself.*

e.   In referring to situations of close proximity, **sam sama samo** translates 'very' or 'itself':

Mieszkamy nad samą rzeką. *We live by the very river (by the river itself).*

Zmarł w samą północ. *He died at the very stroke of midnight.*

f.   In the plural, **sami / same** can have the meaning 'nothing but':

Tam byli sami chłopcy. *There were nothing but boys there.*

Pokazywali nam same stare filmy. *They showed us nothing but old movies.*

ów owa owo *that* (bookish demonstrative pronoun)

	Sg.			Pl.	
	Masc.	Neut.	Fem.	Masc. pers.	Other
NV	ów	owo	owa	owi	owe
G	owego	←	owej	owych	←
D	owemu	←	owej	owym	←
A	= N/G	owo	ową	owych	owe
I	owym	←	ową	owymi	←
L	owym	←	owej	owych	←

The word **ów owo owa** *that* is not much used in colloquial Polish other than in the expression **to i owo** *this and that.*

jeden jedna jedno *one; (pl.) some* (indefinite pronoun)

	Sg.			Pl.	
	Masc.	Neut.	Fem.	Masc. pers.	Other
NV	jeden	jedno	jedna	jedni	jedne
G	jednego	←	jednej	jednych	←
D	jednemu	←	jednej	jednym	←
A	= N/G	jedno	jedną	jednych	jedne
I	jednym	←	jedną	jednymi	←
L	jednym	←	jednej	jednych	←

NOTES ON *JEDEN JEDNA JEDNO*

a.   In the sg., **jeden jedna jedno** is the word for the number 'one', for the uses of which see the following chapter. It may also be used in roughly the same sense as **pewien** *a certain:*

   Znam jedną kobietę, która na pewno ci pomoże. *I know a (certain) woman who will surely help you.*

b.   In the plural, **jedni/jedne** can mean 'some', as opposed to 'others' (the latter being usually expressed with **inny**):

   Jedni studenci są lepsi, inni gorsi. *Some students are better, others worse.*

   Jedne okulary są tańsze, inne droższe. *Some eyeglasses are chepaer, others more expensive.*

c.   The plural of **jeden** is used to express the singular of plural-only nouns, as **jedne drzwi** *one door,* **jedne sanie** *one sleigh;* see also the following chapter, on numerals and the counting of plural-only nouns.

d.   Along with various other pronominal adjectives, **jeden jedna jedno** is often followed by a prepositional phrase with **z**+G '(out) of':

   Jeden student (jeden ze studentów) wyszedł z egzaminu wcześniej. *One student (one of the students) left the examination earlier.*

Also:

Każdy z nas jest zadowolony. *Each of us is satisfied.*

Niektórzy ludzie (niektórzy z ludzi) spóźniają się. *Some (of the) people are running late.*

Która z tych książek będzie interesująca? *Which of those books would be interesting?*

e. The word **niejeden niejedna niejedno** means 'more than one':

Niejedna kobieta za nim oglądała się. *More than one woman would turn around to look at him.*

Unlike **jeden jedna jedno, niejeden,** being logically plural, does not have a separate plural use.

(wszystek wszystka) wszystko *all, every(thing)* (encompassing pronoun)

	Sg.			Pl.	
	Masc.	Neut.	Fem.	Masc. pers.	Other
NV	(wszystek)	wszystko	(wszystka)		
G	(wszystkiego)	←	(wszystkiej)	The formal plural	
D	(wszystkiemu) ←		(wszystkiej)	**wszystek** functions as	
A	(= N/G)	wszystko	(wszystką)	the de facto plural of	
I	(wszystkim)	←	(wszystką)	**każdy**; see further	
L	(wszystkim)	←	(wszystkiej)	below.	

NOTES ON *(WSZYSTEK WSZYSTKA) WSZYSTKO*

a. Except for forms of neuter **wszystko** in the sense 'everything', this pronominal adjective has mostly gone out of use in the singular.

b. As a modifying pronominal adjective, **wszystek wszystka wszystko** can theoretically be used in the singular in the sense of 'all' when referring to mass nouns (nouns naming a substance of which one may have more or less):

Wszystka woda jest skontaminowana. *All the water is contaminated.*

Wszystek piasek został wysypany. *All the sand was poured out.*

In practice, forms of **cały cała całe** are usually used instead: **cała woda** *all the water*, **cały piasek** *all the sand*, **cały rozum** *all of one's intelligence.*

b. The neuter form **wszystko** has the meaning 'everything':

Czy wszystko jest gotowe? *Is everything ready?*

Mimo wszystko nadal go szanuję. *Despite everything, I still respect him.*

Przyglądał się wszystkiemu. *He examined everything.*

Miał wszystkiego dosyć. *He had had enough of everything.*

c. The masculine-personal form **wszyscy** functions in the meaning 'everyone, everybody':

Czy wszyscy już są? *Is everyone here yet?*

See also below under **każdy**.

d. The word **wszelki wszelka wszelkie** *each and every sort*, obsolete **wszelaki**, is used most often in phrases of the sort **na wszelki wypadek** *for any eventuality*, **wszelkimi sposobami** *by any and all means*. Some other examples:

Wszelka pomoc była odrzucona. *Every sort of assistance was rejected.*

Chętnie odpowiem na wszelkie pytania. *I'll gladly answer any and all questions.*

Stało się to wbrew wszelkim oczekiwaniom. *That happened despite all expectations.*

e. An obsolete contracted form of **wszystko** based on the stem **wsz-** occurs mainly in phrases: **po wsze czasy** *for all times*, **ze wszech stron** *from all sides*. Singular forms are largely hypothetical.

3. *Pronominal adjectives with a regular adjectival inflection* (including some with short Nsg. masc. in -Ø) include the following:

pewien pewna pewne *a certain* (indefinite pronoun)

	Sg.			Pl.	
	Masc.	Neut.	Fem.	Masc. pers.	Other
NV	pewien	pewne	pewna	pewni	pewne
G	pewnego	←	pewnej	pewnych	←
D	pewnemu	←	pewnej	pewnym	←
A	= N/G	pewne	pewną	pewnych	pewne
I	pewnym	←	pewną	pewnymi	←
L	pewnym	←	pewnej	pewnych	←

When used as a pronominal adjective, the Nsg. masc. form **pewien**, instead of adjectival **pewny** *sure, certain*, is usual (although **pewny** is not wrong); see **pewien człowiek** *a certain man*, as opposed to **pewny człowiek** *a man who is certain*. More frequent in the sense 'a certain' is **jakiś jakaś jakieś: jakiś człowiek** *some man or other*. Sometimes combinations may be ambiguous; see **pewna sensacja** *a sure sensation* or *something of a sensation*. See also the phrase **kobieta w pewnym wieku** *a woman of a certain age*. In position right after the noun, the short form may be used in the sense 'sure, certain':

To człowiek bardzo pewien (pewny) siebie. *That's a man very sure of himself.*

każdy każda każde *each, every* (distributive pronoun)

	Sg. Masc.	Neut.	Fem.	Pl. Masc. pers.	Other
NV	każdy	każde	każda	wszyscy	wszystkie
G	każdego	←	każdej	wszystkich	←
D	każdemu	←	każdej	wszystkim	←
A	= N/G	każde	każdą	wszystkich	wszystkie
I	każdym	←	każdą	wszystkimi	←
L	każdym	←	każdej	wszystkich	←

NOTES ON *KAŻDY KAŻDA KAŻDE*, PL. *WSZYSCY WSZYSTKIE*

a. The plural of **każdy** is usually expressed with **wszyscy/wszystkie** *all:*

Każdy kot jest czarny. *Every cat is black.*

Wszystkie koty są czarne. *All cats are black.*

Wszyscy moi znajomi są żonaci. *All my acquaintances are married.*

b. In reference to people, the words **każdy/wszyscy** are often used by themselves in the sense 'each person' or, in the plural, 'everyone', 'everybody':

Każdy jest zajęty własnymi sprawami. *Each person is busy with his own affairs.*

Wszyscy są zadowoleni z rezultatów. *Everyone is (all are) satisfied with. the results.*

c. The plural form **każde** occurs in special constructions only. For example, it may be used with plural-only nouns: **każde drzwi** *all doors.* See also

Na każde trzy osoby przypada tylko jedna kula. *For every three persons there is only one bullet.*

?Z każdych czterech miast trzy uległy zniszczeniu. *Out of every four towns, three were destroyed.*

The last sentence is an example of how there is sometimes no elegant way to say certain logical things because of the awkwardness of the syntax.

d. When in the indirect-object position, **każdy** is often accompanied by distributive **po** 'each':

Dałem każdemu dziecku po cukierku. *I gave each child a candy (i.e. one candy per child).*

żaden żadna żadne *none, no, not any* (negative quantifying pronoun)

	Sg. Masc.	Neut.	Fem.	Pl. Masc. pers.	Other
NV	żaden	żadne	żadna	żadni	żadne
G	żadnego	←	żadnej	żadnych	←
D	żadnemu	←	żadnej	żadnym	←
A	= N/G	żadne	żadną	żadnych	żadne
I	żadnym	←	żadną	żadnymi	←
L	żadnym	←	żadnej	żadnych	←

NOTES ON *ŻADEN ŻADNA ŻADNE*

a. **Żaden** functions as the negative of **jeden** *one*, **każdy** *each, every*, **pewien** *a certain*, **wszyscy/wszystkie** *all*, and **wszelki** *any sort of*. The use of **żaden** requires that the verb be negated:

   Każdy chłopiec jest zdolny. *Every boy is talented.*

   Żaden chłopiec nie jest zdolny. *No boy is talented.*

b. In the predicate, the usual English correspondent is *any*:

   Nie mam żadnych dobrych przyjaciół. *I don't have any good friends.*

   When in the subject position, the translation is usually 'no, none, not any':

   Żaden film nie jest dobry. *No (not any) film is good.*

   Żadni ludzie nie przyszli. *None of the people came.*

c. **żaden żadna żadne** occurs less easily in the plural than in the singular. In the plural it does not usually stand alone, without a modified noun. In the sentence

   Żadne osoby nie były zadowolone. *No persons were satisfied.*

   The noun **osoby** may not easily be omitted.

4. In addition to the foregoing items, sequencing adjectives like **pierwszy** *first*, **drugi** *second*, **następny** *next*, and **ostatni** *last* are often used pronominally:

   Kto jest następny (pierwszy, ostatni)? *Who is next (first, last)?*

5. **jaki** *what kind*, **taki** *that kind* and **który** *which*. These items are both questioning and relativizing adjectives, and have a regular adjectival declension. Under the heading of **jaki** and **taki** may also be treated similarly declined **nijaki** *no kind (of no particular sort)*, **niejaki** *some sort of*, and **jednaki** *identical* = **jednakowy**.

jaki jaka jakie *what kind* (qualitative pronoun)

	Sg.			Pl.	
	Masc.	Neut.	Fem.	Masc. pers.	Other
NV	jaki	jakie	jaka	jacy	jakie
G	jakiego	←	jakiej	jakich	←
D	jakiemu	←	jakiej	jakim	←
A	= N/G	jakie	jaką	jakich	jakie
I	jakim	←	jaką	jakimi	←
L	jakim	←	jakiej	jakich	←

NOTES ON *JAKI JAKA JAKIE* AND *TAKI TAKA TAKIE*

a. **Jaki** and **który** are close in meaning, the more specific and contrastive being **który** *which (of several choices)*; see below. **Jaki** usually translates either questioning *what, what kind of, which,* or relative *that*:

Jaki to jest samochód? *What (kind of) car is that?*

To jest najlepszy materiał, jaki mam. *That's the best material that I have.*

The relative pronoun may not be omitted in Polish, as it usually is in English. Contrast the use of **który** and **jaki** in a situation like the following:

Proszę o ser. *I'd like some cheese.*

Jaki? *What kind?* or: **Który?** *Which one?*

The second version implies that the choices are in front of one for choosing.

b. **Jaki** often appears exclamatorily:

Jaki piękny kapelusz! *What a pretty hat!*

Jaka ty jesteś cudowna! *How marvelous you are!*

c. The indefinite form **jakiś jakaś jakieś** *some kind of* has great frequency of use:

Myślę, że kupię jakiś sernik. *I think I'll buy some kind of cheesecake.*

Czeka na ciebie jakiś mężczyzna. *Some man is waiting for you.*

d. Colloquially, **taki taka takie** is often used in more or less the same sense as **jakiś jakaś jakieś**:

Burmistrzem jest taki pan, co przed wojną miał sklep apteczny. *The mayor is some gentleman who before the war had a pharmacy.*

e. The combinations **taki..., jaki...** or **taki..., jak...** are used in the sense 'as..., as...':

Chcę mieć taką samą bluzką, jaką ty masz (or: **jak ty**). *I want to have the same kind of blouse that you have (as you).*

Wynik nie był taki, jakiego (or **jak**) **oczekiwałem.** *The result was not as I expected.*

Chcę żebyś był taki, jak (or **jaki**) **byłeś dawniej.** *I'd like you to be the same as before.*

See also expressions like **Jaki ojciec, taki syn.** *Like father, like son.*

f. The use of **taki taka takie** and **jaki jaka jakie** before an adjective is more natural than **tak, jak** :

Zobacz, jaka malutka (instead of **!jak malutka**)! *Look, how tiny it is (e.g. a mouse)!*

To pytanie nie jest takie ważne (instead of **!tak ważne**). *That question is not so important.*

The items **tak** and **jak** are more often used in comparisons: **To nie jest tak ważne, jak najpierw myślałem.** *That's not as important as I first thought.*

g. **Jaki taki** means 'some sort of', as in

Zbudowali sobie jaki taki dom. *They built some sort of house for themselves.*

który która które *which, who* (identifying pronoun)

	Sg.			Pl.	
	Masc.	Neut.	Fem.	Masc. pers.	Other
NV	który	które	która	którzy	które
G	którego	←	której	których	←
D	któremu	←	której	którym	←
A	= N/G	które	którą	których	które
I	którym	←	którą	którymi	←
L	którym	←	której	których	←

NOTES ON *KTÓRY KTÓRA KTÓRE*

a. **Który** is more specific than **jaki**; it implies that the choices are already visible and known:

Który to jest samochód? *Which car is that (out of specific cars under discussion)?*

Compare to **Jaki to jest samochód?** What kind of car is that, i.e., what brand, or what is it like?

b. In relative clauses, **który** translates English *which* and *who(m)*:

Gdzie jest ta książka, którą czytałem? *Where is that book (the specific one) which I was reading?*

Kto to była ta pani, z którą rozmawiałeś? *Who was that woman with whom you were were talking?*

c. In Nominative-case constructions, interrogative (questioning) pro-nomi-
nal adjectives like **jaki** and **który** usually occur first in the sentence; the
modified noun occurs in final position:

Jaki to jest samochód? *What kind of car is that?*

Która to jest studentka? *Which student-f. is that?*

Czyja to jest książka? *Whose book is that?*

In such constructions, the verb **jest/są** is often omitted: **Czyja to
książka?, Która to dziewczyna?,** etc. In oblique-case constructions, the
interrogative pronoun will more often occur next to the modified noun:

Z którą dziewczyną idziesz do kina? *With which girl are you going to the
movies?*

Nad jakim artykułem tak ustawicznie pracujesz? *On what sort of article
are you working on so diligently?*

O czyje interesy dbasz? *Whose interests are you concerned about?*

(niektóry niektóra) niektóre *some, not all* (indefinite pronoun)

	Sg. Masc.	Neut.	Fem.	Pl. Masc. pers.	Other
NV				niektórzy	niektóre
G	(The singular is regular,			niektórych	←
D	but not often used)			niektórym	←
A				niektórych	niektóre
I				niektórymi	←
L				niektórych	←

Niektóry *some, not all* is used most often in the plural, especially in the
sense 'some, a certain number':

Niektóre samochody trąbiły. *Some of the automobiles were honking.*

Niektórzy są niezadowoleni. *Some (people) are dissatisfied.*

Use in the singular is avoided, as in ***niektóry człowiek** *some man or other;*
use **jakiś jakaś jakieś** instead.

inny inna inne *other, another, different* (contrastive pronoun)

	Sg. Masc.	Neut.	Fem.	Pl. Masc. pers.	Other
NV	inny	inne	inna	inni	inne
G	innego	←	innej	innych	←
D	innemu	←	innej	innym	←
A	= N/G	inne	inną	innych	inne
I	innym	←	inną	innymi	←
L	innym	←	innej	innych	←

Notes on *INNY INNA INNE*

a. **Inny** often contrasts with either **ten sam** *the same one* or **taki sam** *the same sort:*

   To nie jest ten sam film, jest inny. *It's not the same film; it's a different one.*

   Dlaczego jesteś inny niż dawniej? *Why are you (so) different than formerly?*

   Pani jest taka inna. *You are so different (from everyone else).*

b. 'Different from/than' is expressed with either **inny niż** (usual with clausal comparison) or **inny od**+G (usual with nominal comparison):

   On jest zupełnie inny niż pamiętałem (or: **inny od ojca**). *He is completely different than I remembered (from his father).*

c. 'Something different' is rendered by **coś innego**:

   Dzisiaj mam coś kompletnie innego dla ciebie. *I have something completely different for you today.*

   In oblique (non-Nominative/Accusative) uses, **inny** occurs in the same case as the noun:

   Myślę o czymś innym. *I'm thinking about something else.*

   'Someone different/else' is rendered by **ktoś inny**:

   Miałem cię za kogoś innego. *I took you for someone else.*

d. In the plural, **inni/inne** is often coordinated with **niektórzy/niektóre, jedni/jedne,** or **pewni/pewne**:

   Niektórzy (jedni, pewni) ludzie wyszli, inni zostali. *Some people left, others stayed.*

   The masc. pers. plural form **drudzy** (from **drugi** *second, other*) is occasionally used in a similar function:

   Jedni śpiewali, drudzy (usually, **inni**) **tańczyli.** *Some were singing, others were dancing.*

e. The adverbial form of **inny** is **inaczej** *otherwise, differently*, and is used to contrast with **tak samo** *in the same way:*

   Staram się to zrobić jakoś inaczej. *I'm trying to do this somehow differently.*

   The adverbial form **indziej** *else* combines with **gdzie** and **kiedy**:
   gdzie indziej *somewhere else*   **kiedy indziej** *some other time.*

Preposed Fixed Genitive Phrases in a Pronominal Adjectival Function

In formal writing and speech, the unchanging Genitive phrases **tego rodzaju** (or **typu**) *of that type (sort)*, **wszelkiego rodzaju** *of all sorts*, **innego rodzaju** *of a different sort* and others, usually preposed, can occur in a pronominal adjectival function:

Nie powinni mu pozwalać na tego typu wybryki. *They shouldn't allow him this kind of outburst.*

Tego rodzaju wizje rzadko nas nawiedzają. *Visions of this sort visit us infrequently.*

W tym sklepie sprzedzają każdego rodzaju sprzęt narciarski. *They sell every sort of ski equipment in that store.*

Pies przynosi do domu śmieci wszelkiego rodzaju. *The dog brings home all sorts of trash.*

THE USE OF THE NEUTER PRONOMINAL-ADJECTIVAL FORM IN MIXED-GENDER REFERENCE

Pronominal adjectives can use the neuter singular form in situations of clearly mixed sexual reference. Agreement on the verb is usually neuter singular, but on occasion may be masculine personal plural. Such constructions are most natural when referring to male-female partners. The following sentence said of a married couple, is correct, if old-fashioned:

Każde z nas jest zajęte własnymi sprawami. *Each of us is engaged with his/her own affairs.*

More contemporarily, and especially if talking about a group of people, one would say **Każdy z nas jest zajęty własnymi sprawami.** Other examples:

Żadne z tych ludzi nie jest w pełni kompetentne. *None of these (mixed-sex) people is entirely competent.* Probably better: **Żaden z tych ludzi...**

Które z państwa przyszło jako pierwsze? *Which of you men and women was the first to arrive?* More often: **Kto z państwa przyszedł pierwszy?**

The neuter construction is always correct with the noun **rodzice** *parents*:

Jedno z twoich rodziców ma przyjść na wywiadówkę. *One of your parents has to come to a parent-teacher's conference.*

Któreś z twoich rodziców weszło do mieszkania przed chwilą. *One or the other of your parents entered the apartment a moment ago.*

PRO-ADVERBS

By a pro-adverb is meant one of the words that pose or answer the sorts of questions adverbial phrases in a sentence can answer. Typical English pro-adverbs are 'how', 'where', 'when', 'why'. The main Polish pro-adverbs are the following:

Questions:	Answers:	Negatives:
dlaczego *why*	**dlatego** *for that reason*	
kiedy *when*	**wtedy** *then*	**nigdy** *never*
jak *how*	**tak** *that way, thus*	**nijak** *no way*

którędy *which way*	tędy *that way*, tamtędy *that way there*	
gdzie *where*	tam *there*, tu *here*	nigdzie *nowhere*
dokąd *to where*	dotąd *to here*	donikąd *to nowhere*
skąd *from where*	stąd *from here*, stamtąd *from there*	znikąd *from nowhere*

Notes on pro-adverbs:

a. The system of universalistic pro-adverbs is not well developed. It includes **zawsze** *always;* **wszędzie** *everywhere,* **zewsząd** *from everywhere.*

b. **Gdzie** is often used instead of **dokąd** *where to:*

   Dokąd (gdzie) idziesz? *Where are you going?*

c. The most objective and impersonal sense of 'why?' is rendered by **dlaczego**. Other phrases for 'why' in various nuances include (suggesting fruitlessness or accusation) **po co** *what for?;* (expressing sympathy) **czemu** *how come?;* (very accusatorily) **co**; (abruptly) **czego** *what for* (rude)?:

   Po co tu przyszedłeś? *What did you come here for?*

   Czemu tak mizernie wyglądasz? *How come you look so poorly?*

   Co tak siedzisz? *What are you sitting there like that for?*

   Czego się tak gapisz? *What are you staring like that for?*

d. As the negative of **dlaczego** *why*, phrases like **bez powodu** *without cause* or **bez przyczyny** *without reason* are used. Instead of **nijak** *nohow*, the phrase **w żaden sposób** *in no way* is more often used.

e. The occurrence of negative pro-adverbs requires that the verb be negated:

   Nigdy cię nie zapomnę. *I'll never forget you.*

   Nigdzie go nie widzę. *I don't see him anywhere.*

f. Note the expression **ni stąd, ni zowąd** *from neither here nor there, i.e. out of nowhere, for no very good reason.*

g. In informal speech, the item **jak** has taken on the career of a virtually universal conjunction of condition or comparison (in such meanings as 'if', 'when', 'as', 'than'):

   Jak (instead of **kiedy**) **tylko będziesz na miejscu, to zadzwoń.** *As soon as you arrive, call.*

   Jak (instead of **jeśli**) **tam źle trafisz, to nie moja wina.** *If you lose your way, it's not my fault.*

   Rozumiem takie rzeczy lepiej, jak (instead of **niż**) **ty.** *I understand things better than you.*

The use of **jak** instead of **niż** *than*, as in the third example, is not recommended by most stylisticians, but is popular nevertheless.

INDEFINITE PRONOUNS AND ADVERBS

Indefinite adverbs and pronouns are formed by adding -(o)ś or -kolwiek either to a question adverb or to a declined form of a question pronoun or pronominal adjective. The suffix -ś refers to something specific but unknown; the suffix -kolwiek refers to something both non-specific and unknown, i.e., to anything. The corresponding difference in English is rendered by the prefixes *some-* (= -ś) and either *any-* or *-ever* (= -kolwiek).

1. Indefinite adverbs

Specific:	Non-specific:
gdzieś *somewhere*	**gdziekolwiek** *anywhere, wherever*
jakoś *somehow*	**jakkolwiek** *anyhow, however*
kiedyś *sometime*	**kiedykolwiek** *anytime, whenever*
dokądś *to somewhere*	**dokądkolwiek** *to anywhere*
skądś *from somewhere*	**skądkolwiek** *from anywhere*
dlaczegoś *for some reason*	**dlaczegokolwiek** *for any reason, for whatever reason.*

The above forms based on **dlaczego** and **dokąd** are used only infrequently. The suffix -**inąd** occurs mainly in the word **skądinąd** *from elsewhere, otherwise*:

2. Indefinite pronouns

Specific:	Non-specific:
coś *something*	**cokolwiek** *whatever, anything*
ktoś *someone*	**ktokolwiek** *whoever, anyone*
któryś *some*	**którykolwiek** *any, whichever*
jakiś *some kind*	**jakikolwiek** *whatever kind, any kind*
czyjś *someone's*	**czyjkolwiek** *anyone's, whosesoever.*

Notes on indefinite pronouns:

a. The particles -**ś** and -**kolwiek** are added after the inflected form of the pronoun or pronominal adjective: **coś, czegoś, czemuś; ktokolwiek, kogokolwiek, komukolwiek,** and so on. Examples:

—**Kup mi coś.** *Buy me something.*
—**Co, mianowicie?** *What, namely?*
—**Cokolwiek. Cokolwiek mi kupisz, będę zadowolony.** *Anything. Whatever you buy me, I'll be satisfied.*

b. The particle -**ś** is sometimes omitted with **kto** and **co** in existential uses, but the effect without -**ś** can sound a trifle rude:

Jest tam kto(ś)? *Is anybody there?*

Przynieść ci co(ś)? *Is there anything I can bring you?*

c. The particles **-ś** and **-kolwiek** may sometimes be combined with each other to express extreme vagueness of reference: **coś kolwiek** *something or other*, **ktoś kolwiek** *someone or other*, **gdzieś kolwiek** *someplace or other*; and so on.

d. The literary word **ongiś** *at one time, in its day* is isolated among the system of indefinites.

3. The prefix **nie-** added to certain pronominal adjectives and question adverbs creates an indefinite expression in more or less the same meaning as **-ś**:

niektóry *some*   **niejaki** *some sort*
nieco *something*   **niegdyś** *once, formerly*
niekiedy *sometimes*   **niejako** *sort of*

Note also **gdzieniegdzie** *here and there*. **Nieco** also means 'somewhat', as in **On jest nieco tępy** *He's a trifle obtuse.*

4. The particle **bądź** sometimes appears in the meaning '-ever', as in **co bądź** *whatever*, **jaki bądź** *any kind at all*, **kto bądź** *whoever*. The particle **byle** is used in the meaning 'any-' in a pejorative sense:

byle co *any old thing*   **byle kto** *any old person*
byle jaki *any old sort*   **byle jak** *any old way.*

5. The word **mało** can be used with personal pronouns and pro-adverbs in the sense 'hardly any':

Mało kto miałby ochotę. *Hardly anyone would have the desire.*

Mało kiedy chodzę na filmy. *I hardly ever to the movies.*

Mało co można kupić w tym sklepie. *You can hardly get anything in this store.*

SUPPLETIVE PRO-ADVERBIAL CONSTRUCTIONS

a. Constructions with **sposób** *way, manner* often substitute for **tak** *that way* or **jak** *what way*; see , **w jaki sposób** *in what way*, **w taki sposób** *in such manner*, **w ten sposób** *in that way.*

b. Constructions with **strona** *direction, way* can function as de facto pro-adverbs of direction, substituting for **którędy, tędy, tamtędy, skąd**; see **w którą stronę** *in which direction*; **w jaką stronę** *in what direction*, **z jakiej strony** *from what direction*, **z której strony** *from which direction*, **w tę stronę** *in that direction.*

c. Constructions with **powód** *cause* and **przyczyna** *reason* function in de facto pro-adverbial phrases of cause: **z jakiego powodu** or **z jakiej** przyczyny *for what reason*, z tego powodu or z tej przyczyny *for that reason*.

THE EMPHATIC PARTICLE -Ż(E)

The particle -ż (-że after consonants) may be added to certain interrogative or other expressive words for emphasis or in order to express surprise:

cóż? *what?!*	któż *but who?!*
gdzież *but where?!*	kiedyż *but when?!*
dlaczegoż or dlaczegóż *but why?!*	jakże(ż) *but how?!*
czyż *really?!*	ależ *come now!*
skądże *from where?! what do you mean?*	proszęż *come now!*

On occasion, the particle -ż(e) can be reduplicated: **Niechżeż pan pozwoli!** *Please allow me!*

SUBORDINATING PRONOUNS AND ADVERBS

1. In Polish, as in English, question words, whether pronominal or adverbial, may also be used to introduce subordinate clauses. In Polish writing, subordinate clauses are set off from the introducing clause by a comma:

    Czy wiesz, czyj to jest samochód? *Do you know whose car that is?*

    Nie pamiętam, kto to jest. *I don't remember who that is.*

    Nie rozumiem, dlaczego go lubisz. *I don't understand why you like him.*

    On pyta, czy jestem zajęty. *He's asking whether I'm busy.*

2. Indicative and relative adverbs and pronouns are usually obligatorily co-ordinated with each other. By contrast, English normally omits the indicative member of the pair:

tam, gdzie *the place where*	wtedy, kiedy *the time when*
to, co *the thing that*	tak, jak *the way that, as... as*
ten, kto *the one who*	taki, jaki *the same sort as*

    Examples:

    Obudziłem się dopiero wtedy, kiedy począł mnie szarpać za ramię. *I only awoke when he began tugging me by the shoulder.*

    Spotykamy się tam, gdzie zawsze. *We'll meet in the same place as always.*

    Z tego, co wiem, on jest już na emeryturze. *From what I know, he's already retired.*

    Niech pójdzie ten, kto ma ochotę. *Whoever wants to go, let him.*

TAK, JAK, AND *AŻ* AS MODIFIERS

The adverbs **tak** and **jak** may be used to modify either adjectives or adverbs, either separately or in tandem:

Jak dobrze być wreszcie w domu! *How good to be home at last!*

On nie jest tak stary, jak przypuszczałem. *He's not as old as I supposed.*

On nie umie pływać tak dobrze, jak ja. *He doesn't know how to swim as well as I .*

As discussed earlier, **tak** is more often used in clausal modifications, **taki taka takie** in adjectival ones:

On nie jest tak stary, jak przypuszczałem. *He's not as old as I suspected.*

On nie jest taki stary. *He's not that old.*

By itself, **tak(i)** is often preceded by the emphatic particle **aż**:

Zresztą on nie jest aż taki stary. *For that matter he's not all that old.*

Ona nie śpiewa aż tak dobrze. *She doesn't sing all that well.*

Chapter 8

Numerals

Numerals are a kind of determiner (a word which modifies a noun other than lexically) whose declension and use in Polish are complex enough to merit special treatment. In Polish one may distinguish cardinal, ordinal, collective, and reified numerals, as well as fractional, frequentative, multiplicative, and combinatory numerical expressions.

CARDINAL NUMERALS

Cardinal numerals are the basic numerals with which most things are counted. The Polish cardinal numerals are the following:

0	zero	26	dwadzieścia sześć
1	jeden jedna jedno	27	dwadzieścia siedem
2	dwa, f. dwie	28	dwadzieścia osiem
3	trzy	29	dwadzieścia dziewięć
4	cztery	30	trzydzieści
5	pięć	40	czterdzieści
6	sześć	50	pięćdziesiąt
7	siedem	60	sześćdziesiąt
8	osiem	70	siedemdziesiąt
9	dziewięć	80	osiemdziesiąt
10	dziesięć	90	dziewięćdziesiąt
11	jedenaście	100	sto
12	dwanaście	200	dwieście
13	trzynaście	300	trzysta
14	czternaście	400	czterysta
15	piętnaście	500	pięćset
16	szesnaście	600	sześćset
17	siedemnaście	700	siedemset
18	osiemnaście	800	osiemset
19	dziewiętnaście	900	dziewięćset
20	dwadzieścia	1000	tysiąc
21	dwadzieścia jeden	10,000	dziesięć tysięcy
22	dwadzieścia dwa	1,000,000	milion
23	dwadzieścia trzy	1,000,000,000	miliard
24	dwadzieścia cztery		
25	dwadzieścia pięć		

When enumerating a series, the word **raz** *once* is used instead of **jeden**: **raz, dwa, trzy,** etc.

CARDINAL NUMERAL DECLENSION

1. The number one, **jeden jedna jedno**, is declined like a pronominal adjective. It agrees with the modified noun in gender, number, and case: **jeden kot** *one cat*, Gsg. **jednego kota; jedno dziecko** *one child*, Gsg. **jednego dziecka; jedna krowa** *one cow*, Gsg. **jednej krowy**; and so on. The plural form **jedne** is used with plural-only nouns: **jedne drzwi** *one door*. The word **jeden jedna jedno** is also used in the sense 'a certain': **jeden człowiek** *a certain man*. On the pronominal use of **jeden jedna jedno**, see the preceding chapter.

2. The item **żaden żadna żadne** *no, none, not any*, with a declension similar to that of **jeden** (except for the NAsg. neuter) functions as a numeral of null amount. Its use is treated in the preceding chapter. The noun for 'zero' is **zero** G **zera**.

3. Numbers two, three, four, and 'both'

dwa, f. **dwie** *two*

	M., N.	F.	M.p.pl.
NV	dwa	dwie	dwaj
GL		dwóch, dwu	
D		dwom, dwóm, dwu	
A	dwa	dwie	dwóch
I	dwoma	(dwiema)	dwoma

(or, in all Inst. uses, **dwu**)

trzy *three*

	M., N., F.	M.p.pl.
NV	trzy	trzej
GL	trzech	
D	trzem	
A	trzy	trzech
I	trzema	

cztery *four*

	M., N., F.	M.p.pl.
NV	cztery	czterej
GL	czterech	
D	czterem	
A	cztery	czterech
I	czterema	

oba *both*

	M., N.	F.	M.p.pl.
NV	oba	obie	obaj
GL		obu	
D		obu	
A	oba	obie	obu
I	oboma	obiema	oboma

(or, in all Inst. uses, **obu**)

Notes on *dwa, trzy, cztery, oba*:

a. The forms **dwaj, trzej, czterej** are male-only forms, as are the Accusatives **dwóch, trzech, czterech, obu**. When referring to male-female combinations, the collective numeral is commonly used; see further below.

b. The form **dwu** is a possible form in the GDLI, and it is optional in the Accusative of masc. persons alongside **dwóch**.

c. **dwom** is the recommended written Dative form of **dwa** (in all genders), but **dwóm** also frequently occurs, and **dwu** is also acceptable.

c. **dwiema** and **obiema** are usual in the feminine Instrumental, alongside optional **dwoma, oboma** and **dwu, obu.**

d. In Nominative-case functions, the forms **dwóch** (or **dwu**), **trzech, czterech** plus the Genitive case may be used as alternatives to **dwaj, trzej, czterej**; hence either **dwaj chłopcy** or **dwóch (dwu) chłopców** *two boys*. The forms **dwaj, trzej, czterej** tend to be used more in writing.

e. For 'both', the forms **obydwa obydwie obydwaj** are more frequently used than forms of **oba obie obaj**, but the latter occurs often enough. The declension of **obydwa obydwie obydwaj** is like that of **dwa dwie dwaj,** except that with masculine persons only the Nominative-case construction with **obydwaj** is used (not **obydwóch** or **obydwu** plus the Genitive).

f. Before Locative forms **dwóch** and **czterech** one may use either **w** or **we**: **w(e) dwóch (czterech).**

3. Numbers five–ninety

pięć *five*

	M., N., F.		M.p.pl.
NV	pięć		pięciu
GDL		pięciu	
A	pięć		pięciu
I		pięcioma (pięciu)	

Like **pięć** are declined **sześć sześciu** *six*, **siedem siedmiu** *seven*, **osiem ośmiu** *eight*, **dziewięć dziewięciu** *nine*, **dziesięć dziesięciu** *ten.*

jedenaście *eleven*   **dwanaście** *twelve*

	M., N., F.	M.p.pl.		M., N., F.	M.p.pl.
NV	jedenaście	jedenastu	NV	dwanaście	dwunastu
GDL		jedenastu	GDL		dwunastu
A	jedenaście	jedenastu	A	dwanaście	dwunastu
I	jedenastoma (jedenastu)		I	dwunastoma (dwunastu)	

Note the change of **dwa-** to **dwu-** in oblique case-forms of **dwanaście** (and of **dwadzieścia** *twenty* described below). Like **jedenaście** are declined **trzynaście trzynastu** *thirteen*, **czternaście czternastu** *fourteen*, **piętnaście piętnastu** *fifteen*, **szesnaście szesnastu** *sixteen*, **siedemnaście siedemnastu** *seventeen*, **osiemnaście osiemnastu** *eighteen*, **dziewiętnaście dziewiętnastu** *nineteen.*

dwadzieścia *twenty*   **trzydzieści** *thirty*

	M., N., F.	M.p.pl.		M., N., F.	M.p.pl.
NV	dwadzieścia	dwudziestu	NV	trzydzieści	trzydziestu
GDL		dwudziestu	GDL		trzydziestu
A	dwadzieścia	dwudziestu	A	trzydzieści	trzydziestu
I		dwudziestoma (dwudziestu)	I		trzydziestoma (trzydziestu)

Like **trzydzieści trzydziestu** is declined **czterdzieści czteredziestu** *forty*.

pięćdziesiąt *fifty*

	M., N., F.	M.p.pl.
NV	pięćdziesiąt	pięćdziesięciu
GDL		pięćdziesięciu
A	pięćdziesiąt	pięćdziesięciu
I		pięćdziesięcioma (pięćdziesięciu)

Like **pięćdziesiąt** are declined **sześćdziesiąt** "szeździesiąt" **sześć-dziesięciu** *sixty,* **siedemdziesiąt siedemdziesięciu** *seventy,* **osiemdziesiąt osiemdziesięciu** *eighty,* **dziewięćdziesiąt dziewięćdziesięciu** *ninety.*

4.   Numbers 100–900.

sto *hundred*   **dwieście** *two hundred*

	M., N., F.	M.p.pl.		M., N., F.	M.p.pl.
NAV	sto	stu	NAV	dwieście	dwustu
GDIL		stu (I stoma)	GDIL		dwustu (I dwustoma)

trzysta *three undred* **czterysta** *four hundred*

	M., N., F.	M.p.pl.		M., N., F.	M.p.pl.
NAV	trzysta	trzystu	NAV	czterysta	czterystu
GDIL		trzystu (I trzystoma)	GDIL		czterystu (I czterystoma)

The Instrumental forms in -**oma** above are optional alongside forms in -**u**. **Czterysta** has the accent on the first syllable: "CZTE-ry-sta".

pięćset *five hundred*

	M., N., F.	M.p.pl.
NAV	pięćset	pięciuset
GDIL		pięciuset

Note that the I of **pięćset** is *not* *pięciomaset: **z pięciuset pasażerami** *with five hundred passengers.* The item -**set** does not trigger stress advancement to the next-to-last syllable; see **pięciuset** "PIĘ-ciu-set", **siedemset** "SIE-dem-set", and so on. Similarly to **pięćset** are declined **sześćset sześciuset** *six hundred,* **siedemset siedmiuset** *seven hundred,* **osiemset ośmiuset** *eight hundred,* **dziewięćset dziewięciuset** *nine hundred.*

tysiąc *thousand*

	Sg.	Pl.
NV	tysiąc	tysiące
G	tysiąca	tysięcy
D	tysiącowi	tysiącom
A	tysiąc	tysiące
I	tysiącem	tysiącami
L	tysiącu	tysiącach

milion *million*

	Sg.	Pl.
NV	milion	miliony
G	miliona	milionów
D	milionowi	milionom
A	milion	miliony
I	milionem	milionami
L	milionie	milionach

Notes on Numbers 5 and above:

a. With numbers 5-900, the Nominative-case function of masculine-personal gender combinations is expressed with a construction that is identical to the Genitive-Accusative. The ending is always **-u**. The quantified noun occurs in the Gpl., and verb agreement is neuter-singular; see further below under cardinal-numeral syntax. The Masculine-personal construction in **-u** usually refers to male-only groups. When referring to male-female combinations, the collective numerals are commonly used (see further below under collective numerals).

b. With numbers 5-400, the ending **-u** may occur in the Instrumental instead of **-oma** (numbers 500-900 have only **-u**). The ending **-u** occurs most often in compound numeral expressions where repeated overt Instrumental marking might be felt to be excessive, as in **z pięćdziesięciu dwiema osobami** instead of **z pięćdziesięcioma dwiema osobami**. However, the latter is not incorrect.

c. The numbers 1,000, 1,000,000, and so on are declined as regular masculine nouns in both singular and plural, including when reference is to a masculine-personal group: **dwa tysiące zeszytów** *2000 notebooks,* **pięć milionów ludzi** *5,000,000 people.* In oblique cases, **tysiąc** and **milion** as head numerals always take the Gpl.: **Ta książka wyszła w kilku tysiącach egzemplarzy.** *That book came out in several thousand copies-Gpl.*

d. The regular Dsg. of **tysiąc** is **tysiącowi**. However, especially in longer numeral expressions, the ending **-u** can occur, although most grammarians consider it substandard. Dative-case numeral expressions are in any case rare.

e. When referring to money, **tysiąc** and **milion** have optional Accusative forms in **-a**: **Daj mi tysiąc(a).** *Give me a thousand-spot.*

f. Feminine-like endings on numerals five and above are archaic, occurring into the early part of the 19th century; see Isg. in **-ą** (with different respective rection) in:

[**Słońce**] **siedmią barw błyszczy razem.** *The sun shines forth with seven colors-Gpl at once.*

przed dziesięcią laty *ten years-Ipl ago*

Both examples are from A. Mickiewicz, *Pan Tadeusz* (1834).

INDEFINITE NUMERALS

The following indefinite and questioning numerals have a declension and syntax similar to that of **pięć**:

> **ile ilu iloma** *how many, how much, as much*
> **wiele wielu wieloma** *many, much*
> **kilka kilku kilkoma** *several*
> **parę paru paroma** *a few*
> **tyle tylu tyloma** *so much, as much.*

Notes on Indefinite Numerals:

a. Belonging functionally to this group, but lacking in inflection, are **mało** *a little*, **dużo** *a lot* (and their comparatives **mniej** *less* and **więcej** *more*), **niemało** *quite a bit*, and **sporo** *a goodly amount or number*. These items usually occur only in NA or G functions, and are followed by the Genitive:

> **Mam mało doświadczenia.** *I have little experience.*

> **Nie widzę tu zbyt dużo materiałów.** *I don't see very much by way of materials here.*

These items may occur colloquially in the DIL as well: **z dużo ludźmi** *with a lot of people* (better: **z wieloma (wielu) ludźmi**).

b. With indefinite numerals (which have no gender-neutral collective form; see below), the forms **ile, tyle, wiele, kilka,** and **parę** are often used in Nominative-case functions in combination with masculine personal nouns; hence either **ilu ludzi** or, just as often, **ile ludzi** *how many people*.

c. The items **tyle…, ile…** may be coordinated to express 'as many/much…, as…': **Nie mam tylu pieniędzy, ile ty masz** *I don't have as much money as you do.*

d. **kilka-** and **parę-** are used to form indefinite numerals of the following sort:

> **kilkanaście kilkunastu kilkunastoma** *a dozen or so; from eleven to nineteen*
> **kilkadziesiąt kilkudziesięciu kilkudziesięcioma** *several dozen, from twenty to ninety.*
> **kilkaset kilkuset** *several hundred, from 200 to 900*
> **parenaście parunastu parunastoma** *a couple dozen*
> **parędziesiąt parudziesięciu parudziesięcioma** *several dozen*
> **pareset paruset** *a couple hundred*

e. An indefinite numeral construction in the sense 'or so, give or take a few' may be formed by post-posing **parę** to the numeral: **pięćdziesiąt parę jabłek** *fifty apples or so.*

f. The numbers **setki** *hundreds* and **tysiące** *thousands* can be used as de facto indefinites with neuter sg. verb agreement:

Setki wozów pędziło do mety. *Hundreds of cars were rushing to the finish.*

Tysiące osób uczciło pamięć wielkiego pisarza. *Thousands of persons honored the memory of the great writer.*

Tysiące kobiet samotnie wychowuje swoje dzieci. *Thousands of women bring up their children by themselves.*

Plural syntax in the above instances (e.g., **Setki wozów pędziły do mety** is also possible, but is becoming less frequent.

g. The indefinite numeral **szereg** *a number of* is considered inelegant by some. Normative grammars recommend instead the use of **sporo, niemało, kilka,** or **wiele.** As a quantifier, **szereg** in NA expressions governs the Gpl., and can take neuter sg. verb agreement:

Spotkałem tam szereg osób. *I met a number of persons there.*

Szereg ludzi odchodziło z pracy. *A number of people quit work.*

In oblique cases, **szereg** as a quantifier sometimes takes numeral endings and syntax, hence **przeciw szeregu osobom** *against a number of people-Dpl.* instead of **przeciw szeregowi osób.**

h. The word **kopa** *threescore (sixty)* is also used in the sense 'bunch, pile', especially in the phrase **kopę lat** *it's been ages.* the noun **gromada** *team, herd, group* can have the meaning of a relatively large number: **Było ich cała gromada.** *There was a whole bunch of them.* In dialects or slang, the indeclinable word **siła** may be used in the sense 'a lot': **Mamy siła gości** *We have a lot of guests.* **siła złego na jednego** *a lot of misfortune for a single person* (proverb).

i. Numerical approximations are expressed with **(o)koło** *around, about* plus the Genitive: **(o)koło pięciu samochodów** *around five cars;* or with the phrase **mniej więcej** *more or less:* **mniej więcej tysiąc ludzi** *a thousand people more or less.* The preposition **z(e)+A** is also used in this function: **z pięćdziesiąt kilometrów** *some fifty kilometers,* **ze trzy dni** *some three days.* The use of undeclined numerals after prepositions like **(o)koło** is considered substandard, hence use **koło siedmiu godzin** *around seven hours,* not ***koło siedem samochodów.** This tendency is suggestive of the Accusative-like nature of numerals in Polish (if already Accusative, then this case should resist being over-ridden by a preposition requiring another case).

Cardinal-Numeral Syntax

1. Numbers one, two, three, four follow a straightforward determiner, i.e.
    adjectival, syntax. They agree with the quantified noun in gender,
    number, and case. The following phrases may serve as illustrations:

	jeden chopiec *one boy*	jedna krowa *one cow*	jedno zwierzę*l* *one animal*
N	jeden chłopiec	jedna krowa	jedno zwierzę
G	jednego chłopca	jednej krowy	jednego zwierzęcia
D	jednemu chłopcu	jednej krowie	jednemu zwierzęciu
A	jednego chłopca	jedną krowę	jedno zwierzę
I	jednym chłopcem	jedną krową	jednym zwierzęciem
L	jednym chłopcu	jednej krowie	jednym zwierzęciu
(V	jeden chłopcze	jedna krowo	jedno zwierzę*

* Vocative uses for most numerical expressions are difficult or impossible to imagine.

	dwaj chłopcy *two boys*	dwie krowy *two cows*	dwa zwierzęta *two animals*
NV	dwaj chłopcy	dwie krowy	dwa zwierzęta
G	dwóch chłopców	dwóch krów	dwóch zwierząt
D	dwom chłopcom	dwom krowom	dwom zwierzętom
A	dwóch chłopców	dwie krowy	dwa zwierzęta
I	dwoma chłopcami	dwiema krowami	dwoma zwierzętami
L	dwóch chłopcach	dwóch krowach	dwóch zwierzętach

See earlier discussion regarding the optional occurrence of **dwu** in
oblique case forms. With numbers one, two, three, four, verb agreement is
logical: singular with one and plural with two, three, four:

Jeden chłopiec śmiał się. *One boy was laughing.*

Dwaj chłopcy śmiali się. *Two boys were laughing.*

Jedna krowa zdechła. *One cow died.*

Dwie krowy zdechły. *Two cows died.*

Optional Genitive-like expressions in Nominative-case functions take the
quantified noun in the Genitive case and take neuter singular verb
agreement:

Było nas trzech. *There were three of us.*

Dwóch chłopców leżało na plaży. *Two boys were lying on the beach.*

2. Numbers 5-900, as well as standard indefinite numerals like **ile, kilka,
    wiele**, etc., follow adjectival syntax only in the GDIL; in the NAV these
    numerals are quasi-nouns, and take the quantified noun in the Gpl.:

pięciu studentów *five students*	sześć kobiet *six women*	sto drzew *100 trees*
NAV pięciu studentów	sześć kobiet	sto drzew
G pięciu studentów	sześciu kobiet	stu drzew
D pięciu studentom	sześciu kobietom	stu drzewom
I pięcioma studentami	sześcioma kobietami	stoma drzewami
L pięciu studentach	sześciu kobietach	stu drzewach

See also, with indefinite numerals: **po paru minutach** *after several minutes,* **z wieloma uchyleniami** *with many evasions,* **w kilku wypadkach** *in several instances,* **we wszystkich dziesięciu filmach** *in all ten movies,* and so on.

When the subject of a sentence, numerical expressions five and above take neuter singular verb agreement:

Pięć kobiet szło. *Five women were walking.*

Pięciu studentów zaśmiało się. *Five students laughed out loud.*

It is difficult to demonstrate that Nominative-case numeral phrases five and above are not actually Accusative instead, as though this were an instance of the "Accusative of quantity". This fact would help explain the neuter singular verb agreement (the neuter singular is the default form, used when there is nothing specific for the verb to agree with). When feminine nouns of quantity (which distinguish formally between Nominative and Accusative) become "numeralized", they do tend to take the form of the Accusative; see substandard

Połowę **miast zostało zniszczonych.** *Half of the towns were destroyed.* (based on **połowa** *half*)

3. **Tysiąc** and **milion** always take the Gpl. of the quantified noun, even when they themselves are quantified:

tysiąc osób *1000 persons*	dwa tysiące osób *2000 persons*
NAV tysiąc osób	dwa tysiące osób
G tysiąca osób	dwóch (dwu) tysięcy osób
D tysiącowi (-u) osób	dwom (dwóm, dwu) tysiącom osób
I tysiącem osób	dwoma (dwu) tysiącami osób
L tysiącu osób	dwóch (dwu) tysiącach osób

When used in the singular, **tysiąc**, despite its masculine-like form, takes neuter singular verb agreement unless modified by an adjective:

Tysiąc żołnierzy zginęło. *A thousand people perished.*

Compare to: **Cały tysiąc żołnierzy zginął.** *An entire thousand soldiers perished.*

In the plural, constructions involving **tysiąc** almost always take neuter singular verb agreement. Neuter singular agreement is used in particular when the number is used to indicate an indefinitely large number, and with masculine personal nouns, as in

Tysiące ludzi wyemigrowało. *Thousands of people emigrated.*

Dziesiątki tysięcy Belgów uczestniczyło w pogrzebie. *Tens of thousands of Belgians took part in the funeral.*

A sentence like

Trzy tysiące książek zostało zniszczonych. *3000 books were ruined.*

where the referent is inanimate, will occasionally be found expressed in the plural, although normative grammars consider this incorrect. See

?Trzy tysiące książek zostały zniszczone. *(idem)*

The first version applies the rule that any construction in which the quantified noun appears in the Genitive takes neuter singular agreement. The second version, not unreasonably, views **tysiące** as the Npl. subject of the sentence, with which the verb agrees in number. When unquantified, **tysiące** can take Npl. agreement without problem, hence either of the following is correct:

Tysiące spraw jeszcze mnie tu zatrzymuje. *Thousands of things still keep me here.*

Tysiące spraw jeszcze mnie tu zatrzymują. *(idem)*

COMBINING PRONOMINAL ADJECTIVES WITH NUMERAL EXPRESSIONS

With combinations of a pronominal adjective and a numeral, various orders are possible in the Nominative-case function. If the pronominal adjective appears before the numeral, it most often appears in the Nominative, not the grammatically expected Genitive:

moje pięć sióstr *my five sisters*

alongside possible, but less frequent: **moich pięć sióstr** *(idem)*

pięć moich sióstr *(idem)*

Similarly, **wszystkie dziesięć filmów** *all ten movies* will be preferred over possible **wszystkich dziesięć filmów** *ibid.* Regardless of the choice, an agreeing verb will be in the neuter singular; a predicate adjective will appear in the Genitive:

Moje pięć sióstr *było* **rozpieszczonych.** *My five sisters were spoiled.*

Ostatnie kilka miesięcy *było* **bogatych w wydarzenia.** *The last several months were rich in occurrences.*

Note that the phrase **pięć z moich sióstr** *five out of my sisters*, also possible, implies that one has more than five sisters. The addition of another pronominal adjectival modifier to the phrase 'my five sisters' creates an almost irresoluble syntactic conundrum:

> ??**Wszystkie moje pięć sióstr chce być bogatych.** *(idem)*

> ??**Wszystkich moich pięć sióstr chce być bogatych.** *All five of my sisters want to be rich.*

One could say instead:

> **Moje pięć sióstr bez wyjątku chce być bogatych.** *My five sisters without exception want to be rich.*

COMPOUND NUMERALS

1. Compound numerals follow the syntax of the last member. If the compound ends in two, three, four, the quantified noun will appear in the Nominative plural, and the compound numeral expression will require plural verb agreement:

   > **Dwadzieścia trzy koty bawiły się.** *23 cats were playing.*

2. If the compound ends in five–nine, the quantified noun will occur in the Genitive plural and the expression will take neuter singular verb agreement:

   > **Trzydzieści pięć kotów bawiło się.** *35 cats were playing.*

3. The masculine-personal plural numerals **dwaj, trzej, czterej** do not occur in compound numeral expressions; only **dwóch** (or **dwu**), **trzech**, and **czterech** are used, with corresponding Genitive-case, neuter-singular syntax:

   > **Dwudziestu trzech chłopców bawiło się.** *23 boys were playing.*

4. Compound numerals ending in 1 use **jeden**, which does not change according to gender or case, and which takes the Genitive plural and neuter singular verb agreement:

   > **Czterdzieści jeden dziewczyn uczestniczyło.** *41 girls took part.*

   > **Czterdziestu jeden mężczyzn czekało.** *41 men were waiting.*

   See also in oblique cases:

   > **autobus z dwudziestu jeden pasażerami** *bus with 21 passengers-Ipl.*
   > **dom o trzydziestu jeden oknach** *house with 31 windows-Lpl.*

5. In longer compound numerals, in principle all items are declined:

NA   tysiąc pięćset siedemdziesiąt dwie koszule *1572 shirts*
G   tysiąca pięciuset siedemdziesięciu dwóch koszul
D   tysiącu pięciuset siedemdziesięciu dwom koszulom
I   tysiącem pięćset siedemdziesięciu dwiema koszulami
L   tysiącu pięciuset siedemdziesięciu dwóch koszulach.

However, especially in contexts requiring the frequent recitation of numbers, the thousands and hundreds may not be declined; hence possible L **Zarobiłem na tysiąc pięćset siedemdziesięciu dwóch koszulach** *I made a profit on 1572 shirts*. When counting inventory and livestock, the word **sztuka** *piece, item* often substitutes for the name of the item being counted:

Sprzedano siedemdziesiąt sztuk bydła. *Seventy head of cattle were sold.*

In long numeral expressions, as above, the Dative of **tysiąc** tends to be **tysiącu** instead of **tysiącowi**; with tens and hundreds the I ending -**oma** is often replaced by -**u**.

COLLECTIVE NUMERALS

     dwoje *two*

NV   **dwoje**
G   **dwojga**
DL   **dwojgu**
A   **dwoje**
I   **dwojgiem**

The stem shows an anomalous -**g-** in the oblique forms. Like **dwoje** are declined **oboje obojga** (or **obydwoje obydwojga**) *both*, **troje trojga** *three*, **czworo czworga** *four*, **pięcioro pięciorga** *five*, **sześcioro sześciorga** *six*, **siedmioro siedmiorga** *seven*, **ośmioro ośmiorga** *eight*, **dziewięcioro dziewięciorga** *nine*, and so on, up to **dziewięćdziesięcioro dziewięćdziesięciorga** *ninety* (note: **dwanaścioro** *twelve*, **dwadzieścioro**). In addition, there is an indefinite collective **kilkoro kilkorga** *several*.

Contemporary speakers of Polish are slowly losing command of the collective numeral. Cardinal numerals are often substituted for collectives five and above; collectives higher than nineteen are especially infrequent.

    Collective numerals are used:

1.   with nouns that have no singular (plural-only nouns; see Chapter 5):

troje drzwi *three doors*
czworo sań *four sleighs*
pięcioro skrzypiec *five violins*

When the singular of such a noun is to be expressed, the formal plural of **jeden** is used: **jedne drzwi** *two doors*, **jedne sanie** *one sleigh*. With plural-only "paired" nouns, one usually uses **para** plus the Genitive plural instead of the collective: **pięć par spodni** *five pairs of trousers,* **dwie pary nożyczek** *two pairs of scissors,* **jedne okulary** or **jedna para okularów** *1 pair of eyeglasses,* even **dwie pary sań** *two (pair of) sleighs.* Creations such as **pięć sztuk szkrzypiec** *five items of violins* are the subject of ridicule, but they indicate the difficulty many speakers have when counting plural-only nouns.

2. With paired parts of the body, especially eyes. With **ręka** *hand,* the regular cardinal numeral may be used instead:

dwoje oczu *two eyes* (or even: **troje oczu** *three eyes*)
dwoje rąk *two arms* (or **dwie ręce,** but usually: **oboje rąk** *both arms*)

3. With personal groups of indeterminate gender. The collective almost always occurs with the nouns **ludzie** *people* and, especially, **dzieci** *children:*

dwoje ludzi (alongside **dwóch** or **dwu ludzi**) *two people*
czworo dzieci *four children* (or: **czwórka dzieci,** see below under reified numerals
kilkoro (kilku, kilka) ludzi *several people*

With other nouns, the use of the collective suggests that the group consists of both men and women; hence

pięciu studentów *five male students*
pięć studentek *five female students*
pięcioro studentów *five students of either gender*

4. With groups of animal young, although with larger numbers non-collective numerals are usually used. Sometimes the tens will be repre-sented by the regular (always non-masculine personal) form of the nume-ral, while the unit will be expressed collectively:

dwoje źrebiąt *two foals*
sześcioro orląt *six eaglets*
trzydzieścioro dwoje (or **trzydzieści dwoje**) **kurcząt** *thirty-two chicks* (or even **trzydzieści dwa kurczęta**)
czterdzieści dwoje ludzi *42 people*

5. Collective numerals (with the partial exception of **oboje**; see below, 10) follow a Genitive syntax in the Nominative, Accusative, and Instrumental (!) cases; in the other cases, they follow a modifying syntax:

NAV	**pięcioro kurcząt**
G	**pięciorga kurcząt**
D	**pięciorgu kurczętom**
I	*pięciorgiem kurcząt* (note the Genitive on the noun)
L	**pięciorgu kurczętach**

6. The collective numeral ordinarily takes neuter singular verb agreement:

    Było ich pięcioro. *There were five of them.*

    Troje dzieci bawiło się. *Three children were playing.*

    Dwoje ludzi przyszło. *Two people arrived.*

    Verb agreement is plural when the collective is modified by a pronominal adjective:

    Wszyscy czworo byli zajęci. *All four (people) were busy.*

7. With personal pronouns one places the pronoun before the collective, and uses either singular or plural agreement; or one places the collective plus z+G or **spośród** +G before the pronoun, the sense varying in one case and the other.

    My pięcioro szliśmy (szło) razem. *We five went together.*

    Pięcioro z nas szło razem. *Five of us went together.*

    Troje spośród nas przeziębiło się. *Three from among us caught cold.*

8. Nominative-case pronominal adjectives referring to nouns counted collectively occur in the neuter sg.:

    Tam było dwadzieścia pięcioro ludzi, z których *każde* **miało jakieś braki.** *There were twenty people there, out of whom each one had some kind of shortcomings.*

    For further discussion, of such agreement, see in Chapter 7 under **każdy każda każde.**

SYNTAX OF OBOJE (OBYDWOJE)

10. Unlike the other collectives, **oboje** (or **obydwoje**) takes Npl. agreement when used with masculine personal nouns:

    Oboje goście wyszli. *Both guests-Npl. left-masc.pers.3.p.pl.*

    Contrast with: **Oboje dzieci spało.** *Both children-Gpl. were sleeping-neut.3.p.sg.*

    The Npl. construction with **oboje** is especially frequent in combination with **rodzice** *parents:*

    Oboje moi rodzice urodzili się w Warszawie. *Both my parents were born in Warsaw.*

    In combination with personal pronouns, one finds the same alternatives as with the other collectives, but without a difference in semantic import. One may say either

    Czy oboje z państwa przyleciało (przylecieli) tym samym lotem? *Did both you people arrive on the same flight?*

---

or **Czy państwo oboje przylecieli tym samym lotem?** *(idem)*

My oboje byliśmy zajęci. *We both were tired.*

or **Oboje z nas było zajętych (byliśmy zajęci).** *(idem)*

REIFIED NUMERALS

When a number is referred to by its own name, or when a number is used pronominally, substituting for a room in a hotel, a streetcar, playing card, grade, clothing or tool size, and the like, the reified numeral is usually used, which is a feminine-gender noun ending in **-ka**:

jedynka *a one*

N	**jedynka**
G	**jedynki**
DL	**jedynce**
A	**jedynkę**
I	**jedynką**
V	**jedynko**

Like **jedynka** are declined **dwójka** *two*, **trójka** *three*, **czwórka** *four*, **piątka** *five*, **szóstka** *six*, **siódemka** *seven*, **ósemka** *eight*, **dziewiątka** *nine*, **dziesiątka** *ten*, **jedenastka** *eleven*, **dwunastka** *twelve*, **dwudziestka** *twenty*, **trzydziestka** *thirty*, **czterdziestka** *forty*, **pięćdziesiątka** *fifty*, **sześćdziesiątka** *sixty*, **siedemdziesiątka** *seventy*, **osiemdziesiątka** *eighty*, **dziewięćdziesiątka** *ninety*, **setka** *hundred*, **pięćsetka** *five hundred*. For thousand, the masculine noun **tysiączek** *thousand* is in colloquial use, although ordinarily facultatively animate **tysiąc** is used in reified uses, for example in the card game: **Nie chce mi się grać w tysiąca.** *I don't feel like playing "tysiąc".* Before both **dwójka** and **czwórka** one may use either **w** or **we** in.

Examples:

Wyłożył dwójkę. *He laid down a two (playing card).*
Mam trzy szóstki. *I have three sixes (in cards).*
Dostałem piątkę. *I received a five (grade).*
Mieszkam w jedynce. *I live in (room number) one.*
Jedziemy jedenastką. *We are taking (car number) eleven.*
Podaj mi ósemkę. *Pass me an eight (say, a wrench).*
Czy masz setkę? *Do you have a hundred (zlotys)?*

OTHER USES OF REIFIED NUMERALS

1. A frequent use of the reified numeral is as a kind of collective, analogous to English expressions in *-some*, especially common when referring to sports teams. 'In a group' is expressed with **w** plus the Accusative: **w(e) dwójkę** *in a twosome*. The reified numeral is also used colloquially, alongside the collective, to refer to groups of children or younger adults:

Gramy w(e) dwójkę (w(e) czwórkę). *We're playing as a twosome (foursome).*

Mieszkamy w szóstkę. *The six of us are living together.*
Gra polska jedenastka. *The Polish eleven (soccer team) is playing.*
Mam dwójkę (alongside **dwoje**) **dzieci.** *I have two kids.*

2. The reified numeral is used to refer to age-groups by tens:

   Ona jest już po sześćdziesiątce. *She is already past sixty.*
   On ma pod siedemdziesiątkę. *He is pushing seventy.*

3. Reified numerals **dziesiątka** and **setka** are used in the plural in rough estimations where English uses *dozens* and *hundreds*:

   Dziesiątki (setki) ludzi zostało zabitych. *Dozens (hundreds) of people were killed.*

   Note here the neuter-singular verb and Genitive plural adjective (**zabitych**) in the predicate, used especially when reference is masculine-personal-plural, and when the numbers are approximations only, as is inherently the case with such quantifiers. A sentence such as

   Setki kobiet żyło w biedzie. *Hundreds of women were living in poverty.*

   could just as easily, if not preferably, be expressed with plural agreement:

   Setki kobiet żyły w biedzie. *(idem)*

   See earlier discussion over a similar agreement problem in connection with **tysiąc** where, however, neuter singular agreement is preferred. The implication is that items like **dziesiątka** and **setka** are more nouns than numerals, while **tysiąc** is more a numeral than a noun.

4. As with **tysiąc**, a quantified noun after **dziesiątka** and **setka** will always be in the Genitive plural, regardless of case:

   Można powiedzieć to samo o setkach tysięcy innych ludzi. *One could say the same thing about hundreds of thousands of other people.*

5. The Instrumental case is used to express 'by the dozen', 'by the hundred', etc.:

   Ludzie padali setkami z głodu. *People were falling by the hundreds from starvation.*

6. Another use of the reified numeral is in reference to banknotes and certain other measurements:

   Mam tylko pięćsetkę. *I only have a 500(-zloty note).*

   In more formal usage, constructions of the type **pięćsetzłotówka** *500-zloty note* are used. Cf. also:

   Prosimy o dwie setki. *We'd like two 100s (milliliters of vodka).*

7. Unlike collective numerals, reifed numerals may not be compounded, even in theory. The cardinal numeral is used instead, often next to **numer** *number:*

Jedzie tramwaj numer trzydzieści dziewięć. *Here comes streetcar number 39.*

8. Increasingly, the reified numeral is used in cases of indecision as to the correct numerical form related to lack of knowledge about the gender make-up of a group of people; see the discussion immediately to follow.

SUMMARY: FIVE WAYS TO SAY "THREE STUDENTS"

Numeral use in Polish is most complex when referring to groups of people. The counting of things is mostly straightforward. The widest variety of choices is afforded by the "paucal" numerals 2, 3, 4, so the practical import of numeral choice may be summarized by examining various ways of saying "three students", as an answer to the questions "How many students are in class today?" or "How many students do you have this year?" In Polish, there are two ways of asking these questions, with **ilu** or with **ile**:

Ilu (ile) studentów jest dziś na zajęciach? *How many students are in class today?*

Ilu (ile) masz studentów w tym roku? *How many students do you have this year?*

The grammatically most correct question-numeral here, in both instances, is the masculine-personal form **ilu**. However, the form **ile** functions as a kind of substitute for the missing collective **iloro* in the sense "how many students regardless of sex?", and it is not at all wrong to use it. The form **ilu** is preferred in the second of the two questions, because the question is asked more in the abstract. By contrast, the first question may have been asked with a preconception as to the sexual composition of the group. If the person asking the question already knows that the group consists of both men and women, he or she would be more justified in using **ile**.

Potential mixes of the sexes in a group of three students, as far as Polish grammar is concerned, are the following, where +m or +f means 'at least one male or female, respectively'; –m or –f means 'no male or female, respectively'; and ±m or ±f means 'a male (or female, respectively) may be present, but does not have to be'. In sum, possible groupings are:

a. +m, –f all male
b. –m, +f all female
c. +m, +f some are male, some are female
d. +m, ±f at least one is male, possibly all are male
e. ±m, ±f no sexual identity (obviously, at least one is +).

Note that we use the term 'sex' here in the sense 'perceived as belonging to one of the two sexes'.

The possibility ±m, +f (at least one female) is not pertinent to Polish numeral choice; and the choice –m, –f (neither male nor female) is excluded on logical grounds. The answer to the first question "How many students are in class today?") may be influenced by whether or not one knows the sexual composition of the group in advance. All of the following responses mean 'There are three students in class' and 'This year I have three students':

–m, +f   **Na zajęciach są trzy studentki.**
           W tym roku mam trzech studentów (trzy studentki).

If the students are all female, and we see so or know so, it is correct to use the female-specific form, **trzy studentki**. Otherwise, if the persons are mentioned in the abstract, it is also correct to use the masculine-personal expression **trzech studentów**. To call attention to the female sex of the students involved in answer to an abstract inquiry might be considered to be beside the point.

±m, ±f   **Na zajęciach jest trzech studentów.**
+m, ±f   **W tym roku mam trzech studentów.**

If one has no knowledge of the sexual composition of the group, and if it is beside the point (as it usually is), then the masculine-personal form is correct. This is also the correct choice for +m, ±f, that is, when one knows for certain that at least one member is male, but is not sure about the composition of the whole.

+m, +f   **Na zajęciach jest troje studentów.**
           W tym roku mam trzech (troje) studentów.

If one knows that the group is of mixed sex, then it is correct to use the gender-inclusive form **troje**. In answering the question "How many students do you have?", the responder could answer equally well with **trzech** (at least one male) or **troje** (at least one male and female), as long as this is true.

+m, –f   **Na zajęciach są trzej studenci (jest trzech studentów).**
           W tym roku mam trzech studentów.

Somewhat less onus attaches to identifying a group as all-male, even if the fact is irrelevant, than to identifying a group as all-female. If one knows that the group is all male, then the form **trzej** is correct, but the masculine personal form **trzech** would be more common. In the Accusative case (in the second sentence), the distinction between all-male and masculine-personal (i.e., at least one male) is neutralized in the single form **trzech**.

±m, ±f   **Na zajęciach jest trójka studentów.**
           W tym roku mam trójkę studentów.

In colloquial Polish, especially if the age-group is fairly young, one may use the reified numeral (here, **trójka**) as a gender-neutral and somewhat familiar form. This use is expanding, probably because it fills a logical need.

Because of the complexity of numeral choice when referring to people, the word **osoba** *person*, which is neutral as to sexual reference, is often used to refer to personal groups: **trzy osoby** *three persons*.

ORDINAL NUMERALS

Ordinal numerals are numerical adjectives used to qualify a noun as to its order in a series. The Polish ordinal numerals are as follows:

1st	**pierwszy**	13th	**trzynasty**
2nd	**drugi**	14th	**czternasty**
3rd	**trzeci**	15th	**piętnasty**
4th	**czwarty**	16th	**szesnasty**
5th	**piąty**	17th	**siedemnasty**
6th	**szósty**	18th	**osiemnasty**
7th	**siódmy**	19th	**dziewiętnasty**
8th	**ósmy**	20th	**dwudziesty**
9th	**dziewiąty**	21st	**dwudziesty pierwszy**
10th	**dziesiąty**	22nd	**dwudziesty drugi**
11th	**jedenasty**	23rd	**dwudziesty trzeci**
12th	**dwunasty**	24th	**dwudziesty czwarty**, and so on

Also: **trzydziesty** *30th*, **czterdziesty** *40th*, **pięćdziesiąty** *50th*, **sześćdziesiąty** *60th*, **siedemdziesiąty** *70th*, **osiemdziesiąty** *80th*, **dziewięćdziesiąty** *90th*, **setny** *100th*, **dwusetny** or **dwóchsetny** *200th*, **trzechsetny** *300th*, **czterechsetny** *400th*, **pięćsetny** *500th*, **tysięczny** *1000th*, **dwutysięczny** *2000th*, **trzechtysięczny** *3000th*, **czterechtysięczny** *4000th*, **pięciotysięczny** *5000th*, **milionowy** *1,000,000th*, **miliardowy** *1,000,000,000*.

Notes on the Use of Ordinal Numerals

1. Compound ordinal numerals place only the last two items in the ordinal form: **dwa tysiące trzysta** *pięćdziesiąty drugi* 2351st.

2. Adverbial expressions having the meaning "in the first place", etc. are formed with **po** plus the Accusative sg. neuter form of the ordinal:

   po pierwsze *in the first place*   **po trzecie** *in the third place*
   po drugie *in the second place*   and so forth.

"For the *n*th time" is expressed by **po raz *n*-ty** *for the nth time*, as in **po raz pierwszy** (**drugi, trzeci**) *for the first (second, third) time*. The word **wtóry** *second* sometimes occurs instead of **drugi** in such expressions: **po wtóre** *in the second place*, **po raz wtóry** *for the second time*.

3. The word **pierwszy** *1st* is often coordinated with **ostatni** *last*:

   On nie przyszedł ani jako pierwszy, ani jako ostatni. *He was neither the first nor the last to arrive.*

Note expressions such as the following:

On pierwszy podniósł rękę. *He was the first to raise his hand.*

4. Ordinal numerals are "absolute", i.e. inherently non-comparable; that is, there is no 'more first' or 'firster', for example. Ordinal numerals other than **pierwszy, drugi, trzeci** are rarely used in the plural, hence there is no good way to say directly 'They were the fifth to arrive'. One might say, **Oni przyszli jako piąta para** *They were the fifth couple to arrive.* However, the plural form of the ordinal may be found with plural-only nouns, as in **piąte drzwi po prawej stronie** *fifth door on the right.*

EXPRESSING DATES

1. Case-forms of calendar years are expressed as follows, using the ordinal:

    NA **rok tysiąc dziewięćset dziewięćdziesiąty siódmy** *(the year) one thousand, nine hundred ninety-seven (1997)*

    G **roku tysiąc dziewięćset dziewięćdziesiątego siódmego**

    L **w roku tysiąc dziewięćset dziewięćdziesiątym siódmym** and so on.

    In such expressions, the word for 'year' may either go at the beginning or at the end of the expression.

2. Days of the month appear in the masculine form of the ordinal, as if in agreement with the missing word **dzień** *day:* **dwudziesty piąty marca** *the 25th of March,* **od pierwszego do pierwszego** *from the 1st (of one month) to the 1st (of the next).*

3. Placing an entire expression for a date in the bare Genitive case answers the question **Kiedy to się stało (zdarzyło się, miało miejsce)?** *When did that happen (occur, take place?).* This usage is called the Genitive of Time:

    Pierwszego września, roku tysiąc dziewięćset trzydziestego dziewiątego, wojska niemieckie wkroczyły na terytorium Polski.
    On September 1, 1939, German armies encroached upon Polish territory.

EXPRESSING CLOCK TIME

1. When referring to the time of day, the feminine ordinal numeral is used, agreeing with a usually omitted **godzina** *hour:*

    Jest (godzina) pierwsza. *It is one o'clock.*

    Była (godzina) druga. *It was two o'clock.*

    and so on. Such expressions answer the question **Która jest (była) godzina?** *What time is (was) it?*

2. In expressions involving prepositions, the word for 'hour' is commonly omitted:

o drugiej *at two o'clock*	**o**+L
po trzeciej *after three o'clock*	**po**+L
przed czwartą *before four o'clock*	**przed**+I
do piątej *till, by five o'clock*	**do**+G
od szóstej *beginning after six o'clock*	**od**+G
na siódmą *for seven o'clock*	**na**+A

3. When indicating minutes after or before the hour, the following expressions are used:

pięć po ósmej *five after eight, 8:05*	**po**+L
za kwadrans dziewiąta *quarter till nine, 8:45*	**za**+A, N
(w)pół do dziesiątej *half till ten, 9:30*	**do**+G

'Two till or after' is expressed with the feminine form **dwie**, in agreement with omitted **minuty** *minutes*:

dwie po czwartej *two after four*
za dwie szósta *two till six*

These constructions answer the question "what time is it?" Most may themselves take a preposition (e.g. **od za dziesięć siódma** *from 6:50*). These constructions do not usually take **o** *at*, except that **o** often occurs before **wpół**:

Spotykamy się pięć po drugiej. *We are meeting at five after two.*

Przyjdę za kwadrans (piętnaście) trzecia. *I'll come at a quarter till three.*

Mam bilety na kwadrans (piętnaście) po czwartej. *I have tickets for a quarter past four.*

Będę gotowy (o) wpół do piątej. *I'll be ready at four-thirty.*

4. The construction with **do**+G to express time before the hour is in all instances incorrect, other than in the phrase **wpół do**; hence never

*****Jest kwadrans do czwartej.** *It's quarter to four.* but only

Jest za kwadrans czwarta. *(idem)*

5. In some parts of the country or with some speakers, time orientation may also be toward the half-hour, as in

za pięć wpół do dziewiątej *8:25* ("in five minutes half till nine")
pięć po wpół do ósmej *7:35* ("five after half till eight")

6. In official communications like timetables, and often also in speech, a 24-hour clock is used. Hours 13-24 refer to 1:00 p.m. to 12:00 midnight. Minutes are given following the hour. A radio announcer might say:

Minęła godzina dwudziesta zero pięć. *The hour 20:05 has just passed.*

FRACTIONALS

1. Ordinary fractions are expressed with a cardinal number in the numerator and an ordinal in the denominator. The ordinal modifies a missing noun **część** *part*, hence will be feminine in instances where the matter of gender agreement arises:

jedna trzecia *one third*   **cztery piąte** *four fifths*
dwie siódme *two sevenths*   **pięć szóstych** *five sixths*
siedem setnych *seven hundredths*   and so on

2. When declined, fractional expressions follow regular numeral+noun syntax; the fractioned object, if present, will be in the Gsg.

   NA   **siedem setnych kilograma** *seven/hundredths of a kilogram.*
   GL   **siedmiu setnych kilograma**
   D   **siedmiu setnym kilograma**
   I   **siedmioma setnymi kilograma**

3. 'Half'. The word **połowa** *half* is not normally used other than in descriptions such as

   Połowa miasta leżała w gruzach. *Half of the town lay in ruins* (towns not normally being fractionally measured).

   In measurements, one usually expresses 'half' with **pół** plus the Genitive case:

   pół godziny *half an hour*   **pół chleba** *a half-loaf of bread*
   pół litra *half a liter*   **pół procentu** *half of a percent.*

   The item **pół** functions as an indeclinable quantifier: **około pół godziny** *around half an hour.* In Instrumental uses the noun after **pół** may be subject to government: **przed pół rokiem** (or **roku**) *a half year ago*, **z pół kilogramem** (or **kilograma**) **cukru** *with half a kilogram of sugar.* Otherwise, government is Genitive: **po pół godziny** *after half an hour.* When modified, expressions with **pół** take neuter agreement: **każde pół godziny** *every half hour.*
       After **pół** the Gsg. is usually used with measures, whatever the main number. The Gpl. is sometimes used with other things when the main number is higher than 5. Hence: **trzy i pół litra** *3 1/2 liters-Gsg.*, **pięć i pół litra** *5 1/2 liters-Gsg.*, **trzy i pół miesiąca** *3 1/2 months-Gsg.*, but, after numbers 5 and above, often **pięć i pół miesięcy** *5 1/2 months-Gpl.*, although **pięć i pół miesiąca**-*Gsg.* is considered better by normative authorities. Among measurements of time, **sekunda** *second*, **minuta** *minute*, and **godzina** *hour* count as measures, hence occur in the Gsg. no matter what the main number, while time-periods like **dzień** *day*, **noc** *night*, **tydzień** *week*, **miesiąc** *month*, and **rok** *year* are often treated as

countable; hence **sześć i pół sekundy** *6 1/2 seconds-Gsg.*, but **sześć i pół roku** (or, possibly, **lat**) *6 1/2 years-Gpl.*

4. One-and-a-half is expressed with the indeclinables **półtora** (m. and n.), **półtorej** (f.) plus the Gsg. of the fractioned object:

półtora roku *1 1/2 years*   **półtorej godziny** *1 1/2 hours.*

The combinatory form is **półtora-**, regardless of the gender of the noun; compare **półtoragodzinny** *one-half hour's.* Both **półtora** and **półtorej** take neuter sg. verb agreement:

Minęło półtorej godziny. *One and a half hours passed.*

In oblique-case uses, masculine and neuter uses allow case government to pass through, at least in the Instrumental, while feminine uses do not: **przed półtora rokiem** *a year and a half ago* vs. **przed półtorej godziny** *an hour and a half ago.*

5. The word **ćwierć** (f.) *quarter* is not especially common. It is used most often in fractional weights, as in

ćwierć kilo *quarter kilo(gram)*   **ćwierć deka** *quarter deca(gram)* = *2.5 grams*

The word **ćwiartka** functions as a kind of reified fractional, referring to goods that come in quarter-measures, as

ćwiartka wódki *quarter (liter) of vodka*
ćwiartka kartofli *quarter (bushel) of potatoes.*

6. The decimal place is indicated in Polish with a comma, not a period. Decimal expressions are read as follows:

7,2 kg.   **siedem i dwie dziesiąte kilograma**
or **siedem koma** (or **przecinek**) **dwa kilograma**

7. The word **procent** *percent*, exceptionally for measurements, has the Gsg. form **procentu**, although **procenta** can be heard. In fractional expressions this word usually does not take endings: **trzy i pół procent** *3 1/2 percent*, **pięć i siedem dziesiątych procent** *5 7/10 percent.* In oblique cases, **procent** is often declined in the plural:

Rozdano książki tylko dziesięciu procentom dzieci. *Books were distributed to only ten percent of the children.*

Percentile expressions of all sorts usually take neuter sg. verb agreement:

Cztery procent ludności spożywa obiady poza domem. *Four percent of the population consumes dinner outside the home.*

ARITHMETIC OPERATIONS

Expressions referring to basic arithmetic operations are illustrated below:

$3 + 5 = 8$ **Trzy dodać pięć jest osiem.** or: **Trzy i/a pięć jest osiem.**

$7 - 5 = 2$ **Siedem odjąć pięć jest dwa.** or: **Pięć od siedmiu jest dwa.**

$4 \times 7 = 28$ **Cztery razy siedem jest dwadzieścia osiem.**

$12 \div 2 = 6$ **Dwanaście podzielić przez dwa jest sześć.**

It is possible to substitute **plus** for **dodać** and **minus** for **odjąć**.

FREQUENTATIVE AND MULTIPLICATIVE NUMERICAL EXPRESSIONS

1. To express frequency of occurrence, the noun **raz** NGpl. **razy** *once, one time* is used:

    Byłem tam raz. *I was there one time.*

    On dzwonił kilka razy. *He phoned a number of times.*

2. Alternatively, the adverb-forming suffix **-krotnie** may be employed, preceded by the combinatory form of the numeral (see below).

    Dzwonił kilkakrotnie. *He phoned several times.*

    Podaż wzrosła czterokrotnie w zeszłym kwartale. *Supply grew four-fold in the past quarter.*

3. Correspondents to English 'double', 'triple', 'quadruple', or 'two-fold', 'three-fold', 'four-fold' may also be formed with the prefix **po-** plus stems somewhat similar to the collective numeral. The adverbial form in **-nie** occurs frequently.

    podwójny -nie *double, two-fold*   **poczwórny -nie** *four-fold, four-fold*

    potrójny -nie *triple, three-fold*

    See **potrójny cheeseburger** *triple cheeseburger* (from McDonald's menu).

4. Combinations with **-nasób** *-fold* consist of **dwójnasób** *two-fold*, **trójnasób** *three-fold*, **czwórnasób** *four-fold*, used in construction with **w**, as in **powiększyć się (pomnożyć się) w dwójnasób** *increase (multiply) by two-fold.*

5. "Per" may be expressed with **na+A**: **cztery razy na godzinę** *four times an hour*, **raz na rok** (or **do roku**) *once a year*. Often one simply uses **w+L**, as in **dwa razy w tygodniu** *twice a week.*

DISTRIBUTIVE USE OF NUMERALS

Polish takes care to distinguish between 'I gave the children a candy (i.e. there was only one candy to divide among them)' and 'I gave the children a candy each (for as many children as there were, each one got a candy)'. Without numeral modification and with the number 1 the distributive sense is expressed with **po+L**; numbers 2, 3, 4, 5 and above take **po+A**.

Dałem dzieciom po (jednym) cukierku. *I gave the children a candy each.*

Dałem dzieciom po dwa (trzy, cztery) cukierki (pięć cukierków). *I gave the children two (three, four) candies (five candies) each.*

Te znaczki są po złotówce. *Those stamps are a zloty apiece.*

In the following kind of sentence, **po** acts as a distributive replacement for za+A:

Kupiłem dziesięć znaczków po dwadzieścia złotych. *I bought ten 20-zloty stamps.*

Contrast to **Kupiłem dziesięć znaczków za dwadzieścia złotych.** *I bought ten stamps for 20 zlotys (in all).*

COMBINATORY FORMS OF NUMERALS

Polish cardinal numerals may have special combinatory forms for forming constructions with certain adjectives and nouns. With most numbers, the link-vowel -o- is used:

1 **jedno-**	3 **trzy-** or **trój-**	5 **pięcio-**	7 **siedmio-**
2 **dwu-**	4 **cztero-** or **czworo-**	6 **sześcio-**	10 **dziesięcio-**, and so on.

Examples:

dwustronny *bilateral*
dwuwęglan *bicarbonate*
trójskok *triple jump*
trzykonny *three-horse (e.g. cart)*

czteroosobowy *four-person*
czworokątny *quadrangular*
pięciobój *pentathlon*
dwumiesięczny *bimonthly*

In making compounds with **set-** 100-, the combinatory forms **trzech-, czterech-, pięć-,** etc., are used to make words such as the following:

trzechsetny *300th* **czterechsetlecie** *400th aniversary*
pięćsetletni *500-year-old*, and so on

Indefinite numerals also have combinatory forms:

kilkugodzinny postój *a several-hour layover*
wieloletnie doświadczenie *many-years experience*

The Emphatic Particle *aż*

The particle **aż** *as far as, as much as, as many as* may be preposed to various kinds of numeral expressions in order to stress that the amount is large:

Produkcja wzrosła aż dziesięciokrotnie. *Production rose by as much as ten fold.*

Spędziliśmy w Warszawie aż dziesięć dni. *We spent in Warsaw as many as ten days.*

The more-or-less opposite of **aż** is **zaledwie** *barely:*

Produkcja wzrosło zaledwie o jeden procent. *Production grew by barely one percent.*

A somewhat related phrase is **razem** *together* in the sense 'all told':

Spędziliśmy tam razem dwa tygodnie. *We spent there two weeks altogether.*

'More than' is rendered with **przeszło**; 'upwards of' is expressed with **z górą**:

W spotkaniach z Ojcem Świętym udział wzięło przeszło dziesięć milionów osób. *More than 10 million people took part in meetings with the Holy Father.*

Z górą sześćset osób powołano karnie do wojska. *Upwards of six hundred people were punitively conscripted into the army.*

WEIGHTS AND MEASURES

długość *length,,* **głębokość** *depth,* **grubość** *thickness,* **miara** *measure,* **odległość** or **dystans** *distance,* **szerokość** *width,* **temperatura** *temperature,* **waga** *weight,* **wysokość** *height,* **wzrost** *height (of a person),*

cal -a Gpl. **cali** *inch*
centymetr -a *centimeter, .39 inches*
dekagram (deko) *ten gram, .353 ounces*
galon -a *gallon*
gram -a *gram, .035 ounces*
hektar -a *hectare, 10,000 m2, 2.47 acres*
kilogram -a *kilogram, 2.2046 pounds*
kilometr- a *kilomete, .62 miles*
korzec korca *bushel*
litr -a *liter, 1.057 quarts*
metr -a *meter, 39.37 inches*
mila Gpl. **mil** *mile*

milimetr -a *millimeter, .04 inches*
morga Gpl. **mórg** or **morg** *morg of land, 5,600 m²*
pół litra *half a liter*
kwarta *quart*
setka Gpl. **setek** *100 milliliters*
stopień stopnia *degree (of temperature)*
stopnie pożywej (poniżej) zera *degrees above (below) zero.* **stopnie mrozu** *degrees of frost (= below zero).* **stopnie Celcjusza (Fahrenheita)** *degrees Celcius (Fahrenheit)*
tona *ton, 1,000 kg., 1.1 US ton*

COMMON EUROPEAN CURRENCY

dolar -a *dollar*
frank -a *franc*
funt *pound*
grosz -a *grosh, 1/100 zloty*

lir -a *lire*
marka Gpl. **marek** *mark*
rubel rubla *ruble*
złoty -ego *zloty*

The word **euro** *euro* is currently indeclinable (as in **siedem tysięcy euro** 7000 *euros*), but colloquially one can hear Gsg. **eura**, Isg. **eurem**, NApl. **eura**. In the future one can expect this noun to be adapted to declension in the other cases.

THE INFINITIVE

The citation form of the verb (the form traditionally used by dictionaries) is the infinitive, which in Polish ends either in **-ć** or, rarely, in **-c**. In combination with each infinitive, the corresponding 1st person sg. ("I") and 2nd person sg. ("you") forms are sufficient for classifying the verb as to conjugational type. Although there are fairly regular relationships between the infinitive and the present tense forms, in the end it is simplest to cite and learn each verb in three forms rather than to learn rules for predicting the present tense from a technically analyzed or diacritically or numerically annotated version of the infinitive. In this way the listing **brać biorę bierzesz** comprises the citation forms for the imperfective of the verb 'take'. A system for predicting the present tense from an annotated infinitive is given in an addendum to this chapter.

Dictionaries sometimes use only the 3rd pers. sg. as a second memorization form alongside the infinitive, partly to save space and partly because not all verbs occur in the 1st and 2nd-person sg., for example **grzmieć** *thunder*, **mżyć** *drizzle*. The 1st and 2nd pers. sg. forms are used here because a) these are the logically sequential forms after the infinitive; b) these are the two most useful everyday speech forms for the majority of verbs; c) these two forms give helpful information about stem-changes which can occur in the verb's conjugation (hence less overall rule-memorization is required); d) this strategy allows one to use the 3rd pers. sg. ending by itself to indicate those verbs which do not occur in the 1st and 2nd persons, as **mżyć mży** *drizzle*.

NEGATED VERB-FORMS

The negative particle **nie** is, from the standpoint of pronunciation, part of the verb-form being negated. The particle **nie** may not be separated from the verb-form by any intervening word or particle. If the verb-form is one syllable in length, stress will fall on the negative particle: **nie chcę** "NIE chcę" *I don't want*, **nie dam** "NIE dam" *I won't give*, **nie wiem** "NIE wiem" *I don't know*.

THE FORMAL VERSUS THE PRAGMATIC POLISH CONJUGATIONAL SYSTEM

The Polish finite conjugational system appears superficially similar to the systems of related languages like, say, Russian, consisting of the cross-cutting categories of person (1st, 2nd, 3rd) and number (sg. and pl.). In Russian and a

number of other languages, the 2nd pers. pl. form functions as a form of polite address, whether singular or plural. However, the Polish system is distinct in an important respect from systems like Russian. Instead of the 2nd
pers. pl. form of the verb, Polish uses the titles **pan, pani** (sg.) and **panowie,
panie, państwo** (pl.), in combination with 3rd person forms of the verb, as
pragmatic 2nd-person forms of polite (formal, titled) address. A Russian verb-
form like читаете (čitajete) *read-2nd pers. pl.*, then, has as a minimum the
following six correspondents in Polish, depending on context and sexual
reference:

> **czytacie** *literal 2nd pers. pl. informal address*
> **pan (pani) czyta** *pragmatic 2nd-pers. sg. formal address*
> **państwo (panowie, panie) czytają** *pragmatic 2nd-pers. pl. formal address*

The pragmatic Polish finite conjugational system looks as follows. The
illustration is in the present tense, but analogous observations hold for the
past and future as well. The verb of illustration is **czytać czytam czytasz** *read:*

	Sg.	Pl.
1st person	(ja) czytam	(my) czytamy
2nd person informal	(ty) czytasz	(wy) czytacie
Pragmatic 2nd person formal	(pan, pani) czyta	(państwo) czytają
3rd person	(on, ona, ono) czyta	(one, oni) czytają

THE FOUR PRESENT-TENSE CONJUGATIONS

Technically speaking, the present tense is known as the "non-past",
because the present-tense of perfective verbs typically has future reference. In
this chapter we will treat verbs without reference or regard to aspect
(perfectivity or imperfectivity; see Chapter 11), and refer to the tense as
"present". There are four conjugations, amounting to slightly different sets of
present-tense endings. If one counts the ending of the 3.p.sg. as **-Ø** preceded
by a link vowel, endings are the same for all conjugations in the 2.p.sg.,
3.p.sg., 1.p.pl., and 2.p.pl.:

	Sg.	Pl.
1st p.	-ę or -m	-my
2nd p.	-sz	-cie
3rd p.	-Ø	-ą or -ją

The First and Second conjugations have 1.p.sg. in **-ę** and -3.p.pl. in **-ą**. The
Third and Fourth conjugations have 1.p.sg. in **-m** and 3.p.pl. in **-ją**. In older
poetry, especially for the sake of meter, one occasionally encounters the
1.p.pl. ending **-m**: **To tylko nasze, co dziś zjemy i** *wypijem*! *Only that which
we eat and drink is truly ours!* (A. Mickiewicz). Dialectally and in substandard
speech, one occasionally encounters 2.p.pl. **-ta**, especially in dual use: **Jak nie
chceta, to nie** *musita. If you want, you don't have to.*

A. FIRST CONJUGATION: VERBS IN -Ę -ESZ

Present endings:

1st p.	-ę	-emy
2nd p.	-esz	-ecie
3rd p.	-e	-ą

R2 replacements may occur before the "middle four" endings in -e- (-esz -e -emy -ecie), creating the possibility of a stem-consonant alternation before these endings on the one hand, and before the "outside" endings (-ę and -ą) on the other. In practice, many or most 1st-conjugation stems end in j or in some other functionally soft consonant to begin with, so that no surface alternation results. This is the case, for example, with the following 1st-conjugation verb, whose stem ends in -j-:

psuć psuję psujesz *spoil* (present stem **psu-j-**)

psuję *I spoil*	**psujemy** *we spoil*
psujesz *you spoil*	**psujecie** *you spoil*
psuje *he, she, it spoils*	**psują** *they spoil*

The present stem of many 1st-conjugation verbs is formed with -j- added to a primary consonant, creating a surface R3 stem consonant throughout the present:

pisać piszę piszesz *write* (present stem: underlying **pis-j-**, or surface **pisz-**)

piszę *I write*	**piszemy** *we write*
piszesz *you write*	**piszecie** *you write*
pisze *he, she, it writes*	**piszą** *they write*

If there is a change in the stem consonant between the 1st pers. sg./3rd pers. pl. stem and the stem of the four other present forms, it will be evident from the 1st and 2nd-person forms (this being the reason for citing these two forms); see

iść idę idziesz *go (on foot)*. Note the **d: dź** (spelled **dzi-**) alternation:

idę *I go* **idziemy** *we go*	
idziesz *you go*	**idziecie** *you go*
idzie *he, she, it goes*	**idą** *they go*

móc mogę możesz *be able*. Note the **g: ż** alternation:

mogę *I can*	**możemy** *we can*
możesz *you can*	**możecie** *you can*
może *he, she, it can*	**mogą** *they can*

brać biorę bierzesz *take:* Note the **r: rz** alternation (also the **e: o** alternation):

biorę *I take*	**bierzemy** *we take*
bierzesz *you take*	**bierzecie** *you take*
bierze *he, she, it takes*	**biorą** *they take*

The **e: o** alternation in the stem here occurs before the soft/hard dental **r**.

SURVEY OF VERBS OF THE 1ST CONJUGATION

1. Present stems formed with **-j-**. This general type consists of at least nine subtypes.

   a. Type **-a-ć -j-ę**

   mazać mażę mażesz *smear*

mażę	**mażemy**
mażesz	**mażecie**
maże	**mażą.**

In this subtype, the present-stem **-j-** is added to a primary consonant-stem, producing a surface R3 stem consonant throughout the present. Similarly: **bazgrać bazgrzę bazgrzesz** *scribble*, **chlastać chlaszczę chlaszczesz** *splash*, **chłostać chłoszczę chłoszczesz** *flog*, **chrapać chrapię chrapiesz** *snore*, **chrupać chrupię chrupiesz** *munch*, **ciosać cioszę** or **cieszę, cioszesz** or **cieszesz** *hew*, **czesać czeszę czeszesz** *comb*, **dłubać dłubię dłubiesz** *pick*, **drzemać drzemię drzemiesz** *doze*, **głaskać głaszczę głaszczesz** *stroke*, **karać karzę karzesz** *punish*, **kazać każę każesz** *order*, **kąpać kąpię kąpiesz** *bathe*, **klaskać klaszczę klaszczesz** *clap*, **kłamać kłamię kłamiesz** *tell a lie*, **kopać kopię kopiesz** *kick*, **lizać liżę liżesz** *lick*, **łamać łamię łamiesz** *break*, **łgać łżę łżesz** *fib*, **obrzezać obrzeżę obrzeżesz** *circumcise*, **orać orzę orzesz** *plow*, **pisać piszę piszesz** *write*, **płakać płaczę płaczesz** *cry*, **posłać poślę poślesz** *send*, **rąbać rąbię rąbiesz** *chop*, **skakać skaczę skaczesz** *jump*, **skrobać skrobię skrobiesz** *scrape*, **szarpać szarpię szarpiesz** *wrench*, **trzepać trzepię trzepiesz** *beat*, **wiązać wiążę wiążesz** *tie, bind*, and others.

   Many verbs of this type in **-t-a-ć** refer to sounds or movements. The stem consonant **t** is changed to either regular R3 **c** or, anomalously but more frequently, to **cz**:

   deptać depc(z)ę depc(z)esz *trample*

depc(z)ę	**depc(z)emy**
depc(z)esz	**depc(z)ecie**
depc(z)e	**depc(z)ą**

Similarly: **bełkotać** *stammer,* **chrobotać** *scratch,* **druzgotać** *crush,* **gruchotać** *crash,* **kołatać** *rattle,* **łaskotać** *tickle,* **łechtać** *titillate,* **mamrotać** *mumble,* and many others.

Verbs of this type with roots in **j** show the collapse of potential **jj** to **j** in the present:

krajać kraję (kraj-j-ę) krajesz *slice*

kraję	krajemy
krajesz	krajecie
kraje	krają

Similarly: **bajać** *tell tales,* **łajać** *scold,* **tajać** *thaw*

b. Type **-w-a-ć -j-ę**

dawać daję dajesz *give*

daję	dajemy
dajesz	dajecie
daje	dają

In this subtype, which contains three verb roots ending in **a**, **w** is inserted between the root **a** and the suffixal **-a-** of the infinitive. Roots belonging to this type include the above **da-** as well as **zna-** and **sta-**, both of the last two always prefixed, as in **uznawać uznaję uznajesz** *recognize,* **wstawać wstaję wstajesz** *get up, arise.*

c. Type **-ow-a-ć -u-j-ę**

dziękować dziękuję dziękujesz *thank*

dziękuję	dziękujemy
dziękujesz	dziękujecie
dziękuje	dziękują

In this subtype, the suffix **-ow-** before **-a-** in the infinitive alternates with **-u-** before **-j-** in the present. Similarly: **brakować** *be lacking,* **budować** *build,* **darować** *grant,* **fałszować** *falsify,* **gotować** *cook,* **ilustrować** *illustrate,* **irytować** *irritate,* **krępować się** *feel constrained,* **kupować** *buy,* **lądować** *land,* **ładować** *load,* **malować** *paint,* **marnować** *waste,* **panować** *reign,* **pilnować** *look after,* **planować** *plan,* **pakować** *pack,* **pasować** *fit,* **pracować** *work,* **prasować** *press, iron,* **ratować** *save,* **rysować** *sketch,* **stosować** *employ,* **szanować** *respect,* **wędrować** *wander,* **żałować** *regret,* **żartować** *joke,* and very many more. Among verbs in **-ować** may be found a few vowel-stems like **kreować** *create,* **studiować** *study.* The suffix **-ow-a-:-u-j-** is quite productive in forming new verbs from nouns; see **telefonować** *telephone,* **komputeryzować** *computerize,* and many others.

d. Type -yw-a-ć -u-j-ę

dokonywać dokonuję dokonujesz *accomplish*

dokonuję	dokonujemy
dokonujesz	dokonujecie
dokonuje	dokonują.

Before the infinitive suffix **-yw-, ch** softens to **ch': wymach-yw-ać: wymachiwać** *wave;* **zakoch-yw-ać się: zakochiwać się** *fall in love.* Similarly to **dokonywać** are conjugated **odnajdywać** *discover,* **wyskakiwać** *jump out,* **wywiązywać** *acquit oneself,* **wdeptywać** *trample,* **wywoływać** *develop,* **zachowywać** *maintain,* **zapytywać** *ask,* and a great many other verbs derived from prefixed perfective verbs, especially verbs in -ować: **opracowywać** *elaborate,* **przypilnowywać** *watch, mind,* **przygotowywać** *prepare,* **rozbudowywać** *build on,* **rozszyfrowywać** *decipher,* **zahamowywać** *brake,* and so forth. A few verbs of this class have optional 3rd-conjugation inflections: **dokonywać dokonuję -esz** or **dokonywam -asz; oddziaływać oddziałuję -esz** or **oddziaływam -asz.**

e. Type -eć -eję   (-ě-ć -ě-j-ę)

mdleć mdleję mdlejesz *faint*

mdleję	mdlejemy
mdlejesz	mdlejecie
mdleje	mdleją

The identity of the infinitive vowel as morphophonemic **-ě- (ě$_2$)** is evident from past tense forms showing the **e: a** alternation (e.g. **mdlał mdleli**; see Chapter 10). Many verbs of this type are verbs of state derived from adjectives. Similarly: **blednieć** *grow pale,* **dnieć** *become day,* **drętwieć** *grow stiff,* **grubieć** *grow thick,* **kuleć** *limp,* **jaśnieć** *become light,* **łagodnieć** *grow milder,* **łysieć** *grow bald,* **siwieć** *grow gray,* **tanieć** *become cheaper,* **twardnieć** *harden,* **zdrowieć** *become healthy,* and many others.

f. Type -a-ć -e-j-ę

grzać grzeję grzejesz *warm*

grzeję	grzejemy
grzejesz	grzejecie
grzeje	grzeją

The **-a-** in the infinitive stem derives from the historical contraction of **-ě-j-a-** to **-a-**. Similarly: **chlać chleję chlejesz** *swill* (alternatively, **chlać chlam chlasz**), **dziać się dzieje się** *happen,* **lać leję lejesz** *pour,* **piać pieję piejesz** *crow,* **siać sieję siejesz** *sow,* **śmiać się śmieję się śmiejesz się** *laugh,* **wiać wieję wiejesz** *blow,* **ziać zieję ziejesz** *gape,* and not many others. Verbs of this type do not usually participate in the ě: a alternation in the past: **grzali**, but regionally **grzeli**; and similarly for most of the above verbs.

g. Type -y-ć -y-j-ę

myć myję myjesz *wash*

myję	myjemy
myjesz	myjecie
myje	myją

Similarly: **szyć** *sew*, **kryć** *cover, hide*, **ryć** *dig*, **tyć** *grow fat*, **wyć** *howl*, **żyć** *live*.

h. Type -i-ć -i-j-ę

pić piję pijesz *drink*

piję	pijemy
pijesz	pijecie
pije	piją

Similarly: **bić** *beat*, **gnić** *rot*, **wić** *wind*

i. Type -u-ć -u-j-ę

żuć żuję żujesz *chew*

żuję	żujemy
żujesz	żujecie
żuje	żują

Similarly: **czuć** *sense*, **kłuć** *stab*, **kuć** *forge*, **pruć** *unstitch*, **psuć** *spoil*, **snuć** *dream up*, **pluć** *spit*, **szczuć** *sic (a dog)*, **truć** *poison*, **wyzuć** *dispossess*.

2. Various partially irregular 1st-conjugation verbs, most with infinitives in -a-ć:

brać biorę bierzesz *take*

biorę	bierzemy
bierzesz	bierzecie
bierze	biorą

słać ścielę ścielesz *make bed*

ścielę	ścielemy
ścielesz	ścielecie
ściele	ścielą

chcieć chcę chcesz *want*

chcę	chcemy
chcesz	chcecie
chce	chcą

ssać ssę ssiesz *suck*

ssę	ssiemy
ssiesz	ssiecie
ssie	ssą

jechać jadę jedziesz *ride, drive*

jadę	jedziemy
jedziesz	jedziecie
jedzie	jadą

stać się stanę się staniesz się *become*

stanę się	staniemy się
staniesz się	staniecie się
stanie się	staną się

prać piorę pierzesz *launder*

piorę	pierzemy
pierzesz	pierzecie
pierze	piorą

nazwać nazwę nazwiesz *name*

nazwę	nazwiemy
nazwiesz	nazwiecie
nazwie	nazwą

rwać rwę rwiesz *tear, rip*

rwę	rwiemy
rwiesz	rwiecie
rwie	rwą

być będę będziesz *be-future tense*

będę	będziemy
będziesz	będziecie
będzie	będą

The verb **słać ścielę ścielesz** *make bed*, with optional infinitive **ścielić**, is not to be confused with **słać się ślesz** *send*. The infrequently used unprefixed verb **zwać** has the 3.p.sg. form **zowie** in the set phrase **co się zowie** *out-and-out*. Similarly to **stać się** is conjugated **zostać zostanę zostaniesz** *be left behind*. The infinitives **brać, chcieć, rwać, słać**, and **zwać** elicit mobile vowels from preceding consonantal prefixes; see **odebrać** *take back*, **odechcieć** *cease liking*, **zerwać** *tear off*, **odezwać** *respond*, **zeprać** (or, more often, **sprać** *wash off*). `

3. Type **-n-ą-ć -n-ę**

   ciągnąć ciągnę ciągniesz *tug*

ciągnę	ciągniemy
ciągniesz	ciągniecie
ciągnie	ciągną

   Similarly: **blednąć** *pale*, **błysnąć** *flash*, **braknąć** *become wanting*, **dźwignąć** *lift*, **huknąć** *rumble*, **jęknąć** *moan*, **kichnąć** *sneeze*, **krzyknąć** *shout*, **kwitnąć** *blossom*, **marznąć** "mar-znąć" *freeze*, **milknąć** *grow silent*, **garnąć** *gather*, **pachnąć** *smell*, **płynąć** *swim*, **puchnąć** *swell*, **rosnąć** (alongside less common **róść**) *grow*, **stygnąć** *cool*, **uschnąć** *dry up*, and many others. While most such verbs add **-n-** to consonant-stems, in a few instances **-n-** occurs after a vowel: **frunąć** *fly*, **ginąć** *perish*, **lunąć** *pour down*, **plunąć** *spit*, **płonąć** *burn*, **runąć** *tumble down*, **sunąć** *glide*. From the semantic point of view, verbs of this type belong to two main varieties: change-of-state verbs like **gasnąć** *become extinguished-impf.* and semelfactive verbs (verbs of instantaneous action) like **trzasnąć** *slam-pf.* Some verbs of this type in consonant plus **-ną-** drop **-ną-** when forming the past; see Chapter 10.

4. *Consonant stems.* These include verbs whose infinitive is formed by adding **-ć** (or, with velar stems, **-c**) directly to the stem consonant, without an intervening vowel. Invariably, the stem consonant undergoes some kind of change before the infinitive ending. The present-tense endings are usually added directly to the stem consonant, although some form present-tense stems in the suffix **-n-**. There are no labial-stems among the consonant-stems. Historical glide-stems are represented by the **myć** *wash*,

pić *drink,* and **czuć** *sense* types, already treated above. All other consonant-types are represented, although none in great number.

a. Dental stems (**t, d, s, z**). The infinitive will end in **-ść** or, in the instance of **z**-stems, in **-źć** (still pronounced "ść"). If the root contains **e**, the **e: o** shift will be operant, with **e** preserved before the softened dental in the 2.p.sg. through 2.p.pl. forms.

t-stem: **pleść plotę pleciesz** *braid*

plotę	pleciemy
pleciesz	pleciecie
plecie	plotą

Similarly: **gnieść gniotę gnieciesz** *crush*

d-stem: **wieść wiodę wiedziesz** *lead*

wiodę	wiedziemy
wiedziesz	wiedziecie
wiedzie	wiodą

Similarly: **bóść** (or **bość**) **bodę bodziesz** *gore,* **kłaść kładę kładziesz** *lay, place,* **(u)siąść (u)siądę (u)siądziesz** *sit down.* The verbs **kraść kradnę kradniesz** *steal,* and **paść padnę padniesz** *fall* have present stems in **-n-**; **róść** follows the conjugation of **rosnąć**; see

paść padnę padniesz *fall*

padnę	padniemy
padniesz	padniecie
padnie	padną

s-stem: **nieść niosę niesiesz** *carry*

niosę	niesiemy
niesiesz	niesiecie
niesie	niosą

Similarly: **paść pasę pasiesz** *feed, pasture.* An **ę: ą** shift is visible between the infinitive and the present in **trząść trzęsę trzęsiesz** *shake.*

z-stem: **gryźć gryzę gryziesz** *bite*

gryzę	gryziemy
gryziesz	gryziecie
gryzie	gryzą

Similarly: **leźć lezę leziesz** *crawl,* **wieźć wiozę wieziesz** *transport.* The verb **znaleźć znajdę znajdziesz** *find* has a suppletive present stem in **d**. The verb **grząźć grzęznę grzęźniesz** *sink* has a present stem in **n** (and a change from **ą** in the infinitive to **ę** in the present).

b. Velar stems (**k, g**). The infinitive will end in **-c**, this ending being a sign that the stem-consonant is underlying **k** or **g**.

k-stem: **piec piekę pieczesz** *bake*

piekę	**pieczemy**
pieczesz	**pieczecie**
piecze	**pieką**

Similarly: **siec siekę sieczesz** *hack,* **tłuc tłukę tłuczesz** *crush,* **wlec wlokę wleczesz** *drag along.* The **e: o** shift in the stem of **wlec** is not expected, but nevertheless occurs, before the velar consonant. A couple of **k**-stems have present stem in **-n-**:

ciec cieknę ciekniesz *flow*

cieknę	**ciekniemy**
ciekniesz	**ciekniecie**
cieknie	**ciekną**

Similarly: **wściec się wścieknę się wściekniesz się** *grow angry,* **rzec rzeknę rzekniesz** *say, utter*

g-stem: **móc mogę możesz** *be able*

mogę	**możemy**
możesz	**możecie**
może	**mogą**

Similarly: **strzyc strzygę strzyżesz** *clip.* Some **g**-stems have present stems in **-n-**:

biec biegnę biegniesz *run*

biegnę	**biegniemy**
biegniesz	**biegniecie**
biegnie	**biegną**

Similarly: **przysiąc przysięgnę przysięgniesz** *take oath,* **ulec ulegnę ulegniesz** *yield,* **zaprząc zaprzęgnę zaprzęgniesz** *harness*

c. Nasal stems (**n, m**). Verbs of this type have superficial infinitives ending in **-ąć** deriving from underlying stems in **'n** or **Øm** (see Chapter 2 under Mobile **ę** and **ą**).

n-stem: **piąć się pnę pniesz** *clamber* (stem **p'n-**)

pnę się	**pniemy się**
pniesz się	**pniecie się**
pnie się	**pną się**

Similarly: **ciąć tnę tniesz** *cut* (stem **t'n-**), **giąć gnę gniesz** *bend,* **kląć klnę klniesz** *swear* (stem **kl'n-**), **miąć mnę mniesz** *crumple* (stem **m'n-**), **począć pocznę poczniesz** *initiate* (stem **pocz'n-**), **zacząć zacznę zaczniesz** *begin* (stem **zacz'n-**), **żąć żnę żniesz** *reap* (stem **ż'n-**). Consonantal prefixes before verbs in **C'n-** show mobile vowels before stem-forms in **Cn-**: **rozpiąć rozepnę rozepniesz** *unpin*.

m-stem: **dąć dmę dmiesz** *puff* (stem **dØm-**)

dmę	dmiemy
dmiesz	dmiecie
dmie	dmą

Similarly: **żąć żmę żmiesz** *press*.

The stem **j Ø m-**, belonging to this type, deserves special mention. The unprefixed form of this verb, whose infinitive is **jąć** (usually occurring with **się**) *start*, no longer occurs in the present tense (which was, historically, ***imę *imiesz**, etc.). Prefixes ending in a consonant will show a mobile **e** before this stem in the present, as in **objąć obejmę obejmiesz** *embrace*:

objąć obejmę obejmiesz *embrace*

obejmę	obejmiemy
obejmiesz	obejmiecie
obejmie	obejmą

Similarly: **nająć najmę najmiesz** *hire*, **odjąć odejmę odejmiesz** *subtract*, **przejąć przejmę przejmiesz** *take over*, **przyjąć przyjmę przyjmiesz** *accept*, and others. The word **wziąć wezmę weźmiesz** *take* also shows this root:

wziąć wezmę weźmiesz *take*

wezmę	weźmiemy
weźmiesz	weźmiecie
weźmie	wezmą

The commonly encountered infinitive form **wziąść** for **wziąć** is considered substandard and should be avoided, whether in writing or in speech.

d. Liquid stems (**r, ł**). Verbs of this type are **r-** and **ł-**stems mainly in a historical sense. Such a small number of verbs is involved that it does not make sense to defend the analysis as **r-** and **ł-**stems from the synchronic point of view, by formulating sound-change rules.

r-stem: **umrzeć umrę umrzesz** *die*

umrę	umrzemy
umrzesz	umrzecie
umrze	umrą

Similarly: **drzeć** *tear*, **przeć** *urge*, **trzeć** *rub*, **wrzeć** *seethe*. The verb **żreć żrę żresz** *devour* belongs here but does not exhibit R2 **rz** in the 2.p.sg.-2.p.pl.: **żresz żre żremy żrecie**.

ł-stem: **pleć pielę pielesz** *weed*

pielę	**pielemy**
pielesz	**pielecie**
piele	**pielą**

The hard **ł** of the underlying stem appears in the past tense; cf. **pełł** *he weeded* (see Chapter 10). A frequently heard alternative infinitive is **pielić**. The only other verb of this type is **mleć mielę mielesz** *grind*. Both verbs have more frequently occurring second-conjugation forms: **pielić pielę pielisz, mielić mielę mielisz**; and mixed conjugations are also encountered, e.g. **mielić mielę mielesz**.

B. SECOND CONJUGATION: VERBS IN *-J-Ę -ISZ*

	Basic endings		Often spelled:	
1st p.	**-j-ę**	**-imy**	**-ę**	**-ymy**
2nd p.	**-isz**	**-icie**	**-ysz**	**-ycie**
3rd p.	**-i**	**-j-ą**	**-y**	**-ą**

The **-j-** in the 1st pers. sg. and 3rd pers. pl. can be viewed as the result of adding the vowels **-ę** or **ą** to **i**: **-ię, -ią: -ję, -ją**. Because of this **-j-**, the endings of the 2nd conjugation afford the opportunity for a stem-consonant alternation in the present if the stem consonant is an underlying dental (**t, d, s, z, st, zd**), with R3 (**c, dz, sz, ż, szcz, żdż**) occurring before **-j-ę** and **-j-ą**, and R2 (**ć, dź, ś, ź, ść, źdź**) occurring before other endings, in **-i-**. Since the link vowel in the 2nd-conjugation infinitive will be either **-i-** or **-e-** (**-ě₂-**), R2 will occur in the infinitive stem as well. The primary stem consonant will be found only in other words (usually nouns) sharing the same root. Endings beginning in **-i-** (**-isz -i -imy -icie**) are subject to the **i/y** spelling rule. All relevant sound changes and spelling rules are evident from the three citation forms.

SURVEY OF VERBS OF THE 2ND CONJUGATION

Structurally, verbs of the extremely numerous 2nd conjugation are similar to one another, and differ mainly in whether the infinitive-vowel suffix is **-i-** or (much less often) **-e-** (morphophonemic **-ě₂-**). The present endings are added directly to the stem without any intervening formants. Here we will arrange 2nd-conjugation verbs according to the kind of stem-consonant. The resulting types amount for the most part to different spelling varieties.

1. Labial-stems (**p, b, f, w, m**). R2 and R3 are represented by the same soft labial sound (**p', b', f', w', m'**) throughout. To the same spelling type belong stems in the dental nasal **n** (R2/3 **ń**).

p-stems: kupić kupię kupisz *buy*   Analysis of sg.:

kupię	**kupimy**	**kup-j-ę: kup'-ę**, spelled **kupię**
kupisz	**kupicie**	**kup-isz: kup'-isz**, spelled **kupisz**
kupi	**kupią**	**kup-i: kup'-i**, spelled **kupi**

The primary root consonant **p** is visible in **wykup** *ransom*. Similarly, with infinitive in **-i-**: **chełpić się** *brag*, **gapić się** *stare*, **kpić** *mock*, **krzepić** *strengthen*, **lepić** *fashion*, **łupić** *plunder*, **potępić** *condemn*, **oślepić** *blind*, **topić** *drown*, **trapić** *worry*, **tropić** *track*. With infinitive in **-ě-**: **chrypieć** *speak hoarsely*, **cierpieć** *suffer*, **kipieć** *seethe*, **skrzypieć** *squeak*.

The verb **spać** *sleep* is a 2nd-conjugation verb with stem in **p** whose infinitive vowel is entirely exceptional for this conjugation:

spać śpię śpisz *sleep*

śpię	**śpimy**
śpisz	**śpicie**
śpi	**śpią**

b-stems: **lubić lubię lubisz** *like* Analysis of sg.:

lubię	**lubimy**	**lub-j-ę**: lub'-ę, spelled **lubię**
lubisz	**lubimy**	**lub-isz**: lub'-isz, spelled **lubisz**
lubi	**lubią**	**lub-i**: lub'-i, spelled **lubi**

The primary root consonant **b** is visible in the adjective **luby** *pleasant*. Similarly, with infinitive in **-i-**: **chybić** *miss*, **garbić** *hunch*, **gnębić** *depress*, **grabić** *plunder*, **gubić** *lose*, **hańbić** *disgrace*, **ozdobić** *decorate*, **robić** *do*, **rzeźbić** *sculpt*, **ślubić** *wed*, **trąbić** *trumpet*, **uszczerbić** *harm*, **wabić** *entice*. With infinitive in **-ě-**: **świerzbieć** *itch*.

f-stems: **trafić trafię trafisz** *hit upon* Analysis of sg.:

trafię	**trafimy**	**traf-j-ę**: traf'-ę, spelled **trafię**
trafisz	**traficie**	**traf-isz**: traf'-isz, spelled **trafisz**
trafi	**trafią**	**traf-i**: traf'-i, spelled **trafi**

The uncommon primary root consonant **f** is visible in **traf** *blind luck*. Similarly, also with infinitive in **-i-**: **potrafić** *be able*, **trefić** *make ritually unclean*.

w-stems: **łowić łowię łowisz** *hunt* Analysis of sg.:

łowię	**łowimy**	**łow-j-ę**: łow'-ę, spelled **łowię**
łowisz	**łowicie**	**łow-isz**: łow'-isz, spelled **łowisz**
łowi	**łowią**	**łow-i**: łow'-i, spelled **łowi**

The primary root consonant **w** is visible in **łów** *catch*. Similarly, with infinitive in **-i-**: **barwić** *dye*, **bawić** *amuse*, **ciekawić** *interest-3.p.sg*, **dławić** *throttle*, **drwić** *mock*, **dziurawić** *make hole in*, **głowić się** *ponder*, **jawić się** *appear*, **krzywić** *bend*, **krwawić** *bleed*, **łzawić się** *shed tears*, **mówić** *say*, **martwić** *worry*, **naprawić** *fix*, **sławić** *praise*, **sprawić** *cause*, **tkwić** *stick*, **trawić** *digest*, **trzeźwić** *make sober*.

m-stems: tłumić tłumię tłumisz *stifle*   Analysis of sg.:

tłumię	**tłumimy**	**tłum-j-ę: tłum'-ę**, spelled **tłumię**
tłumisz	**tłumicie**	**tłum-isz: tłum'-isz**, spelled **tłumisz**
tłumi	**tłumią**	**tłum-i: tłum'-i**, spelled **tłumi**

The primary root consonant **m** is visible in **tłum** *throng*. Similarly, with infinitive in **-i-**: **dymić** *smoke*, **gromić** *defeat, rout*, **karmić** *feed*, **mamić** *deceive*, **oszołomić** *dumbfound*, **oznajmić** *apprise*, **plamić** *stain*, **ujarzmić** *put under the yoke*, **zawiadomić** *inform*. With infinitive in **-ě-**: **brzmieć** *sound*, **grzmieć** *rumble*, **szumieć** *make noise*.

n-stems: bronić bronię bronisz *defend*   Analysis of sg.:

bronię	**bronimy**	**bron-j-ę: bron'-ę**, spelled **bronię**
bronisz	**bronicie**	**bron-isz: bron'-isz**, spelled **bronisz**
broni	**bronią**	**bron-i: bron'-i**, spelled **broni**

The primary root consonant **n** is visible in **obrona** *defense*. Similarly, with infinitive in **-i-**: **bębnić** *drum*, **bluźnić** *blaspheme*, **cenić** *evaluate*, **czynić** *do*, **dudnić** *pipe*, **dzwonić** *ring*, **ganić** *censure*, **gonić** *hunt, pursue*, **lenić się** *dilly-dally*, **mocnić** *strengthen*, **olśnić** *bedazzle*, **pełnić** *fill* **pienić się** *foam*, **promienić się** *radiate*, **opróżnić** *empty*, **różnić** *differentiate*, **ranić** *wound*, **rozluźnić** *loosen*, **rumienić się** *blush*, **skłonić** *incline*, **strwonić** *dissipate, waste*, **ślinić** *moisten with saliva*, **śnić** *dream*, **tlenić** *oxidize* **tętnić** *throb*, **tumanić** *fool, stupefy*, **ulotnić się** *decamp*, **uwolnić** *free*, **uwydatnić** *enhance*, **winić** *blame*, **zamienić** *exchange*, **zatrudnić** *hire*, **żenić się** *be wed*.

The following verb, with infinitive in **-ě-**, fails to undergo softening in the 1.p.sg. and 3.p.pl.:

zapomnieć zapomnę zapomnisz *forget*

zapomnę	**zapomnimy**
zapomnisz	**zapomnicie**
zapomni	**zapomną**

2. Stems in underlying **ł** show surface **l** everywhere, and take spelled endings similar to those of labial and **n**-stems except for the lack of **i** before **ę** and **ą** in the 1st pers. sg. and 3rd pers. pl.:

l-stems: palić palę palisz *smoke*   Analysis of sg.:

palę	**palimy**	**pał-j-ę: pal-ę**, spelled **palę**
palisz	**palicie**	**pał-isz: pal-isz**, spelled **palisz**
pali	**palą**	**pał-i: pal-i**, spelled **pali**

The primary root consonant **ł** is visible in **niewypał** *dud, misfire*. Similarly: **chwalić** *praise*, **chylić** *bend*, **doskonalić** *improve*, **dzielić** *divide*, **golić się** *shave*, **gramolić się** *clamber*, **kwilić** *whimper*, **mdlić** *be sick*, **modlić się** *pray*, **mydlić się** *sudse*, **mylić się** *be mistaken*, **naglić** *urge*, **niewolić** *deprive of liberty*, **oświetlić** *light up*, **obalić** *overthrow*, **ocalić** *rescue*, **pobielić** *whiten*,

podkreślić *underscore, emphasize*, **pozwolić** *allow*, **pylić** *dust*, **rozczulić się** *be moved*, **smolić** *tar*, **solić** *salt*, **strzelić** *shoot*, **szklić** *glaze*, **szkolić** *school*, **tlić się** *smolder*, **tulić** *cuddle*, **ustalić** *determine*, **utrwalić** *make permanent*, **weselić** *cheer up*, **wydalić** *send far away*, **wymyślić** *think up*, **zawalić** *knock down*, **żalić się** *lament*. Infinitive in -ĕ-: **boleć** *pain*, **myśleć** *think*, **skomleć** *whine*, **woleć** *prefer*.

3. Stems in **j** are subject to the spelling rule which drops **j** after a vowel before **i** (in the infinitive and 2.p.sg. through 2.p.pl.). In the 1.p.sg. and 3.p.pl., the **j** of the stem and the **j** of the ending contract into one **j** (e.g. **stroj-ję: stroję**).

j-stems: **stroić stroję stroisz** *trim, tune*   Analysis of sg.:

stroję	**stroimy**	**stroj-j-ę: stroj-ę**, spelled **stroję**
stroisz	**stroicie**	**stroj-isz**, spelled **stroisz**
stroi	**stroją**	**stroj-i**, spelled **stroi**

The root-final **j** may be seen in **strój** *attire*. Similarly: **czaić się** *lie in wait*, **doić** *milk*, **dwoić** *double*, **gnoić** *rot*, **goić się** *mend*, **kleić** *glue*, **kroić** *slice*, **łoić** *wallop*, **oswoić** *tame*, **poić** *give to drink*, **przyzwyczaić** *accustom*, **roić się** *swarm*, **troić** *triple*, **uspokoić** *calm down*, **uzbroić** *arm*, **zataić** *conceal*, **znoić się** *drudge*. Stems in **oj** with infinitives originally in -ĕ- have been contracted into contemporary infinitives in -ać (**stoj-ĕ-ć: stać**):

stać stoję stoisz *stand*   Analysis of sg.:

stoję	**stoimy**	**stoj-j-ę: stoj-ę**, spelled **stoję**
stoisz	**stoicie**	**stoj-isz**, spelled **stoisz**
stoi	**stoją**	**stoj-i**, spelled **stoi**

Similarly: **bać się boję się boisz się** *be afraid*.

4. Dental stems (**t, d, s, z, st, zd**). R2 and R3 of dental consonants have different realizations:

Primary	R2	R3
t	ć	c
d	dź	dz
s	ś	sz
z	ź	ż
st	ść	szcz
zd	źdź	żdż

t-stems: **rzucić rzucę rzucisz** *throw*   Analysis of sg.:

rzucę	**rzucimy**	**rzut-j-ę: rzuc-ę**, spelled **rzucę**
rzucisz	**rzucicie**	**rzut-isz: rzuć-isz**, spelled **rzucisz**
rzuci	**rzucą**	**rzut-i: rzuć-i**, spelled **rzuci**

The primary root consonant **t** is visible in **rzut** *cast*. Similarly, with infinitive in **-i-**: **błocić** *make muddy*, **bogacić** *enrich*, **gwałcić** *rape*, **kłócić się** *quarrel*, **karcić** *rebuke*, **kręcić** *twist*, **kształcić** *form*, **nęcić** *tease*, **nucić** *hum*, **oświecić** *illuminate*, **płacić** *pay*, **pocić się** *sweat*, **polecić** *recommend*, **skrócić** *shorten*, **szpecić** *impair*, **śmiecić** *litter*, **trącić** *jostle*, **tracić** *lose*, **wiercić** *drill*, **wrócić** *return*, **złocić** *gild*. With infinitive in **-ě-**: **lecieć** *fly*.

d-stems: chodzić chodzę chodzisz *walk*   Analysis of sg.:

chodzę	chodzimy	chod-j-ę: chodz-ę, spelled chodzę
chodzisz	chodzicie	chod-isz: chodź-isz, spelled chodzisz
chodzi	chodzą	chod-i: chodź-i, spelled chodzi

The primary root consonant **d** is visible in **chód** *gait*. Similarly: **błądzić** *err*, **bredzić** *rave*, **brudzić** *soil*, **brzydzić** *disgust*, **budzić** *rouse*, **cedzić** *strain*, **chłodzić** *cool*, **słodzić** *sweeten*, **gładzić** *smooth*, **godzić** *please*, **łagodzić** *mollify*, **łudzić** *deceive*, **marudzić** *tarry*, **nudzić** *bore*, **odwiedzić** *visit*, **oszczędzić** *put aside, save*, **płodzić** *procreate*, **pędzić** *rush*, **prowadzić** *lead*, **rządzić** *govern*, **sądzić** *judge*, **sprawdzić** *cause*, **szkodzić** *harm*, **szydzić** *mock*, **śledzić** *follow*, **trudzić** *trouble*, **wędzić** *smoke*, **wodzić** *lead*. Infinitive in **-ě-**: **siedzieć** *sit*, **widzieć** *see*:

s-stems: nosić noszę nosisz *carry*   Analysis of sg.:

noszę	nosimy	nos-j-ę: nosz-ę, spelled noszę
nosisz	nosicie	nos-isz: noś-isz, spelled nosisz
nosi	noszą	nos-i: noś-i, spelled nosi

The primary root consonant **s** is visible in **wynos** *carry-out*. Similarly: **dusić** *strangle*, **gasić** *extinguish*, **głosić** *proclaim*, **grymasić** *be fussy*, **kosić** *mow*, **krasić** *flavor*, **krztusić** *choke*, **kusić** *tempt*, **miętosić** *crumple*, **prosić** *request*, **wskrzesić** *rekindle*, **wymusić** *force*, **wywiesić** *hang out*, **zakąsić** *snack*. With infinitive in **-ě-**: **musieć** *have to*, **wisieć** *hang*.

z-stems: wozić wożę wozisz *transport*   Analysis of sg.:

wożę	wozimy	woz-j-ę: woż-ę, spelled wożę
wozisz	wozicie	woz-isz: woź-isz, spelled wozisz
wozi	wożą	woz-i: woź-i, spelled wozi

The primary root consonant **z** is visible in **wóz** *cart*. Similarly: **grozić** *threaten*, **mrozić** *freeze*, **odgałęzić się** *branch off*, **razić** *offend*, **skazić** *corrupt*, **uwięzić** *imprison*.

st-stems: czyścić czyszczę czyścisz *clean*   Analysis of sg.:

czyszczę	czyścimy	czyst-j-ę: czyszcz-ę: czyszczę
czyścisz	czyścicie	czyst-isz: czyść-isz spelled czyścisz
czyści	czyszczą	czyst-i: czyść-i, spelled czyści

The primary consonant cluster **st** is visible in **czysty** *clean*. Similarly: **gęścić** *thicken*, **gościć** *entertain*, **mścić** *avenge*, **mieścić** *contain*, **mościć** *cushion*, **namaścić** *anoint*, **pieścić** *pet*, **puścić** *release*, **rościć sobie** *have pretensions*, **szeleścić** *rustle*, **tłuścić** *smear with grease*, **uiścić** *remit*, **zachwaścić** *let run to weeds*. The verbs **czcić** *worship* is a historical **st**-stem, related to **cześć** *honor*. The potential present stems *czszcz-, *czść- have been simplified to **czcz-, czć-**:

czcić czczę czcisz *worship*

czczę	czcimy
czcisz	czcicie
czci	czczą

Similarly: **chrzcić chrzczę chrzcisz** *christen, baptize*.

zd-stems: **jeździć jeżdżę jeździsz**   Analysis of sg:
    ride, drive

jeżdżę	jeździmy	jezd-j-ę: jeżdż-ę: jeżdżę
jeździsz	jeździcie	jezd-isz: jeźdź-isz, spelled jeździsz
jeździ	jeżdżą	jezd-i: jeźdź-i, spelled jeździ

The primary consonant cluster **zd** is visible in **jazda** *ride*. Similarly: **bruździć** *furrow*, **gwoździć** *nail*, **gnieździć się** *nest*, **rozgwieździć się** *be starlit*.

5. With underlying velar stems (**k, g, ch**) R3 and R2 are represented by the same hushing consonant (**cz, ż,** or **sz,** respectively) throughout, after which **i** will be respelled as **y**:

k-stems: **uczyć uczę uczysz** *teach*   Analysis of sg.:

uczę	uczymy	uk-j-ę: ucz-ę: uczę
uczysz	uczycie	uk-isz: ucz-isz, spelled uczysz
uczy	uczą	uk-i: ucz-i, spelled uczy

The primary root consonant **k** is visible in **samouk** *self-taught scholar*. Similarly: **ćwiczyć** *train*, **dotyczyć** *concern*, **dręczyć** *torment*, **kończyć** *finish*, **kurczyć** *contract, shrink*, **liczyć** *count*, **łączyć** *connect*, **majaczyć** *loom*, **męczyć** *tire*, **moczyć** *moisten*, **mroczyć się** *grow dark* **niszczyć** *destroy*, **niweczyć** *annihilate*, **odstręczyć** *repel*, **partaczyć** *botch*, **pożyczyć** *loan*, **przeinaczyć** *alter*, **raczyć** *deign*, **ręczyć** *vouch*, **sączyć** *ooze*, **skoczyć** *leap*, **ślęczyć** *drudge*, **świadczyć** *witness to*, **tłoczyć** *press, print*, **toczyć się** *roll*, **tuczyć** *fatten*, **ubezpieczyć** *insure*, **uczestniczyć** *take part*, **włóczyć się** *roam*, **wykluczyć** *exclude*, **wystarczyć** *be enough*, **zahaczyć** *hook*, **zawdzięczyć** *be indebted*, **zbroczyć** *steep in blood*, **znaczyć** *mean*, **zobaczyć** *see*. The verbs **przeistoczyć** *transform* and **zjednoczyć** *unify* seem related to nouns in **t**; see **istota** *essence*, **jednota** *unity*. K-stems with infinitive in **-ě-** are mostly sound-words, but still mostly related to nouns in **k**: **beczeć** *bleat*, **brzęczeć** *clang,* **burczeć** *rumble,* **dźwięczeć** *ring,* **huczeć** *roar,* **krzyczeć** *shout,* **jęczeć** *moan,* **kwiczeć** *squeal,* **milczeć** *be silent,* **ryczeć** *roar,* **syczeć** *hiss,* **warczeć** *snarl.*

Stems in underlying **-sk-** can be recognized in a few verbs with infinitives in **-szczyć** or **-szczeć**: **troszczyć się** *be concerned* (**troska** *concern*), **piszczeć** *squeal* (**pisk** *squeal*), **polszczyć** *polonize,* (**Polska**); however, **przywłaszczyć** *appropriate* seemingly comes from a root in **st-**; cf. **właściwy** *proper.* A few verbs of this type are related to words in **-c** (itself historically related to **k**), as **ograniczyć** *limit* (**granica** *border,* **tańczyć** *dance* (**taniec** *dance*), **uwieńczyć** *crown* (**wieniec** *wreath*). sk-stems with infinitive in **-ě-** include **błyszczeć** *flash,* **treszczeć** *crackle,* **wrzeszczeć** *bellow.*

g-stems: **ulżyć ulżę ulżysz** *relieve*   Analysis of sg.:

ulżę	**ulżymy**	**ulg-j-ę: ulż-ę: ulżę**
ulżysz	**ulżycie**	**ulg-isz: ulż-isz,** spelled **ulżysz**
ulży	**ulżą**	**ulg-i: ulż-i,** spelled **ulży**

The primary root consonant **g** is visible in **ulga** *relief,* although not all 2nd-conjugation verbs in **-żyć** can be related to Polish roots in **g**. For example, **świeżyć** *freshen;* cf. **świeży** *fresh,* seems to have a stem in basic **ż**. Other 2nd-conjugation verbs in **-żyć** include **barłożyć** *litter,* **ciążyć** *weigh down,* **dążyć** *head for,* **drążyć** *hollow out,* **dzierżyć** *wield power,* **krążyć** *circle,* **mitrężyć** *dawdle,* **mnożyć** *multiply,* **mrużyć** *wink,* **mżyć** *drizzle,* **natężyć** *strain,* **obnażyć** *lay bare,* **odprężyć się** *relax,* **oskarżyć** *accuse,* **położyć** *lay,* **pogrążyć** *sink,* **prażyć** *grill,* **smażyć** *fry,* **ważyć** *weigh,* **wróżyć** *augur,* **wydłużyć** *stretch out,* **wyposażyć** *outfit,* **zadłużyć** *involve in debt,* **zasłużyć** *deserve,* **zaśnieżyć** *cover in snow,* **zauważyć** *notice,* **zdążyć** *manage,* **zniżyć** *lower,* **znużyć** *weary.* The verb **zbliżyć się** *draw nearer* is related to a root in **z** (**bliz-ki: bliski** *near*); the **ż** may be modeled on the comparative stem of **bliższy** *nearer.* Stems in **-żdż** include **miażdżyć** *mash* (**miazga** *mash*), **dżdżyć** *rain.* Infinitive in **-ě-**: **drżeć** *tremble,* **leżeć** *lie,* **rżeć** *neigh.*

ch-stems: **płoszyć płoszę płoszysz** *startle*   analysis of sg:

płoszę	**płoszymy**	**płoch-j-ę: płosz-ę: płoszę**
płoszysz	**płoszycie**	**płoch-isz: płosz-isz** spelled **płoszysz**
płoszy	**płoszą**	**płoch-i: płosz-i,** spelled **płoszy**

The primary root consonant **ch** is visible in **popłoch** *panic.* Other 2nd-conjugation verbs in **-szyć**: **cieszyć się** *be glad,* **ciszyć** *silence,* **grzeszyć** *sin,* **kruszyć** *crumble,* **naruszyć** *break (law),* **ośmieszyć** *ridicule,* **panoszyć się** *run rampant,* **pustoszyć** *lay waste,* **rozjuszyć** *infuriate,* **rozprószyć** *dissipate,* **ruszyć** *move,* **straszyć** *frighten,* **suszyć** *dry,* **śpieszyć się** *hurry,* **towarzyszyć** *accompany,* **węszyć** *sniff,* **zagłuszyć** *stifle (a sound).* Some verbs in **sz** seem based on comparative stems: **powiększyć** *increase,* **przewyższyć** *surpass,* **ulepszyć** *improve,* **upiększyć** *beautify,* **zmniejszyć** *decrease.* Infinitive in **-ě-**: **dyszeć** *pant,* **słyszeć** *hear.*

5. Stems in **r** (for which R2/3 is **rz**) take the same spelled present endings as underlying velar stems:

r-stems: **parzyć parzę parzysz** *scorch*

		Analysis of sg.:
parzę	**parzymy**	par-j-ę: parz-ę: **parzę**
parzysz	**parzycie**	par-isz: parz-isz, spelled **parzysz**
parzy	**parzą**	par-i: parz-i, spelled **parzy**

The primary root consonant **r** is visible in **para** *steam*. Similarly: **gwarzyć** *chat*, **iskrzyć się** *sparkle*, **marzyć** *daydream*, **odkurzyć** *dust off, vacuum-clean*, **powtórzyć** *repeat*, **przechytrzyć** *outsmart*, **przymierzyć** *try on*, **rozszerzyć** *widen*, **srebrzyć** *silver*, **szczerzyć** *grin*, **tchórzyć** *turn coward*, **tworzyć** *create*, **umorzyć** *amortize*, **warzyć** *brew beer*, **wierzyć** *believe*, **wywietrzyć** *air out*, **zaburzyć** *disturb*, **zachmurzyć się** *become cloudy*, **zanurzyć** *sink, dip*, **zdarzyć się** *happen*. Infinitive in **-ě-**: **obejrzeć** *look at*, **patrzeć** (alongside **patrzyć**) *look*.

C. THIRD CONJUGATION: VERBS IN -*AM* -*ASZ*

Present endings:

1st p.	-am	-amy
2nd p.	-asz	-acie
3rd p.	-a	-ają

Except for one verb (**mieć** *have*), the infinitive always ends in **-a-ć** and, if one knows that the verb is 3rd-conjugation, the infinitive provides sufficient information by itself for forming the present. One could, then, alternatively conclude that the endings are **-m -sz -Ø -my -cie -ją**, added to the infinitive stem.

czekać *wait*

czekam *I wait*	**czekamy** *we wait*
czekasz *you wait*	**czekacie** *you wait*
czeka *he, she, it waits*	**czekają** *they wait*

Similarly: **błąkać się** *be lost*, **błagać** *beseech*, **biegać** *run*, **chować** *keep*, **cmokać** *smack lips*, **czytać** *read*, **dbać** *take care*, **ganiać** *run about*, **gęgać** *gaggle*, **grać** *play*, **kichać** *sneeze*, **kochać** *love*, **konać** *die*, **korzystać** *take advantage*, **kukać** *cuckoo*, **latać** *fly*, **łatać** *patch*, **łuskać** *shell, husk*, **mieszać** *mix*, **mieszkać** *live, dwell*, **mijać** *pass*, **mrugać** *wink*, **narzekać** *complain*, **obiecać** *promise*, **padać** *fall*, **pamiętać** *remember*, **parać się** *be busy with*, **pełzać** *creep*, **polegać** *depend*, **pomagać** *help*, **pętać** *fetter*, **pukać** *knock*, **pytać** *ask*, **skakać** *jump*, **szukać** *search*, **ściskać** *squeeze*, **śpiewać** *sing*, **tkać** *weave*, **trwać** *last*, **trzymać** *hold*, **ufać** *trust*, **urągać** *abuse*, **władać** *possess*, **wahać się** *vacillate*, **wołać** *call*, **wymiotać** *vomit*, **zgrzytać** *grate*, **żądać** *demand*. While not many basic verbs belong to the 3rd conjugation, in fact this type numbers in the thousands as the result of processes of imperfective derivation; see Chapter 11.

One 3rd-conjugation verb has 3.p.pl. in **-dzą** instead of **-ją** (the effect of adding **-ją** directly to the underlying root in **d**):

dać *give*

dam *I'll give*	**damy** *we'll give*
dasz *you'll give*	**dacie** *you'll give*
da *he, she'll give*	**dadzą** *they'll give*

One 3rd-conjugation verb has an infinitive in **-eć** (**-ě-ć**):

mieć *have*

mam *I have*	**mamy** *we have*
masz *you have*	**macie** *you have*
ma *he, she, it has*	**mają** *they have*

D. FOURTH CONJUGATION: VERBS IN *-EM -ESZ*

Present endings:

1st p.	**-em**	**-emy**
2nd p.	**-esz**	**-ecie**
3rd p.	**-e**	**-eją** (**-dzą**)

Only a few verbs belong to the 4th conjugation. They include the following:

umieć *know how*

umiem *I know how*	**umiemy** *we know how*
umiesz *you know how*	**umiecie** *you know how*
umie *he, she, it knows how*	**umieją** *they know how*

Similarly: **rozumieć rozumiem rozumiesz** *understand,* **śmieć śmiem śmiesz** *dare.* Note: the pronunciation or writing of 3.p.pl. **umieją** or **rozumieją** as *umią or *rozumią is incorrect and should be avoided. A couple of 4th-conjugation verbs have **-dzą** in the 3.p.pl., produced by adding **-ją** to underlying roots in **d**:

wiedzieć *know (information)*

wiem *I know*	**wiemy** *we know*
wiesz *you know*	**wiecie** *you know*
wie *he, she, it knows*	**wiedzą** *they know*

Similarly:

powiedzieć powiem powiesz powiedzą *say*
jeść jem jesz jedzą *eat*

The Irregular Verb *być* 'be'

This is the only truly irregular Polish verb. Its present forms are as follows:

być *be*

jestem *I am*	**jesteśmy** *we are*
jesteś *you are*	**jesteście** *you are*
jest *he, she, it is*	**są** *they are.*

The verb 'be' is the only verb to have a specifically future form:

będę *I will be*	**będziemy** *we will be*
będziesz *you will be*	**będziecie** *you will be*
będzie *he, she, it will be*	**będą** *they will be*

Będę also functions as a future-tense auxiliary verb; see Chapter 10.

THE DETACHABILITY OF THE 1ST AND 2ND PERSON ENDINGS OF *BYĆ*

In very colloquial speech, the 1st and 2nd person endings of the present tense of **być** may be detached and fixed to other words:

Jam nieszczęśliwy! *I am unhappy!*

Głupiś! *You are stupid!*

Present-tense endings of **być** are detached much less often than the same endings with past-tense verb forms; see Chapter 10. The property of the endings **-m, -ś, -śmy, -ście** to be detached while maintaining the effect of the verb 'be' raises the question as to whether certain Polish nouns and adjectives may be "conjugated"; see the quasi-conjugations of **świnia** *swine*, **szczęśliwy** *happy*:

świniam *I am a swine*	**świnieśmy** *we are swine*
świniaś *you (sg.) are a swine*	**świnieście** *you (pl.) are swine*
świnia *he, she, it is a swine*	**świnie** *they are swine.*
szczęśliwym *I am happy*	**szczęśliwiśmy** *we are happy*
szczęśliwyś *you are happy*	**szczęśliwiście** *you are happy*
szczęśliwy *he is happy`*	**szczęśliwi** *they are happy*

See Z. Saloni and M. Świdziński (1985), *Składnia języka polskiego* (Warszawa: PWN). p. 89, who decide that these are, nevertheless, contractions of lexically independent items.

RULES OF THUMB FOR INTERPRETING THE CITATION FORMS OF VERBS OF THE 1ST AND 2ND CONJUGATIONS

The following routine will ensure that all present-tense forms are produced correctly, whether the verb is 1st or 2nd-conjugation (both with 1.p.sg. in **-ę**). The verb of illustration is 1st-conjugation **nieść niosę niesiesz** *carry.*

a. The 1st pers. sg. and 2nd per. sg. form will generate the following matrix, to be filled in:

Sg.	Pl.
niosę	
niesiesz	

b. The 3rd person pl. is filled in by looking at the 1st person sg., and by re-placing -ę with -ą:

Sg.	Pl.
niosę	
niesiesz	
	niosą

c. The 3rd pers. sg. and 1st and 2nd pers. pl. are filled in by looking at the 2nd pers. sg. In order to obtain the 3rd pers. sg. from the 2nd pers. sg., drop the ending **-sz: niesie-sz: niesie**. The 1st and 2nd pers. pl. endings are then added to this stem: **niesie-my, niesie-cie**.

Sg.	Pl.
niosę	**niesiemy**
niesiesz	**niesiecie**
niesie	niosą

The same routine applies to the 2nd conjugation, as in **chodzić chodzę chodzisz** *walk*:

Sg.	Pl.
chodzę	
chodzisz	

b.

Sg.	Pl.
chodzę	
chodzisz	
	chodzą

c.

Sg.	Pl.
chodzę	**chodzimy**
chodzisz	**chodzicie**
chodzi	chodzą

RULES OF THUMB FOR INTERPRETING THE CITATION FORMS OF VERBS OF THE 3RD AND 4TH CONJUGATIONS

With the 3rd and 4th conjugations, having 1st person sg. in **-m**, it is usually possible to rely on the form of the 1st person sg. alone; the other forms follow from it. However, for the sake of uniformity with the first and second conjugations, it makes sense to cite and learn such verbs in the first two forms of the present as well.

a. The stem may be obtained by dropping **-m** from the 1st person sg. or **-sz** from the 2nd person sg.:

Sg.	Pl.
pyta-m	
pyta-sz	

b. To this stem, add the endings:

Sg.	Pl.
pyta-m	**pyta-my**
pyta-sz	**pyta-cie**
pyta-ø	**pyta-ją**

The endings are the same as for conjugations 1 and 2, except that the 3rd person plural ending is **-ją**, which is added to the stem, which ends in a vowel (**a** or **e**). Observe that in the 3rd and 4th conjugations, the plural forms are each one syllable longer than the corresponding singular forms.

The few verbs of conjugation 3 and 4 with 3rd pers. pl. in **-dzą** instead of in **-ją** must be cited in four forms: **dać dam dasz dadzą** *give pf.,* **wiedzieć wiem wiesz wiedzą** *know (information),* **jeść jem jesz jedzą** *eat.*

ANNOTATING THE INFINITIVE TO PREDICT THE PRESENT TENSE

A simple system is available for marking the infinitive of verbs in such a way as to make its conjugation and conjugation-type clear. The following are verbs of the major conjugational types, illustrating this notation:

An infinitive marked	Implies:
pis I ać	**piszę piszesz pisze**
da I wać	**daję dajesz daje**
dzięk I ować	**dziękuję dziękujesz dziękuje**
dokon I ywać	**dokonuję dokonujesz dokonuje**
mdle I ć -j-	**mdleję mdlejesz mdleje**
dzia I ć -j-	**dzieję dziejesz dzieje**
my I ć	**myję myjesz myje**

An infinitive marked	Implies:
pi | ć	piję pijesz pije
żu | ć	żuję żujesz żuje
ciąg | nąć	ciągnę ciągniesz ciągnie
pleść -t-	plotę pleciesz plecie
wieść -d-	wiodę wiedziesz wiedzie
paść -dn-	padnę padniesz padnie
nieść -s-	niosę niesiesz niesie
gryźć -z-	gryzę gryziesz gryzie
piec -k-	piekę pieczesz piecze
ciec -kn-	cieknę ciekniesz cieknie
strzyc -g-	strzygę strzyżesz strzyże
biec -gn-	biegnę biegniesz biegnie
piąć -n-	pnę pniesz pnie
dąć -m-	dmę dmiesz dmie
umrzeć -r-	umrę umrzesz umrze
pleć -l-	pielę pielesz piele
kup | ić	kupię kupisz kupi
słysz | eć	słyszę słyszysz słyszy
stać -oj-	stoję stoisz stoi
czeka | ć	czekam czekasz czeka
umie | ć	umiem umiesz umie.

Observe that the consonant-stems are indicated by giving the stem-consonant to the right. Under this system, only truly exceptional verbs (like **dać**, **wiedzieć, jeść**, with 3.p.pl. in **-dzą**) need to be listed in more than one form.

THE IMPERATIVE

The Formal versus the Pragmatic Imperative System

As with the indicative conjugational forms of the verb, the formal imperative (command-form) system differs from the system of its pragmatic implementation. Formally speaking, there are three imperative forms, the 2nd pers. sg., 2nd pers. pl., and 1st pers. pl. However, because of the use of the hortatory particle **niech** with 3rd-person pronouns, and occasionally with 1st-person sg. pronouns, the pragmatic system is considerably more complex than the formal system:

Formal system:

	Sg.	Pl.
1st person	—	**zróbmy** *let's do!*
2nd person	**zrób** *do!*	**zróbcie** *do!*

Pragmatic system:

	Sg.	Pl.
1st person	niech zrobię	zróbmy
2nd person	zrób	zróbcie
Pragmatic 2nd person formal	niech pan zrobi	niech państwo zrobią
3rd person	niech on zrobi	niech oni zrobią

The endings of the formal imperative are as follows:

2.p.sg   -ø   2.p.pl.   -cie   1.p.pl.   -my.

The imperative is formed differently in the case of the 1st and 2nd conjugations on the one hand, and the 3rd and 4th conjugations on the other.

Verbs of the 1st and 2nd conjugations add the imperative endings to a stem that is the same as the stem of the "middle-four" present endings. To obtain the stem, one may subtract **-e** from the 3.p.sg. form of 1st-conjugation verbs or **-i/y** from the 3.p.sg. form of 2nd-conjugation verbs, keeping the stem-consonant as it was (except that labial consonants harden). Keeping the stem-consonant as it was may involve tracing a spelling rule in reverse, instating a kreska, as in **jechać jadę jedziesz** *ride,* imperative stem **jedź-**.

1st conjugation

Infinitive	3.p.sg.	Imper.stem	Imperative forms
pisać	pisze	pisz-	pisz piszcie piszmy
kąpać	kąpie	kąp-	kąp kąpcie kąpmy
pracować	pracuje	pracuj-	pracuj pracujcie pracujmy
lać	leje	lej-	lej lejcie lejmy
pić	pije	pij-	pij pijcie pijmy
pluć	pluje	pluj-	pluj plujcie plujmy
zostać	zostanie	zostań-	zostań zostańcie zostańmy
nieść	niesie	nieś-	nieś nieście nieśmy

Exceptions and irregularities in the 1st conjugation:

a. Verbs in **-awać -aje**, as well as the verb **chcieć**, form the imperative by adding **j** to the infinitive stem:

wstawać	wstaje	wstawa-	wstawaj wstawajcie -jmy
chcieć	chce	chcie-	chciej chciejcie chciejmy

b. **wziąć wezmę weźmiesz** *take*   **weź weźcie weźmy**

c. **być** *be*   **bądź-**   **bądź bądźcie bądźmy**

2nd conjugation

Infinitive	3.p.sg.	Imper. stem	Imperative forms
chwalić	chwali	chwal-	chwal chwalcie chwalmy
kupić	kupi	kup-	kup kupcie kupmy
wrócić	wróci	wróć-	wróć wróćcie wróćmy
nosić	nosi	noś-	noś noście nośmy
leżeć	leży	leż-	leż leżcie leżmy
myśleć	myśli	myśl-	myśl myślcie myślmy
patrzeć	patrzy	patrz-	patrz patrzcie patrzmy

The imperative of the last verb, **patrzeć**, serves as a suppletive imperative for **widzieć** *see*, which otherwise does not form the imperative.

The vowel **o** in a stem before a voiced stem-consonant may go to **ó**, especially before **j**. For example, **o** goes to **ó** in

bać się	boi się	boi się	(nie) bój się bójcie się bójmy się
godzić	godzi	godź-	gódź gódźcie gódźmy
odmłodzić	odmłodzi	odmłodź-	odmłódź odmłódźcie odmłódźmy
otworzyć	otworzy	otworz-	otwórz otwórzcie otwórzmy
pozwolić	pozwoli	pozwol-	pozwól pozwólcie pozwólmy
robić	robi	rob-	rób róbcie róbmy
stać	stoi	stoj-	stój stójcie stójmy
stroić	stroi	stroj-	strój strójcie strójmy
uspokoić	uspokoi	uspokoj-	uspokój uspokójcie uspokójmy

while **o** remains **o** in

chodzić	chodzi	chodź-	chodź chodźcie chodźmy
wodzić	wodzi	wodź-	wodź wodźcie wodźmy
wozić	wozi	woź-	woź woźcie woźmy

Some verbs have alternative forms:

głodzić *starve*	głodzi	głodź-	głódź or głodź
golić *shave*	goli	gol-	gol, regionally gól
grozić *threaten*	grozi	groź-	groź, less often gróź
słodzić *sweeten*	słodzi	słodź-	słódź or słodź

IMPERATIVES WITH THE STEM EXTENSION -Y/IJ-

First- and second-conjugation verbs lacking a vowel in the present-tense stem, as well as verbs whose stems end in a consonant plus **n** or **m**, take the stem extension **-y/ij-** before the imperative endings:

Infinitive	3.p.sg.	Imper.stem	Imperative forms
biegnąć	biegnie	biegń-yj-	biegnij biegnijcie biegnijmy
brzmieć	brzmi	brzm'-yj-	brzmij brzmijcie brzmijcie
czcić	czci	czć-yj-	czcij czcijcie czcijmy
chrzcić	chrzci	chrzć-yj-	chrzcij chrzcijcie chrzcijmy
drwić	drwi	drw'-yj-	drwij drwijcie drwijmy
drzeć	drzy	drz-yj-	drzyj drzyjcie drzyjmy
kpić	kpi	kp'-yj-	kpij kpijcie kpijmy
kraść	kradnie	kradń-yj-	kradnij kradnijcie kradnijjmy
mścić	mści	mść-yj-	mścij mścijcie mścijmy
pomnieć	pomni	pomń-yj-	pomnij pomnijcie pomnijjmy
spać	śpi	śp'-yj-	śpij śpijcie śpijmy
wysłać	wyśle	wy-śl-yj-	wyślij wyślijcie wyślijmy
wytrzeć	wytrze	wy-trz-yj-	wytrzyj wytrzyjcie wytrzyjmy
zacząć	zacznie	zaczń-yj-	zacznij zacznijcie -zacznijmy

Occasionally doublets may arise. For example, the regular imperative of **zdjąć zdejmę zdejmie** *take off* and other verbs with this root is **zdejmij zdejmijcie zdejmijmy**, etc. However, some people say **zdejm zdejmcie zdejmmy**. The above rules suggest that the imperative of **obejrzeć obejrzę obejrzysz** *look at* will be **obejrz obejrzcie obejrzmy**, and these forms can be heard, but the recommended imperative forms are **obejrzyj obejrzyjcie obejrzyjmy**. As a rule, even the most challenging consonant clusters other than those in consonant plus **n** will not take the extension **-ij-**. Compare, for example, **rozluźnić rozluźnię rozluźnisz** *loosen*, imperatives **rozluźnij rozluźnijcie rozluźnijmy** with **wątpić wątpię wątpi** *doubt*, imperative forms **wątp wątpcie wątpmy** (although **wątpij wątpijcie wątpijmy** can be heard). Similarly, the recommended imperative of **jeździć jeżdżę jeździsz** *ride* is **jeźdź jeźdźcie jeźdźmy**, not the often encountered substandard **jeździj jeździjcie jeździjmy**. The verb **wziąć wezmę weźmiesz** *take* forms the imperative irregularly: **weź weźcie weźmy**, although substandard **weźmij weźmijcie weźmijmy** can also be heard.

Verbs of the 3rd and 4th conjugations add the imperative endings to a stem that is like the 3.p.pl. minus ą:

Infinitive	3.p.sg.	Imper.stem	Imperative forms
czekać	czekają	czekaj-	czekaj czekajcie czekajmy
pytać	pytają	pytaj-	pytaj pytajcie pytajmy
umieć	umieją	umiej-	umiej umiejcie umiejmy
śmieć	śmieją	śmiej-	śmiej śmiejcie śmiejmy
powiedzieć	powiedzą	powiedz-	powiedz powiedzcie powiedzmy
jeść	jedzą	jedz-	jedz jedzcie jedzmy

Exceptions:

a. The imperative of **dać dam dasz dadzą** *give* and of **mieć mam masz mają** *have* is formed on the infinitive stem: **daj dajcie dajmy; miej miejcie miejmy.**

b. The usual imperative of Imperfective **rozumieć rozumiem rozumieją** *understand* is regular: **rozumiej rozumiejcie rozumiejmy.** However, the Perfective **zrozumieć** usually forms the imperatives **zrozum zrozumcie zrozummy.**

Notes on Imperative Use

a. For the use of the imperative in connection with the Perfective and Imperfective aspect, see Chapter 11, p. 274.

b. The 2.p.sg. and 2.p.pl. imperatives are forms of informal address and, as such, follow the same rules of social use as the pronouns **ty** and **wy**; see Chapter 7. The imperative has a high frequency of use in situations among close friends and family members. Examples:

Podaj mi twój numer telefonu. *Give me your phone number.*

Siadaj, Tomek, dawno cię nie widziałem. *Sit down, Tomek, I haven't seen you for ages.*

Żałuj, że nie byłaś wczoraj na przyjęciu. *You should be sorry that you weren't at the party yesterday.*

Nie bójcie się, wszystko będzie dobrze. *Never fear, everything will go fine.*

Chodźmy do mnie na kawę. *Let's go to my place for coffee.*

c. The 1.p.pl. form has the meaning of an exhortative, including the speaker and his audience: **chodźmy** *let's go,* **poczekajmy** *let's wait a bit.* The 1.p.pl. form connotes somewhat informal address, but not as informal as the 2nd-pers. forms.

d. The imperative of formal address is obtained by combining the exhortative particle **niech** 'let' (obsolete or very high-style **niechaj**) with the pronouns of formal address (**pan, pani, państwo**) to form a 3rd-person expression:

Niech państwo się nie śmieją. *Don't laugh, people.*

Niech pani odpowie. *Please answer, madam.*

Niech pan zdejmie kożuch. *Take off your coat, sir.*

The construction with **niech** is broader than an imperative. It often has the sense of a suggestion or encouragement, especially in its 3rd person use:

Niech on dzwoni do mnie o każdej porze dnia i nocy. *Have him call me at any time of day or night.*

Niech may be used with some verbs which otherwise do not form an imperative:

Niech widzi (lubi, woli). *Let him see (like, prefer) it.*

Niech is often used in imprecations:

Niech go gęś kopnie. *May a goose kick him.*

Niech go czort trafi. *May the devil take him.*

Niech occasionally occurs with 1st-person verbs:

Niech ja to zrobię za ciebie. *Why don't I do that in place of you?*

e. Both formal and informal imperatives are often accompanied by **proszę** *please:*

Proszę niech pan wejdzie. *Please come in.*

Proszę powtórz to. *Please repeat that.*

f. The use of **proszę** plus the infinitive is not often used in making requests outside formal situations, where someone is "in charge", for example teacher-to-student:

Proszę mówić wyraźniej. *Please speak more clearly.*

Such usage (i.e. **proszę** plus the infinitive) is avoided in everyday conversation as being excessively formal and even rude. Use **proszę** plus the imperative instead.

g. A generic prohibitive command, used especially with children and pets, is **Nie wolno!** *Don't!, You mustn't!*

h. In military and similarly peremtory commands, and when giving orders to pets, the infinitive may serve as an imperative:

Stać! *Stand up!*

Leżeć! *Lie down!*

Nie wychylać się! *Don't lean out!* (sign on trolley).

PRAGMATIC AVOIDANCE OF THE IMPERATIVE

i. The practical effect of an imperative (getting someone to do something for one) is often achieved indirectly, by using means other than the imperative. Depending on circumstances, the following remarks could be taken as requests for the same action on the part of the listener:

Pościel łóżko. *Make your bed.* (imperative)

A może pościelisz łóżko, co? *How about making the bed, huh?* (future)

Mógłbyś pościelić łóżko. *You might make your bed.* (conditional)

Pamiętaj, że masz pościelić łóżko. *Remember to make your bed.* (reminder)

Przecież łóżko jest niepościelone. *But the bed isn't made.* (oblique comment).

Trzeba pościelić łóżko. *The bed needs to be made.* (modal of obligation).

Chapter 10

Past Tense, Compound Future Tense, Conditional, Modals

FORMATION OF THE PAST TENSE

The forms of the past tense are based on the stem of the infinitive; they are much simpler to produce than the forms of the present tense. If the infinitive ends in a vowel plus -ć, as is usually the case, the 3rd person past tense is formed by dropping -ć and adding -ł (masculine), -ła (feminine), -ło (neuter) -li (masculine personal plural), or -ły (other plural). 1st and 2nd-person endings are added to the 3rd-person forms. The 1st and 2nd-person endings are as follows:

	Sg.	Pl.
1st pers.	-(e)m	-śmy
2nd pers.	-(e)ś	-ście

In the masculine, the singular endings are joined to the 3rd person form with the link vowel -e-, creating the endings -em, -eś. The 1st and 2nd-pers. neuter endings (-om, -oś) are sometimes cited, but for all practical purposes do not occur. In sum, the endings of the past tense are these:

	Sg.			Pl.	
	Masc.	Fem.	Neut.	Masc. pers.	Other pl.
1.p.	-łem	-łam	—	-liśmy	-łyśmy
2.p.	-łeś	-łaś	—	-liście	-łyście
3.p.	-ł	-ła	-ło	-li	-ły

1. Verbs in -ać, -ić, -uć, -yć. Most verbs with infinitives ending in a vowel plus -ć form the past tense like dać *give:*

dać dam dasz dadzą *give*

Singular:

1.p.	dałem (m.)	dałam (f.) *I gave*	
2.p.	dałeś (m.)	dałaś (f.) *you (sg.) gave*	
3.p.	dał *he gave*	dała *she gave*	dało *it gave*

Plural:

1.p.	daliśmy (m.p.)	dałyśmy (f.) *we gave*
2.p.	daliście (m.p.)	dałyście (f.) *you (pl.) gave*
3.p.	dali (m.p.)	dały (f., n.) *they gave*

2. Verbs in **-eć**. Verbs ending in **-eć** change **e** to **a** (an instance of the **ě: a** shift) before 3rd-person endings other than the masc. pers. pl., where **e** is retained. The 1st and 2nd-person endings are then added to the 3rd-person forms; see

mieć mam masz *have*

Singular:

1.p.	**miałem** (m.)	**miałam** (f.) *I had*	
2.p.	**miałeś** (m.)	**miałaś** (f.) *you (sg.) had*	
3.p.	**miał** *he gave*	**miała** *she had*	**miało** *it had*

Plural:

1.p.	**mieliśmy** (m.p.)	**miałyśmy** (f.) *we had*	
2.p.	**mieliście** (m.p.)	**miałyście** (f.) *you (pl.) had*	
3.p.	**mieli** (m.p.)	**miały** (f., n.) *they had*	

3. Verbs in **-ąć** exhibit the **ę: ą** shift in the 3rd-person forms, with **ą** occurring in the closed syllable of the 3rd pers. masc. sg., and in the 1st and 2nd pers. forms based on it. In effect, **ę** appears everywhere except in the masc. sg., where **ą** occurs, as with

zacząć zacznę zaczniesz *begin (pf.)*

Singular:

1.p.	**zacząłem** (m.)	**zaczęłam** (f.) *I began*	
2.p.	**zacząłeś** (m.)	**zaczęłaś** (f.) *you (sg.) began*	
3.p.	**zaczął** *he began*	**zaczęła** *she began*	**zaczęło** *it began*

Plural:

1.p.	**zaczęliśmy** (m.p.)	**zaczęłyśmy** (f.) *we began*	
2.p.	**zaczęliście** (m.p.)	**zaczęłyście** (f.) *you (pl.) began*	
3.p.	**zaczęli** (m.p.)	**zaczęły** (f., n.) *they began*	

4. Verbs in dropping **-nąć**. Some verbs ending in a consonant plus **-nąć** drop this entire segment and add endings to the resulting consonant-stem. This kind of verb may be indicated by citing the masc. past form. Here is the past of **zbladnąć** *grow pale (pf.)*:

zbladnąć zbladnę zbladniesz zbladł *grow pale (pf.)*

Singular:

1.p.	**zbladłem** (m.)	**zbladłam** (f.) *I paled*	
2.p.	**zbladłeś** (m.)	**zbladłaś** (f.) *you (sg.) paled*	
3.p.	**zbladł** *he paled*	**zbladła** *she paled*	**zbladło** *it paled*

Plural:

1.p.	**zbladliśmy** (m.p.)	**zbladłyśmy** (f.) *we paled*	
2.p.	**zbladliście** (m.p.)	**zbladłyście** (f.) *you (pl.) paled*	
3.p.	**zbladli** (m.p.)	**zbladły** (f., n.) *they paled*	

Note: this verb is alternatively **zblednąć**, for whose past tense see illustrations to follow. Often with such verbs, the masculine sg. is formed with **-ną-**, while the other forms will lack **-nę-**:

kwitnąć kwitnę kwitniesz kwitnął kwitła *blossom*

Singular:

1.p.	**kwitnąłem** (m.)	**kwitłam** (f.) *I blossomed*
2.p.	**kwitnąłeś** (m.)	**kwitłaś** (f.) *you (sg.) blossomed*
3.p.	**kwitnął** *he b'd*	**kwitła** *she blossomed* **kwitło** *it blossomed*

Plural:

1.p.	**kwitnęliśmy** (m.p.)	**kwitłyśmy** (f.) *we blossomed*
2.p.	**kwitnęliście** (m.p.)	**kwitłyście** (f.) *you (pl.) blossomed*
3.p.	**kwitnęli** (m.p.)	**kwitły** (f., n.) *they blossomed*

Alternate forms like **kwitł, kwitliśmy, kwitnęła, kwitnęłyśmy**, etc. are not incorrect, merely less frequent. A good dictionary should be consulted on a verb-individual basis. For more illustrations, see further below.

5. Verbs in **-ść, -źć, -c.** Consonant-stem verbs, with infinitives in **-ść, -źć,** and **-c**, add past-tense endings to the underlying infinitive stem, which is usually the same as the stem of the 1.p.sg. present. Verbs with **e** in the root usually retain **e** only in the masculine personal plural, and show **o** in the other forms, changing to **ó** in the 3rd pers. sg. masc. (an example of the **e: o** shift, feeding into the **o: ó** shift). Here are the past-tense forms of **wieść wiodę wiedziesz** *lead* (past stem **wied-**) and **strzyc strzygę strzyżesz** *cut, clip* (past stem **strzyg-**). Note in the former the change of **e** to **o** in past forms other than the masc. pers. pl., and the change of **o** to **ó** in the 3rd pers.masc. sg.:

wieść wiodę wiedziesz *lead*

Singular:

1.p.	**wiodłem** (m.)	**wiodłam** (f.) *I led*
2.p.	**wiodłeś** (m.)	**wiodłaś** (f.) *you (sg.) led*
3.p.	**wiódł** *he led*	**wiodła** *she led* **wiodło** *it led*

Plural:

1.p.	**wiedliśmy** (m.p.)	**wiodłyśmy** (f.) *we led*
2.p.	**wiedliście** (m.p.)	**wiodłyście** (f.) *you led*
3.p.	**wiedli** (m.p.)	**wiodły** (f., n.) *they led*

strzyc strzygę strzyżesz *cut, clip*

Singular:

1.p.	**strzygłem** (m.)	**strzygłam** (f.) *I clipped*
2.p.	**strzygłeś** (m.)	**strzygłaś** (f.) *you (sg.) clipped*
3.p.	**strzygł** *he clipped*	**strzygła** *she clipped* **strzygło** *it clipped*

Plural:

1.p.	**strzygliśmy** (m.p.)	**strzygłyśmy** (f.) *we clipped*
2.p.	**strzygliście** (m.p.)	**strzygłyście** (f.) *you (pl.) clipped*
3.p.	**strzygli** (m.p.)	**strzygły** (f., n.) *they clipped*

6. **ł-** and **r-**stems. Verbs of the not-numerous **drzeć** *tear* and **pleć** *weed* types have past-tense forms as follows, using stems in **ar-** and **eł-**, respectively:

drzeć drę drzesz *tear*

Singular:

1.p.	**darłem** (m.)	**darłam** (f.) *I tore*
2.p.	**darłeś** (m.)	**darłaś** (f.) *you (sg.) tore*
3.p.	**darł** *he tore*	**darła** *she tore* **darło** *it tore*

Plural:

1.p.	**darliśmy** (m.p.)	**darłyśmy** (f.) *we tore*
2.p.	**darliście** (m.p.)	**darłyście** (f.) *you tore*
3.p.	**darli** (m.p.)	**darły** (f., n.) *they tore*

Exceptionally, **wrzeć wrę wrzesz** *boil, seethe* forms the past on the stem **wrzě-**:

wrzeć wrę wrzesz *seethe*

Singular:

1.p.	**wrzałem** (m.)	**wrzałam** (f.)*I seethed*
2.p.	**wrzałeś** (m.)	**wrzałaś** (f.) *you (sg.) seethed*
3.p.	**wrzał** *he seethed*	**wrzała** *she seethed* **wrzało** *it seethed*

Plural:

1.p.	**wrzeliśmy** (m.p.)	**wrzałyśmy** (f.) *we seethed*
2.p.	**wrzeliście** (m.p.)	**wrzałyście** (f.) *you seethed*
3.p.	**wrzeli** (m.p.)	**wrzały** (f., n.) *they seethed*

The verb **zawrzeć zawrę zawrzesz** in the sense 'contain, conclude' forms the past like **drzeć: zawarł zawarła zawarli zawarły**, while the similarly shaped verb in the sense 'begin to boil' forms its past like **wrzeć: zawrzał zawrzała zawrzeli zawrzały**.

pleć (or **pielić**) **pielę pielesz** *weed*

Singular:

1.p.	**pełłem** (m.)	**pełłam** (f.) *I weeded*
2.p.	**pełłeś** (m.)	**pełłaś** (f.) *you (sg.) weeded*
3.p.	**pełł** *he weeded*	**pełła** *she weeded* **pełło** *it weeded*

Plural:

1.p.	**pełliśmy** (m.p.)	**pełłyśmy** (f.) *we weeded*
2.p.	**pełliście** (m.p.)	**pełłyście** (f.) *you weeded*
3.p.	**pełli** (m.p.)	**pełły** (f., n.) *they weeded*

The only other verb of the ł-type is **mleć** (or **mielić**) **mielę mielesz** *grind*, past **mełł**, etc. Observe that softening affects only the final ł of the cluster **łł: pełli**. Both of these verbs are uncommon and tend to occur mainly in grammatical descriptions, as here. Alternative past-tense forms abound, for example, masc. 3.p.sg. **mielił, mleł, mlił,** or even **mioł**.

7. Irregular. Verbs with irregular past-tense stems include
iść idę idziesz *go, be going*, past **szedł szłam szli**

Singular:

szedłem (m.)	**szłam** (f.) *I went*	
szedłeś (m.)	**szłaś** (f.) *you (sg.) went*	
szedł *he went*	**szła** *she went*	**szło** *it went*

Plural:

szliśmy (m.p.)	**szłyśmy** (f.) *we went*	
szliście (m.p.)	**szłyście** (f.) *you (pl.) went*	
szli (m.p.)	**szły** (f., n.) *they went*	

Similarly: **podejść podejdę podejdziesz** *approach (pf.)*, past **podszedł podeszła podeszli**; **pójść pójdę pójdziesz** *go (pf.)*, past **poszedł poszłam poszli,** and other prefixed versions of this root.

Mixed masculine-feminine forms like *poszłem *poszłeś or, much less often, *poszedłam *poszedłaś, frequent in the speech of the very young, are usually rooted out in the first year of school. Among adults, they mainly survive among adults in Polish spoken abroad.

jeść jem jesz jedzą *eat*, past **jadł jadła jedli**
Singular:

jadłem (m.)	**jadłam** (f.)*I ate*	
jadłeś (m.)	**jadłaś** (f.) *you (sg.) ate*	
jadł *he ate*	**jadła** *she ate*	**jadło** *it ate*

Plural:

jedliśmy (m.p.)	**jadłyśmy** (f.) *we ate*	
jedliście (m.p.)	**jadłyście** (f.) *you (pl.) ate*	
jedli (m.p.)	**jadły** (f., n.) *they ate*	

Similarly irregular:

znaleźć znajdę znajdziesz *find (p.)*, past **znalazł znalazła znaleźli**
usiąść usiądę -dziesz *sit down (p.)*, past **usiadł usiadła usiedli**

FURTHER EXAMPLES OF PAST TENSE FORMS

Although past-tense formation does not vary by conjugational type or subtype but rather according to the type of infinitive, the examples below are arranged according to conjugation so as to give a broad representative sample. Verbs are taken from among those used for present-tense illustrations in the preceding chapter.

First Conjugation:

mazać mażę mażesz *smear*

mazałem	mazałam	mazaliśmy	mazałyśmy	
mazałeś	mazałaś	mazaliście	mazałyście	
mazał	mazała	mazało	mazali	mazały

łajać łaję łajesz *scold*

łajałem	łajałam	łajaliśmy	łajałyśmy	
łajałeś	łajałaś	łajaliście	łajałyście	
łajał	łajała	lajało	łajali	łajały

dziękować dziękuję dziękujesz *thank*

dziękowałem	dziękowałam	dziękowaliśmy	dziękowałyśmy	
dziękowałeś	dziękowałaś	dziękowaliście	dziękowałyście	
dziękował	dziękowała	dziękowało	dziękowali	dziękowały

dokonywać dokonuję dokonujesz *accomplish*

dokonywałem	dokonywałam	dokonywaliśmy	dokonywałyśmy	
dokonywałeś	dokonywałaś	dokonywaliście	dokonywałyście	
dokonywał	dokonywała	dokonywało	dokonywali	dokonywały

mdleć mdleję mdlejesz *faint*

mdlałem	mdlałam	mdleliśmy	mdlałyśmy	
mdlałeś	mdlałaś	mdleliście	mdlałyście	
mdlał	mdlała	mdlło	mdleli	mdlały

dziać dzieję dziejesz *knit*

działem	działam	dzialiśmy	działyśmy	
działeś	działaś	dzialiście	działyście	
dział	działa	działo	dziali	działy

myć myję myjesz *wash*

myłem	myłam	myliśmy	myłyśmy	
myłeś	myłaś	myliście	myłyście	
mył	myła	myło	myli	myły

pić piję pijesz *drink*

piłem	piłam	piliśmy	piłyśmy	
piłeś	piłaś	piliście	piłyście	
pił	piła	piło	pili	piły

żuć żuję żujesz *chew*

żułem	żułam	żuliśmy	żułyśmy	
żułeś	żułaś	żuliście	żułyście	
żuł	żuła	żuło	żuli	żuły

brać biorę bierzesz *take*

brałem	brałam	braliśmy	brałyśmy	
brałeś	brałaś	braliście	brałyście	
brał	brała	brało	brali	brały

chcieć chcę chcesz *want*

chciałem	chciałam	chcieliśmy	chciałyśmy	
chciałeś	chciałaś	chcieliście	chciałyście	
chciał	chciała	chciało	chcieli	chciały

jechać jadę jedziesz *ride, drive*

jechałem	jechałam	jechaliśmy	jechałyśmy	
jechałeś	jechałaś	jechaliście	jechałyście	
jechał	jechała	jechało	jechali	jechały

stać się stanę się staniesz się *become*

stałem się	stałam się	staliśmy się	stałyśmy się	
stałeś się	stałaś się	staliście się	stałyście się	
stał się	stała się	stało się	stali się	stały się

być jestem jesteś są *be.* future tense:

byłem	byłam	byliśmy	byłyśmy	
byłeś	byłaś	byliście	byłyście	
był	była	było	byli	były

ciągnąć ciągnę ciągniesz *tug*

ciągnąłem	ciągnęłam	ciągnęliśmy	ciągnęłyśmy	
ciągnąłeś	ciągnęłaś	ciągnęliście	ciągnęłyście	
ciągnął	ciągnęła	ciągło	ciągnęli	ciągnęły

blednąć blednę bledniesz *grow pale.* The usual past-tense forms are:

bladłem	bladłam	bledliśmy	bladłyśmy	
bladłeś	bladłaś	bledliście	bladłyście	
bladł	bladła	bladło	bledli	bladły

więdnąć więdnę więdniesz *fade.* The usual past-tense forms are:

wiądłem	więdłam	więdliśmy	więdłyśmy	
wiądłeś	więdłaś	więdliście	więdłyście	
wiądł	więdła	więdło	więdli	więdły

zniknąć zniknę znikniesz *disappear.* Acceptable past-tense forms are either:

zniknłem	zniknłam	znikliśmy	zniknłyśmy	
zniknłeś	zniknłaś	znikliście	zniknłyście	
zniknł	zniknła	znikło	znikli	zniknły

or

zniknąłem	zniknęłam	zniknęliśmy	zniknęłyśmy	
zniknąłeś	zniknęłaś	zniknęliście	zniknęłyście	
zniknął	zniknęła	zniknęło	zniknęli	zniknęły

marznąć marznę marzniesz (r-z) *freeze.* The usual past-tense forms are:

marzłem	marzłam	marzliśmy	marzłyśmy	
marzłeś	marzłaś	marzliście	marzłyście	
marzł	marzła	marzło	marzli	marzły

Note the absense of **z : ż** in the masc. pers. pl. (**marzli**), despite the optional present forms **marźniesz marźniesz**, etc.

pleść plotę pleciesz *braid*

plotłem	plotłam	plotliśmy	plotłyśmy	
plotłeś	plotłaś	plotliście	plotłyście	
plótł	plotła	plotło	pletli	plotły

paść padnę padniesz *fall*

padłem	padłam	padliśmy	padłyśmy	
padłeś	padłaś	padliście	padłyście	
padł	padła	padło	padli	padły

nieść niosę niesiesz *carry*

niosłem	niosłam	nieśliśmy	niosłyśmy	
niosłeś	niosłaś	nieśliście	niosłyście	
niósł	niosła	niosło	nieśli	niosły

gryźć gryzę gryziesz *bite*

gryzłem	gryzłam	gryźliśmy	gryzłyśmy	
gryzłeś	gryzłaś	gryźliście	gryzłyście	
gryzł	gryzła	gryzło	gryźli	gryzły

piec piekę pieczesz *bake*

piekłem	piekłam	piekliśmy	piekłyśmy	
piekłeś	piekłaś	piekliście	piekłyście	
piekł	piekła	piekło	piekli	piekły

ciec ciekę ciekniesz *flow*

ciekłem	ciekłam	ciekliśmy	ciekłyśmy	
ciekłeś	ciekłaś	ciekliście	ciekłyście	
ciekł	ciekła	ciekło	ciekli	ciekły

móc mogę możesz *be able*

mogłem	mogłam	mogliśmy	mogłyśmy	
mogłeś	mogłaś	mogliście	mogłyście	
mógł	mogła	mogło	mogli	mogły

biec biegnę biegniesz *run*

biegłem	biegłam	biegliśmy	biegłyśmy	
biegłeś	biegłaś	biegliście	biegłyście	
biegł	biegła	biegło	biegli	biegły

piąć się pnę się pniesz się *clamber*

piąłem się	pięłam się	pięliśmy się	pięłyśmy się	
piąłeś się	pięłaś się	pięliście się	pięłyście się	
piął się	pięła się	pięło się	pięli się	pięły się

dąć dmę dmiesz *puff*

dąłem	dęłam	dęliśmy	dęłyśmy	
dąłeś	dęłaś	dęliście	dęłyście	
dął	dęła	dęło	dęli	dęły

objąć obejmę obejmiesz *embrace*

objąłem	objęłam	objęliśmy	objęłyśmy	
objąłeś	objęłaś	objęliście	objęłyście	
objął	objęła	objęło	objęli	objęły

wziąć wezmę weźmiesz *take*

wziąłem	wzięłam	wzięliśmy	wzięłyśmy	
wziąłeś	wzięłaś	wzięliście	wzięłyście	
wziął	wzięła	wzięło	wzięli	wzięły

umrzeć umrę umrzesz *die*

umarłem	umarłam	umarliśmy	umarłyśmy	
umarłeś	umarłaś	umarliście	umarłyście	
umarł	umarła	umarło	umarli	umarły

mleć mielę mielesz *grind*

mełłem	mełłam	mełliśmy	mełłyśmy	
mełłeś	mełłaś	mełliście	mełłyście	
mełł	mełła	mełło	mełli	mełły

Second Conjugation:

kupić kupię kupisz *buy*

kupiłem	kupiłam	kupiliśmy	kupiłyśmy
kupiłeś	kupiłaś	kupiliście	kupiłyście
kupił	kupiła	kupiło	kupili kupiły

spać śpię śpisz *sleep*

spałem	spałam	spaliśmy	spałyśmy
spałeś	spałaś	spaliście	spałyście
spał	spała	spało	spali spały

zapomnieć zapomnę zapomnisz *forget*

zapomniałem	zapomniałam	zapomnieliśmy	zapomniałyśmy
zapomniałeś	zapomniałaś	zapomnieliście	zapomniałyście
zapomniał	zapomniała	zapomnieło	zapomnieli zapomniały

woleć wolę wolisz *prefer*

wolałem	wolałam	woleliśmy	wolałyśmy
wolałeś	wolałaś	woleliście	wolałyście
wolał	wolała	wolało	woleli wolały

stroić stroję stroisz *trim, tune*

stroiłem	stroiłam	stroiliśmy	stroiłyśmy
stroiłeś	stroiłaś	stroiliście	stroiłyście
stroił	stroiła	stroiło	stroili stroiły

stać stoję stoisz *stand*

stałem	stałam	staliśmy	stałyśmy
stałeś	stałaś	staliście	stałyście
stał	stała	stało	stali stały

jeździć jeżdżę jeździsz *drive*

jeździłem	jeździłam	jeździliśmy	jeździłyśmy
jeździłeś	jeździłaś	jeździliście	jeździłyście
jeździł	jeździła	jeździło	jeździli jeździły

uczyć uczę uczysz *teach*

uczyłem	uczyłam	uczyliśmy	uczyłyśmy
uczyłeś	uczyłaś	uczyliście	uczyłyście
uczył	uczyła	uczyło	uczyli uczyły

leżeć leżę leżysz *lie*

leżałem	leżałam	leżeliśmy	leżałyśmy
leżałeś	leżałaś	leżeliście	leżałyście
leżał	leżała	leżało	leżeli leżały

Third Conjugation:

czekać czekam czekasz *wait*

czekałem	czekałam	czekaliśmy	czekałyśmy	
czekałeś	czekałaś	czekaliście	czekałyście	
czekał	czekała	czekało	czekali	czekały

mieć mam masz *have*

miałem	miałam	mieliśmy	miałyśmy	
miałeś	miałaś	mieliście	miałyście	
miał	miała	miało	mieli	miały

Fourth Conjugation:

umieć umiem umiesz *know how*

umiałem	umiałam	umieliśmy	umiałyśmy	
umiałeś	umiałaś	umieliście	umiałyście	
umiał	umiała	umiało	umieli	umiały

wiedzieć wiem wiesz wiedzą *know (information)*

wiedziałem	wiedziałam	wiedzieliśmy	wiedziałyśmy	
wiedziałeś	wiedziałaś	wiedzieliście	wiedziałyście	
wiedział	wiedziała	wiedziało	wiedzieli	wiedziały

DETACHABLE PAST-TENSE PERSONAL VERB ENDINGS

In colloquial and dialectal Polish, more often in the south than in other parts of the country, the 1st and 2nd-person past-tense verb endings may be detached from the verb and attached to a word toward the beginning of the clause, especially to conjunctions and personal pronouns, but in principle to any word. If **-m** or **-ś** are detached and attached to a word ending in a consonant, they are joined to it with the help of non-softening **-e-** (e.g. **jakem pisał** *as I was writing*). Combinations such as **jużem, jakem, żem**, etc. sound archaic or odd; they should not be imitated by a non-native speaker. Plural endings are somewhat more naturally detached than singular. Examples:

Kiedyś wróciła? *When did you return?*

Dlaczegoś tak wcześnie wstała? *Why did you get up so early?*

Trochęśmy się niepokoili. *We were somewhat concerned.*

Jużem ci powiedział. *I've already told you.*

W co wyście się bawili? *What were you playing at?*

Gdzieście byli cały dzień? *Where have you been all day?*

On był pewien, żem go zdradzała. *He was certain that I was being unfaithful to him.*

THE COMPOUND FUTURE OF IMPERFECTIVE VERBS

Verbs may be either Perfective or Imperfective (Chapter 11). The future tense of Imperfective verbs is produced by combining the future tense forms of być, i.e. będę będziesz, etc., with the 3rd pers. past forms of the verb. Here is the compound, or periphrastic, future of the verb czytać *read* :

Singular

	Masculine	Feminine
1.p.	będę czytał	będę czytała *I am going to read*
2.p.	będziesz czytał	będziesz czytała *you are going to read*
3.p.	będzie czytał	będzie czytała *he/she is going to read*

3rd-pers. neuter: będzie czytało *it is going to read.*

Plural

	Masc. pers.	Other
1.p.	będziemy czytali	będziemy czytały *we are going to read*
2.p.	będziecie czytali	będziecie czytały *you-pl. are going to read*
3.p.	będą czytali	będą czytały *they are going to read*

Notes on będę:

a. Forms of będę will most often translate English 'going to' in the sense of 'intend to': będę czytał *I am going to read, I intend to read*. However, in appropriate contexts, będę czytał can also be used to mean 'I will be reading' or 'I will (often) read'. Będę can also have the meaning of persistence in the face of reason, good taste, etc.: Jak długo będziesz dłubać w nosie? *How long are you going to pick your nose?*

b. Instead of the past-tense forms, one may also use the infinitive; hence będę czytać *I am going to read* may be used instead of either będę czytał or będę czytała. The use of the past-tense forms is much more frequent in colloquial Polish, especially with personal subjects, and is somewhat more frequent with male reference than with female.

c. When the order of będę and the main verb is reversed for special effect, usually emphatic and often negative, only the infinitive is used:

Ja tego filmu oglądać nie będę. *I am not going to see that film.*

My w takich warunkach pracować nie będziemy. *We are not going to work under such conditions.*

The following order in stage introductions is quite frequent:

Teraz śpiewać będzie Maryla Rodowicz. *Now Maryla Rodowicz will sing.*

d. Polish never uses forms of iść idę idziesz *go* as a future-tense auxiliary. Idę kupić film has the literal meaning 'I am on my way to buy film'. 'I am going to buy film' in the sense 'I intend to buy film' will be translated as **będę kupować (kupował, kupowała) film.**

e. The auxiliary **będę** does not combine with forms of **być.** In other words, ***będę być** is not used. The form **będę** by itself expresses the future of 'be': **Będę zajęty.** *I am going to be busy.* **Będę tam o ósmej.** *I'll be there at 8:00.*

f. The auxiliary **będę** may not under any circumstances be combined with perfective verbs. Such a combination produces a serious grammatical error. Hence only **będę przyjmować** *I will accept,* never ***będę przyjąć.**

g. **Będę** rarely combines with Determinate verbs of motion, the present form having prospective meaning by itself. Hence one normally says **Dziś wieczorem my z Edkiem idziemy** (not: **będziemy iść**) **do teatru.** *This evening Edek and I are going to the theater.* In the sense specifically of 'walk', however, Determinate verbs do naturally combine with **będę;** see **Będziemy iść powoli.** *We are going to walk slowly.*

CONDITIONAL MOOD

The Polish conditional mood expresses what in English is usually expressed with modal verbs like *would, could, might.* In its basic form, it is produced by inserting the conditional particle **by** just before past-tense personal verb endings:

	Sg.			Pl.	
	Masc.	Fem.	Neut.	Masc. pers.	Other pl.
1.p.	pisałbym	pisałabym		pisalibyśmy	pisałybyśmy
2.p.	pisałbyś	pisałabyś		pisalibyście	pisałybyście
3.p.	pisałby	pisałaby	pisałoby	pisaliby	pisałyby

The meaning of **pisał(a)bym** is 'I would write', 'I could write', 'I might write'. If the personal pronouns or a personal name are present, then **by** plus personal endings are usually detached and placed between the pronoun (or name) and the main verb:

	Sg.	Pl.
1.p.	ja bym pisał (pisała)	my byśmy pisali (pisały)
2.p.	ty byś pisał (pisała)	wy byście pisali (pisały)
3.p.	on (ona) by pisał (pisała)	oni (one) by pisali (pisały)

Also: **Janek by pisał** *Janek would write;* **Maria by pisała** *Maria would write.*

The particle **by** plus personal endings obligatorily becomes detached from the main verb and attached to such clause-initiating conjunctions as **choć/chociaż** *although,* **gdy** *if,* **jak** *as, how, if,* **jeśli** *if* (literary **jeżeli**), **to** *then,* **że** *that:*

Singular

	Masc.	Fem.	Neut.
1.p.	**gdybym pisał**	**gdybym pisała**	
2.p.	**gdybyś pisał**	**gdybyś pisała**	
3.p.	**gdyby pisał**	**gdyby pisała**	**gdyby pisało**

Plural

	Masc. pers. pl.	Other pl.
1.p.	**gdybyśmy pisali**	**gdybyśmy pisały**
2.p.	**gdybyście pisali**	**gdybyście pisały**
3.p.	**gdyby pisali**	**gdyby pisały**

In colloquial speech, other words can attract the particle **by**: **Bardzo bym chciał** *I'd really like to.* In less formal speech, if a personal pronoun or name and a clause-initiating conjunction is present, the pronoun can split the conjunction and **by**:

Singular

	Masc.	Fem.	Neut.
1.p.	**jeśli ja bym pisał**	**jeśli ja bym pisała**	
2.p.	**jeśli ty byś pisał**	**jeśli ty byś pisała**	
3.p.	**jeśli on by pisał**	**jeśli ona by pisała**	**jeśli ono by pisało**

Plural

	Masc. pers. pl.	Other pl.
1.p.	**jeśli my byśmy pisali**	**jeśli my byśmy pisały**
2.p.	**jeśli wy byście pisali**	**jeśli wy byście pisały**
3.p.	**jeśli oni by pisali**	**jeśli one by pisały**

Alternatively: **jeślibym ja pisał, jeśli ja pisałbym**, etc.

USES OF THE CONDITIONAL

1. *Clauses of purpose.* The conditional is often used in clauses of purpose, in which case the conditional particle is usually attached to the subordinating conjunction **że** *that*, producing what amounts to the purposive conjunction **żeby** *in order to* (or, more literary, **aby**). Sometimes **by** is used by itself.

    Piszę ci, żebyś (abyś, byś) wiedziała, co tutaj się dzieje. *I'm writing you so that you will know what is going on around here.*

    Pożycz mi pięć dolarów, żebym (abym, bym) miał na obiad. *Lend me five dollars, so I'll have enough for dinner.*

    If the subjects of the main and subordinate clause are the same, the purposive clause may be infinitival:

Pracuję po to, żebym miał (or żeby mieć) pieniądze. *I'm working so that I might have (in order to have) money.*

Żeby is often followed by an infinitive in generalized statements such as the following:

Żeby znaleźć dobrą pracę, trzeba mieć dużo szczęścia. *In order to find a good job, one must have a lot of luck.*

2.   *Contrary-to-fact clauses.* If an if-then sentence coordinates two states or events that are hypothetical or contrary to the way things are, then both clauses will be in the conditional:

Gdybym był bogaty, nie musiałbym tak ciężko pracować. *If I were rich, I wouldn't have to work so hard.*

Poszedłbym do kina, gdyby tylko było co oglądać. *I'd go to the movies if there were only something to watch.*

Co byś zrobił, gdybym umarła? *What would you do if I died?*

3.   *After verbs of permission, warning, request, command, desire, concern, hope, preference.* Complements of such verbs are placed in the conditional, the clause being introduced by **żeby (aby, by)**:

On prosi nas, żebyśmy mniej hałasowali. *He's asking us to make less noise.*

Błagam was, żebyście nie zwlekali z decyzją. *I beg you not to put off your decision.*

Ona powiedziała mi, żebym do niej dzwonił codziennie. *She told me to phone her every day.*

Ostrzegam was, abyście tego nie robili. *I warn you not to do that.*

Nie życzę ci, żebyś kiedykolwiek musiała coś podobnego przeżyć. *I don't wish that you might ever have to live through such a thing.*

Nie chcę, żebyście się spóźnili. *I don't want for you-pl. to be late.*

Chcę, żeby mi na nagrobku podobny napis wyryto. *I want a similar inscription to be written on my grave.*

Żądam, żeby pan oddał te pieniądze. *I demand that you give back that money.*

Będziemy dbali o to, żeby wszystko było w odpowiednim stanie. *We will see to it that everything is in proper shape.*

Trudno wymagać od czytelnika, by się znał na wszystkim. *It's difficult to demand of the reader that he be an expert on everything.*

Chodzi o to, żeby być przygotowanym na wszystko. *It's a matter of being prepared for everything.*

SO-CALLED SUBJECT-RAISING AND THE CONDITIONAL

"Subject-raising" refers to the conversion of a subject of a subordinate clause to an object of the main clause, as in English *I want that he go: I want him to go* or, colloquially, *I want for him to go*. In this example, *he*, the subject in the first sentence, becomes *him*, the object of the second sentence. Polish has very limited possibilities for subject-raising, preferring instead either a conditional clause or, sometimes, a prepositional phrase.

Subject-raising is usually not allowed if the verb of a main clause takes the Accusative; instead, the subordinate clause will appear in the conditional:

Profesor wymagał, *żebym powtórzył* cały kurs. *The professor demanded that I repeat the entire course.*

With verbs that are more causal in meaning, one often finds **do** plus a verbal noun:

Profesor zmusił mnie *do powtórzenia* całego kursu. *The professor forced me into repeating the entire course.*

Subject-raising is allowed if the verb takes the Dative:

Profesor kazał mi powtórzyć cały kurs. *The professor ordered me to repeat the entire course.*

Pozwoliłem mu tam mieszkać. *I allowed him to live there.*

Zabraniam wam tam chodzić. *I forbid you to go there.*

Kazał nam czekać. *He asked us to wait.*

4. *Optionally after verbs of hope, doubt, fear.* The conditional is often instead of the indicative to express a greater degree of uncertainty or doubt regarding a conceptualized state of affairs introduced by some kind of subordinating verb like **bać się** *fear*, **myśleć** *think*, **przypuszczać** *suppose*, **sądzić** *judge*, **wątpić** *doubt*, **wierzyć** *believe*, **wyobrażać sobie** *imagine*:

Wątpię, czyby on mógł to zrozumieć. *I doubt whether he would be able to understand that* (instead of also possible **..., czy on to zrozumie** *whether he'll understand that*).

Nie myślę, aby to było tak łatwo. *I don't think that would be so easy* (instead of also possible **..., że to będzie tak łatwo** *that that will be so easy*).

Boję się, żebyśmy nie zdążyli. *I'm afraid lest we not make it on time* (instead of also possible **..., że nie zdążymy** *that we'll not make it on time*).

Similar to this use is the use of the conditional with **chyba** to express "wild imaginings":

Przyjadę, chyba żebym zachorował. *I'll come unless I get sick* (instead of also possible **..., jeśli nie zachoruję** *if I don't get sick*).

5. *oblique commands.* The conditional may be used to express an insinuating command, often conveying impatience:

Mógłbyś mi trochę pomóc. *You might help me a little.*

Mogłabyś już skończyć makijaż. *You might finish your makeup already.*

Mógłby się trochę zainteresować tym tematem. *He might show a little interest in this subject.*

6. *Optatives.* The conditional can be used to express a hope for something to happen or not to happen:

Żeby on nie zapomniał ciepłego ubrania. *Just so he didn't (= I hope he didn't) forget his warm clothing.*

Żeby to się nie powtórzyło. *Just so that doesn't happen again.*

This construction is also used in oaths and imprecations such as

Żeby go diabli wzięli. *May the devils take him.*

Wishes, oaths, and imprecations can also be expressed with **bodaj(że)**, historically **Bog daj** *God grant*, which attracts personal endings, and which can either occur with the conditional particle **by** or not:

Bodajś ty świata bożego nie widział! *I wish you had never seen the light of God (= had never been born).*

Bodajbyśmy nigdy nie musieli tu wracać. *May we never have to return here.*

> The syntactically required use of the conditional is quite frequent in spoken Polish. However, optional uses of the conditional are decidedly less frequent in Polish than is the use of *could, should,* and *might* in English. English-speaking learners of Polish tend to overuse the conditional in the translation of sentences like *Could you help me?*, which in Polish will usually be **Czy możesz mi pomóc?** See also *I could go with you.* **Mogę z tobą pójść.** *This tie would be nice.* **Ten krawat będzie dobry.** And so on.

PAST PERFECT TENSE

The past perfect refers to a past state or action relative to another past state or action, similarly to the English past perfect: "By the time he called *I had already left.*" In contemporary Polish, the past perfect has all but dropped out of use, the simple past being used instead. The past perfect is formed by compounding past-tense forms of the main verb with 3rd-person forms of **być: poszedłem był** *I had gone.* The auxiliary follows the main verb. Here are some examples taken from Jerzy Andrzejewski's 1948 novel *Popiół i diament* 'ash and diamond'. As the examples show, this construction may be used in either Perfective or Imperfective aspect:

Front jeszcze w styczniu *przeszedł był* **przez te strony.** *The front had already passed (pf.) through these parts in January.*

Podgórski przedtem już *zauważył był* **zbiegowisko.** *Podgorski had already noticed (pf.) the gathering earlier.*

Teraz dopiero spostrzegała, że miał gazetę, którą *czytał był* **pilnie z samego rana.** *Only now did she notice that he had a newspaper which he had been reading (impf.) assiduously since early morning.*

Ulewa *musiała była przejść. The downpour must have passed (pf.).*

The past perfect is associated with literary style and does not often occur in the 1st and 2nd persons. More possible in speech than the past perfect itself is the past perfect conditional, formed by combining the past tense with conditional forms of **być**. Here is the imperfective (the perfective would be similar, replacing forms of **czytać** with forms of **przeczytać**):

Singular:
1.p. **byłbym czytał** (f. **byłabym czytała**) *I would have been reading.*
2.p. **byłbyś czytał** (f. **byłabyś czytała**) *you would have been reading*
3.p. **byłby czytał** (f. **byłaby czytała**) *he (she) would have been reading*

Plural:
1.p. **bylibyśmy czytali** (f. **byłybyśmy czytały**) *we would have been reading*
2.p. **bylibyście czytali** (f. **byłybyście czytały**) *you would have been reading*
3.p. **byliby czytali** (f. **byłyby czytały**) *they would have been reading*

"FUTURE PERFECT TENSE"

Very infrequently, the form of the perfective past may be found used in the meaning of a future perfect ('will have done'). This usage is alien to many or most speakers, and is made fun of by Zofia Grodzieńska in a humorous sketch with lines like the following:

Zanim *wszedłeś,* **przynieś mi z przedpokoju klucz.** *Before you will have come in, bring me the key from the hallway.*

Zanim *włożyłeś* **plaszcz, wejdź na drabinę i zdejmij walizkę z antresoli.** *Before you will have put on your coat, climb the ladder and bring down a suitcase from the entresol.*

Standard usage here would replace **wszedłeś** and **włożyłeś** with perfective futures **wejdziesz** and **włożyłeś**, respectively.

MODALS

By "modals" are meant words used to modify a verb with such senses as possibility, probability, capability, obligation, necessity, commitment, and the like. This is not so much a part of speech as it is a collection of various lexical means of modal modification. In Polish most modals are verbs, and take the modified verb in the infinitive.

1. *Modals of obligation.* Although there is a good deal of overlap in the use of modals of obligation, by and large useful one-to-one correspondences may be established between English and Polish usages.

a. *ought.* The half-adjective, half-verb **powinien, f. powinna** plus the infinitive of the main verb expresses both 'ought' and 'should' in the sense of 'ought'. Its forms are as follows; note that the endings are similar to those for the present tense of **być**:

Sg.	Masc.	Fem.	Neut.
1.p.sg.	**powinienem**	**powinnam** *I ought*	
2.p.sg.	**powinieneś**	**powinnaś** *you (sg.) ought*	
3.p.sg.	**powinien** *he ought*	**powinna** *she ought*	**powinno** *it ought*
Pl.	Masc. pers.	Other pl.	
1.p.pl.	**powinniśmy**	**powinnyśmy** *we ought*	
2.p.pl.	**powinniście**	**powinnyście** *you (pl.) ought*	
3.p.pl.	**powinni**	**powinny** *they ought*	

Note the usual stress: "po-wi-NIE-nem, po-wi-NIE-neś" (instead of also heard "po-WI-nie-nem, po-WI-nie-neś"; "po-WIN-ni-śmy, po-WIN-ni-ście". The increasingly less often used past tense is produced by compounding these forms with forms of **być**, which comes after the modal: **powinienem był pójść** *I ought to (should) have gone,* **powinniśmy byli pójść** *we ought to (should) have gone,* and so on. There is no future tense. An impersonal may be formed by adding **się** to the neuter: **powinno się pójść** *one ought to go.*

Examples:

On nie powinien wypuszczać psa samego na dwór. *He shouldn't (ought not to) let his dog out alone into the yard.*

Powinniście mniej narzekać i więcej pracować. *You all ought to complain less and work more.*

Oni powinni być teraz w domu. *They ought to be at home now.*

Ona nie powinna była tego powiedzieć. *She shouldn't (ought not to) have said that.*

Nie powinno się było tego powiedzieć. *One ought not to have said that.*

The specifically past tense forms of **powinien** are becoming purely literary. A past-tense marker occurring elsewhere in the sentence allows a form of **powinien** to stand by itself in the past:

Dyrektor bardzo źle to rozegrał, powinien (był) nas uprzedzić. *The director handled that very badly, he should have warned us.*

b. *should.* In its normal sense of expressing that something is a "good idea", 'should' is ordinarily expressed impersonally with **trzeba** *it is* *necessary* plus the infinitive. The identity of the intended subject is inferred from the context:

Trzeba się śpieszyć. *We should hurry.*

Trzeba było go posłuchać. *You should have listened to him.*

Trzeba będzie to zrobić jeszcze raz. *It will be necessary to do that again.*

In order to express a specific subject, **trzeba** may be used to introduce a personalized conditional clause:

Trzeba, żebyś wyjechał na parę dni. *It's necessary that you leave town for a couple of days.*

Alternatively, one may use the impersonal 3.p.sg. **należeć** *one should:*

Należy być wrażliwy na nuanse. *One should be receptive to nuances.*

Należałoby trochę poczekać. *It would be a good idea to wait a bit.*

c. *must, need to.* The idea of both of these English modals may be expressed with **musieć muszę musisz** *must, need to* plus the infinitive:

Muszę ci coś powiedzieć. *I have to tell you something.*

Czy musisz mi zawsze przerywać? *Do you always have to interrupt me?*

Musimy poświęcić więcej czasu temu zagadnieniu. *We need to devote more time to this question.*

Musieć often appears in the compound future tense:

Będziesz musiał(a) uważać. *You will have to watch out.*

Oni będą musieli brać korepetycje. *They will have to get tutoring.*

d. *have to, supposed to.* These English modals are usually expressed with **mieć mam masz** *have (to), supposed (to)* plus the infinitive:

Mam być w domu o ósmej. *I'm supposed to be at home at eight.*

Miałeś kupić dzisiejszą gazetę. *You were supposed to buy today's paper.*

Pamiętaj, że masz wynieść śmieci. *Remember that you're supposed to take out the trash.*

Observe that this use of **mieć** corresponds approximately to the English modal *have to* "hafta".

2. *Modals of ability.*

a. *may, can, be able, might, could.* Notions of both permission and ability may be expressed with **móc mogę możesz** *can, be able, may* or impersonally with the verbals **można** *one can, one may*, **niepodobna** *there is no way (bookish)*, **nie sposób** *it's impossible* plus an infinitive. Other modals of ability include **potrafić potrafię potrafisz** *manage, be able*, **zdążyć zdążę zdążysz** *manage to do (on time)*, **zdołać zdołam zdołasz** *manage.* Examples:

Czy mogę ci pomóc? *May I help you?*

Można wejść? *May I enter?*

Mów głośniej, nie można cię zrozumieć. *Talk louder, one can't understand you.*

Niepodobna (nie sposób) tego wysłuchać. *There is no way to listen to this to the end.*

Zaledwie zdążył zakręcić gaz. *He barely managed to turn off the gas.*

Nie zdołałem skończyć twojego artykułu. *I didn't manage to finish your article.*

Ona potrafi być bardzo uparta. *She is able to be very stubborn.*

Might and *could* are usually expressed with the conditional of **móc**:

Mógłbyś trochę odpocząć. *You might take a little rest.*

Czy mógłbym ci coś kupić? *Could I buy anything for you?*

b. To 'be allowed to' do something is expressed with **wolno** *one may* plus the infinitive, together with a possible Dative-case subject:

Wolno tu palić? *May one smoke here?*

Nie wolno ci było tego robić. *You shouldn't have done that.*

Wolno is often used without any specific verb:

Nie wolno! *You mustn't (do that)!*

c. *can* in the sense *know how* (learned ability) is expressed with **umieć umiem umiesz** *know how:*

Czy umiesz grać w brydża? *Do you know how to play bridge?*

Ona już umie pływać. *She already knows how to swim.*

This verb is used with the verb 'speak' implied to express language ability:

Nie umiemy (mówić) po francusku. *We don't know (how to speak) French.*

Umieć may take a direct pronominal object:

Co umiesz? *What do you know how to do?*

3. *Modals of desire, intent, and emotional attachment.*

a. Notions of desire and intent are expressed with **chcieć chcę chcesz** *want to,* **mieć ochotę** *have the desire, feel like;* **woleć wolę wolisz** *prefer;* **zamierzać zamierzam zamierzasz** *intend* (also: **mieć zamiar** *have the intention*); and **będę** in the sense 'intend to continue doing'.

Gdzie chcesz wyjechać na wakacje w tym roku? *Where do you want to go for vacation this year?*

Mam ochotę pójść na kawę. *I feel like going out for coffee.*

Wolę nie pracować w niedzielę. *I prefer not to work on Sunday.*

Co masz zamiar dziś robić? *What do you intend to do today?*

Zamierzam dziś napisać kilka listów. *I intend to write several letters today.*

Czy będziesz cały dzień oglądać telewizję? *Are you going to (do you intend to) watch television all day?*

b. The notion of 'liking to do' may be expressed with **lubić lubię lubisz** *like*, but probably more often with the adverb **chętnie** *willingly:*

Lubię tu siedzieć i patrzeć w niebo. *I like to sit here and gaze at the sky.*

Chętnie ci pomogę w lekcjach. *I'd be glad to help you with your lessons.*

Note that the verb **kochać** *love* is *not* a modal verb, and may *not* be followed by an infinitive as it may in English.

The adjective **rad rada** *glad* is occasionally used in conjunction with the conditional as an equivalent to **chętnie**:

Rad(a) bym ci pomógł (pomogła) w lekcjach. *I'd be glad to help you with your lessons.*

This construction has all gone out of use in contemporary Polish, the construction with **chętnie** being used instead.

4. *Modals of possibility and probability* are usually expressed with adverbs like **chyba** *probably, I suppose*, **może** (or **być może**) *maybe*, **prawdopodobnie** *probably*. The verb **móc mogę możesz** can also be used in the possibilistic sense of 'may' or 'might':

On może nie przyjść w porę. *He may (might) not come in time.*

Prawdopodobnie wkrótce się ożenię. *I'll probably get married soon.*

Jutro chyba będzie deszcz. *It will probably rain tomorrow.*

Może/chyba/prawdopodobnie Janek będzie chciał ci towarzyszyć. *Maybe/I suppose/probably Janek will want to accompany you.*

5. *Modals of effort or attempt* include **(po)starać się** *try*, **(s)próbować** *attempt*, **usiłować** *endeavor:*

Postaraj się być bardziej wyrozumiały. *Try to be more understanding.*

On nawet nie próbuje mnie zrozumieć. *He doesn't even try to understand me.*

Usiłuję naprawić radio, ale jakoś mi nie wychodzi. *I'm trying to fix the radio, but somehow I'm not getting it right.*

6. *Modals of evaluation.*
a. The phrases **niestety** *unfortunately* and **na szczęście** *fortunately* are often used to editorialize about a described state or event:

Niestety jestem dziś po południu zajęty. *Unfortunately I'm busy this afternoon.*

Na szczęście już nie muszę gotować obiadów. *Fortunately I don't have to cook dinners any longer.*

b. The 3rd-person verbs **należy** *one ought* and **wypada** *it is right or fitting* are often used to accompany "good or bad ideas":

Należy obejrzeć ten program. *One ought to watch that program.*

Nie wypadało nalegać. *It wasn't right to insist.*

VERBALS

By a "verbal" is meant an uninflected word which nevertheless acts like a verb in that it has predicative force and can introduce a subordinate clause. Typically, verbals express opinions about a statement introduced in a subordinate clause, and they are followed by a verb in the infinitive. The tense of a verbal is expressed with neuter singular forms of **być**, whether past or future. In the present, **jest** will usually be omitted. Many or most verbals may take a Dative-case subject; however, some, like **można** *one may* and **trzeba** *one must*, usually do not. Among Polish verbals are the following:

czas *time* (often in the phrase **najwyższy czas** *high time*)

grzech *it is a sin*	**trzeba** *it is necessary*
można *it is possible*	**warto** *it is worthwhile, proper*
niepodobna *there is no way*	**wolno** *it is permitted*
nie sposób *there is no way*	**wstyd** *it is a shame*
strach *it is a fright*	**wszystko jedno** *it's all the same*
szkoda *it is too bad, it's a shame*	**żal** *it is a pity*

Examples:

Jemu wszystko wolno. *For him everything is allowed.*

Wszystko mi jedno. *It makes no difference to me.*

Trzeba będzie jeszcze raz sprawdzić. *It will be necessary to check again.*

Nie można było czekać. *It was impossible to wait.*

Nie sposób było go zrozumieć. *There was no way to understand him.*

Wstyd/strach było tego słuchać. *It was a shame/a fright to listen to that.*

Będzie ci tego żal. *You'll regret it.*

Warto przeczytać tę książkę. *It'll be worthwhile reading that book.*

Szkoda mówić. *It's pointless to talk about it.*

One may encounter either

Był **najwyższy czas wracać.** *It was high time to return.*

or *Było* **najwyższy czas wracać.** *It was high time to return.*

depending on whether **czas** is inteprpreted as the masculine-gender noun subject or as a verbal.

Many adverbs can function as de facto verbals, especially **dobrze** *it's good*, **miło** *it's nice*, **próżno** *it is fruitless*, **przykro** *it's unpleasant*, **trudno** *it's difficult*.

Tomek, dobrze/świetnie/doskonale, że jesteś. *Tomek, it's good/great/excellent that you're here.*

Miło było spędzić wieczór z państwem. *It was pleasant to spend the evening with you -m.p.pl.*

Próżno narzekać. *It's fruitless to complain.*

Trudno będzie wrócić do studiów po wakacjach. *It will be hard to return to one's studies after vacation.*

Trudno is often used as a self-sufficient comment: **Trudno** *It's tough (too bad, nothing you can do about it).*

Notes on the Syntax of Verbals

a. Many verbals can occur under some circumstances with Dative pronouns: **Wstyd mi było** *I was ashamed*, **Żal mu będzie** *He'll regret it*, **Nie wolno ci** *You mustn't*. However, some, like **można** or **warto**, almost never occur with Dative pronouns, even though they might seem appropriate. One should check with a dictionary to be sure.

b. **Trzeba, wstyd,** and **żal** can take Dative+Genitive complements:

Żal mu było straconej szansy. *He regretted the lost opportunity.*

Trzeba mi światła. *I need some light.*

Wstyd mi swojej głupoty. *I'm ashamed of my stupidity.*

With infinitive complements, **trzeba** does not normally take the Dative; hence usually not !**Trzeba nam tam pojechać** but rather **Trzeba tam pojechać** *We should go there,* with 'we' being interpolated from context.

c. **Szkoda** can take a Dative with an infinitive, as in **Szkoda mi was opuszczać.** *I'm sorry to have to leave you.* More often, it is used with infinitives without a Dative: **Szkoda marzyć.** *No use dreaming.* **Szkoda** can also take Genitive complements, normally without an accompanying Dative, as in **Szkoda pieniędzy.** *It's a waste of money.* **Szkoda** can be used to introduce subordinate clauses introduced by **że,** as in **Szkoda, że nic nie mówiłeś** *It's too bad you didn't say anything.*

Chapter 11

THE POLISH TENSE-ASPECT SYSTEM

Verbal aspect has to do with how an action or event is conceived and portrayed—chiefly, whether as completed; as generic-habitual; or as on-going; see the following chart, with illustrations in English:

Aspectuality:

Tense:	On-going	Generic-habitual	Completed
Present	I am writing	I often write	
Past	I was writing	I often wrote	I just wrote
Future	I will be writing	I will often write	I will write now

Observe that the box [present + completed] is empty: an event taking place in the real present cannot logically be finished. The English verb signals an on-going event with the suffix *-ing: I am writing.* Polish, by contrast, adds a special nuance to the basic aspectual picture by paying attention not only to whether an action is completed or not but, also, to whether a completed action has caused a change in the state of affairs. Consequently, most verbs in Polish have two aspect forms. The PERFECTIVE form refers to completed events which result in changes in states of affairs. The IMPERFECTIVE refers to all other kinds of actions, which may be a) on-going, b) generic-habitual, or c) complete but not resulting in a changed state of affairs. In Polish, it makes a difference whether *I wrote* means simply 'I am no longer writing' (Imperfective) or 'I wrote through to the end, I finished writing, resulting in a final product' (Perfective).

By nature, perfectively construed actions and events have either occurred in the past or will occur in the future, and either at or as of a specific point in time. As a consequence, Perfective verbs have only a past and a future tense. They cannot refer to action unfolding in the present, and they cannot refer to future or past events which, although complete, did not have an effect at or as of a specific time. Here is how a typical action-verb, **pisać** *(impf)* **napisać** *(pf) write* looks when viewed according to the cross-cutting categories of tense and aspect:

	Imperfective	Perfective
Present	**piszę** *I am writing, I write*	
Past	**pisałem (pisałam)** *I was writing, I wrote*	**napisałem (napisałam)** *I wrote (to the end)*
Future	**będę pisał (pisała)** *I will write, be writing*	**napiszę** *I'll write (to the end)*

From the point of view of aspectuality, the Polish verb system adds another dimension to the system, not shared with English, that of action which is both completed and resultative:

←————— Imperfective ————→   Perfective

	On-going	Generic-habitual	Completed	Resultative
Present	**piszę**	←		
Past	**pisałem -am**	←	←	**napisałem -am**
Future	**będę pisał(a)**	←	←	**napiszę**

Observe that the future tense of an Imperfective verb is expressed with the compound future, using **będę** plus either the Imperfective 3rd-person past forms or the Imperfective infinitive, while the future tense of a Perfective verb is expressed with the present-tense form of the Perfective verb. The Perfective aspect is often formed from simplex (unprefixed) verbs like **pisać** by adding prefixes (here, **na-**), specific to the given verb. Aspect formation is described further below.

GUIDELINES FOR ASPECT CHOICE

Here are some rules of thumb for choosing between the Imperfective and Perfective form of a verb:

1. Perfective verbs refer to actions or events which lead to something, advance the narrative, or change the state of affairs. They usually answer the question 'what has happened?'. Imperfective verbs often answer the question 'what was going on?'. Since the Imperfective is the more semantically encompassing of the two aspects, the less specific in meaning, it is usually a good guess to use it in cases of indecision. The Imperfective is rarely totally wrong.

2. The following kinds of adverbs tend to be compatible with one or the other aspect; generally speaking, the Imperfective-compatible adverbs answer the questions **jak często** *how often?*, **jak długo** *how long?*, **ile razy** *how many times?*:

Imperfective-compatible adverbs	Perfective-compatible adverbs
całymi dniami *for days on end*	**dopiero co** *only just*
ciągle *often*	**nagle** *suddenly*
czasami, czasem *sometimes*	**nareszcie, wreszcie** *finally, at last*
często *often*	**natychmiast** *immediately*
długo *for a long time*	**niechcąc** *unintentionally*
jeszcze *still*	**nieoczekiwanie** *unexpectedly*
nieraz, niekiedy *sometimes*	**od razu** *forthwwith*
nigdy *never*	**przed chwilą** *a moment ago*
od czasu do czasu *from time to time*	**w końcu** *in the end*
regularnie *regularly*	**wkrótce** *shortly, in a bit*
rzadko *seldom*	**właśnie** *only just*
wciąż *continually*	**za chwilę** *in a moment*
zawsze *always*	**zaraz** *right away*
zwykle *usually*	**znowu** *again*

Contrast:

On nigdy nie wraca późno do domu. *He never returns home late.*
On właśnie wrócił z pracy. *He's just returned from work.*

3. The Perfective aspect often occurs after conjunctions like **aż** *until,* **jak tylko** *as soon as,* **zanim** *before*:
Powiem mu jak tylko go zobaczę. *I'll tell him as soon as I see him.*
Zgaś światło zanim wyjdziesz. *Turn out the light before you leave.*

Further, one often finds the Imperfective after **jeszcze** *still,* and the Perfective after **już** *already*:

Czy jeszcze się ubierasz? *Are you still dressing?*
Nie, już skończyłam. *No, I'm finished already.*

4. The choice between the aspects occurs either in the future or, usually, in the past tense. Consequently, attention may be profitably directed to the question of which aspect to use in the past tense when referring to completed action. The following rules of thumb will be of help:

a. Verbal notions associated with unprefixed Imperfective verbs naturally occur in the past Imperfective unless one wishes to stress the successful completion of the action:
Wczoraj czytałem nową powieść. *Yesterday I read-impf a new novel.* (no suggestion as to whether the novel was finished or not).
By contrast,
Wczoraj przeczytałem nową powieść. *(same meaning-pf)*
suggests that the novel was either finally finished or read more-or-less in a single sitting.

Similarly,

Dzwoniłem do niego wczoraj. *I called-impf him yesterday.*
does not imply one way or the other whether the call was completed and
a conversation took place. By contrast,

Zadzwoniłem do niego wczoraj. *(same meaning-pf)*
suggests that the call went through and that a conversation did take
place.

b. Verbal notions expressed by prefixed Perfective verbs having suffixally
    derived Imperfective forms tend to be naturally associated in the past
    tense with the Perfective aspect. These will generally be notions whose
    performance by itself implies a successful result. For example, under
    ordinary circumstances, if one orders dinner (**zamówić** *order-pf, impf*
    zamawiać), one will have passed information to a waiter who will
    eventually bring the dinner. It is natural, then, to say

Zamówiłem obiad dla nas obojga. *I ordered -pf dinner for the both of us.*

The use of the Imperfective aspect here would imply either that the ordering was interrupted in mid-course ("I was ordering dinner, when the
lights went out.") or that the action was an unsuccessful attempt ("I tried
to order dinner, but the waiter never brought it.")

c. A useful rule to follow is that if the question the past-tense statement an-
    swers can possibly be translated by an English verb in *-ing*, then the
    Imperfective aspect should be used:

Wczoraj uczyłem się nowych polskich czasowników. *Yesterday I*
    studied/was studying-impf some new Polish verbs.

Contrast this with

Wczoraj nauczyłem się dziesięciu nowych polskich czasowników.
    Yesterday I learned-pf ten new Polish verbs.

Only the first, not the second, sentence may be logically queried with
"What were you doing yesterday when I called?" The lexical difference
between English *study* and *learn* corresponds in this instance to a difference in aspect: the former implies an activity without a necessary result,
while the latter implies a definite result.

5. Polish is more sensitive than English to whether an event is present or fu-
    ture. In logically future reference, Polish will use the Imperfective or
    Perfective future. The contrast between English and Polish arises espe-
    cially often after clauses beginning with "if" or "when":

Imperfective:

English: If he *has* any reservations, we will have to modify our strategy.

Polish: **Jeśli on *będzie miał* jakieś zastrzeżenia, to będziemy musieli
           zmienić taktykę.** (Imperfective verb)

Perfective:

English: If he *answers* that question correctly, I will be surprised.

Polish: **Jeśli on dobrze *odpowie* na to pytanie, to się zdziwię.**
(Perfective verb).

In these examples the italicized Polish future corresponds to the italicized present tense in English.

6. Questions merely inquiring whether or not an action has occurred, isolated from any immediate consequence, will usually be asked and answered in the Imperfective aspect:

Czy jadłeś już śniadanie? *Have you eaten-impf breakfast yet?*

This is the normal polite inquiry. On the basis of a negative answer, the speaker might be expected to offer the listener something to eat. By contrast,

Czy zjadłeś już śniadanie? *(same meaning-pf)*

might be spoken in a scolding tone by a mother to a child having trouble eating its breakfast. The child has either been dilly-dallying, or the breakfast needs to be taken care of so that something else can happen (for example, going to school).

7. Generalized questions in the Imperfective aspect are often accompanied at least implicitly by the adverb **kiedykolwiek** *ever, at any time:*

Czy (kiedykolwiek) oglądałeś ten film? *Have you (ever) seen that film?*

8. If in a string of events the accomplishment of each one is the prerequisite for the occurrence of the next one, the verbs will be in the Perfective aspect:

Obudziłem się, wstałem, wziąłem prysznic i ogoliłem się. *I awoke, got up, took a shower, and shaved.*

9. So-called phasal verbs, referring to the beginning, continuation, or end of an action, obligatorily take an Imperfective infinitive. Phasal verbs include **zacząć zaczynać** *begin (pf/impf)*, **kończyć skończyć** *finish (impf/pf)*, **przestać przestawać** *stop (pf/impf)*, **kontynuować** *continue (impf):*

Przestań dokuczać siostrze. *Stop teasing your sister!*

Zaczynasz łysieć. *You're beginning to get bald.*

Wreszcie skończyłem czytać tę książkę. *I finally finished reading that book.*

10. Positive imperatives of verbs referring to simple acts are usually Perfective, and negative imperatives are usually Imperfective, since they suggest "not now, and not ever":

Powiedz mi coś. *Tell-pf me something.* (positive Perfective command)

Zrób mi przysługę. *Do me a favor.* (positive Perfective command)

Nie mów tego. *Don't say-impf that.* (negative Imperfective command)

Nie opowiadaj bzdur! *Don't talk-impf nonsense!* (negative Imperfective command).

Notes on the Aspect of Imperatives:

a. With activity verbs, a positive Imperfective imperative can have the sense of beginning the action or, if the action is already begun, of continuing it:

   Proszę, czytaj! *Please begin reading* (or, under appropriate circumstances, *Please keep reading*).

   Siedź, siedź! *Sit, sit!* (i.e., *don't get up!*)

b. One should take care when putting positive imperatives in the Imperfective, because they are apt to sound rude; see the naturally rude, hence Imperfective

   Zwiewaj! *Beat it-impf!* **Uciekaj!** *Get out of here!* **Idź stąd!** *Go away from here!*

c. After repeating a normal positive command in the Perfective, it may be followed up by repetition in the Imperfective, conveying insistence:

   Weź parasol, będzie deszcz. *Take-pf your umbrella, it's going to rain.*

   Bierz parasol, mówię ci! *Take-impf your umbrella, I tell you.*

d. Negative Perfective commands are normally interpreted as warnings not to do something by accident:

   Nie jedz tego. *Don't eat-impf that* (normal negative Imperfective command).

   Nie zjedz tego! *Don't eat-pf that!* (or something bad will happen).

   Nie przekręć kontaktu, bo cię prąd porazi. *Don't turn on-pf the switch, or you'll get a shock.*

   Uważaj, nie poślizgnij się! *Watch out, don't slip-pf!*

   Contrast:

   Nie pij mojej herbaty! *Don't drink my tea!* (a general prohibition)

   Nie wypij mojej herbaty! *(idem),* spoken to someone about to make a wrong choice).

e. In friendly speech, imperatives that are invitations, and imperatives calling for a change in body position, are often expressed in the Imperfective:

   No wstawaj już! *Come on, get up-impf already!* The Perfective imperative **wstań** here might be considered too abrupt.

Siadaj i opowiadaj, co słychać u ciebie! *Have a seat-impf and tell-impf me what's new with you.*

11. Verbs after the modals **czas** *it's time* and **pora** *it's time* occur in the Imperfective:

Robi się późno. Pora już iść. *It's getting late. It's high time to go.*

Już czas wracać. *It's already time to return (to be getting back).*

ENGLISH PERFECT TENSES AND THE POLISH ASPECTS

12. It is important to bear in mind that English present- and past-perfect verb constructions using *have* and *had*, as *I have written* (present-perfect) *I had written* (past perfect) may be expressed with either Polish aspect, depending on the meaning. If an English expression can possibly be expressed with the *-ing* form of the verb, then the Polish Imperfective form will be used:

Present and past perfect translated by Polish Imperfective:

We have lived (have been living) here for ten years.

Mieszkamy tu dziesięć lat. Note: *present* Imperfective.

We had lived (had been living) there for ten years when the war broke out).

Mieszkaliśmy tam dziesięć lat, kiedy wojna wybuchła. Note: *past* Imperfective.

Present and past perfect translated by Polish Perfective:

We have just returned from Poznań.

Dopiero co wróciliśmy z Poznania. Note: *past* Perfective.

We had just returned from Poznań when we learned of father's death.

Dopiero co wróciliśmy z Poznania, kiedy dowiedzieliśmy się o śmierci ojca. Note: *past* Perfective.

THE INTERACTION OF THE ASPECTS WITH SEMANTIC CLASSES OF VERBS

13. When assessing aspect use, it is often helpful to determine the semantic class of the verb, whether (a) STATIVE, i.e., refering to an open-ended condition not under the control of the speaker, e.g., **lubić** *like*, **mieć** *have*; (b) ACTIONAL, i.e., referring to an open-ended activity not directed at a goal, e.g. **bawić się** *play*, **śmiać się** *laugh*; (c) GOAL-DIRECTED, i.e., action that lasts for a while but tends toward a logical conclusion or result, e.g., **czytać** *read*, **pisać** *write*; (d) ACCOMPLISHMENTS, i.e., actions whose normal performance results in a change in the state of affairs, e.g., **kupić** *buy*, **zamówić** *order (dinner, etc.)*; (e) LOGICAL RESULTS, i.e., actions whose very meaning incorporates the idea of an end result, e.g., **przyjechać** *arrive*, **umierać** *die*. Finally, one may distinguish verbs of (f) INSTANTAN-

EOUS ACTION, for which performance and outcome are viewed as simultaneous, e.g., **wybuchnąć** *explode*, **runąć** *collapse*, **stuknąć** *whack*.

In the past and future tenses, the Perfective of a stative, actional, or goal-directed verb needs to be justified; that is, the action needs to be both singulative and to have changed the state of affairs. With accomplishment or logical-result verbs, which usually do result in changed states of affairs, it is the Imperfective which needs to be justified: the action, even if singulative, must have failed to produce the expected result for one to use the Imperfective. The sentence

Wczoraj kupowałem nowy samochód. *I bought-impf a new car yesterday.*

sounds slightly surprising, since one expects the process of buying to result in a transfer of ownership; the use of the Imperfective here suggests that the expected purchase did not take place. In such instances, the use of the Imperfective adds a sense of unsuccessful attempt: 'I tried to buy a car yesterday'.

The Perfective form of a stative, actional, or goal-directed verb usually adds a shade of meaning to the basic meaning of the verb; thus, **polubić** *like-pf* means 'come to like'; **posiedzieć** *sit-pf* means 'sit a bit'; **przeczytać** *read-pf* means 'read through to the end, finish reading'. Many verbs have either an actional or a goal directed interpretation. For example, 'reading' may be considered to be an activity in itself or an activity directed toward an end. The Perfective and Imperfective forms of alternative actional/goal-directed verbs are often used contrastively against each other:

Zdawałem ten egzamin, ale kto wie, czy zdałem? *I took the exam, but who knows whether I passed it?*

Uczyłyśmy się tego materiału cały tydzień, ale czy nauczyłyśmy się go, to dopiero się okaże. *We studied the material for a whole week, but it's an open question whether we learned it.*

In these two examples, the perfective verb lends a nuance of action leading to success. See also **błagać** *beseech-impf*, **ubłagać** *successfully beseech, induce-pf*. In this sense, the verbs **szukać** *look for-impf* and **znaleźć** *find-pf* become de facto aspectual pairs.

VERBS OF MOTION constitute a special sub-class of actional/goal-directed verbs, in that these verbs have different forms for referring to pure action on the one hand (the INDETERMINATE form), and for referring to goal-directed motion on the other hand (the DETERMINATE form), cf. **chodzić** *go, walk-indet. (often or in general)* vs. **iść** *go, walk-det. (somewhere, with a purpose)*. See further below, under The Aspect of Verbs of Motion.

The semantic class of a verb is often reflected in its outer form. Stative, actional, and goal-directed activity verbs tend to be simplex (unprefixed), and to form the Perfective through prefixation (see **grać zagrać** *play impf/pf,* **pisać napisać** *write impf/pf,* **robić zrobić** *do, make impf/pf*). With natural accomplishment and logical-result verbs, the structually and semantically basic form of the verb is almost always the Perfective, whether prefixed or not, and the Imperfective form will be derived from it by suffixation (see **kupić kupować** *buy pf/impf,* **zamówić zamawiać** *order pf/impf*), **ubrać ubierać** *dress pf/impf* Verbs of instantaneous action often occur in suffixally differentiated pairs: **stuknąć stukać** *whack pf/impf,* **wybuchnąć wybuchać** *explode pf/impf,* **kichnąć kichać** *sneeze pf/impf.* Dictionaries usually cite a verb in the Imperfective form first, although it makes as much sense to cite accomplishment-, logical-result, and instantaneous-action verbs first in the derivationally primary Perfective form, as is done here in subsequent chapters.

Speakers of English will usually be correct by following the above rules and, where the rules do not suggest a solution, by relying on one's natural inclination based on one's general understanding of the Perfective aspect. Obviously it may be confusing to a Polish listener if one uses the present-tense form of a Perfective verb when referring to actual present time, because typically the present Perfective has future meaning. Such a sentence will not be ungrammatical, merely illogical and hence possibly contextually incomprehensible. It is important not to over-use the compound future with **będę** simply because it reminds one of the English future tense with *will*. With the majority of verbs referring to contemplated future action, the Perfective future is the correct choice. The compound future with **będę** is statistically less frequent than the English *will* construction.

THE MORPHOLOGY OF ASPECT

In general, each Polish verb has two forms, Imperfective and Perfective. For the most part, simplex (unprefixed) verbs are Imperfective, for example, **czytać** *read,* **grać** *play,* **pisać** *write,* **robić** *do,* and so on. Only a few simplex verbs in Polish, like **zdołać** *manage to do,* are inherently Perfective with no Imperfective counterpart. Most simplex Perfectives end in **-ić** and are related to simplex Imperfective verbs belonging to a different conjugation:

Simplex Perfective	Corresponding Imperfective
chwycić chwycę chwycisz *seize*	**chwytać chwytam chwytasz**
chybić chybię chybisz *miss*	**chybiać chybiam chybiasz**
czepić się czepię się czepi się *get at s.o.*	**czepiać się czepiam się czepiasz się**
dać dam dasz dadzą *give*	**dawać daję dajesz**
kupić kupię kupisz *buy*	**kupować kupuję kupujesz**
obiecać obiecam obiecasz	**obiecyvać obiecuję obiecujesz**
puścić puszczę puścisz *let go*	**puszczać puszczam puszczasz**
ruszyć ruszę ruszysz *move*	**ruszać ruszam ruszasz**
rzucić rzucę rzucisz *throw*	**rzucać rzucam rzucasz**

(u)siąść (u)siądę (u)siądziesz *sit down**   siadać siadam siadasz
skoczyć skoczę skoczysz *jump*   skakać skaczę skaczesz
stać stanę staniesz *become*   stawać staję stajesz
stąpić stąpię stąpisz *tread*   stąpać stąpam stąpasz
strzelić strzelę strzelisz *shoot*   strzelać strzelam strzelasz
szczepić szczepię szczepisz *graft*   szczepiać szczepiam szczepiasz
trafić trafię trafisz *hit, strike*   trafiać trafiam trafiasz
trącić trącę trącisz *jostle*   trącać trącam trącasz
wrócić wrócę wrócisz *return*   wracać wracam wracasz

*The verb **siąść siądę siądziesz** almost always occurs in the prefixed form **usiąść**.

Many simplex Perfective verbs ending in **-nąć -nę -niesz**, most referring to instantaneous (semelfactive) acts or occurrences, correspond to simplex Imperfectives of some other conjugation, often 3rd (**-am -asz**), but sometimes 1st (**-ę -esz**) or 2nd (**-ę -y/isz**):

Perfective in **-nąć -nę -niesz**:	Corresponding Imperfective:
brząknąć *strum*	**brząkać brząkam brząkasz**
chlusnąć *splash*	**chlustać -am -asz** or **chluszczę chluszczesz**
frunąć *fly, flutter*	**fruwać fruwam fruwasz**
gwizdnąć *whistle*	**gwizdać gwiżdżę gwiżdżesz**
jęknąć *moan*	**jęczeć jęczę jęczysz**
kichnąć *sneeze*	**kichać kicham kichasz**
klepnąć *pat*	**klepać klepię klepiesz**
krzyknąć *shout*	**krzyczeć krzyczę krzyczysz**
milknąć *be silent*	**milczeć milczę milczysz**
minąć *go by, pass*	**mijać mijam mijasz**
mrugnąć *wink*	**mrugać mrugam mrugasz**
plunąć *spit*	**pluć pluję plujesz**
sięgnąć *reach*	**sięgać sięgam sięgasz**
stanąć *stand up*	**stawać staję stajesz**
stuknąć *knock*	**stukać stukam stukasz**
sypnąć *pour, spill*	**sypać sypię sypiesz**
szarpnąć *yank*	**szarpać szarpię szarpiesz**
szczęknąć *clang*	**szczękać szczękam szczękasz**
szczypnąć *pinch*	**szczypać szczypię szczypiesz**
ścisnąć *press*	**ściskać ścikam ściskasz**
tknąć *touch*	**tykać tykam tykasz**
trzasnąć *slam*	**trzaskać trzaskam trzaskasz**
westchnąć *sigh*	**wzdychać wzdycham wzdychasz**
zerknąć *squint*	**zerkać zerkam zerkasz**
ziewnąć *yawn*	**ziewać ziewam ziewasz**

and many others. Before the suffix **-nę-/-ną-**, consonant simplifications may take place (**st: s, sk: s, zg: z, pt: p, w: Ø**); the full stem may be seen before **-a-ć**: **świsnąć** *świstać whistle*, **bryznąć** *bryzgać splash*, **szasnąć** *szastać rustle*,

szelesnąć szeleścić (*szelest-ić*) *rustle,* **szepnąć** *szeptać whisper,* **trzasnąć trzaskać** *slam.*

PERFECTIVE PREFIXATION

Most simplex verbs are Imperfective and, when prefixed, become Perfective. As a rule, these will be stative, actional, or goal-directed verbs. A number of prefixes have the function of creating Perfective verbs without appreciably changing the meaning of the base verb. It is impossible to predict which "empty" prefix will be used with which verb; the perfectivizing prefix must be memorized for each one. The commonest empty perfectivizing prefixes are **po-, u-, z-, za-**. Here are some examples of semantically empty perfectivizing prefixes:

Imperfective	Prefixed Perfective	Prefix
analizować -zuję -zujesz *analyze*	**przeanalizować**	prze-
budować -duję -dujesz *build*	**zbudować**	z-
całować -łuję -łujesz *kiss*	**pocałować**	po-
czekać -am -asz *wait*	**zaczekać**	za-
czynić *do*	**uczynić**	i-
czytać -am -asz *read*	**przeczytać**	prze-
dziękować -kuję -kujesz *thank*	**podziękować**	po-
dzwonić -nię -nisz *ring*	**zadzwonić**	za-
emigrować -ruję -jesz *emigrate*	**wyemigrować**	wy-
golić się -lę się -lisz się *shave*	**ogolić się**	o-
gotować -tuję -tujesz *cook*	**ugotować**	u-
jechać jadę jedziesz *ride*	**pojechać**	po-
kończyć -czę -czysz *finish*	**skończyć**	z- (s-)
myć myję myjesz *wash*	**umyć**	u-
mylić się -lę się -lisz się *be mistaken*	**pomylić się**	po-
płacić -cę -cisz *pay*	**zapłacić**	za-
pić piję pijesz *drink*	**wypić**	wy-
pisać piszę piszesz *write*	**napisać**	na-
prosić -szę -sisz *request*	**poprosić**	po-
pytać -am -asz *ask*	**zapytać**	za-
robić -bię -bisz *do*	**zrobić**	z-
rozumieć -em -esz *understand*	**zrozumieć**	z-
słyszeć -szę -szysz *hear*	**usłyszeć**	u-
śpiewać -am -asz *sing*	**zaśpiewać**	za-
tracić -cę -cisz *lose*	**stracić**	z- (s-)
uczyć uczę uczysz *teach*	**nauczyć**	na-

A few of the above Perfective verbs do form secondary Imperfectives, suggesting either that the prefix is less than totally empty, or that it has both empty and meaning-modifying versions; see **wypić wypijać** *drink up,* **zapytać zapytywać** *question.*

THE SPELLING OF Z- *AND ROZ-*

The perfectivizing prefix **z-** is written mostly as pronounced:

z before vowels and voiced consonants:	**zgrubieć** *grow fat-pf*, **zobowiązać** *oblige-pf*
s before hard voiceless consonants:	**stopić** *melt-pf*, **spalić** *burn-pf*
ś before **ć (ci):**	**ściszyć** *quieten-pf*, **ściąć** *cut down-pf.*
z but pronounced "ź" before **dź (dzi):**	**zdziczeć** "źdźiczeć" *go wild*

The perfectivizing prefix **roz-** is written **roz-** everywhere, no matter what the pronunciation: **rozwinąć** *develop-pf*, **rozdzierać** "roźdźerać" *tear apart*, **rozpaczać** "rospaczać" *despair*, **rozcieńczać** "rośćeńczać" *dilute*.

IMPERFECTIVES WITHOUT PERFECTIVES

A good number of Imperfective verbs do not have Perfective counterparts, at least in given senses. Some examples would be **borykać się** *struggle*, **bredzić** *rave*, **czuwać** *be vigilant*, **domagać się** *demand*, **dolegać** *afflict*, **domagać się** *demand*, **dotyczyć** *concern*, **mieć** *have*, **móc** *be able*, **musieć** *have to*, **nadzorować** *oversee*, **nalegać** *insist*, **należeć** *belong to*, **narzekać** *complain*, **naśladować** *invite*, **parać się** *dabble in*, **pastwić się** *torment*, **podejrzewać** *suspect*, **pochodzić** *derive from*, **podróżować** *travel*, **przewodniczyć** *preside over*, **służyć** *serve*, **sprzyjać** *favor*, **sterować** *steer*, **ścigać** *pursue*, **towarzyszyć** *accompany*, **usiłować** *endeavor*, **wtórować** *accompany*, **ubiegać się** *solicit, try for*, **uczestniczyć** *take part*, **uganiać się** *chase after*, **umieć** *know how*, **woleć** *prefer*, **współczuć** *sympathize with.*, **zazdrościć** +D +G *envy*, **znoić się** *toil*.

BIASPECTUAL VERBS

Only a few verbs are biaspectual, able to express either aspect, for example, **pitrasić** *cook (colloquial)*, **potrafić** *be able, manage*, **powozić** *drive (horse-drawn vehicle)*. Dictionaries often list **ranić** *wound* as biaspectual, although in today's Polish this verb is Imperfective, having the Perfective partner **zranić**. Borrowed verbs in **-ować** may be slightly less well integrated into the simplex-imperfective vs. prefixed-perfective system than other verbs. For example, while **emigrować** *emmigrate* forms **wyemigrować**, no common suffix occurs for perfectivizing **imigrować** *immigrate*. Often dictionaries may simply fail to register the prefixed Perfective. Speakers may have no hesitation about forming, say, **zaingerować** from **ingerować** *interfere*, but dictionaries are hesitant to give this information. Polish verbs in **-ować** have not developed biaspectuality, as is often the case with analogous verbs in Russian.

THE SEMANTICS OF PREFIXATION

Most Perfective verbs are created by adding a prefix to an Imperfective verb, changing at the same time the base verb's meaning. Although the semantic contribution of the prefix may often be understandable ex post facto, it is not possible to provide rules for predicting the semantic result of adding a given prefix to a given verb. Only a limited number of prefixes are used with any specific verb. Consider that while **mówić** (*impf*) and **powiedzieć** (*pf*) can both mean 'say', **odmówić** means 'refuse', while **odpowiedzieć** means 'answer'. Consider also the various idiomatic meanings produced by adding prefixes to the base word **kazać** *order*: **nakazać** *demand*, **pokazać** *show*, **przekazać** *hand over*, **przykazać** *enjoin*, **rozkazać** *command*, **skazać** *condemn*, **ukazać** *show, indicate*, **wskazać** *point to*, **wykazać** *exhibit*, **zakazać** *forbid*.

Typically, the addition of a prefix to a simplex verb changes a stative or actional verb to a verb of accomplishment or logical result. Observe, for example, how the base actional verb **mówić** *say* becomes prefixally transformed into various accomplishment-verbs: **namówić** *persuade*, **odmówić** *refuse*, **omówić** *talk over*, **przemówić** *give a speech*, **umówić** *arrange*, **wmówić** *try to make to believe*, **wymówić** *pronounce*, **zamówić** *order*.

Prefixes used in Perfective prefixation include **do-, na-, nad-, o-/ob-, od-, po-, pod-, prze-, roz-, w-, wy-, wz-,** and **z-/s- (ś-).** Of these, only **roz-, wy-** and **wz-** are not related to independent prepositions. As with prepositions, prefixes ending in a consonant may be followed by a mobile vowel before certain consonant clusters, especially before verb roots interpreted as asyllabic: **obeznać** *acquaint*, **poderwać** *snatch*, **roześmiać się** *break out in laughter*, **zetrzeć** *wipe off*.

With some verbs, especially verbs of motion, perfectivizing prefixes tend to retain their literal spatial meaning; cf. **obejść** *go around*, **odejść** *go away*, **nadejść** *approach*, **najść** *come upon*, **przejść** *pass over*, **wejść** *go in*, **wyjść** *go out*, **wzejść** *rise*, **zejść** *go down*, and others. Verbs whose action involves the processing of substances, like **sypać** *sprinkle, pour (granular substances)* and **lać** *pour (liquid substances)* are also instructive for basic concrete meanings:

dosypać *sprinkle or pour into*	**dolać** *pour into*
nadsypać *sprinkle too much*	**nadlać** *pour too much*
nasypać *heap up, pour on or over*	**nalać** *pour in or on*
obsypać *sprinkle all over*	**oblać** *drench*
odsypać *sprinkle or pour from*	**odlać** *pour from*
podsypać *strew*	**podlać** *water, sprinkle*
posypać *sprinkle a bit*	**polać** *pour over*
przesypać *sprinkle from, into*	**przelać** *transfer by pouring*
usypać *pile up (sand, etc.)*	**ulać** *pour off, decant*
wysypać *sprinkle or pour out*	**wylać** *pour out*
zasypać *cover up by pouring, bury*	**zalać** *flood, inundate*
zsypać *pour down into*	**zlać** *pour out onto*

Verbs of process often have a basic Perfective in **po-** and two alternative Perfectives, one in **na-**, indicating a larger amount, and another in **u-**, indicating a lesser amount. The prefixed Perfectives themselves will usually form derived Imperfectives. See, for example,

Base verb	Main Perfective	Large amount	Small amount
brudzić *soil*	**pobrudzić**	**nabrudzić nabrudzać**	**ubrudzić ubrudzać**
ciąć *cut*	**pociąć**	**naciąć nacinać**	**uciąć ucinać**
siec *chop*	**posiec posiekać**	**nasiec nasiekać**	**usiec usiekać**
and others			

With most verbs, the semantic contribution of prefixes is more abstract and idiomatic. Often prefixes function in the rendering of loan translations (calques) from other languages, especially Latin. For example, **wy-** can render Latin *ex-*, as in **wyciągnąć** *extract,* **wydać** *expend,* **wykonać** *execute,* **wykopać** *exhume,* **wykroczyć** *exceed,* and so on. Here is a summary of the perfectivizing prefixes; the meanings commonly associated with them; and some illustrative examples:

do- motion to, addition, aim, attainment, adaptation, completion; Latin *ad-*

> **dojść** *arrive at,* **dodać** *add,* **doczekać się** *live to see,* **dogonić** *catch up with,* **dokończyć** *finish off,* **dopalić** *finish burning,* **doprowadzić** *lead to,* **dorobić** *adapt, make to fit,* **dostosować** *adapt*

na- motion toward or into, application to surface, accumulated result

> **nabrać** *take on,* **naciąć** *cut an amount,* **nadąć** *inflate,* **nadeptać** *trample on,* **nagromadzić** *pile up,* **nagrzać** *warm up,* **najechać** *run into,* **najść** *come upon,* **nakleić** *stick to,* **namazać** *smear on,* **namówić** *induce,* **nanieść** *bring to*

na- się to surfeit or satisfaction

> **najeść się** *eat one's fill,* **naczytać się** *read up on,* **napić się** *quench one's thirst*

nad- approach, over, superfluously, partially

> **nadłamać** *break off,* **nadejść** *approach,* **naderwać** *tear partially,* **nadgryźć** *gnaw,* **nadlecieć** *come flying,* **nadpłacić** *overpay,* **nadrobić** *make up*

o-, ob- action around, all around, thoroughly, downward, separation

> **obłamać** *break off,* **obejść** *go around,* **obmyć** *sponge down,* wash off, **obniżyć** *lower,* **obrzucić** *throw, pelt,* **obsadzić** *plant, stock,* **ograć** *fleece* (in cards), **ograbić** *rob, plunder,* **opaść** *fall,* **opracować** *elaborate,* **oskarżyć** *accuse,* **oszklić** *glaze,* **otoczyć** *surround.* Other than for the occurrence of **ob-** before vowels (**obumierać** *waste away*), the occurrence of **o-** vs. **ob-** cannot be perfectly predicted (**ob-** is more frequent). Occasionally, both prefixes will occur with the same verb in different meanings, as **omówić** *discuss,* **obmówić** *speak ill of,* **osadzić** *plant,* **obsadzić** *fill a post,* **oszukać** *deceive,* **obszukać** *search thoroughly*

od- motion from, off, away, back to, replication, recompense, annulment, restoration, action lasting for a period of time; Latin *re-*

> **odłożyć** *put off,* **odbudować** *rebuild,* **odczekać** *wait a period of time,* **odczytać** *recite,* **odejść** *depart,* **odkurzyć** *dust off,* **odmówić** *refuse,* **odnieść** *take to,* **odpaść** *fall off,* **odpłacić** *pay back,* **odpisać** *write back,* **odpowiedzieć** *respond,* **odpracować** *work off,* **odprawić** *send away,* **odrobić** *make up,* **odrosnąć** *grow back,* **odwrócić** *restore*

po- for a while, a bit, a single execution, enter a state

> The prefix **po-** comes close to being an empty Perfectivizing prefix in **pocałować** *kiss,* **pójść** *go,* **pokryć** *cover,* **połączyć** *join,* **połknąć** *swallow,* **posłać** *send,* **powiększyć** *enlarge,* and others. The sense 'a bit' may be seen in verbs like **poczekać** *wait a bit,* **pograć** *play a while,* **poleżeć** *lie a bit,* **pomówić** *speak a bit,* **posiedzieć** *sit a while,* **posiwieć** *grow a bit gray,* **posłuchać** *listen a bit,* **pospać** *have a bit of sleep,* **posprzątać** *tidy up,* etc. The sense 'enter the state' is visible with the verbs **polubić** *take a liking to,* **poczuć** *come to feel,* **popatrzeć** *have a look at,* **porozumieć się** *come to an understanding,* **poweseleć** *be cheered up*

pod- under, support, toward, in secret

> **podsunąć** *push up,* **podjechać** *approach,* **podłączyć** *hook up, attach,* **podnieść** *lift,* **podpatrzyć** *spy,* **podpiąć** *pin up,* **podpisać** *sign,* **podskoczyć** *hop up,* **podsłuchać** *eavesdrop,* **podsumować** *sum up*

prze- across, over, through, thoroughly, in order, to the end, through and through, from one state to another, anew, overly; Latin *trans-*

> **przeanalizować** *analyze,* **przebudować** *rebuild,* **przechować** *store,* **przechwalić** *overpraise,* **przeciąć** *cut through,* **przedrukować** *reprint,* **przegrać** *lose,* **przejechać** *run over,* **przejrzeć** *look through,* **przekazać** *hand over, convey,* **przekształcić** *transform,* **przelecieć** *fly past,* **przemówić** *make a speech,* **przenieść** *transfer,* **przeniknąć** *penetrate,* **przepalić** *overheat,* **przepisać** *transcribe,* **przerobić** *reshape, do over,* **przerwać** *interrupt*

prze- się with verbs of motion: random activity

> **przejść się** *stroll,* **przejechać się** *take a ride*

przy- arrival at destination, leveling, attachment, somewhat

> **przygasić** *dim,* **przygnieść** *press down, flatten,* **przygwoździć** *nail to,* **przyjść** *come,* **przykręcić** *screw down,* **przylepić** *stick to,* **przymierzyć** *try on,* **przynieść** *bring,* **przypalić** *scorch, burn slightly,* **przypiec** *toast,* **przyprowadzić** *lead to,* **przystąpić** *approach,* **przyszyć** *sew to,* **przyśpieszyć** *hasten,* **przywrócić** *restore*

roz- in various directions, destruction, expansion, dissipation, into bits, throughout or all-encompassing, undo; Latin *dis-*, *un-*

> **rozcieńczyć** *dillute*, **rozdać** *hand out*, **rozdzielić** *divide*, **rozebrać** *undress*, **rozerwać** *rip to shreds*, **rozgniewać** *enrage*, **rozgryźć** *crack open*, **rozgrzeszyć** *remit sins*, **rozjaśnić** *illuminate*, **rozlać** *pour out*, **rozliczyć** *reckon up*, **rozładować** *unload*, **rozpętać** *unleash*, **rozwiązać** *untie, (dis)solve*, **rozwinąć** *develop*

roz- się dispersal

> **rozejść się** *disperse, go separate ways*, **rozliczyć się** *settle accounts with*, **rozstać się** *be separated, part*, **rozwieść się** *get divorced*

u- partially, ability, aside, intensity, loss, cause to, simple performance

> **ubezpieczyć** *insure*, **ubawić** *divert, amuse*, **ubrać** *dress*, **ubyć** *subside*, **uchować** *save*, **uchronić** *protect*, **uchwycić** *take hold of*, **uchylić** *leave ajar*, **uciąć** *cut off a bit*, **uczulić** *sensitize*, **udzielić** *impart*, **udźwignąć** *manage to lift*, **upić** *drink a little*, **usunąć** *move aside*, **utonąć** *drown*, **utrzymać** *maintain*

The prefix **u-** often forms simple Perfectives: **ugryźć** *bite*, **uprać** *launder*, **ucieszyć** *gladden*, **ugrupować** *form into groups*, **urodzić** *give birth*.

w- into, inclusion; Latin *in-*

> The literal meaning of **w-** 'in' is retained in most derivations: **wejść** *enter*, **wkroczyć** *encroach*, **wliczyć** *include*, **wnieść** *carry in, introduce*, **wpłacić** *pay in*, **wpaść** *fall in*, **wpędzić** *drive in*, **wpisać** *write in, enter*, **wprowadzić** *introduce*, **wstawić** *interpose*

w- się intensity

> **wczytać się** *become well read in*, **wpatrzyć się** *stare at*

wy- away from, out, final product, over a surface, completely, identification; Latin *ex-*

> **wychylić** *lean out*, **wyciągnąć** *pull out*, **wytrzeć** *wipe off*, **wycisnąć** *squeeze out*, **wydać** *hand over*, **wydzielić** *secrete*, **wygrać** *win*, **wyjechać** *leave*, **wykorzystać** *exploit*, **wykrzyczeć** *cry out*, **wykształcić** *form, shape*, **wykuć** *hammer into shape*, **wykupić** *buy up*, **wylać** *pour out*, **wyliczyć** *enumerate*, **wyładować** *unload*, **wyłączyć** *exclude*, **wypracować** *elaborate*, **wyrwać** *tear out, extract*

wz-, ws- motion upwards, increase

> **wskazać** *point to*, **wskrzesić** *resuscitate*, **wspiąć się** *climb*, **wzbogacić** *enrich*, **wzbudzić** *arouse*, **wzdąć** *inflate*, **wzejść** *rise*, **wziąć** *grasp*, **wzgardzić** *disdain*, **wzlecieć** *fly up*, **wzmocnić** *strengthen*

z-, s-, ś- together, down from, to point of change or destruction

> **zejść** *come down*, **zepsuć** *ruin*, **zetrzeć** *wipe off*, **zjeździć** *ride into the ground*, **zmienić** *change*, **zmusić** *force*, **zmyć** *wash off*, **znieść** *cancel*, **zniszczyć** *de-*

stroy, **zrównać** *make even*, **związać** *tie together*, **zwolnić** *slow*. No doubt because of the sense 'to the point of change', this prefix is one of the most productive in the creation of semantically empty Perfective partners, especially with verbs ending in -ować: **spakować** *pack*, **spolszczyć** *polonize*, **spróbować** *try*, **ściemnieć** *become dark*, **zrobić** *do*, **zanalizować** *analyze*, **zbudować** *build*, **zdenerwować się** *become upset*, **zjeść** *eat*, **zmarnować** *waste*, **znudzić** *bore*, **zorientować się** *become oriented*, **zranić** *wound*, **zrealizować** *realize*, **zrezygnować** *resign*, **zrobić** *do*, **zrozumieć** *understand*, **zwariować** *go crazy*; and many more.

z- się with verbs of motion: from all around

> **zejść się** *come together, assemble*, **zjechać się** *convene*, **zlecieć się** *come flying from all around*

za- beginning, all over, arrival, readiness, closure, to death or destruction

> **zabić** *kill*, **zabrudzić** *soil*, **zachorować** *fall ill*, **zadeptać** *trample*, **zagryźć** *bite to death*, **zajechać** *reach, get to*, **zakręcić** *turn shut*, **zakryć** *conceal*, **zakrzyczeć** *begin shouting*, **zakurzyć** *cover with dust*, **zakwitnąć** *burst into bloom*, **zalać** *inundate*, **zamknąć** *shut*, **zanieść** *deliver*, **zastrzelić** *shoot to death*, **zaśpiewać** *(start to) sing*, **zatruć** *poison to death*, **zatrzymać** *stop*. Wide use as perfectivizing prefix in idiomatic meanings: **zachować** *maintain*, **zamówić** *order*, **zakazać** *forbid*, **zarobić** *earn*. The prefix za- forms many simple Perfectives from verbs in -ować: **zablokować** *blockade*, **zanudzić** *bore to death*, **zaobserwować** *observe*, **zaprojektować** *plan*, **zasugerować** *suggest*, and many others.

za- się thoroughly, to excess

> **zagadać się** *talk the time away*, **zagalopować się** *gallop past*, **zakochać się** *fall in love*, **zasiedzieć się** *overstay one's visit*

IMPERFECTIVE SUFFIXATION: OVERVIEW OF THE SUFFIXES

When a perfectivizing prefix creates a Perfective verb in a meaning that is substantially different from the meaning of the base verb, the need arises to derive from it an Imperfective verb in the new meaning. This is usually done by suffixation, most often by creating a verb of the 3rd conjugation (in -ać -am -asz), whatever the conjugation of the base verb. The most important Imperfective suffixes are the following (for a detailed examination of their distribution, see further below):

1. **-ać -am -asz** is added to consonant-stem verbs of the 1st conjugation (see **przegryźć przegryzać** *gnaw through*, **ulec ulegać** *yield*); to many verbs in -nąć (see **zaciągnąć zaciągać** *drag*); and to most 2nd-conjugation verbs in -y/ić (see **zapalić zapalać** *light*).

2. **-wać -wam -wasz** is added to monosyllabic infinitive stems ending in -eć, -'ać, -uć, -yć; see **zachcieć zachciewać** *want*, **ogrzać ogrzewać** *warm*, **zatruć**

zatruwać *poison*, **przeżyć przeżywać** *survive*, **wylać wylewać** *pour out*. By "monosyllabic" is meant that the stem consists of a single syllable after possible prefixes are subtracted.

3. Minor suffixes:

   a. **-jać -jam -jasz** occurs with monosyllabic stems in **-ić**, as in **zabić zabijać** *kill*.

   b. **-ować -uję -ujesz** occurs with only a couple of verbs, for example, **znaleźć znajdować** *find*.

   c. **-wać -ję -jesz** occurs with three roots in **-ać**; see **dać dawać** *give*.

4. **-ywać (-uję -ujesz** or, sometimes, **-ywam -ywasz)**, the most productive Imperfective suffix, is added to all other verbs, in the process replacing the final vowel of the infinitive; see **wymazać wymazywać -uję** *efface*.

Stem and root changes. The addition of Imperfective suffixes is accompanied by certain changes to the stem or root:

   a. Verbs of the 2nd conjugation show R3 in the Imperfective stem consonant, i.e. the same consonant as in the 1st pers. sg. of the base verb. This change is visible when the root consonant is an underlying dental consonant:

Primary	t	d	s	z	st	zd
R1/2	ć	dź	ś	ź	ść	źdź
R3	c	dz	sz	ż	szcz	żdż

Cf. **odpłacić** (ć) **odpłacać** *pay back*, **zanudzić** (dź) **zanudzać** *bore*, **zaprosić** (ś) **zapraszać** *invite*, **zagrozić** (ź) **zagrażać** *threaten*, **wypuścić** (ść) **wypuszczać** *let out*, **zagnieździć** (źdź) **zagnieżdżać** *nest*.

   b. With most verbs the root-vowel **o** (including **ó**) will be replaced with **a**; covert ' will be replaced by **i**; and covert Ø by **y**:

Examples of **o: a: ozdobić ozdabiać** *decorate*, **pomóc pomagać** *help*, **przerobić przerabiać** *do over*, **skrócić skracać** *shorten*, **ugościć ugaszczać** *entertain*, **umocnić umacniać** *strengthen*, **umówić umawiać** *appoint*, **upoić upajać** *intoxicate*, **zaprosić zapraszać** *invite*, **zagrozić zagrażać** *threaten*, **zamrozić zamrażać** *freeze*, **zatopić zatapiać** *immerse*. This rule encompasses **o** originating from shifted **e: spleść (splotę spleciesz) splatać** *weave*, **ugnieść (ugniotę ugnieciesz) ugniatać** *knead* can both be considered to reflect **o: a**, the **o** deriving from **e** before a hard dental. If there are two vowels **o**, only the second will be replaced by **a: upodobnić upodabniać** *liken*.

The suffix **-ywać (-uję -ujesz** or **-ywam -ywasz)** does not usually condition the change of the root-vowel **o** to **a**; see **dostosować dostosowywać**

-uję *adapt,* **wyskrobać wyskrobywać** -uję *scrape out,* **zakochać się zakochiwać się** -uję *fall in love.* However, **o** does go to **a** in **wyskoczyć wyskakiwać** -uję *leap out.*

Examples of **'** **i**: **przekląć** (prze-kl'n-) **przeklinać** *curse,* **ugiąć** (u-g'n-) **uginać** *bend,* **wyciąć** (wy-t'n-) **wycinać** *cut out,* **zacząć** (za-cz'n-) **zaczynać** (y/i rule) *begin,* **zapiąć** (za-p'n-) **zapinać** *pin shut.* Before **r** or **ł**, **'** becomes **'e**: **umrzeć** (u-m'r-) **umierać** *die,* **wybrać** (wy-b'r-) **wybierać** *choose,* **wypleć** (wy-p'ł-, although usually **wypielić**) **wypielać** *weed out.*

Examples of **Ø**: **y**: **nadąć** (na-dØm-) **nadymać** *inflate,* **nazwać** (na-zØw-a) **nazywać** *name,* **przerwać** (prze-rØw-a-) **przerywać** *interrupt,* **spotkać** (spotØk-a-) **spotykać** *meet,* **tknąć** (tØk-) **tykać** *touch,* **zaspać** (za-sØp-a-) **zasypiać** *oversleep,* **westchnąć** (wØz-dØch-) **wzdychać** *sigh* (the spelling **westchnąć** reflecting the assimilation in voicing of **zd** to **st** before **ch**).

The **'e**: **'a** alternation occurring in Imperfective derivation in some roots is an example not of a vowel replacement but of the **'e** : **'a** alternation before soft-vs.-hard dentals; see **odpowiedzieć odpowiadać** *answer.*

DETAILS ON THE DISTRIBUTION OF THE IMPERFECTIVE SUFFIXES

1. **-ać -am -asz**

   a. This suffix is added to the underlying consonant of consonant-stems: **paść padać** *fall,* **przypiec przypiekać** *scorch,* **pomóc pomagać** *help,* **spleść splatać** *weave,* **wykraść wykradać** *pilfer,* **wypaść wypasać** *pasture,* **wypleć wypielać** *weed out,* **wyprząc wyprzęgać** *unharness,* **wytrzeć wycierać** *wipe off,* **zagryźć zagryzać** *bite to death.*

   b. This suffix is also added to the consonant-stem of most prefixed Perfective verbs in **-ną-ć**, in the process replacing **-ną-**: **posunąć posuwać** *push,* **zaciągnąć zaciągać** *drag,* **zasięgnąć zasięgać** *seek information,* **zawilgnąć zawilgać** *become moist,* **zerknąć zerkać** *squint,* and many others. Possibly lost consonants before **-nąć** are replaced before **-ać**; see **prześliz(g)nąć się prześlizgać się** *glide past,* **wycis(k)nąć wyciskać** *squeeze,* and others.

   c. Most 2nd-conjugation verbs form derived Imperfectives in this suffix, for example, **dokuczyć dokuczać** *annoy,* **nagrodzić nagradzać** *reward,* **nastroić nastrajać** *tune,* **oprawić oprawiać** *frame,* **opuścić opuszczać** *let down,* **pozwolić pozwalać** *permit,* **przemówić przemawiać** *give a speech,* **rozdzielić rozdzielać** *divide,* **wkroczyć wkraczać** *encroach,* **wypłacić wypłacać** *pay out,* **wyprowadzić wyprowadzać** *lead out,* **wyrzucić wyrzucać** *throw out,* **zapewnić zapewniać** *assure,* **zarobić zarabiać** *earn,* and very many others.

   d. A few monosyllabic verbs in **-a-ć** with stems containing covert **'** or **Ø** form Imperfectives in this suffix: **nazwać nazywać** *name,* **przerwać**

przerywać *interrupt,* **wybrać wybierać** *choose;* **wysłać wysyłać** *send;* irregular: **zasłać zaścielać** *cover with a spread.*

2. **-wać -wam -wasz**

    This suffix is added to monosyllabic vowel-stems with roots in **u** and **y**, and to a few non-2nd-conjugation verbs in **-e-**: **dojrzeć dojrzewać** *ripen,* **odczuć odczuwać** *sense,* **przebyć przebywać** *stay,* **umyć umywać** *wash off,* **zachcieć zachciewać** *feel like.* Verbs of the **grzać grzeję grzejesz** *warm* type add this suffix to a stem in **e**: **ogrzać ogrzewać** *warm,* **wyśmiać się wyśmiewać się** *mock,* **zalać zalewać** *inundate.*

3. Minor suffixes

    a. **-jać -jam -jasz.** Monosyllabic verbs with roots in **i** form Imperfectives in **-jać -jam -jasz**: **rozbić rozbijać** *shatter,* **wypić wypijać** *drink up.* Also **rozwinąć rozwijać** *develop.*

    b. **-ować -uję -ujesz.** Verbs using the root **j'm-** form Imperfectives in **-ować -uję -ujesz**: **zdjąć zdejmować** *take off,* **objąć obejmować** *embrace.* This suffix is occasionally used elsewhere, as with **wystąpić występować** *occur* and other compounds of **-stąpić**, **znaleźć znajdę znajdziesz znajdować** *find* (but usually **odnaleźć odnajdywać -uję -ujesz** *discover*).

    c. **-wać -ję -jesz.** Three monosyllabic roots in **a**: **da-, sta-, zna-,** take the suffix **-wać -ję -jesz**: **przyznać przyznawać (przyznaję przyznajesz)** *admit,* **rozdać rozdawać (rozdaję)** *hand out,* **wstać wstawać (wstaję)** *get up,* **zostać zostawać (zostaję)** *be left.*

4. **-ywać (-uję -ujesz** or, much less often, **-ywam -ywasz)**

    This is the most productive of the Imperfective suffixes. A dictionary should be consulted on an individual basis concerning whether the present is usually formed in **-uję -ujesz** or, much less often, **-ywam -ywasz**. This suffix occurs with the following classes:

    a. Verbs of the **pisać piszę piszesz** *write* type (1st conjugation): **okłamać okłamywać -uję** *deceive,* **pokazać pokazywać -uję** *show,* **przepisać przepisywać -uję** *write over,* **rozdrapać rozdrapywać -uję** *scratch,* **zamazać zamazywać -uję** *smear.*

    b. Verbs of the very numerous **-ować -uję -ujesz** type: **dostosować dostosowywać -uję** *adapt,* **wypracować wypracowywać -uję** *elaborate,* **obdarować obdarowywać -uję** *bestow,* **załadować załadowywać -uję** *load down.*

    c. Verbs of the **pytać pytam pytasz** *ask* type (3rd conjugation): **obiecać obiecywać -uję** *promise,* **odczytać odczytywać -uję** *recite,* **przekonać przekonywać -uję** or **-ywam** *persuade,* **wygrać wygrywać -ywam** *win,* wyrównać wyrównywać -uję or -ywam *level*, zamieszkać zamieszkiwać -uję *inhabit*, zatrzymać zatrzymywać -uję or -ywam *stop*.

d. 2nd-conjugation verbs in -eć take this suffix and show a reversion to the primary root consonant, in connection with which a possible ě in the root changes to a: przypatrzeć się przypatrywać się -uję *have a look at*, odsiedzieć odsiadywać -uję *sit out*, odlecieć odlatywać -uję *fly away*; przewidzieć przewidywać -uję *foresee*; also 4th-conjugation dowiedzieć się dowiadywać się -uję *find out*.

e. Various other verbs, especially velar stems, take this suffix instead of the suffix that might be expected on the basis of the above rules: obsłużyć obsługiwać -uję *service*, wykrzyknąć wykrzykiwać -uję *shout*, wyleżeć wylegiwać -uję *lie abed*, wtrysnąć wtryskiwać -uję *inject*, wyskoczyć wyskakiwać -uję *leap out*, zatrzasnąć zatrzaskiwać -uję *slam*.

DISTRIBUTIVE USE OF *PO-*

The prefix **po-** is the only prefix which may perfectivize a derived prefixed Imperfective verb. When added to such a verb, **po-** both perfectivizes the verb and adds the distributive meaning 'one by one':

Pozajmowali wszystkie miejsca. *One by one, they occupied all the places.*

Nie zdążył porozmieszczać kartek przy nakryciach. *He didn't manage to set out the cards by the table settings.*

Porozrzucała wszystkie koszule na podłodze. *She threw each and every one of the shirts on the floor.*

SUPPLETIVE ASPECT PAIRS

Occasionally, two different verbs will become associated with each other in an aspectual relationship. This is the case, for example, with the following pairs:

Imperfective	Perfective
brać biorę bierzesz	wziąć wezmę weźmiesz *take*
kłaść kładę kładziesz	położyć położę położysz *lay, place, put*
mówić mówię mówisz	powiedzieć powiem -wiesz -wiedzą *say*
oglądać oglądam oglądasz	obejrzeć obejrzę obejrzysz *watch, view*
widzieć widzę widzisz	zobaczyć zobaczę zobaczysz *see*

Of the above Imperfective verbs, **brać**, **mówić**, and **widzieć** can form prefixed Perfectives in new meanings, which will form corresponding back-derived Imperfectives. Here are various compounds of **brać**:

nabrać nabierać *take in*
odebrać odbierać *take back*
pobrać pobierać *receive, take*
przebrać przebierać *change clothes*

rozebrać rozbierać *undress*
ubrać ubierać *dress*
wybrać wybierać *choose*
zabrać zabierać *take along*

Here are various compounds of **mówić**:

namówić namawiać *induce*
odmówić odmawiać *refuse*
omówić omawiać *discuss*
przemówić przemawiać *give speech*
umówić umawiać *arrange, settle*

wmówić wmawiać *try to convince*
wymówić wymawiać *pronounce*
zamówić zamawiać *order*
zmówić się zmawiać się *conspire with*

Here are compounds of **widzieć**:

przewidzieć -widywać *foresee*   przywidzieć się przywidywać się *appear*

By contrast, compound Imperfectives and Perfectives of **kłaść** are formed on the two stems **-kładać** and **-łożyć**:

nakładać nałożyć *impose*
odkładać odłożyć *put off*
przedkładać przedłożyć *prefer*
przekładać przełożyć *translate*

układać ułożyć *compose*
wkładać włożyć *put into*
wykładać wyłożyć *lay out*
zakładać założyć *bet*

Compound Imperfectives and Perfectives of **-glądać** are based on **-glądać** and **-jrzeć**:

doglądać dojrzeć *supervise*
oglądać obejrzeć *examine*
podglądać podejrzeć *spy on*
przeglądać przejrzeć *look through*

przyglądać się przyjrzeć się *observe*
rozglądać się rozejrzeć się *look about*
wyglądać wyjrzeć *peer out*
zaglądać zajrzeć *peek in on*

Also suppletive for all intents and purposes are

znaleźć znajdę znajdziesz *find*
odnaleźć odnajdę -dziesz *discover*

znajdować znajduję znajdujesz
odnajdywać odnajduję odnajdujesz

FREQUENTATIVE VERBS

The suffixes **-ywać -ywam -ywasz** and **-ać -am -asz** can be used to form frequentative (iterative, habitual) verbs from certain simplex Imperfectives, with root changes similar to those occurring under imperfectivization:

Base verb:	Frequentative:
być (jestem jesteś) *be*	bywać bywam bywasz
czytać czytam czytasz *read*	czytywać czytuję czytujesz
grać gram grasz *play*	grywać grywam grywasz
jeść jem jesz jedzą *eat*	jadać jadam jadasz
mówić mówię mówisz *say*	mawiać mawiam mawiasz
mieć mam masz *have*	miewać miewam miewasz

pić piję pijesz *drink*	pijać pijam pijasz
pisać piszę piszesz *write*	pisywać pisuję pisujesz
siedzieć siedzę siedzisz *sit*	siadywać siadywam siadywasz
służyć służę służysz *serve*	sługiwać sługuję sługujesz
słuchać słucham słuchasz *listen to*	słuchiwać słuchuję słuchujesz
spać śpię śpisz *sleep*	sypiać sypiam sypiasz
szyć szyję szyjesz *sew*	szywać szywam szywasz
widzieć widzę widzisz *see*	widywać widuję widujesz

The frequentative is used more often in the south of Poland than in the north. It may almost always be replaced with the regular Imperfective. Examples:

Czytuję codziennie gazetę. *I read the paper every day.*

Zięć czasami grywa na fortepianie. *My son-in-law sometimes plays the piano.*

To jest miejsce, gdzie siadywała mama. *That's the place where mama used to sit.*

Zwykle jadam śniadanie o ósmej. *I usually eat breakfast at eight.*

Jak mawia przysłowie: gość w dom, Bóg w dom. *As the proverb says: guest in the house, God in the house.*

Nasi przodkowie miewali podobne problemy. *Our forebears used to have similar problems.*

Dawno już przestałem ją widywać. *I stopped seeing her a long time ago.*

THE ASPECT OF VERBS OF MOTION

The Polish basic verbs of motion 'go' and 'carry' distinguish between motion under one's own power and motion by vehicle or other conveyance. In addition, these and certain other Imperfective basic verbs of motion make a distinction as to whether the action is on-going (Determinate) or habitual (Indeterminate). To an extent, the Determinate form corresponds to the English verb form in *-ing*. The full set of contrasts may be illustrated only by verbs of 'going' and 'carrying':

'go':	Imperfective:	
Meaning:	Determinate:	Indeterminate:
go on foot, walk	**iść idę idziesz**	**chodzić chodzę chodzisz**
go by vehicle, ride	**jechać jadę jedziesz**	**jeździć jeżdżę jeździsz**

'carry':	Imperfective:	
Meaning:	Determinate:	Indeterminate:
carry	**nieść niosę niesiesz**	**nosić noszę nosisz**
carry by vehicle, transport	**wieźć wiozę wieziesz**	**wozić wożę wozisz**

Examples:

Gdzie teraz idziesz? *Where are you going now?*

Często chodzę do teatru. *I often go to the theater.*

Jedziemy do Krakowa o ósmej. *We are going to Cracow at eight.*

Jeździmy najchętniej pociągiem. *We like best to go by train.*

Możesz nieść głowę wysoko. *You can carry your head high.*

Ona nosiła dziecko na rękach. *She used to carry her child in her arms.*

Schody ruchome wiozą nas na górę. *An escalator carries us upstairs.*

Wożę córkę do szkoły codziennie o siódmej. *I drive my daughter to school
every day at seven.*

The verb **nosić** also means 'wear':

Nie wiedziałem, że nosisz okulary. *I didn't know you wore glasses.*

Nosisz zawsze tę samą koszulę. *You're always wearing the same shirt.*

Verbs displaying the Determinate-Indeterminate distinction include:

Determinate:
biec biegnę biegniesz *run*
iść idę idziesz *go*
jechać jadę jedziesz *ride*
lecieć lecę lecisz *fly*
leźć lezę leziesz *crawl**
nieść niosę niesiesz *carry*
płynąć płynę płyniesz *swim*
wieść wiodę wiedziesz *lead**
wieźć wiozę wieziesz *transport*

Indeterminate:
biegać biegam biegasz
chodzić chodzę chodzisz
jeździć jeżdżę jeździsz
latać latam latasz
łazić łażę łazisz
nosić noszę nosisz
pływać pływam pływasz
wodzić wodzę wodzisz
wozić wożę wozisz

* The verbs **leźć** *crawl* and **wieść** *lead* are uncommon in their unprefixed forms, **pełzać**
and **prowadzić**, respectively, being used instead.

NOTES ON THE USE OF DETERMINATE AND INDETERMINATE VERBS

a. The words **teraz** *now* and **często** *often*, will usually elicit the Determinate
and Indeterminate forms, respectively, of the verb:

Teraz idę (jadę, niosę, wiozę). *Now I am going (riding, carrying,
transporting).*

Często chodzę (jeżdżę, noszę, wożę). *I often go (ride, carry, transport).*

b. In the imperative, the verbs **iść idę idziesz** *go, be going* and **chodzić
chodzę chodzisz** *go (often)* are specialized in the senses of 'go' and 'come',
respectively:

Idź stąd! *Go away!*

Chodź tu! *Come here!*

c. Determinate verbs are by nature purposive and directed toward a single aim. If motion is random, diffuse, or cut into different segments, the Indeterminate will be used, even though the action is on-going:

On lata po wszystkich sklepach. *He is running around to all the stores.*

Po południu pływam w klubie. *In the afternoon I swim at the club.*

d. Determinate verbs of motion are essentially the only Polish verbs for which the present-tense form may be used with prospective future implication, as in

Jutro jadę do domu. *I'm going home tomorrow.*

My z Jurkiem idziemy dziś wieczorem do kina. *Jurek and I are going to the movies this evening.*

Because the present tense of motion verbs may be used with future meaning, the compound future with **będę** plus the Determinate verb (e.g. **będę szedł/szła/iść, będziemy jechali/jechały/jechać**) is infrequently used.

e. Polish tends to be literal about using 'fly' with airplanes and 'sail' with boats and ships, rather than the generalized verb 'go, travel', even when the means of transportation is not emphasized in the sentence:

Do Warszawy z Nowego Jorku leci się (not: jedzie się) osiem godzin. *It takes eight hours to fly from New York to Warsaw.*

Płyniemy (not: jedziemy) statkiem do Gdańska jutro rano o ósmej. *We're sailing by ship to Gdansk tomorrow morning at eight.*

PERFECTIVE PREFIXATION WITH VERBS OF MOTION

Prefixed Perfective verbs of motion lose the Determinate-Indeterminate distinction. The basic Perfectives of **iść/chodzić** and **jechać/jeździć** are formed with the prefix **po-** plus the Determinate verb: **pójść pójdę pójdziesz, pojechać pojadę pojedziesz.** Po- is also used with other verbs of motion, but with **nieść** and **wieźć** the more frequent prefixes are **za-** or sometimes **od-**:

	Imperfective		Perfective
	Determinate	Indeterminate	
go on foot	iść	chodzić	**pójść**
go by vehicle	jechać	jeździć	**pojechać**
carry on foot	nieść	nosić	**zanieść, odnieść**
carry by vehicle	wieźć	wozić	**zawieźć, odwieźć**
lead	wieść	wodzić	**powieść**
fly	lecieć	latać	**polecieć**
crawl	leźć	łazić	**poleźć, wleźć**
swim, sail	płynąć	pływać	**popłynąć**
run	biec	biegać	**pobiec**

PREFIXED VERBS OF MOTION IN NEW MEANINGS

Verbs of motion are among the most liberal of verbs in forming Perfective compounds in concrete spatial meanings with prefixes. Here are Perfective compounds of **iść**:

dojść *go as far as*``	**rozejść się** *disperse*
nadejść *draw near*	**ujść** *get by, go a certain distance*
najść *come upon*	**wejść** *enter, go up*
obejść *go around*	**wyjść** *go out, leave*
odejść *go away*	**wzejść** *rise (of sun)*
podejść *approach*	**zajść** *set (of sun)*
przejść *pass by or through*	**zejść** *come down*
przyjść *come, arrive*	

Corresponding Imperfective forms of prefixed verbs of motion in new meanings are often obtained by combining the prefixes with the Indeterminate form of the verb:

Prefixed Perfective	Prefixed Imperfective
dojść *go as far as*``	**dochodzić**
nadejść *draw near*	**nadchodzić**
obejść *go around*	**obchodzić**
odejść *go away*	**odchodzić**
podejść *approach*	**podchodzić**
przejść *pass by or through*	**przechodzić** and so on

Also:

wynieść *carry out*	**wynosić**
zawieść *mislead*	**zawodzić**
wywieźć *cart out*	**wywozić**
odpłynąć *sail away*	**odpływać**
ubiec *run off*	**ubiegać**
wyleźć *crawl out*	**wyłazić** and so on

However, Imperfective counterparts of prefixed Perfectives formed on **jechać** and **lecieć** are formed on the stems **-jeżdżać** and **-latywać**, respectively:

dojechać *arrive at*	**dojeżdżać dojeżdżam dojeżdżasz**
odjechać *drive away*	**odjeżdżać odjeżdżam odjeżdżasz**
odlecieć *fly away*	**odlatywać odlatuję odlatujesz**
przylecieć *arrive by flying*	**przylatywać przylatuję przylatujesz**

INDETERMINATE VERBS WITH INDEPENDENT MEANINGS

A few verbs that are Indeterminate in form also function as independent verbs and, to a limited expent, may themselves be perfectivized with prefixes, for example, **nosić** *wear,* **ponosić** *wear for a while-pf,* **wynosić** *wear out-pf,* **znosić** *wear down or out-pf* The forms **wynosić** and **znosić** may function as either Perfective or Imperfective, according to meaning. Perfectives formed on the verb **jeździć** take back-derived Imperfectives using **-jeżdżać**:

zajeździć zajeżdżać *over-ride (e.g. a horse)*
zjeździć zjeżdżać *visit; ride into the ground*

VERBS OF PLACEMENT AND BODY POSITION

Polish has a fairly complex set of verbs for expressing body position (verbs of putting, standing, sitting, hanging), made the more difficult for speakers of English by the fact that the traditional English system of body-position verbs is changing and causes English speakers themselves a good deal of difficulty. In principle, for each each body position there should be a CAUSATIVE verb (put something into the position), an AUTOCAUSATIVE verb (assume the position oneself), and a STATIVE verb (be in the position), each with its own Imperfective and Perfective aspect forms. In practice, the system is not perfectly exemplified, partly for semantic, and partly for pragmatic reasons.

LIE

put in the position	assume the position	be in the position
kłaść kładę kładziesz *put, place, lay-impf*	**kłaść się** *lie down- impf*	**leżeć leżę leżysz** *lie, be lying-impf*
położyć położę położę *place, lay-pf*	**położyć się -ę -ysz** *lie down-pf*	**poleżeć -ę -ysz** *lie for a while-pf*

STAND

put in the position	assume the position	be in the position
stawiać -am -asz *put, stand-impf*	**wstawać wstaję wstajesz** *get up-impf*	**stać stoję stoisz** *stand, be standing-impf*
postawić -wię -wisz *put, stand-pf*	**wstać wstanę wstanę** *get up-pf*	**postać** *stand for a while-pf*

SIT

put in the position	assume the position	be in the position
sadzić sadzę -dzisz *plant, set-impf*	**siadać -am -asz** *sit down-impf*	**siedzieć siedzę -dzisz** *sit, be sitting-impf*
posadzić *plant, set-pf*	**usiąść usiądę -dziesz** *sit down-pf*	**posiedzieć** *sit for a while-pf*

HANG

put in the position	assume the position	be in the position
wieszać -am -asz *hang up- impf*	**wieszać się** *hang oneself-impf*	**wisieć wiszę wisi** *hang, be hanging-impf*
powiesić powieszę powiesi *pf*	**powiesić się** *hang oneself-pf*	**powisieć** *hang for a while-pf*

In practical situations, 'put' is most often translated by **postawić stawiać** *put in a standing position*, **nastawić nastawiać** *put on*, **wstawić wstawiać** *put in*, and **położyć kłaść** *lay*. The usual case after **na** here is the Locative, but the Accusative can be used to emphasize dynamism or accuracy of placement:

Postaw książkę na półce (półkę). *Put the book on the shelf.*

Wstaw piwo do lodówki. *Put the beer in the refrigerator.*

Połóż nóż na stole (stół). *Put the knife on the table.*

The verb **nastawić** *put on* does not usually take a second complement:
Nastaw herbatę. *Put the tea on.*

VERBS OF CONVERSE ACTION

Some common verbs of converse action include

Imperfective   Perfective

otwierać -am -asz *open*	**otwórzyć -rzę -rzysz**
zamykać -am -asz *shut, close*	**zamknąć -nę -niesz**
zaczynać -am -asz *begin*	**zacząć zacznę zaczniesz**
kończyć -ę -ysz *finish, end*	**skończyć** *finish, end*
włączać -am -asz *connect, turn on*	**włączyć -czę -czysz**
wyłączać -am -asz *disconnect*	**wyłączyć -czę -czysz**

Imperfective forms in **-łączać** (**wyłączać, odłączać, włączać,** etc.) are often pronounced as **"-lanczać"**, rather than **"-łonczać"**, as though an **o: a** change had taken place in the root. This pronunciation, though widespread, is considered substandard.

Imperfective   Perfective

odkręcać -am -asz *turn on (water)*	**odkręcić odkręcę odkręcisz**
zakręcać -am -asz *turn off*	**zakręcić zakręcę zakręcisz**
wkładać -am -asz *put on (clothing)*	**włożyć włożę włożysz**
zdejmować -uję -ujesz *take off*	**zdjąć zdejmę zdejmiesz**
ubierać się -am -asz *get dressed*	**ubrać się ubiorę ubierzesz**
rozbierać się *get undressed*	**rozebrać się -biorę -bierzesz**

THE CITATION OF ASPECT PAIRS

Few, if any, dictionaries of Polish, whether designed for foreigners or for native Poles, have entirely consistent and efficient ways of citing and relating aspect pairs. In subsequent chapters the following routine is observed:

a.   Verbs cited without further indication as to *pf* (Perfective) or *impf* (Imperfective) will be assumed to be Imperfective: **grać** *play*, **usiłować** *endeavor*, but **kupić** *buy (pf)*.

b.   Empty perfectivizing prefixes may be set off before the simplex verb, with alphabetization following the simplex verb: **(za)demonstrować** *demonstrate*, **(na)pisać** *write*.

c.   If possible, suffixally differentiated verbs are combined into a single citation with the help of parentheses: **wyda(wa)ć** *expend*, **rozkaz(yw)ać** *command*, **zmieni(a)ć** *change*. In all such instances the shorter of the two will be Perfective, the longer Imperfective.

d.   When suffixally or lexically differentiated aspectually paired verbs are placed next to each another, the first verb will be Perfective, the second Imperfective, regardless of length or alphabetical order: **polecić polecać** *recommend*, **wziąć brać** *take*.

e.   When two verbs are cited next to one another and the first has the suffix **-nąć**, the first will be Perfective, the second Imperfective: **klepnąć klepać** *pat*.

Participles, Verbal Nouns, and Grammatical Voice

THE POLISH PARTICIPLE SYSTEM

Polish participles are of two kinds, adjectival and adverbial (the latter also called gerunds). ADJECTIVAL PARTICIPLES are declined like adjectives and, like adjectives, agree with a modified noun in gender, number, and case. At the same time they retain certain syntactic properties of the verb on which they are based. ADVERBIAL PARTICIPLES are not declined. They are used to take the place of a regular conjugated verb in a subordinate clause when the subject of the verb in the subordinate and main clauses is the same. In effect, an adverbial participle is an uninflected verb form, which retains the syntactic properties of the verb on which it is based. Adjectival and adverbial participles are characteristic of a formal written style. In casual speech one more often uses alternative constructions involving conjugated verb forms instead. The difference between an adjectival and an adverbial participle, and the substitution in colloquial speech of regular verb forms for both one and the other, is illustrated below:

Adjectival:

Kobieta *wracająca* (= **która wracała) z pola już nie była tą samą kobietą, którą pamiętał.** *The woman returning (= who was returning) from the field was no longer the same woman he remembered.*

Adverbial:

Wracając (= **jak wracała) do domu, Maria przemyślała wszystko, co usłyszała.** *Returning (= as she returned) home, Maria thought over everything she had heard.*

The above participles are Imperfective; observe that they refer to unfolding action. The Polish participle system distinguishes among the categories of a) adjectival vs. adverbial participles; c) participles of Imperfective vs. Perfective aspect; and c) active vs. passive participles. Active participles refer to an action that the modified noun is undertaking, for example **piszący** *(one who is) writing.* Passive participles refer to an action which the modified noun is undergoing, for example **napisany** *(something which has been) written.* The system as a whole looks like this (illustrated with the verb **pisać napisać** *write impf/pf).* There are several gaps in the system; mainly, for logical reasons, there is no such thing as a passive gerund.

	Imperfective		Perfective	
	Adjectival	Adverbial	Adjectival	Adverbial
Active	piszący	pisząc		napisawszy
Passive	pisany		napisany	

THE ACTIVE ADJECTIVAL PARTICIPLE

The ACTIVE ADJECTIVAL PARTICIPLE may be formed by adding **-c-** plus adjective endings to the 3rd person pl. present form of an Imperfective verb:

Infinitive	3rd person plural	Active adjective participle
chcieć *want*	**chcą**	**chcący -a -e** *wanting*
witać *greet*	**witają**	**witający -a -e** *greeting*
mówić *say*	**mówią**	**mówiący -a -e** *saying*
płonąć *burn*	**płoną**	**płonący -a -e** *burning*
iść *go*	**idą**	**idący -a -e** *going*, and so on

NOTES ON THE ACTIVE ADJECTIVAL PARTICIPLE

a. The active adjectival participle refers to an on-going action, process, or state. It often occupies the position of a modifying adjective, usually placed before the noun (here and following from J. Andrzejewski, *Popiół i diament*):

W *ciemniejącym* **pokoju zaległo milczenie.** *In the darkening room silence fell.*

Poczęli dawać *zjeżdżającemu* **wozowi rozkaz zatrzymania się.** *They began to give the approaching vehicle the order to stop.*

Z pewną ulgą przyglądała się tej *milczącej* **furii.** *With a certain satisfaction she observed this silent fury.*

b. The active adjectival participle may follow the noun to form an abbreviated relative clause:

Obaj policjanci *zajmujący* **miejsca w tyle wozu wyskoczyli.** *Both policemen occupying places in the back of the vehicle leaped out.*

On stał za biurkiem z twarzą nie *wyrażającą* **żadnego uczucia.** *He stood behind the desk with a face not expressing any feeling.*

Nad łóżkiem wisiał oleodruk *przedstawiający* **świętego Krzysztofa.** *Above the bed hung an oil reproduction representing Saint Christopher.*

In the above examples, observe how the participle takes complements like any verb: **policjanci zajmujący miejsca** *policemen occupying places,* **twarz nie wyrażająca żadnego uczucia** *a face not expressing any emotion,* and so on.

c. In the relative-clause function the active adjectival participle can also precede the modified noun. In such use the participle is usually separated from the noun by an intervening phrase serving to restrict or specify the action of the participle:

Kopnął *leżący na ścieżce* **kamień.** *He kicked a stone lying on the path.*

Coś mówił do *towarzyszącej mu* **kobiety.** *He said something to the woman accompanying him.*

Przebiegli *dzielącą ich od wejścia* **przestrzeń.** *They ran past the space which separated them from the entrance.*

d. The active adjectival participle is often used as an ad hoc personal noun:

Mówiący **ciagle zmieniał temat.** *The speaker constantly changed the subject.*

Dla *chcącego* **nie ma nic trudnego.** *For someone who is willing, nothing is impossible (= where there's a will there's a way).*

Opłakując zmarłych *żyjący* **opłakują samych siebie.** *In mourning the dead, the living mourn themselves.*

e. Some active adjectival participles have acquired the status of regular adjectives, for example, **interesujący** *interesting*, **olśniewający** *dazzling*, **przygnębiający** *depressing*, **rażący** *offensive*, **śpiący** *sleepy*, **wymagający** *demanding*, and many others.

f. Some active adjectival participles have acquired the status of independent adjectival nouns: **palący** *smoker*, **przewodniczący** *chairman*, **służący** *servant*, **strajkujący** *striker*, **wierzący** *believer*, and many others.

g. The adverbial form of the active adjectival participle occurs frequently:

Wódka działała na niego *krzepiąco.* *The vodka acted on him invigoratingly.*

Lustro odbijało kilka *drwiąco* **uśmiechniętych twarzy.** *The mirror reflected a number of mockingly laughing faces.*

Barman spojrzał *pytająco* **w jego stronę.** *The bartender glanced questioningly in his direction.*

THE ACTIVE ADVERBIAL PARTICIPLE

The ACTIVE ADVERBIAL PARTICIPLE (present gerund) may be formed by adding **-c** to the 3rd person pl. present form of an Imperfective verb:

Infinitive	3rd person plural	Active adverbial participle
żyć *live*	**żyją**	**żyjąc**
czekać *wait*	**czekają**	**czekając**
pisać *write*	**piszą**	**pisząc**
kłaść *place, lay*	**kładą**	**kładąc**
widzieć *see*	**widzą**	**widząc**
wstawać *arise*	**wstają**	**wstając**, and so on

a. The active adverbial participle refers to an action or state that is simultaneous to another action or state having the same subject. If both actions are Imperfective, it is sometimes a matter of personal preference as to which verb will be treated as main, and which as subordinate:

Czekając siedzieli i rozmawiali, pijąc piwo i zagryzając kiełbasą. *While waiting, they sat and conversed, while drinking beer and nibbling sausage.*
Or: **Czekali siedząc i rozmawiając, pijąc piwo i zagryzając kiełbasą.** *They waited while sitting and conversing, drinking beer and nibbling sausage.*

Wchodząc na schody kłóciły się. *Ascending the stairs, they were quarreling.*
Or: **Kłócąc się wchodzili na schody.** *Quarreling, they ascended the stairs.*

Dłuższą chwilę klęczał, namyślając się. *For a longish time he kneeled, thinking things over.* Or: **Dłuższą chwilę namyślał się, klęcząc.** *For a longish time he thought things over, kneeling.*

b. Often the main verb will be Perfective:

Przecierając chustką oczy, skinęła głowę. *Wiping his eyes with a handkerchief, she nodded-pf her head.*

Poszedł pierwszy, kulejąc. *He went-pf first, limping.*

Czekając na jego przyjazd, ludzie zeszli ku rzece. *Waiting for his arrival, the people went-down-pf toward the river.*

Będąc w Londynie, poszedłem do porządnego krawca. *Being in London, I went-pf to a good tailor.*

ADVERBIAL PARTICIPLE OF PRIOR ACTION

The ADVERBIAL PARTICIPLE OF PRIOR ACTION (past gerund) refers to action that has already been completed by the time of the main action. Like adverbial participles in general, it replaces one of two verbs sharing the same subject. This participle is limited almost exclusively to formal written style, and even there it is encountered less and less frequently. It is formed only from Perfective verbs; despite its resemblance to an adjective, this form is not declined.

1. If the masculine sg. past-tense stem of the verb consists of a vowel plus -ł, the suffix **-wszy** is added to the stem obtained by subtracting -ł:

3rd pers. sg. masc. past:	Adverbial participle of prior action:
napisał *he wrote*	**napisawszy** *having written*
poczuł *he sensed*	**poczuwszy** *having sensed*
powiedział *he said*	**powiedziawszy** *having said*
zaczął *he began*	**zacząwszy** *having begun*
zbił *he beat up*	**zbiwszy** *having beaten up*

2. If the masculine sg. past tense form consists of a consonant plus **-ł**, the
    suffix **-szy** is added to the **-ł**:

3rd pers. sg. masc. past:	Adverbial participle of prior action:
poszedł *he went*	**poszedłszy** *having gone*
spostrzegł *he observed*	**spostrzegłszy** *having observed*
upiekł *he baked*	**upiekłszy** *having baked*
oparł *he leaned*	**oparłszy** *having leaned*
zgniótł *he crushed*	**zgniótłszy** *having crushed*

Note that the English translation will often utilize the progressive
participle instead of the perfect participle.

a. If the main verb is Perfective, the adverbial participle of prior action
    usually precedes it, often occurring in sentence-initial position:

    Opuściwszy **rękawy koszuli, nałożył marynarkę.** *Having rolled down
    (rolling down) the sleeves of his shirt, he put on his jacket.*

    Podszedłszy **do okna stanął tam, odwrócony plecami.** *Having approached
    (approaching) the window, he stood there with his back turned.*

    Oparłszy **but o kamień, zaciągnął się dymem.** *Resting his shoe against a
    rock, he inhaled the smoke.*

b. The adverbial participle of prior action may also follow the main verb,
    especially if it is Imperfective:

    Siedział za biurkiem, jedną dłonią *podparłszy* **głowę.** *He sat behind the
    desk, supporting his head on one palm.*

    Chodził po pokoju, *założywszy* **ręce do tyłu.** *He walked around the room,
    clasping his hands behind him.*

    Pani skręciła w prawo, nie *przeczekawszy* **pierwszej fali pieszych.** *You
    made a right turn without waiting for the first wave of pedestrians.*

THE PASSIVE PARTICIPLE

The PASSIVE PARTICIPLE is an adjectival participle referring to action
which a noun undergoes, for example, **gotowane jajko** *boiled egg.* It is the
most complicated of the participles to form and, at the same time, the most
often used. The formative suffix is either **-t-** or **-(e/o)n-**, added to a stem best
described relative to each verb-group. The passive participle may be formed
from either Perfective or Imperfective verbs, although the formation from
Perfective verbs is more frequent. It is most often formed from transitive
(Accusative-requiring verbs), although not all transitive verbs do form a
passive participle (**mieć** *have* and **woleć** *prefer,* for example, do not). Many
oblique-case verbs do form a passive participle; for example, **unikać** +G *avoid,*
pf **uniknąć** forms **unikany, unikniępy.** Whether or not a given verb forms a
declinable passive participle, almost any verb can form an impersonal passive

in **-o**, formed on the same stem. For more information on the possibility of passive formation, see below under Passive Voice: Irregularities in the Possibility for Passivization. For the use of impersonal passive forms in **-no/ -to**, see below under Impersonal Passive.

1. First-conjugation verbs of the **pić, myć, psuć, dąć, ciąć, osiągnąć**, and **trzeć** types take the formant **-t-**. Verbs ending in **-ąć** change **ą** to **ę**. Verbs of the **-nąć** type soften **-n-**. Except for the last type, the stem-form is similar to what one finds in the fem. past. In the examples below, the passive participle is cited in the Nsg. masc., fem., and neut., and in the NV masc. pers. pl.:

Infinitive:	3p.sg.fem.past:	Passive participle:
pić *drink*	**piła**	**pity -a -e, *pici** *drunk*
szyć *sew*	**szyła**	**szyty -a -e, *szyci** *se*
psuć *spoil*	**psuła**	**psuty -a -e, *psuci** *spoiled*
dąć *puff*	**dęła**	**dęty -a -e, *dęci** *puffed*
ciąć *cut*	**cięła**	**cięty -a -e, *cięci** *cut*
osiągnąć *attain* (pf)	**osiągnęła**	**osiągnięty -a -e, *osiągnięci** *attained*
trzeć *rub*	**tarła**	**tarty -a -e, *tarci** *rubbed*

* Masculine personal forms for certain passive participles are hard to imagine. This comment holds for various forms both here and below, whether starred or not.

2. First-conjugation obstruent consonant-stems (having infinitives in **-ść, -źć, -c**) take the formant **-en-**, shifting to **-on-** except in the NV masc pers. pl. The stem is similar to the one which occurs in the 2.p.sg. present (C2).

Infinitive:	1-2. p. sg. pres.:	Passive participle:
nieść *carry*	**niosę niesiesz**	**niesiony -a -e, niesieni** *carried*
wieźć *transport*	**wiozę wieziesz**	**wieziony -a -e, wiezieni** *transported*
piec *bake*	**piekę pieczesz**	**pieczony -a -e, pieczeni** *baked*

An exceptional R3 consonant replacement takes place before **-en-** in the NV masc. pers. pl. of verbs having underlying stems in **-t-** or **-d-**:

pleść *braid*	**plotę pleciesz**	**pleciony -a -e, pleceni** *braided*
kłaść *place*	**kładę kładziesz**	**kładziony -a -e, kładzeni** *placed*

3. Second-conjugation verbs with infinitives in **-i/y-** take **-en-/-on-**. If the infinitive stem ends in C2, the formant is added to a stem in C3. In practice, this will be the same stem that occurs in the 1.p.sg. present:

Infinitive	1. p. sg. pres.:	Passive participle:
czyścić *clean*	**czyszczę**	**czyszczony -a -e, czyszczeni** *cleaned*
kupić *buy* (pf)	**kupię**	**kupiony -a -e, kupieni** *bought*
nosić *carry*	**noszę**	**noszony -a -e, noszeni** *carried*

palić *smoke*	palę	palony -a -e, paleni *smoked*
płacić *pay*	płacę	płacony -a -e, płaceni *paid*
prowadzić *lead*	prowadzę	prowadzony -a -e, prowadzeni *led*
tworzyć *create*	tworzę	tworzony -a -e, tworzeni *created*
wozić *cart*	wożę	wożony -a -e, wożeni *carted*
and so on		

4. With verbs with infinitive stems ending in -a- or -e- (morphophonemic -ě-), of whatever conjugational type, the formant -n- is added to the infinitive stem. The infinitive suffix -ě- changes to -a- in all forms, including in the NV m.p.pl. form before ń:

Infinitives in -a-:

brać *take*	brany -a -e, brani *taken*
malować *paint*	malowany -a -e, malowani *painted*
pisać *write*	pisany -a -e, pisani *written*
czytać *read*	czytany -a -e, czytani *read*
lać *pour*	lany -a -e, lani *poured*

Infinitives in -ě-:

widzieć *see*	widziany -a -e, widziani *seen*
ujrzeć *glimpse (pf)*	ujrzany -a -e, ujrzani *glimpsed*
myśleć *think*	myślany -a -e, myślani *thought*

5. Irregular passive-participle formations include

chrzcić *christen*	chrzczony -a -e, chrzczeni *christened*
czcić *honor*	czczony -a -e, czczeni *honored*
mleć *grind*	mielony -a, -e, mieleni *ground*, alongside more regular, but archaic mełty -a -e, mełci
natchnąć *inspire (pf)*	natchniony -a -e, natchnieni *inspired*
otworzyć *open (pf)*	otwarty -a -e, otwarci *opened*. Regular otworzony -a -e also occurs.
pleć *weed*	pielony -a, -e, pieleni *weeded*, alongside more regular, but archaic pełty -a -e, pełci
zjeść *eat (pf)*	zjedzony -a -e, zjedzeni *eaten*
znaleźć *find (pf)*	znaleziony -a -e, znalezieni *found*

USES OF THE PASSIVE PARTICIPLE NOT RELATED TO GRAMMATICAL VOICE

For the use of the passive participle in the expression of passive voice, see later in this chapter under Grammatical Voice.

a. Passive participles are most often used as attributive deverbal adjectives:

Starsza *tleniona* kobieta weszła z ulicy. *An older peroxided woman entered from the street.*

Stał za biurkiem z *opuszczonymi* **oczami.** *He stood behind the desk with eyes lowered.*

Miał przed sobą *rozłożoną* **gazetę.** *He had in front of him an unfolded newspaper.*

b.   Passive participles often follow the noun, with the effect of a condensed relative clause:

List *wysłany* **dziś z Warszawy będzie jutro w Krakowie.** *A letter sent today from Warsaw will be in Krakow by tomorrow.*

W pokoju *pozbawionym* **pełnego oświetlenia panował półmrok.** *In the room, deprived of full illumination, there reigned a semi-darkness.*

Trzymał laskę *zakończoną* **gałką z kości słoniowej.** *He held a cane topped with a knob of ivory.*

c.   A participle expressing a relative clause is placed in front of the modified noun if separated from the noun by an intervening verbal complement:

Zsunął *zawinięty* **powyżej łokcia rękaw.** *He pushed back his sleeve, rolled above his elbow.*

Wojska wycofały się z zajętych przez nie *terytoriów.* *The armies withdrew from the territories occupied by them.*

Obaj milczeniem pominęli *umówione* **na wtorek** *spotkanie.* *Both passed over in silence the meeting scheduled for Tuesday.*

d.   Passive participles often follow a verb of mental or physical state or activity, in the function of an appositive predicate adjective:

Ona milczała, do głębi *poruszona* **tym gestem.** *She remained silent, touched to the depths by this gesture.*

Marcin leżał na łóżku, *wsparty* **o poduszki.** *Marcin lay on the bed, supported against the pillows.*

On ciągle siedział *pochylony* **nad papierami.** *He continued sitting bent over the papers.*

e.   Passive participles are frequently used as ad hoc personal nouns:

Niezadowoleni **uchylali się od pracy.** *The dissatisfied (ones) held back from work.*

Skazany **wrócił do celi.** *The condemned man returned to his cell.*

f.   Many passive participles, especially Perfective ones, have become independent adjectives, for example, **doświadczony** *experienced,* **niewyspany** *sleepy,* **obłąkany** *insane,* **ograniczony** *limited,* **ożywiony** *lively,* **rozchełstany** *disheveled,* **szalony** *crazy,* **ulubiony** *favorite,* **uzdolniony** *gifted,* **wrodzony** *innate,* **wyszukany** *recondite,* **zajęty** *busy,* **zepsuty** *ruined,* **złożony** *complex,* **znużony** *weary,* and many others. Noteworthy are passive-participle adjectives related to perfective verbs of emotion and other verbs in **się**: **zadowolony** *satisfied* (see **zadowolić się** *become satisfied pf*), **ucieszony** *consoled* (see **ucieszyć się** *be consoled pf*), **zachwycony** *enthralled* (see **zachwycać się** *become enthralled pf*), **zdziwiony** *surprised* (see **zdziwić się** *be surprised pf*), **zmęczony** *tired* (see **zmęczyć się** *grow weary pf*), **zapalony** *avid* (see **zapalić się** *become enthusiastic pf*), and others.

g. Some words which are passive participles by origin have acquired the status of independent personal nouns: **deputowany** *delegate*, **internowany** *internee*, **narzeczony** *fiancée*, **oskarżony** *the accused*, **przełożony** *superior*, **uczony** *scholar*, and many others.

THE VERBAL ADJECTIVE OF CHANGED STATE

Perfective change-of-state verbs sometimes form an adjective of resultant state with the suffix **-ł-**. The formation is similar to the past tense in **-ł-**; in practice, the Nsg. masc. of this adjective has the same shape as the 3.p.pl. non-masc. pers. past:

Base verb (all pf):	3.p.pl. non-masc. past:	Verbal adjective of changed state:
dojrzeć *ripen*	**dojrzały**	**dojrzały** *ripe*
osiwieć *grow gray*	**osiwiały**	**osiwiały** *grizzled*
przyblednąć *pale*	**przybladły**	**przybladły** *faded*
umrzeć *die*	**umarły**	**umarły** *dead*
zgnić *rot*	**zgniły**	**zgniły** *rotten*
zgrubieć *grow thick*	**zgrubiały**	**zgrubiały** *thickened*

Observe that with verbs whose infinitive ends in the suffix -ě-, the **e** is everywhere replaced by **a**, including in the NVpl. masc. pers. form: **dojrzali**, **osiwiali**, **zgrubiali**, and so on. With intransitive **zmoknąć** *get soaked*, the superficially passive form **zmoknięty** *soaked* has the same effect as an adjective of resultant state: **zmoknięte ubranie** *soaked-through clothing*.

VERBAL ADJECTIVES OF ABILITY

Many derived prefixed Imperfective verbs in **-a-** can form an adjective of ability or inability in **-alny**:

Infinitive	Verbal adjective of ability
sprawdzać *verify*	**sprawdzalny** *verifiable*
wymieniać *exchange*	**wymienialny** *exchangeable*
odwołać *revoke (pf)*	**nieodwołalny** *irrevokable*
przemakać *seep through*	**nieprzemakalny** *waterproof*

Occasionally verbs of the second conjugation in **-i-**, and of the first conjugation in **-nę-**, will use the negated form of the Perfective passive participle as an adjective of *in*ability:

Occasionally verbs of the second conjugation in -i-, and of the first conjugation in -nę-, will use the negated form of the Perfective passive participle as an adjective of *in*ability:

okiełznać *bridle (pf)*	**nieokiełznany** *unbridled, irrepressible*
prześcignąć *surpass (pf)*	**nieprześcigniony** *unsurpassable*
ukoić *appease (pf)*	**nieukojony** *unappeasable*
uniknąć *avoid (pf)*	**nieunikniony** (*sic*) *unavoidable*
zwyciężyć *conque (pf)*	**niezwyciężony** *unconquerable*, and others

The sense of negative ability is also conveyed by the phrase **nie do** plus a Perfective verbal noun: **projekt nie do wykonania** *undoable project*, **sytuacja nie do wyobrażenia** *unimaginable situation*, **postawa nie do zrozumienia** *incomprehensible attitude*, and so forth.

VERBAL NOUNS

Most verbs can derive a noun for use in nominal positions in a sentence:

Ona pisze pracę doktorską. *Pisanie* **pracy doktorskiej zajmuje jej dużo czasu.** *She is writing a doctoral dissertation. The writing of the doctoral dissertation is taking up lots of her time.*

The verbal noun is of neuter gender. It is formed by adding the softening formant -*´* plus neuter-gender noun endings to a stem like that of the passive participle (whether or not that participle itself is formed). Before stem-final -**t**- or -**n**- (which softens to **ć** or **ń**, respectively), a preceding -**e**- or -**ě**- will remain unshifted, as in the NVpl. masc. pers. form of the passive participle:

Verb:	Passive participle:	Verbal noun:
nosić *carry*	**noszony noszeni**	**noszenie** *carrying*
pić *drink*	**pity pici**	**picie** *drinking*
piec *bake*	**pieczony pieczeni**	**pieczenie** *baking*
pisać *write*	**pisany pisani**	**pisanie** *writing*
robić *do*	**robiony robieni**	**robienie** *doing*
ściąć *cut down (pf)*	**ścięty ścięci**	**ścięcie** *cutting down*
uczyć *teach*	**uczony uczeni**	**uczenie** *teaching*
znaleźć *find*	**znaleziony znalezieni**	**znalezienie** *finding*

and so forth. Unlike in the NV masc. pers. pl. form of the passive participle, root-final **t** (**ć**) or **d** (**dź**) will go to **c, dz**, respectively:

chcieć *want*	**chciany chciani**	**chcenie** *wanting*
widzieć *see*	**widziany widziani**	**widzenie** *seeing*

Nominalizations of **iść** *go* are formed exceptionally:

pójść *go (pf)*	(pass. part. lacking)	**pójście** *going*
przejść *pass (pf)*	(pass. part. lacking)	**przejście** *passage*
przyjść *come (pf)*	(pass. part. lacking)	**przyjście** *arrival*, etc.

NOTES ON VERBAL NOUNS

a. Verbal nouns tend to retain the Dative, Instrumental, or Prepositional syntax of the verb from which they are derived. Additionally, if the base verb occurs with the particle **się**, then the verbal noun will generally retain **się**:

Base construction:	Nominalization:
nasycić się mięsem *sate oneself on meat-I*	**nasycenie się mięsem**
pisać ołówkiem *write with a pencil-I*	**pisanie ołówkiem**
rządzić krajem *rule a country-I*	**rządzenie krajem**
pomagać koledze *help a colleague-D*	**pomaganie koledze**
przeszkadzać handlowi *hinder trade-D*	**przeszkadzanie handlowi**

If the verb has Accusative syntax, the object noun will appear in the Genitive case:

czytać książkę *read a book-A*	**czytanie książki**
zająć miejsce *occupy a place-A*	**zajęcie miejsca.**

b. The subject of a nominalized verb may also appear in the Genitive, creating the possibility of ambiguity: **przekupienie prezydenta** *the bribing of/by the president.* If both subject and object are present, the second phrase will be expressed with **przez+A**: **zajęcia kraju przez wojsko** *the occupation of the country by the army.*

c. Some verbs, for example **iść** *go,* **mieć** *have,* **móc** *be able,* **usiąść** *sit down,* **umieć** *know how,* **woleć** *prefer,* do not form verbal nouns. Verbs which occur only in the 3rd pers. sg. impersonal tend not to form verbal nouns, for example **brakować** *be lacking,* **grzmieć** *thunder,* **wystarczyć** *be enough.* Often the existence of an independent noun in about the same meaning of the potential verbal noun will for all practical purposes prevent the formation of the verbal noun except in special circumstances.

Verb:	Possible verbal noun:	Noun usually used instead:
atakować *attack*	**atakowanie**	**atak** *attack*
biegać *run*	**bieganie**	**bieg** *race, course*
chcieć *want*	**chcenie**	**chęć** *desire,* **ochota** *willingness*
dotykać *touch*	**dotykanie**	**dotyk** *touch*
gwizdać *whistle*	**gwizdanie**	**gwizd** *whistle*
krzyczeć *shout*	**krzyczenie**	**krzyk** *shout*
lękać się *dread*	**lękanie się**	**lęk** *fear, dread*
lecieć *fly*	**lecenie**	**lot** *flight*
pracować *work*	**pracowanie**	**praca** *work, job*
rozwinąć *develop (pf)*	**rozwinięcie**	**rozwój** *development*

walczyć *struggle*	**walczenie**	**walka** *battle, struggle*
kupić *buy (pf)*	**kupienie**	**kupno** *purchase*
jechać *drive, ride*	**jechanie**	**jazda** *ride*
rekomendować	**rekomendowanie**	**rekomendacja** *recommendation*

and many more. The independent noun will still usually display the syntax of the original verb: **handlować zbożem** *trade in grain*, hence **handel zbożem.**

d. As noted above, the reflexive particle is often kept along with with the formation of the verbal noun:

Gwałtowne *zatrzymanie się* **samochodu obudziło wszystkich śpiących pasażerów.** *The violent stopping of the car awakened all the sleeping passengers.*

Po *zameldowaniu się* **poszliśmy do swoich pokoi.** *After signing in, we went to our rooms.*

However, **się** is not usually kept with verbs of personal grooming (as **myć się** *wash*, **czesać się** *comb*, **golić się** *shave*, **ubrać się** *dress*):

Golenie nie zajmuje mi zbyt dużo czasu. *Shaving doesn't take up too much of my time.*

The loss of **się** with the verbal noun suggests that the form has completely passed over to the status of a noun. Compare

Noun:	Verbal noun:
martwienie *worry*	**martwienie się** *worrying*
poświęcenie *dedication*	**poświęcenie się** *devoting oneself*
rozstanie *parting*	**rozstanie się** *taking leave of one another*

e. The prepositions **po+L** *after*, **przed+I** *before*, and **przy+L** *during* are often used with verbal nouns (usually Perfective after **po** and **przed**, Imperfective after **przy**) to form tense-expressions: **po wyjściu** *after leaving*, **przy wychodzeniu** *while leaving*, **przed wyjściem** *before leaving*.

f. A great many verbal nouns have acquired the status of independent nouns, for example, **cięcie** *surgical section*, **krzyżowanie** *intersection*, **mieszkanie** *apartment*, **odznaczenie** *honor, distinction*, **odzwierciedlenie** *reflection*, **promieniowanie** *radiation*, **przejście** *passage*, **spostrzeżenie** *observation*, **wyjaśnienie** *explanation*, **wyjście** *exit*, **wzniesienie** *promontory*, **zarządzenie** *edict*, **zdanie** *opinion*, **zgięcie** *bend, inflection*, **zgnębienie** *depression*, **życie** *life*, and many, many more.

g. The frequent use of verbal nouns is characteristic of heavy academic, journalistic, or bureaucratic style:

Powinniśmy poczuwać się do obowiązku *pójścia* **za głosem rodzącej się wątpliwości,** *rozejrzenia* **się w faktach,** *przemyślenia* **ich i** *zdobycia* **własną pracą własnego punktu** *widzenia.* *We ought to feel it our obligation to follow the voice of our burgeoning doubt, to cast about for the facts, to think them through and obtain by our own effort our own point of view.*

Jest rzeczą rzadką, aby nauka w stadium *powstawania* **nie była zmuszona do** *filozofowania* **dla** *wykrojenia* **sobie miejsca: ona się ustala przez** *odróżnianie się.* *It is a rare thing for a science in the stage of its development not to be forced to philosophize in order to carve out a place for itself: it is delineated through its being differentiated.*

Nevertheless, colloquial speech often employs verbal nouns. Many common syntactic constructions utilize verbal nouns as complements, for example, **trudny do wykonania** *difficult to execute*, **łatwe do zrealizowania**, *easy to realize*, **gotowy do wyjścia** *ready to leave*, **wart naśladowania** *worth imitating*; **nie do zrozumienia** *incomprehensible*, and so on. Additionally, see point e. above regarding the use of **przed** *before*, **przy** *during*, **po** *after*.

h.   Many verbs of offering, proposing, advising, forcing, etc. take verbal nouns in the complement, often substituting for a conditional phrase, for example:

Zaproponował mi zostanie do jutra. *He proposed that I stay until the next day.*

Zleciłem mu przetłumaczenie artykułu. *I commissioned to him the translation of the article.*

Odradzał mi zwlekanie z decyzją. *He advised me not to delay my decision.*

i.   Verbal nouns often occur in Polish after the preposition **do**, in situations where, based on English, one might expect the infinitive:

Zmusił mnie do powtórzenia całego kursu. *He forced me to repeat the entire course.*

To nie osobiste pobudki skłoniły go do zawarcia ze mną znajomości. *It wasn't personal motives that inclined him to strike up an acquaintance with me.*

Zachęcał mnie do uczestniczenia w konferencji. *He encouraged me to take part in the conference.*

j.   A common English use of the verbal noun tends to be avoided in Polish:

I'm surprised at his coming so late. **Dziwię się (mu), że tak późno przyszedł.**

Not: **!Dziwię się jego tak późnemu przyjściu.**

k. For some verbal nouns, the existence of a base verb is mainly hypothetical (even if sometimes given in dictionararies); see especially verbal nouns of installation: **zadrzewienie** *planting with trees,* **oflagowanie** *putting up flags,* **zwodociągowanie** *putting in sewer lines,* etc.

GRAMMATICAL VOICE

Overview

Grammatical voice refers to sentence point of view in sentences containing verbs that ordinarily are active-transitive, i.e. consist of a Nominative subject and an Accusative object. There are three derived voices in Polish (alongside the basic ACTIVE VOICE): passive, impersonal passive, and middle. Under PASSIVE VOICE, the former object becomes the subject; the former subject, if it is retained, is expressed with a preposition- or-case phrase. An example would be:

Active: **Profesor opublikował artykuł.** *The professor-N published the article-A.*

Passive: **Artykuł został opublikowany (przez profesora).** *The article-N was published (by the professor).*

Under IMPERSONAL PASSIVE VOICE, the object remains in the object position (and is expressed with the Accusative case), but there is no former subject. An example would be:

Przeczytano książkę. *The book-A was read; someone read the book.*

In such a sentence, because there is no underlying subject, it is impossible to express a subject with any kind of preposition-or-case phrase like **przez studenta** *by the student.*

MIDDLE VOICE is similar to impersonal passive voice in that there is no underlying subject; under middle voice, however, the former object becomes the present subject of the sentence. An example would be:

Lekcja się zaczyna. *The lesson-N is beginning.*

Note the use of **się** here as a marker of intransitivity. In this sentence, no one is "beginning" the lesson; the lesson is depicted as beginning on its own, according to such circumstances as a schedule of classes. The sentence qualifies as middle because the verb may also be used active-transitively without **się**, as in **Zaczynamy lekcję.** *We're beginning the lesson-A.*

Active, passive, impersonal-passive, and middle sentences are all employed to say pretty much the same kinds of things. There is no necessary difference in real-world states of affairs that would cause one to choose a passive construction over an active one. The choice among the voices is primarily regulated by stylistic considerations related to narrative strategy, i.e., to what one has just said or is about to say, or what one wishes to emphasize.

Passive Voice

Passive voice refers to a shift in the perspective of a transitive sentence (a sentence with a subject and a direct object), whereby the former object becomes the subject of a passive participle. The former subject, if it not simply omitted because its identity is obvious or non-essential, is expressed with a preposition- or case-phrase:

Active: *John wrote this article.* **Jan napisał ten artkuł.**
Passive: *This article was written by John.* **Ten artykuł został napisany przez Jana.**

Polish distinguishes between actional and statal passives, and also frequently makes use of changes in word order to effect a change in sentence perspective which is the rough stylistic equivalent of passive voice.

The Actional Passive

The canonical passive in Polish is the ACTIONAL, utilizing the link verb **zostać zostanę zostaniesz** *get, become (pf)* plus the Perfective passive participle (in Perfective uses), or forms of **być** *be* plus the Imperfective passive participle (in Imperfective uses). According to the standard description, each of the three tenses of an active Imperfective sentence, and each of the two tenses of an active Perfective sentence, have corresponding passive constructions. The Perfective is used more often than the Imperfective.

Imperfective

	Active:	Passive
Pres.	**Jan czyta książkę.**	**Książka jest czytana przez Jana.**
	Jan reads (is reading) a book.	*The book is read (is being read) by Jan.*
Fut.	**Jan będzie czytał książkę.**	**Książka będzie czytana przez Jana.**
	Jan is going to read the book.	*The book is going to be read by Jan.*
Past	**Jan czytał książkę.**	**Książka była czytana przez Jana.**
	Jan read (was reading) a book.	*The book was (was being) read by Jan.*

Perfective

	Active:	Passive
Fut.	**Jan przeczyta książkę.**	**Książka zostanie przeczytana przez Jana.**
	Jan will read the book.	*The book will be read by Jan.*
Past	**Jan przeczytał książkę.**	**Książka została przeczytana przez Jana.**
	Jan read the book.	*The book was read by Jan.*

The canonical system may be elaborated on in various ways. For example, **bywać bywam bywasz** *be (iterative)* may be used as a link verb with Imperfective passive participles to convey the idea of repetitive action:

Te zwierzęta bywają regularnie poddawane eksperymentom. *These animals are regularly subjected to experiments.*

The imperfective link verb **zostawać zostaję zostajesz** *(impf), get, become* can be used with a passive participle, usually Imperfective, to describe a process:

Ten plan zostaje stopniowo realizowany. *That plan is gradually being realized.* Equals: **Ten plan jest w procesie stopniowego realizowania się.** *That plan is in the process of gradual realization.*

See also the distinction between:

Ci pracownicy zostają zwolnieni. *These workers are in the process of being released-perf. (all at once).*

Ci pracownicy zostają zwalniani. *These workers are being released-imperf. (in stages).*

The Statal Passive

The STATAL PASSIVE, which is inherently Imperfective in meaning (even though the participle itself is Perfective), utilizes **być** *be* as a link verb plus the Perfective passive participle. The sense is that of a resultant state, often the equivalent of perfect tenses in English. In the past tense, there is a suggestion that the state is no longer in effect:

Present: **Ten kraj jest zajęty.** *That country is (has just been) occupied.*
Past: **Ten kraj był zajęty.** *That country was (had been) occupied.*
Future: **Ten kraj będzie zajęty.** *That country will be (will have been) occupied.*

Compare the difference in import between the actional and statal passives in the following past-tense sentences:

Ten dom został pomalowany. *That house was painted; i.e. before it wasn't, now it is* (actional passive).

Ten dom był pomalowany. *That house was painted; i.e. it was once painted, but now it needs repainting* (statal passive).

Similarly, statal **Most był przerzucony przez rzekę** *A bridge had been thrown across the river* implies that the bridge is no longer in operation. By contrast, the same sentence expressed actionally, **Most został przerzucony przez rzekę**, suggests that the bridge is still standing and carrying traffic.

Irregularities in the Possibility for Passivization

Not every verb which takes the Accusative case can be used passively. For example, **mieć** *have* and **woleć** *prefer* have no passive participles; however, the roughly synonymous **posiadać** *possess* and **preferować** *prefer* do form passive participles. Many non-**się** Genitive-requiring verbs may form passive participles, for example, **nienawidzić** *hate*, **odmówić** *refuse*, **zabraniać** *forbid*. Dative-requiring verbs do not as a rule form passive participles. For example, from **zaimponować** + D *impress* one may not form **zaimponowany** *impressed*. Instrumental verbs of control (**kierować** *direct*, **manipulować** *manipulate*, **sterować** *steer*, **rządzić** *govern*) may, but other Instrumental verbs do not. Few dictionaries give such information.

Expressing the Original Subject

In a passive sentence, an original agentive subject is expressed with a prepositional phrase using **przez+A**:

Kennedy został zastrzelony przez Oswalda. *Kennedy was shot by Oswald.*

Lalka została napisana przez Prusa. *"Lalka" (The Doll) was written by Prus.*

Forces of nature and, especially, substances can be expressed with the Instrumental case:

Dom został obalony *wiatrem* (better: ***przez wiatr***). *The house was knocked over by the wind.*

Pola były pokryte *śniegiem*. *The fields were covered with snow.*

The Inverse-Word-Order, or de facto Passive

Alongside the above-described methods of expressing passive voice, in practice the effect of passive voice in Polish is most often created by reversing the order of subject and object, leaving the original grammar of the sentence intact. In this construction, called the INVERSE, the subject phrase is of necessity retained; it is placed in sentence-final position, while the complement phrase becomes placed in sentence-initial position. The verb continues to agree with the original subject:

Tę cechę posiada dużo czasowników. *This characteristic-A is possessed by many-N verbs.*

To samo powiedziała mi moja mama. *The same thing-A was told me by my mother-N.*

Okręt sprzedał zespół jego zubożałych właścicieli. *The ship-A was sold by the group of its impoverished owners.*

In the last sentence, in view of the masculine inanimate gender and hence the identical Nominative/Accusative forms of both subject and object, Polish relies on the logic of the real world to suggest who is selling what. Similarly, in **Wynik zdecydował przypadek**, one reasons that probably 'an accident determined the outcome' rather than the other way around.

For semi-transitive (oblique-case or prepositional) verbs, the inverse is often the only available means for achieving the stylistic effect of passivization, i.e., the exchange in narrative prominence of subject and complement:

Tym problemem zajmowało się już wielu uczonych. *This problem has already been taken up by many scholars.*

Nad tym zagadnieniem już nie będziemy zastanawiać się. *Over this question we will no longer linger.*

The Impersonal Passive

The impersonal passive falls into the category of impersonal or subjectless expressions in general (see Chapter 14). The impersonal passive is a construction for which there is no straightforward formal correspondent in English. It is usually translated in English as a passive, but it has the stylistic effect of an active, if subjectless, construction. In the Polish construction, the subject is intrinsically absent; the object remains in the Accusative, and does not become promoted to the position of subject. There are three kinds of impersonal passive constructions in Polish, the **się** construction, the **-no/-to** construction, and a construction using the neuter sg. past indicative.

1. In the impersonal passive **się** construction, the particle **się** takes the place, as it were, of the missing subject. The verb occurs in the 3rd pers. sg., and the object occurs in the Accusative case (or, if the verb is negated, in the Genitive). The verb is usually Imperfective:

    Tworzy się **tu wielkie dzieła sztuki.** *Great works of art are being created here.*

    Już *nie ogląda się* **tego filmu.** *That film is not watched any longer.*

    Verbs which occur with **się** in the given meaning of the verb cannot be used in the impersonal passive. For example, if the verb is **martwić się**, one may not say *Dużo się martwi o stopnie. One worries a lot about grades.*

2. The impersonal passive **-no/-to** construction is inherently past-tense in reference. It is formed by adding the ending **-o** to the stem of the passive participle, whether Imperfective or, usually, Perfective (and whether or not the verb otherwise forms a passive participle):

    Dawano **wiele przykładów.** *Many examples were given.*

    Przekręcono **klucz w drzwiach.** *The key was turned in the door.*

    Poinformowano **nas za późno.** *We were informed too late.*

    Wzięto **go pod przybranym nazwiskiem.** *He was apprehended under an assumed name.*

    Wyłączono **radio.** *The radio was turned off.*

    Teraz dopiero *otwarto* **letnią werandę.** *Only now had the summer porch been opened.*

The form in **-no/-to** may be made from almost any verb, even from most modal verbs:

Musiano już jechać. It was already necessary to leave (from **musieć** *have to*).

Miano czekać. One had to wait (from **mieć** *have, be supposed to*).

Chciano uczestniczyć. One wanted to participate (from **chcieć** *want*).

Among the few verbs which do not form the impersonal passive are **móc** *be able* and **pomóc** *help.*

In the past tense, the choice between the **się** and the **-no/-to** construction is often a matter of free choice:

Wymieniło się kilka nazwisk. Several names were mentioned.

or: *Wymieniono kilka nazwisk. (same meaning)*

There is a slight suggestion with the **-no/-to** construction that the implicit subject is masculine personal plural. Hence the second of the above sentences would not normally be used to refer to a real-life situation where it could be expected that a singular person or plural women had mentioned the names.

3. A neuter sg. past-tense indicative verb can be used to describe an event, usually violent in nature, in an impersonal passive way: **kopnęło go** *he was knocked against*, **sparaliżowało go** *he became paralyzed*, **szarpnęło go** *something jerked him*, and so on. See

Przechodnie chcieli zobaczyć, kogo przejechało. *The pedestrians wanted to see who had been run over.*

The underlying agent, typically representing some kind of natural force (not a car, as in the foregoing example), may appear in the Instrumental:

Okrętem trząsnęło falą. *The boat was shaken by a wave.*

Robotników poraziło prądem. *The workers were hit by an electric current.*

Drogi zasypało śniegiem. *The roads were covered in snow.*

4. Both the **się** and the **-no/-to** constructions can occur with semi-transitive (oblique-case and prepositional) verbs:

Długo czekano (czekało się) na taksówkę. *A taxi was waited-for for a long time.*

Niechętnie pomagano (pomagało się) ludziom. *People were being helped unwillingly.*

Verbs already occurring with **się** must choose the **-no/-to** construction in the past tense:

Martwiono się (not **martwiło się*) **o nas.** *We were being worried about.*

Middle Voice

Under MIDDLE VOICE, a usually inanimate object becomes the subject of a derived **się** verb, as in

Koncert już się zaczął. *The concert has already begun.*

Burza się zbliża. *The storm is drawing close.*

Mecz kończył się remisem. *The match finished in a tie.*

Pociąg powoli się zatrzymywał. *The train was slowly coming to a stop.*

In all the above instances, the verb exists in its basic form without **się**. In the middle construction, there is no implicit subject. No one is moving the storm or the train forward; they are moving under their own power. The difference between the middle and the impersonal passive may be seen in the following comparison:

Middle:	**Woda się gotuje.** *Water is boiling.*
Impersonal passive:	**Wodę się gotuje.** *Water is being boiled.*

Note the use of the Nominative case in the first sentence, and the Accusative in the second. See also

Middle:	**Ta brama się nie otwiera.** *This gate doesn't open.*
Impersonal passive:	**Tej bramy się nie otwiera.** *One doesn't open this gate.*

The Genitive complement **tej bramy** after the negated verb in the impersonal passive sentence contrasts with the Nominative subject **ta brama** in the middle. The middle construction is mostly limited to verbs of physical process and change of state. Middle-voice candidates like

Ta książka dobrze się sprzedaje. *This book is is selling well.*

Ta praca szybko mi się pisze. *Writing this assignment is going quickly for me.*

can also, and probably better, be expressed as impersonal passives **Tę książkę dobrze się sprzedaje.** or **Tę pracę szybko mi się pisze.**

Middle Verbs of Mental Agitation

A fairly large number of verbs referring to mental agitation usually occur with **się**, to such an extent that the form with **się** can be considered basic with them, while the form without **się** can be considered derived. Some examples:

bać się *be afraid*	**nudzić się** *be bored*
cieszyć się *be glad*	**rozczarować się** *be disappointed (pf)*
denerwować się *get upset*	**śmiać się** *laugh*
dziwić się *be surprised*	**wstydzić się** *be ashamed*
martwić się *worry*	**zachwycać się** *be enthralled*
obrażać się *be offended*	**żalić się** *complain*
niepokoić się *be concerned*, and many others	

Of the above, **bać się** *be afraid* and **wstydzić się** *be embarrassed* never occur without **się**. Such verbs have developed their own individual ways of connecting with complements. For example, **bać się** and **wstydzić się** take the Genitive; **cieszyć się** and **śmiać się** take z+G; **dziwić się** takes the Dative; **martwić się** and **niepokoić się** take either the Instrumental or o+A; **obrazić**

się takes **na**+A; **rozczarow(yw)ać się** takes the Instrumental; and so on. Compare:

Martwię się stopniami syna. *I'm worried by my son's grades.*

Martwią mnie stopnie syna. *My son's grades worry me.*

The active-transitive construction, without **się**, sounds slightly more formal or distant and less engaged.

Functions of *SIĘ*

Some of the following functions of **się** have also been been treated above under the discussion of grammatical voice.

The verbal particle **się**, literally meaning 'self', occurs in many different functions, the most important of which are listed below. The particle **się** may not appear in clause-initial position; in colloquial Polish, it resists occurring in clause-final position as well. The less formal the style, and the shorter the verb, the more likely it is that **się** will appear before the verb. When in the vicinity of an enclitic (unstressed) personal pronoun, **się** will usually follow the pronoun: **On *mi się* nie podoba.** *I don't like him.* On occasion, two proximate occurrences of **się** will be collapsed into one:

Staram się ogolić (się). *I'm trying to shave.*

W zimie dużo się jeździ na nartach i (się) czyta. *In the winter one skis and reads a lot.*

Jak się jej bliżej przypatrzy (się), sytuacja zupełnie inaczej wygląda.
When one looks at it more closely, the situation appears completely different.

The following types of formal reflexives are not semantically hermetic, but flow into one another.

1. LITERAL REFLEXIVES. This is the main use in which **się** may be replaced for emphasis with the long-form reflexive **siebie**.

   Kot się myje. *The cat is washing itself.*

   Skaleczyłem się w palec. *I hurt my finger.*

   Najpierw wykąpię się, później się ogolę. *First I'll bathe, later I'll shave.*

   One could also say: **Kot myje siebie** *The cat is washing itself;* etc.

2. Reciprocal-action reflexives, where **się** has the sense of 'each other':

   Spotykamy się w tej samej kawiarni, co zawsze. *We're meeting in the same cafe as always.*

   Nie kłóćmy się, dobrze? *Let's not quarrel, all right?*

   Poznaliśmy się na konferencji w Szczyrku. *We met at a conference in Szczyrk.*

   Poznali się latem, pobrali się w jesieni, a rozwiedli się na wiosnę. *They met in the summer, got married in the fall and divorced in the spring.*

3. Figurative reflexives, in which the **się** may no longer felt to be literally reflexive, but one can still see the semantic basis of the derivation:

   Budzę się o szóstej. *I wake at 6:00.*

   Czuję się dobrze w jego towarzystwie. *I feel good in his company.*

   Przewróciłem się jadąc rowerem. *I took a spill while riding my bike.*

   Uczę się historii i biologii. *I'm studying history and biology.*

   Ona poświęciła się nauce. *She devoted herself to science.*

   That these uses are figurative can be detected from the inability to replace **się** with **siebie. Ona poświęciła siebie nauce** could possibly mean that she donated her body to science.

4. UNDERGOER AND IMPERSONAL REFLEXIVES, similar in sense to passives:

   Nie da się tego zrobić. *That can't be done.*

   Lekarz zawze się znajdzie. *A doctor can always be found.*

   Nazywam się Paweł Warski. *I am called Paweł Warski.*

   Zraniłem się o gwóźdź. *I got injured on a nail.*

5. REFLEXIVES OF SIGNING IN OR IDENTIFICATION:

   Niech państwo się tu podpiszą. *Please sign here.*

   Pan musi się najpierw zameldować. *You have to register first.*

   Wylegitymowałem się prawem jazdy. *I identified myself by showing my driver's license.*

6. MIDDLE REFLEXIVES, where a transitive verb has become intransitive by the addition of **się**. See also above under Middle Voice. The subject is typically inanimate:

   Godzina wyjazdu już się zbliża. *The hour of departure is drawing close.*

   Pociąg nagle zastrzymał się. *The train suddenly came to a stop.*

   Przedstawienie zaczyna się (kończy się) wpół do dziewiątej. *The performance begins (ends) at 8:30.*

   Sytuacja wreszcie wyjaśniła się. *The situation finally cleared up.*

   Ten wykład wydłuża się w nieskończoność. *This lecture is stretching out into eternity.*

7. REFLEXIVE MIDDLES OF APPEARANCE OR PROPERTY:

   Ten rzeczownik nie odmienia się. *This noun doesn't decline.*

   Śnieg się topi a drzewa się zielenią. *The snow is melting and the trees are turning green.*

   Jej poezja cechuje się pozorną prostotą. *Her poetry is characterized by an illusory simplicity.*

   Sylwetki domów wyłaniały się z mroku. *The silhouettes of the houses emerged from the darkness.*

Lampa się pali (dymi). *A lamp is burning (smoking).*

8. REFLEXIVE MIDDLES OF MENTAL AGITATION (see also above under Grammatical Voice: Middle Verbs of Mental Agitation).

Cieszę się, że wreszcie przyjechałam. *I'm glad I've finally arrived.*

Dziwię się, że możesz tak spokojnie tam siedzieć. *I'm surprised that you can sit there so calmly.*

Wszyscy zachwycają się jego najnowszą poezją. *Everyone is enthralled by his latest poetry.*

Obraziła się na wszystko, co powiedziałem. *She took offense at everything I said.*

9. DEPERSONALIZED REFLEXIVES. The particle **się** may be added to essentially any non-**się** verb, including the verb **być** *to be*, to create a verb with an indefinite, although implicitly personal, subject. Grammatically speaking, it is as though **się** becomes the subject of a 3rd-pers. sg. neuter verb. A verb, if transitive, remains transitive, i.e. takes Accusative complements (or, if negated, Genitive complements). Note the difference between

Middle: **Kawa się gotuje.** *The coffee-N is boiling.*
Negated: **Kawa się nie gotuje.** *The coffee-N is not boiling.*

Impersonal: **Kawę się gotuje.** *Coffee-A is being boiled.*
Negated: **Kawy się nie gotuje.** *One doesn't boil coffee-G.*

Za moich czasów dużo się mówiło o tym. *In my day there was a lot of talk about that.*

Przyjemnie się pracuje w tym zakładzie. *One works pleasantly (it's pleasant to work) in this shop.*

Ciężko się z nim rozmawia. *It's difficult having a conversation with him.*

Jak się nie ma co się lubi, to się lubi, co się ma. *If you don't have what you like, then you like what you have.*

The depersonalized **się** construction is used especially frequently in forming questions of the type:

Jak tam się jedzie? *How does one get there?*

Jak się wymawia (pisze) to słowo? *How does one pronounce (spell) that word?*

Co się mówi w takiej sytuacji? *What does one say in such a situation?*

This construction translates both English impersonal *one* and the English informal impersonal *you*:

Przy takiej chorobie nie daje się zimnych okładów. *With such an illness one doesn't administer cold compresses.*

Jak się zaniedba katar, to można dostać zapalenie płuc. *If you neglect a cold, you can get pneumonia.*

10. REFLEXIVE VERBS OF SEEMING OR APPEARANCE, usually impersonal:

Wydawało się, że była gotowa wyjść. *It seemed she was ready to leave.*

Okazuje się, że ona ma niezwykły talent. *It turns out that she has an exceptional talent.*

The depersonalized **się** construction occurs especially often in combination with a "Dativized" subject. This construction sounds best when referring to involuntary acts or when disclaiming responsibility:

Dobrze dzisiaj spałem. *I slept well today* → **Dobrze mi się dzisiaj spało.**

Tak tylko powiedziałem. *I only said that (i.e., I didn't mean it)* → **Tak mi się tylko powiedziało.**

11. VERBS OF DISPERSAL OR CONGREGATION:

Goście zaczynają się schodzić. *The guests are beginning to gather.*

Sława jej rozeszła się szeroko. *Her fame was widely disseminated.*

Rozstajemy się na zawsze. *We are parting forever.*

12. VERBS OF SURFEIT IN **na- + się**:

W młodości naczytałem się powieści historycznych. *I read plenty of historical novels in my youth.*

On doszczętnie się nachlał. *He got roaring drunk.*

Naprawdę najadłem się. *I'm really stuffed.*

No, nagadałem się u ciebie. *Well I guess I've talked your ear off.*

13. The addition of **prze- się** to a verb of motion creates a verb in the sense of motion for its own pleasure:

Przejdźmy się w kierunku miasta. *Let's take a walk in the direction of town.*

Chętnie bym się przejechał na koniu. *I'd gladly go horseback riding.*

14. Many verbs occur only, or almost exclusively, with **się**. Here is a partial list. Observe that a number of these verbs refer to diffuse actions (**gramolić się** *clamber*, **mizdrzyć się** *cajole*, **rozpłakać się** *burst into tears*, etc.). Verbs are cited in the Imperfective, except where noted.

bać się *be afraid*	**jąkać się** *stammer*
błąkać się *wander around*	**kłaniać się** *bow, greet*
czaić się *lurk*	**kwapić się** *be eager for*
domagać się *demand*	**lenić się** *dilly-dally*
domyślać się *guess*	**lęgnąć się** *breed, hatch*
dowiedzieć się *find out (pf)*	**lękać się** *fear*
dziać się *happen*	**lubować się** *delight in*
gnieździć się *nest*	**łajdaczyć się** *lead dissolute life*
gramolić się *clamber*	**mizdrzyć się** *cajole*
iskrzyć się *sparkle*	**modlić się** *pray*

nachlać się *get soused (pf)*
nadąsać się *put on airs (pf)*
napić się *have a drink (pf)*
obawiać się *fear*
odzywać się *respond*
opiekować się *take care of*
panoszyć się *lord it over someone*
parać się *dabble in*
pastwić się *wreak malice on*
piąć się *climb*
podobać się *be pleasing*
pojawiać się *appear*
porozumieć się *come to an understanding (pf)*
posługiwać się *make use of*
potykać się *slip, stumble*
pozbywać się *get rid of*
przyglądać się *observe*
przypatrzeć się *have a look at (pf)*
przysłuchiwać się *listen carefully*
przysłużyć się *render a service (pf)*
rozglądać się *look around*
rozpłakiwać się *burst into tears*
rozpływać się *flow away*
rozsiąść się *settle down comfortably (pf)*
rozsłuchać się *listen attentively (pf)*
skarżyć się *complain*
spodziewać się *expect*
spóźniać się *be late*

srożyć się *rage*
stać się *become (pf)*
starać się *try*
śmiać się *laugh*
śnić się *appear in dream*
tlić się *smoulder*
troszczyć się *care about*
trudnić się *be engaged in*
tułać się *rove, wander*
ulotnić się *decamp (pf)*
upierać się *be stubborn, persist*
uśmiechać się *smile*
wahać się *vacillate*
wałęsać się *wander*
wdzięczyć się *be alluring*
wpatrywać się *stare at*
wstydzić się *be embarrassed*
wygłupiać się *make fool of self*
wyspać się *have a good sleep (pf)*
zakochać się *fall in love (pf)*
zapalić się *become enthusiastic (pf)*
zdarzyć się *happen (pf)*
zderzać się *collide*
zgadzać się *agree*
zjawić się *turn up (pf)*
znoić się *toil*
zżyć się *grow accustomed to (pf)*
zżymać się *flinch*
żalić się *complain*, and many more

SOME VERBAL PARADIGMS

Following are some verbal paradigms for a) the prefixally Perfective verb **pisać napisać** *write (impf/pf)* and b) the suffixally Imperfective verb **zająć zajmować** *occupy (pf/(impf)*. These paradigms omit possible formations with the particle **się** (such as reflexives, middles, impersonals, verbal nouns), which would roughly double the number of forms.

pisać napisać *write (impf/pf)*

Imperfective

	Present			Imperative	
	Sg.	Pl.		Sg.	Pl.
1.p.	piszę	piszemy			piszmy
2.p.	piszesz	piszecie		pisz	piszcie
3.p.	pisze	piszą			

Past

Sg.		Pl.	
Masc.	Fem.	Masc. pers.	Other pl.
1.p. pisałem	pisałam	pisaliśmy	pisałyśmy
2.p. pisałeś	pisałaś	pisaliście	pisałyście
3.p. pisał	pisała	pisali	pisały

Neut. **pisało**

Future

Sg.	Pl.		
Masc.	Fem.	Masc. pers.	Other pl.
1.p. będę pisał*	będę pisała	będziemy pisali	będziemy pisały
2.p. będziesz pisał	będziesz	będziecie pisali	będziecie pisały
3.p. będzie pisał	będzie pisała	będą pisali	będą pisały

Neut. **będzie pisało**

* Optionally: **będę pisać**, etc.

Conditional

Masc.	Fem.	Masc. pers.	Other pl.
1.p. pisałbym	pisałabym	pisalibyśmy	pisałybyśmy
2.p. pisałbyś	pisałabyś	pisalibyście	pisałybyście
3.p. pisałby	pisałaby	pisaliby	pisałyby

Neut. **pisałoby**

Perfective

Present		Imperative	
Sg.	Pl.	Sg.	Pl.
1.p. napiszę	napiszemy		napiszmy
2.p. napiszesz	napiszecie	napisz	napiszcie
3.p. napisze	napiszą		

Past

Sg.		Pl.	
Masc.	Fem.	Masc. pers.	Other pl.
1.p. napisałem	napisałam	napisaliśmy	napisałyśmy
2.p. napisałeś	napisałaś	napisaliście	napisałyście
3.p. napisał	napisała	napisali	napisały

Neut. **napisało**

Conditional

	Masc.	Fem.	Masc. pers.	Other pl.
1.p.	napisałbym	napisałabym	napisalibyśmy	napisałybyśmy
2.p.	napisałbyś	napisałabyś	napisalibyście	napisałybyście
3.p.	napisałby	napisałaby	napisaliby	napisałyby

Neut. napisałoby

Participles and verbal substantives

Imperfective adjectival
piszący -a -e

Imperfective verbal	Perfective verbal
piszac	napisawszy

Imperfective passive	Perfective passive
pisany -a -e	napisany -a -e

Imperfective impersonal	Perfective impersonal
pisano	napisano

Imperfective verbal noun	Perfective verbal noun
pisanie	napisanie

zająć zajmować *occupy (pf/impf)*

Perfective

	Future		Imperative		
	Sg.	Pl.	Sg.	Pl.	
1.p.	zajmę	zajmiemy			zajmijmy
2.p.	zajmiesz	zajmiecie	zajmij	zajmijcie	
3.p.	zajmie	zajmą			

Past

	Sg.		Pl.	
	Masc.	Fem.	Masc. pers.	Other pl.
1.p.	zająłem	zajęłam	zajęliśmy	zajęłyśmy
2.p.	zająłeś	zajęłaś	zajęliście	zajęłyście
3.p.	zajął	zajęła	zajęli	zajęły

Neut. zajęło

Conditional

	Masc.	Fem.	Masc. pers.	Other pl.
1.p.	zająłbym	zajęłabym	zajęlibyśmy	zajęłybyśmy
2.p.	zająłbyś	zajęłabyś	zajęlibyście	zajęłybyście
3.p.	zająłby	zajęłaby	zajęliby	zajęłyby

Neut. zajęłoby

Imperfective

Present

	Sg.	Pl.
1.p.	**zajmuję**	**zajmujemy**
2.p.	**zajmujesz**	**zajmujecie**
3.p.	**zajmuje**	**zajmują**

Imperative

	Sg.	Pl.
1.p.		**zajmujmy**
2.p.	**zajmuj**	**zajmujcie**

Past

	Sg.		Pl.	
	Masc.	Fem.	Masc. pers.	Other pl.
1.p.	**zajmowałem**	**zajmowałam**	**zajmowaliśmy**	**zajmowałyśmy**
2.p.	**zajmowałeś**	**zajmowałaś**	**zajmowaliście**	**zajmowałyście**
3.p.	**zajmował**	**zajmowała**	**zajmowali**	**zajmowały**

Neut. **zajmowało**

Future

	Sg.		Pl.	
	Masc.	Fem.	Masc. pers.	Other pl.
1.p	**będę zajmował***	**będę zajmowała**	**będziemy zajmowali**	**będziemy zajmowały**
2.p.	**będziesz zajmował**	**będziesz zajmowała**	**będziecie zajmowali**	**będziecie zajmowały**
3.p.	**będzie zajmował**	**będzie zajmowała**	**będą zajmowali**	**będą zajmowały**

Neut. **będzie zajmowało**

*Optionally: **będę zajmować**, etc.

Conditional

Sg. Pl.

	Masc.	Fem.	Masc. pers.	Other pl.
1.p.	**zajmowałbym**	**zajmowałabym**	**zajmowalibyśmy**	**zajmowałybyśmy**
2.p.	**zajmowałbyś**	**zajmowałabyś**	**zajmowalibyście**	**zajmowałybyście**
3.p.	**zajmowałby**	**zajmowałaby**	**zajmowaliby**	**zajmowałyby**

Neut. **zajmowałoby**

Participles and substantives

Imperfective adjectival
zajmujący -a -e

Imperfective verbal
zajmując

Perfective verbal
zająwszy

Imperfective passive
zajmowany -a -e

Perfective passive
zajęty -a -e

Imperfective impersonal
zajmowano

Perfective impersonal
zajęto

Imperfective verbal noun
zajmowanie

Perfective verbal noun
zajęcie

Chapter 13

Uses of the Cases

KINDS OF CASE USES

There are too many possible noun-functions in sentences, and too few Polish cases, for each noun-function to be associated with a specific case. Instead, the same case may be used to express different functions, and different functions may be expressed not only by case-endings alone but also with prepositions plus cases. By and large, prepositions serve to make general case meanings more specific. As a rough characterization, one may distinguish among (a) "bare" or basic syntactic uses of cases; (b) governed uses of cases, including especially uses after prepositions and verbs; (c) idiomatic uses of cases, often figurative extensions of the basic case-use, used to express adverbial ideas. For example, the Genitive case is used BASICALLY to express noun-to-noun relationships, as in **dom** *ojca* *house of father, father's house.* Additionally, the Genitive is GOVERNED (required) after certain prepositions and verbs, as in **bez** *wody without water-G*, or **słucham** *muzyki I'm listening to music-G.* Finally, the Genitive occurs IDIOMATICALLY, as in the expressions of dates; see **pierwszego maja** *on the first of May.*

SURVEY OF THE CASES AND THEIR MAIN USES

THE NOMINATIVE CASE

Because of its basic naming function, the Nominative case is used as the form of noun citation in dictionaries and glossaries. It has the following main uses:

1. Subject of a sentence:

   Adam słucha. *Adam is listening.*

   Pada deszcz. *Rain is falling.*

   Gdzie jest moja książka? *Where is my book?*

2. Complement of the introducing or naming phrases **to jest** *that is*, **to są** *those are*, and **oto** *here is/are* (the last item usually without **jest/są**):

   To jest mój brat. *That is my brother.*

   To są moje okulary. *Those are my eyeglasses.*

   To był ciekawy referat. *That was an interesting talk.*

   To będzie najlepsza sztuka sezonu. *That will be the best play of the season.*

   Oto nasza kuchnia. *Here's our kitchen.*

3. Both sides of a **to (jest)/to (są)** or **oto** equational sentence:

    Ten pan to (jest) mój znajomy. *That man is my acquaintance.*

    Maria to moja najlepsza przyjaciółka. *Maria is my best friend.*

    Oto is summative in meaning:

    Być albo nie być: oto pytanie. *To be or not to be: that's the question.*

    > For most intents and purposes, the constructions with **to jest/to są/oto** are the only ones in which two separate noun phrases in the Nominative case will be found under the domination of the same verb (usually, **być**). Predicate nouns are normally expressed with the Instrumental case; see further below.

4. Predicate adjectives (mainly, adjectives following **być** *be,* **wydawać się** *seem,* **robić się** *turn, become,* **stawać się** *become*):

    Twoja córka jest bardzo zdolna. *Your daughter is very talented.*

    Czy to krzesło jest zajęte? *Is this chair taken?*

    Wydajesz się dziś inny. *You seem different today.*

    Ostatnio zrobiłeś się okropnie nerwowy. *You've become awfully nervous lately.*

5. Adjectives appositive to the subject:

    On przyszedł jako pierwszy. *He was the first to arrive.*

    Siedział nieruchomy, głęboko dotknięty jej słowami. *He sat motionless, deeply touched by her words.*

    > In general, appositive nouns and adjectives agree in case with the referred-to noun. See
    >
    > **Znaleźli go leżącego na podłodze.** *They found him-A lying-A on the floor.*
    > **Zabijaki bały się jej jak ognia.** *Rabble-rousers feared her like fire-G.*
    > **Ufam mu jak własnemu bratu.** *I trust him like my own brother-D.*
    > **Mówicie o nim jako o już nie żyjącym.** *You speak about him as if no longer alive.*

6. In single-word sentences used to set a scene:

    Szarość. *Grayness (reigns everywhere).*

    Jesień. Desczcz. *It's autumn. It's raining.*

    Nuda. *Boredom (fills the scene).*

7. In predicative questioning sentences beginning with **jaki** *what kind,* **który** *which,* **czyj** *whose:*

Jaki to jest samochód? *What kind of car is that?*
Czyja to była owca? *Whose sheep was that?*
Który to był rok? *Which year was that?*

Note also the use of the Nominative in the phrase **co za** *what sort of*:

Co to za człowiek (ludzie)? *What sort of man is that (people are they)?*
Co to było za zebranie? *What kind of meeting was that?*
Co za kompromitacja. *What a disgrace.*

8. In exclamations like

Jaki piękny wikok! *What a pretty sight!*
Jaki ty jesteś mądry! *How smart you are!*
Wspaniały pomysł! *Excellent idea!*
Cud! *It's a miracle!*

9. In comparisons after **jak**:

Ona nie jest tak wymagająca, jak ja. *She is not as demanding as I am.*

10. As a form of direct address, instead of the Vocative:

Marek! Chodź tu! *Marek! Come here!*
Maria! Tak się cieszę, że cię widzę. *Maria-! I'm so happy to see you.*

11. In titles, names, and other quotation forms:

Mam na imię Marek (or: **Jestem Marek**). *My name is Marek (I'm Marek).*
Nazywam się Zenon Zieliński. *My name is Zenon Zielinski.*
Przezywamy go Grubas. *We nickname him Fatso.*
Czytamy powieść "Trędowata". *We're reading the novel The Leper-N.*
but: **Czytamy "Trędowatą".** *We're reading The Leper-A.*
Przybył do wyspy Formoza. *He arrived at the island of Formosa.*
but: **Przybył do Formozy.** *He arrived at Formosa.*

THE GENITIVE CASE

The Genitive is possibly the Polish case most diversified as to use. It is the most frequently occurring of the cases after the Nominative and Accusative. Its basic use is to express various meanings of "of" in noun-to-noun relations, including most importantly the notion of possession broadly speaking. Here is a review of the most important uses of the Genitive case:

ADNOMINAL GENITIVE

1. The Genitive expresses various senses of "of" in noun-to-noun relations. This is called the "adnominal" use, because the noun in the Genitive oc-

curs next to another noun, which the noun in the Genitive modifies in some way.

a. Possession, ownership, authorship:

książka studenta *student's book*
artykuł profesora *professor's article*
mieszkanie Państwa Śliwińskich *Mr. and Mrs. Sliwinski's apartment*
film nieznanego reżysera *film of (by) an unknown director*

b. Familial or friendly relationship:

mąż siostry *sister's husband*
przyjaciel Jurka *Jurek's friend*
narzeczony mojej siostry *my sister's fiancé*
syn brata sąsiada *neighbor's brother's son*

It is considered much less elegant to place the Genitive of possession before the noun possessed, as in English; hence one should say

To jest aparat Krysi. *That's Krysia's camera.*

not: **!To jest Krysi aparat.**

Placement before the noun is possible, although not obligatory, when emphasis is intended, as in

To jest Krysi aparat, a nie Zosi. *That's Krysia's camera, and not Zosia's.*

---

c. Part or component of:

ściany domu *walls of the house*
ostrze noża *blade of the knife*
brzeg rzeki *bank of river*
sedno rzeczy *heart of the matter*
pierwsza część powieści *first part of the novel*
koniec filmu *end of the film*

d. Aspect or feature of:

perła Adriatyku *pearl of the Adriatic*
szczyt impertynencji *the height of impertinence*
blask słońca *flash of sunlight*
cecha charakteru *trait of character*

e. Characteristic of:

marzenia młodości *aspirations of youth*
sen letniej nocy *dream of a summer's night*
typowa postawa mieszczucha *typical attitude of a Philistine*

f. Time of:

data urodzenia *date of birth*

wiek Oświecenia *age of the Enlightenment*
dni klęski *days of defeat*
pierwszy stycznia *1st of January*

g. Trait of:

człowiek charakteru *man of character*
osoba różnych talentów *a person of many talents*
ludzie złej woli *people of ill will*

> Traits are also expressed with **o** plus the Locative: **człowiek o wspaniałym charakterze** *man of an excellent character* and with **z** plus Instrumental: **człowiek z długą brodą** *man with a long beard.*

h. Rank or quality of:

koń wysokiej klasy *high-class horse*
wino najniższego gatunku *wine of the poorest sort*
pianista światowej sławy *pianist of world renown*

i. Kind of, about:

Dom Kultury *House of Culture*
gramatyka języka polskiego *grammar of the Polish language*
historia Rzymu *history of Rome*

j. Underlying subject of action:

szczekanie psów *barking of dogs*
rozwój gospodarki *development of the economy*
szum drzew *rustling of trees*
przemówienie ministra *minister's speech*

k. Underlying object of action:

czytanie książki *reading of the book*
objęcie władzy *assumption of power*
obalenie rządu *overthrow of the government*
wygranie meczu *winning of the match*

l. In phrases of the following type, related to the Genitive after quantifiers (see further below).

dużo interesującego *a lot of interest (that is interesting)*
coś ładnego *something pretty*
nic nowego *nothing new*

GENITIVE OF QUANTITY AND AMOUNT

2. Related to its use in expressing 'part of' is the use of the Genitive to express amount or number of:

a. Quantity or amount of (in either Gsg. or Gpl., depending on whether the noun is countable):

kawałek chleba *piece of bread-Gsg.*
kilo jabłek *kilogram of apples-Gpl.*
litr wódki *liter of vodka-Gsg.*

With food items caught or harvested in quantity, the Gsg. is traditionally used instead of the Gpl., hence **dziesięć ton śledzia** *ten tons of herring* (**buraka cukrowego** *sugar beet,* **porzeczki** *currant,* etc.), although the use of the Gpl. here is on the rise.

b. Container of:

szklanka mleka *glass of milk-Gsg.*
butelka wina *bottle of wine-Gsg.*
pudełko zapałek *box of matches-Gpl.*
kubek kawy *mug of coffee-Gsg.*

c. The Genitive, sg. or pl., is used after words like **dużo** *a lot,* **trochę** *a little,* **mało** *not much,* **dosyć** *enough,* **sporo** *a good number of,* **jeszcze** *some more,* **więcej** *more of,* **mniej** *less of:*

dosyć czasu *enough time*
dużo roboty *a lot of work*
jeszcze piwa *some more beer*
mało pieniędzy *not enough money*
mniej pieprzu *less pepper*
trochę masła *a little butter*
więcej rozsądku *more common sense*

d. The Genitive singular is usually used after fractionals like **pół** *half,* **półtora** *one and a half,* **procent** *percent* (see Chapter 8 for details):

pół jabłka *half an apple*
półtorej godziny *one and a half hours*
czterdzieści procent wolnego czasu *forty percent of free time*

e. The Genitive plural is used after indefinite numerals like **kilka** *several,* **wiele** *many,* **parę** *a couple:*

kilka pytań *several questions*
wiele dziedzin *many areas-of-study*
parę sztuk *a couple of pieces*

f. The Genitive plural is used after numbers 5 and above, and in all Genitive-like masculine-personal numerical expressions:

pięć jabłek *five apples*
sto egzemplarzy *a hundred copies*
trzech studentów *three students*

For more on numeral expressions, see Chapter 8.

PARTITIVE GENITIVE

g. The Genitive is often used with substances instead of the Accusative to indicate "a little" of the substance, as though **trochę** *a little* were present before the noun:

Nalać ci herbaty? *May I pour you some tea?*
Dodać cukru? *Should I add some sugar?*
Łyknij wody. *Swallow some water.*
Przywieźć piasku? *Should I bring some sand?*

GENITIVE OF NEGATION

3. The Genitive is obligatory instead of the Accusative after negated Accusative-requiring verbs:

Positive, with Accusative:	Negative, with Genitive:
Oglądam telewizję.	**Nie oglądam telewizji.**
I watch televison.	*I don't watch television.*
Mam pieniądze.	**Nie mam pieniędzy.**
I have money.	*I don't have money.*
Lubię banany.	**Nie lubię bananów.**
I like bananas.	*I don't like bananas.*
Pamiętam tę piosenkę.	**Nie pamiętam tej piosenki.**
I remember that song.	*I don't remember that song.*
Proszę otworzyć książki.	**Proszę nie otwierać książek.**
Please open your books.	*Please don't open your books.*

The Genitive is required even when the verb itself is not negated, but only an auxiliary:

Nie mogę sobie przypomnieć jego nazwiska. *I can't recall his name.*

Nie chcemy oglądać tego programu. *We don't want to watch that program.*

Nie mam czasu przeczytać twojego artykułu. *I don't have time to read your article.*

Nie wystarczy otworzyć listy, żeby chętni zaczęli się zapisywać. *It's not enough to start a list for volunteers to begin to sign up.*

Only in the instance of great distance from the negated auxiliary is the Accusative allowable, as possibly in

Gdybym nie musiał ciągle budzić w nim poczucie (better: **poczucia**) **odpowiedzialności...** *If I didn't constantly have to inspire in him a sense of responsibility...*

Nie uważałem za konieczne poznać ją (better: **jej**). *I didn't consider it necessary to meet her.*

Amerykanin nie czuje żadnej potrzeby znać język obcy. *An American does not feel any need to know a foreign language.*

In the last example, one could say that the Genitive is already "used up" in **potrzeby**, hence does not carry over to **język cudzy**.

The Genitive of Negation applies only to items felt to be direct objects. The Accusative pronoun in the expression **Głowa ją boli** *Her head hurts her* is not felt by all to be a direct object, hence **Głowa ją już nie boli** *Her head doesn't hurt her any longer* is acceptable. Similarly, Accusatives in complements of amount like **trwać dwie godziny** *to last two hours*, **przejechać dziesięć kilometrów** *to travel ten kilometers*, **ważyć tonę** *weigh a ton*, and so on, are not necessarily taken to be direct objects; hence possible:

Ta sztuka nie trwa nawet dwie godziny (instead of **dwóch godzin**). *That play doesn't last even two hours.*

Nie siedziałem tam nawet minutę (instead of **minuty**). *I didn't sit there for even a minute.*

Ten wóz nie waży nawet tonę (instead of **tony**). *That car doesn't even weigh a ton.*

If the verb ordinarily takes a case other than the Accusative, the case does not change under negation:

Ufam (nie ufam) tym ludziom. *I trust (don't trust) those people-D.*

Gardzę (nie gardzę) nimi. *I despise (don't despise) them-I.*

The complement of a negated Genitive-requiring verb will also be in the Genitive:

Używam (nie używam) soli. *I take (don't take) salt-G.*

GENITIVE AFTER NEGATED EXISTENTIALS

4. The Genitive is required after the negated existentials **nie ma** *there isn't any*, **nie będzie** *there won't be any*, **nie było** *there wasn't any*:

Nie ma mleka. *There is no milk.*

Nie było Jana. *Jan was not there.*

Nie będzie czasu. *There won't be enough time.*

Existential 'be' continues to take the Genitive after negated auxiliaries:

nie może być lepszego dowodu *there can't be any better proof*
nie powinno być żadnych trudności *there shouldn't be any difficulties*

Along with various other verbals (see further below), the existential verbal **brak** *there is a lack of* takes the Genitive:

Brak dobrych ludzi. *There aren't enough good people.*

Brak tu doświadczenia. *There's a lack here of experience.*

Brak piwa. *Out of beer.*

VERBS REQUIRING THE GENITIVE

5.   The Genitive is the second most frequent case of verbal complement after the Accusative. The Genitive is required after the following kinds of verbs. These categories are for convenience in arrangement only. In the end, each verb must be examined individually as for whether or not it takes the Genitive, and, occasionally, in which nuance.

a. Impersonal verbs of addition, loss, lack, sufficiency:

brakować *be lacking (3.p.only)*	**przysporzyć przysparzać** *add to*
pozby(wa)ć się *get rid of*	**uby(wa)ć** *decrease (3.p.only)*
przyby(wa)ć *gain (3.p.only)*	**wystarczyć** *be enough (pf, 3.p.only)*

As the first two of the following examples show, these verbs often occur in combination with the Dative of affected person:

Brakuje mi jeszcze jakiejś części. *I'm still lacking some part.*

Ta konstrukcja przysparza cudzoziemcom poważnych kłopotów *This construction causes foreigners serious difficulties.*

Wody przybywa w rzece. *Water's rising in the river.*

Naszych sił powoli ubywa. *Our forces are slowly waning.*

Wystarczy piwa na stu ludzi. *There's enough beer for a hundred people.*

b. Verbs of avoidance, fear, dislike, regret, some with **się**:

bać się *be afraid of*	**wstydzić się** *be ashamed*
nienawidzić *hate, loathe*	**wyrzec się wyrzekać się** *renounce*
lękać się *fear*	**zabronić zabraniać** *forbid*
obawiać się *dread*	**zaprzeć się zapierać się** *disavow*
odmówić odmawiać *refuse*	**żałować** *regret*
uniknąć unikać *avoid*	

Pies boi się ognia. *The dog is afraid of fire.*

Nienawidzę całej jego rodziny. *I hate his entire family.*

Nie trzeba lękać się prawdy. *There's no need to fear the truth.*

Obawiam się konsekwencji. *I dread the consequences.*

Mój mąż odmawia mi wszystkiego. *My husband refuses me everything.*

On wstydzi się swojej rodziny. *He's ashamed of his family.*

Zabraniam ci palenia w moim domu. *I forbid you to smoke in my house.*

Żałuję prawie wszystkiego w swoim życiu. *I regret almost everything in my life.*

c. Related to the foregoing use, a number of verbs in **się** expressing approach or avoidance take the Genitive, for example

chwytać się *grab for*   **strzec się strzegać się** *avoid*
spodziewać się *expect*   **trzymać się** *hold to.*

Tonący chwyta się brzytwy. *A drowning man will grasp at a razor.*
Ona spodziewa się dziecka. *She is expecting a child.*
Strzeż się go jak ognia. *Avoid him like fire.*
W tym domu trzymamy się tradycji. *In this house we maintain traditions.*

d. Verbs of need, want, desire, demand:

chcieć *want*   **pragnąć** *desire*
domagać się *demand*   **wymagać** *demand*
łaknąć *thirst for*   **żądać** *demand*
potrzebować *need*   **życzyć** *wish*

Czego jeszcze chcesz? *What else do you want?*
Ludzie domagają się swoich praw. *The people demand their rights.*
Potrzebuję twojej pomocy. *I require your assistance.*
Każdy pragnie szczęścia. *Everyone desires happiness.*
Wymagam absolutnej ciszy. *I demand absolute silence.*
Policjant zażądał prawa jazdy. *The policeman demanded my driver's license.*
Życzę ci powodzenia. *I wish you luck.*

e. Verbs of testing, trying, tasting, using:

doświadczyć *experience*   **uży(wa)ć** *use*
(s)kosztować *taste*   **zaczerpnąć** *draw an amount (pf).*
(s)próbować *try*

Skosztuj tych ciastek. *Taste these pastries.*
Spróbuj tego wina. *Try this wine.*
Czy używasz soli? *Do you use salt?*
Chcę zaczerpnąć świeżego powietrza. *I want to catch a breath of fresh air.*

f. A good number of verbs in **do-**, for example:

doby(wa)ć *gain by effort, extract*   **dołożyć dokładać** *lay on, add to*
dochodzić *arrive at by effort*   **dopuścić się dopuszczać się** *commit*
dochować *keep, preserve (pf)*   **dosiąść dosiadać** *mount a horse*
doczekać *live to see (pf)*   **dosięgać dosięgnąć** *reach up to*
doda(wa)ć *lend, impart*   **dotrzym(yw)ać** *keep, uphold*
doglądać *look after, supervise*   **dotyczyć** *concern*
dokazać *(pf) show off*   **dotykać dotknąć** *touch*
dokon(yw)ać *perform, execute*   **dozna(wa)ć** *experience (pf)*
dolać dolewać *pour on*   **dożyć** *live to see (pf)*, and others

Nareszcie dobyłem głosu. *At last I was able to speak.*

Powoli dochodzimy prawdy. *We're slowly getting at the truth.*

Czy możesz dochować tajemnicy? *Can you keep a secret?*

On nie doczeka (or **dożyje**) **starości.** *He won't live to see old age.*

Jego obecność dodała jej odwagi. *His presence gave her courage.*

Doglądam chorej matki. *I'm looking after my sick mother.*

Profesor dokonał czegoś naprawdę rewolucyjnego. *The professor accomplished something truly revolutionary.*

Dolej mi wody do wanny. *Pour me water for a bath.*

Dołożyć ci sznycla? *Can I give you another cutlet?*

Dopuszczasz się grzechu. *You're committing a sin.*

On zawsze dotrzymuje obietnicy. *He always keeps his promise.*

Doznałem prawdziwego rozczarowania. *I experienced true disappointment.*

g. Verbs of surfeit or completion in **na- się**, for example

naczytać się *read one's fill (pf)*   **napić się** *have a drink (pf)*
najeść się *eat one's fill (pf)*   **nauczyć się** *learn (pf)*

Napij się wody. *Have a drink of water.*

Najedliśmy się słodyczy. *We had our fill of sweets.*

Czego się dziś nauczyłeś w szkole? *What did you learn in school today?*

h. Verbs of accumulation in **na-**, for example

nab(ie)rać *gather, take on*   **nagad(yw)ać** *say plenty*
naby(wa)ć *acquire*   **nakupić** *buy up (pf)*

Statek powoli nabrał szybkości. *The ship slowly gathered speed.*

Trzeba nabyć należytego doświadczenia. *It's necessary to gain the necessary experience.*

Nagadał mi samych głupstw. *He told me nothing but a pile of nonsense.*

Nakupiłem jabłek. *I bought lots of apples .*

i. Various other verbs:

bronić *defend*   **szukać** *look for*
gratulować *+D +G congratulate on*   **udzielić udzielać** *give, impart, loan*
nabawić *+A +G (pf) be the cause of* **(na)uczyć** *+A +G teach*
pilnować *look after*   **(na)uczyć się** *study, learn*
poszukiwać *look for*   **ujść uchodzić** *escape, avoid (notice,*
słuchać *listen to, follow, obey*   *capture)*
                                         winszować *congratulate on +D +G.*

Muszę bronić swojego punktu widzenia. *I have to defend my point of view.*

To dotyczy ciebie i twojej rodziny. *It concerns you and your family.*

Gratuluję pani nowej posady. *I congratulate you on your new position.*

Pilnuj swojego dziecka. *Mind your child.*

Chętnie słucham muzyki klasycznej. *I like to listen to classical music.*

Życzę sobie, żebyś słuchała moich rad. *I recommend that you follow my advice.*

Szukam swojej torebki. *I'm looking for my handbag.*

Uczę się historii nowożytnej. *I'm studying modern history.*

Uczę Marię muzyki. *I'm teaching Maria music.*

Wątpię, czy ten bank udzieli nam kredytu. *I doubt whether that bank will give us credit.*

Złodziej uszedł sprawiedliwości. *The criminal escaped justice.*

VERBS WITH ALTERNATIVE GENITIVE/ACCUSATIVE SYNTAX

j. A number of verbs, including some listed above, allow complements in either the Genitive or the Accusative, sometimes differentiated according to meaning or level of formality. As a general trend, Accusative syntax is spreading at the expense of Genitive. One hears many instances of Accusative where prescriptive grammar still requires the Genitive. For example, one may encounter incorrect ***udzielić naganę** for **udzielić nagany** *deliver a reprimand*. Here are some examples:

bronić *defend* takes the Genitive according to grammar books, but in colloquial speech the Accusative is commonplace:

Muszę bronić swojego punktu widzenia (or, colloquially, **swój punkt widzenia**). *I have to defend my own point of view.*

The Accusative is normal in the sense 'defend in court', as in **bronić przestępcę** *defend a criminal*.

chcieć *want* tends to take the Accusative with specific objects and the Genitive with vague and abstract objects:

Czego chcesz? *What do you want (anyway)?*

Co chcesz? *What (specific thing) do you want?*

dosta(wa)ć *get* often takes the Genitive when referring to illnesses and states of mind, but otherwise takes the Accusative:

Dostałam znowu migreny. *I got a migraine-G again.*

Dostałem piątkę na egzaminie. *I got a five (an A) on the exam.*

Dostaniesz lanie. *You'll get a whipping-A.*

dostarczyć dostarczać *provide,* like **dostać,** normally takes the Accusative but often takes the Genitive when the object refers to an amount of something:

Miasto dostarcza mieszkańcom wody i gazu. *The city provides water-G and gas-G to the inhabitants.*

Compare with

Lisica dostarcza pożywienie młodym. *The mother fox provides food-A for its young.*

A number of verbs prefixed with **na-** take the Accusative with count or defininite nouns and the Genitive with substances and abstractions; see

nabyć nabywać *acquire, purchase:* **nabyć majątek** *acquire a fortune* but **nabyć doświadczenia** *acquire experience*

nabrać nabierać *gather in:* **nabrać siano** *gather in the hay,* **nabrać siana** *gather in some hay*

naciąć nacinać *nick+A, cut off a large amount+G:* **naciąć trzonek młotka** *put a nick in the hammer handle,* **naciąć kwiatów** *cut off a large amount of flowers*

and various other verbs in **na-**

oszczędzić oszczędzać *save* and **ustąpić ustępować** *yield* usually take the Accusative, but may take the Genitive in certain phrases:

W ten sposób oszczędzamy czas. *That way we'll save time-A.*

Oszczędź mi wstydu. *Spare me your embarrassment-G.*

Wieś powoli ustępuje miejsce (miejsca) miastu. *The countryside is slowly yielding its place to the town.*

prosić *ask* usually takes the Accusative: **Prosić gości do stołu.** *Ask one's guests to the table.* As a polite turn of phrase in the sense 'if you please', **proszę** properly takes the Genitive: **proszę sądu** *if the court pleases,* **proszę pani** (less elegantly: **panią**) *if you please, ma'am.*

przestrzec przestrzegać can take the Genitive in the sense 'observe rules'; it takes the Accusative in the sense 'warn'; hence **przestrzegać przepisów** *observe regulations-G* but **przestrzegać dziecko** *warn the child-A.*

słuchać *listen to* with the Accusative, although sometimes heard, is considered to be a serious grammatical error, outside of the frequently encountered (e.g. in stores) **Słucham panią?** *May I help you, madam?* The Genitive is normal: **Słucham muzyki.** *I'm listening to music.*

uchylić uchylać *tip, leave open halfway* is used with the Genitive when referring to hats and eyeglasses, but otherwise usually occurs with the

Accusative: **uchylić okno** *leave the window ajar,* **uchylić firankę** *draw back the curtain,* but **uchylić kapelusza (czapki)** *tip one's hat (cap),* **uchylić okularów** *put one's eyeglasses aslant.*

uży(wa)ć *use* tends to take the Genitive with substances and abstract nouns, but the Accusative with concrete nouns:

Trzeba będzie użyć siły. *It'll be necessary to use force-G.*

Czy mogę użyć twój ołówek? *May I use your pencil-A?*

or, stressing temporary use: **Czy mogę użyć twojego ołówka?** *May I make use of your pencil-G?*

The Genitive with this verb is never incorrect.

zapomnieć zapominać *forget* . In dictionaries and grammars one may encounter examples such as **Zapomniałem swojej łaciny.** *I've forgotten my Latin-G.* However, this verb increasingly is used with the Genitive only in the sense 'leave behind, forget to take', as in **zapomnieć pieniędzy** *forget one's money.* Its use with the Accusative in the sense 'be unable to remember' is becoming more frequent, as in

Zapomniałem swoją łacinę. *I've forgotten my Latin.*

Zapomniałem jego imię. *I've forgotten his first name.*

GENITIVE AFTER CERTAIN VERBALS

6. The Genitive is used as the case of complement after certain verbals (uninflected words with verbal force), for example, **brak** *there's a lack,* **szkoda** *it's a waste,* **trzeba** *it is necessary, one needs,* **potrzeba** *one will need,* **wstyd** *it's a shame,* **żal** +D+G *sorry for:*

Brak tu dobrej woli. *There's a lack of good will here.*

Szkoda pieniędzy i czasu. *It's a waste of money and time.*

Trzeba tu rozsądku. *We need a little common sense here.*

Potrzeba nam nowych inicjatyw. *We need some new initiatives.*

Wstyd mu swoich kłamstw. *He's ashamed of his lies.*

Nawet mi jej żal. *I even feel sorry for her.*

GENITIVE AFTER CERTAIN ADJECTIVES

7. The Genitive is used as the case of complement after certain adjectives, for example **chciwy** *greedy for,* **godny** *worthy of,* **pozbawiony** *deprived of,* **świadomy** *conscious of,* **wart** *worth,* **winien winna** *responsible for,* **żądny** *desirous of:*

To jest syn godny ojca. *That's a son worthy of his father.*

On jest chciwy pieniędzy. *He is greedy for money.*

Jestem świadom swoich braków. *I am conscious of my shortcomings.*

To śmiechu warte. *That's worth a laugh (i.e. that's ridiculous).*
Wszyscy artyści są żądni sukcesu. *All artists are desirous of success.*
On był winien nieszczęścia. *He was responsible for the misfortune.*

Note that **winien winna** may take the Accusative, the Genitive, or the Dative, depending on the nuance: 'owe', 'because of', 'responsible for', respectively.

GENITIVE AFTER PREPOSITIONS

8. The Genitive is required after more prepositions than any other case. Prepositions requiring the Genitive include the following:

a. Many basic prepositions:

bez *without*	**mimo** *despite*
blisko *near*	**naokoło** *all around*
dla *for (the good of)*	**naprzeciw(ko)** *across from*
do *to, up to, until*	**spośród** *from among, out of*
dokoła (dookoła) *(all) around*	**u** *at (someone's), near*
koło *around, about*	**według** *according to*
obok *next to, alongside*	**wobec** *regarding, in the face of*
od *from, away from, than*	**wokół, wokoło** *round, about*
oprócz, prócz *besides*	**wskutek** *as the result of*
podczas *during*	**wśród** *among, in the midst of*
podług *according to*	**z** *out of, from, down from, off, because of*
pośród *amongst*	**za** *in the sense during the time or reign of*

Here are some notes on certain Genitive-requiring prepositions:

dla+G

The preposition **dla** translates the 'for' of benefit: **Zrobiłem to dla ciebie.** *I did it for you.* **przejście dla pieszych** *passageway for pedestrians.* This preposition is expanding at the expense of the Dative case, which can also express benefit. Thus one may use either **łatwo ci** *it's easy for you* (usually without **jest**) or **to łatwe dla ciebie** (same meaning). Besides 'benefit', **dla** may be used to express emotion in regard to, or purpose: **podziw dla kogoś** *admiration for*, **szacunek dla rodziców** *respect for one's parents;* aim: **dla przyjemności** *for pleasure,* **dla zabawy** *for entertainment,* **dla urozmaicenia** *for variety,* **dla pieniędzy** *for money.*

A few adjectives combine naturally with **dla**: **dobry dla zdrowia** *good for the health,* **trudny dla cudzoziemca** *hard for a foreigner,* **pożyteczny dla większości** *useful for the majority;* **szkodliwy dla otoczenia** *harmful to the environment,* **wygodny dla nas** *comfortable for us.*

do+G

Besides the normal sense of directional 'to' (some place or someone) and 'into', **do**+G translates 'until': **do nocy** *until nightfall*, **do godziny pierwszej** *until one o'clock;* 'as many as': **do dwudziestu ludzi** *up to as many as 20 people;* and 'as far as': **dojechać do celu** *arrive at a destination.* **Do**+G can also translate 'for' in various senses: **chętny do roboty** *eager for work*, **gotowy do egzaminu** *ready for the exam*, **uczyć się do egzaminu** *study for an exam*, **woda do picia** *water for drinking*, **maszyna do szycia** *sewing machine.*

Many verbs and a few adjectives occur in phrasal combination with **do**+G, most of them logically, for example, **bliski do** *near to*, **dostosować się do** *adapt to*, **należeć do** *belong to*, **przyczynić się do** *contribute to*, **przygotować się do** *prepare oneself for*, **przyzwyczaić się do** *become accustomed to*, **telefonować do** *telephone to*, **wrócić do** *return to*, **zawołać do** *call to.*

od+G

Besides its normal uses in the senses 'from', 'away from', **od**+G translates 'for' in the sense 'for a time just past': **od miesiąca** *for (the past) month*, as well as 'since': **od najdawniejszych czasów** *since the oldest times.* **Od**+G also translates 'than' in comparisons like **wyższy od drzewa** *taller than a tree*, **starszy od siostry** *older than one's sister*, and so on. See also such uses as **odbiegać od normy** *depart from the norm*, **umierać od głodu** *die from starvation*, **lekarstwo od bólu głowy** *headache medicine*, **klucz od** (or **do**) **drzwi** *key to the door.*

A number of verbs and a few adjectives occur naturally with complements in **od**+G, for example **daleki od** *far from*, **ocalić od** *save from*, **wrócić od** *return from*, **odchodzić od** *leave from*, **odsunąć się od** *move away from*, **otrzymać od** *receive from*, and so on.

u+G

The preposition **u**+G is used most frequently to express 'at a person's house or place of business': **u rodziców** *at on's parents;* **u Marty** *at Marta's*, **u siebie w domu** *in one's own home*, **u fryzjera** *at the hairdresser's*, **u adwokata** *at the lawyer's.* It can also mean 'according to one's ways': **u nas** *in our country, in our parts;* **u Anglików** *among the English;* 'attached to': **u pasa** *at one's belt;* 'toward the end of': **u schyłku wieku** *near the end of the century;* in oaths: **co u licha?** *what the devil?.*

z+G

Besides its more normal uses in the senses 'out of, off, down from', **z** is often used figuratively in expressions such as **z ciekawości** *out of curiosity*, **z natury** *by nature*, **z całego serca** *from one's whole heart*, **z grzeczności** *out of politeness*, **ze złości** *out of anger*, **z przemęczenia** *from overwork*, **z przerażenia** *out of fear*, **z pamięci** *from memory*, and so on. **Z**+G translates 'for' in the sense of 'known for': **znany ze swoich książek** *known for his books*, **znana ze swojego**

głosu *known for her voice*, etc.; **egzamin z biologii** *biology exam;* etc. For other uses, see below under Spatial Prepositions.

A number of verbs and a couple of adjectives occur in phrasal combination with z+G, for example **cieszyć się z** *be glad of,* **korzystać z** *avail self of,* **kpić sobie z** *mock,* **składać się z** *be composed of,* **śmiać się z** *laugh at,* **wyjechać z** *drive away from,* **wyprowadzić się z** *move out of,* **wysiąść z** *get out of (bus, etc.),* **być zadowolony(m) z** *be satisfied with,* **żartować z** *make fun of.*

b. To the Genitive-requiring prepositions may be added the motion-from correspondents of the Instrumental-requiring prepositions

+Instrumental:

między *between, among*
nad *above, over*
pod *under, beneath*
poza *on the other side of*
przed *before*
za *behind, beyond*

+Genitive:

spomiędzy *from among*
znad *from above*
spod *from beneath*
spoza *from the other side of*
sprzed *from before*
zza *from beyond, from behind*

c. The majority of phrasal prepositions take the Genitive, including

na kształt *modeled after*
na mocy *on the strength of*
na podstawie *on the basis of*
na rzecz *on behalf of*
na temat *on the subject of*
na zasadzie *on the basis of*
nie opodal *not far off from*
pod pozorem *on the pretext of*
pod warunkiem *on the condition of*
pod wpływem *under the influence of*
pod względem *as far as X is concerned*
przy pomocy, za pomocą *with the help of*
z powodu *because of*

siłą *on the strength of*
w celu *with the aim of*
w charakterze *in shape of*
w ciągu *during (the course of)*
w czasie *during (the time of)*
w imieniu *in the name of*
w miarę *to the extent of*
w myśl *by way of*
w obliczu *in the face of*
w obrębie *in the framework of*
w postaci *by way of*
w pobliżu *in the vicinity of*
w przeciągu *in the course of*
w wyniku *as the result of*
względem *as regards*, and others

d. To the phrasal prepositions taking the Genitive may be added certain spatial adverbs and adverb-phrases functioning as prepositions:

blisko *near to* (but **daleko od** *far from*)
wewnątrz *inside*
wszerz *along the breath of*
na zewnątrz *on the outside of*
z przodu *from the front of*

z tyłu *from the rear of*
na środku *in the center of*
poniżej *lower than, below*
pośrodku *in the middle of*
powyżej *higher than, above*

GENITIVE OF TIME

9. The Genitive is used to express dates and to answer questions as to time of occurrence, as in **następnego dnia** *on the next day*, **tej nocy** *on that night*, **pewnego razu** *one time*, etc.

   To się stało zeszłego roku. *That happened last year.*

   Wojna wybuchła pierwszego września. *War broke out on September 1st.*

   Dnia dwudziestego dziewiątego kwietnia rozpoczęto prace przy budowie portu. *On the 29th day of April work was begun on the construction of the port.*

   While years by themselves, without an accompanying date, take **w+L** (**Urodziłem się w roku tysiąc dziewięćset siedemdziesiątym drugim.** *I was born in 1972*), the Genitive of time with a day of the month will be followed by the Genitive of time of the year:

   List dedykacyjny został napisany (dnia) dwudziestego drugiego grudnia tysiąc siedemset sześćdziesiątego siódmego roku. *The letter of dedication was written on December 22, 1767.*

GENITIVE OF WISH

10. The Genitive is used in expressions calling for or wishing for something, as if after missing Genitive-requiring verbs like **chcieć** *want*, **potrzebować** *need*, or **życzyć** *wish*: **Pomocy!** *Help!*, **Ratunku!** *Rescue (me)!*, **Cierpliwości!** *Have patience!*, **Wody!** *Water!* **Szczęśliwej podróży!** *Bon voyage!*, **Wesołych Świąt!** *Happy Holidays!*, **Wszystkiego najlepszego** *All the best!* and so on. The verb **życzyć** appears on greeting cards:

   Miłych i pogodnych Świąt Wielkanocnych życzy Magda. *Magda wishes (you) pleasant and peaceful Easter Holidays.*

THE DATIVE CASE

The Dative case is traditionally the case of indirect object, that is, the person or other animate being for whom or which something is done, or to whom or which something is given. In practice, the Dative case in Polish is used most often with personal pronouns and personal names. Despite its many and subtle uses, the Dative is, after the Vocative, the least commonly encountered of the Polish cases in speech, at least with nouns. Its use with nouns is encountered somewhat more frequently in writing. Some of the traditional uses of the Dative have been taken over by the prepositions **do+G** *to* and **dla+G** *for*. The Dative has the following main uses:

INDIRECT OBJECT

1. The Dative is the case of indirect object, expressing the recipient of a transfer of property or the person to whom something is said:

   Dałem paszę koniowi. *I gave fodder to the horse.*

Kupuję narzeczonemu prezent. *I'm buying my fiancé a present.*

Sprzedaję samochód swojej sąsiadce. *I'm selling my car to my neighbor.*

Pożycz mi tę książkę. *Lend me that book.*

Mówiłem ci już, że jestem zajęty. *I already told you I'm busy.*

Matka lubi, kiedy czytam jej gazetę. *Mother likes it when I read her the paper.*

Related to this use is the use of the Dative to refer to the recipient of a greeting or naming:

Dzień dobry panu (pani)! *Hello, sir/madam!*

Also somewhat related is the phrase **na imię** +D:

Na imię mi Marek. *My name is Marek; call me Marek.*

BENEFICIARY

2. The Dative can be used to refer to the person who profits from an action. This use is similar to and often semantically blends into the indirect-object use:

Uszyję córce nową sukienkę. *I'll sew my daughter a new dress.*

Ustępuję swoje miejsce następnemu mówcy. *I'm yielding my place to the next speaker.*

Chopiec narąbał drzewa dwu starcom. *The boy chopped some wood for the two old people.*

Herbata z cytryną dobrze ci zrobi. *Tea with lemon will do you good.*

The Dative of beneficiary is frequently used with the reflexive pronoun **sobie**:

Zamawiam sobie nowy płaszcz. *I'm ordering myself a new coat.*

COMMISSIONED WORK

3. The Dative is used after 'give', 'commission', and 'order' in constructions corresponding to English 'have something done by someone':

Oddałem samochód mechanikowi do naprawy. *I took my car to be fixed at the mechanic's.*

Zleciłem mu namalowanie swojego portretu. *I commissioned him to paint my portrait.*

INALIENABLE (BODY-PART) POSSESSION

4. The Dative is occasionally used to express the possessor of a (frequently negatively) responding part of the body. This use, traditionally called the Dative of inalienable possession, is not as frequent as one might expect from its use in related languages.

Drgnęły jej plecy. *Her shoulders trembled.*

Serce mu bije jak młot. *His heart is beating like a hammer.*

Włosy mi stanęły dęba. *My hair stood on end.*

Mojemu oponentowi mina zbladła. *My opponent's face blanched.*

Są tacy ludzie, którym ucho zdrętwiało. *There are some people who have become hard of hearing.*

LOSER, PERSON INCONVENIENCED

5. The Dative is frequently used to express the person who loses or is inconvenienced by an action:

Zdechł mi pies. *My dog died.*

Zepsułem ci samochód. *I've ruined your automobile.*

Amputują mu nogę. *They're amputating his leg.*

Zginął mi zegarek. *My watch has disappeared.*

Zabrali mi telewizor. *They took away my television set.*

Odbił mi dziewczynę. *He stole away my girl.*

Odbierasz nam nadzieje. *You are taking away from us our hopes.*

Ukradli mi portfel. *They stole my wallet.*

Wlazł nam w drogę. *He got in our way*

Psujesz mi humor. *You're ruining my humor.*

Takie sprawy zatruwają człowiekowi życie. *Things like that poison a person's life.*

PERSONAL VERBS REQUIRING THE DATIVE

6. The Dative is used after verbs which logically require or allow for a personal subject and indirect object or beneficiary, for example:

(po)darować *grant, concede*
da(wa)ć *give*
dostarczyć dostarczać *provide*
gratulować +D +G *congratulate on*
kupić kupować *buy*
nada(wa)ć *lend, imbue*
odda(wa)ć *give back, hand over*
(za)ofiarować *grant*
(za)płacić *pay*
pożyczyć pożyczać *loan*
poda(wa)ć *give, serve*
pokaz(yw)ać *show*
poświęcić poświęcać *dedicate*
(za)prezentować *present*

przedstawi(a)ć *introduce*
przynieść przynosić *bring*
przypis(yw)ać *ascribe*
(z)robić *do*
sprzeda(wa)ć *sell*
udzielić udzielać *impart*
ujawnić ujawniać *reveal*
wskaz(yw)ać *indicate*
zarzucic zarzucać *reproach*
zlecić zlecać *commission*
złożyć składać *(fig.) give (vow, etc.)*
zwrócić zwracać *return, direct*
życzyć *wish*

Zapomniałem oddać Zbyszkowi marynarkę. *I forgot to give Zbyszek his jacket back.*

Kup mi coś ciekawego. *Buy me something interesting.*

On dobrze płaci swoim pracownikom. *He pays his workers well.*

Pożycz mi sto złotych do pierwszego. *Lend me 100 zlotys till the 1st.*

Ona zrobiła nam wielką przykrość. *She did a great unkindness to us.*

Chciałbym panu zwrócić na coś uwagę. *I'd like to direct your attention to something.*

Królowa Wanda złożyła ślub bogom słowiańskim. *Queen Wanda made a vow to the Slavic gods.*

An important subcategory of such verbs are those of communication:

kazać *order*
(za)meldować *report*
mówić *say, tell*
obiec(yw)ać *promise*
odpowiedzieć odpowiadać *answer*
opowiedzieć opowiadać *narrate*
powiedzieć *say (pf)*
pozwolić pozwalać *allow, permit*
przekaz(yw)ać *convey*
przyzna(wa)ć (się) *confess*

przepowiedzieć przepowiadać *foretell*
przypomnieć przypominać *remind*
przyzna(wa)ć *admit*
(po)radzić *advise*
skarżyć się *complain*
tłumaczyć *explain*
zwierzyć się zwierzać się *confide*
żalić się *complain*

Minister kazał nam długo czekać. *The minister had us wait a long time.*

Przekaż matce pozdrowienia. *Convey my greetings to your mother.*

Opowiedz nam o swojej podróży. *Tell us about your trip.*

Przypomnij mi, że mam pójść jutro do dentysty. *Remind me that I have to go to the dentist tomorrow.*

Radzę ci, żebyś poszła do specjalisty. *I advise you to go to a specialist.*

Note that the verbs **ostrzegać** *warn*, **(po)informować** *inform*, **uprzedzić uprzedzać** *forewarn*, and **zawiadomić zawiadamiać** *inform* take the Accusative.

7. The Dative is used after verbs expressing bother, help, threat, harm, or hindrance, including:

dociąć docinać *tease*
dokuczyć dokuczać *tease, bother*
dolegać *afflict, ail*
(za)grozić *threaten*
pomóc pomagać *help*
przeszkodzić przeszkadzać *hinder*
przeczyć *refute*

skąpić *grudge*
sprzyjać *be conducive to, favor*
(za)szkodzić *harm.*
ubliżyć ubliżać *insult*
wymyślić wymyślać *berate*
zagrozić zagrażać *threaten*
zaprzeczyć zaprzeczać *contradict*

Twoja obecność przeszkadza mi w pracy. *Your presence hinders me in my work.*

Przestań dokuczać siostrze. *Stop teasing your sister.*

Indianom groziła zagłada. *The Indians were threatened with extinction.*

Co dolega twojemu psu? *What's ailing your dog?*

Często sobie pomagamy. *We often help one another.*

Los sprzyja śmiałym. *Fortune favors the bold.*

Palenie szkodzi zdrowiu. *Smoking harms one's health.*

8. The Dative is required after a number of verbs of resistance and opposition:

odmówić odmawiać +D +G
   deny, refuse
podołać *stand up to (pf)*
przeciwstawi(a)ć się *be against*

sprzeciwi(a)ć się *object to*
stawiać upór *put up a resistance to*
zapobiec zapobiegać *prevent, forestall*
zaprzeczyć zaprzeczać *contradict*

Nogi odmawiały mu posłuszeństwa. *His legs refused to obey him.*

Nie zaprzeczaj mi. *Don't contradict me.*

Takie posunięcia nie zapobiegły wybuchowi wojny. *Such measures did not forestall the outbreak of war.*

Czy podołasz temu wszystkiemu? *Can you deal with all of that?*

9. The Dative is required after certain verbs referring to belief, trust, subordination, gratitude, concern, relation, sympathy:

(po)dziękować *thank*
kłaniać się *bow to, nod to*
odpowiadać *correspond to*
podda(wa)ć się *yield to*
podlec podlegać *submit to*
podporządkow(yw)ać się *be subordnate to*
poświęcić poświęcać *dedicate, devote*

służyć *serve*
sprostać *be equal to*
towarzyszyć *accompany*
ufać *trust*
udostępni(a)ć *make accessible to*
ulec ulegać *undergo, be subject to*
(u)wierzyć *believe*
współczuć *sympathize with*
wtórować *accompany, second*

Dziękuję ci za pamięć. *Thanks for remembering.*

Taka postawa nie służy żadnemu celowi. *Such an attitude doesn't serve any purpose.*

Zawsze kłaniam się kobietom, starcom i dzieciom. *I always nod to women, old men, and children.*

Leksykalne znaczenie słowa może ulec zmianie. *The lexical meaning of a word can undergo change.*

Udostępniono profesorowi wszystkie zbiory. *They opened all the collections to the professor.*

Nie można ufać tym ludziom. *One cannot trust those people.*

Oni wierzą wszystkiemu i wszystkim. *They believe everything and everyone.*

Naprawdę współczuję twojej matce. *I really sympathize with your mother.*

Ten towar nie odpowiada naszym potrzebom. *That product doesn't meet our needs.*

Muszę poświęcić swoim uczniom trochę czasu. *I have to devote a little time to my pupils.*

Rżenie koni wtórowało wyciu wilków. *The neighing of the horses accompanied the howling of the wolves.*

10. In addition to the above larger semantic classes, the Dative is required after a few verbs referring to

a. attitude toward:

dziwić się *be surprised at*   **zazdrościć** +D +G *envy*

Dziwię się jego zachowaniu się. *I'm surprised at his behavior.*

Zazdroszczę ci twojej równowagi. *I envy you your calm.*

b. attentiveness (verbs in **przy- się**):

przyglądać się *look at, observe*   **przysłuchiwać się** *listen to*
przypatrywać się *take a close look at*

Policjant uważnie przyglądał się pieszemu. *The policeman watched the pedestrian attentively.*

Z przyjemnością przysłuchiwaliśmy się jej grze. *We listened to her playing with pleasure.*

c. presiding:

patronować *be patron over*   **przewodniczyć** *preside over*

Prus patronował młodym pisarzom. *Prus was the patron of younger writers.*

Idea wolności przewodniczyła wszystkim ich przedsięwzięciom. *The idea of freedom presided over all their undertakings.*

Note that **nadzorować** *oversee* takes the Accusative.

d. The verb **imponować** *impress* takes the Dative:

On imponował wszystkim słuchaczom swoją erudycją. *He impressed all the listeners with his erudition.*

3RD-PERSON VERBS TAKING THE DATIVE

11. The Dative is used after various verbs usually occurring in the 3rd pers. Such verbs may be divided into those that can take a specific 3rd-person subject, and those that do not. The following verbs often take specific subjects:

należeć się *deserve*   **uda(wa)ć się** *be successful*
podobać się *be pleasing to*   **ujść uchodzić** *pass by, escape*
przysługiwać *deserve, be owed to*   **wyjść wychodzić** *work out for*

Należy mi się podwyżka. *I deserve a raise.*

Przysługuje mi urlop. *I have a vacation coming to me.*

Nie uda ci się ta wyprawa. *That expedition of yours won't succeed.*

Ten błąd łatwo może uchodzić naszej uwadze. *That mistake can easily escape our notice.*

Te skarpetki nie podobają mi się. *I don't like these socks.*

Podobasz mi się, i myślałem, że ja ci się też podobam. *You appeal to me, and I thought that I appeal to you too.*

12. These verbs occur without specific subjects:

brakować *be lacking*	**uda(wa)ć się** *succeed (for someone)*
być *be (the matter with someone)*	**ujść uchodzić** *escape someone's*
iść *go (for someone)*	*responsibility*
powodzić się *go well (for someone)*	**wyda(wa)ć się** *seem*
przejść przechodzić *pass by get*	**wystarczyć** +D +G *be enough of*
over	**zda(wa)ć się** *appear*

Brakuje mi czasu. *I'm out of time.*

Co im jest? *What's the matter with them?*

Jak panu idzie? *How's it going with you?*

Dobrze mu się powodzi. *He's doing well.*

Udało mi się znaleźć tę książkę. *I managed to find that book.*

Wydaje mi się, że skądś panią znam. *It seems to me that I know you from somewhere.*

Tak ci się tylko zdaje. *It only appears that way to you.*

13. Various 3rd-person impersonal verbs of mental state or physical sensation occur with a Dative subject:

burczeć *rumble*	**kręcić się** *be dizzy*
chcieć się *feel like*	**odbi(ja)ć się** *belch, burp*
dzwonić *ring*	**szumieć** *ring, hum,* and others
nudzić się *be boring*	

Pić mi się chce. *I'm thirsty.*

Nie chce mi się iść do kina dzisiaj. *I don't feel like going to the movies today.*

Nudzi mi się. *I'm bored.*

Kręci mi się w głowie. *I feel dizzy.*

Burczało mu w brzuchu. *His stomach grumbled.*

14. The Dative occurs as the case of complement after a few impersonal verbs of concern or interest:

chodzić komuś o coś *be concerned about something*	**zależeć komuś na czymś** *be of importance to someone*
nie wychodzić komuś *not work out for someone*	

Chodzi nam o jak najszybsze rozwiązanie tego problemu. *We are anxious to have this matter resolved as soon as possible.*

Bardzo mi zależy na twoim zdaniu. *Your opinion is of great importance to me.*

15. For the Dativized subject of sentences depersonalized with **się**, see Chapter 12, p. 321.

16. The Dative is the case of complement after impersonal adverbial expressions referring to feelings and sensations, including:

chłodno *chilly*
ciepło *warm*
duszno *stifling, stuffy*
gorąco *hot*
krucho *frail*
łatwo *easy*
mdło *sick, nauseated*
miło *nice*
przyjemnie *pleasant*

ponuro *gloomy*
przykro *unpleasant*
smutno *sad*
trudno *difficult*
wesoło *merry, gay, jolly*
wygodnie *comfortable*
zimno *cold*
źle *bad*

Duszno mi. *I feel stuffy.*

Nie będzie ci tak łatwo. *It won't be so easy for you.*

Mojej żonie nie jest tu zbyt wygodnie. *My wife doesn't feel very comfortable here.*

Dość krucho ze mną dzisiaj. *I'm feeling pretty poorly today.*

Bardzo nam przykro. *We're very sorry.*

Jest zawsze tak ponuro na jego zabawach. *It*'s always so gloomy at his parties.*

Zimno mi. *I feel cold.*

Mojemu kotu jest mdło. *My cat is sick to its stomach.*

17. The Dative is used after various modals such as **brak** *lack of* **szkoda** *waste of,* **potrzeba** *need for,* **wstyd** *ashamed of,* **żal** *sorry for:*

Szkoda mi pieniędzy. *It's a waste of my money.*

Brak mu współczucia. *He lacks sympathy.*

For further information and examples, see Chapter 10.

THE DATIVE AFTER PREPOSITIONS

18. Only a few prepositions require the Dative case; they include

dzięki *thanks to, due to*
ku *toward*
na przekór *to spite, in defiance of*

przeciw(ko) *against*
wbrew *despite*

Dzięki tobie udało mi się zdać egzamin. *Thanks to you I was able to pass my exam.*

Wszystko zmierza ku lepszej przyszłości. *Everything is tending toward a better future.*

Wyszła za mąż na przekór rodzinie. *She married to spite her family.*

Wbrew oczekiwaniom, wszystko skończyło się jak najlepiej. *Despite expectations, everything ended as well as possible.*

Robotnicy protestują przeciwko podwyżce cen. *The workers are protesting against the rise in prices.*

ku

Of the above prepositions, **ku** *toward* is infrequently used other than in expressions of the sort **ku mojemu zaskoczeniu** *to my surprise,* **ku mojemu ździwieniu** *to my amazement,* **ku swojej uchwale** *to his/her credit;* and so on. See also **ku górze** *upward,* **ku wieczorowi** *toward evening,* **ku lasowi** *in the direction of the forest,* **ku słońcu** *toward the sun,* **zmierzać ku zagładzie** *head toward extinction.* The notion of 'toward(s)' tends usually to be expressed with **do**+G *to;* **w kierunku**+G *in the direction of ;* or **w stronę**+G.

przeciw

The preposition **przeciw** is used in the sense of being against a particular opinion or position: **Czy jesteś za nami czy przeciw nam?** *Are you for us or against us?* **Przeciw** possibly has its most frequent use in the phrase **mieć coś przeciwko komuś** *have something against someone.* Phrases of the sort **płaszcz przeciw deszczowi** *coat against the rain,* **parasol przeciw słońcu** *parasol against the sun,* and the like, are often replaced with adjectival constructions of the sort **tabletki przeciwbólowe** *pain-pills,* **okulary przeciwsłoneczne** *sun-glasses,* and so on. The notion 'in opposition to' is often expressed with **w przeciwieństwie do** plus the Genitive.

ADJECTIVES REQUIRING THE DATIVE

19. The Dative may be used as a case of complement following a number of adjectives, including

bliski *near*	**wdzięczny** *grateful*
dłużny *indebted*	**wiadomy** *known*
drogi *dear*	**wierny** *faithful*
obcy *alien*	**winny** *to blame*
przeciwny *opposed*	**wrogi** *hostile*
przychylny *favorably disposed*	**wspólny** *common, shared*
przyjazny *friendly*	**współczesny** *contemporary*
rad *glad*	**znany** *known*
równy *equal*	**zobowiązany** *obliged*
właściwy *proper*	**życzliwy** *kindly disposed*

Będziesz zawsze bliska mojemu sercu. *You'll always be near my heart.*

Honor to pojęcie drogie każdemu Polakowi. *Honor is a concept dear to every Pole.*

Jego sposób zachowania się jest mi zupełnie obcy. *His manner of behavior is completely alien to me.*

Byliśmy radzi jego przyjściu. *We were happy about his arrival.*

Jestem wam bardzo wdzięczny. *I'm very grateful to you.*

To jest przeciwne naturze. *That's against nature.*

Poczucie humoru to cecha wspólna wszystkim narodom. *A sense of humor is a trait common to all peoples.*

Kawał ten jest dobrze znany wszystkim studentom. *That joke is well known to all students.*

Nic mi o tym nie wiadomo. *I don't know anything about that.*

In the sense of physical proximity, **bliski** *near* takes the Genitive: **restauracja bliska hotelu** *restaurant close to the hotel.*

SPECIFYING DATIVES

20. A use of the Dative, traditionally called the "ethical" Dative, but better termed "specifying", consists in adding to the sentence the reflexive pronoun **sobie** which is not controlled by any item in the sentence, and which specifies the subject in some way. **Sobie** typically adds the sense of random, diffuse, carefree, or idiosyncratic action, without regard for others or for appearances:

Chodźmy sobie. *Let's be on our way.*

Idź sobie. *Go on your way.*

Pomyślę sobie. *I'll give it some thought.*

21. The reflexive pronoun **sam sama samo** in the Dative forms **samemu, samej samym** may specify 'by oneself', 'on one's own' in sentences where the main verb is represented by an infinitive, especially in sentences which imply the presence of a Dative-case subject:

Trudno mu mieszkać samemu. *It's difficult for him to live on his own.*

SUBJECT OF INFINITIVE

22. The Dative can theoretically occur as the subject of an infinitive in a clause inside an existential construction. In practice, in contemporary speech the Nominative occurs:

Jest komu (kto) to zrobić. *There's someone who can do that.*

Nie ma komu (kto) nim się zajmować. *There's no one one to look after him.*

THE ACCUSATIVE CASE

The Accusative case is the usual case of verbal complement in the function of 'direct object'. It also has many uses after prepositions as well as a number of independent idiomatic uses.

DIRECT OBJECT

1. When a verb's meaning is not complete without both a subject and a second noun, the second noun appears in the Accusative case unless some other case or preposition-plus-case is specifically required by the verb. The number of verbs which take the Accusative case is quite large, numbering in the thousands. Here is a list of common Accusative-requiring verbs, given in the Imperfective except where noted:

bić *hit, strike*	**składać** *fold*
brać *take*	**słyszeć** *hear*
budować *build*	**spotykać** *meet*
budzić *wake up*	**sprzedawać** *sell*
całować *kiss*	**stawiać** *place, stand, set*
czytać *read*	**tracić** *lose*
dawać *give*	**traktować** *treat*
gotować *cook*	**trzymać** *hold*
jeść *eat*	**tworzyć** *create*
kłaść *lay down*	**widzieć** *see*
kochać *love*	**witać** *greet, welcome*
kupować *buy*	**woleć** *prefer*
lubić *like*	**wołać** *call*
łamać *break*	**wybierać** *choose*
łapać *catch*	**wydawać** *publish*
mieć *have*	**wygrywać** *win*
nieść *carry*	**wyjaśniać** *explain*
oceniać *evaluate*	**wynosić** *carry out*
odwiedzać *visit a person*	**wyrzucać** *throw out*
oglądać *view*	**wysyłać** *send*
otrzymywać *receive*	**zabierać** *take along*
otwierać *open*	**zabijać** *kill*
pamiętać *remember*	**zajmować** *occupy*
pełnić *fill*	**zamykać** *close, lock*
pić *drink*	**zatrzymywać** *stop*
pisać *write*	**zauważać** *notice*
płacić *pay*	**zawierać** *contain*
pokazywać *show*	**zbierać** *collect*
położyć *place, lay (pf)*	**zdobywać** *acquire*
przedstawiać *present*	**zmieniać** *change*
przegrywać *lose*	**znać** *know*

przygotowywać *prepare*
psuć *spoil, ruin*
robić *do*
rozumieć *understand*
ruszać *move*

znajdować *find*
zniszczyć *destroy (pf)*
zobaczyć *glimpse (pf)*
zostawiać *leave behind*
zwiedzać *visit a place*

Znam tę książkę. *I know that book.*

Przeczytałem twój artykuł. *I read your article.*

Muszę kupić butelkę wina. *I have to buy a bottle of wine.*

Znalazłem nasze miejsce. *I found our place.*

Dobrze pamiętam twoją siostrę. *I remember your sister well.*

Poznałem twojego męża wczoraj. *I made the acquaintance of your husband yesterday.*

Recall that negated Accusative-requiring verbs take Genitive complements: **Nie znam tej książki.** *I don't know that book-G;* **Nie przeczytałem twojego artykułu** *I haven't read your article-G;* etc. See above under uses of the Genitive case.

The adjective **winien winna** *own* takes an Accusative complement: **On jest winien nam tysiąc złotych.** *He owes us one thousand zlotys.*

This word may take personal endings similar to **powinien** (Chapter 10): **Winniśmy mu życie.** *We owe him our life.*

THE ACCUSATIVE AFTER PREPOSITIONS

2. The Accusative is used after a number of prepositions, many of which take some other case in a more basic use:

a. Prepositions which occur only with the Accusative include:

ponad *over and above, more than,* as in **ponad godzinę** *more than an hour*

poprzez *across, throughout,* and **przez** *through, across, for a period of time*

Of these, only **przez** requires commentary:

przez

Przez plus the Accusative expresses 'through, across, through the agency of, for a time': **przez błoto** *through the mud,* **przez miesiąc** *during the course of a month,* **przez most** *across the bridge,* **przez park** *through the park.* **Przez** often expresses the cause of a negative circumstance (positive circumstances being expressed with **dzięki** +D *due to*):

Nie mogę spać przez twoje chrapanie. *I can't sleep because of your snoring.*

A frequent syntactic use of **przez** is to express the demoted subject in a passive sentence:

Kot został przejechany przez samochód. *The cat was run over by a car.*

Radio zostało zepsute przez dziecko. *The radio was ruined by the child.*

For more on the passive voice, see Chapter 11.

b. Prepositions which occur with both Locative and Accusative include

na +L *on; with A, onto, toward, for*   **po** +L *after; with A, for*

o +L *about, with A, against*   **w** +L *in; with A, into*

Here are some notes on specific of the above prepositions in their Accusative uses. Of necessity, these notes give only a glimpse into the varied uses of these four prepositions with the Accusative.

na+A. The preposition **na** plus the Accusative is used as the complement of motion verbs with nouns for which location is expressed with **na** plus the Locative. Hence, because one says **na lotnisku** *at the airport-L,* one also says **na lotnisko** *to the airport-A.* This principle also holds for words referring to events: **na obiedzie** *at dinner,* hence **na obiad** *to dinner;* **na przedstawieniu** *at the performance,* hence **bilet na przedstawienie** *ticket for the performance.* With towns, **na** +A indicates 'toward': **droga na Kraków** *road in the direction of Krakow.* For more information on **na**, see below, under the Locative Case: The Choice Between **na** and **w**; and in Chapter 14 under Complements of Motion Verbs. **Na+A** occasionally translates 'onto': **wyjść na ulicę** *go outdoors,* **wskoczyć na krzesło** *jump up onto the chair,* **wstąpić na tron** *ascend the throne.* Usually, 'onto' is translated by **na+L: postawić na półce (stole, podłodze,** etc.) *put on the shelf (table, floor).* **Na+A** expresses 'for' in the sense of anticipation of, readiness for, response to, or intended purpose: **czekać na autobus** *wait for a bus,* **gotowy na wszystko** *ready for anything;* **odporny na zmęczenie** *resistant to fatigue,* **pieniądze na jedzenie** *money for food,* **skrzynka na listy** *letter-box;* as well as 'for' in the celebration of occasions: **prezent na urodziny** *present for one's birthday.* **Na+A** also expresses 'for how long': **wyjechać na miesiąc** *leave for a month,* as well as the idea of 'per' in expressions like **czterdzieści kilometrów na godzinę** *40 km. per hour,* **raz na rok** *once a year.* **Na+A** may also express an exact period of time before, instead of the simple Accusative of time: **na tydzień przed Bożym narodzeniem** *a week before Christmas.*

Various expressions exhibit **na** +A, for example, **na Boga!** *by God!,* **na dodatek** *to boot,* **na domiar złego** *to make matters worse,* **na dobre** *for good,* **na dobry rozum** *as far as common sense is concerned,* **na gapę** *without paying,* **na odwrót** *vice versa,* **na pewno** *for certain,* **na pokaz** *for show,* **na przemian** *by turn,* **na przestrzał** *from end to end,* **na przykład** *for example,* **na rozkaz** *at a command,* **na stałe** *permanently,* **na stare lata** *in one's old age,* **na szczęście** *fortunately,* **na widok** *at the sight of,* **na wynos** *carry-out,* **na zakończenie** *in conclusion,* **na zawsze** *forever,* **na złość** *out of spitefulness,*

na zmianę *for a change,* **ze względu na zdrowie** *in view of one's health;* and many others.

A large number of verbs, and a few adjectives, form Accusative-requiring phrasal combinations with **na**, including **chorować (być chory) na grypę** *be sick with the flu,* **cierpieć na anginę** *suffer from angina,* **czekać na pociąg** *wait for a train,* **czuły na poezję** *sensitive to poetry,* **gniewać się na męża** *be angry at one's husband,* **liczyć na pomoc** *count on help,* **natrafić na przykrość** *encounter an unpleasantry,* **namówić na kawę** *persuade one to have coffee,* **narazić się na niebezpieczeństwo** *expose oneself to danger,* **narzekać na przepisy** *complain about regulations,* **obrazić się na cały świat** *take offense at the whole world,* **oddziaływać na** *have an affect on,* **odpowiedzieć na pytanie** *answer a question,* **patrzeć na słońce** *look at the sun,* **pozwolić na wyjazd** *allow to leave,* **reagować na światło** *react to light,* **skarżyć się na sąsiada** *complain about one's neighbor,* **spóźnić się na zebranie** *be late to a meeting,* **spojrzeć na dziewczynę** *glance at a girl,* **stać kogoś na samochód** *someone can afford a car,* **wpływać na zdrowie** *have an influence on one's health,* **wrażliwy na słońce** *sensitive to the sun,* **wskazać na lepszą drogę** *indicate a better way,* **wściekać się (być wściekły) na sekretarkę** *be enraged at one's secretary,* **zamknąć na klucz** *lock up,* **zaprosić na obiad** *invite for dinner,* **zdany na pastwę losu** *cast into the jaws of fate,* **zdążyć na spektakl** *make it to a performance on time,* **zdecydować na operację** *decide on an operation,* **zgadzać się na propozycję** *agree to a proposal,* **zły na brata** *be angry at one's brother,* **zmarły na gruźlicę** *dead of tuberculosis,* **zwracać uwagę na** *direct attention to,* and many others. Note that while **liczyć na** *count on* takes the Accusative, **polegać na** *depend on* takes the Locative.

o+A. The preposition **o** occurs with the Accusative in the sense of leaning, hitting, or knocking against a surface: **opierać się o drzewo** *lean against a tree,* **uderzyć się o ścianę** *knock into a wall.* O+A occurs in phrases of measure like **Jestem wyższy od ciebie o całą głowę.** *I'm taller than you by a whole head.* **Jestem o wiele bardziej zajęty niż on.** *I'm a lot busier than he is.* O+A also occurs in senses of 'for' and 'about' after verbs of asking, striving, or concern, and in various idiomatic verb-preposition combinations: **bać się o przyszłość** *be afraid about the future,* **chodzi o życie i śmierć** *it's a matter of life and death,* **dbać o czystość** *be concerned about cleanliness,* **kłócić się o pieniądze** *quarrel over money,* **martwić się o stopnie** *worry about grades,* **podejrzewać o przestępstwo** *suspect of a crime,* **prosić o pomoc** *ask for help,* **przyprawić o złość** *make angry,* **starać się o stypendium** *try for a scholarship,* **troszczyć się o zdrowie** *be concerned about one's health,* **ubiegać się o prezydenturę** *run for the presidency,* **walczyć o pokój** *strive for peace,* **zazdrosny o męża** *jealous of one's husband.* See also the phrases **łatwo o, trudno o** +A *it's difficult (to get):* **Trudno jest o dobrą pracę.** *It's hard to find good work.*

po+A. With the Accusative, **po** occurs in the sense of 'up to' or 'as far as': **po kolana** *up to one's knees*, **aż po osiemnasty wiek** *all the way up until the 18th century*, **po szyję** *up to one's neck*, **po horyzont** *as far as the horizon*. **Po+A** also occurs in the sense of the 'for' of fetching after verbs of motion: **pójść po lekarza** *go for the doctor*, **przyjść po dziecko** *come for one's child*, **wyjść po zakupy** *go out shopping*, **zajechać po gościa** *come by to pick up a guest*.

w(e)+A. With the Accusative, **w** occurs in the sense of 'into' with abstractions and objects of vague proportions, less often with concrete nouns: **w dal** *into the distance*, **w przyszłość** *into the future*, **w świat** *into the world*, **we mgłę** *into the fog*, **w tę stronę** *in that direction*, **w tłum** *into the crowd*, **wpaść w depresję** *fall into a depression*, etc. Usually, 'into' is expressed with **do+G: do pokoju** *into the room*, **do wody** *into the water*, etc. With days of the week, **w+A** expresses 'on the day': **w poniedziałek** *on Monday*, **w środę** *on Wednesday*, etc.; also: **w biały dzień** *in broad daylight*. **W+A** may be used to express motion in a given direction, especially up or down: **w górę** *upwards*, **w dół** *downwards*. Action by a deadline or in the course of a time period may be expressed with **w+A: zrobić coś w jeden dzień** *do something in a single day*, **w mig** *in a trice*, **w godzinę** *in (only) an hour*, **w porę** *in time*, **umrzeć w tydzień po żonie** *die within a week of one's wife*. See also the expressions **słowo w słowo** *word for word*, **w miarę** *to the extent*.

When part of a verb-preposition phrasal combination, the preposition **w** usually takes the Accusative. Most commonly encountered are complements of verbs of physical contact. Some examples are **bawić się w chowanego** *play hide and seek*, **bić w twarz** *hit in the face*, **całować w rękę** *kiss on the hand*, **dotykać w policzek** *touch on the cheek*, **grać w tenisa** *play tennis*, **ingerować w tekst** *force changes in a text*, **kopać w kolano** *kick in the knee*, **obfitować (być bogaty) w lasy** *be abundant (rich) in forests*, **obrócić w żart** *turn into a joke*, **patrzyć w okno** *look through the window*, **spojrzeć w niebo** *glance into the sky*, **strzelić w plecy** *shoot in the back*, **uczesać włosy w koński ogon** *comb one's hair into a pony-tail*, **uderzyć w drzewo** *hit a tree*, **trafić w sedno rzeczy** *hit on the essence of the matter*, **ubrać się w sukienkę** *put on a dress*, **wdawać się w szczegóły** *go into details*, **wierzyć w Boga** *believe in God*, **zmienić się w bestię** *turn into a beast*.

c. Prepositions which occur with both the Instrumental and Accusative include

między +*I between, among; with A, into the midst of*

nad +*I over, above; with A (after verbs of motion), over, (to) above*

pod +*I under, beneath; with A (after verbs of motion), up to the foot of, ((to) under*

poza +*I beyond; with A (after verbs of motion), to beyond*

przed +I *before, in front of; with A, to in front of.* **iść przed siebie** *go straight ahead*

za +I *beyond, in back of; with A, to behind, beyond; by (the hand, etc.); for (of exchange); after a period of time; in someone's place*

For uses after verbs of motion, see in Chapter 14 under Complements of Verbs of Motion. Here are some notes on specific uses of **za**:

za+A. Besides its concrete use after verbs of motion to express 'to beyond', the preposition **za** plus the Accusative expresses the 'for' of exchange after various verbs: **dziękować za pomoc** *thank for help*, **kupić/sprzedać za sto złotych** *buy/sell for 100 zlotys*, **odpowiadać za uczciwość kogoś** *be responsible for someone's honesty*, **pić za zdrowie kogoś** *drink to one's health*, **przeprosić za przewinienie** *ask forgiveness for an offence*, **ręczyć za dobre wyniki** *vouch for good results*, **umrzeć za wolność** *die for freedom*, **wstydzić się za czyjeś zachowanie się** *be ashamed for someone's behavior*. See also **Za jaką cenę?** *At what cost?* **Kto pójdzie za niego?** *Who will go in his place?* Especially common is the use of **za** in the sense 'after a period of time': **Będę gotowy za godzinę** *I'll be ready in an hour*. This construction is found in clock-time expressions (see Chapter 8): **Jest za dziesięć siódma.** *It's ten till seven.*

Za+A is used in the sense of holding something 'by' something and mistaking someone for something or someone: **trzymać za rękę** *hold by the hand*, **złapać za kołnierz** *catch by the collar*. A few verb-plus-preposition combinations in the sense 'in the guise of' involve **za**+A: **brać za ekspertę** *take for an expert*, **przebrać się za klauna** *dress up as a clown*, **służyć za przykład** *serve as an example*, **uchodzić za geniusza** *pass for a genius*, **uważać za idiotę** *consider an idiot*.

ACCUSATIVE OF TIME AND AMOUNT

3. The Accusative may be used by itself to express a period of time or an amount of something:

Czekam tu godzinę. *I've been waiting here for an hour.*

Jestem cały dzień zajęty. *I'm busy the entire day.*

Jesteśmy w Polsce pierwszy raz. *We are in Poland for the first time.*

Restauracja jest czynna całą dobę. *The restaurant is open day-and-night.*

Chwileczkę! *Just a moment!*

A few verbs take Accusative complements of amount, felt to be different from Accusatives of direct object:

Te papierosy kosztowały dolara. *Those cigarettes cost a dollar.*

Okręt waży trzydzieści tysięcy ton. *The ship weighs 30,000 tons.*

After verbs prefixed with **prze-**, Accusative complements of time are more clearly felt to be direct objects, as judged by the use of the Genitive after negation:

On ma przesiedzieć dziesięć lat w więzieniu. *He gets to serve ten years in prison.*

Compare:

On jeszcze nie przesiedział swoich dziesięciu lat. *He hasn't served out his ten years-G yet.*

THE INSTRUMENTAL CASE

The Instrumental is probably the semantically most variegated of the cases. Its basic use has to do with expressing the means by which something is done. Additionally, it has many figurative uses, most of which are based on the Instrumental of means. The various free uses of the Instrumental are difficult to distinguish one from another. It has an important syntactic use in the expression of predicate nominals, and it is required after a fair number of prepositions and verbs.

INSTRUMENTAL OF MEANS

1. The Instrumental is used to express the means by which something is done, especially with tools, body parts, and substances, but also with actions. It is frequently used figuratively. This use is extremely common; here is a mere smattering of examples: **dotykać palcem** *touch with one's finger*, **pzebić strzałą** *stick with an arrow*, **karmić piersią** *breast-feed*, **myć szamponem** *wash with shampoo*, **obudzić krzykiem** *rouse with a shout*, **odżywiać się orzechami** *feed on nuts*, **pisać długopisem** *write with a ball-point*, **przekonać argumentacją** *persuade with a line of reasoning*, **rozbawić anegdotą** *amuse with an anecdote*, **smarować olejem** *smear with oil*, **rysować kredkami** *draw with chalk*, **spłukać ciepłą wodą** *rinse with warm water*, **uderzyć pięścią** *strike with one's fist*, **walić młotem** *beat with a hammer*, **widzieć gołymi oczami** *see with one's bare eyes*, **wycierać ręcznikiem** *wipe with a towel*, **wymusić siłą** *compel by force*, **zawiązać sznurem** *tie up with twine*, **zdumiewać bogactwem** *amaze with wealth*, **zwrócić uwagę swoją uczonością** *call attention to oneself with one's learning*, **zrobić starą technologią** *do by means of old technology*, **żyć wspomnieniami** *live on one's memories*.

This use of the Instrumental is often exhibited after passive participles: **dotknięty palcem** *touched by a finger*, **olśniony rozmową** *dazzled by the conversation*, **osiągnięty żmudną pracą** *attained by drudge work*, **zachwycony wspaniałą kolekcją** *entranced by the marvelous collection*, **zaszokowany stanowiskiem** *shocked by someone's position*, **zawiązany sznurem** *tied up with twine*, and so on.

The sense 'with the aid or help of' is not usually expressed with the Instrumental case but rather with the phrasal prepositions **przy pomocy**+G or **za pomocą**+G: **Zrobił to przy pomocy kolegów.** *He did it with the assistance of his colleagues.* **On chodzi przy pomocy laski.** *He walks with the help of a cane.* **Ona czyta za pomocą szkiełka** *She reads with the help of a magnifying glass.*

INSTRUMENTAL OF CONVEYANCE

2. The Instrumental is used to express means of conveyance: **jechać taksówką (autobusem, koleją, windą)** *travel by taxi (bus, rail), take the elevator;* **lecieć samolotem** *fly by plane,* **płynąć statkiem (łodzią)** *sail by ship (boat).* Usually: **jechać na rowerze** *ride on a bike-L* (or **rowerem**).

INSTRUMENTAL OF CAUSE

3. The Instrumental is used with passive participles to express elemental causes: **zmoczony deszczem** *soaked by the rain,* **obalony wiatrem** *knocked over by the wind,* **grzany słońcem** *warmed by the sun.* The instrumental is also used after passive participles to refer to abstract causes: **opanowany żądzą zemsty** *ruled by the desire for revenge,* **pochłonięty pracą** *absorbed in work,* **trapiony sumieniem** *plagued by one's conscience,* **wstrząśnięty wiadomością** *stunned by the news,* **zaskoczony nagłym przyjściem** *surprised by the sudden arrival,* **zmęczony wysiłkiem** *exhausted from the exertion,* **zmartwiony stopniami** *worried by one's grades.*

Note that the Instrumental is not used to express the demoted agent or concrete subject in a passive construction, this being expressed with **przez**+A:

Powieść została napisana przez Prusa. *The book was written by Prus.*

Ten przypadek jest implikowany przez czasownik. *This case is connoted by the verb.*

INSTRUMENTAL OF COVER AND SUBSTANCE

4. The Instrumental is used to express the application of something to the surface of something or the filling up of something with something: **nakryć obrusem** *cover with a tablecloth,* **obrosnąć mchem** *become overgrown with moss,* **owinąć papierem** *wrap with paper* (or: **owinąć w paper**), **napełnić wodą** *fill with water,* **pokryć farbą** *cover with paint,* **nakryć naczyniami** *set (the table) with dishes,* **napełnić (zalać) wodą** *fill up (inundate) with water,* **przesiąknięty krwią** *soaked in blood,* **pokropić octem** *sprinkle with vinegar,* **pobrudzić błotem** *soil with mud;* **posypać piaskiem** *sprinkle with sand,* **przykryć kocem** *cover with a blanket,* **zasłonić firankami** *shade with curtains.* Figuratively in **szpikowany obcymi wyrazami**

permeated with foreign expressions, **otoczyć tajemnicą** *surround with mystery,* etc.

INSTRUMENTAL OF PATH

5. The Instrumental is used to express route-by-which: **iść drogą (lasem, polem, ulicą, doliną)** *go along the road (through the forest, field, along the street, across the valley);* **iść śladem (tropem)** *follow the trace (trail) of,* **jechać szosą (autostradą)** *drive along the highway (freeway),* **biec korytarzem** *to run down the corridor,* **płynąć Bałtykiem** *ply the Baltic,* **wieść torem** *lead along a path,* **włazić drzwiami i oknami** *crawl in through the doors and windows,* **wściskać się wszystkimi szparami** *press in through all cracks,* **zejść schodami** *descend the stairs.*

INSTRUMENTAL OF BODY-PART OR HELD OBJECT

6. The movement of a body-part or held object is expressed with the Instrumental: **bębnić palcami** *drum with one's fingers,* **machać ręką (laseczką)** *wave one's hand (a stick),* **kiwać głową** *nod one's head,* **kręcić głową** *shake one's head,* **skinąć głową** *nod one's head,* **trząść głową** *shake one's head,* **wzruszyć ramionami** *shrug one's shoulders,* **rzucić kamieniem** *throw a rock,* **mrugać oczami** *blink one's eyes,* **rzucić okiem** *cast an eye,* **ruszyć palcem** *move one's finger,* **ruszać kołyską** *rock a cradle,* **zawijać kierownicą** *turn the steering wheel,* **wywijać laseczką** *wave one's walking stick.* The verb 'throw' takes an Instrumental complement in the sense 'throw in a general direction, pelt', but Accusative in the sense of 'throw to':

Rzuć czymś we mnie, może ci będzie lepiej. *Throw something at me, maybe you'll feel better.*

Rzuć mi zapałki. *Toss me the matches*

INSTRUMENTAL OF ACCOMPANYING ACTION, GESTURE, OR EMOTION

7. The Instrumental may be used to express an accompanying gesture, reaction, or emotion: **odpowiedzieć uśmiechem** *respond with a smile,* **pominąć milczeniem** *pass over in silence,* **przywitać piosenkami** *greet with songs,* **reagować niezadowoleniem** *react with dissatisfaction,* **mówić szeptem** *speak in a whisper,* **iść szybkim krokiem** *walk at a brisk pace,* **kipieć złością** *seethe with anger,* **zapłonąć rumieńcem** *blush.*

INSTRUMENTAL OF MANNER, SPECIFICATION, COMPARISON

8. The Instrumental can be used to further specify an action. See **kończyć się fiaskiem** *end in a fiasco.* The Instrumental may also be used to specify further the idea of the verb: **umrzeć gwałtowną śmiercią** *die a violent death,* **listy płynęły całą falą** *letters flowed in an entire wave,* **robota szła**

pełną parą *work went on at full steam*, **woda lała się strumieniami** *water flowed in streams*.

Close to this use are expressions such as **jechać galopem (kłusem)** *ride at a gallop (trot)*, **dziesiątkami** *by the tens (= dozens)*, **iść parami** *go in pairs*. The Instrumental may be used to make comparisons, as in **czuję się panem sytuacji** *I feel like master of the situation*, **paść trupem** *fall a corpse (= down dead)*, **biec lotem strzały** *fly like an arrow shot*; etc.

INSTRUMENTAL OF RESPECT

9. The Instrumental may be used to express bodily or mental attitude, or to express with respect to what an action stands out: **błysnąć inteligencją** *sparkle with intelligence*, **odwrócony plecami** *with his back turned*, **odznaczać się odwagą** *distinguish oneself by one's valor*, **ubogi duchem** *poor in spirit*, **stać bokiem** *stand sidewise*, **siedzieć twarzą do okna** *sit with one's face toward the window*.

INSTRUMENTAL OF TIME

10. The Instrumental is used in certain more-or-less set expressions to express time of year or day: **zimą** *in the winter* (alongside **w zimie**), **jesienią** *in the fall* (alongside **w jesieni**), **latem** *in the summer* (alongside **w lecie**), but usually **na wiosnę** *in the spring* (alongside **wiosną**), **późną nocą** *late at night*, **dniem** *during the day*, **rankiem** *in the morning*, **dziś wieczorem** *this evening*. See also phrases such as **chwilami** *at times*, **czasami** *sometimes*, **całymi godzinami (latami)** *for hours (years) on end*, **dawnymi czasy** *in olden days*, **innym razem** *another time*, **miesiącami** *month after month*.

INSTRUMENTAL OF PREDICATE NOMINAL

11. By predicate nominal is meant a noun complement linked to the subject noun with the verb 'be', 'seem', 'become', 'turn out'. Predicate nominals in Polish more or less obligatorily take the Instrumental case:

On jest Polakiem (Ona jest Polką). *He (she) is a Pole.*

On był moim najlepszym przyjacielem. *He was my best friend.*

Ona będzie najlepszą kandydatką. *She will be the best candidate.*

On został prezydentem. *He became president.*

Jesteśmy dobrymi przyjaciółmi. *We are good friends.*

On stał się świetnym adwokatem. *He became an excellent lawyer.*

Ona okazała się zdolną skrzypaczką. *She turned out to be a talented violinist.*

This rule may be broken only rarely, for example with insults of the sort:

Jesteś kompletny idiota (or **kompletnym idiotą**)! *You're a complete idiot!*

Additionally, other nouns which have an adjective-like, characterizing quality to them may optionally be used in the Nominative, as though they were predicate adjectives:

Jestem byk. *I'm a Taurus (with the personality that implies).*

On jest po prostu geniusz. *He's simply a genius.*

Jesteśmy szlachta. *We are nobility.*

In all these instances, the Instrumental is a less expressive possibility.

INSTRUMENTAL OF SECOND OBJECT

12. After verbs which take two objects, the second will be in the Instrumental:

Wybrano go prezesem towarzystwa. *He was elected president of the society.*

Piast został obrany księciem. *Piast was elected prince.*

Mianowali pułkownika generałem. *They named the colonel a general.*

Ochrzczono go rzecznikiem rządu. *He was dubbed the government's spokeman.*

Trzeba go brać takim, jakim jest. *One must take him as he is.*

Akcja ta uczyniła chorych zakładnikami protestu. *That action made those who were sick the hostages of the protest.*

Somewhat related is the Instrumental of 'endowment':

Natura obdarzyła go dyszkantem. *Nature endowed him with a tenor voice.*

INSTRUMENTAL WITH PREDICATE ADJECTIVES

13. Predicate adjectives normally take the Nominative case, in agreement with the subject (see above under the Nominative case). However, verbs of 'seeming' and 'becoming' may occasionally be found with the Instrumental, especially in older literature, although today the Nominative is usual:

Ona okazała się bardzo zdolna (or **zdolną**). *She turned out to be very talented.*

On wydaje się (być) roztargniony (or **roztargnionym**). *He seems (to be) distracted.*

The Instrumental may be found with adjectival complements after the infinitive **być** *be;* after the impersonal **jest się** *one is;* after the verbal noun **bycie** *being,* and after the gerund **będąc** *(while) being,* especially when referring to states that no longer exist:

Trzeba być odważnym. *One must be brave.*

Nie powinno się podejmować decyzji, kiedy się jest podenerwowanym. *One oughtn't to make decisions when one is upset.*

Będąc młodym, marzył o zawodzie adwokata. *Being young (when he was young), he dreamed about a career as an attorney.*
Bycie wyrozmiałym nic cię nie kosztuje. *Being understanding doesn't cost you anything.*

Fairly frequent is the Instrumental with adjectives used sententially:

Jasnym (alongside **jasne**) **jest, że takie słabe struktury nie mogą podejmować poważnych decyzji.** *It is clear that such weak structures cannot undertake serious decisions.*

See also under Sentential Adjectives in the following chapter.

VERBS REQUIRING THE INSTRUMENTAL

14. The following verbs, many with **się**, take complements in the Instrumental case (cited in the Imperfective except where noted). Note that although a number of these verbs express 'control over', the verb **kontrolować** *control* itself takes the Accusative.

bawić się *play with*
brzydzić się *be disgusted by*
cieszyć się *enjoy*
częstować *(+A +I) treat to*
denerwować się *be upset by*
dysponować *have at one's disposal*
dowodzić *lead (e.g. troops)*
dyrygować *direct (orchestra)*
dzielić się *share*
gardzić *despise*
gospodarować *run, manage*
handlować *trade, deal in*
interesować się *be interested in*
kierować *direct*
kończyć się *end in*
manipulować *manipulate*
martwić się *be worried by*
obdarzać *bestow with*
operować *operate with*
opiekować się *look after*
pachnąć *smell of*

parać się *dabble in*
posługiwać się *make use of*
rozczarować się *be disappointed by*
rozporządzać *have to offer*
rządzić *govern*
sterować *steer*
śmierdzić *stink*
trapić się *worry one's head over*
trudnić się *be engaged in*
władać *have mastery over*
wzruszać się *be moved by*
zachwycać się *be enthralled with*
zaciągać się *inhale*
zagryzać *nibble on*
zajmować się *be engaged in*
zakończyć się *end with (pf)*
zarażać się *be infected by*
zatrącać *smell of, hint o*
zarządzać *managef*
zatruwać się *be poisoned by*

Examples:

Janek cieszy się dobrym zdrowiem. *Janek enjoys good health.*
Dzieci bawią się lalkami. *The children are playing with dolls.*
Janusz zajmuje się chemią. *Janusz's business is chemistry.*

Interesuję się przyrodą. *I'm interested in nature.*

Czasownik ten rządzi dopełniaczem. *This verb governs the Genitive.*

Gardzę każdą ideologią. *I despise every ideology.*

Generał dowodzi wojskiem. *The general is leading the army.*

Głęboko wzruszyłem się jego słowami. *I was deeply moved by his words.*

Mecz zakończył się fiaskiem. *The game ended in a fiasco.*

Wszędzie śmierdziało węglem. *It stank of coal everywhere.*

Zaraziłem się katarem. *I caught a cold.*

Rozczarowałem się jego najnowszą powieścią. *I was disappointed with his latest novel.*

Pachnie tu liliami. *It smells here of lilies.*

To już zatrąca fałszem. *That already smacks of falsehood.*

To tyle, co rzucanie grochem o ścianę. *That's like throwing peas at a wall (= a fruitless effort).*

Nie trap się tym. *Don't worry your head over it.*

On zarządza całym gospodarstwem. *He oversees the whole estate.*

Zatruliśmy się grzybami. *We got sick on mushrooms.*

Rozporządzamy wielkim asortymentem różnych towarów. *We have on offer a large assortment of various goods.*

INSTRUMENTAL AFTER PREPOSITIONS

15. The following prepositions take the Instrumental case in their basic spatial meanings (for possible Accusative uses, see above). In addition, all of these prepositions have associated figurative meanings.

między *between, among*
nad *over, above; with bodies of water: at*
pod *beneath, under; with towns: near*
pomiędzy *amidst*
poza *on the other side of, besides*
przed *before, in front of; ago*
z *together with*
za *beyond, beyond, after, in favor of*

Here are some illustrative phrases with Instrumental-requiring prepositions:

między+I 'between, among': **między nami** *between us*, **między sufitem a podłogą** *between the floor and the ceiling*, **między piątą a szóstą** *between five and six o'clock*, **między innymi** *among other things*.

nad+I. Literally, 'above, over': **nad nami** *over us*, **nad głową** *overhead*, **świętość nad świętościami** *holy of holies*. Location next to bodies of water: **nad Wisłą** *on the Vistula*, **nad morzem** *at the seaside*, **nad jeziorem** *by the lake*. The phrase **nad ranem** *toward morning*. With verbs and nouns meaning 'work on or consideration of': **praca nad dysertacją** *work on one's* *dissertation*, **badania nad środkami przeciwbólowymi** *research on anaesthetics*, **zastanawiać się nad problemem** *consider a problem*, **wahać się nad decyzją** *vacillate over a decision*. After verbs of pity and lament: **litować się nad ofiarami** *have pity for the victims*, **płakać nad zmarłymi** *lament over the dead*. With verbs of domination: **panować nad sytuacją** *master the situation*, **górować nad krajobrazem** *dominate the landscape*, **pastwić się nad bezbronnymi** *wreak one's rage on the defenseless*.

pod+I. Literally, 'beneath, at the foot of': **pod budynkiem** *at the foot of the building*, **pod ciężarem** *under the weight*, **pod dachem** *under the roof*, **pod drzewem** *under a tree*, **pod kocem** *under a blanket*, **pod pomnikiem** *at the foot of the monument*, **pod schodami** *below stairs*, **pod światłem** *under the light*. With towns, **pod+I** means 'on the outskirts of': **pod Warszawą** *near Warsaw*. Figuratively: **pod kontem** *at the doorstep of*, **pod adresem** *aimed at*, **pod kontrolą** *under the control of*, **pod naciskiem** *under pressure*, **pod napięciem** *under stress*, **pod opieką** *under the care*, **pod panowaniem** *under the reign of*, **pod parasolem** *under an umbrella*, **pod ostrzałem** *under fire*, **pod tytułem** *under the heading of*, **pod warunkiem** *under the condition*, **pod wpływem** *under the influence*, **pod zarzutem** *on the charge*.

przed+I. Literally, 'before, in front of': **przed domem** *in front of the house*, **przed koncertem** *before the concert*, **przed wojną** *before the war*, **przed wyjazdem** *before departure*, **przed godziną szóstą** *before six o'clock*, **przed ludźmi** *in front of people, in the public view*, **przed kolegami** *in front of one's co-workers*, **przed czasem** *prematurely*, **przede wszystkim** *especially*, **przed nami** *in front of us, awaiting us*. Often with perfective verbal nouns: **przed pójściem** *before going*, **przed zakończeniem** *before the end*. With periods of time **przed** may express 'ago': **przed chwilą** *a moment ago*, **przed laty** *years ago*, **przed paroma godzinami** *a few hours ago*. With verbs of defense, warning, or escape: **bronić się przed krytyką** *defend oneself from criticism*, **przestrzegać przed pożarem** *warn against fire*, **uciekać przed burzą** *take shelter from the storm*, **uchronić się przed słońcem** *protect oneself from the sun*.

z+I 'together with': **chleb z masłem** *bread and butter*, **kawa z cukrem** *coffee with sugar*, **kontakt z rodziną** *contact with one's family*, **mieszkać z rodzicami** *live with one's parents*, **my z Ewą** *Ewa and I*, **obcować ze złodziejami** *have to do with criminals*, **pracować z bólem głowy** *work with a headache*, **problem z pieniędzmi** *problem with money*, **przyjść z prośbą** *come with a request*, **razem z narodem** *together with the people*, **razem z nią** *together with her*, **sklep z winem** *wine-shop*, **torebka z ryżem** *bag of rice*, **współpraca z zagranicą** *cooperation with abroad*, **z każdą chwilą** *with each passing moment*, **z początkiem miesiąca** *with the beginning of the month*, **z przyjaciółmi** *with one's friends*, **z uporem** *stubbornly*.

Z+I often expresses identifying marks or accoutrements: **pan z brodą** *gentleman with a beard*, **kobieta z klasą** *woman of class*, **osoba z tytułem**

person with a title, **człowiek z poczuciem humoru** *person with a sense of humor.* **Z+I** also expresses an accompanying emotion: **czekać z niecierpieniem** *wait impatiently,* **reagować z entuzjazmem** *react with enthusiasm,* **patrzeć z ciekawością** *watch with curiosity,* **słuchać z przyjemnością** *listen with pleasure.* See also phrases like **Co jest z nią?** *What's wrong with her?* **Co ze zdrowiem?** *How's your health?* **Co się dzieje z moim podaniem?** *What's happening with my request?*

Z+I occurs after verbs of struggle and conflict: **dać sobie radę z walizką** *manage with a suitcase,* **kłócić się z mężem** *quarrel with one's husband,* **uporać się z jakąś trudnością** *struggle with some kind of difficulty,* **walczyć z wrogami** *do battle with one's enemies.* After verbs of reciprocal action: **całować się z ciocią** *exchange kisses with one's aunt,* **kochać się z kimś** *make love with someone,* **mocować się z czymś** *grapple with something,* **porozumieć się z sobą** *come to an understanding with one another,* **pożegnać się z przeszłością** *say goodbye to one's past,* **przywitać się z gośćmi** *greet one's guests,* **rozmawiać ze sobą** *talk with one another,* **spotykać się z klęską** *meet with defeat,* **umówić się z przyjaciółką** *make a date with one's girlfriend,* **wiązać się z kimś** *be connected to someone,* **widzieć się z kimś** *be seeing someone,* **zgadzać się z decyzją** *agree with a decision,* **żenić się z kuzynką** *marry one's cousin,* **zderzyć się z ciężarówką** *collide with a truck.*

za+I 'behind, beyond': **za biurkiem** *behind one's desk,* **za górami** *beyond the mountains,* **za kulisami** *behind the scenes,* **za nami** *behind us,* **za oknem** *outside the window,* **za plecami** *behind one's back,* **za rzeką** *on the other side of the river,* **za stołem** *at table,* **za ścianą** *behind the wall.* Expressions such as **jeden za drugim** *one after the other,* **samochód za samochodem** *car after car,* **tęsknić za rodziną** *pine for one's family,* **za chlebem** *in search of bread,* **za każdym razem** *each time,* **za pomocą** *with the help of,* **za sprawiedliwością (reformą)** *in favor of justice (reform),* **za twoim pozwoleniem** *with your permission.*

THE LOCATIVE CASE

The Locative case always occurs in combination with one or another of the following prepositions in the approximately indicated senses:

na *on, on top of, at*　　　　　**przy** *during, at, near*
o *about (concerning), at (a time)*　　**w** *in, at*
po *after, along, all over*

Here are a few illustrative phrases illustrating Locative-requiring prepositions:

na+L 'on': Literally in **na dachu** *on the roof,* **na lądzie** *on land,* **na morzu** *at/on the sea,* **na piśmie** *in writing,* **na plaży** *on the beach,* **na podłodze** *on the floor,* **na rogu** *on the corner,* **na roli** *on the land,* **na rowerze** *on a bike,* **na spacerze** *on a walk,* **na stole** *on the table,* **na ścianie** *on the wall,* **na ulicy** *on* *the street;* figuratively in phrases like **na podstawie** *on the basis,* **na stopniu rozwoju** *at the stage of development.* **Na** is used for wide open places: **na basenie** *at the swimming pool,* **na boisku** *on the playing field,* **na cmentarzu** *at the cemetery,* **na dworze** *outside,* **na lotnisku** *at the airport,* **na placu** *on the square,* **na rynku** *at the marketplace.* **Na** is used for presence at events: **na demonstracji** *at a demonstration,* **na egzaminie** *at an examination,* **na koncercie** *at a concert,* **na kolacji (obiedzie, śniadaniu)** *at supper (dinner, breakfast),* **na konferencji** *at a conference,* **na lekcji** *at the lecture,* **n a przedstawieniu** *at a performance,* **na przyjęciu** *at the party,* **na wykładzie** *at a lecture,* **na zebraniu** *at the meeting,* **na zjeździe** *on the congress;* with compass directions: **na północy** *in the north,* **na południu** *in the south,* **na wschodzie** *in the east,* **za zachodzie** *in the west;* 'in a state or stage', especially work-related: **na chorobie** *on sick leave,* **na delegacji** *on a business trip,* **na emeryturze** *in retirement,* **na ukończeniu** *in the final stage,* **n a zwolnieniu** *laid off.* See also the verb-phrases **polegać na czymś** *depend on,* **zależeć komuś na czymś** *be important for someone,* **znać się na czymś** *know something about something.* For more information, see below under The Choice Between **na** and **w**.

o+L 'about': **o pracy** *about work,* **o tej książce** *about that book.* To express clock time: **o godzinie czwartej** *at 4 o'clock,* **o świcie** *at dawn,* **o tej porze** *at that time.* O+L is frequently found after verbs of knowledge such as **czytać** *read,* **przekonać się** *find out, determine,* **marzyć** *(day)dream,* **pamiętać** *remember,* **słyszeć** *hear,* **wiedzieć** *know,* **zapomnieć** *forget,* and so on. A special use is in the expression of traits: **dziewczyna o jasnych włosach** *girl with light hair,* **dom o białych ścianach** *house with white walls,* **człowiek o dziwnym usposobieniu** *man with a strange disposition,* **osoba o chorej fantazji** *person with a sick imagination,* etc.

po+L 'after, along, all over, according to': **po pracy** *after work,* **po miesiącu** *after a month,* **po śmierci** *after death,* **po mieście** *all over town,* **po rzece** *along the river,* **po nocach** *night after night,* **butelka po mleku** *milk-bottle,* **noc po nocy** *night after night,* **gładzić po włosach** *stroke someone's hair,* **poznać po głosie** *recognize by one's voice.* Often with perfective verbal nouns: **po wyjściu** *after leaving,* **po obudzeniu się** *after waking up.* A special use of **po** is in distributive numeral expressions like **Dałem dzieciom po jabłku.** *I gave the children an apple each.* **Zjedliśmy po kanapce.** *We ate a sandwich each.* **Wypijemy po (jednym) kieliszku.** *We'll drink a glass each.* In the distributive use, **po** is used with the Accusative after numerals other than 'one': **Zjedliśmy po sześć bananów.** *We ate six bananas each.*

przy+L 'at, during, near to, in the presence of': **przy muzyce** *to the accompaniment of music,* **przy pracy** *during/while at work,* **przy rodzinie** *by/with one's family,* **przy stole** *at the table,* **przy ścianie** *next to the wall,* **przy świadkach** *in the presence of witnesses,* **przy świetle** *in the light,* **przy tej okazji** *on that occasion,* **przy ulicy Miodowej** *next to Miodowa Street.*

Attachment: **frędzla przy poduszce** *tassel on a pillow,* **wojskowy przy ambasadzie** *military man attached to the embassy,* **upierać się przy zdaniu** *insist on one's opinion.* Often with imperfective verbal nouns: **przy wychodzeniu** *while leaving.*

w+L 'in': Literally in **w bibliotece** *in the library,* **w fotelu** *in an armchair,* **w hotelu** *in a hotel,* **w kapeluszu** *in (wearing) a hat,* **w okularach** *in (wearing) glasses,* **w krześle** *in a chair,* **w łóżku** *in bed,* **w muzeum** *in the museum,* **w pokoju** *in the room,* **w pracy** *at work,* **w pudełku** *in a box,* **w szafie** *in the cupboard,* **w szkole** *at/in school,* **w szufladzie** *in the drawer,* **w Warszawie** *in Warsaw.* In time periods: **w semestrze** *in the semester,* **w styczniu** *In January,* **w tym momencie** *at that moment,* **w tym tygodniu (miesiącu, roku)** *in this week (month, year),* **w życiu** *in one's life.* Figuratively in: **w dobrym nastroju** *in a good mood,* **w druku** *in print,* **w gospodarce** *in the economy,* **w modzie** *in fashion,* **w moim guście** *to my taste,* **w moim typie** *in my type,* **w obiegu** *in circulation,* **w odosobnieniu** *in isolation,* **w pamięci** *in one's memory,* **w podróży** *en route,* **w porządku** *in order, all right,* **w rezultacie** *as a result,* **w tym stylu** *in this style,* **w szoku** *in shock,* **w zdumieniu** *in amazement.* The phrase **kochać się w kimś** *be in love with.*

THE CHOICE BETWEEN *NA* AND *W(E)*

The preposition **w** means literally 'in', and **na** means 'on'; 'at' a place is for the most part split between **w** and **na**. Dictionaries often turn out to be of little help in instances of indecision. The following guidlelines are in addition to those contained in the examples of uses of **na** and **w** above. Many nouns allow either **w** or **na** according to logic see **w/na pudełku** *in/on the box,* **w/na jeziorze** *in/on the lake,* **w/na powietrzu** *in/on the air,* **w/na środku** *in/on the middle.* Sometimes the difference in meaning will be other than simply literal: **na uniwersytecie** *at the university (e.g. attending)* vs. **w uniwersytecie** *(visiting or working);* **w fabryce** *in the factory* vs. **na fabryce** *on the factory grounds;* **w zatoce** *in the bay* vs. **na zatoce** *in the bay area,* **na operze** *at the opera* vs. **w operze** *(singing) in the opera.* **W mieście** means 'in the town', while, colloquially, **na mieście** means 'in town'. One hears, with little if any difference in meaning, either **w sali** or **na sali** *in the lecture hall;* **w świetlicy** or **na świetlicy** *in the clubroom;* **w zakładzie** or **na zakładzie** *in the shop, plant,* **w kopalni** or **na kopalni** *in the mine,* **w świecie** or **na świecie** *in the world, on the Earth.* **Na** is idiomatically determined in **na dworcu** *at the station,* **na klatce schodowej** *in the stairwell,* **na korytarzu** *in the corridor,* **na swoim miejscu** *in it's place,* **na poczcie** *at the post office.*

Countries usually take **w** (**w Anglii** *in England,* **we Francji** *in France,* **w Niemczech** *in Germany*); however, a few countries either require or allow **na**: **na/w Litwie** *in Lithuania,* **na/w Słowacji** *in Slovakia,* **na Ukrainie** *in Ukraine,* **na Węgrzech** *in Hungary.* Islands and peninsulas usually take **na**: **na Wyspach Hawajskich** *on the Hawaiian Islands,* **na Cejlonie** *on Ceylon,* **na Alasce** *in Alaska,* **na Florydzie** *in Florida.* Regions within a country take either na or w: na **Mazowszu** *in the Mazowsze Region,* na **Kurpiach** *in the Kurpie Region,* w **Małopolsce** *in Little Poland,* w **Galicji** *in Galicia.* Town districts take na: na **Mokotowie** *in Mokotow,* **Na Śródmieściu** *In Srodmiescie (district)* vs. **w śródmieściu** *downtown.* However: **w centrum** *in the center part of town.*

THE VOCATIVE CASE

The Vocative case is used for direct address; it usually has an accompanying affectionate or respectful emotional connotation. By the nature of things, the Vocative is used almost exclusively with titles and first names for people and pets. However, in principle any noun may form a Vocative in the singular. In the plural, the Vocative is always like the Nominative and so cannot be easily distinguished other than according to the way a name or title is used.

The Vocative is used in greetings such as the following; its use after the Vocative titles **panie** and **pani** is obligatory:

Dzień dobry, panie dyrektorze! *Hello, director!*

Witam, panie Janie (pani Heleno)! *Greetings, Jan (Helena)!*

Szanowny Panie (Szanowna Pani)! *Dear Sir (Lady)!*

Zaraz to zrobię, panie ministrze! *I'll do that right away, Your Excellency!*

Słusznie, panie sierżancie! *Right you are, Sergeant!*

Witam serdecznie, profesorze! *A sincere welcome, professor!*

Kochany Bracie (Kochana Siostro)! *Dear Brother (Sister)* (at the head of a letter).

The Vocative of relation-names is the rule when addressing someone around the home: **Mamo!** *Mother!* **Tato!** *Dad!* **Babciu!** or **Babuniu!** *Grandma!* **Ciociu!** *Aunt!* **Synku!** or **Syneczku!** *Sonnie!* **Córeczko!** or **Córuniu!** *Dear daughter!* and so on. In use outside the home, the Vocative form is slightly more common with names for women than for men; and with affectionate names than with formal names. Thus, **Mario!** *Mary!* sounds slightly affected, while **Marysiu!** (diminutive of the same name) sounds normal. **Marysiu!** for its part will be encountered somewhat more frequently than, say, **Rysiu!** *Rick!* from **Ryszard** (the Nominative forms **Rysiek, Ryś,** or **Rysio** often being used instead). The Vocative is regularly used with the religious names and titles **ksiądz** V **księże** *priest,* **siostra** V **siostro** *sister/nurse,* **ojciec** V **ojcze** *father,* **Bóg** V **Boże** *God,* **Jezus** *Jesus,* irregular V **Jezu** (or **Jezusie**). The Vocative of most non-diminutive relation-names is highly unusual or impossible; hence one will almost never encounter such forms as **!babko, !ciotko, !córko, !wuju,** and so on.

In formal situations, one may use the Vocative of a title combined with the last name (but note that the last name itself does not take the Vocative): **Nie ujdzie panu to, doktorze Śliwczuk!** *You won't get away with it, doctor Sliwczuk!* One occasionally hears strangers addressed at a distance in public with the Vocative: **Dziewczyno!** *Girl!* **Człowieku!** *Man!* **Kobieto!** *Woman!* **Kolego!** *Buddy!* **Obywatelu!** *Citizen!*, although such use should be consideed uncouth. It is better to use **przepraszam pana/panią** or **proszę pana/pani**.

The Vocative is used in insults following the model: **Brudasie!** *You slob!*, **Ty gnoju!** *You scum!* **Kundlu!** *You cur!* **Kretynie!** *Moron!* **Głupku!** *Dolt!* Equally as often it is used with mocking endearment, as **Głuptasie!** *You silly!* **Stary byku!** *You old bull (= goat)!* In poetry, the Vocative may be encountered with a wide variety of nouns, especially abstract: **Wolności!** *O Freedom!*, **Młodości!** *O Youth!*, **Ojczyzno moja!** *O my fatherland!* **Ziemio moja ukochana!** *O my native land!* **Mój nieszczęśliwy losie!** *O my unhappy fate!*, **O zła godzino!** *O evil hour!* **O polska krwi!** *O Polish blood!*, and so on.

A comparatively recent development is the colloquial use of the Vocative in certain Nominative functions as in **Rysiu się spóźnia.** *Rysio is running late.*

POLISH TRANSLATIONS OF 'FOR'

The English preposition *for* has a wide variety of translations into Polish, using various prepositions, several cases, and even the conditional of the verb. The most important correspondences of English *for* are given below:

1. **dla+G** 'for the benefit of': **Czy te kwiaty są dla mnie?** *Are those flowers for me?*; 'easy/hard for': **To łatwe dla mnie.** *That's easy for me.*; 'for the sake of': **sztuka dla sztuki** *art for art's sake.*

2. **za+A** 'in exchange for': **Ile zapłaciłeś za ten zegarek?** *How much did you pay for that watch?*, **Sprzedałem za grosze.** *I sold it for pennies.*; 'responsible for': **Nie odpowiadam za jego zachowanie.** *I'm not responsible for his behavior*; 'in place of': **Niech ja to zrobię za ciebie.** *Let me do that for (instead of) you.*; 'on behalf of': **za wolność** *for freedom*; 'mistake for': **Wziąłem go za lekarza.** *I took him for a doctor.* **Uchodził za akrystokratę.** *He tried to pass for an aristocrat*; 'thank for, ask pardon for': **Dziękuję za pomoc.** *Thanks for the help.*, **Przepraszam za kłopot.** *Excuse me for the bother.*

3. **na+A** 'intended for': **bilet na samolot** *ticket for the airplane*, **podręcznik na użytek cudzoziemców** *textbook for the use of foreigners*, 'desire for': **Mam ochotę na coś zimnego.** *I feel like having something cold.*; 'for naught': **To wszystko pójdzie na nic.** *That'll all go for nothing.*; 'for an event or time': **bilet na godzinę ósmą** *ticket for 8 o'clock*, **spóźniać się na przedstawienie** *be late for the performance*; 'for a time yet to come': **Wyjeżdam na rok.** *I'm leaving for a year.* **Rozstajemy się na zawsze.** *We're parting forever.* Also see exclamations like **na miłość boską** *for God's sake!*

4. **od+G** 'for (a time just past)': **Mieszkam w Warszawie od siedmiu lat.** *I've been living in Warsaw for the past seven years'.*

5. **przez+A** 'for a period of time': **Przez ostatnie miesiące pracujemy pełną parą.** *We've been working at full steam for the last (several) months.* This sense

of 'for' may also be expressed by the bare Accusative case: **Noszę ten kapelusz już jedenaście lat.** *I've been wearing that hat for eleven years already.* The expression 'for periods of time on end' can be expressed by the bare Instrumental: **całymi dniami** *for days on end,* although **całe dnie** or **przez całe dnie** is also correct.

6. **po+A** 'go for': **Wyskoczę po piwo.** *I'll dash out for some beer.* **Zajądę po ciebie o ósmej.** *I'll drop by for you at eight o'clock.*

7. **do+G** 'for (of specific application)': **woda do picia** *water for drinking,* **maszynka do ogolenia** *machine for shaving, electric razor,* **pasta do zębów** *paste for teeth, toothpaste.*

8. **o+A** '(ask, fight) for': **prosić o pomoc** *ask for help,* **walczyć o istnienie (równouprawnienie)** *fight for existence (equality).*

9. **u+G** 'for (be employed by a person)': **Ona pracuje u dentysty.** *She works for a dentist.* 'Work for a company or firm' is translated by **w+L: Pracuję w banku.** *I work for a bank.*

10. **jak na+A** 'for (of belittling comparison)': **On nieźle mówi jak na cudzoziemca.** *He speaks not badly for a foreigner.*

11. **z(e)+G** 'known for': **On jest znany ze swoich wcześniejszych prac.** *He is known for his earlier works.*

12. **za+I** 'long for': **Tęsknię za tobą.** *I miss you, long for you.* In older Polish, **po + L: Tęsknię po tobie.**

13. **jeśli chodzi o+A, co do+G** 'as for': **Jeśli chodzi o brata, to on jest jeszcze w szkole.** *As for my brother, he is still in school.* **Co do twojego pomysłu, on jest zupełnie nierealny.** *As for your idea, it is totally impractical.*

14. The conditional. The English use of *for* after a verb of request has a correspondent in the Polish conditional:

Prosili, żebyśmy mniej hałasowali. *They asked for us to make less noise.*

NOUN ROLES

Different languages have different ways of expressing the roles nouns can play vis-à-vis the verb and the other nouns in a sentence. NOUNS, whose basic function is to refer to objects in the world, are ontologically primary with respect to VERBS which, by referring to the actions, states, and events in which nouns can participate, are inherently at least somewhat abstract, and dependent on nouns and noun roles. By way of illustration, take the primary nouns *dog, man, ball*. It is possible to think of various abstract relations, expressed by verbs, which can coordinate these three nouns, each in different ways. With each verb, the nouns assume different roles.

Verb: *throw*:   The *man* threw the *dog* the *ball*.

Noun roles: *man*: actor   *dog*: recipient   *ball*: object

Verb: *hit*   The *man* hit the *dog* with the *ball*.

Noun roles: *man*: actor   *dog*: object   *ball*: instrument

Verb: *bring*   The *dog* brought the *ball* to the *man*.

Noun roles: *dog*: actor   *ball*: object   *man*: goal; and so on

The number of roles which can be delineated in this way, by looking at different verbs and the different kinds of roles that can occur with them, are several dozen in number at least. In order to make the role of a noun clear in a sentence, Polish uses mainly (a) case endings on nouns, and (b) prepositions in combination with case endings on nouns. By contrast, English mainly uses (a) the order of the nouns in the sentence, and (b) prepositions plus the nouns.

SUBJECT, COMPLEMENT, OBJECT, ADJUNCT

Both English and Polish usually elevate, as it were, a single noun in the sentence, typically the actor (or, if there is only one noun in the sentence, then that noun) to the status of GRAMMATICAL SUBJECT, this being the main noun, and the noun with which the verb of the sentence grammatically agrees and around which the sentence is usually oriented. In the first two sentences above, *man* is the subject; in the third sentence, the subject is *dog*. Many verbs are not complete without specifying more than just a subject. Material that is required in addition to a verb and its subject is termed the COMPLEMENT of the verb. In *The man threw the dog a ball*, the segment *the dog a ball* comprises the complement (the segment *the man threw* would not be complete by itself).

The most frequent kind of complement is the DIRECT OBJECT, referring to a noun toward which the verb's action is directed. By convention, direct objects in Polish are considered to be verb-required nouns occurring in the Accusative case, as **piłkę** in **Pan rzucił psu piłkę** *The man threw the dog a ball.*

Verbs that take direct objects are called TRANSITIVE. Verbs that take complements which are not direct objects are called SEMITRANSITIVE, and the complements themselves are called OBLIQUE COMPLEMENTS. Oblique complements divide into BARE-CASE complements and PREPOSITIONAL complements. An example of a bare-case oblique complement would be the Instrumental form **domem** in **Matka zajmuje się domem** *Mother takes care of the house.* An example of an oblique prepositional complement would be **do sklepu** in **Idę do sklepu** *I'm going to the store.*

A noun phrase (a noun and its possible modifiers) which occurs relatively optionally in a sentence, and is not required or strongly connoted by the verb, is called an ADJUNCT. Adjuncts typically perform an adverbial function; that is, they answer one of the adverbial questions: how, when, why, where, how long, how often, and so on. In the sentence **Pójdę do teatru po obiedzie.** *I'm going to the theater after dinner*, the phrase **po obiedzie** *after dinner* is an adverbial adjunct, answering the question 'when'. An example of a non-adverbial adjunct would be **z Julią** in **Idę do teatru z Julią** *I'm going to the theater with Julia.* Here, the adjunct answers the question "with whom", and is called a 'comitative' or 'accompanying' adjunct.

Two important types of noun phrases straddle the border between being complements and adjuncts, and are accordingly termed INDIRECT COMPLE-MENTS These are (a) *indirect objects*, usually expressed in Polish either with the Dative case or with **do** *to* plus the Genitive case, as in **Kupię ci coś** *I'll buy you something*, or **Mówię do ciebie** *I'm talking to you;* and (b) the INSTRUMENTAL PHRASE, which expresses means-by-which, as in **Piszę tę pracę ołówkiem** *I'm writing this assignment with a pencil* or **Jadę do Warszawy pociągiem.** *I'm traveling to Warsaw by train.* Indirect complements may occur either by themselves as a complement or with another complement. However, Dative and Instrumental complements rarely occur together.

Finally, one may mention DOUBLE COMPLEMENTS, which are required after various kinds of verbs; first, after verbs of placement like **dodać** *add*, as in **Dodać mleka do ciasta.** *Add some milk to the dough.* Secondly, double complements occur after verbs of selection like **wybrać** *elect*, as in **Wybrali Wałęsę prezydentem.** *They elected Walesa president.* Thirdly, verbs of motion may take double complements, as in **Idę do teatru na przedstawienie.** *I'm going to the theater to a performance.* Lots of other verbs, not always easy to classify, also take double complements, for example **częstować** +A, +I *treat to:* **Poczęstował nas tokajem.** *He treated us to Tokay.*

THE FUNCTION OF WORD-ORDER

WORD ORDER plays a fundamentally different role in Polish on the one hand and English on the other. Consider the English sentence

The man threw the dog a ball.

In this sentence, according to the rules of English, the first noun in the sentence, *man*, because it is placed before the verb *threw*, is interpreted as actor. Grammatically speaking it is the sentence's subject. The second noun, *dog*, by being placed both after the verb and before the third noun *ball*, is interpreted as the recipient. Grammatically, it is an indirect object. The third and final noun, *ball*, is interpreted as object (also called a 'patient'). Grammatically, it is a direct object. All of these role- and grammatical-relation assignments are made partly on the basis of logic but, mainly, on the basis of word order. Changing the word order changes the way the role of the noun is interpreted, even in the face of logic. In English, *The man threw the dog a ball* is a completely different sentence from *The man threw the ball a dog*. In English even logic cannot intervene to help make sense out of a sentence with incorrect word order. In any language, the practical limits of word order as an indicator of a noun's role are quite circumscribed. In practice, English delimits mainly these three roles—actor, recipient, and object—(grammatically: subject, indirect object, direct object) with word order alone. Other roles are usually indicated with prepositions.

Polish, which has a highly formalized case-ending system for indicating noun-roles and grammatical relations, does not primarily make use of word order for indicating noun roles. Instead, it uses case-endings on nouns, and prepositions in combination with case-endings on nouns. Differences in word order are used to express not roles of nouns, but emphasis on nouns, something which in English is usually expressed with differences in intonation, or at least in some other way than with word order. In sentences containing three nouns, such as the man-dog-ball sentence, the following word-orders are common in Polish, all expressing the same basic proposition "The man (**pan**-Nominative) threw (**rzucił**) the dog (**psu**-Dative) the ball (**piłkę**-Accusative)". Each of these orders answers a slightly different question, the key to the interpretation being the last word in the sentence:

Statement made:

Pan rzucił psu *piłkę.*   *The man threw the dog a BALL.*

Piłkę rzucił pan *psu.*   *The ball was thrown by the man TO THE DOG.*

Psu rzucił piłkę *pan.*   *To the dog a ball was thrown BY THE MAN.*

Question answered:

Pan rzucił psu *piłkę.*   *WHAT did the man throw to the dog?*

Piłkę rzucił pan *psu.*   *TO WHOM did the man throw the ball?*

Psu rzucił piłkę *pan.*   *WHO threw the ball to the dog?*

In Polish, word order is determined by the principle: *the closer the item is to the end of the sentence, the more informative the item is, and the more logical emphasis it carries.* The item placed at the beginning of a declarative sentence tends to be the sentence's TOPIC, the thing commented on by the verb and possible following items. The item placed at the end contains the COMMENT, the answer to the question the statement implicitly responds to. Peripheral adverbial phrases, referring to the general circumstances of an action, often occur in sentence-initial position, before the topic:

Dzisiaj wolę zostać w domu. *I prefer to stay at home today.*

W połowie czerwca Natalia postanowiła przeprowadzić kontrolę czytelni. *In the middle of June Natalia decided to conduct an inventory of the reading room.*

When all items in a sentence are equally new, a non-direct-object complement often precedes the verb, with the subject following the verb:

Na jednej ścianie wisiał portret prezydenta. *On one wall hung a portrait of the president.*

W dole po szynach toczył się powoli pociąg. *Below along the tracks a train slowly rolled.*

In cases of formal ambiguity between subject and object, the choice is made on the basis of logic:

Wejście-*entrance* **stanowiło**-*comprised* **kilka**-*several* **desek**-*boards*. *Several boards comprised the entrance.*

If logic does not avail, then the left-hand noun phrase will be interpreted as the most likely subject. Thus, the following sentence will most naturally be interpreted as 'children-N subj. like elves-A obj.', rather than the semantically and grammatically possible inverse proposition.

Dzieci-*children* **lubią**-*like* **krasnoludki**-*elves*.

MAJOR POLISH SENTENCE TYPES

'Be' Sentences

The verb 'be' occurs in a wide range of uses, including introduction; equation; membership in a set; location; existence; and state. For impersonal 'be' sentences (of the type 'it's cold', etc.), and for the 'be' of time (as in 'it's five o'clock') see under Impersonal Sentences.

1. INTRODUCING AND NAMING 'BE' SENTENCES. In order to introduce a noun into a discussion, to identify it, or to give its name, the **to jest** (pl. **to są**) construction is used:

To jest zeszyt (lampa, krzesło). *That is a notebook (lamp, chair).*

To są moje okulary. *Those are my eyeglasses.*

In this construction, the item **to** is constant, but does not condition agreement on the verb. The verb agrees in gender and number with the noun being introduced, which occurs in the Nominative case. In the present tense, the verb may be omitted:

To (jest) nasz lektor. *That is our lecturer.*

To (są) nasi sąsiedzi. *Those are our neighbors.*

To była moja żona. *That was my wife.*

To byli moi studenci. *Those were (or: that was) my students.*

See also the expression: **To jest to.** That's the ticket, that's the thing, that's the idea.

When introducing persons, one uses personal forms of **być** plus the name:

Jestem Adam Bobrowski. *I am Adam Bobrowski.*

Czy pani przypadkiem jest Anna Bobrowska? *Are you by chance Anna Bobrowska?*

2. EQUATIONAL OR IDENTIFYING 'BE' SENTENCES. When two nouns are stated as being the equivalent of one another, **to jest/to są** (with present-tense **jest** or **są** being optional and often omitted) is used. Both nouns occur in the Nominative:

Ten pan to mój znajomy. *That man is my acquaintance.*

Ci ludzie to nasi przyjaciele. *Those people are our friends.*

Warszawa to stolica Polski. *Warsaw is the capital of Poland.*

Ich dom to szczyt przepychu. *Their house is the height of ostentation.*

Notes on Identifying *to*

a. The construction with **to** can be dismissive or summative in effect. See:

Magda to bardzo atrakcyjna dziewczyna. *Magda is a very attractive girl.*

This sentence means that 'being an attractive girl' is a good summative characterization of Magda.

b. The particle **to** is often used to point attention to identity or responsibility:

To ja wziąłem twoje papiery. *It was I that took your papers.*

To nie on był odpowiedzialny za kryzys fiskalny. *It was not he that was responsible for the fiscal crisis.*

c. **To** may be used to link an infinitive to a noun:

Powiedzieć, że jestem zadowolony, to byłaby przesada. *To say that I'm happy would be an exaggeration.*

3. INCLUSIONAL 'BE' SENTENCES. 'Be' in the sense of inclusion in a set is expressed with forms of **być** linking two nouns, the member-noun and the set-noun. The set-noun appears in the Instrumental:

Mój brat jest oficerem. *My brother is an officer.*

Moja siostra była nauczycielką. *My sister was a school-teacher.*

Największym polskim miastem jest Warszawa. *The largest Polish town is Warsaw.*

Użycie tej formy jest błędem gramatycznym. *The use of this form is a grammatical error (= belongs to the class of grammatical errors).*

The Instrumental is often used even when the set-noun is unique:

Jestem jego matką i mnie to bardzo boli. *I am his mother, and it hurts me a lot.*

(in the first person, this sounds better than possible **To ja jestem jego matka...**).

To an extent, equational and inclusional 'be' sentences are in competition with one another. Especially if the set is small or amounts to one item, the same idea may be expressed either one way or the other. Thus, the first two sentences above sound good mainly when expressed inclusionally (my brother belongs to the set of officers; my sister belongs to the class of school-teachers). However, the third sentence sounds quite normal when expressed equationally: **Największe polskie miasto to Warszawa.**

In theory, generic or innate membership in a set may be expressed by putting the set-noun in the Nominative instead of the Instrumental. In practice, this happens only rarely, and only when the noun has virtually adjectival force or refers to a character trait, as in

On jest geniusz! *He's a genius (= he's brilliant).*

Pan jest partacz! *You're a bungler!*

Compare

On jest lwem. *He's a Leo (= he was born under that sign).*

On jest lew. *He's a Leo (= he has the qualities typical of a Leo).*

Ona jest Polką. *She's a Pole (= she's a native of Poland).*

Zresztą ona jest Polka. *After all, she's a Pole (= that's the behavior one might expect of her).*

It is rarely, if ever, incorrect to use the Instrumental in such instances.

4. LOCATIONAL 'BE' SENTENCES AND OTHER LOCATION-VERBS. 'Be' in the sense of 'be physically present' somewhere is one of various verbs that can be followed by locational complements, and which may also be

treated here. Some common location-verbs include **mieszkać** *reside, live in a place,* **przebywać** *stay,* **rosnąć** *grow,* **występować** *appear,* **zatrzymywać się** *stay, tarry* and others. Activity verbs like **pracować** *work,* **czytać** *read,* **grać** *play,* **śpiewać** *sing,* **występować** *appear, occur,* and so on, often function as location-verbs. Some examples of locational sentences are:

Janek jest dzisiaj w Warszawie. *Janek is in Warsaw today.*

Maria pracuje w Warszawie ale mieszka w Łodzi. *Maria works in Warsaw but lives in Lodz.*

Brat przebywa za granicą. *My brother is staying abroad.*

Pod domem rośnie dąb. *Next to the house an oak is growing.*

Anna śpiewa w operze. *Anna is singing in the opera.*

Zatrzymujemy się w Hotelu Europejskim. *We're staying at the Hotel Europejski.*

Especially important among location-verbs are verbs of physical attitude like **leżeć** *lie,* **stać** *stand,* **siedzieć** *sit,* **wisieć** *hang* which, in Polish, are more often used with inanimate things than in English:

W kącie stoi lampa. *A lamp is standing in the corner.*

Warszawa leży nad Wisłą. *Warsaw is situated on the Vistula.*

Na ścianie wisiały trzy portrety. *Three portraits were hanging on the wall.*

Babcia siedzi w swoim krześle. *Grandma is sitting in her chair.*

For further information on verbs of body position, see Chapter 11.

5. EXISTENTIAL 'be' sentences are used to state the presence (or absence) of a thing in a location and, as such, they are similar to, though not the same as, locational 'be' sentences.

   a. POSITIVE EXISTENTIAL 'be' sentences, like locational 'be' sentences, consist of a subject, a form of **być**, and a location-phrase:

Profesor jest w gabinecie. *The professor is in his office.*

W hotelu są wolne pokoje. *There are vacant rooms in the hotel.*

Anna była wczoraj w pracy. *Anna was at work yesterday.*

Existential 'be' sentences are often used to query or describe the presence or absence of people in given places, or the presence or absence of items in stores:

Czy jest Janek? *Is Janek there?*

Czy dyrektor już jest? *Is the director there yet?*

Czy jest dziś świeży chleb? *Is there fresh bread today?*

Czy są świeże bułki? *Are there any fresh rolls?*

As the examples show, this kind of sentence is often matched in English with *there is, there are*; note the absence in Polish of any correspondent of *there*.

b. NEGATIVE EXISTENTIAL sentences replace **być** with **nie ma** in the present tense, and with **nie było** and **nie będzie** in the past and future tenses, respectively. The complement (the person or thing missing) appears in the Genitive case:

Nie ma Jana w domu. *Jan is not at home.*

W niedzielę nie ma świeżego chleba w sklepach. *On Sunday there is no fresh bread in the stores.*

Anny nie będzie jutro w pracy. *Anna will be absent at work tomorrow.*

W całym mieście nie było ani jednego otwartego sklepu. *In the entire town there wasn't a single store open.*

The difference between a locational 'be' sentence and an existential sentence may be seen under negation. The negation of a locational 'be' sentence does not prompt the use of **nie ma** or any other changes. Compare:

Locational: **Janek nie był w Warszawie dzisiaj.** *Janek was not in Warsaw today.*

Existential: **Janka nie było w Warszawie dzisiaj.** *(approximately same meaning)*

The negative locational sentence is implicitly contrastive, and suggests volition on the part of the subject: Janek has chosen to be not in Warsaw today, but somewhere else. The negated existential sentence has no such connotation: Janek is simply absent from Warsaw. A sentence like

W lodówce jest piwo. *There is some beer in the refrigerator.*

is most naturally apt to be taken as existential (since the beer is not there of its own volition). Accordingly, its negation will be expressed existentially:

Nie ma piwa w lodówce. *There is no beer in the refrigerator.*

c. When the item being existentially negated occurs in its own clause, the syntax of that clause takes precedence over the Genitive:

Jest (nie ma) o co się martwić. *There's something (nothing) to worry about.*

Jest (nie ma) komu (or **kto**) **tam pojechać.** *There's someone (no one) to drive there.*

Jest (nie ma) czemu się dziwić (czego się bać). *There's something nothing) to be surprised at (to be afraid of).*

Było (nie było) co powiedzieć. *There was something (nothing) to say.*

Będzie (nie będzie) czym się przejmować. *There will be (won't be) anything to concern oneself about.*

d. In Polish, other verbs besides **być** with existential force (including the frequentative **bywać**) do *not* take the Genitive of the missing item when the sentence is negated; hence only the following are possible:

W tym jeziorze węgorze nie bywają. *Eels-N don't occur in this lake.*

Nie istnieją żadne inne możliwości. *No other possibilities-N exist.*

Takie problemy nie występują u nas. *Such problems-N do not occur here.*

Additionally, the negated infinitive of existential 'be' (**nie być**) does *not* take the Genitive:

On może nie być w domu o tej porze. *He-N may not be at home at this time of day.*

6. QUANTITATIVE 'BE' SENTENCES. Related to locational and existential 'be' sentences are 'be' and other sentences describing the amount of something:

Tu jest pięć jabłek. *Here are five apples.*

Tu są moje dwie najlepsze przyjaciółki. *Here are my two best girl-friends.*

W tym domu mieszka siedem osób. *Seven persons live in this house.*

7. 'BE' SENTENCES OF TIME OF DAY. Polish sentences expressing time of day, day of the week, and so on, often use forms of **być** which agree with the hour or day:

Jest godzina piąta po południu. *It's five o'clock in the afternoon.*

Była już noc. *It was already night.*

Jutro będzie czwartek, szóstego maja. *Tomorrow will be Thursday, the sixth of May.*

Sentences of the type 'it's late', 'it's early', and so on, are expressed "ambiently" (see further below under Impersonal Sentences):

Jest już późno (jeszcze wcześnie). *It's already late (still early).*

8. PREDICATE ADJECTIVAL 'BE' SENTENCES. Predicate adjectives (attributive adjectives linked to a subject with the verb 'be') occur in the Nominative case:

Twoja matka jest bardzo miła. *Your mother is very nice.*

Góry są wysokie, a rzeki szerokie. *The mountains are tall, and the rivers wide.*

Społeczeństwo jest leniwe. *Society is lazy.*

Used of people, predicate adjectives based on participles often substitute for what can otherwise be said with a verb:

On jest spóźniony. *He is late.* = **On spóźnia się.**

Ona jest zadowolona. *She is happy.* = **Ona się cieszy.**

Jestem zdziwiony. *I'm surprised.* = **Dziwię się.**

Jesteśmy zachwyceni. *We are enthralled.* = **Zachwycamy się.**

Some adjectives can take further complements, whether bare-case or prepositional:

On jest pochłonięty własnymi sprawami. *He is absorbed in his own affairs-Instrumental.*

Oni są żądni władzy. *They are desirous of power-Genitive.*

Pies jest wierny swojej pani. *The dog is faithful to his mistress- Dative.*

Szef był bardzo zadowolony z mojej pracy. *The boss was very pleased with my work-Genitive.*

Ona jest w dalszym ciągu zła na mnie. *She continues to be angry with me-Accusative.*

A special class of such adjectives are comparatives, which may take complements in **od**+G:

Jan jest o wiele starszy od Janiny. *Jan is a lot older than Janina.*

After the infinitive **być**; after the gerund **będąc** *being*; after the verbal noun **bycie** *being*; or after an impersonal use of **być**, the Instrumental case may be found, corresponding to a sense of change in or contradiction of state. However, the Nominative is becoming more frequent, especially after **być**:

On chciałby być bardziej *interesujący(m)*. *He'd like to be more interesting.*

Będąc *młodą*, **poświęciła dużo czasu czytaniu powieści.** *When she was young she devoted a lot of time to reading novels.*

Dobrze jest, kiedy się jest naprawdę *zmęczonym* **pracą fizyczną.** *It's good when one is really tired from physical labor.*

Bycie *młodą* **i** *piękną* **na zawsze to mój główny cel.** *Being young and beautiful forever is my main goal.*

The Nominative is usually found with adjectives after link-verbs other than **być**:

Ona wydaje się jakoś *zaniepokojona*. *She seems somehow upset.*

On staje się coraz *grubszy*. *He's getting fatter and fatter.*

Czy mam się czuć *zaproszony*? *Am I to consider myself invited?*

Ona zrobiła się bardzo *zazdrosna*. *She's gotten very jealous.*

Factive Predicate Adjectives, Adverbs, and Nouns

When an introducing adjective directs attention to the factual aspect of a state of affairs, introduced by że(by), the adjective usually occurs in the neuter singular:

Jest wysoce *podejrzane*, że ostatnio spędza wieczory poza domem. *It's highly suspicious that lately she spends her evenings outside the house.*

Ciekawe, że dopiero teraz podnosisz tę sprawę. *It's curious that you're only raising this issue now.*

To *niemożliwe*, żebyś tego wcześniej nie zauważył. *It's impossible that you didn't notice that earlier.*

However, adjectives expressing a more direct emotional response to a state of affairs may occur in the adverbial form:

To *wspaniale*, że dostałeś nowe mieszkanie. *It's great that you got a new apartment.*

To *okropnie*, że on mógł coś podobnego zaproponować. *It's s terrible that he could suggest something like that.*

If the subordinate clause is introduced by **co**, then the adjective occurs in the neuter singular, emotional or not:

To *okropne*, co on powiedział. *That's terrible what he said.*

A few nouns functioning as verbals have a factive function, for example **szkoda** *too bad,* **cud** *a miracle,* **dziw** *wonder:*

Szkoda, że nie mogłaś przyjść wcześniej. *It's too bad you weren't able to come earlier.*

Dziw, że jego to dotąd nie ominęło. *It's a wonder that it hadn't escaped him up till then.*

Impersonal ('It') Sentences

By "impersonal" sentences are meant sentences with no specific subject. The ontological subject of such sentences is to be found, if anywhere, in the surrounding environment or state of affairs. In English, such sentences typically utilize non-referential *it*. In Polish, such sentences *never* use the pronoun **ono.**

1. AMBIENT SENTENCES. An ambient sentence makes a statement about the weather, time, atmosphere, situation. Many verbs occur ambiently, using the 3rd pers. sg. neut.:

Błyska się i grzmi. *It's lightning and thundering.*

Pada już czwarty dzień pod rząd. *It's been raining for the fourth day in a row.*

Na wschodzie zaczęło dnieć. *It began to grow light in the east.*

2. Often the verb **być** will be used ambiently in combination with a weather or atmosphere adverb:

Jutro będzie słonecznie. *It will be sunny tomorrow.*

Strasznie tu jest duszno. *It's terribly stuffy in here.*

Było tak samo gorąco w nocy jak w dzień. *It was just as hot at night as during the day.*

Robi się późno. *It's getting late.*

In artistic prose and stage directions, one may encounter single-noun ambient sentences of the type

Noc. Cisza. *It's night. Silence reigns.*

3. Many impersonal sentences imply the presence of an affected person, expressed by the Dative case. There are two main types: 3rd-person verbs with **się** and adverbial.

a. 3RD. PERS. VERB WITH *SIĘ* PLUS DATIVE:

Wydaje mi się, że już pora wyjść. *It seems to me that it's already time to leave.*

Śniło mi się, że byłem na Alasce. *I dreamed I was in Alaska.*

Nie chce mi się iść na operę. *I don't feel like going to the opera.*

Robi mi się mdło. *I feel nauseated.*

Zdaje ci się. *You're imagining it.*

Dobrze mi się spało. *I slept well.*

Nie opłaca się nam tego robić. *It's not worthwhile for us to do that.*

b. ADVERB PLUS 3RD PERS. FORM OF **być** PLUS DATIVE:

Jest nam nudno (smutno). *It's boring (sad) for us. = We feel bored (sad).*

Trudno (łatwo) mu. *It's difficult (easy) for him.*

Bardzo mi przykro. *It's unpleasant for me. = I'm very sorry.*

Było nam bardzo miło. *It was very nice for us.*

Ambient adverbs often occur in this construction:

Nam jest ciepło (gorąco, zimno, duszno). *We are/feel warm (hot, cold, stuffy).*

The difference between, for example,

On jest smutny. *He is sad.*

and **Jemu jest smutno.** *(idem)*

is that the former implies a character trait, whereas the latter implies a temporary state, a momentary feeling. It is perfectly logical to say, for example, **On jest nudny, ale nie jest mu nudno.** *He is boring, but he's not bored.*

c. The items **wiadomo** *it is known* and **nie wiadomo** *it is not known* are used either by themselves or with a Dative complement:

Wiadomo, że z nim nie można rozmawiać. *It's known that one cannot have a conversation with him.*

Nic mi o tym nie wiadomo. *I don't know anything about that.*

DEPERSONALIZED SENTENCES

"Depersonalized" sentences are sentences with personal subjects where the identity of the subject is not clarified. There are three main ways to depersonalize a sentence:

1. The particle **się** may be combined with the 3rd pers. sg. neuter form of almost any verb to make a depersonal sentence:

    Dużo się mówi ostatnio o tym poecie. *There's a lot being said lately about that poet.*

    Jak się jedzie do Kielc? *How does one get to Kielce?*

2. In the past tense, the impersonal passive participle (see Chapter 12) competes with the depersonal use of **się**:

    Dużo mówiono o nim (or: **Dużo się mówiło o nim**). *A lot was said about him.*

3. Occasionally **człowiek** is used in the sense of 'one' to form a depersonalized sentence of the sort

    Człowiek lepiej pracuje z pełnym żołądkiem. *One works better with a full stomach.*

    Żeby człowieka dobrze poznać, trzeba z nim zjeść beczkę soli. *In order to get to know a person well, it's necessary to eat a barrel of salt with him.*

    Na wiosnę człowiekowi lżej na sercu. *In the springtime one is lighter of heart.*

SENTENCES WITH INFINITIVES

There are various kinds of infinitival sentences, a loose category consisting of: sentences whose central part consists of: an infinitive by itself; those where the infinitive is governed by a "verbal"; those where the infinitive is governed by an adverb serving as an ad hoc verbal; those where the infinitive is governed by a modal; those where the infinitive is phasally modified (by a verb referring to the start, end, or middle of an action); those containing a purposive verb of motion. A separate type concerns sentences where the infinitive is introduced by a lexically fuller verb.

1. PURE INFINITIVAL SENTENCES are usually used in making proposals, and in asking whether something is a good idea or not. The identity of the subject is determined by context:

   Przyjść jutro? *Should I come tomorrow?*

   Nalać ci herbaty? *May I pour you some tea?*

   Zdjąć ten obraz? *Should we take down that picture?*

   Kupić czy nie? *Should I buy it or not?*

   Umyć umyję. *As for washing, I can do that.*

   Sometimes an infinitive may be used to express 'time to', 'no other choice but to', usually in the form of an exclamation:

   Wszysto było gotowe—tylko siadać i jechać! *Everything was ready. Nothing remained but to saddle up and ride.*

   Nic, tylko siąść i płakać. *Nothing to do but sit down and cry.*

   Wozy zaprzęgać! *Time to harness the wagons!*

   Przebierać się i do domu! *Time to change clothes and go home!*

   See also sentences like the following, where the infinitive is used to entertain an idea:

   Ja!? Sprzątać? *What, me clean!?*

   Observe in the above examples the use of the Imperfective aspect.

2. Infinitival sentences are often used in recipes, instructions on labels, in public warnings, and peremptory commands, such as

   Nie dotykać (wychylać się, wchodzić)! *Don't touch (lean out, enter)!*

   Po praniu dobrze wypłukać. *Rinse well after washing.*

   Świeżą marchew umyć, oskrobać, opłukać i zetrzeć na tarce. *Wash, peel, rinse, and grate some fresh carrots.*

3. INFINITIVE-ONLY VERBS. Two verbs relating to sense perceptions are always used impersonally and in the infinitive: **widać** *to be seen*, **słychać** *to be heard*. The past and future tense is formed with **było, będzie:**

   Jej męża ostatnio nie widać. *Her husband isn't to be seen lately.*

   Wszędzie było słychać gdakanie kur. *Everywhere the crowing of chickens was to be heard.*

   Co słychać z moim podaniem? *What's the news on my application?*

   The infinitive **czuć** *to be sensed or smelled* can also be used in this way:

   Od Irki czuć było wódką. *Irka smelled of vodka.*

The verb **znać** *know* and **wiedzieć** *know information*, can also be used infinitivally:

Tego nie będzie znać. *One won't be able to recognize that.*

Wczorajszej nocy, nie wiedzieć czemu, śniły mu się szczyty gór. *The preceding night for some reason he had dreamt of mountain peaks.*

The infinitive **stać** +A, **na**+A *afford* can also be mentioned here:

Nie stać mnie na nowy samochód. *I can't afford a new car.*

4.   INFINITIVES AFTER VERBALS. Among common verbals which can take the infinitive are the following:

czas *it's time*	**szkoda** *it's too bad*
grzech *it's a shame*	**trzeba** *it is necessary*
można *it is possible*	**warto** *it is worthwhile*
nie sposób *it is impossible*	**wolno** *it is permitted*
pora *it's time*	**wstyd** *it's a shame*
strach *it's a fright*	**żal** *it's a pity.*

Trzeba się śpieszyć. *It's necessary to hurry (= we ought to hurry).*

Czas było wracać. *It was time to be getting back.*

Pora była wstawać. *It was time to be getting up.*

Można to zrozumieć w zupełnie inny sposób. *One can understand that in a completely different way.*

Grzech było spędzić tam tyle czasu. *It was a sin to spend so much time there.*

Nie sposób zrozumieć, o co im chodzi. *There's no way to figure out what they're getting at.*

Warto przeczytać tę książkę. *It's worth reading this book.*

Note the neuter sg. verb use with **czas** *it's time*, **grzech** *it's a sin*, and most other verbals; **pora** *time*, however, takes feminine agreement. The word **trzeba** has a short colloquial form **trza**, not spelled except in imitation of live speech.

5.   INFINITIVES AFTER ADVERBS functioning as an ad hoc verbal:

Miło pana poznać. *It's nice to meet you.*

Przyjemnie jest słuchać takiej muzyki. *It's pleasant to listen to this kind of music.*

Trudno jest sobie wyobrazić, jak on wszystkiemu podoła. *It's difficult to imagine how he'll manage everything.*

6. INFINITIVES AFTER MODAL VERBS. Among common modal verbs (verbs and phrases referring to want, duty, obligation, and the like) followed by infinitives are the following:

chcieć *want*	**musieć** *must, have to*
lubić *like*	**potrafić** *manage*
móc *be able*	**powinien** (and its forms) *ought*
mieć *be supposed to, have to*	**pragnąć** *desire*
mieć ochotę *feel like*	**umieć** *know how*
mieć zamiar *intend*	**woleć** *prefer*

Examples:

Wolę tam nie iść. *I prefer not to go there.*

Czy możesz mi pomóc? *Can you help me?*

Mam ochotę wyjść na spacer. *I feel like going out for a walk.*

Masz być gotowy na wszystko. *You are to be prepared for anything.*

Powinniśmy zostać. *We ought to stay.*

Naprawdę powinno się było zostać. *One really ought to have stayed.*

To these may be added the impersonal modals
należeć *one ought*   **wypadać** *it is correct*

Należy oszczędzać pieniądze na czarną godzinę. *One should save money against a dark hour (= rainy day).*

Nie wypadało narzekać. *It wouldn't have been right to complain.*

Negated modal expressions take direct objects in the Genitive:

Nie powinniśmy byli *tego* **robić.** *We shouldn't have done that.*

Nie chcemy ci *tego* **pokazać.** *We don't want to show you that.*

Nie należało *tego* **robić.** *One ought not to have done that.*

7. INFINITIVES AFTER CERTAIN ADJECTIVES. A few adjectives may be followed by infinitival complements, for example **godny (godzien)** *worthy*, **gotowy (gotów)** *ready, prepared*, **rad** *glad*, **skłonny** *inclined*:

Ona jest gotowa pomyśleć Bóg wie co. *She is prepared to believe God knows what.*

Jestem skłonny zgodzić się z tobą. *I'm inclined to agree with you.*

8. INFINITIVES AFTER PHASAL VERBS. The infinitive is required by a verb referring to the beginning, end, or continuation of an action. Phasal verbs include **zaczynać** *begin*, **kończyć** *end*, **przestać** *stop*, **rozpoczynać** *initiate*, **kontynuować** *continue*. All of these verbs require that the following infinitive be Imperfective:

Zaczynasz łysieć. *You're beginning to get bald.*

Przestań mnie draźnić. *Stop irritating me.*

Skończ wreszcie śpiewać. *Stop singing at last.*

9. INFINITIVES AFTER PURPOSIVE MOTION-VERBS. In this construction, the conjunction **żeby** *in order to,* usually used in clauses of purpose, is not used:

Musimy pójść zobaczyć tę wystawę. *We have to go and see that exhibition.*

Idę kupić chleb. *I'm going to buy bread.*

Jadę do Warszawy odwiedzić moją starą ciocię. *I'm going to Warsaw to visit my old aunt.*

Śpieszymy się zobaczyć pożar. *We're hurrying to see a fire.*

10. INFINITIVES AFTER VERBS OF ORDERING, COMMAND, HINDRANCE. In this construction, the subject of the main verb and of the infinitive are different. The subject of the introduced clause often appears in the Dative:

Zabronił nam palić. *He forbade us to smoke.*

Przeszkadzasz mi czytać. *You're preventing me from reading.*

Kazał nam czekać. *He ordered us to wait.*

If the verb takes an Accusative object, the infinitive will normally not be employed, but either **do** plus a verbal noun, or a conditional clause; see

On zmusił (namówił) mnie do wyjścia. *He forced (persuaded) me to leave.*

On prosił nas, żebyśmy opuścili salę. *He asked us to leave the hall.*

11. OTHER VERBS INTRODUCING INFINITIVES. The infinitive may be introduced by a wide range of verbs in constructions in which the subject of the introducing verb and of the infinitive is the same. Here is a small list of such introducing verbs:

bać się *be afraid*	**(po)starać się** *try*
obawiać się *fear*	**śmieć** *dare*
obiec(yw)ać *promise*	**(na)uczyć się** *study*
odważyć odważać *dare*	**umożliwi(a)ć** *enable*
(za)planować *plan*	**usiłować** *endeavor*
przyrzec przyrzekać *swear*	**wstydzić się** *be embarrassed*
przyzwyczaić się *become accustomed (pf)*	**zapomnieć zapominać** *forget*
(s)próbować *try*	**zgodzić się zgadzać się** *agree*

Wstydzę się to powiedzieć. *I'm afraid to say it.*

Staram się to zrozumieć. *I'm trying to understand that.*

Uczę się pływać. *I'm learning to swim.*

Jak śmiesz mi zaprzeczyć! *How dare you contradict me!*

Zapomnieliśmy przynieść piwo. *We forgot to bring the beer.*

Obiecam zwrócić do pierwszego. *I promise to return it by the first.*

12. INFINITIVES ARE NOT NECESSARILY NOUNS. Infinitives cannot be automatically used in a nominal function. If an infinitive seems to require occurrence in a nominal position in a sentence, some other construction will usually be used:

a. Often the infinitive will be replaced by a verbal noun, or possibly introduced by a modal or modally used adverb:

Rozmowa z nim jest trudna. *It's difficult to have a talk with him.*

or: **Trudno jest z nim rozmawiać** or: **Trudno się z nim rozmawia.**

In other words, there is no straightforward way to say such things as 'To talk with him is difficult', unless one would wish to argue that in sentences such as the following, **przyjemnie** is acting as a predicate adjective in an unmarked, adverbial form:

Siedzieć tu jest przyjemnie. *To sit here is pleasant.*

b. The conditional mood is often used to avoid an infinitive in a nominal position after verbs which do not take an infinitival complement in personal interpretations:

Proponuję, żebyśmy tu zostali na jeszcze jeden tydzień. *I propose to stay (that we stay) here for another week.*

or: **Proponuję pozostanie tu na jeszcze jeden tydzień.** *I propose staying here for one more day.*

The sentence **Proponuję zostać tu na jeszcze jeden tydzień** *I propose to stay here for one more day* is fine in the sense 'I propose that I stay...'; likewise, **Proponuję ci zostać tu na jeszcze jeden dzień.** *I propose to you to stay for another day.* is acceptable, since the verb is used with the Dative case in connection with subject-raising (see discussion in Chapter 12).

c. Infinitives can be used as the subject of an equational 'be' sentence:

Przecież wyłysieć to byłaby dla mnie tragedia. *After all, to grow bald would be for me a tragedy.* Alternatively, with a verbal noun and an inclusional 'be' sentence:

Wyłysienie byłoby dla mnie tragedią. *Balding would be for me a tragedy.*

'NORMAL' SENTENCES

By 'normal' sentences are meant 'non-be' sentences with a Nominative-case subject, an agreeing verb, and, possibly, a verbal complement. Such sentences may be divided into (1) those without a complement (= intransitive); (2) those with Accusative complements (= transitive); (3) those with oblique-case complements (= semitransitive oblique); (4) those with prepositional complements (= semitransitive prepositional). A special instance of the last type is (5) verbs of motion with directional complements. Here we will give only a few illustrative examples of these various sentence types. More information may be found in Chapter 13 on case and preposition uses.

1. INTRANSITIVE SENTENCES (Nominative + verb):

   Adam czeka. *Adam is waiting.*

   Ewa się śmieje. *Ewa is laughing.*

   Dzieci się bawią. *The children are playing.*

   Dziecko już śpi. *The child is already sleeping.*

   Okręt tonie. *The ship is sinking.*

2. TRANSITIVE SENTENCES (Nominative + verb + Accusative complement). The number of verbs which can take an object in the Accusative case is quite large. For a partial list, see in Chapter 13 under Verbs Taking the Accusative.

   a. SIMPLE TRANSITIVES:

   Jerzy czyta dzisiejszą gazetę. *Jerzy is reading today's paper.*

   Nasza córka studiuje germanistykę. *Our daughter is studying Germanistics.*

   Kupiliśmy nowy samochód. *We bought a new car.*

   Pies ugryzł chłopca. *The dog bit the boy.*

   Hodujemy owce i krowy. *We raise sheep and cows.*

   Negated transitive verbs take complements in the Genitive case. See in Chapter 13 under uses of the Genitive.

   b. TRANSITIVES WITH INDIRECT OBJECTS (Nominative + verb + Dative + Accusative complement):

   Ekspedientka dała klientowi kwit. *The salesperson gave the customer the receipt.*

   Julian zwrócił koledze pieniądze. *Julian returned the money to his friend.*

   Proponowałem żonie podróż do Włoch. *I proposed to my wife a trip to Italy.*

   c. VERBS WITH INSTRUMENTAL PHRASES Nominative + verb + Instrumental ± Accusative or other complement):

   On pisze czerwonym ołówkiem. *He writes with a red pencil.*

   Zaskoczył nas swoim talentem. *He surprised us by his talent.*

   Zwykle dojeżdam do Warszawy autobusem. *I usually commute to Warsaw by bus.*

d. VERBS WITH DOUBLE COMPLEMENTS. The canonical double-object construction consists of (Nominative + verb + Accusative + Instrumental):

Mianowano go prezesem. *He was appointed presiding officer.*

Wybrali Wałęsę prezydentem. *They elected Walesa president.*

With **wybrać** *elect*, the construction with **na+A** is more colloquial:

Wybrali Wałęsę na prezydenta.

Double-complement sentences may sometimes be created by using the conjunction **jako** *in the function of* to join the first and second objects. The second object copies the case of the first object:

Nie przyjąłem tego jako żartu. *I didn't take that as a joke.*

A great many other verbal actions logically call for two complements:

Zamieniam stare narty na nowe. *I'm trading in my old skis for new ones.*

Gratuluję panu otrzymania nagrody. *I congratulate you on receiving the award.*

Dziękuję ci za poparcie. *Thank you for your support.*

Proszę was o spokój. *I request you to be quiet.*

Chłopiec przedstawił dziewczynie swoich kolegów. *The boy introduced his friends to his girl-friend.*

Uczę Zosię muzyki. *I'm teaching Zosia music.*

Wymieniam złotówki na dolary. *I'm exchanging zlotys for dollars.*

and many more.

3. SEMITRANSITIVE SENTENCES (subject + verb + oblique-case or prepositional complement). By oblique-case complements are usually meant bare-case complements in the Genitive, Dative, or Instrumental cases. Additionally, Accusative complements which are not direct objects can also be considered to be semitransitive. For lists of verbs taking these cases, see in Chapter 13 under the respective cases. Here are a few examples of oblique-case-complement sentences:

a. GENITIVE COMPLEMENTS.

Potrzebujemy wyobraźni i inicjatywy. *We need imagination and initiative.*

Szukamy nowych rozwiązań starych problemów. *We are looking for new solutions to old problems.*

Chętnie słucham wszystkiego, co mówisz. *I gladly listen to everything you say.*

b. DATIVE COMPLEMENTS.

Nie ufam żadnym adwokatom. *I don't trust any lawyers.*

Krzysztof zawsze pomaga swoim kolegom. *Krzysztof always helps his colleagues.*

Dziwię się jego postawie. *I'm surprised at his attitude.*

c. INSTRUMENTAL COMPLEMENTS.

Pan Szymański zarządza całym przedsiębiorstwem. *Mr. Szymanski manages the entire business.*

Interesuję się zbieraniem znaczków. *I'm interested in collecting stamps.*

Zachwycam się jego sposobem mówienia. *I'm fascinated by his manner of speaking.*

d. OBLIQUE ACCUSATIVE COMPLEMENTS.

Ten twój pies waży tonę. *That dog of yours weighs a ton.*

Czekamy na ciebie całą godzinę. *We've been waiting for you a whole hour.*

The test of an oblique Accusative complement is that negating the verb does not trigger the Genitive instead of the the Accusative.

e. PREPOSITIONAL COMPLEMENTS (subject + verb + prepositional complement). This is an extremely large class of sentences. For more information, see under individual preposition+case uses in Chapter 13. Here are some examples:

Martwię się o ciebie. *I'm worried about you.*

Czekam na autobus. *I'm waiting for the bus.*

Liczę na waszą dyskrecję. *I'm counting on your discretion.*

Wierzę w wartość pracy. *I believe in the value of work.*

Ta torebka należy do Wandy. *That handbag belongs to Wanda.*

Anna rozmawia z jakimś mężczyzną. *Anna is conversing with some man.*

Polegam na waszym rozsądku. *I rely on your common sense.*

THE SYNTAX OF VERBS OF MOTION

f. VERBS OF MOTION (SEMI-TRANSITIVE PREPOSITIONAL SENTENCES WITH DIRECTIONAL COMPLEMENTS). Polish exhibits a three-way system of preposition use for expressing whether an object or person is (a) statically located relative to a place of orientation; (b) on the way toward being at the position of static location; or (c) on the way away from (out of, off) the position of static location. Consider the three sentences:

Location at: **Samolot leci nad Francją.** *The airplane is flying over France-Instrumental.*

Motion toward: **Samolot leci nad Francję.** *The airplane is heading to over France-Accusative.*

Motion from: **Samolot leci znad Francji.** *The airplane is flying from over France-Genitive.*

In expressing location-at, motion-to, and motion-from, the nature of the point of static orientation (in, on, over, before, behind, etc.) is of primary importance for determining the motion-to and motion-from prepositions. Here are the most important considerations involved in this system:

In Polish, the basic spatial prepositions, 'in', 'on', and 'at', take the Locative case, while the peripheral spatial prepositions 'in front of', 'under', 'over', 'behind', and 'between' take the Instrumental case. The notions of 'at', 'to', or 'from' a person's place or sphere of influence take the Genitive. Bodies of water, towns, monuments, and certain other kinds of nouns require separate treatment. In sum, spatial prepositions form a three-fold system, depending on the dimensions of AT, TO, FROM, the basic and orientational relation being AT.

Location AT	Movement TO	Movement FROM

Containers, most places, surrounding environments:

w+L *in*	**do**+G	**z**+G

w pokoju *in the room*, **do pokoju** *to, into the room*, **z pokoju** *from, out of the room*

w Warszawie *in Warsaw*, **do Warszawy** *to Warsaw*, **z Warszawy** *from Warsaw*

w wodzie *in the water*, **do wody** *into the water*, **z wody** *out of the water*

Abstractions or amorphous objects or spaces:

w+L *in*	**w**+A *into*	**z**+G *from*

w dali *in the distance*, **w dal** *into the distance*, **z dali** *from out of the distance*

w tłumie *in the throng*, **w tłum** *into the throng*, **z tłumu** *out of the throng*

Surfaces, events, wide open places:

na+L *on, at*	**na**+A	**z**+G

na stole *on the table*, **na stół** *onto the table*, **ze stołu** *off the table*

na koncercie *at the concert*, **na koncert** *to the concert*, **z koncertu** *from the concert*

na wsi *in the country*, **na wieś** *to the country*, **ze wsi** *from the country*

Even when the location-at meaning is determined idiomatically, the movement-to and movement-from prepositions are still based on the static-location use. Thus, because of **na poczcie** *at the post-office*, one says **na pocztę** *to the post-office*.

Persons, peoples, professional offices:

u+G *at*	do+G	od+G

u Jana *at Jan's place,* **do Jana** *to Jan's,* **od Jana** *from Jan's*

u dentysty *at the dentist's,* **do dentysty** *to the dentist's,* **od dentysty** *from the dentist's*

Bodies of water:

nad+I *on, near, at*	nad+A	znad+G

nad Wisłą *on (by) the Vistula,* **nad Wisłę** *to the Vistula,* **znad Wisły** *from the Vistula*

nad morzem *by the sea,* **nad morze** *to the sea,* **znad morza** *from the sea*

Towns:

pod+ I *near*	pod+A	spod+G

pod Warszawą *near Warsaw,* **pod Warszawę** *to near Warsaw,* **spod Warszawy** *from near Warsaw*

za+I *outside*	za+A	zza+G

za Warszawą *outside Warsaw,* **za Warszawę** *to outside Warsaw,* **zza Warszawy** *from outside Warsaw*

za granicą *abroad,* **za granicę** *abroad,* **zza granicy** *from abroad*

poza+I *outside*	poza+A	spoza+G

poza Warszawą *outside Warsaw,* **poza Warszawę** *to the other side of Warsaw,* **spoza Warszawy** *from the other side of Warsaw*

Monuments, buildings, large objects:

pod+I *near*	pod+A	spod+G

pod pomnikiem *by the monument,* **pod pomnik** *up to the monument,* **spod pomnika** *from by the monument*

pod gmachem *by the building,* **pod gmach** *up to the building,* **spod gmachu** *from next to the building*

Up

na górze *at the top*	**do góry** *upwards*	**od góry** *from on high*
	na górę *to the top*	**z góry** *from uphill*
	w górę *uphill*	

ku górze is commonly used alongside **do góry**

Down

na dole *at the bottom*	do dołu *downwards*	od dołu *from under*
	na dół *to the bottom*	z dołu *from the bottom*
	w dół *downhill*	

Forward/Back

na przodzie *in front*	do przodu *to the front*	z przodu *from the fr.*
w tyle *in the back*	do tyłu *to the back*	z tyłu *from the back*

na przodzie is more often used than w przodzie; naprzód means 'forward, ahead'

Right/Left/Straight

na prawo *on the right*	w prawo *to the right*	z prawa *from the right*
na lewo *on the left*	w lewo *to the left*	z lewa *from the left*
prosto *straight*	wprost *head on*	

Way, direction, side

po stronie *on the side*	w stronę *toward*	ze strony *from the dir.*

The word **strona** is used in such constructions as **W którą stronę jedziemy?** *Which way do we go?* **w obie strony** *in both directions,* **w jedną i drugą stronę** *in one direction and the other,* and so on. This word is often combined with **prawy** *right* and **lewy** *left* in the phrases **po prawej (lewej) stronie** *on the right (left) hand side,* **z prawej (lewej) strony** *from the right (left) hand side.*

Center, middle

w środku *in the middle*	do środka *to the m.*	ze środka *from the m.*

Inside, outside

wewnątrz *inside*	do wewnątrz *to the i.*	od wewnątrz *from i.*
zewnątrz *outside*	na zewnątrz *to the o.*	z zewnątrz *from o.*

DOUBLE-DIRECTIONAL COMPLEMENTS

g. When two motion-to phrases occur in the same sentence, both tend to be expressed with motion-to prepositions, unlike in English, in which one phrase is often expressed statically:

Jedziemy do Szczyrku na konferencję. *We are going to a conference in Szczyrk.*

Jesteśmy zaproszeni do Walczaków na obiad. *We're invited to the Walczak's for dinner.*

THE COMPLEMENTS OF VERBS OF PLACEMENT

h. Verbs of placement take double complements, consisting of a moved
object and a place of eventual location. In most concrete uses, the
preposition used with the place of eventual location will take the case
of location, not the possibly expected case of motion-to. See

Książka leży na stole. *The book is lying on the table-L.*

Połóż książkę na stole. *Put the book on the table-L.*

A sentence like **Połóż książkę na stół.** *Put the book on the table-A*, with the
Accusative, is not incorrect, merely emphatic. See also

Płaszcz wisi w szafie. *The coat is hanging in the closet-L.*

Powieś płaszcz w szafie. *Hang the coat up in the closet-L.*

Miotła stoi za drzwiami. *The broom is standing behind the door-I.*

Postaw miotłę za drzwi(ami). *Stand the broom up behind the door-A(I).*

Kocioł stoi na piecu. *The pot is sitting on the stove-L.*

Nastaw kocioł na piec(u). *Put the kettle on the stove-A(L).*

Because of the more specific destination in the last sentence, Accusative
na piec is possibly preferable to Locative **na piecu.**

As an exception, the verb **nałożyć nakładać** *lay-pf/impf* usually takes
the Accusative:

Nałóż towar na furę. *Load the goods onto the cart-A.*

The Accusative may be found in figurative expressions, as in

Profesor wyrzucił studenta za drzwi. *The professor kicked the student out of
class-A.*

Prezes ponownie poddał sprawę pod dyskusję. *The chairman once again
submitted the matter to discussion.*

The Accusative stresses the accuracy, definiteness, and effectiveness of
the placement:

Czasami mam ochotę podłożyć bombę pod Biały Dom. *Sometimes I feel
like putting a bomb beneath the White House-A.*

The sense of 'in' or 'into' after a verb of placement is usually expressed by
do+G:

Piwo jest w lodówce. *The beer is in the refrigerator-L.*

Wstaw piwo do lodówki. *Put the beer in the refrigerator-G.*

For more information, see under Verbs of Placement and Body Position in
Chapter 11.

PHRASES OF TIME

Most essential information concerning adjunctive (non-required, adverbial) phrase-types is covered under the uses of cases and prepositions in

Chapter 13. The most important kind of adjunctive phrase is that of 'time'. Phrases of time are best described through illustration. The following examples illustrate possible constructions with the word **rok** *year*. Similar expressions may be formed with other names for periods of time such as **tydzień** *week*, **dzień** *day*, **wiek** *century*, **godzina** *hour*, **miesiąc** *month*. Many or most of these phrases have distinct senses depending on whether the time-period is viewed as a duration or as a reference point.

rok (bare Accusative) *for a year('s length of time)*. **Byłem w Polsce jeden rok.** *I was in Poland a year.*

do roku₁ (do+G) *up to the (specific) year*. **Do zeszłego roku mieszkałem u rodziców.** *Up until last year I lived with my parents.*

do roku₂ (do+G) *up to a year('s length of time)*. **Dostał do roku więzienia.** *He got up to a year in prison.*

na rok₁ (na+A) *for a year (looking ahead)*. **Wyjeżdżam do Polski na rok.** *I'm going to Poland for a year.*

na rok₂ (na+A) *exactly a year before*. **Zbieramy się na rok przed obchodami.** *We're gathering a year before the commemoration.*

o rok (o+A) *by a year*. **Przegapiliśmy jubileusz o cały rok.** *We missed the anntversay by an entire year.*

od roku₁ (od+G) *for the year (just past)*. **Od roku pracuję jako kelner.** *For the past year I've been working as a waiter.*

od roku₂ (od+G) *since the (specific) year*. **Pracuję tam od zeszłego roku.** *I've been working there since last year.*

po roku (po+L) *after a year (usually looking back)*. **Po tylko jednym roku mówisz zupełnie dobrze po polsku.** *After only one year you speak Polish quite well.* Compare with **za+A**.

przed rokiem₁ (przed+I) *a year ago*. **Przeprowadziliśmy się tu przed rokiem.** *We moved here a year ago.*

przed rokiem₂ (przed+I) *before the (specific) year*. **Przed rokiem siedemdziesiątym szóstym nie pracowałem.** *Before 1976 I didn't work.* More or less the equivalent of: **do zeszłego roku** *up to last year.*

przez rok (przez+A) *through the course of a year*. **Byłem chory przez cały rok.** *I was sick the whole year through.* This construction usually amounts to an emphatic version of the bare Accusative.

w rok (w+A) *in the space of a year*. **Wszystko zdążyłem zrobić w rok.** *I managed to do everything in the space of a year.* More frequently used in about the same meaning is **w ciągu roku** *in the course of a year.*

w roku (w+L) *in the (specific) year*. **Mam pojechać do Polski w tym roku.** *I'm supposed to go to Poland this year.*

za rok (za+A) *after a year (looking ahead)*. **Za jeszcze jeden rok będziesz już mówił po polsku zupełnie płynnie.** *After one more year you will speak Polish completely fluently.*

Days of the week take **w** +A: **w środę** *on Wednesday*. Dates are expressed with the Genitive of time: **piątego stycznia** *on the fifth of January*.

NOTES ON NEGATION

1. If the verb in a sentence is negated, the negative particle **nie** is placed immediately before the verb. Otherwise, negation attaches to the item before which **nie** occurs:

   Jan nie wstąpił do wojska. *Jan didn't join the army.*

   Jan wstąpił nie do wojska. *It wasn't the army that Jan joined.*

   Nie Jan wstąpił do wojska. *It wasn't Jan that joined the army.*

2. Negative polarity items, especially items beginning with **ni-**, require that the verb be negated, no matter whether the item appears in subject or object position:

   Nic nie widzę. *I don't see anything.*

   Nikt nie ma parasola. *No one has an umbrella.*

   The items **żaden żadna żadne** and **wcale** *at all* are negative polarity items (require a negated verb):

   Żaden pies nie podoba mi się. *I don't like any dog.*

   Nie widzę tu żadnych moich przyjaciół. *I don't see any of my friends here.*

   Wcale się nie dziwię. *I'm not at all surprised.*

NOTES ON AFFIRMATION AND DENIAL

Yes-no questions are answered with **tak** *yes,* or **nie** *no.* Polish does not use the verb **robić** *do* as a pro-verb in affirmations and denials, similar to the English use of *do.* The verb from the question-sentence must be repeated:

   —**Czy pamiętasz Annę?** *Do you remember Anna?*
   —**Tak, pamiętam.** *Yes, I do.*

   — **Widzisz ten dom?** *Do you see that house?*
   — **Tak, widzę.** *Yes, I do.*

   — **Lubicie pływać?** *Do you like to swim?*
   — **Lubimy, lubimy.** *We do, we do.*

and so on. When an affirmation contradicts an expectation, **owszem** *of course, why yes* is often used:

   — **To nie przeszkadza, prawda?** *This doesn't bother you, does it?*
   — **Owszem, przeszkadza.** *Why yes, it does.*

This word is also used to express reserved affirmation:

— **Czy wy się znacie?** *Do you two know each other?*
— **Owszem.** *Yes (I suppose we do).*

The word **no** has the function in colloquial affirmations similar to English *yeah*. It conveys a slight sense of 'obviously' or 'so what?', and is apt to sound rude and surly:

—**To twoja piłka?** *That your ball?*
—**No.** *Yeah (so?).*

NOTES ON INTERROGATION

1. Yes-no questions (questions expecting either a confirmative or disconfirmative answer) are formed by placing the question particle **czy** at the beginning of the sentence. The order of elements remains unchanged:

    Declarative: **Jestem wolny dziś wieczorem.** *I am free this evening.*
    Interrogative: **Czy będziesz wolny dziś wieczorem?** *Will you be free this evening?*

    The particle **czy** may be omitted provided sentence intonation (see further below) makes the interrogative nature of the sentence clear:

    Będziesz wolny? *Will you be free?*

    Chcesz pójść ze mną? *Do you want to go with me?*

2. Adverbial and pronominal questions are formed similarly to English, by placing the question word at the beginning of the sentence:

    Gdzie mieszkasz? *Where do you live?*

    Dlaczego pytasz? *Why do you ask?*

    Co robisz? *What are you doing?*

    O co pytasz? *What are you asking about?*

    Czym się interesujesz? *What are you interested in?*

    Kim on właściwie jest? *Who is he exactly?*

3. The pronominal question words **jaki** *what kind*, **który** *which*, **czyj** *whose* are often separated from the items they modify and placed at the beginning of the sentence:

    Który to jest już dzwonek? *Which bell is that already?*

    W jakim ty mieszkasz budynku? *What building do you live in?*

    W czyim byliście domu? *Whose house were you in?*

Notes on Conjunctions

1. The most important coordinating conjunctions are **i** *and*, **a** *and, but*, and **ale** *but*. The item **i** primarily coordinates items within a phrase; it is a conjunction of pure addition: **Adam i Ewa** *Adam and Ewa*, **Warszawa i Kraków** *Warsaw and Krakow*, **nauka i życie** *science and life*, **tu i tam** *here and there*.

The "*My z Ewą*" Construction

2. When the subject of a sentence consists of two compounded items belonging to different grammatical persons, the first of them a singular pronoun, the matter of verb agreement is often resolved by pluralizing the singular pronoun and putting the second pronoun or name in the Instrumental following **z** *with*. In this way, **ja i Ewa** optionally becomes **my z Ewą (jesteśmy)** *Ewa and I (are)*; **ty i Adam** optionally becomes **wy z Adamem (jesteście)** *you and Adam (are)*; **ja i ty** becomes **my z tobą (jesteśmy)** *you and I*; and so on. Examples:

    My z Ewą (or: **ja i Ewa**) **jesteśmy starymi przyjaciółmi.** *Ewa and I are old friends*

    Okazuje się, że wy z Adamem (or: **ty i Adam**) **pracujecie w tej samej dziedzinie.** *It turns out that you and Adam work in the same field.*

    My z tobą (or: **ty i ja**) **jesteśmy sąsiadami.** *You and I are neighbors.*

    It is possible, but not necessary, to express two coordinated 3rd-person subjects with this construction. If so, the verb may be either plural or, if the Nominative-case noun is next to the verb, singular:

    Już jest (są) Adam z Ewą. *Adam and Ewa are already here.*

    Adam z Ewą już są. (same meaning)

    Adam i Ewa już są. (same meaning).

3. Where English uses an *and* which could conceivably be replaced by *but* or *while*, Polish uses **a**, particularly as a sentence conjunction:

    Adam poszedł, a Ewa została. *Adam left, and/but/while Ewa remained.*

    Mama pracuje w szkole, a ojciec w biurze. *Mama works in a school, and/while/but father works in an office.*

    The conjunction **a** is usually used when coordinating two items governed by **między** *between*: **między pierwszą a trzecią** *between one and three o'clock.*

4. **Ale** is used to join two strongly contrasting items, especially clauses:

    On jest głupi ale miły. *He is stupid but nice.*

    On lubi mnie, ale nie wiem dlaczego. *He likes me, but I don't know why.*

In negative statements such as the following, **tylko** *only* is used more often than **ale**:

To nie jest Adam, tylko (or ale) Janusz. *That is not Adam but Janusz.*

To nie jest wejście, tylko (or ale) wyjście. *That's not the entrance but the exit.*

5. Some coordinated conjunctions are

   a. **i..., i...** *both... and...*

   Jest i piwo, i wino. *There is both beer and wine.*

   b. **albo..., albo...** *either... or...*

   Albo ty pójdziesz, albo ja pójdę. *Either you will go or I will.*

   c. **ani..., ani...** *neither... nor...* The item **ani** requires that the verb be negated:

   Na stole nie ma ani pieprzu, ani soli. *There is neither pepper nor salt on the table.*

LIST OF THE MOST IMPORTANT CONJUNCTIONS

Here is a list of the most important Polish conjunctions. Selected conjunctions are illustrated with sentences. In addition to other subordinating conjunctions, subordinate clauses may be introduced by adverbial question words like **czy, gdzie, dlaczego, kiedy,** etc.:

Nie wiem, *czy* **on będzie mnie pamiętał.** *I don't know whether he'll remember me.*

Nie wiem, *kiedy* **będę gotowy.** *I don't know when I will be ready.*

Nie rozumiem, *dlaczego* **mnie lubisz.** *I don't understand why you like me.*

On nie powiedział, *gdzie* **on mieszka.** *He didn't say where he lives.*

➤ *all the more that* **tym** +comparative, **że**

Sytuacja jest *tym* **trudniejsza, że tak nieoczekiwanie powstała.** *The situation is all the harder that it arose so unexpectedly.*

➤ *although* **chociaż; choć; (po)mimo że**

Nie zdałem egzaminu *pomimo,* **że byłem dobrze przygotowany do niego.** *I didn't pass the exam, even though I felt well prepared for it.*

Mimo, że na dworze upał, w mieszkaniu jest dość zimno. *Even though it's hot outside, it's fairly cool in the apartment.*

➤ *and* **i, a**

➤ *anyway* **mimo to**

Nie zaprosiła go, a mimo to przyszedł. *She didn't invite him, but he came anyway.*

➤ *as, while* **jak**

Patrzył przez okno, *jak* **dziecie bawią się na podwórzu.** *He looked through the window while the children played in the yard.*

➤ *as far as* **o ile**

O ile **wiem, on jest dzisiaj w Poznaniu.** *As far as I know, he's in Poznan today.*

➤ *as long as, provided* **skoro; pod warunkiem, że**

Zajrzyjmy do tego sklepu, *skoro* **już tu jesteśmy.** *Let's have a look at this shop, as long as we're already here.*

Pójdziesz do kina *pod warunkiem, że* **najpierw odrobisz lekcje.** *You'll go to the movies provided you first do your homework.*

➤ *as soon as* **jak/gdy/kiedy tylko; skoro tylko**

Zadzwoń do mnie *jak tylko* **wrócisz.** *Phone me as soon as you return.*

➤ *as though* **jak gdyby, jakby**

Ten obraz wygląda *jakby* **był nie z tej epoki.** *That picture looks as though it were out of another century.*

➤ *as well as* **oraz**

W konferencji uczestniczyli wybitni specjaliści oraz przedstawiciele związków zawodowych. *In the conference were taking part prominent academic specialists as well as representatives of trade unions.*

➤ *at the time when* **wtedy, kiedy...**

Przepraszam, ale nie miałam czasu na rozmowę *wtedy, kiedy* **zadzwoniłaś wczoraj.** *I'm sorry, but I didn't have time for a chat when you saw me yesterday.*

➤ *because* **dlatego, że; bo; bowiem; ponieważ; gdyż**

Zrobię to tylko *dlatego, że* **mnie o to prosisz.** *I'll do that only because you're asking me to.*

Spóźniła się na pociąg, gdyż (ponieważ, bo, dlatego że) za późno wyszła z domu. *She was late for the train because she left the house too late.*

➤ *before* **zanim; nim; przedtem jak**

Zanim **pójdę do pracy, zadzwonię do dyrektora.** *Before I go to work, I'll phone to director.*

➤ *both... and...* **i... i...**

Rano musiała *i* obiad przygotować, *i* odprowadzić dzieci do szkoły. *In the morning she had both to make dinner and to take the children to school.*

➤ *but, and* **ale; a; lecz**

Chcę czytać, *a* ty mi przeszkadzasz. *I want to read, and you're bothering me.*

Pójdę na zabawę, *ale* nie będę tańczył. *I'll go to the party, but I won't dance.*

➤ *either... or...* **albo... albo...**

➤ *especially since* **zwłaszcza, że**

Dzisiaj wolę zjeść obiad w domu, *zwłaszcza, że* nie mam pieniędzy. *I prefer to eat dinner at home today, especially since I don't have any money.*

➤ *even if, even though* **choćby**

Muszę mieć ten sweter, *choćbym* miała wydać na niego sto dolarów. *I have to have that sweater, even if I have to spend 100 dollars for it.*

➤ *except that* **z tym, że**

Chętnie ci pomogę w sprzątaniu *z tym, że* okien nie będę myć. *I'll gladly help you clean, except that I won't wash windows.*

➤ *for, because, since* **bo; gdyż; ponieważ**

Zostanę dzisiaj w domu, *bo* źle się czuję. *I'll stay at home today, because I feel bad.*

➤ *however* **jednak** (in Polish, a possible conjunction)

Kocham swoje dzieci, nie chcę *jednak* ich rozpieszczać. *I love my children; however, I don't want to spoil them.*

➤ *if* **jeśli; jeżeli; jak; o ile**

➤ *if only* **jeśli tylko**

➤ *if... then...* **jeśli (or gdy)... to...;**
jeśliby (or gdyby)... toby...

***Jeśli* dobrze pamiętam, *to* pracujesz w banku.** *If I remember rightly, you work in a bank.*

***Gdybyś* mnie naprawdę kochał, *tobyś* nie spędzał tyle czasu poza domem.** *If you really loved me, you wouldn't spend so much time outside the house.*

➤ *just as* **tak, jak**

***Tak, jak* myślałem, nie zastałem go w domu.** *Just as I thought, I didn't find him at home.*

➤ *like* **jak; niby**

Marcin czuł się *jak (niby)* **zaszczute zwierzę.** *Marcin felt like a chased animal.*

➢ *neither... nor...* **ani... ani...**

➢ *nevertheless* **niemniej** (in Polish, a conjunction)

Właściwie sytuacja nie była niebezpieczna, *niemniej* **postanowiłem coś zrobić.** *The situation wasn't actually dangerous; nevertheless, I decided to do something about it.*

➢ *no sooner... than...* **ledwie..., kiedy...**

Ledwie wyszliśmy, *kiedy* **zaczął padać deszcz.** *No soonerhad we gone out out than it began to rain.*

➢ *on the other hand* **za to; natomiast** (in Polish, occasional conjunctions)

Rano będziemy zwiedzać muzea, za to popołudnie będziemy mieli wolne. *In the morning we'll visit museums; by contrast, we'll have the afternoon free.*

Siostra jest jeszcze w szkole, brat natomiast skończył politechnikę i pracuje jako inżynier. *My sister is still in school; my brother, by contrast, has finished engineering school and works as an engineer.*

➢ *or* **lub; czy**

Chcesz kawę *czy* **herbatę?** *Do you want coffee or tea?* (i.e., Which do you want?)

Rano piję kawę *lub* **herbatę.** *In the morning I drink coffee or tea.*

➢ *or else* **bo**

Stój *bo* **strzelę!** *Stop or I'll shoot!*

➢ *otherwise* **bo inaczej**
➢ *provided* **pod warunkiem, że**

Powiem ci, co on powiedział, *pod warunkiem, że* **będziesz to trzymała w tajemnicy.** *I'll tell you what he said, provided you keep it a secret.*

➢ *since, as long as* **skoro; kiedy**

Proszę, wejdź, *skoro* **tu już jesteś.** *Please, come in, as long as you're already here.*

➢ *since, for* **ponieważ; bo; gdyż**
➢ *so* **dlatego; (a) więc; zatem; toteż**

Razem będzie nam łatwiej, *dlatego* **proszę cię, zostań tu.** *It'll be easier for us together, so I beg you, stay here.*

Nie wnikam w twoje sprawy, *a więc* **i ty nie wnikaj w moje.** *I don't pry into your affairs, so don't you pry into mine either.*

➤ *than* **niż; aniżeli; jak**

Ten problem jest trudniejszy, *niż* myślałem. *That problem is more difficult than I thought.*

➤ *that, so that, in order to* **żeby; ażeby**

➤ *that (subordinating conj.)* **że**

➤ *then* **wtedy**

➤ *therefore* **dlatego; zatem**

➤ *unless* **chyba, że; jeśli nie**

Wyjedziemy jutro na wieś, *chyba, że* będzie deszcz. *We'll drive out into the country tomorrow, unless there's rain.*

Przyjdę z pewnością, *chyba żebym* miała gości. *I'll come fore sure, unless I have guests.*

➤ *until* **aż; dopóki nie; (do)póty... (do)póki...**

Będziemy tu czekali, (*tak długo, dotąd*) *aż* pociąg się wyruszy. *We'll wait here until the train starts moving.*

Słuchaj uważnie, *aż* zrozumiesz. *Listen carefully, until you understand.*

Nigdzie nie pójdziesz, *dopóki nie* wyniesiesz śmieci. *You're not going anywhere until you take out the trash.*

***Dopóty* dzban wodę nosi, *dopóki* mu się ucho nie urwie.** *The pitcher carries water until its ear breaks off* (proverb).

➤ *when* **kiedy; jak**

➤ *whenever* **kiedy tylko**

➤ *whether... or...* **czy... czy...**

Jeszcze nie wiadomo, *czy* wyjadę nad morze, *czy* też zostanę w domu. *It's still not known whether I'll go to the seashore or instead stay at home.*

➤ *while* **podczas gdy; przy czym; jak; tymczasem**

***Podczas gdy* wolę to zrobić jak najszybciej, nie wiem, czy teraz są najlepsze warunki.** *While I'd like to do that as soon as possible, I don't know whethe the circumstances are best at present.*

On spędza cały czas na towarzyskich rozmowach, *przy czym* robota wciąż leży i czeka. *He's spending all his time talking with friends, while the work is still there sitting there waiting.*

Słuchałam radia *jak* on czytał gazetę. *I listed to the radio while he read the paper.*

THE CHOICE BETWEEN *ŻE* AND *CZY* AFTER REPORTING VERBS

Polish is strict as to whether one uses **że** *that* or **czy** *whether* after reporting verbs (verbs used to introduce indirectly conveyed speech or thought). **Czy** occurs after verbs or phrases of 'not knowing'. As a rule, if one may possibly use *whether* in English, then one obligatorily uses **czy** in Polish. Note the reciprocity of **wiedzieć** *know* and **wątpić** *doubt*= 'don't know' under negation:

Wiem, że ma najlepsze zamiary. *I know that he has the best intentions.*

Nie wiem, czy on ma najlepsze zamiary. *I don't know whether he has the best intentions.*

Wątpię, czy on się na to zgodzi. *I doubt whether he'll agree to that.*

Nie wątpię, że on się na to zgodzi. *I don't doubt that he'll agree to that.*

Similarly, one says **jestem pewien, że...** *I'm certain that*, but **nie jestem pewien, czy...** *I'm not certain whether*. Verbs of judgment and expectation (e.g. **myśleć** *think*, **oczekiwać** *expect*, **przypuszczać** *suppose, expect*, **sądzić** *judge*, **wyobrażać sobie** *imagine*) take only **że**:

Nie oczekiwałem, że ta wycieczka będzie tyle kosztowała. *I didn't expect that that excursion would cost so much.*

Recall that negative verbs of knowledge and thought may optionally take conditional complements: **Wątpię, czyby się na to zgodził.** *I doubt whether he would agree to that.* For further discussion see Chapter 10.

FACTIVE *TO*

When one sentence becomes incorporated into another, the neuter demonstrative pronoun **to**, used factively and followed by either **że** or **czy**, is often used to join the two together. The item **to** is inflected for case, in accordance with the syntax of the introducing clause:

Nie zaprzeczam temu, że ta muzyka robi wrażenie. *I don't dispute that that music makes an impression.*

Nie chodzi mi o to, że bierze łapówki. *I'm not concerned about that fact that he's taking bribes.*

Zawsze interesuję się tym, co piszesz. *I'm always interested in what you're writing.*

SIMPLE SENTENCE INTONATION

Polish is not spoken with a great deal of up-and-down modulation. Nevertheless, it is important to deliver sentences with the correct intonation for the general types: declarative, yes-no interrogative, adverbial/pronominal interrogative, and imperative. Polish and English make use, by and large, of the same intonational patterns, but not necessarily for achieving the same results.

1. DECLARATIVE SENTENCES. The neutral declarative sentence intonation pattern begins at mid or slightly high pitch level and ends on a low falling pattern:

Mie-szkam w Kra-$_{ko\text{-}wie}$. *I live in Krakow.*

Emphatically, the declarative sentence may rise on the final word, then drop at the end:

Mie-szkam w Kra-$^{ko\text{-}}_{wie}$.

Declarative sentences expressing a contrast show a rise on the first main word being contrasted:

Miesz-kam w Kra-$^{ko\text{-}wie}$, a-le pra-cu-ję w Wa-do-$^{wi\text{-}}_{cach}$.

2. YES-NO INTERROGATIVE SENTENCES (sentences which expect yes or no for an answer). The neutral intonation pattern for yes-no questions consists of a mid pitch onset leading into a slight down-and-up-to-mid-high dip at the end of the sentence:

Czy je-steś go-$_{to}$-^{wy}? *Are you ready?*

3. ADVERBIAL OR PRONOMINAL INTERROGATIVE SENTENCES (questions beginning with question-words like **gdzie, jak, kiedy, kto, co**, and so on). The neutral intonation pattern for adverbial or pronominal questions is to begin with a slightly high pitch on the question-word, shifting to a slightly low pitch for the rest of the sentence:

O $^{któ\text{-}}$rej kon-cert się za-czy-na? *When does the concert begin?*

For emphasis, pitch may instead slowly rise to the stressed syllable of the last word, then fall:

O któ-rej kon-cert się za-^{czy}-$_{na}$?

Importantly, adverbial and pronominal questions do *not* end on a rise.

4. IMPERATIVE SENTENCES (commands). A common command intonation begins on a high pitch and slowly falls toward the end of the sentence:

^{O}-budź się! *Wake up!*

Zdej-mij ka-pe-$_{lusz}$! *Take off your hat!*

Alternatively, the same intonation may be used as in an emphatic declarative sentence:

Zdej-mij ka-$^{pe\text{-}}_{lusz}$!

SENTENCE TAGS

5. Declarative sentences are often followed by a tag aimed at enlisting the attention or response of the listener. Among common sentence tags in Polish are **tak?** *yes?* **nie?** *no?*, **prawda?** *right?*, **nieprawdaż?** *isn't that so?*, **co?** *what?*. All of these tags mean about the same thing, but some are more polite than others; it is safest to use **prawda**; **nie** is apt to be taken as rude. The intonation of tags requires a dip at the end of the sentence, followed by a rise to a somewhat high pitch on the tag:

Po-go-da jest o-ᵇʳᶻʸ-dli_-wa, nie (prawᵈᵃ)? *The weather is horrible, isn't it?*

CLITICS AND THEIR PLACEMENT

By "clitic" is meant a word without independent stress which forms an accentual unit with some other word. "Proclitics" are placed before a word, while "enclitics" are placed after a word. The only clitics in Polish in this full sense are the *proclitic* negative verbal particle **nie** and basic prepositions which, when placed before a word, form a phonological unit with that word to the extent that the place of stress will be affected; see **nie dał** "NIE dał", **ode mnie** "o-DE mnie". *Enclitics* in Polish include (a) detachable past-tense verb endings **-(e)m, -(e)ś, -(e)śmy, -(e)ście** (Chapter 10); (b) the conditional particle **by** (Chapter 10); (c) the emphatic particle **-ż(e)** (Chapter 7); (d) the exhortative particle **no** (as in **Chodź no!** *come on, will you?*); and (e) the no-longer used interrogative particle **li**, as in **Znasz li ten kraj?** *Do you know that land?* (contemporary: **Czy znasz ten kraj?**). In standard educated Warsaw speech, none of the foregoing enclitics, a.-e., affect the place of the stress of the word to which they are attached.

Notes:

a. The reflexive particle **się** (Chapter 12) and the unstressed personal pronouns **mi, mu, go** (including also unstressed versions of Genitives **go, jej, ich,** unstressed Datives **jej, im** and unstressed Accusatives **ją** and **je;** Chapter 7) have clitic-like properties in that they cannot occur in clause-initial position, and they tend to avoid occurrence in clause-final position. They tend not to occur too far away from the verb. When they occur after the verb, they occur immediately after it. When Dative and Accusative unstressed pronouns co-occur, Dative pronouns tend to precede Accusative pronouns:

Daj mi go natychmiast! *Give it-masc.-A to me-D immediately!*

Unstressed Dative pronouns tend to occur before **się**, while unstressed Accusative or Genitive pronouns tend to occur after **się**:

Dziwię ci się. *I'm surprised at you.* (compare with **Dziwię się panu.** *I'm surprised at you-m. formal*).

Twoja siostra bardzo mi się podoba. *Your sister appeals to me a lot.*

Boję się go. *I'm afraid of him.*

Bardzo się ich wstydzę. *I'm very ashamed of them.*

Violations of these ordering tendencies do not produce ungrammatical sentences, merely less felicitous ones.

b. In a variety of speech considered semi-educated and emphatically condemned by normative authorities, the past-tense enclitics **-śmy** and **-ście** are allowed to affect a shift in stress; hence **mie-LI-śmy** instead of **MIE-li-śmy, mie-LI-ście** instead of **MIE-li-ście.**

c. The particle **no** can either appear in clitic position or in clause-initial position, as in **No, chodź!** (or **Chodź no!**) *Well come on!* **No** has many other functions besides its use as an exhortative. Many are comparable to English *well*, as in **No, to będziemy musieli wezwać hydraulika.** *Well, then, we'll have to call the plumber.* Consult a dictionary for details. See earlier discussion for the use of **no** as an affirmative particle.

LIST OF IMPORTANT 'LITTLE WORDS'

By 'little words' are meant words with reduced lexical content that often have an emphatic, contrastive, or merely stalling function. Rather than present a detailed classification or description, we will simply list such words here as a (rather large) group.

a bit, slightly	**o mało, nieco, trochę**
above all; primarily	**nade wszystko; przede wszystkim**
absolutely	**absolutnie**
actually	**właściwie; w rzeczywistości**
admittedly	**wprawdzie**
after all	**przecież, zresztą**
again	**jeszcze raz, znowu**
all kinds of	**różnego rodzaju**
almost	**prawie; o mało nie**
almost = by just a little	**bez mała; o mało nie**
already	**już**
also	**też; także; również; i**
among other things	**między innymi**
and so on	**i tak dalej (itd.)**
and things like that	**i tym podobnie (itp.)**
any (moment, day, hour)	**lada (chwila, dzień, godzina)**
any longer	**już nie**
any old	**byle**
anyway, even so	**i tak**
as; so	**tak**
as a whole, on the whole	**ogołem biorąc; na ogół**
as if, as it were	**niby, jak gdyby**

as many/much as	**aż**
at all (as in *not at all*)	**wcale nie**
at last	**wreszcie; nareszcie**
at least (of amount)	**co najmniej**
at least	**przynajmniej; chociażby**
at the bottom of things	**w gruncie rzeczy**
at the same time	**jednocześnie; tymczasem; zarazem**
awfully	**strasznie, okropnie, szalenie**
barely	**zaledwie; ledwie; ledwo**
basically	**w zasadzie**
better not	**lepiej nie**
briefly put	**krótko mówiąc**
but, why	**przecież; wszak**
but after all	**przecież**
by no means	**bynajmniej**
by the way	**a propos, nawiasem mówiąc**
chiefly	**głównie, przeważnie**
completely	**kompletnie; zupełnie; całkiem; całkowicie**
constantly	**wciąż; ciągle**
continually	**ciągle; nadal**
doubtless	**niewątpliwie, śmiało**
downright	**wręcz; zgoła**
either (as in *not either*)	**też nie**
else	**jeszcze; indziej; inaczej**
entirely	**całkiem; całkowicie**
especially	**zwłaszcza; szczególnie; przede wszystkim**
essentially	**istotnie; w zasadzie**
even	**nawet; i**
even so	**i tak**
evidently	**widocznie**
exactly	**właśnie, otóż to**
exceedingly	**nadzwyczaj**
excessively	**zbytnio; nader**
exclusively	**wyłącznie**
fairly	**dość; raczej**
finally	**wreszcie; nareszcie**
first of all	**najpierw**
for all that; for that matter	**zresztą**
for example	**na przykład** (less elegant: **przykładowo**)
for sure	**na pewno**
for the moment	**na razie**
finally	**nareszcie**
fortunately	**na szczęście**
fundamentally	**zasadniczo**

generally	na ogół, ogólnie rzecz biorąc
gladly	chętnie
great, excellent, wonderful	wspaniale; doskonale; świetnie
hardly (anyone, etc.)	mało (kto)
here	tu
here and there	tu i ówdzie
here is	oto
here you are	proszę
hither and thither	tędy i owędy
honestly	szczerze mówiac
however	jednak
in a way	poniekąd
in a word, briefly	jednym słowem; krótko mówiąc
in advance	z góry
in any case	w każdym razie
in general, at all	w ogóle
in other words	innymi słowy
in the end	w końcu
in the first (second, etc.) place	po pierwsze (po drugie, etc.)
in the meantime	tymczasem
in turn	z kolei
indeed; actually	rzeczywiście; zaiste
just (= only)	tylko
just (= exactly); precisely	właśnie; akurat
just a minute	chwileczkę
least	najmniej
less	mniej
let	niech
let's say	dajmy na to; powiedzmy
like	niby
likely	prawdopodobnie; chyba; pewnie
likewise	również
marvelous	cudownie
maybe, perhaps	może; być może
more (degree/amount)	bardziej; więcej
more and more	coraz
more or less	mniej więcej
more than	przeszło
moreover	na dodatek; mało tego
most	najwięcej
most likely	najprawdopodobniej
namely	mianowicie
necessarily	koniecznie

neither here nor there	ni stąd ni zowąd
next; subsequently	następnie; potem
no; not	nie
no doubt	zapewne
no matter	mniejsza z tym
no more; no longer	już nie
nonetheless	tym niemniej jednak
not at all	wcale; bynajmniej
not completely	niezupełnie
not just any	nie lada
not necessarily	niekoniecznie
not quite	niespełna; niezupełnie
not really	raczej nie; nie bardzo
not too	niezbyt
not yet	jeszcze nie
obviously	oczywiście
of course	oczywiście; owszem
of course not	oczywiście, że nie
o.k.	w porządku
on the one hand	z jednej strony
on the other hand	z drugiej strony; za to; zaś; natomiast
only just	dopiero co
only	tylko; in time expressions, dopiero
or, in other words	czyli
otherwise	skądinąd; inaczej
over and above that	ponadto
overly	nader
particularly	szczególnie; w szczególności; zbyt
perhaps	chyba; pewnie; może
please	proszę
possibly	ewentualnie
practically	praktycznie
practically = almost	o mało; omal; niemal
precisely; just; just so	właśnie; akurat
predominantly	przeważnie
presently	obecnie
primarily	przede wszystkim
probably	chyba; prawdopodobnie
rather	raczej; dość
really	naprawdę; doprawdy; rzeczywiście
simply	po prostu
sincerely speaking	szczerze mówiąc
so	tak; więc
so, well	otóż

so-called	tak zwany
solely	jedynie
sooner or later	przędzej czy później
sort of; rather	raczej; dość
still	jeszcze; nadal
superfluously	zbytecznie
supposedly	podobno
surely	pewnie
terribly	strasznie; szalenie
thank you	dziękuję
that is, that means, i.e.	to jest; to znaczy
then (afterwards)	potem
then (= so)	więc
there	tam
thus; so	tak; więc
to be sure	wprawdzie; na dobrą sprawę; owszem
to boot	na dodatek; i to
to make matters worse	na domiar złego
too; too much	zbyt; za
too bad	szkoda
totally	całkowicie; kompletnie; całkiem
undoubtedly	niewątpliwie
unfortunately	niestety
upwards of	z górą
very	bardzo
well; yeah	no
well then	tak więc
what a...	co za...
what is more	co więcej
what now?	co znowu?
whatever	bądź co bądź
what's worse...	co gorsza...
why... (of protest)	ale, przecież
why yes	owszem
willingly	chętnie
with pleasure	z przyjemnością
yes	tak
yet	jeszcze; już (see notes below)
you're welcome	proszę

Notes on Particular "Little Words":

1. **już** *already* and **jeszcze** *still*. The key to understanding the use of these two words is to understand that **już nie** is the practical opposite of **jeszcze**, while **jeszcze nie** is the practical opposite of **już**:

Czy *już* tam pracujesz? *Are you already working there?*

Nie, *jeszcze* tam *nie* pracuję. *No, I'm not working there yet.*

Czy *jeszcze* tam pracujesz? *Are you still working there?*

Nie, *już* tam *nie* pracuję. *No, I'm not working there any longer.*

Occasionally, **już** can be translated as either 'already' or 'still', depending on emphasis; see

Czy *już* jesteś gotowy? *Are you ready yet?*

Czy *już* jesteś zmęczony? *Are you tired already?*

The first sentence expresses impatience, the second surprise.

2. **bardziej, więcej, jeszcze, coraz** (translations of 'more')

   a. 'more' of degree is expressed with **bardziej: bardziej zajęty** *busier.*

   b. 'more' of amount is expressed with **więcej: Potrzebuję więcej czasu.** *I need more time.*

   c. 'more' in the sense of 'some more', 'another' is expressed with **jeszcze: Chcesz jeszcze piwa?** *Do you want some more beer?*

   d. 'more and more' is expressed with **coraz** plus the comparative form of the adjective or adverb: **coraz większy** *bigger and bigger,* **coraz szybciej** *faster and faster.*

3. **tylko** and **dopiero.** While 'only' is usually translated by **tylko**, in contexts relating to time and age, 'only' in the sense of 'only just' or 'barely' is expressed with **dopiero.**

   Twój list przyszedł dopiero wczoraj. *Your letter arrived only yesterday.*

   Ona będzie miała dopiero pięć lat. *She will be only five years old.*

   When immediately modifying a verb, 'only just' is often expressed with **dopiero co**:

   Twój list dopiero co przyszedł. *Your letter only just arrived.*

4. **dość** *rather* and **nie zbyt** *not too* often function as reciprocals:

   Ona jest *dość* miła. *She is rather nice.*

   Ona *nie* jest *zbyt* miła. *She is not especially nice.*

   Nie zbyt also often functions as the negative of **bardzo** *very:*

   Jestem dziś *bardzo* zajęty. *I am very busy today.*

   Nie jestem dziś *zbyt* zajęty. *I'm not too busy today.*

5. **co najmniej, przynajmniej, bynajmniej**

   a. 'At least' of numbers is expressed with **co najmniej**:

Tam będzie co najmniej tysiąc ludzi. *There will be at least 1000 people there.*

b. 'At least' in the silver-lining sense of 'oh, well' is expressed with **przynajmniej**:

Przynajmniej nic poważnego ci się nie stało. *At least nothing serious happened to you.*

c. **Bynajmniej (nie)** means 'not at all', and is more or less equivalent to **wcale nie**:

Bynajmniej nie jestem zmęczony. *I'm not at all tired.*

On bynajmniej nie jest tu najgorszym zawodnikiem. *He's not at all the worst athlete here.*

6. **właśnie** *precisely, just,* **akurat** *precisely, just.* These are favorite Polish fillers, more or less equivalent in meaning.

Właśnie chciałem to powiedzieć. *I was just about to say that.*

Twój mąż właśnie przyszedł. *Your husband has just arrived.*

A jak akurat nie ma dla nas miejsc? *And just what if there are no places for us?*

7. **przecież** *but (of protest),* **zresztą** *for that matter.* These words, subject to overuse by many, function in a kind of reciprocal relationship, the former expressing protest, the latter resignation:

Przecież dopiero wróciłaś. Jak możesz już wyjeżdżać? *But you only just returned. How can you already leave again?*

Dobrze, zostanę. Zresztą, nie mam innego wyboru. *Fine, I'll stay. For that matter, I don't have any other choice.*

A phrase similar in meaning to **zresztą** is **i tak** *even so.*

Nie szkodzi, że zepsułeś mi samochód. I tak chciałem kupić nowy. *It doesn't matter that you ruined my car. I wanted to buy a new one anyway.*

8. **proszę** *please,* **dziękuję** *thank you.*

a. **Proszę** is potentially a verb in the sense 'I request'. Although it usually functions as an adjunct in a sentence, it occasionally does take an infinitive or an Accusative object; and it is often used in the 1st pers. pl.:

Proszę nie rób tego. *Please don't do that.*

Proszę przyjąć moje wyrazy ubolewania. *Please accept my expressions of sympathy.*

Prosimy was, uspokójcie się! *We beg you, calm down.*

b. **Proszę** also occurs in the encouraging or offering senses of 'here you are', 'by all means', 'help yourself', 'after you'. In this sense, it often is followed by **bardzo**. Additionally, **proszę** is the correspondent of English *you're welcome* after **dziękuję** *thank you*. The latter word is a verb, not merely a particle, and it often occurs in the 1st pers. pl.:

—**Proszę, siadajcie.** *Please, have a seat!*

—**Dziękujemy.** *We thank you.*

—**Proszę bardzo.** *You're very welcome.*

c. To attract someone's attention or initiate a conversation with a stranger, one may use **proszę pana/pani.**

Proszę pana/pani, czy pan/pani się orientuje, gdzie jest najbliższy postój taksówek? *Excuse me sir/madam, do you know where the nearest taxi stand is?*

The excessive use in conversation of **proszę pana/pani** or, especially, of the informal **proszę ciebie** *I ask you, I say*, is manneristic. Expressions such as **proszę kolegi/koleżanki** *I say, colleague* are remnants of the rapidly receding past.

COMMON GREETINGS

dzień dobry *hello.* The normal formal and polite greeting, **dzień dobry** is spoken at all times of the day, including in the morning and into the early evening.

dobry wieczór *good evening.* A formal and polite greeting used in the night-time.

do widzenia *good bye.* The standard formal and polite phrase of parting.

dobra noć *good night.*

witam! (pl. **witamy!**) *Welcome!*

cześć *hi, bye.* An informal friendly greeting used among people on a first-name basis. **hej** is still more informal than **cześć**.

do zobaczenia *see you.* A relaxed and informal phrase of parting.

na razie *so-long.* Informal and colloquial.

hej! *So-long!* Extremely informal.

słucham (halo) *hello?* Normal ways of answering a telephone. **Słucham** is used more in offices, **halo** at home.

COMMON EXCLAMATIONS

ach! *ah! (rapture).* **Ach jaki piękny widok!** *Oh what a beautiful sight!*

aha! *aha! (realization).* **Aha, to tak się sprawy mają?** *Aha, so that's how things are?*

au! *ouch! (pain).* **Au, jak okropnie boli!** *Oh, how it hurts!*

ba! *nay!* **Te uczucia dorównują, ba, przerastają uczucia tych wielkich miłośników.** *Those feelings equal, nay, surpass, the feelings of those great lovers.*

bęc! *bang! bonk! smack!*

biada +D! *woe to!* **Biada temu, kto tego nie słucha.** *Woe to him who doesn't listen.*

Boże! *God!* The word carries less expressive force than in English. **Broń Boże!** *God forbid!* **Boże, jakem jest zmęczony!** *God how tired I am.*

brawo! *bravo! that's the way! attaboy!*

cholera! *damn!* Carries more expressive force than the rough equivalent in English. Not to be used in polite company.

e tam! *oh come on! give me a break! cut it out!*

ech! (e!) *ah!, aw! (contempt)* **Ech, to akurat jest wyssane z palca.** *Aw,that's completely made up.*

fe! (fi!) *fie! pooh!*

ha! *humph!, ha! (triumph).* **Ha, a nie mówiłem?** *Ha, didn't I say so?*

halo! *hey (you)!* **Halo, gdzie pan idzie?** *Hey, where do you think you're going?*

he!? *huh!? so!? well!?*

hej! *hey!* **Hej, czy mógłby pan pomóc?** *Hey, could you lend a hand?* **Hej** is also used in the sense 'hi' or 'bye', rather like **cześć.**

heta! *gee up!*

hm *hmm.*

hola! *hey, wait up!*

hop hop! *yoo-hoo! (calling at a distance).* **Hop hop! Poczekajcie chwilkę!** *Hey up there, wait a moment!*

hopla! *upsy-daisy!* **Hopla, teraz skoczymy przez ognisko.** *Up we go, now we jump over the campfire.*

hur(r)a! *hurray! hurrah!*

jej(ku)! *my!*

Jezu! *Jesus!* The word carries less expressive force than in English. **Jezu, Tomku, mówisz to już piąty raz.** *Jesus, Tomek, you're saying that for the fifth time already.*

Matko boska! *Mother of God!*

niestety! *alas!*

no no! *well I never, you don't say!*

nuże *come on! get going!*

o! *there!, you see!* **O, widzisz, znowu się denerwujesz.** *There, you see, you're getting upset again.*

och! *oh! (complaint)* **Och, kiepsko się czuję.** *Oh, but I feel lousy.*

oh! *oh! (surprise).* **Oh, ty tutaj!** *Oh, YOU'RE here.*

oho! *ahh! (discovery).* **Oho, ktoś już się zorientował!** *Oho! Someone finally figured things out!*

oj! *oh my! (unpleasant surprise, pain).* **Oj, przestań, to boli!** *Ow, stop that, it hurts.*

ojej! *oh dear!, whoops!* **Ojej, ojciec miał znowu atak?** *Oh dear, father had another attack?*

(p)fe!, tfu! *phooey!, ugh! (distaste).* **Pfe, cóż to za maniery!** *Ugh, what kind of manners are those?*

(p)fu!, fuj! *ugh!* **Pfu, jak tu cuchnie!** *Ugh, how it stinks here!*

phi! *pshaw! aw! (disdain, indifference).* **Phi, może sobie gadać, co zechce.** *Aw, he can say what he likes.*

pif paf! *bang bang!*

psiakrew *confound it! damn!*

rany boskie! *good heavens*

szkoda! *a pity! too bad!*

uf! *whew!* **Uf, ale ciężka ta walizka!** *My but that suitcase is heavy!*

y... *uh... (hesitation).* **Y... trudno mi dokładnie powiedzieć.** *Uh... it's difficult for me to say.*

NOTES ON PUNCTUATION

These notes convey only the most basic information regarding Polish punctuation (**interpunkcja**), a subject of considerable complexity and subjective interpretation.

CAPITALIZATION

1. Polish *does* capitalize:

   a. First and last names of people: **Maria Dąbrowska, Julian Tuwim, Zofia Nałkowska.**

   b. Proper geographical and ethnic or national names: **Albania** *Albania,* **Albańczyk** *Albanian (person),* **Morze Bałtyckie** *The Baltic Sea,* **Góry Świętokrzyskie** *Holy Cross Mountains,* **Stany Zjednoczone** *United States,* **Cygan** *Gypsy,* **Polak** *Pole.*

   c. The first letter of the first word only of book and article titles: *Ludzie stamtąd People from the Other Side,* ***Kwiaty polskie*** *Polish Flowers.*

d. Periodicals (the first letters of the main words): **Nauka i Życie** *Science and Life*, **Ekspres Wieczorny** *Evening Express*, **Gwiazda Polarna** *Evening Star*, **Życie Literackie** *Literary Life.*

e. Names of organizations, societies, companies (the first letters of the main words): **Armia Krajowa** *National Army*, **Wiedza Powszechna** *Universal Knowledge* (a publisher); **Polskie Towarzystwo Językoznawcze** *Polish Linguistics Society*, **Polska Kasa Oszczędności** *Polish Savings Bank.*

f. The first letter of proper acronyms spelled out: **Pekao** *PKO.*

g. Second-person pronouns and titles used in direct address in correspondence (and advertising): **Drogi Panie!** *My Dear Sir*, **Kochany Bracie** *Dear Brother.* From an advertisement: **Czy to możliwe, że Twój nowy robot kuchenny wytwarza także wolny czas?** *Is it possible that your new food processor can also create free time?*

h. Many sacred words: **Bóg** *God*, **Kościół** *The Church*, **Pan** *The Lord.*

2. Polish *does not* capitalize:
   a. Proper adjectives: **amerykański** *American*, **polski** *Polish*, **rafaelowski** *Raphaelian.*

   b. Inhabitants of towns: **warszawiak** *citizen of Warsaw*, **krakowiak** *citizen of Krakow.* Observe the difference between **poznaniak** *resident of the town Poznan* and **Poznaniak** *inhabitant of the Poznan region* (capitalized because used ethnically).

   c. Derivations from acronyms: **pegerowiec** *member of a PGR* (from **PGR Państwowe Gospodarstwo Rolnicze**= *State Agricultural Enterprise, i.e. collective farm*).

   d. Brand names when used as nouns in their own right: **Jechał fiatem.** *He was driving a Fiat.* Compare to **Jechał samochodem marki "Fiat"** *He was driving a car of the Fiat brand.*

   e. Names of the months or days of the week: **styczeń** *January*, **poniedziałek** *Monday.*

COMMAS, PERIODS, SPACES

1. Polish uses a comma before a subordinate conjunction: **Obiecał, że to zrobi.** *He promised that he would do it.* **Wątpię, czy on to zrozumie.** *I doubt whether he'll understand it.*

2. Polish does not use a comma before **i** as a coordinating conjunction: **Jedliśmy obiad i słuchaliśmy radia.** *We ate dinner and listened to the radio.*

3. Polish does *not* use a comma before the last item in a series: **Adam, Marek i Ewa** *Adam, Marek, and Ewa.*

4. Polish usually uses a comma where English uses a semicolon, i.e., to separate two clauses not joined by a conjunction: **Znał wszystkie style retoryki, posługiwał się nimi swobodnie.** *He knew all the styles of rhetoric; he made use of them freely.*

5. Polish does *not* write a period after abbreviations ending on the last letter of the word. Compare **prof. profesor** *profesor*, **doc. docent** *docent*, **gen. generał** *general*, **inż. inżynier** *engineer*, **red. redaktor** *editor* to **bp biskup** *bishop*, **dr doktor** *doctor*, **mgr magister** *master*, **z-ca zastępca** *deputy*. Additionally, one does not use periods after abbreviations for weights and measures: **kg kilogram** *kilogram*, **zł złoty** *zloty*; **ha hektar** *hectare*.

6. The question as to whether to write a space in prepositional phraseologisms can only be resolved by consulting a dictionary; see **na pewno** *for sure* vs. **naprawdę** *really*; **na przekór** *in defiance of* vs. **naprzeciwko** *across from*.

7. The matter of whether to treat **nie** as a prefix or as a separate negative particle often occasions difficulty, especially before participles. If the combination is felt to be an established word, independent from the deriving verb, the items are written together: **nieokiełzany** *exuberant, unbridled*, **nieoswojony** *untamed*, **niezadowolony** *dissatisfied*, etc.

8. The names of the major marks of punctuation are as follows:

cudzysłów *quotation mark*	**przecinek** *comma*
dwukropek *colon*	**pytajnik** *question mark*
kropka *period*	**średnik** *semicolon*
myślnik *dash*	**wielokropek** *dots (...)*
nawias *parenthesis*	**wykrzyknik** *exclamation mark.*

Note the phrases **w nawiasach** *in parentheses*, **w cudzysłowie** (not the frequently heard ***w cudzysłowiu**) *in quotes.*

ABBREVIATIONS

Polish relies on a reader's familiarity with a great many more abbreviations than does English. A representative list would go on for many pages (and items are constantly changing and increasing in number due to changing socio-political reality and the creation of ever new institutions and other entities). Here is a mere smattering of abbreviations in common use in the press, omitting weights and measures, names of institutions and organizations, and self-evident abbreviations:

bm. bieżącego miesiąca *of the current month*	**płn. połnoc, północny** *north(ern)*
	pr. porównaj *compare, cf.*
br. bieżącego roku *of the current year*	**pt. pod tytułem** *entitled*
c.d. ciąg dalszy *continuation*	**RP Rzeczpospolita Polska** *Polish Republic*

d/s do spraw *concerning*
im. imienia *named after*
inż. *engineer*
itd. i tak dalej *and so forth*
j.n. jak niżej *as below*
jw. jak wyżej *as above*
ks. ksiądz *the Reverend*
m. mieszkanie *apartment*
m.in. *among other things*
m.st. miasto stołeczne *capital city*
n.e. naszej ery *of our era, A.D.*
np. na przykład *for example*
n.p.m. nad poziomem morza
 above sea level
ob. obywatel *citizen*
ok. około *about, circa*
p. or P. pan *Mr.* **(pani** *Ms.***)**
pp. panowie, panie, państwo
p. patrz *see, vid.*
p.n. patrz niżej *see below*
p.n.e. przed naszą erą *before our*
 era, B.C.
p.wyż. patrz wyżej *see above*
płd. południe, południowy

SA spółka akcyjna *corporation*
sp. z o.o. spółka z ograniczoną
odpowiedzialnością *limited*
 liability company
str. strona *page*
śp. świętej pamięci *the late*
 (deceased)
św. święty *saint*
tj. to jest *that is, i.e.*
tow. towarzystwo *society*
tzn. to znaczy *that means, i.e.*
tzw. tak zwany *so-called*
ul. ulica *street*
ur. urodzony *born*
wg według *according to*
woj. województwo *voivodeship*
wsch. wschód, wschodni *east(ern)*
w/w wyżej wymieniony *above-*
 mentioned
z-ca zastępca *deputy*
z. zobacz *see*
zach. zachód, zachodni *west(ern)*
zm. zmarły *deceased*
 south(ern)

Glossary of Grammatical Terms

Although this work is directed at the general user, and does not require a knowledge of technical linguistic concepts or terminology, a familiarity with some basic linguistic terms may prove useful for following certain discussions.

ACRONYM: a word composed of the first syllables or letters of a complex proper name, as **CDT** (cedete), abbreviated from **Centralny Dom Towarowy** *central department store;* or **Cepelia**, from **CPLiA** (**Centrala Przemysłu Ludowego i Artystycznego** *Folk and Art Industry Exchange*).

ACTIVE VOICE: the normal sentence perspective in which the doer is also the subject of the sentence, as in **Jan śpiewa piosenkę.** *Jan is singing a song.* Usually opposed to passive voice, as in **Piosenka jest śpiewana przez Jana.** *The song is being sung by Jan,* where the subject of the sentence is the object acted on. See MIDDLE VOICE, PASSIVE VOICE, VOICE.

ADJECTIVAL NOUN: An adjectival form functioning on a regular basis as a noun, for example, **znajomy** *acquaintance*, **narzeczony** *fiance*. Compare SUBSTANTIVIZED ADJECTIVE.

ADJECTIVE: a part of speech whose function is to qualify nouns according to some property or type, whether intrinsic or acquired. The items **biały** *white*, **nudny** *boring*, **ciepły** *warm*, **polski** *Polish*, and so on, are adjectives.

ADJUNCT: a word or phrase which is not required by a verb and its syntax, but which fills out the meaning of the sentence in some way. Usually adjuncts are adverbial, i.e. answer an adverb question such as 'how, why, when, where, how long'. In **Może on przyjdzie jutro** *Maybe he'll come tomorrow,* **może** *maybe* and **jutro** *tomorrow* are adverbial adjuncts. Adjuncts are a kind of MODIFIER.

ADVERB: a word which, in a sentence, modifies a verb, adjective, or other adverb. Most adverbs are derived from adjectives (for example **ładnie** *prettily* from **ładny** *pretty*). Adverbs answer questions like 'how, when, where, why, how long'. Some adverbs are primary (non-derived), for example, **teraz** *now*, **zawsze** *always*, **jeszcze** *still*, **tylko** *only*. Adverbs are a kind of ADJUNCT and MODIFIER.

AFFECTIVE: said of a derivation with emotional rather than grammatical content. For example, affectionate first-names like **Basia** from **Barbara** may be said to be affective.

AFFIX: in Polish, either a prefix or a suffix; by convention, not an ending (see those terms).

AFFRICATE: a consonant consisting of a stop followed by a spirant sound; in Polish, the affricates are **c, ć, cz, dz, dź, dż**. See Chapter 1.

AGREEMENT: the property of a class of words to change form in accordance with a feature of another class of words. For example, adjectives agree as to ending with the nouns they modify in gender, number, and case.

AMBIENT: said of a state that characterizes the surrounding environment, such as **Jest ciepło.** *It is hot,* **Robi się późno.** *It is getting late.*

ANAPHORIC PRONOUN: a pronoun which stands for a noun mentioned earlier in a text.

ASPECT: a verbal category referring to whether a situation referred to is a state or an action; and, among actions, how it unfolds: progressively, completively, habitually, or generically. Polish grammatical aspect refers to whether a verb is PERFECTIVE or IMPERFECTIVE. Perfective verbs refer to completive acts in either past or future time which result in a change of state or situation; Imperfective verbs refer to states, actions or events in progress; habitual or generic states, actions, and events; and to completive actions and events that do not result in a change of state or situation. Some verbs of motion distinguish special DETERMINATE and INDETERMINATE forms. Determinate verbs refer to simple, purposeful, on-going action, while Indeterminate verbs refer to diffuse or repeated action.

AUGMENTATIVE: a derivation consisting in the adding of a semantic component 'big', 'large', or 'out-sized', for example, the derivation of **ciacho** 'really big pastry' from **ciasto** *cake, pastry.*

AUXILIARY VERB: a loose category of verbs which may be followed by another verb in the infinitive, as **chcę** *I want* in **Chcę wyjść.** *I want to leave.*

BASE: the word which forms the basis of a derivation. For example, **Warszawa** is the derivational base of the adjective **warszawski**. A BASE FORM is the form of the word used for citation in dictionaries, together with accompanying notation for determining the word's inflection.

CARDINAL NUMERALS: the basic forms of the numbers, with which things are counted (one, two, three, etc.). Opposed to ORDINAL NUMERALS, which are used to arrange things as to order of precedence in a series (first, second, third, etc.).

CASE: a formal grammatical category of nouns, indicated by inflectional endings added to the noun, helping to signal the function of the noun in a sentence. Polish nouns exhibit Nominative, Genitive, Dative, Accusative, Instrumental, Locative, and Vocative case forms, in both singular and plural.

CLAUSE: usually taken to mean a sub-sentence, one of the main parts of a complex or compound sentence. Like sentences, clauses usually consist of a subject, a verb, and a possible verbal complement. Clauses are either independent or dependent (subordinate, introduced by another clause). In **Nie wiem, gdzie on mieszka.** *I don't know where he lives,* **Nie wiem...** is the independent clause, and **gdzie on mieszka** is the dependent clause.

CLITIC: a stressless word which depends for its position in a sentence on the placement of other words. PROCLITICS go in front of other words, while ENCLITICS go after other words. In Polish, basic prepositions are proclitic. Items such as the past-tense verb endings (**-em, -eś**, etc.) and the conditional particle **by** are enclitic. The reflexive particle **się** is a clitic in that it must follow some other word in its clause.

COLLOQUIAL: used here mainly in the sense "spoken" as opposed to "written". The language of spoken and written discourse have different norms of appropriateness. Many words, phrases, and constructions are acceptable colloquially, i.e. in casual speech, but are not used in formal writing or in speech based on the written norm. For example, the detachment of past-tense endings from the verb is a characteristic of colloquial speech. See also formal and informal.

COMMON-GENDER (EPICENE) NOUN: a noun which may vary in gender in referring to persons of either sex, as **sierota** *orphan (masculine or feminine).*

COMPLEMENT: the part of a sentence that contains the material that makes the verb and its subject (if the sentence has a subject) complete. In **Idę do sklepu** *I'm going to the store,* **do sklepu** is the complement.

COMPLEMENTARY DISTRIBUTION: the predictably mutually exclusive occurrence of two items. For example, the masculine-neuter Locative sg. endings -**u** and -**e** are in complementary distribution: -**u** occurs after functionally soft and velar consonants, -**e** elsewhere.

CONDITIONAL MOOD: a sentence whose content refers to hypothetical, possibly desired but not yet realized states of affairs is said to be in the conditional mood. In Polish, this term is normally used to refer to an inflectional category of verb produced by adding -**by**, plus personal endings, to 3rd-person past-tense forms, as in **wolałbym** *I'd prefer-masc.* See also MOOD.

CONJUGATION: the inflection or inflectional type of a verb.

CONJUNCTION: a part of speech whose function is to link similar items to one another (whether nouns to nouns, verbs to verbs, clauses to clauses, etc.). Conjunctions may be coordinating (used to conjoin and possibly contrast items, like i *and*, **ale** *but*); or subordinating (used to introduce subordinate clauses, like **czy** *whether*, **bo** *because*, **skoro** *since*).

CONSONANT: a sound (phoneme) with no syllabic value. Opposed to VOWEL.

CONSONANTAL: of, relating to, or consisting of a consonant. Opposed to VOCALIC.

DECLENSION: the inflection or inflectional type of a noun, adjective, pronoun, or numeral.

DEEP FORM: see UNDERLYING FORM.

DEFECTIVITY: in an inflection, the lack of a form or range of forms for no apparent reason. For example, the verb **móc** *be able* is unable to form a verbal noun, and so is defective in this respect.

DEPERSONAL: said of a sentence which has a logically personal subject whose identity remains unclear. English THEY is often used to depersonalize a sentence, as in *They're tearing down the old Sears building.*

DERIVATION: usually, the production of one word based on another. For example, the adjective **iglasty** *needle-like* is derived from **igła** *needle.*

DERIVATIONAL MORPHOLOGY: opposed to INFLECTIONAL MORPHOLOGY, derivational morphology refers to processes of forming one word from another. For example, the production of **wózek** *baby carriage* from **wóz** *cart, carriage*, or of **krakowski** *Cracovian* from **Kraków** *Cracow* is a matter of derivational morphology. The description of the individual forms of inflected words belongs to INFLECTIONAL MORPHOLOGY.

DERIVED CONSONANT: in Polish morphophonemics, a consonant which bears an etymological relationship to another consonant. See PRIMARY CONSONANT.

DETERMINATE VERB: an imperfective verb of motion whose form refers to unidirectional, purposeful action, as **nieść** *carry*, opposed to indeterminate **nosić**. See ASPECT.

DETERMINER: a word which modifies a noun non-lexically, usually as to scope of reference. The most important determiners are numerals and pronominal modifers, as **ten budynek** *that building.*

DIACHRONIC: from the historical point of view; opposed to SYNCHRONIC.

DIMINUTIVE: a derivation consisting in the addition of a semantic component 'little', 'small', 'tiny', 'cute', for example, the derivation of **wózek** *baby carriage* from **wóz** *cart, carriage.*

DIRECT CASES: the Nominative and the Accusative cases together are often referred to as direct cases, as opposed to the other, or OBLIQUE CASES.

DIRECT OBJECT: a noun phrase connoted by a (by definition, transitive) verb and its subject and, in Polish, occurring in the Accusative case. In **Widzę żarówkę** *I see a lightbulb*, the Accusative form **żarówkę** is the direct object.

ENCLITIC: a stressless particle dependent for its place of occurrence on a word which it follows. For example, the emphatic particle **-że** as in **jakże** *but how?* is an enclitic.

ENDING: in inflection, the mutually exclusive morphemes with predominantly grammatical function which are added to the end of a stem as the final element in word formation, for example the Nominative singular ending **-o** added to **słow-** to form **slowo** *word.*

ETYMOLOGY: the study of the origin of words and their meanings.

FACULTATIVE: optional, according to how one wants to view a thing or situation. For example, the word **papieros** *cigarette* is facultatively animate, meaning that it can take the animate Accusative sg. ending **-a**.

FINITE VERB: a verb that occurs in a clause and takes personal endings. In Polish, this amounts to a verb in the present, past, future, or imperative. A finite verb form is opposed to NON-FINITE VERB FORMS: the infinitive, participles, gerunds, and the verbal noun.

FORMAL AND INFORMAL SPEECH: different norms of speech behavior may apply when addressing relative strangers as opposed to persons one is close to and familiar with. In Polish, formal and informal speech primarily has to do with the selection of appropriate pronouns, titles, and forms of greeting.

FORMANT: a suffix with mainly word-formative function, with weak or non-existant semantic content, for example, the suffix **-a-** in **pisać** *write.*

FUNCTIONALLY HARD CONSONANT: same as PRIMARY CONSONANT, plus **j**.

FUNCTIONALLY SOFT CONSONANT: the same as DERIVED CONSONANT, except for **j**, which is functionally soft but not derived. See PRIMARY CONSONANT, SOFT CONSONANT.

GENDER: in Polish, a class of noun which can be defined according to whether one may substitute for the noun the anaphoric pronoun **on** (masculine), **ona** (feminine), **ono** (neuter), **oni** (masculine-personal plural), or **one** (other plural). To be distinguished from: biological sex; sex as categories to which people assign other people; culturally conditioned sex-roles ("gender" in the sociological-anthopological sense); and from morphosyntactic categories such as "animacy" and "personal".

GERUND: also called an adverbial participle or a verbal adverb, a gerund in Polish is an uninflected verb form, often translated as 'while doing' or 'after having done'. An example would be **Nie** *widząc* **innego wyjścia, poddał się.** *Not seeing any other alternative, he gave in.*

GOVERNMENT: the ability of one part of speech to condition a particular form of another part of speech, which the first part of speech dominates in some way. For example, some verbs govern Dative complements, as **pomagać** *help*; other verbs govern Genitive complements, for example **słuchać** *listen to*; and so on. Prepositions govern various cases. For example, **od** *from* governs the Genitive case.

HARD CONSONANT: see under SOFT CONSONANT.

HYPOTHETICAL FORMS: seemingly possible forms which, for whatever reason, do not actually occur, for example, the passive participles **szyci sewn-masc.pers.pl.* or **pici drunk-masc.pers.pl.* Here the impediment to the formation is logical-pragmatical (one does not usually sew or drink people). Hypothetical forms may be indicated by an asterisk.

IMPERATIVE: the command form of a verb, as **chodź tu** *come here!* See also under MOOD.

IMPERFECTIVE VERB: in Polish, a verb belonging by its form and meaning to the imperfective aspect, referring to on-going, repeated, or ineffectual actions or events. Opposed to PERFECTIVE VERB. See ASPECT.

IMPERSONAL: a term used in various senses in linguistics; here it will be used to designate sentences relating experiences expressed indirectly, as **Jest mi zimno.** *It is cold to me = I am cold.*

INCHOATIVE (INCEPTIVE): a verbal process referring to the beginning of an action. For example, one meaning of **pojechać** *ride, drive (pf.)* is inchoative: 'get going'.

INDETERMINATE VERB: an Imperfective verb of motion whose form refers to diffuse or repeated action, as **nosić** *carry*, opposed to Determinate **nieść**. See ASPECT.

INDICATIVE MOOD: the basic factual mode of narration. See also MOOD.

INDIRECT OBJECT: the noun naming the being for whom or to whom something is done, or to whom something is said. In **Dałem psu kość.** *I gave the dog a bone*, **psu** *dog-Dative* occupies the position of indirect object.

INFINITIVE: the semantically and formally most neutral form of a verb, the form under which, in Polish, verbs are listed in dictionaries. The infinitive is usually translated in English with TO: **śpiewać** *to sing*, **czekać** *to wait.*

INFLECTION: the process of adding endings to stems; or the combined body of forms produced by adding all of the endings to a stem.

INFLECTIONAL MORPHOLOGY: opposed to DERIVATIONAL MORPHOLOGY, inflectional morphology is concerned with the description of a word in all its forms. Inflectional morphology may be subdivided into CONJUGATION (the study of the forms of verbs) and DECLENSION (the study of the forms of nouns, adjectives, pronouns, and numerals).

INTERROGATIVE: questioning; see mood.

INTRANSITIVE: referring to a verbal action which, in a given sentence, does not carry over to an object. In **Ewa śpiewa** *Ewa is singing* the verb is intransitive, because the matter of what Ewa is singing is not mentioned. The verb **śpiewać** *sing* is optionally TRANSITIVE, as in **Ewa śpiewa piosenkę** *Ewa is singing a song.* The verb **spać** *sleep* is inherently intransitive.

LEXICAL: relating to words, whether word-forms or word-meanings. More narrowly, "lexical" refers to words with full referential meaning, as opposed to words with substantially grammatical meaning or function.

MASCULINE ANIMATE: in Polish, a designation for a noun of masculine gender, almost always referring to an animate being, which exhibits certain characteristic morphological or syntactic properties in the singular. For example, masculine-declension animate nouns have Genitive-Accusative sg. in **-a.**

MASCULINE PERSONAL: in Polish, a gender distinction in the plural. Masculine personal gender refers to groups of people at least one of whom is male. Masculine-personal-plural groups are referred to with the pronoun **oni**, as opposed to **one**, which is used to refer to other than masculine-personal-plural groups. Masculine personal distinctions are made in the verbal, nominal, and adjectival inflectional systems.

MIDDLE VOICE: a sentence point-of-view whereby an object undergoes an action from its own perspective, regardless of who or what is causing the action, as in **Samochód zatrzymał się.** *The car came to a stop.* See ACTIVE VOICE, PASSIVE VOICE, VOICE.

MOBILE VOWEL: in Polish, a vowel (**e**) which alternates with zero (nothing) in different forms of the same word. Usually, the mobile vowel appears in stems before a zero ending, as in NAsg. **mech** *moss,* compare Gsg. **mchu.**

MODAL VERB: a kind of auxiliary verb (a verb taking an infinitive) used to modify the verbal idea as to such things as will, intent, attitude, ability, etc. In **Lubię jeść** *I like to eat*, **lubię** is a modal verb.

MODIFIER: a word or phrase which restricts in some way, making more precise, the interpretation of another word or phrase in the sentence is said to MODIFY that word or phrase. For example, in the phrase **ten łagodny pies** *that gentle dog*, **ten** modifies **pies** as to its scope of reference, and **łagodny** modifies it as to its character. Modifiers of nouns include adjectives, numerals, and determiners. Adverbs modify verbs, adjectives, and other adverbs. For example,in the phrase **szybko leci** *quickly fly*, the adverb **szybko** modifies the verb **leci** as to its manner.

MOOD: mood refers to the underlying intent or factuality of the contents of a sentence, according to whether the implicit intent of the speaker is to relate (indicative mood); to command (imperative mood); to question (interrogative mood); to speculate (hypothetical or conditional mood); or to desire (optative mood).

MORPHEME: a meaningful part of a word which cannot be analyzed into smaller meaningful parts. Suffixes, prefixes, endings, and roots are examples of morphemes. In **prze-kaz-yw-a-ć** *to transfer*, **prze-** is a prefix, **kaz-** is the root, **-yw-** and **-a-** are suffixes, and **-ć** is an ending.

MORPHOLOGY: the study of a language's word-forms, word-parts, and word formation. See DERIVATIONAL MORPHOLOGY, INFLECTIONAL MORPHOLOGY.

MORPHOPHONEME: a distinctive basic sound unit or abstract operator in word formation, with one or more different interpretations on the phonemic level. In practice, a morphophoneme is usually a phoneme capable of changing to another phoneme. For example, the Polish morphophoneme **k** yields either phonemic **k, c**, or **cz**, according to sound-change rules, as in **ręka** *hand*, **ręce** *hands*, **ręczny** *manual.*

MORPHOPHONEMIC OPERATOR: an item which has no direct sound realization, but which otherwise acts like a morphophoneme in that it can condition or undergo phonemic change, as the ending **-∅**.

MORPHOPHONEMICS: the study of phonemically relevant sound-changes related to changes in the grammatical shape of words. For example, when a grammatical ending in **-e-** is added to the stem **mog-**, **g** is replaced by **ż**, as in **mog-e-sz: możesz** *you can.* Since this is a phonemically relevant sound-change (the phoneme **g** goes to the phoneme **ż**) activated by the grammar, the change is termed morphophonemic.

MORPHOSYNTAX: the study of the interplay between morphology and syntax. For example, the replacement of the Accusative by the Genitive on the direct object of a negated transitive verb (**Mam czas.** *I have time-A.* vs. **Nie mam czasu** *I don't have time-G.*) is a matter of morphosyntax.

NOMINAL: pertaining to nouns and noun categories.

NON-FINITE VERB FORMS: in Polish, these consist of the infinitive, participles, gerunds, and the verbal noun.

NON-LEXICAL: not having full referential meaning; opposed to LEXICAL. Such parts of speech as particles, prepositions, conjunctions, and determiners may be said to be non-lexical.

NOUN: a word that refers to people, places, things, or abstract entities; and which typically fills in a sentence one of the grammatical roles connoted by a verb, for example, subject, direct object, indirect object, instrument, location, among others.

NULL: a morphophonemic operator consisting of literally nothing, sometimes used to describe absolute word-final position, not followed by a ZERO ENDING. Symbol: #.

NUMBER: in Polish, the property of a noun to refer either to a single item (singular number) or to more than one item (plural number). Some Polish forms reflex a historical dual number, usually referring to a matched couple (eyes, hands, etc.).

NUMERAL: a part of speech whose function is to qualify a noun as to its quantity or as to its order in a sequence. Types of Polish numerals include cardinal, ordinal, collective, reified, indefinite, multiplicative, fractional, and combinatory. See Chapter 8.

OBJECT: see DIRECT OBJECT, INDIRECT OBJECT.

OBLIQUE CASES. any case other than Nominative or Accusative, which are termed DIRECT CASES. In practice, "oblique" usually means the Genitive, Dative, Instrumental, or Locative. The Vocative case is usually considered to be outside the direct-oblique distinction.

OBLIQUE COMPLEMENT: any COMPLEMENT that is not a DIRECT OBJECT.

ORDINAL NUMERAL: an adjectival numeral, used to refer to the order of something in a series, like **pierwszy** *first*, **drugi** *second*, and so on.

ORTHOGRAPHY: the letters used to spell words and the principles governing them.

PARADIGM: broadly speaking, all the inflected forms of a word in all of its categories. For example, the paradigm of a verb comprises the forms of the present, past, infinitive, imperative, the opposite aspect, the imperfective future, the verbal noun, the various verbal adjectives and adverbs, and all of their forms.

PART OF SPEECH: a class of words as determined by its combined referential-syntactic function. See CONJUNCTION, NOUN, PRONOUN, VERB, ADJECTIVE, ADVERB, NUMERAL, QUANTIFIER, PREPOSITION, PARTICLE. Parts of speech are sometimes divided into LEXICAL (noun, verb, adjective, most adverbs) and NON-LEXICAL or functional (conjunction, numeral, quantifier, preposition, particle, some adverbs).

PARTICLE: a non-lexical part of speech whose function is emphatic, contrastive, or logical-grammatical. For example, the particle -**by** is used in forming the conditional mood; the particle -**ś** is used in the formation of indefinite pronouns like **ktoś** *someone;* the particle **nie** is used to negate an item; and so on.

PARTICIPLE: usually, an adjective derived from a verb which retains some of the syntactic properties of the verb; for example, **zajęte przeze mnie krzesło** *the occupied-by-me chair* (from **z a j ą ć** *occupy-pf.*). The term 'participle' may also be used to designate an adverb derived from a verb, as **zajmując** *while occupying,* from **zajmować** *occupy-impf.*).

PASSIVE VOICE: a sentence perspective which views the action of the sentence from the point of view not of the actor but of the person or thing being acted on. The sentence **Książka została zmoczona przez deszcz.** *The book was soaked by the rain* is passive, because the action is seen from the point of view of the book instead of the rain, as in **Deszcz zmoczył książkę.** *The rain soaked the book.* See ACTIVE VOICE, MIDDLE VOICE, VOICE.

PEJORATIVE: a negative coloration attaching to certain word-usages or derivations, especially of nouns, is said to be pejorative. For example, in Polish **glina** (literally, 'mud, clay') may be used as a pejorative designation of 'policeman'.

PERFECTIVE VERB: in Polish, a verb belonging by its form and meaning to the Perfective aspect, referring to actions or events that are both complete and effect a significant change in state, hence are either in the past or future tense, or are abstract exemplifications of a state-changing action or event. Opposed to IMPERFECTIVE VERB. See ASPECT.

PHASAL VERB: a kind of auxiliary verb referring to the beginning, ending, or continuation of an action, as **kończyć** *end,* **zacząć** *begin.*

PHONEME: one of the basic sounds of a language, by means of which words in a language are constructed. The crucial notion is that phonemes are distinct one from another for purposes of distinguishing word-forms from one another. For example, the sounds u and o are used to distinguish between **tu** *here* and **to** *that,* hence **u** and **o** are phonemes. Phonemes are divided into vowels and consonants.

PHONETICS: the study of how the sounds of a language (its phonemes) are pronounced in fact, with subtle variations according to sound environment.

PHONOLOGY: the study of a language's system of sounds.

PHRASE: any string of words, shorter than a clause, with an inner structure. For example, a prepositional phrase consists of a preposition, the noun it is used with, and any modifiers of the noun. A sentence is made up of its component phrases.

PRAGMATICS: a paralinguistic discipline dealing with how forms are actually used in real situations, as opposed to their purely formal description.

PREDICATE: The part of the sentence that is left after subtracting the grammatical subject. In **Anna śpiewa w operze.** *Anna is singing in the opera,* **śpiewa w operze** is the predicate.

PREDICATE ADJECTIVE: an adjective occurring in the predicate of a sentence, linked to the subject noun with such verbs as 'be', 'seem', 'become'. In **Ten pies jest bardzo grzeczny.** *That dog is very well-behaved,* **grzeczny** is a predicate adjective.

PREDICATE NOUN: a noun occurring in the predicate of a sentence, linked to the subject noun with such verbs as 'be', 'seem', 'become'. In **Marta jest sprzątaczką.** *Martha is a cleaning-lady,* **sprzątaczką** is a predicate noun.

PREFIX: a morpheme added to the beginning of a stem, e.g. **za-** in **zaprosić** *invite.*

PREPOSITION: A non-lexical part of speech added before a noun in order to help specify its function in a sentence. For example, in the phrase **w ogrodzie** *in the garden,* the preposition **w** *in* helps to specify **ogród** *garden* as the place where a given action or state occurs or obtains. Prepositions perform the same kind of functions as case endings, but are more specific as to their meaning.

PRIMARY CONSONANT: in Polish morphophonemics, one of the consonants which can change to another consonant according to morphophonemic rules. In **mucha** *fly,* **ch** is a primary consonant which changes to **sz** in the dative-locative sg. form **musze.** Opposed to DERIVED or FUNCTIONALLY SOFT consonants.

PRODUCTIVE: when a process can be applied in the creation of new formations, the process is said to be productive. For example, the suffix **-yw-a-** is relatively productive in the creation of new imperfective verbs from prefixed perfective verbs.

PRONOUN: a word which takes the place of a noun in a sentence, often according to the gender of the noun, when the noun is clear from context.

For example, **kto** *who*, **co** *what*, **on** *he*, are pronouns. Pronouns are of various sorts: personal, interrogative, relative, indefinite, and others. See Chapter 7.

PROPER NOUN: a noun with individual reference and naming function, as **Ewa** *Ewa*, **Warszawa** *Warsaw*, **Ziemia** *The Earth*.

QUANTIFIER: a DETERMINER which refers to the number or amount of something, either specifically as in the case of NUMERALS, or generally, as in the instance of words like **kilka** *several*.

REFLEXIVE: an action where the subject and the object of an action are the same. In English *I wash* has an optional reflexive interpretation: 'I wash myself'. In Polish, the term usually describes verbs which take the reflexive particle **się**, whether or not they are literally reflexive in meaning. For example, **ranić się** has both a literal and a figurative reflexive meaning: 'wound oneself' or 'get wounded'; **bać się** *be afraid* is reflexive only in a formal sense.

ROOT: the central morpheme in an inflected word, usually containing the word's deepest lexical content. In the word **pokazać** *show*, the root is **kaz-**; **po-** is a prefix, **-a-** is a suffix, and **-ć** is an ending. This word shares the same root with such words as **wskazać** *indicate*, **zakazać** *forbid*, **zakaz** *prohibition*, **wykazać** *exhibit*, **wykaz** *invoice*, and so on.

SEMANTIC: having to do with the interpretation of meaning.

SEMELFACTIVE: a verbal action that takes place instantaneously, as for example **burknąć** *grunt*.

SEMI-TRANSITIVE: neither wholly transitive nor wholly intransitive; used to refer to verbs which take OBLIQUE-CASE COMPLEMENTS, as **pomagać komuś** *help someone*, or PREPOSITIONAL COMPLEMENTS, as **patrzeć na coś** *look at something*.

SEMIVOWELS: also referred to as glides; in this work, the bilabial glide **ł** and the palatal glide **j**.

SIMPLEX VERB: a verb without a prefix, for example, **nieść** *carry*, as opposed to a prefixed verb like, say, **odnieść** *carry back*.

SOFT CONSONANT: Polish consonants may be either PHONETICALLY SOFT (pronounced with the tongue held against the soft palate) or PHONETICALLY HARD (not so pronounced). Among hard consonants, some are HISTORICALLY OR FUNCTIONALLY SOFT and contrast in grammatical rules with FUNCTIONALLY HARD consonants. See Chapter 2.

SOFTENING: in Polish grammar this generally means functional softening, that is, replacing a primary consonant with a corresponding palatal or affricate consonant, as in the replacement of **k** with **c** in **ręka** *hand* **ręce-**Lsg.

SONANT: also called sonorant, one of the nasal or liquid consonants, consisting of a steadily resonanting voiced sound: **m, m', n, ń, (ŋ), (ŋ'), r, l.** See Chapter 1.

SPIRANT: in the present work, one of the consonants **f, w, ch, s, z, sz, ż, rz.** See Chapter 1.

STEM: in inflection and word-formation, the part of the word to which affixes (whether prefixes or suffixes) are added, or to which endings are added. For example, in **zdanie** *opinion*, the stem is **zdań-**.

STRESS: the pronunciation of a syllable of a word with greater emphasis than other syllables. In Polish, almost all full words have stress on the next-to-last syllable.

SUBJECT: a noun with which the verb of a sentence agrees, and which usually constitutes the focus of the sentence's import. In **Jan zostaje pod aresztem.** *Jan remains under arrest*, **Jan** is the subject .

SUBJECTLESS: a sentence which does not have a referentially identifiable subject. In English, the sentence IT IS FIVE O'CLOCK is subjectless, even though the item IT acts as a grammatical, or "dummy", subject. In Polish, such sentences are subjectless both semantically and literally; see **Jest godzina piąta.**

SUBORDINATE CLAUSE: a clause introduced by another, main clause. In **Skąd wiesz, że nadchodzi burza?** *How do you know that a storm is approaching?* the segment **skąd wiesz...** is the main clause, and **że nadchodzi burza** is the subordinate clause.

SUBSTANDARD: in any language with a rich cultural and literary history, certain forms and expressions will be considered less proper and correct, i.e. less reflective of so-called educated speech, than others, for largely arbitrary reasons. An example in English would be saying *he don't* instead of *he doesn't*. In Polish, supposedly less educated speakers place stress on the next-to-last syllable of 1st and 2nd-person plural past-tense verb forms like **pytaliśmy** *we asked*, **pytaliście** *you asked*, whereas stress on the preceding syllable is considered correct (**pytal*iś*my, pytal*iś*cie**). Similarly, the standard infinitive of 'take-perfective' is **wziąć**, not substandard **!wziąść**. There is nothing inherently wrong about substandard speech. However, matters of standard-language correctness have social importance, in that one's person and the contents of one's speech are apt to be judged, fairly or not, on the basis of the forms of speech one chooses.

SUBSTANTIVAL: more or less the equivalent of NOMINAL.

SUBSTANTIVIZED ADJECTIVE: An adjective used as an ad hoc noun, for example, **chory** *sick*, used in the sense 'patient'. Compare ADJECTIVAL NOUN.

SUFFIX: a morpheme added to the end of a stem, e.g. **-nik-** in **ogrodnik** *gardener*. By convention, endings are not considered to be suffixes.

SUPPLETIVITY: when two historically distinct items function as forms belonging to the same synchronic word, the relationship between them is said to be suppletive. For example, **ludzie** *people* serves as the suppletive plural of **człowiek** *man*.

SURFACE (OR SHALLOW) STEM: a stem-form adequate only to the prediction of the forms occurring in the immediate inflection of a word, not necessarily to the prediction of all derivational relations contracted by it. For example, **kość-** is the surface stem of **kość** *bone*. The deep stem of this word is **kost-**, a form which shows better the relationship of **kość** to words like **skostniały** *ossified*. See also UNDERLYING FORM.

SYLLABLE: a non-meaningful stretch of sound consisting of a vowel plus possible preceding or following consonants. A spoken word is composed of its syllables. In Polish, syllables usually consist of a vowel by itself, or of one or more initial consonants plus a vowel. A syllable ending with a consonant is called a CLOSED SYLLABLE, opposed to an OPEN SYLLABLE, which ends with a vowel. In **Warszawa** *Warsaw*, **War-**, **-sza-**, and **-wa** are syllables, the first closed, the second two open.

SYNCHRONIC: from the contemporary point of view; opposed to DIACHRONIC.

SYNTAX: the study of phrase, clause, and sentence structure; often, in practice, the study of verbs and the kind of noun phrases with which they can occur.

TENSE: the indication, usually by grammatical means (typically, by endings on the verb), of the time of an action or state described by a sentence. There are three basic tenses: present (action AT or DURING the current time); past (action BEFORE the current time); and future (action AFTER the current time).

TRANSITIVE: the property of a verb to take direct objects, that is, noun complements in the Accusative case. Other verbs are considered to be INTRANSITIVE. Verbs which take prepositional or bare-case non-Accusative complements can be termed SEMITRANSITIVE. For example, **pisać** *write* is transitive, since it takes Accusative complements (**pisać książkę** *write a book*); **zajmować się** is Semitransitive, since it takes Instrumental complements: **zajmować się domem** *take care of the house;*

czekać *wait* is semi-transitive and takes Prepositional complements: **czekać na pocztę** *wait for the mail.* The verb **spać** *sleep* is Intransitive.

TRUNCATION: the removal of the end of a stem during the course of word formation. For example, **ciacho** *pastry-augmentative* is formed by truncating **ciasto** *cake, pastry* before the stem-final **st** and replacing **st** with **ch.**

UNDERLYING (OR DEEP) FORM: an abstract form of a word, different from its SURFACE (or SHALLOW) FORM, used for explaining certain eytmological relationships. For example, the underlying form of **suszyć** *to dry* may be said to be **such-i-ć**, showing root-final **ch** before its change to **sz**, demonstrating the relationship of this word to such other words as **suchy** *dry.*

VERB: the central part of speech in most sentences, coordinating the roles of the noun phrases and adjuncts with which it occurs. Verbs refer to actions, occurrences, processes, states, identities, and relationships. The items **pisać** *write,* **czekać** *wait,* **rozumieć** *understand,* **być** *be,* and so on, are verbs.

VERBAL: pertaining to verbs and verb categories. Additionally, in Polish, a VERBAL is a minor uninflected part of speech consisting of words with a verb-like function or force. In **Trzeba go zapytać** *It's necessary to ask him,* **trzeba** is a verbal.

VOCALIC: of, relating to, or consisting of a vowel. Opposed to CONSONANTAL.

VOICE: the technical word for sentence perspective, as determined by whether the sentence takes the point of view of its subject or its object. Voice can be ACTIVE (as in **Jan gotuje wodę** *Jan is boiling water.*); PASSIVE (**Woda jest gotowana przez Jana.** *The water is being boiled by Jan.*); or MIDDLE (as in **Woda się gotuje.** *The water is boiling.*) A special kind of voice in Polish is the IMPERSONAL PASSIVE, as in **Wodę się gotuje.** *Water is being boiled.*

VOWEL: a sound (phoneme) with syllabic value. Opposed to CONSONANT.

VOWEL-SHIFT: a morphophonemic change consisting in the replacement of one vowel with another in different forms of a word, as in **stół** *table,* Gsg. **stołu, mąż** *husband,* Gsg. **męża**, showing the shift of **o** to **ó**, and of **ę** to **ą**, respectively.

ZERO ENDING: an ending consisting of nothing, in contrast to other endings in the same inflection which are not zero. Symbol: **0.** For example, the Nominative sg. of 'notebook' is **zeszyt0**; compare with Gsg. **zeszytu,** Dsg. **zeszytowi,** and so on. Compare with NULL.

Some Polish Grammatical Terms

głoska *sound*
samogłoska *vowel*
spółgłoska *consonant*

końcówka *ending*
przedrostek *prefix*
rdzeń *root*
suffiks *suffix*
temat *stem*
odmiana *inflection*

słowo *word*
część mowy *part of speech*
czasownik *verb*
liczebnik *numeral*
  główny *cardinal*
  porządkowy *ordinal*
  zbiorowy *collective*
partykuła *particle*
przyimek *preposition*
przymiotnik *adjective*
przysłówek *adverb*
rzeczownik *noun*
spójnik *conjunction*
zaimek *pronoun*
  osobowy *personal*
  dzierżawczy *possessive*

deklinacja *declension*
rodzaj *gender*
  męski *masculine*
  żeński *feminine*
  nijaki *neuter*
  męskoosobowy *masculine personal*
  żywotny *animate*
  nieżywotny *inanimate*

koniugacja *conjugation*
osoba *person*
  pierwsza *first*
  druga *second*
  trzecia *third*
czas *tense*
  przeszły *past*
  przyszły *future*
  teraźniejszy *present*
  zaprzeszły *past perfect*
aspekt *aspect*
  dokonany *Perfective*
  niedokonany *Imperfective*
  jednokierunkowy *Determinate*
  niejednokierunkowy *Indeterminate*
  wielokrotny *frequentative*
imiesłów *participle*
  przymiotnikowy *adjectival*
  przysłówkowy *adverbial*
  rzeczownik odczasownikowy *verbal noun*
strona *voice*
  bierna *passive*
  czynna *active*
  zwrotna *reflexive*

zdanie *sentence*
pytanie *question*
stwierdzenie *statement*
zaprzeczenie *negation*
rozkaz *command*

liczba *number*
    pojedyńcza *singular*
    mnoga *plural*

przypadek *case*
    mianownik *Nominative*
    dopełniacz *Genitive*
    celownik *Dative*
    biernik *Accusative*
    narzędnik *Instrumental*
    miejscownik *Locative*
    wołacz *Vocative*

stopniowanie *comparison*
stopień *degree (of comparison)*
    równy *positive*
    wyższy *comparative*
    najwyższy *superlative*

tryb *mood*
    oznajmujący *indicative*
    przypuszający *conditional*
    pytający *interrogative*
    rozkazujący *imperative*

składnia *syntax*
podmiot *subject*
orzeczenie *predicate*
przydawka *modifier*
dopełnienie *complement*
    bliższe *direct object*
    dalsze *indirect object*
okolicznik *adverbial phrase*
    czasu *of time*
    sposobu *of manner*
    miejsca *of place*
    miary *of extent*
    stopnia *of degree*
    warunku *of condition*

Index of Words Cited in a Grammatical Context

450 INDEX OF WORDS

wykonawca 55
wykonawczyni 55
wykopać 282
wykorzystać 284
wykraść wykradać 287
wykroczyć 282
wykrzyczeć 284
wykrzyknąć wykrzykiwać 289
wykształcić 284
wykuć 284
wykup 237
wykupić 284
wylać 281, 284, wylewać 286
wyleźć wyłazić 294
wyleżeć wylegiwać 289
wyliczyć 284
wyładować 284
wyłącznie 412
wyłączyć 284. wyłączyć 296
wymachiwać 220
wymagać 336
wymagający 300
wymazać wymazywać 286
wymieniać 393. wymienialny 307
wymię 118
wymiotać 233
wymówić 281. wymawiać 290
wymusić 230
wymyślić 229. wymyślać 347
wynieść 294. wynosić 294, 295
wynos 230
wynosić 354
wyobrażać sobie 260
wypadać 267, 389
wypaść wypasać 287
wypić wypijać 279, 288
wypleć (wypielić) wypielać 287
wypłacić wypłacać 287
wyposażyć 232
wypracować 284. wypracowywać 288
wyprowadzić wyprowadzać 287
wyprząc wyprzęgać 287
wypuścić wypuszczać 286
wyrównać wyrównywać 289

wyrwać 284
wyrzec się wyrzekać się 335
wyrzucić 287, 398. wyrzucać 287, 354
wyskakiwać 220
wyskoczyć wyskakiwać 287, 289
wyskrobać wyskrobywać 287
wysłać 241. wysyłać 288, 354
wysoki wyższy 144. wysoko, wysoce
146, 14. wyżej 149, wyżej 150
wysokość 214
wysokogórski 141
wyspać się 322
wystarczyć 231, 308, 335, 350
wystąpić występować 288, 380
wysyłać 354
wysypać 281
wyszukany 306
wyśmiać się wyśmiewać się 288
wytrzeć 241, 284. wycierać 287
wytyczna, 57
wywiązywać 220
wywiesić 230
wywietrzyć 233
wywieźć wywozić 294
wywoływać 220
wzbogacić 284
wzbudzić 284
wzdąć 284
wzdychać 278
wzejść 281, 284, 294
wzgardzić 284
względem+G 343
wziąć 225, 239, 253, 284, 289. wziąść 225
wzlecieć 284
wzmocnić 284
wzniesienie 309
wzrost 214
wzruszać się 365

z+I 341, 342, 343, 366, 367, 368, 73
z drugiej strony 414
z górą 214, 415
z góry 413
z jednej strony 414